CAA

Computer Applications
and Quantitative Methods in Archaeology (CAA)

Virtual Reality in Archaeology

Edited by

Juan A. Barceló, Maurizio Forte and
Donald H. Sanders

BAR International Series 843
2000

Published in 2016 by
BAR Publishing, Oxford

BAR International Series 843

Virtual Reality in Archaeology

ISBN 978 1 84171 047 1

BAR Publishing is the trading name of British Archaeological Reports (Oxford) Ltd. British Archaeological Reports was first incorporated in 1974 to publish the BAR Series, International and British. In 1992 Hadrian Books Ltd became part of the BAR group. This volume was originally published by Archaeopress in conjunction with British Archaeological Reports (Oxford) Ltd / Hadrian Books Ltd, the Series principal publisher, in 2000. This present volume is published by BAR Publishing, 2016.

Printed in England

BAR
PUBLISHING

BAR titles are available from:

BAR Publishing
122 Banbury Rd, Oxford, OX2 7BP, UK
EMAIL info@barpublishing.com
PHONE +44 (0)1865 310431
FAX +44 (0)1865 316916
www.barpublishing.com

Contents

Archaeological Applications

Concluding Address

***Please note that the CD referred to above (and in the text) has now been replaced with a download available at www.barpublishing.com/additional-downloads.html**

Presentation

Nick Ryan

Computer Applications in Archaeology (CAA)
President

The twenty-sixth annual conference on Computer Applications and Quantitative Methods in Archaeology (CAA98) took place between the 25th and 28th March 1998 at the Centre de Cultura Contemporània de Barcelona. CAA conference organisers have long been encouraged to innovate, and for this year Juan Barceló as Chairman of the local organising commitee took the bold step of including a public Festival of Virtual Reality in Archaeology as an adjunct to the main conference. Visitors to the festival, including conference delegates, local citizens and media, were treated to an impressive display of some fifty contemporary examples of visualisation in archaeology. The presentations covered a wide range of purposes, production budgets and technical sophistication. Together, they gave a clear impression of the range of possibilities for the application of visualisation techniques in archaeological interpretation, in education and in museums, both physical and virtual.

This volume and its accompanying CD bring many of the visual aspects of the festival together with a collection of some thirty papers, many from the main sessions of the conference, covering technical, methodological and theoretical issues that underpin the creation of archaeological visualisations. The book, like the festival, is a temporal snapshot of ideas, trends and methods, yet many of the papers address fundamental and enduring issues that archaeologists, museum curators and others must confront when using visualisations, whether for restricted professional purposes or as a means of disseminating their ideas to a wider audience.

Several papers address the needs of the archaeologist who is unfamiliar with the techniques but is interested in using visualisation as an aid to analysis, or simply in exploring a particular problem domain. What is possible? How is it done? What techniques are available now? In the future, how might these benefit from current research in computer graphics? What equipment and techniques can we use to ease the task of collecting the often enormous quantities of data needed for a detailed visualisation of an artefact, building or landscape? How can visualisations help archaeologists in interpreting their data, or in exploring the range of possibilities that the, invariably fragmentary, sources might represent?

Beyond these basic technical and methodological questions lie other equally, if not more, important issues. A number of papers address such questions. What does it mean to say that something is "virtually real"? What effect does enhanced realism have on the way that our visualisations are received? How and where might we use highly detailed models, perhaps with realistic lighting, atmospheric effects and even acoustics, yet still retain that message of uncertainty that has often been conveyed so effectively by the use of smoke in "artists' impressions"?

In one sense, these questions are little different from those that have long been addressed by museum curators when they wish to go beyond the mere display of artefacts. Yet we now have not only much wider access to the tools and techniques for producing visualisations and to the means of publication via the Internet, but also far less control over the ways in which much of our work is received and used. Together, these place upon us a considerable responsibility to ensure that we effectively communicate the tentative nature of our models.

As I write this prologue, I am engaged in the production of a large visualisation of Roman Canterbury in which the great majority of features are wholly imaginary or, at best, informed speculation. One aim of this work is to help museum visitors appreciate the tentative nature of much archaeological interpretation. Yet, at the same time, we hope also to demonstrate how much can be inferred from the results of small isolated urban excavations. The final form of the Canterbury model will owe much to ideas discussed here and elsewhere by many of the authors represented in this volume and to techniques illustrated on the CD. In one sense, we are avoiding many of the problems of representing our lack of knowledge and uncertainty by making them an explicit theme of the presentation.

It is to be hoped that this volume will provide a useful source of ideas towards the development of new and refined ways of using visualisation in archaeology.

THE DIVERSITY OF ARCHAEOLOGICAL VIRTUAL WORLDS

Juan A. Barceló, Maurizio Forte and Donald H. Sanders

Editors

The concept of *virtual archaeology* was first proposed by Paul Reilly (1990) to refer to the use of 3D computer models of ancient buildings and artefacts. The key concept is *virtual*, an allusion to a model, a replica, the notion that something can act as a surrogate or replacement for an original. Virtual reality is being used as a generic word to refer to the growing range of dynamic-interactive visualisation (Gillings 1999, Lloret 1999). Virtual reality is such a "hot" concept that many people tend to use it even when its use is logically inappropriate. It should be defined as those environments where the human operator is transported into a new interactive environment by means of devices that display signals to the operator's sense organs and devices that sense various actions of the operator. Consequently, many archaeological three-dimensional representations currently displayed in books and videos are not VR systems because there is not this sensitive interaction.

In this volume, you can read (and see in the accompanying CD-ROM) many different applications. From reconstructions of Megalithic monuments to Medieval churches, from Egyptian musical instruments to Roman pottery. In all cases, archaeological data have been translated into images by means of 3D solid modelling. Images help understanding of the complexities of archaeological concepts in many different ways.

The book is divided into several parts: introductory papers, technical papers and archaeological applications.

The first papers (by Barceló, Sanders, Kantner and Holloway) are more general and have an introductory character. The main objectives of virtual reality are presented, and some of the techniques are explained (see especially Holloway's paper for a technical introduction to 3D modelling).

This book offers a complete overview of virtual reality techniques in archaeology. However, approaches are very different, and somewhat difficult to compare for readers without technical knowledge in this subject. Therefore, J. A. Barceló's introductory paper has been written in order to give a preliminary idea about what a 3D solid model is, what kind of "model" is a "computer model", how to build it, and how to use it. Image construction is a reasoning process. Our brain builds images by processing knowledge in specific ways. Because of the quantity of information computer visual models can explain, we must insist on the procedures of image construction. This is the main subject of this first paper: to explain how a virtual archaeological model can be built, and how this process of model building is, in fact, a reasoning mechanism of explanation. We think by building images instead of writing texts. In the paper, the concept of "visualisation" is first introduced, with a short discussion of the quantitative nature of archaeological data. Different approaches to data acquisition (video-capture, photogrammetry, computer tomography, 3D scanning, and the like) are also presented, and how to build a model once we have obtained real data. Different methodologies are examined, and some relevant archaeological examples are also presented. The difficult concept of "reconstruction" is also shown, especially questions about how to "complete" fragmented archaeological data. A general introduction to rendering, texturing and illumination (but see the papers by Lucet, by Pope and Chalmers, and by De Nicola et al.) gives some clues to the concept of "realism" and why we need "realistic" models. A final presentation of interactivity and the basis of "augmented" reality ends the paper. Throughout the paper, the most current archaeological applications of virtual reality techniques are quoted as examples of different approaches.

In his chapter Donald Sanders reviews some of the drawbacks of traditional methods of publishing, counters with alternatives based on the use of virtual reality, touches on some complications of new media technologies, and concludes with some innovations that may usher in virtual archaeology of the new millennium. The focus of his chapter is how archaeologists can use virtual reality for the dissemination of archaeological material via excavation reports, teaching materials, and research resources. John Kantner considers how decisions in the creation of virtual architecture are further constrained by the goals of the project and the intended audience, the desired product, the quality of archaeological information, and technological capabilities. The chapter examines how to balance realism vs. reality, and ends by examining how these issues have been addressed in 3D reconstructions that the author has made of prehistoric architecture from the southwestern United States. Dennis Holloway offers an architect's perspective on the *shape* of prehistoric buildings and monuments, giving examples and a general framework for building good reconstructions of prehistoric buildings. His examples, taken from the southwestern United States, are related to those presented by Kantner.

A first block of technical papers deals with the problem of data acquisition. In order to solve the realism vs. reality paradox (see Kantner, *this volume*), we need that the model be a representation of real data. The papers by Gillings, Pollefeys et al., and Attardi et al. introduce different methods of data acquisition, and how a 3D model can be created which fits the empirical data.

Gillings' paper is an attempt to answer the question: what does it mean to describe something as virtually real? He presents issues such as the relationship between "model", "reality" and "authenticity". The *Negotiating Avebury* project is also examined, within a broad theoretical framework, emphasising the fluidity and contingency of VR models as fully mimetic modes of representation. The goal of the project has been to integrate VR techniques into the generation of primary archaeological records. In this way the idea that VR simulations could, and should, be seen as a natural and complimentary adjunct to the familiar maps, plans and elevation drawings of traditional archaeological research, is strengthened and reinforced. In the Avebury research, VR models are first and foremost seen as primary records, linked directly to specific archaeological problems. For example, to what extent does the bulk of the stones constrain vision within and across the monument? Rather than the creation of a single monolithic "Virtual Avebury" the aim is to create a large number of highly contingent "Virtual Aveburys" through which it will be possible to examine particular questions and problem areas. Directly related to this theoretical discussion, there is the problem of data acquisition, because the more reliable the data, the more useful is the resulting model. The commercial program PhotoModeler is presented, including a number of archaeological applications. Photogrammetry and direct image capture is the subject presented in the other technical papers. Pollefeys et al. compare two different 3D acquisition techniques which have been applied to reconstructions of objects, monuments and buildings of the archaeological site of Sagalassos (in Turkey). Attardi et al.'s paper is a good example of seeing what cannot be seen because it is hidden. Using remote sensing methods (computer tomography), they explore what is inside a mummy, and offer an hypothetical view of the real face of the person. Also related to photogrammetry is Feihl's paper, in the archaeological applications section.

A second block of technical papers concerns rendering and lighting. Papers by Lucet, De Nicola et al., Pope and Chalmers, Pásztor et al., and Goodrick and Harding, offer a general overview of algorithms and detailed archaeological applications of how to give photo-realism to a 3D computer model. Developing some of the theoretical guidelines presented before (Kantner, Gillings), Genevieve Lucet argues that artistic exploration cannot be the underlying idea of archaeological reconstruction. Archaeology demands exactness and accurate visualisation of architecture, before its aesthetic presentation. In consequence, if one of the aims of a virtual reconstruction of archaeological sites is to obtain a realistic reproduction in order to achieve a close approximation to the original building as it was conceived and constructed by its builders, and if archaeologists want to experiment and live such ancient space, it becomes clear why the precise modelling and simulation of light is a key aspect of realistic reconstruction. De Nicola et al. show how to test and develop a methodology able to fasten and optimise the operations and the times of the photorealistic ray tracing processes. It is exemplified with data from the excavation of an Avarian Age cemetery (7th century AD). Pope and Chalmers present a different rendering algorithm, based on how sound and echoes propagate in closed environments. This methodology is applied to the underground prehistoric Hypogeum at Hal Salfieni, Malta. Pásztor et al. present rendering and lighting algorithms to analyse a specific historical hypothesis: whether the light of the rising sun on the megalithic monument of Stonehenge during a particular occasion interacts with the building in a way that could have been used as an architectural element to enhance proceedings taking place inside it. This computer study deals only with the light and shadow effects generated by the rising summer solstice sun. Very similar is the paper by Goodrick and Harding. They analyse whether the Neolithic monument complex of Thornborough in North Yorkshire was orientated towards stellar constellations, many of which are known to have been so important to other cultures. This could only be achieved with the use of virtual reality or related visualisation techniques, simulating the sky at night with all known stars and constellations in their proper places.

If most VR applications in archaeology intend to reconstruct ancient buildings or monuments, two contributions in this book deal with the replication of archaeological artefacts. C. Steckner analyses the visualisation of ancient pottery artefacts and the estimation of their shape and weight. Here the statistics and geometry of shape meet Artificial Intelligence and Virtual Reality, the one focusing the average object, the other the exemplary shape construction. Brogni et al. offer an example of interactivity between the user and a 3D virtual object. The goal is not only to reconstruct the artefact's shape, volume and texture (an Egyptian flute), but to create an interactive system where the user can "use" a virtual model of the flute.

Especially interesting are the design of interactive systems, where users can become "immersed" into a virtual world. The same paper by Brogni et al. is a good introduction to the subject of interactivity. Their system allows total access to the information about the archaeological artefact by means of an environment with text-windows and buttons (Graphic User Interface), which allows us to interact with the application and guide the consultation. The screen is held by the user and pointed along the line of sight to the real position where the artefact would be located. At present this application is used for the representation of an Egyptian glass flute, but it is a suitable platform for every artefact, and the virtual environment could even be a tomb or an ancient palace. The visitor gives orders by touching the screen on graphic buttons, located on the side of the screen, which are easy to hit with the same fingers thathold the screen. At the same time the tracking sensor gives all the information about the movement in the real space relative to the central system, which can prepare the new image for the screen according to the new point of view. During the virtual exploration, it is possible to retrieve particular information about the figures in the decoration of the flute. By touching a button, the virtual exploration stops and a window opens with a photograph and an explanation text.

A different sense of "interactivity" is explored by Kadobayashi et al. They introduce the idea of Meta-Museum, which is a new environment where experts and novices can easily communicate with each other so that they can share broad knowledge related to all aspects of humans and nature. A practical formation of Meta-Museum would be a combination of traditional museums that have physical objects and virtual museums that have digital information. Kadobayashi et al. have developed the VisTA and VisTA-walk systems based on the Meta-Museum concept. These systems simulate the transition process of an ancient village. Users (here it may refer to experts) can visualise the transition process through real-time 3D computer graphics after they interactively set the value of each building's lifetime. Users intuitively learn the ancient landscape of the site because they can walk through the reconstructed 3D computer graphics village. The systems provide intuitive information access through the selection of objects such as buildings in the 3D computer graphics scene. Hence, VisTA will serve the users as a tool for helping them research and easily make effective presentations. They propose a new interface, a full-body and non-contact gesture interface, for exploring cyberspace that does not require visitors to wear extra devices; it is easy to use and at the same time can provide an immersive walk-through and information accessing capabilities. The name of the system with the new interface is "VisTA-walk." The expected users of VisTA will be archaeologists, and the users of VisTA-walk will be museum visitors, although this is not a strict definition.

It is interesting to compare the Meta-Museum concept with the Nu.M.E. concept in the paper by Bonfigli and Guidazzoli. Here virtual interaction is obtained through the Internet and a series of web documents. Interacting with the Nu.M.E. interface the user begins with the virtual reconstruction of a city as it is nowadays and travels backward in time using the time-bar. As the user travels back in time, recent buildings dissolve into the ground and ancient buildings that no longer exist pop up. To make sure that the visitor understands that he/she is seeing only as much as the historical sources can justify, each building is accompanied by an HTML document compiled by a historian. These hypertexts contain references to the historical resources and can be consulted at any time during the visit. Bonfigli and Guidazzoli offer a detailed examination of the Virtual Historic Museum of the City of Bologna as an example.

Internet interactivity by means of VRML documents is also considered in the introductory papers by Sanders and by Mitchell and Economou. Sanders describes three types of archaeological publications (excavation reports, research resources, and educational materials) that can be created as VRML documents, thus allowing them to be accessed via the Internet. The advantages include their immediate accessiblility as well as the ease with which they can be updated as new data is collected and analysed. In Mitchell and Economou, the Tomb of Menna project is presented to investigate how the Internet can be used to provide access to archival material from the Griffith Institute at the Ashmolean Museum, Oxford. A web site was constructed based on information about the Egyptian noble Menna. The site included a 3D walk-through of the tomb as well as supporting pages containing text and photographs. A related project, also explained in the paper, is the Kahun project. Its aim is to investigate how an Internet-based resource can be used to support the work of the Education Service at Manchester Museum. The project would allow children to make the most of their time in the museum and allow follow-up work after the museum visit. The paper contains an evaluation of users' interactivity with the system. The reader should compare this evaluation of an Internet virtual world with a similar evaluation of a full-body "immersive" interaction in the paper by Kadobayashi et al.

Frischer et al. give an account of the Rome Reborn project. Rome Reborn is producing its model of the ancient city of Rome in reverse chronological order, starting with Late Antiquity, and in concentric circles starting from two centres: the old civic centre in the Roman Forum and the new Christian quarter of the city in the southeast sector of the city, between S. Giovanni in Laterano and Santa Maria Maggiore. The project short-term goal is to connect the individual sites modelled and to recreate an itinerary from the pagan civic centre to the Christian religious centre. In this paper, the Basilica of Santa Maria Maggiore model is presented. The authors explain how they have built the model, integrating all archaeological and art historical information, and the different interactivity approaches designed, from video editing to Internet access. Specially interesting is the CAVE approach to total immersion, very similar to that proposed by Kadobayashi et al.

A different approach to interactivity within a virtual model is Panoramic VR. Here the user is able to induce some movements on a virtual scene, but the model is passive;it is the user who changes points of view: the model remains in its place. Louise Krasniewicz offers in her paper some examples of this technique. The alternative approach, that is, a fly-through of a landscape, is presented in the paper by Ruiz Rodriguez et al. In this case, the user does not move around a static image but sees how a dynamic representation of a landscape model moves in some directions. These computer animations with a photorealistic aspect allow the territory to be overflown. This territory is considered as a three-dimensional space that is the basis of a historical hypothesis based on the interpretation of the archaeological documentation, in this case the Iberian population patterns in the Upper Guadalquivir basin (Spain). *Travel to the time of the Iberians* is based on the design and the implementation of a New Virtual Environment of the landscape of Jaén (Spain) as a virtual multidimensional environment characterised by efficient and effective navigation and orientation tools, using virtual reality and interaction techniques to represent real scenarios (the landscape of archaeological areas of interest as it is nowadays), artificial scenarios (the recreated landscape of the past in 3D reconstruction) and their integration. In particular, the multimedia navigation is based on the 3D reconstruction of the landscape, with the introduction of tools to show 3D reconstructed models interactively by addition or removal.

Josep Gurri and Esther Gurri offer a good example of the current move towards "enhanced" or augmented reality (see also Sanders, in this volume). That is, computer animated models where the user not only "moves" within the model, but obtains information about different aspects of the model. Gurri and Gurri present a virtual model of the Roman city of Baetulo, nowadays Badalona (Spain). The system was approached as a didactic tool that allows the user to acquire textual as well as visual knowledge. It starts with a main menu from which the user can go directly to the ancient buildings (the Roman baths, for example) or to an introductory screen that describes ancient Baetulo. The graphic part is very important in all the screens, although there is always a voice-over that tells users more about what they are seeing. Furthermore there is the possibility of another voice-over and a text that explains the subjects with more detail. This text is referenced with hypertext, associating some concepts to images in order to aidcomprehension. The main goal of this multimedia project was to provide the general public with an idea of what the Roman baths were like, how people lived, how things were done and which objects and tools were used in that historical period—all in all, to reconstruct the different parts of the baths as accurately as possible.

Among the other papers, Feihl explains how to integrate an entire visualization project, beginning with the need to procure on site an image that is as close as possible to reality and to use advanced spatial information acquisition techniques. Further, it is necessary to work out the restitution of space and to produce synthesis images in order to illustrate the results of studies or restoration alternatives. Several Medieval examples are used for this explanation. Hixon et al. use a similar strategy to recreate ancient Yodefat (Israel). Martens et al. proposes a virtual model of Sagalassos (Turkey), from the third century BC until the seventh century AD. Louhivuori et al. offer a model of the Byzantine city of Emmaus-Nicopolis (Israel). Uotila and Sartes deals with the medieval town of Turku (Finland), and Junyent and Lorés present the virtual model of the Iberian hillfort of Els Vilars (Lleida, Spain). In all these cases, the goals of reconstructions and the methodologies are explained.

The paper by Forte and Borra proposes a virtual model to produce images and animations representing the historical evolution of the Castle of Este (Italy). Here not only general objectives and methodologies are presented, but also a general multimedia approach to reconstruction and "augmented reality" approach (compare with Gurri and Gurri). The authors have projected the first virtual 3D reconstruction of the castle, starting from the architectural aspects of the monument (plans, sections, views), analysing and comparing the historical sources, and studying the volumes in order to make detailed three-dimensional models of the monument through time in the four periods of building. Considering the complexity of the project, it was very important to use different 2D-3D metaphors so as to obtain the best cognitive impact compared to many didactic approaches to multimedia information. In fact a visualisation in multiple levels permits every user to choose the best multimedia path in accordance with his own knowledge: therefore the system must school the user, having a high regard for key-concepts and key-words, but using images and animations for communicating information. The project development emphasized the distinct information layers of the architectural periods correlated with the multimedia aims, as well as how to create a model, and the necessary interaction in the development team between the Scientific Tutor, the Modeller and the Communication Manager.

In his concluding paper, Maurizio Forte addresses some general and philosophical questions about virtuality, and the proper meaning of the *virtual archaeology* concept.

Virtual Reality techniques in archaeology as presented in this book—reconstructions, 3D graphics, immersive imaging—promise an accessible, highly visual, and interactive means of representing difficult-to-see data, opening up new ways of presenting research. Virtual Reality models allow us to put all of our contemporary knowledge and thought about an object into a user-interactive presentation. Maurizio Forte points out that such models are important because, "above and beyond its strong popular impact, computer reconstruction allows the presentation of complex information in a visual way that enables it to be used to test and refine the image or model that has been created" (Forte 1997:110).

The advantage of virtual computer models in comparison to traditional analysis is evident. The visualising process resulting from solid modelling can sometimes reveal relationships within an archaeological 'reconstruction' more clearly than any other current methods of display (Fletcher and Spicer 1992, Molyneaux 1992, Miller and Richards 1994). Consequently, those models permit spatial queries such as "what is next to", what surrounds, what is above, below, to the side of, etc. (Harris and Lock 1996), or the provision of complete physical properties (mass, volume, centre of gravity, moments of inertia, radii of gyration etc.), as well as the ability to generate section views, add full visual physical properties, and detect interference between adjacent components (Daniel 1997). By constructing detailed models of the excavated material, archaeologists can re-excavate the site and search for evidence which escaped attention during the actual dig (Reilly 1990). Computer models of archaeological buildings or artefacts can be linked to text, image, and sound databases permitting self-guided educational or research virtual tours of ancient sites in which users can learn about history, construction details, or daily life with a click of the mouse. As suggested by D. Sanders (1999 and *this volume*) alternative publications can supplement or supplant traditional paper-based source material. In this sense, archaeological virtual reconstructions can be used, for instance, to determine how much material would be required to construct walls of an architectural feature, or to evaluate different theories of how a roof might have been built, or to evaluate other archaeological hypotheses, identifying inconsistencies in the actual archaeological data and rectifying incorrect assumptions about the appearance of prehistoric features.

Some virtual models are intended for use in exploration and analysis in which the user has some ideas about what he/she is looking for, but is not fully sure. Other computer representations are often prepared for presentations intended to communicate one's findings to others. The key difference here is between the need to understand the data better, versus the desire to communicate a particular understanding that has already been reached. To date, the catalyst for visualisation in archaeology has not been the search for improved techniques for discovering new knowledge but rather for improved ways for presenting existing knowledge to the public (Miller and Richards 1994), but in the next years we look forward to new applications in many different domains.

References Cited

DANIEL, R., 1997, "The need for the solid modelling of structure in the archaeology of buildings", Internet Archaeology, 2, 2.3 (http://intarch.ac.uk/journal/issue2/daniels_index.html

FLETCHER, M., SPICER, D., 1992, "The display and analysis of ridge-and-furrow from topographically surveyed data". In *Archaeology and the Information Age.* Edited by P. Reilly and S.Rahtz. London: Routledge, pp. 97-122.

FORTE, M (ed), 1997 *Virtual Archaeology: Great Discoveries Brought to Life Through Virtual Reality,* Thames and Hudson, London

GILLINGS, M., 1999, Engaging Place: a Framework for the Integration and Realisation of Virtual-Reality Approaches in Archaeology" In *Archaeology in the age of the Internet.CAA 1997.* Edited by L.Dingwall, S.Exon, V. Gaffney, S. Laflin, M. Van Leusen. Oxford: British Archaeological Reports (Int. Series, S750).

GOLDSTEIN, L., 1996, "Representation and geometrical methods of problem-solving". In *Forms of Representation* Edited by D. Peterson. Exeter. Intellect Books

HARRIS, T.M. LOCK, G., 1996, "Multi-dimensional GIS: exploratory approaches to spatial and temporal relationships within archaeological stratigraphy". *Analecta Praehistorica leidensia* No. 28 (2), pp. 207-316

LLORET, T., 1999, "Arqueología Virtual y audiovisual. Una nueva propuesta en la difusión del conocimiento arqueológico". *Revista de Arqueología* XX, 213, pp. 13-19

LULL, V., 1999, "The new technologies and designer archaeology". In *New Techniques for Old Times. Computer Applications and Quantitative Methods in Archaeology.* Edited by J.A. Barceló, I. Briz and A. Vila. Oxford: British archaeological Reports (S757).

MILLER, P., RICHARDS, J., 1994, "The good, the bad, and the downright misleading: archaeological adoption of computer visualisation". In *Computer Applications in Archaeology 1994.* Edited by Jeremy Huggett & Nick Ryan. Oxford: British Archaeological Reports (Int. Series, 600).pp. 19-22.

MOLINEAUX, B., 1992, "From virtuality to actuality: the archaeological site simulation environment". In *Archaeology and the Information Age.* Edited by P. Reilly and S.Rahtz. London: Routledge, pp.312-322

REILLY, P., 1990, "Towards a virtual archaeology". *Computer Applications in Archaeology 1990,* Edited by K.Lockyear and S.Rahtz. oxford: British Archaeological reports (Int. Series 565), pp., 133-139.

REILLY, P., 1992, "Three-Dimensional modelling and primary archaeological data". In *Archaeology and the Information Age.* Edited by P. Reilly and S.Rahtz. London: Routledge, pp. 147-173

SANDERS, D. H., 1999, "Virtual Worlds for Archaeological Research and Education" In *Archaeology in the age of the Internet.CAA 1997.* Edited by L.Dingwall, S.Exon, V. Gaffney, S. Laflin, M. Van Leusen. Oxford: British Archaeological Reports (Int. Series, S750).

TUK, A., 1994, "Cogent GIS visualisations". In *Visualisation in geographical Information Systems.* Edited by H.M. Hearnshaw & D.J. Unwin. New York: John Wiley.

WOOLEY, B., 1992, *Virtual Worlds.* Oxford: Blackwell.

Introductory Papers

VISUALIZING WHAT MIGHT BE: AN INTRODUCTION TO VIRTUAL REALITY TECHNIQUES IN ARCHAEOLOGY

Juan A. Barceló

Universitat Autónoma de Barcelona
ilphd@blues.uab.es

"Reality is that which is, virtuality is what seems to be" (Nelson 1987).

Is there anything in Virtual Archaeology but wonderful images? General audiences like virtual reconstructions, and maybe there are opportunities for archaeologists and computer scientists to "sell" the Past dressed in beautiful colours, textures and shapes. But are we doing history (or anthropology, or sociology,...) when we reconstruct archaeological sites using VR techniques? This paper is a general introduction to VR techniques. They should not be presented as a way of doing reconstructions, but as a simulation of archaeological reasoning. If "Interactivity" is the key word in Virtual Reality, then we should understand it not as a way of "moving" through a computer representation, but as a "manipulation" of an archaeological interpretation.

Visualizing Archaeological Data

Images are among the most usual primary data for archaeological research.. For years, artists have collaborated with archaeologists in order to "reconstruct" all those wonderful things not preserved in the archaeological record, and they have provided archaeologists with artistic depictions of the past. However, these "illustrations" of the past are not an explicative vision of anything. When the artist represents what cannot be seen, then the artist uses his/her imagination, or partial information provided by an archaeologist, to create the images. The resulting item is not an explanation of the past, but a personal and subjective way of "seeing" it.

A "virtual" model, instead, is a representation of some (not necessarily all) features of a concrete or abstract entity. The purpose of a model of an entity is to allow people to understand the structure or behaviour of the entity, and to provide a convenient vehicle for "experimentation" with and prediction of the effects of input or changes to the model. Graphic models are those that use graphical means for creating and editing the model, to obtain values for its parameters, and to visualize its behaviour and structure. These models allow us to derive quickly and automatically any geometric property or attribute that the object is likely to possess. Geometric models give a precise mathematical description of the shape of a real object to simulate processes according to the inherent geometrical properties of the described object (Mortensen 1985, Fishwick 1995).

Consequently, "visualization" can be defined as the mapping of abstract quantities into graphical representations (geometric representations of lines, surfaces, and solids) as an aid in the understanding of complex, often massive numerical representations of scientific concepts or results (McCormick et al. 1987 , Reilly and Thompson 1992, Bryson 1994, Colonna 1994, Miller and Richards 1994, Fishwick 1995). It is the process of creating a *geometric model* for understanding the regularity present in a data set: joining points with lines, fitting surfaces to lines, or "solidifying" connected surfaces (Gershon 1994, Chen 1999). All that means that "visualizing" the real world it is not the same as "picturing" it, because the model and the graphical means for creating and visualizing the world are distinct (Foley et al. 1996). That is, geometry is used as a visual language to represent a theoretical model of the pattern of contrast and luminance, which is the strict equivalent of perceptual models of sensory input in the human brain (Goldstein 1996).

Archaeological visualization is then a way of modelling past information, and not a photograph of ancient data (Daniel 1997). Suppose we have archaeological data, collected at a set of scattered locations. In almost all cases, these data can be regarded as samples of some underlying entity—an object, an activity area, a building, a territory, a landscape, etc.— and, indeed, it is this underlying entity which we wish to display, not the data. To "visualize" the archaeological record means, then, the building of a geometric model of archaeological data. Input data are spatial variables describing archaeological material ,that is any quantitative or qualitative property of archaeological data varying *spatially* (topologically or according a specific distance measure), and which contributes to explaining the dependency relationships between the locations of the object, activity area, building, territory, or landscape we wish to study (Barceló and Pallarés 1996). If a point is the model of an archaeological entity location, then by joining points with lines, fitting surfaces to lines, and "solidifying" connected surfaces, we try to explain the *shape* and *morphology* of the archaeological entity (Barceló and Pallarés 1998). That is to say, any "visual model" is in some way a spatial model that reflects a decomposition of space in "units" (points, lines, areas, etc.) with the idea that if we can specify the *(spatial)* behaviour of each unit, we can understand the behaviour of the whole system (Fishwick 1995, Bertol and Foell 1996).

Nevertheless, the archaeological record is not a set of points, lines, surfaces, sections or blocks. Neither is it a continuum except in the broadest sense of the term. Every archaeological unit—a vase, a bone, a house, a territory—can be described as an irregular or regular volume with distinguishing characteristics. The boundaries between units create discontinuities that are further complicated by intrinsic archaeological factors, like deposition and post-deposition, for example. Within this heterogeneous complexity we are concerned with *variables,* such as artefact concentrations, activity areas, or, in general, any presence/absence of some archaeological property or other feature that is continuously variable within the volume of a unit, but is discontinuous across boundaries. To adequately represent this complex environment on a computer we must consider a nearly infinite continuum made up of discrete, irregular, discontinuous volumes which in turn control the spatial variation of archaeological features. The possibilities of using geometric elements to visualise archaeological numerical data do not signify that the data in real life correspond directly to abstract geometric elements. We should not create wonderful imaginative illustrations of the past, but should use geometry to explain some properties of the data set, that is, properties related to shape, size, texture, time and location.

Archaeological data are any items transformed by human action. A stone can be an artefact in the same sense as the landscape is also an artefact. Human action is then the main cause of shape, size, texture and location differences in the archaeological record. Any archaeological inference should be based, then, on the observed differences among these categories. Human action cannot be seen in the archaeological record, but it has some material effects that can be investigated by "visualizing" how human action transforms the nature of, and gives shape and size to, artefacts, or modifies the original location of artefacts. This is why archaeological data refer to these categories.

To generate numerical archaeological data to be visualized, we need to identify the independent spatial variables and the dependent ones. In archaeology, like in other disciplines, dependent data are related to the properties of archaeological entities, and independent variables refer to position and location. We have the following possibilities:

1. *Bi-Dimensional Modelling*

T	time location (independent variable)
W_1 ,... W_n	presence/absence/quantity of any archaeological entity (artefact, structure, ecological data, soil type)

In this case, we are involved with two-dimensional data sets which contain only a single value at every point . This is the classical example of archaeological seriation, where a single line or curve explains the relationship between time (as represented by stratigraphic ordering of some archaeological complex) and any other quantitative variable (for example, the quantity of rubbish accumulation, such as pottery sherds).

2. *Three-dimensional Modelling*

X,Y	2D point co-ordinates: longitude, latitude (independent variables)
Z	height or stratigraphic depth (dependent variables)

Here, we deal with the problem of *shape.* It is defined as the information that is invariant under translations, rotations and isotropic rescalings (Small 1996), that is, those aspects of the data that remain after location and scale (size) information are discounted. It is then a quantitative property about spatial location and size. Everything that has *size* and location, has *shape.* Shape is a field for physical exploration: it has not only aesthetic qualities, nor is shape just a pattern of recognition. Shape also is determining the spatial and thus the material and the physical qualities of objects and buildings (Sheppard 1989, Steckner 1996 and *this volume*, Lukesh 1996). Given this definition, we can create geometric models of any archaeological entity: a stone, vase, pit, house or territory. Archaeological numeric data refer to a surface measured at points whose co-ordinates are known. By tracing lines, curves and surfaces between co-ordinates, we create a geometric model of shape.

Shape models are not "photographs" of archaeological data, but visual models of the geometry of three dimensional data (Sheppard 1989, Bertol and Foell 1996, Zampi 1999, Zack 1999, Berry et al., 1998, Steckner, *this volume*). Those data are the three-dimensional co-ordinates of the vase profile, the three-dimensional co-ordinates of different architectonic elements: walls, columns, arches, windows, ceiling, etc., and the three-dimensional co-ordinates of topography. Because they are not single pictures, geometric properties (curvature, length, thickness, height, volume, etc.) can now be measured on these models. We should take into account, that when we are in three-dimensional modelling, we are not reduced only to three parameters *(x, y, z)*, but in addition to *depth* (relative surface height above the *xy* plane), there are: *surface gradient* (the rate of change of depth in the *x* and *y* directions) and *surface normal* (orientation of a vector perpendicular to the tangent plane on the object surface). This last parameter is defined also by means of other parameters: *surface slant* and *surface tilt.* (Zhang et al. 1999)

3. *Four-dimensional Modelling*

X,Y,Z	3D point co-ordinates: longitude, latitude, height/depth (independent variables)
W_1 ,... W_n	presence/absence/quantity of any archaeological entity (artefact, structure, ecological data, soil type, etc.)

We introduce now the time dimension. Here we are trying to "see" how time is involved in the changing pattern of shape modification, that is by changes in the state of an entity. There are not many archaeological applications, although it is, probably, the most interesting area for Virtual Reality in archaeology. Various authors have simulated four-dimensional models, where *time* is the fourth dimension, using animation techniques (Castleford 1991, MacEachren 1994, Johnson 1999, Daly and Lock 1999).

4. *Mixed Models*

X,Y,Z, T	4D point co-ordinates, longitude, latitude, height/depth, time (independent variables)
W_1 ,... W_n	presence/absence/quantity of any archaeological entity (artefact, structure, ecological data, soil type)

We can add a more dimensions to any geometric model. The most typical example is that of a 3D map, showing a visual representation of the relationship between soil type, hydrography (dependent variables) and topographic position (independent variables). This is a *3D+1D model*, where an archaeological spatial variable is draped into a 3D model of the topography. Among other examples, these models can be used to visualise concentrations of material within the landscape (Lock and Daly 1999). The more independent variables the system has, the more complete the resulting model is. We are not limited to 4 variables *(x, y ,z, w)*, but we can in fact relate two or more three-dimensional models (x_1, y_1 ,z_1, w_1), (x_2, y_2 ,z_2, w_2). For instance, we can analyse the dynamics of the interaction between site form (a three-dimensional shape model) and topography (another three-dimensional shape model). Traditional two-dimensional maps do not reveal details of slope and aspect. Although the location of the archaeological features is noted, one cannot easily determine the relationship between these features and the terrain. There are obvious differences between terraces on the slopes of a hill and terraces which are merely slightly flatter areas of an already flat landform. These differences are more easily quantified and assessed from a three-dimensional model (see applications by Lukesh 1996, Reeler 1999, Messika 1999, Leusen 1999 among others).

Building Geometric Models from Observable Data

We will focus here on three-dimensional models, and how to create the model from real world 3D point co-ordinates. The aim is to produce a high-level representation of the shape of the object, in the form of a set of surfaces. Different surface parameters should be estimated, taking into account the geometric relationships of real 3D points, and how they fit to the modelled surfaces and the specific shapes of surfaces as well (Werghi et al. 1999, Varady et al. 1997, Weishar 1998, Chen 1999).

Building a geometrical model is a four-step procedure: data acquisition, pre-processing, parameter estimation, and modelling. There are, however, different approaches to the main steps of data acquisition and modelling. See the specific details of archaeological model building in Holloway (*this volume*).

DATA ACQUISITION

It is relatively easy to obtain a two-dimensional description of any artefact, and represent it in a computer-readable form. Since the invention of drawing and photography, we have known how to create 2D geometric models. An archaeological map is a geometric model of a 2D archaeological record. However, *shape* can only be analysed using three dimensions. Therefore, it is necessary to acquire 3D co-ordinates of archaeological objects and structures to build shape models.

3D co-ordinates can be measured manually and introduced into the computer through a keyboard. In many cases, archaeologists use electronic theodolites to capture 3D information from the real world. However, these approaches are interactive, so that they need the action of the user to provide enough information to translate locational properties of artefacts and structures into numeric data (3D co-ordinates). There is nothing wrong in using archaeological information to *re-create* the third dimension (depth), but in some cases, it requires an automatic data capture procedure. The idea is to derive a geometric model in a domain-independent, bottom-up fashion, in the absence of prior (top-down knowledge) (Baur and Beer 1990). This implies some constraints on the world from which the scene comes, or information supplementary to a single image. Given that the target is a model of 'shape'—that is surfaces and their orientation in three dimensions—it should be clear why this family of techniques became called *shape from X*, where *X* is one of a number of options. These options are those the user clearly uses to assist in determining depth from retinal image (2D). For more details about 3D data acquisition, see Pollefeys et al (*this volume*), Feihl (*this volume*) and Gillings *(this volume*).

From 2D to 3D

In some cases, 3D data are not available, but only 2D elements (plans and sections). These units are converted into 3D by *extrusion.* This technique takes a 2D entity, such as a square, a circle or other closed path, and extends it perpendicularly into the third dimension to produce, in the case of a circle, say, a tube or a cylinder. Some programs also let you extrude a long a curved path to produce more complex-shapes. *Lathing* produces shapes by turning an outline around an axis. Related to lathing is the ability to sweep surfaces, whereby you spin a surface around an axis that extends in three dimensions. After extrusion or lathing, a "lofting" process joins two different polygons together, provided they have the same number of vertices. Since holes can not be cut out of the model, it is necessary to build the 3D model using lots of small segments fitted together. The polygons should be positioned in space interactively, and corresponding vertices joined to form a surface or skin over them. Interaction with the user and prior information is needed, in order to recreate depth.

This approach was one of the most used techniques in the first uses of 3D modelling in archaeology (Eisler et al. 1988, Chapman 1991), and it is still necessary, when we have not access to the data to be modelled, and have only old drawings and old photographs). In some archaeological early examples (like the Langcliffe Limekiln model by Chapman 1991, Wood and Chapman 1992) the input data were 2D shapes (polygons). *X* and *y* co-ordinates were taken from the archaeological plans and sections, and entered via keyboard. Once the two-dimensional shapes were complete, the software manipulated them in various ways to form 3D objects. For example, a simplified kiln was formed from two polygons: one was the cross-section of half the base, including the interior tunnel and the upper curtain wall to its full height; the other was the path taken by the outside edge of the kiln viewed in plan. The software "swept" the cross-section around the path to form the basic 3D shape.

Modern applications of this approach are exemplified in the papers by Holloway (*this volume)*, and Hixon et al. (*this volume*). Gurri and Gurri (*this volume*) have delineated two-dimensionally some parts of the Roman baths of Baetulo, before starting to create the three-dimensional geometry inside the computer. The friezes, the mosaics and the mouldings were some of the things that had to be drawn. Having the digital two-dimensional delineation as a starting point, they created the 3D geometry. The elevation of the walls and the roof were inferred from the remains of the building that had been preserved and taking into account other parallels found. Through the infographic software, the bidimensional shapes were created following the Z parameters according to the archaeologists' hypotheses. In the case of archaeological artifacts, 2D drawings of contour attributes are very usual, while 3D volume with its physical properties may be regained from such a contour by extrusion and lathing. Steckner (*this volume*) explains how to use extruded surfaces and revolution geometry (lathing) to model ancient pottery

These simple methods can also be used for modelling archaeological stratigraphies. Archaeologists have always processed stratigraphic ordering by using bi-dimensional matrices. However, stratigraphy is an intrinsically 3D information. In the Klinglberg-St. Veit Early Bronze Age site excavation, for instance, archaeologists only had plan records of the cuts of archaeological features, the digitized outlines of the cuts were extruded to form solid prisms. Slices were then cut away from the sides (or from the top) of the modelled excavation to reveal the internal details of the trench. By such means archaeologists were able to determine whether there are any visual correlations between the distribution of objects in the features and in the overlying layers (Reilly and Shennan 1989). Beex (1993) has used an alternative approach for a 3D display of artefact concentrations. His idea was to combine all graphical information collected on an excavation into a 3D model of the excavated trenches. It meant that two-dimensional drawings (each separated layer) should be transposed on a three-dimensional surface. Having a geometrical model of the levels and the cross-sections drawn on their original place, it was quite easy to combine these elements into one image. To improve visibility the trench surface was shown without grid lines, and the cross-sections were placed against a plate. In using hidden lines and CAD-layers any viewpoint of a trench at a certain level could be provided (see also Lukesh 1996).

SHAPE FROM SHADING

The approach tries to compute depth based on the grey-level variations of any intensity image if the position of the light source is known (Horn and Brooks 1989, Sonka et al. 1994, Zhang et al. 1999). Detected shadows give a clear orientation of their neighbouring surfaces, and allow depth to be deduced. Here, the computer uses information of an object and its lighting environment (kind of light source, kind of reflective surface, location and quantity of light sources, etc.) to define an association between a tridimensional shape and the parameters of the light environment (Forte and Guidazzoli 1996b). The method has been mostly used to derive Digital Elevation Models from satellite imagery.

More complex is the possibility to achieve depth information by projecting a predefined light pattern onto the surface of the object. The range information is computed from the distortion of the light pattern seen from the camera. The image from the camera consists of a profile line that has information about the position of the surface points observed, if the illumination and scene geometry is known. With the help of the distance between the line observed and the calibrated line one can determine the position of the surface points in the 3D space. Projecting a number of light patterns (lines), the results are serial cross-sections through the object. With the help of these profile sections, a 3D model of the object can be generated. One way to construct the model is to stack up all calculated serial cross-sections at different points along a line and to colour each cross-section with different lightness. Sablatnig and Menard (1996, see also Menard and Sablatnig 1996) have used this method to compute 3D models of pottery sherds. This approach has been used also by Baribeau et al. (1996) for automated replication of museum objects.

SHAPE FROM TEXTURE

Attempts to recapture some 3D information can also be based on the texture gradient—that is, the direction of maximum rate of change of the perceived size of the texture elements, and a scalar measurement of this rate (Sonka et al. 1994). This texture gradient describes the modification of the density and the size of texture elements and so the surface orientation can be determined. From the distortion of the texture the angle to the image plane can be computed. If the texture is not distorted, then the image and the object plane are parallel.

De Nicola et al. (*this volume*) offer an application of this technique. They have used the Heightfields function in the POV-RAY software package. A *heightfield* is an object that has a surface determined by the colour value or palette index number of a graphic image file, designed for that purpose. The maximum height is the one which corresponds to the maximum possible colour or palette index value in the image file. The resolution of the heightfield is influenced by two factors: the resolution of the image and the resolution of the colour/index values. The image size determines the resolution in the X and Z directions. The resolution along the Y direction is determined by colour/index value. Pollefeys et al. (*this volume*) present a different approach. Here a single-shot range sensor pattern is projected with a standard slide projector onto an object. A single image of the illuminated object is then sufficient to obtain a very accurate textured 3D reconstruction of that object. This technique was used to generate models of statues and masks found at Sagalassos. Starting from an image that contains the projected grid, the first step consists of extracting horizontal and vertical lines. From this, an initial grid is constructed. In general this grid still contains some inconsistencies. These are detected and corrected; then the grid is refined to obtain subpixel accuracy. From the deformation of this final grid the shape is computed. At the same time the lines are filtered away to obtain the texture.

This technique can be used to develop a 3D map of the ground surface from radar altimetry data, calculating perspective views using raycasting techniques (DeJong 1994). Alternatively, in underwater archaeology, bathymetric data serve as input to a visualization software, which can be used to obtain 3D perspectives of underwater objects (Blake 1993, Rosenblum and Kamgar-Parsi 1994, Fry 1998, Chapman et al. 1999). Stewart (1991) used a probabilistic model of sonar returns to form a 3D image of the USS Monitor which sank in a storm during the American Civil War in 1862. In this approach, the conical probability distribution is determined for the sonar's beam pattern and angular measurement. Position error and ranging uncertainty further smear the sensing envelopes. Here, a single *ping* is taken to define a region that cannot be precisely determined but can be probabilistically represented using a colour scan whereby warm colours give probability values increasing close to unity.

SHAPE FROM STEREO

The stereo analysis method is similar to the human visual system. Because of the way our eyes are positioned and controlled, our brain usually receive similar images of a scene taken from nearby points of the same horizontal level. Therefore the relative position of the images of an object will differ in the two eyes. Our brains are capable of measuring this disparity and thus estimating the depth. Stereo analysis tries to imitate this principle: we might hope that a 3D scene, if presenting two different views, might permit the recapture of depth information when the information therein is combined with some knowledge of the sensor geometry (eye location). Images that are relatively widely separated are taken, and correspondences between visible features made (Marr 1982, Sonka et al. 1994).

Photogrammetry is one of the most used "shape from stereo" methods. It has been mostly used for the automatic calculation of data inputs for geometric models. When acquiring 3D models of ancient buildings and monuments, the major standing elevations are photographed stereoscopically in black-and-white using a metric camera at a distance of no greater than 10 metres from each wall face. A minimum of three targeted points per stereoscopic model should be surveyed by trigonometric intersection. Both the stereo photography and instrument survey should provide data commensurate with a 1:20 plotting scale, the resulting elevation drawings delineating all visible architectural and stone detail. The return walls at each end of the internal elevations are depicted as vertical cross-sections, and consist of a line defining the principal wall plane, including sections through adjacent openings and voids which broke the wall plane (Binney et al. 1993, Braun et al., 1995, Gisiger et al. 1996, Hsia and Newton 1999, Burton et al. 1999).

In the case of aerial photogrammetry, the computer georeferences two or more consecutive pictures. A series of points are then given common to consecutive pictures, with their respective co-ordinates, so we can get absolute orientation. What is really achieved is that each pixel of the image has its corresponding co-ordinate in the real terrain, and viceversa (Astorqui 1999). A related, but somewhat different approach involves a combination of 2D detection and 3D height extraction. A ground plan is decomposed into 2D rectangles. Each rectangle defines the base of one building primitive. Position, orientation and horizontal extension of each cuboid are already defined by the parameters of the rectangle. In the case of the automatic construction of building models, the remaining unknown parameters are the height of the cuboid, the roof type and the roof slopes. These parameters are estimated by fitting the building primitives to a Digital Surface Model, that is a height model acquired by airborne laser altimeters (Kim and Muller 1998, Hoala and Brenner 1999).

Feihl (*this volume*) offers a good art historical example of photogrammetric data acquisition. In the example presented here, the church of Saint-François, [Switzerland] built in the second half of the thirteenth century, the external photogrammetric pairs were taken from a gondola hanging at the end of a 60 meter arm fixed on a truck; in other cases a helicopter is required for taking the oblique shots necessary for the definition of geometry in plan as well as in elevation. The slides were taken with a Leica R4 S Elcovision metric chamber and a Pentax 6/7 Elcovision. Gillings (*this volume*) gives an account of the commercial software PhotoModeler (EOS Systems Inc.), and how it can be used for acquisition of archaeological geometric data. It creates fully three-dimensional models on the basis of shared points that can be identified in multiple photographs taken of a single object from a variety of different viewing angles.

Menard and Sablatnig have used a similar approach for building geometric models of pottery sherds. Two fixed CCD cameras are used to get intensity images from two different positions. Position parameters are known (distance between the two cameras, the distance between object and the image plane, the focus of the lenses and the resolution of the CCD-Cameras). Then, for a given point in the left image a corresponding point in the right image can be found, and the three-dimensional position can be computed with the additional information about the camera parameters (Sablatnig and Menard 1996, Menard and Sablatnig 1996).

SHAPE FROM MOTION

The relative movement of objects in view, their translation and rotation relative to the observer, and the motion of the observer relative to other static and moving objects all provide very strong clues to shape and depth (Sonka et al. 1994). The extraction of 3D information from moving scenes can be done as a two-phase process: preliminary processing operates on pixel arrays to make correspondences, or calculate the nature of flow, while the shape extraction follows a separate higher level process.

Kampffmeyer developed the ARCOS system for the automatic drawing and simulation of form of pottery vases from video capturing of geometric data from sherds. Ceramic sherds are placed on a rotation plate, recorded by a video camera, then interactively processed and measured, and finally drawn automatically. A computer program extracts the contour of the sherd from the intensity image. The rotation of the sherd determined the shape of the original pot. The shortcoming of this approach is that small inaccuracies in the positioning of the sherd on the rotation plate could therefore cause enormous mistakes in the reconstructed pot (Kampffmeyer et al. 1987). Development of this system was stopped, because of the bad results of the prototype. However, current technology would have contributed to a better implementation (Rowner 1993, Menard and Sablatnig 1996).

Forte and Guidazzoli (1996b) have begun some investigations for the archaeological use of this approach. They use a temporal sequence of frame images (a video movie) of static objects. Those objects (archaeological artefacts, ancient buildings or monuments) have the illusion of being in motion, because of the movement of the camera. Using the pattern of temporal changes in image grey levels or colours, they obtain the tridimensional characteristics (shape) of video captured objects. The third dimension is reconstructed following the temporal sequence of parametric points in the static images.

Pollefeys et al (*this volume*) also present an example of shape from motion. Using nothing other than the images, a textured 3D reconstruction of the recorded scene is obtained in an automated way. The sequence can be taken with a simple hand-held video or still camera. The camera need not be calibrated, and zoom and focus can be used freely. The motion is unconstrained and the system does not make use of any reference points. In addition the method is just as easy to use for small objects as for complete sites. The method therefore offers a lot of flexibility and is easy to use. The authors have obtained a global reconstruction of the whole site of Sagalassos (Turkey), and also of separate monuments.

3D SCANNING

The first 3D scanner machines are being commercialized these days. There are many different mechanisms, but most of them are based on a laser beam triangulation. A stripe of light is emitted onto the scanning surface, then is viewed simultaneously from two locations using an arrangement of mirrors. Viewed from an angle, the laser stripe appears deformed by the object's shape. These deformations are recorded by a CCD sensor and are digitized. The cameras positioned within each of four scanning heads record this surface information as the heads traverse the length of the scanning volume (top to bottom). The separate data files from each scanning head are then combined by software. Using angles and distances between laser, object and detector, the *x, y,*and *z* co-ordinates of each point in the object can be computed in a trigonometric fashion (Bajaj et al. 1995, Wholers 1995, Paquette 1996, Borghese et al., 1998, Petrov et al., 1998).

A good example is the VI-700 digitizing camera system by MINOLTA. Using a quintuple zoom lens and laser beam, it the converts objects into three-dimensional co-ordinate data for input into a computer (http://www.minolta.com/japan/rio/vivid/index.html). 3D data can be acquired in the same way as photographing an object. In addition, zoom and autofocus functions can be used to define the target object and eliminate unwanted objects, such as backgrounds. The functions enable a user to select specific points on the target object to be viewed, modified, modelled, or scaled with ease. MINOLTA's VI-700 segments an object into 200 vertical and 200 horizontal lattices, and into a 400x400 point colour image, detected on 3D co-ordinates in only 0.6 seconds. It uses the light-stripe method to emit a horizontal stripe light through a cylindrical lens to the object. After 1-frame CCD exposure, among the signal charges transferred to the memory only those of the reflected light from the object surface are extracted by block readout whilst the other signal charges are drained at once. The stripe light is scanned on the CCD image plane at one horizontal line per frame and the CCD is driven so that the block readout start position is shifted one line per frame, to acquire a total of approximately 250 frames of the image. The output signal from the CCD is then sent to the analogue processing portion, where it is amplified and subjected to waveform processing. It is then converted into a digital signal (i.e., image data), which and is then converted by triangulation into distance information. This process is repeated by scanning the stripe light vertically on the object surface using a galvano mirror, to obtain a 3-D image data of the object.

These systems are now beginning to be used in archaeology. Zheng (1999) is one of the very first examples. Here, a specifically built 3D scanner has been built to capture both texture and 3D information from ancient sculptures, the Xian Terra-cotta Soldiers, from ancient China.

Computer Tomography Techniques have been used as 3D scanners for medical imaging and in other disciplines. Very few archaeological uses of these automatic 3D model-builders exist, but Attardi et al. (*this volume*) show that they can be used for research on mummies and other types of human-body reconstruction (see also Hughes 1996). The principle underlying the application of this technology is that similar materials have the same radio-opacity and are, consequently, represented in a CT scan by the same densitometric level. In CT slices, the intensity associated with each pixel in the grey scale is proportional to tissue density: black corresponds to air, white to bones. It is therefore possible to process the CT scans sequence so as to obtain a 3D grid, where to each "knot" (control point) is associated with the densitometric value measured by the CT scans. The result is a 3D 256-grey-levels image.

REPRESENTATION METHODS: POLYGON-MODELLING

The easiest way to create a 3D geometric model is by using a wireframe or polygonal scheme. A wireframe model is composed of lines and curves defining the edges of an object, and it is usually constructed interactively. Each line or curve element is separately and independently constructed based on original 3D point co-ordinates. A polygon mesh is a set of connected polygonally bounded planar surfaces. It is represented as a collection of edges, vertices and polygons connected in such a way that each edge is shared by at most two polygons. An edge connects two vertices, and a polygon is a closed sequence of edges (Foley et al. 1996).

The easiest way to create a polygon mesh is by computing an optimised *triangulated network* (TIN) that connects the *x,y,z,* co-ordinate locations of the known observation points. A primary advantage of the TIN approach is that the observed 3D locations of the points are honoured, and neither smoothing nor interpolation is necessary. The resulting surface always includes the observed points. Another advantage is that the observed density of information is maintained; small triangles occur where the point density is high, and correspondingly large triangles occur where the density is low. The final advantage concerns its ability to represent discontinuity in the extent of a surface. There is no necessity for a surface to be continuous throughout the modelling region. The most commonly applied algorithm is Delaunay tessellation. It results in the optimum triangle set, with triangles that are as well-ordered as possible in terms of their equilateralness. The triangles are generated on the basis of the *x,y* locations of the points. The local *z* co-ordinates provide the topological relief. This means that generation and manipulation of TINs must be performed relative to a local reference plane that is approximately parallel to the surfaces considered. (Tsai 1993, Houlding 1994, Margaliot & Gotsman 1995).

In polygon modelling, the obvious errors in the representation of non-planar surfaces can be made arbitrarily small by using more and more polygons to create a better piecewise linear approximation to a real (non-planar) surface. Fractal geometry (Novak 1994) can be used to enhance this procedure. A *fractal* is a geometrically complex object, the complexity of which arises through the repetition of form over some range of scale, that is, just keep repeating the same thing over and over, at different positions (Ebert et al. 1994). For instance, a Digital Elevation Model of a mountain can be initiated with a single triangle positioned in real three dimensional space. The midpoint of each edge of the triangle is contacted to the other midpoints dividing the original triangle into four triangles, The midpoints are then deflected upward or downward (according to real *x,y,z* co-ordinates) to give volume to the form. This process is repeated with the midpoints of the new triangles, so that in the third step we have 16 triangles. The process can be repeated recursively, as many times as one likes, to produce an increasingly detailed mountain that will be made of smaller and smaller triangles. The idea is to let the computer create much of the detail in response to a general instruction in which the basic parameters of an object are described. Such techniques are called "procedural" because the computer produces the detailed geometry of the object by following programmed procedures (Friedhoff and Benzon 1989). This approach can be useful in recursive objects, like a tree, where the same procedure that produce the trunk and first branching structure is employed again to produce successive branches. The branching angle, the length, radius and taper of a branch and number of branches can be randomly determined from certain parameters.

Triangulation methods to create a model of landscape are used by Gillings (*this volume*), Goodrick and Harding (*this volume*), Ruiz Rodriguez et al. (*this volume*), and Martens et al. (*this volume*). Holloway (*this volume*) applies the procedure to the modelling of ancient buildings, and Brogni et al. (*this volume*) explain a detailed example about how to create a geometric model of an artefact using these techniques: they built many circles, on different heights, with different radii, following the geometric data from ancient pictures of the object (an Egyptian flute), then they linked them together with only one surface; as a result, they obtained a strange cylinder, unsymmetrical and irregular, like in the real flute. All the other parts are built like revolution solids, from convenient curves, and fitted together to look like a single object.

REPRESENTATION METHODS: PARAMETRIC MODELLING

Instead of using polygons to approximate surfaces, some algorithms provide ways in which the surface can be mathematically approximated; the approximation becomes greater as the surface becomes more complicated. The general idea is to *interpolate* a given set of points, which means that the curve produced passes exactly through the points. Many methods exist for interpolating 3D co-ordinates to form continuous surfaces. One way to interpolate surface is by parametric polynomial surfaces, which define points on a 3D curve by using three polynomials in a parameter t, one for each of x, y and z. The coefficients of the polynomials are selected such that the surface follows the desired path. Although various degrees of polynomials can be used, the most usual are cubic polynomials.

The *bezier form* of the cubic polynomial surface segment indirectly specifies the endpoint tangent vector by specifying two intermediate points that are not on the interpolated surface. The surface interpolates the two end control points and approximates the other two. The surface is contained in the *convex hull* of the four control points. *B-splines* are a generalisation of bezier surfaces. They consist of surface segments whose polynomial coefficients depend on just a few control points (*local control*) . Thus moving a control point affects only a small part of a surface. A surface segment need not pass through its control points, and the two continuity conditions on a segment come from the adjacent segments. *Uniform B-splines* (URBS) means that control points for each segment are spaced at equal intervals. is an example of interpolated spline surface. The points are interpolated by the spline, which passes through each point in a direction parallel to the line between the adjacent points. The straight line segments indicate these directions. *Non-uniform B-splines* (NURBS) permit unequal spacing between control points for each segment (Mortensen 1985, Park and Kim 1995, Foley et al. 1996, Hoffman and Rossignac 1996, Daniel 1997, Ishida 1997, Piegl and Tiller 1999).

Parametric surface modelling has been used in archaeology for building geometric models of artefacts. It only requires sampling a series of points along the contour (landmarks or profile discontinuities), and then interpolating a polynomial cubic function. The resulting curve is then processed using *lathing* to obtain the final 3D modelling. Steckner (*this volume*, 1996) uses bezier surfaces to build a model of ancient pottery. Other approaches, using different algorithms, to surface interpolation for pottery reconstruction, are those by Smith (1983) and Juhl (1995), using polynomial functions, Hall and Laflin (1984) using B-Spline. Main (1988) adopted tangential profiles, other authors (Lewin and Goodson 1990, Durham, Lewis and Shennan 1993) have opted for generalised Hough transforms. Meucci and Buzzanca (1996) have used NURBS interpolated surfaces to create a geometric model of a Medieval ship. See other relevant applications in Attardi et al. (*this volume*), Gurri and Gurri (*this volume*), Feihl (*this volume)*.

Parametric surface modelling is also the most usual technique for landscape representation. It has been used in this way by Ruiz Rodriguez et al.*(this volume*), among others. Input information is usually presented as an unstructured cloud of *x,y,z* points, and the geometric model is computed as an interpolated surface (Lancaster and Salkauskas 1986, Kvamme 1991, Haigh 1992, Wood 1994, Hsia and Newton 1999). An example of surface interpolation in 3D archaeological visualisation is the Iron Age Danebury site model (Earl 1999). The surfaces themselves were defined by constructing regular rectangular meshes which corresponded to the measurements available. Points within these were then used to define extrapolated surfaces via the AutoCAD edgesurf and rulesurf commands. Different parameters for these commands were compared for particular modelled areas. This identified considerable variation in the final modelled surfaces, dependent upon choices such as the number of ruled lines, which filtered through to the appreciation of the spaces produced in the final analyses. Without this comparison conclusions produced would have seemed far more robust.

Remote Sensing data visualisation is also a good candidate for parametric modelling, because a smoothed surface can be interpolated on the data obtained by geophysical survey. Houlding (1994) reports how to use 3D models for analysing bedrock profiles (geophysically determined) incorporating other geological or archaeological characteristics. Main et al. (1994) have reconstructed pits and trenches detected on the stratigraphic sequence of the prehistoric site at Runnymede Bridge using bicubic interpolated surfaces. This was done by taking each set of four adjacent survey points and generating a surface patch which interpolated the points. Where only three adjacent points exist, a triangular polyface mesh is generated instead. This routine models cut features (typically post-holes or pits) using measurements of position and size, and helps in the visual interpretation by relating the shape and volume of post-holes with their 3D spatial distribution. Bradley and Fletcher (1996) uses an interpolated activity map to visualise the results of ground penetrating radar surveys. In this application, Stapeley Hill, a Bronze age ring cairn is visualised without any excavation. The vertical heights are exaggerated by a factor of three to emphasise features. As a result, the authors have detected the edge of a wide ridge in the foreground of the image caused by the remains of an ancient field wall, and behind it the obvious ring structure with a small central mound. The interpolated surface reveals a rough shaped area of enhanced radar activity (top centre of image) with an irregular central figure. A further area of high activity lies at the bottom right of the image and is probably associated with field wall remains.

The same approach has been developed by other authors. Fletcher and Spicer (1988, 1992) have even created a “virtual” geophysical model by interpolating a parametric surface to simulated geomagnetic data. Eder-Hinterleitner et al. (1996, see also Neubauer et al. 1996) have developed this approach, showing how archaeological structures (ditches) can be reconstructed by a 3D visualization of magnetic anomalies measured in a magnetic prospecting at the Neolithic enclosure of Puch (Austria). The reconstruction starts with a classification of the pre-processed data. The classification is based on the probability for each data value that does not originate from the expected archaeological structure. Then, by using the data and the classification, the expected archaeological structures are reconstructed. No assumptions about the position and shape of the expected archaeological structure are made, except that the result has to be *smooth.* This preliminary free reconstruction is used to determine the nearly exact horizontal positions and a rough estimation of the depth of the expected structures. The detected structures and a modelling of the shape of the expected structures are used to reconstruct the exact position, depth and shape.

Parametric modelling can also be one of the most useful techniques for studying the dynamics of interaction between site formation and topography. Reeler (1999) has shown how terraces, for instance, are constructed along the slopes in order to maximize flat areas for habitation and other activities and also in order to steep the slopes approaching the flat areas. The terraces show up as flattened areas within the interpolated 3D model. The relationship between the terraces and the landform can be examined and the internal arrangement of terraces assessed. The degree of preservation of the terraces is also evident to some degree in the clarity with which these features are defined, although of course the resolution of the survey data is an important influence. The sharpness of all the features in the site can be assessed as long as there is some control over survey resolution. Modelling of the sites in three dimensions can also help to determine how the terrain was modified in order for the terrace to be constructed. There are two main ways in which terraces might have been constructed. They were either cut back into the slope and the soil removed was discarded or reused elsewhere, or they were cut partway into the slope and the soil removed was used to steep the front edge of the terrace. The latter type was partly cut back into the slope and partly built out from the slope. Increasing the steepness of the front edge of the terrace has defensive advantages. It is possible that one method was used for some terraces on a site, and the other method was used for other terraces on the same site. It may be possible to suggest which method of manufacture was used for terraces from the 3D models produced in the computer.

REPRESENTATION METHODS: SOLID MODELLING

Just as a set of 2D lines and curves does not need to describe the boundary of a closed area, a collection of 3D planes and surfaces does not necessarily bound a closed volume. In Archaeology, however, it is important to distinguish between the inside, outside and surface of a 3D object and to be able to compute properties of the object that depend on this distinction. By “solid modelling” meant the representation of volumes completely surrounded by surfaces (Foley et al. 1996). Parametric surfaces and polygon representation discussed in the previous section are also used as low-level geometric components for solid models. Strictly speaking, most are actually "surface models" formed from polygon meshes. "Solid model" really should only be used to describe those that are composed of solid primitives (cube, sphere, torus, cylinder, cone, etc.) and composed using "Constructive Solid Geometry". However this is probably less important than it used to be a few years ago when software either handled one or the other. Nowadays, most of the surface (polygon) rendering software has the capability to do CSG operations such as solid union, intersection and difference, and most CSG systems also handle polygon meshes. See Brogni et al. (*this volume*), and Holloway *(this volume*) for applications of hybrid models, where surfaces and polygons are integrated into a solid model of closed surfaces.

Boundary representation

B-rep models represent solids with boundary faces. They can be described conceptually as a triple (Sonka et al. 1994):

- a set of surfaces of the object
- a set of space curves representing intersections between surfaces
- a graph describing the surface connectivity

Unlike parametric models, b-rep software holds information about the inside of faces as well as the outside. B-rep models achieve topological consistency, although they do not ensure geometrical consistency (e.g. it is possible for a concavity in an object to protrude through the opposite side of the polyhedron). The *boundary* of a closed set of points is the set of its boundary points, whereas the *interior* consists of all of the set's other points. Shape is represented as polyhedral whose faces can be replaced by B-spline or bezier surfaces, i.e., the surfaces are coded by their vertices, edges and faces.

A simple enumeration of the solid's faces (i.e. of its boundary) suffices to distinguish the solid unambiguously from its unbounded complement. Most boundary models, however, store additional connectivity information between the geometric boundary elements (vertices, edges and faces). Objects represented by their topological boundaries. A solid's boundary is the set of its bounding faces, with each face represented by the surface in which it lies and by its bounding edges. The nature of the bounding faces is not restricted to polygons, but extends to trimmed NURBS, quadrics, and other forms. Different applications deal with different geometric entities: solids are used for modelling mechanical components; faces and curves may represent construction regions of contacts between solids; interior faces decompose solids into simpler elements for analysis or into subsets exhibiting different physical properties; internal cracks or missing boundary portions capture information about domain singularities (Rossignac 1994).

Constructive solid geometry

It consists in building objects by using solid primitives (e.g. sphere, box, cone) and Boolean operators. Each primitive represents a real volume. It means that a CSG modeller can determine whether a point is outside or inside a solid object and combine them to create complex shapes. The model is stored as a tree, with leaf models representing the primitive solid, and edges enforcing precedence among the set theoretical operations. To determine physical properties or to make pictures, we must be able to combine the properties of the leaves to obtain the properties of the roots. CSG models often have a hierarchical structure induced by a bottom-up construction process: components are used as building blocks to create higher-level entities, which in turn serve as building blocks for yet higher-level entities, and so on. To simplify the task of building complex objects (and their models), application-specific atomic components can be used as the basic building blocks. In 2D, these components are usually computer-drawn templates of standard symbolic shapes, which in turn are composed of geometric primitives, such as lines, rectangles, polygons, ellipses, arcs and so on. In 3D, shapes such as cylinders, parallelepipeds, spheres, pyramids, and surfaces of revolution are used as basic building blocks. These 3D shapes may be defined in terms of lower level geometric primitives, such as 3D polygons.

By storing a recipe (process) for creating a model from primitive entities and operations, constructive representations capture much of the designer's intent. In this way, common features, such as walls, doorways and columns can be stored as basic objects in libraries of primitive forms for future use. These would take the form of fully defined volumes that could then be adapted to the subject being modelled. An object, once defined as a basic shape, can be copied and modified later. Starting with a basic object, such as a column, it is easy to then change it to include the appropriate base and capital, material, paint colour, fluting, etc. A combination of methods is chosen to create the initial shapes, Boolean operations can then be used to fine-tune the result. Once the basic building blocks have been created it is a fairly simple matter to copy and then position them (see Drew et al. 1990, Chapman 1991, Cornforth et al. 1991, Kemp 1993, Ozawa 1996, Bloomfield and Schofield 1996, Lloret 1999). Holloway (*this volume*), Feihl (*this volume*) and Louhivuori et al. (*this volume*) show examples of this approach. In the latter paper, the basic types of objects created in the 2D and 3D libraries are floors, roofs, walls, doors, windows and lamps. The more refined definitions are like "the still existing blocks of Triapsis", "Nile mosaic", "Corinthian capital of type x", "Solidus of Constantin II", or "Early Islamic oil lamp". All factors can be selected freely in groups or one by one and be seen in almost any imaginable combinations. All features needed are picked up from the libraries and all the other features are hidden. Then the result is lit as required, and shown in 1D, 2D, 3D or 4D, in alphanumeric lists, sections, plans, facades, perspectives and axonometries, virtual models or animations.

In the Furness Abbey 3D computer model it was decided to model the nave and aisles of the church stone-by-stone. To make the piers, for example, one stone was created and then copied and positioned until there were sufficient stones to form the first course around the pier. The course was then copied and the second positioned above it. Once the whole column was complete, it too was copied and the piers positioned to form one side of the nave arcade. The piers of the opposite nave arcade were simply generated by mirror copying of the first arcade (recursive procedural graphics programming) (Delooze and Wood 1990, Wood and Chapman 1992).

In the case of Rievaulx Abbey, the building was initially divided into three-dimensional blocks. Elements which belonged together were grouped on the same layer. Ready-made building blocks (sphere, cube, torus, wedge, cylinder) with user-specified dimensions were used, together with user-defined solids of revolution and solids of extrusion. A combination of methods is chosen to create the initial shapes, Boolean operations can then be used to fine-tune the result. The most complicated modelling tasks were presented by the cross-vaulted ceilings. For the aisles, a shape made by intersecting two cylinders was subtracted twice from a rectangular block (Kemp 1993).

The same approach can be used to decompose a site formation process, where each layer or cut feature is also a component in a CSG model. Grafland is a simulated excavation consisting of a series of layers with various features cut into them (Reilly 1990, 1992). The layers were manufactured by creating hypothetical profiles, which were then digitized. This is equivalent to surveying along a transect. The layer is defined initially as that volume between the measured surface and an arbitrary datum plane at some depth below. The top of the layer(s) immediately underneath from the bottom of the previous layer define its other side. Layers can be isolated using CSG operators. Most of the cut features in the Grafland model are composed of compound CSG shapes, such as cylinders and spheres or parts thereof. However, some of the contexts have been modelled as if a real irregularly shaped feature had been found with artefacts deposited. The model can be linked, therefore, to a Harris Matrix or phasing program, so that context sequences and connectivity can be studied. It becomes possible to devise different exploration scenarios to see how far they can facilitate a reconstruction of the site, the activities on the site and post-depositional process operating at the site. An animation sequence can be generated to illustrate the composition of the model excavation.

REPRESENTATION METHODS: VOLUME MODELLING

Spatial subdivision models decompose the solid into cells, each with a simple topological structure and also often a simple geometric structure. Cell decomposition differs from CSG models in that it is possible to compose more complex objects from simple, primitive ones in a bottom-up fashion by 'gluing' them together. The *glue* operation can be thought of as a restricted form of union in which the objects must not intersect (Foley et al. 1996, Hoffmann and Rossignac 1996). *Spatial-occupancy enumeration* is a special case of cell decomposition in which the solid is decomposed into identical cells arranged in a fixed, regular grid. To represent an object, we need only to decide which cells are occupied and which are not. It is easy to find out whether a cell is inside or outside of the solid, and to determine whether two objects are adjacent. These cells are often called *voxels* (volume elements), in analogy to pixels. Each voxel has values associated with it, which represents some measurable properties or independent variables (e.g. colour, density, opacity, material, coverage). A geometric model is "voxelized" into a set of voxels that best approximate the volumetric input data. A voxel model represents the scene as a set of geometric primitives, but instead of a list of geometric objects, all objects are converted into a uniform meta-object, the voxel. Each voxel is atomic and represents the information about, at most, one object that resides in that voxel. (Kaufman 1990, 1994). For all of its advantages, however, volume modelling has a number of obvious fallings that parallel those representing a 2D shape by 1 bit-deep bitmap.

Volumetric modelling has been used to model geological subsurface data (Houlding 1994, Harris and Lock 1996), and therefore can be used also for modelling archaeological stratigraphic sequences. Houlding (1994) has shown how 2D sections of stratigraphic sequence can be converted into a volumetric model of layers. This includes determination of the volume of any irregular shape, or the volume of its intersection with another irregular shape, or the intersection of an isosurface (three-dimensional contour) of a variable value, or the intersection of an isosurface with an irregular shape, as well as the ability to analyse the contents of any volume or intersection in terms of the volume data structure. The primary objective of this archaeological volume modelling is to provide a means of qualifying subsurface space by assigning characteristic values to discrete, irregular archaeological volumes. However, it should also provide an avenue for interactively imposing control on the characterization process. A complete archeo-stratigraphical characterization may require several archaeological volumes (or models), each consisting of tens of thousands of these volume elements, called components. Archaeological deposits are mostly continuous volumes of material deposited as sediments. Discontinuities, the so-called stratigraphic interfaces, reflect a change in the rate of deposition or the nature of the material being deposited. Alternatively, some intervening event has removed or modified material before the next stage of deposition continues. Between the "changes" are volumes of largely homogenous material. A visualization model might be one that captured the fuzziness of the breaks and changes (in 3D) which characterise many archaeological deposits, but which also allowed the investigator to annotate the data and overlay interpretations concerning the whereabouts of interfaces for instance.

An example of volumetric modelling using *voxels* is presented in Pope and Chalmers (*this volume*). Reilly and Thompson (1992) give another one using data from the Potterne excavation in Wiltshire (UK). The point measurements were transformed into a 3D grid of cells by centring colour-coded translucent cubes over the sample locations. They used voxel replication rather than interpolation to enlarge the representation for viewing.. "Soil type" was displayed in this fashion. With low opacity, one notices several cloudy *layers* extending across regions (but not all) of the viewed data. Harris and Lock (1996) also report the use of volumetric modelling for the study of stratigraphic sequence. Data input comprises *x,y,z* co-ordinates and property values. This varied according to the subject matter as to whether co-ordinates defined leading vertices along horizontal or vertical profiles of an object or were randomly distributed. Minimum tension modelling was used to calculate a three-dimensional grid which formed the basis from which to define specific volumes or solids. In a number of instances the model was constrained in *x,y* or *z* so that the polygonal solid matched the boundaries of predefined stratigraphic units. In this way the boundaries of certain units could be delimited where applicable by curtailing the influence of data values in adjacent layers or volumes. The system, though simple in appearance, conceals numerous complexities in the way in which solid forms are constructed, classified, rendered and displayed.

Building Geometric Models from Simulated Data

The archaeological record is most of the times incomplete: not *all* past material things have remained until today. In addition, most of those few items from the past that we can observe today, are broken. Here, incomplete or partial inputs should be used to build a geometric model. In some cases, however, virtual archaeological models are explicitly "incomplete", because a "reconstruction" is not always necessary. Goodrick and Harding (*this volume*) and Pásztor et al. (*this volume*) show how specific calculations and analysis of a monument's social use can be done without "reconstructions". In another case, Csáki and Redó (1996) use a 3D geometrical model of a Roman villa in Central Italy to separate the architectonic components of a building partially preserved from the structures built upon it. Their purpose is not to reconstruct bad preserved information, but to analyse the temporal ordering of archaeological remains. Kotsakis et al. (1994) are also not interested in reconstructing a site, but in understanding stratigraphic and spatial relationships of preserved material. In the Bronze Age site of Toumba Thessaloniki, an unexpected discovery was a number of earthen constructions, consisting of mudbrick walls forming large boxes filled with clay. Some of these terrace-like constructions were no less than six meters wide. They were spread across the slope at different levels. Normally these features would be interpreted as successive phases of the terraces; however, there was stratigraphic evidence which indicated that at least some of the constructions lying at different levels should belong to a single complex. In order to visualize the relation of these features to each other, a geometric 3D model was constructed. To this end, real co-ordinates of the features were used and were connected according to their stratigraphic evidence producing first a ground plan and then a reconstruction in wireframe . At the lower level there is a wall supported by a line of small retaining terraces. A narrow lane climbs uphill and is flanked by a massive box-like terrace. As the excavation proceeded it became more plausible that these isolated groups actually belonged to a single complex, related stratigraphically to certain occupational phases found at the top of the tel. Here, although the geometrical model is incomplete (there is no information about the height of walls or roofing systems), it enhanced the understanding of spatial organisation and formation process of the site (Kotsakis et al. 1994).

Nevertheless, in most other cases, what we need is to create a "complete" model in order to complete damaged input data. In those circumstances, we can generate *simulated* data "to see what archaeologically cannot be seen". In previous sections, we have discussed how to create geometric models when we have enough information: by using polygons connecting points, by interpolating parametric surfaces or volumetric primitives. In those cases, the procedure is "inductive" or bottom-up: we create geometric shapes and structure by linking already existing points. When we do not have enough points, we should follow the opposite approach, that is, deductive or top-down: we create an hypothetical model, we fit it to the incomplete input data, and then we use the model to simulate the non-preserved data (Baur and Beer 1990). We use the term "simulation" for the process of finding the parameters necessary to infer values at other locations in a 3D surface from the relationship embedded in the data and in other information describing the data and their acquisition (Forte 1992, Guidazzoli 1992, Gottarelli 1995, Nielson 1994, Meucci & Buzzanca 1996).

It is the same procedure used by the human brain to understand incomplete sensory information. Because images are not the raw data of perception, it is theoretically possible to rebuild an altered image, using prior-knowledge in the process of image formation from the pattern of luminance contrasts observed in the empirical world. The fragmented spatial information available must be extrapolated to complete closed surfaces. So, the reconstruction of a given object or a given building structure as an architectural frame is a generalization of fragmented observable data by mathematical object description, representing partially the view of a lost physical world reality. The question is how to add knowledge in a systematic way. As we will see, this process is analogous to scientific explanation, and therefore, it involves *induction, deduction* and *analogy*. This means, that the simulated model will be based on one of the various rebuilding hypotheses described by archaeologists. One of the advantages of virtual reality is the possibility of being able to show many alternative hypotheses therefore making it possible for experts to check their theories and share doubts as well as uncertainties, distinguishing the certain elements from the hypothetical ones.

The easiest approach is by simply adding fragmented input data (Sanders, *this volume*). Kalvin et al. (1999) give another good example, the restoration of a disintegrated ceiling of a building. Within that building, archaeologists have recovered about 3600 pieces, some of them big (10 x 15 cm), some others as small as a thumb-nail. The ceiling pieces were digitized, and the process of restoration was taken over looking for candidate matches between pieces using a "what-if" spreadsheet type of approach. To select a set of pieces for a candidate match the user makes a request such as: "Find all pieces that have the colours red, blue and black, have fragmentary details of a fox and a snake, have a rough texture and were repainted". Once a set of pieces has been selected, they are manipulated on-screen to align them correctly. The orientation and thickness of the cane markings are used at this stage to guide and confirm possible alignments. Higgins introduced a somewhat different approach, by taking some preserved elements and replicating them either deterministically or randomly according to some placement rules. This method has been used to reconstruct badly preserved Aztec mosaics (Higgins 1996). There are many other examples of "reconstruction by means of simple sum of pieces" (see Gottarelli 1996, among others).

Houlding (1994) shows how to create a 3D volumetric model of geological data, using as input incompletely sampled data. In this case, the user has not all relevant 3D information, but a series of 2D sections, irregularly sampled over a 2D area. The purpose is to generalize sampled data into an homogenous 3D model. The first step is to extend the 2D sections normally, so that different samples meet at common planes. This is achieved by assigning fore- and back-thickness to the volume data component. A boundary matching algorithm can be applied so that the pairs of boundaries are modified and matched on the common planes to provide a continuous three dimensional interpretation of the stratigraphic unit (archaeological depositional unit). This is equivalent to a linear interpolation of the boundary profiles between each pair of sections. The initial two-dimensional interpretation boundaries have been stretched and modified in the third dimension, so that they now define an irregular volume, equivalent to the volume of the geological unit between the sections (Houlding 1994: 115-119).

In those cases, however, input information was not really "incomplete". Most input information was available, but the original ordering of pieces was lost. The purpose of modelling was then to rebuild the order of input data, based on information already existing in the preserved data: the narrative (pictorial) logic of the elements represented. When input data is really very incomplete, we should fill the gaps with information that does not proceed from the data. We need to build the model first, and then use it for simulating the real object. In most cases, we create "theoretical" or "simulated" geometric models. Here "theory" means general knowledge about the most probable "shape" of the object to be simulated or prior archaeological knowledge of the archaeological reality to be simulated. This is a classic syllogism:

IF	b (X,Y,Z)	FITS MODEL A
THEN	b (SHAPE)	DERIVES FROM MODEL A

The procedure may be illustrated by the mathematical ovoid and the eggshell compared. The eggshell is a solid formed by a fine closed surface. Continuity and dynamics are bound to the shape of the eggshell, in such a way that it is possible to locate the fragments of a broken eggshell as well as to define the whole by only very few spatial measurements. Evidently, to model the physics of an eggshell, it is sufficient to pick from the fragments of a broken eggshell some spatial world data to simulate the entire eggshell. The spatial continuity and dynamics of the ovoid is included in the mathematical description, to simulate the missing information. The algorithm for the mathematical ovoid serves as a generalized constructive solid geometry, and just some additional information will tell the specification and the modification of the individual eggshell, its capacity and the location of the centre of gravity and the related statics. This kind of fact-based solid simulation by mathematical guidelines is including the physical measurement of a shell, just as a recursive calculation (Steckner 1993, 1996). In other words, we should create a geometric model (the mathematical ovoid) of the interpreted reality, and then use information deduced from the model to fit the partially observed reality.

The easiest reconstruction approach is then "completion". In geometric terms, the fragmented spatial information available must be extrapolated to complete closed surfaces. By definition, a solid is only a solid if its surface is completely closed. Fragmented data are represented as scattered *x,y,z* input data sampled at irregular locations. An interpolated parametric surface is represented by a grid which can be envisioned as a two orthogonal sets of parallel, equally spaced lines representing the co-ordinate system. The points where grid lines intersect are called grid nodes. Values of the surface must be known or estimated at each of these nodes using "gridding" techniques. The method begins with a rough surface interpolating only boundary points, and in successive steps, refines those points (and the resulting surface) by adding the maximum error point at a time until the desired approximation accuracy is reached. (Watson 1992, Park and Kim 1995, Algorri and Schmitt 1996, Ma and He 1998, Piegl and Tiller 1999).

An interesting new direction to computer "reconstruction" comes from the investigation of inferring 3D models from freehand sketches drawn directly on the screen of a pen-based PC. These programs transform the pen strokes as a sequence of points from which it interprets the type of shape, assuming some dependent preference function. Once the type is decided, the closest fit to the stroke is determined using different numerical techniques. The system tries to interpret certain relationships between fitted primitives (e.g. whether two curves are adjacent, or whether two adjacent lines are at a right angle). If such a relationship is found within a tolerance, the parameters of the primitives are altered to establish an exact relationship. Techniques like extrusion, profiling, or lathing can then be used to transform topological relationships between curves and lines (angles) into 3D surfaces (Eggli et al. 1996).

These approaches are only useful when "incompleteness" is more a result of bad sampling than of broken or not preserved material. Completion is then the task of surface interpolation. For instance, a wall can be reconstructed by interpolating a continuous surface which fill the gaps in preserved data. But in other cases, we do not have an irregularly sampled surface, but an interrupted surface. In those cases, we should *add* new geometrical information, instead of merely calculating missing information from nearest neighbour points. This is the situation in pottery analysis, when we try to reconstruct the shape of the vessel from the preserved sherds. Steckner (*this volume*) uses simple interpolation to solve the same problem. Here, a surface is interpolated on some points sampled along the contour of the sherd. Several measurements—like volume, width, maximal perimeter, etc—are computed from sherd data (contour). Reconstructions of pots from sherds are made by comparing the actual contour or interpolated surface with the contour lines and surfaces already computed for complete vessels. The most similar is taken for the complete reconstruction and classification (see also Steckner & Steckner 1987). A similar approach has been developed in the qualitative case by Barceló (1996b) using a fuzzy logic approach to compute the similarity between the sherd information and the complete vase already known. Generalized Hough transformation, instead of surface interpolation has been used by Lewin and Goodson (1990), and by Durham, Lewis and Shennan (1993). Rowner (1993) uses a similar approach for lithic analysis (projectile points). Alternatively, contour reconstruction can be computed from interpoint distances. Berger et al. (1999) presents an algorithm for doing this task, even when the precise location of each point is uncertain. A neural network (see Barceló 1993, 1996a) can be used also to reconstruct a surface. The Neural Network is trained using "complete surfaces" (real objects). Then, given a partially damaged input (incomplete surface), the network generates those points that were not available. An application of this approach is given in Gu and Yan 1995.

Another way of reconstructing the gaps in a surface is by deforming the parameters of a theoretical model of this surface until it fits the known data points. Since preserved data are not arbitrary, a generic model having a known shape is a logical starting point for a curve or surface fitting process. Pertinent features within the data are incorporated into the basic structure of the model. The model is then deformed to fit the unique characteristics of each data set (Dobson et al. 1995). Tsingos et al (1995) use a modification of this approach: implicit iso-surfaces generated by a *skeleton* for shape reconstruction. An initial skeleton is positioned at the centre of mass of the data points, and divided until the process reaches a correct approximation level. Local control for the reconstructed shape is possible through a local field function, which enables the definition of local energy terms associated with each skeleton. The method works as a semi-automatic process: the user can visualize the data, initially position some skeleton thanks to an interactive implicit surfaces editor, and further optimize the process by specifying several "reconstruction windows", that slightly overlap, and where surface reconstruction follows a local criterion. Thalmann et al. (1995) use a similar approach for reconstructing the Xian Terracotta Soldiers. A geometric model of these Chinese sculptures is produced through a method similar to modelling of clay, which essentially consists of adding or eliminating parts of material and turning the object around when the main shape has been set up. They use a sphere as a starting point for the heads of soldiers, and they add or remove polygons according to the details needed and apply local deformations to alter the shape. This process helps the user towards a better understanding about the final proportions of a human's head. Scaling deformations were first applied to the sphere to give an egg shape aspect, then various regions selected with triangles were moved by translation. At this point vertices were selected one by one and then lifted to the desired locations. The modelling of different regions was started, sculpting and pushing back and forth vertices and regions to make the nose, jaws, eyes and various landmarks.

Using a similar approach, Attardi et al. (*this volume)* use a distortion (warping) of the 3D model of a reference scanned head, until its hard tissues match those of the scanned data. The subsequent stage is the construction of the hybrid model composed by the hard tissues of the mummy plus the soft ones of the reference head. Another example of warping to reconstruction is Brogni et al (*this volume*).

In all these approaches, we use general models and particular constraints as mechanisms for modifying a preliminary hypothetical geometrical model into another that satisfies the constraints. Finding the geometric configurations that satisfy the constraints is the crucial issue. There are two strategies: the first strategy, referred as the "instance solver" uses specific values of the constraints and looks for geometric configurations satisfying these constraints. In the second strategy, the generic solver investigates first whether the geometric elements could be placed given the constraints independently of their values. Among the constraints, there are geometric constraints (related to shape) and feature-extrinsic constraints (Algorri and Schmitt 1996, Werghi et al., 1999). The drawbacks of this method is that it only allows reconstructing surfaces of fixed topological type, and archaeological remains are not always easily represented using parametric surfaces. When "shape" and topology are too complex, other kind of models should be used to simulate archaeological realities.

This is the case of ancient buildings. In most cases, preserved remains do not shed light on the structure of vertical walls which therefore remain unknown. Archaeological or art history background information is then needed. In the case of the model of the Roman city of Bath, for instance, it is known from fragments of roofing and ribbing found in the mud when the site was first excavated that the bath was covered by a large masonry vault. This was confirmed by the remains at ground level where the supports to the roof were strengthened to take the weight of this vault. Height of the vault was then estimated using physical principles and an optimal distribution of weight (Lavender et al. 1990). In the Dresden Frauenkirche project (Collins 1993, Collins et al. 1993), detailed architectural drawings and old photographs displaying the church in its original aspect have been preserved. When existing information was not available in the preserved input data, photographs from contemporary churches had to be used. A similar approach was used for the 3D reconstruction of Maltese burials. Chalmers and Stoddart (see Chalmers et al. 1995, Chalmers and Stoddart 1996, Chalmers et al. 1997) had a complete topographic and photogrammetric survey in which accurate watercolours of the monuments by nineteenth-century artists were stretched to fit the real data. The reconstruction of the Hadrianic Baths in Leptis Magna (Rattenburg 1991) is largely based on three types of sources: a) Pictorial evidence from plans and photographs of the building's ruins, b) Descriptive accounts by modern authors on the baths in both their existing condition and in their imagined original state, c) Evidence shown by contemporary buildings in other parts of the Roman empire which gives clues as to likely construction methods and spatial forms.

Many other examples of integrating historical information to simulate archaeological data and building "complete" models of ancient buildings appear in this volume, see the papers by Feihl, Forte and Borra, Frischer et al., Gurri and Gurri, Hixon et al., Louhivuori et al., Martens et al., Mitchell and Economou, and by Uotila and Sartes. A usual problem in all these approaches is that most photographs found in old publications and documents seem not be linkable with modern orthogonal representations. To be used in the construction of a theoretical model, they should be photogrammetrically rectified. This procedure may be supported by numerical data analysis, analyzing and recalculating the metric distances in the photographs and in the preserved archaeological remains.

When old drawings and photographs are not available, external data can be estimated from ethnographic records, as has been used by Ozawa (1992, 1996) for estimating the general shape of a building. The geometric model was based on a contour map of keyhole tomb mounds of ancient Japan. When archaeological information is not enough to produce the contour map, an expert system creates an estimated contour map of the original tomb mound in co-operation with archaeologists. The expert system holds the statistical knowledge for classifying any tomb into its likeliest type and the geometrical knowledge for drawing contour lines of the tomb mound. Shape parameters are introduced by the user for each contour map, and the system classifies the mound as one of the seven types, according to specific parameters (diameter, length, weight, height, etc.). The estimated shape layout is then used as input for the 3D solid modelling and rendering (Ozawa 1992). In the Iron Age enclosed settlement at Navan in Amagh (Northern Ireland), given a list of post-hole locations, a virtual model of the site computed the height of the posts, which would have been planted in the holes, on the basis of certain assumptions regarding a possible roof structure, and then generated the appropriate model definition statements automatically. As the heights of individual posts were under the control of the virtual model, modifications due to even minor alteration to the pitch of the roof, for instance, were straightforward to implement (Reilly 1992). In examples like this one, virtual reality models are hypothesis engines able to study how to accommodate probable shapes into the actual known parameters (see also Small 1996, Baur and Beer 1990).

Although it is not an "expert system" in the real sense of the word, the rule-based program used by N. Ryan (1996, 1997) to create a totally simulated display of a Roman temple is wholly deterministic: you give a couple of parameters and it generates large numbers of dimensions. The program uses a set of rules, derived from the writings of the 1st century AD architect Vitruvius, that define the relative proportions of the many parts of a temple. The only input required from the user is the number of columns across the front and the height of a column.

Florenzano et al. (1999) give a further advance in this artificial intelligence approach. They use an Object-Oriented Knowledge-Base containing a theoretical model of existing architecture. They have chosen classical architecture as the first field of experiment of the process. This architecture can be modelled easily enough. The proportion ratios linking the diverse parts of architectural entities to the module allows a simple description of each entity's morphology. The main hypothesis of this research is about comparing the theoretical model of the building to the incomplete input data (preserved remains) acquired by photogrammetry. Abstract models are organized with the aim of isolating elementary entities that share common morphological characteristics and function, on which rules of composition can be used to re-order the building. The concept of architectural entity gathers in a single class the architectural data describing the entity, the interface with survey mechanisms and the representation methods. Each architectural entity, each element of the predefined architectural corpus, is therefore described through geometrical primitives corresponding to its morphological characteristics: a redundant number of measurable geometrical primitives are added to each entity's definition, as previously mentioned.

1. Splitting of the object into a cloud of points measured on its surface.
2. Linking of the points to architectural entities.
3. Data processing.
4. Definition of geometrical models reconstructed on these points.
5. Definition of the architectural model, which is informed by the geometrical model.
6. Consistency-making on the whole set of entities.

Lewis and Séguin (1998) give another approach to building reconstruction. They have created the Building Model Generator (BMG) which accepts 2D floor plans in a common DXF geometry description format. The program first converts these plans into a suitable internal data structure that permits, not only efficient geometric manipulation and analysis, but also the integration of non geometrical data, as the definition and identity of all rooms, doors, windows, columns, etc. It then corrects small local geometrical inconsistencies and makes the necessary adjustments to obtain a consistent layout topology. This clean floor plan is then analysed to extract semantic information (room identities, connecting portals, the function of columns or arches, etc.). With that information the pure walls are extruded to a specified (by the user) height, and door, window and ceiling geometries are inserted where appropriate. This generates a 3D representation of the building shell, which can then be visualized, and some local adjustment on parts of the building or material properties can be made with an interactive editor.

An interesting future development is the possibility of using visualizations in a case-based reasoning framework (Foley and Ribarsky 1994). The fundamental strategy is to organize a large collection of existing visualizations as *cases* and to design new visualizations by adapting and combining the past cases. New problems in the case-based approach are solved by adapting the solutions to similar problems encountered in the past. The important issues in building a case-based visualization advisor are developing a large library of visualizations, developing an indexing scheme to access relevant cases, and determining a closeness metric to find the best matches from the case library.

"Realistic" Models

What is a *realistic image*? Here "realistic" means "like the real world", and this can be achieved especially by capturing the effects of light interacting with real physical objects.

To represent archaeological artefacts, we should "imitate" the real world, describing an artefact by more than just shape properties. Visual characteristics can be subdivided into sets of marks (points, lines, areas, volumes) that express position or shape and retinal properties (colour, shadow, texture) that enhance the marks and may also carry additional information (Foley and Ribarsky 1994, Astheimer et al. 1994). Texture is usually defined using six different attributes: coarseness, contrast, directionality, line-likeness, regularity and roughness. This is why we should take into account "retinal properties" in the geometric model: each surface appearance should depend on the types of light sources illuminating it, its properties, and its position and orientation with respect to the light sources, viewer and other surfaces. Variation in illumination is a powerful cue to the 3D structure of an object because it contributes to determination of which lines or surfaces of the objects are visible, either from the centre of projection or along the direction of projection, so that we can display only the visible lines or surfaces.

The human brain transforms light intensities into "visual" models. A "visual model" is only a spatial pattern of luminance contrasts that explains how the light is reflected. As models, they are the result of a transformation of *input* data, into a geometric explanation of the input, with light and texture informations (Marr 1982, Watt 1988, Gershon 1994, Wadnell 1995). Consequently, to imitate the real world, a visual model of any object should integrate:

* a pattern of changes in light wavelength and surface-reflectance, that is, *colour.*
* a pattern of changes in edge orientation (curvature), that is, *shape*, where an edge is an abrupt change in luminance values
* a pattern of changes in luminance variations in a scene with non-uniform reflectance, that is *texture* .
* a pattern of discrimination between edges at different spatial positions, that is *topology.*
* a pattern of discrimination between edges at different spatial-temporal positions, that is, *motion.*

To study variation in luminance patterns, we should consider all the set of characteristics (based on physical properties) assigned to a surface or volume model. We use the term *shading* to describe the process of calculating the colour of a pixel or area from surface properties and a model of illumination sources. *Texturing* is a method of varying the surface properties from point to point in order to give the appearance of surface detail that is not actually present in the geometry of the surface. In both cases, the object properties are expressed as intensity values variation of colour, light and reflectance over surface (Sonka et al. 1994, Ebert et al. 1994). We should take into account that the colour assigned to each pixel in a visible surface's projection is a function of the light reflected and transmitted by the objects (Foley et al. 1996), whereas shadow algorithms determine which surfaces can be "seen" from the light source. Phong's illumination (shading) model, for instance, is an algebraic equation relating the intensity of ambient light, the surface ambient reflection coefficient, the object diffuse colour, the atmospheric attenuation factor, the intensity of point light source with specific wavelength, the diffuse reflection coefficient, the specular reflection coefficient and specular colour (Burdea & Coiffet 1994, Foley et al. 1996).

We call "rendering" the procedures that assign to the surfaces of an object their visual physical properties such as colour and shadow. Rendering modes can be understood as specializations of an underlying transport theory model of light propagation in a participating medium. The intensity in the image plane should be described as the emission at each point S along the ray scaled by the optical depth to the eye. The most used rendering methods for illuminating and shading geometric models are the *ray-tracing* algorithm and *radiosity* methods.

Ray-tracing determines the visibility of surfaces by tracing imaginary rays of light from the viewer's eye to the objects in the scene. A centre of projection (the viewer's eye) and a window on an arbitrary view plane are selected. The window may be thought of as being divided into a regular grid, whose elements correspond to pixels at the desired resolution. Then for each pixel in the window, an *eye ray* is fired from the centre of projection through the pixel's centre into the scene. The pixel's colour is set to that of the object at the closest point of intersection (Foley et al. 1996). Although ray tracing does an excellent job of modelling specular reflection and dispersionless refractive transparency, it still makes use of a directionless ambient-lighting term to account for all other global lighting contributions. Approaches based on thermal engineering models for the emission and reflection of radiation eliminate the need for the ambient-lighting term by providing a more accurate treatment of inter-object reflections. All energy emitted or reflected by every surface is accounted for by its reflection from or absorption by other surfaces. The rate at which energy leaves a surface, called *radiosity*, is the sum of the rates at which the surface emits energy and reflects or transmits it from that surface or other surfaces. Unlike conventional rendering algorithms, radiosity methods first determine all the light interactions in an environment in a view-independent way. Then, one or more views are rendered, with only the overhead of visible-surface determination and interpolative shading. Radiosity methods allow any surface to emit light; thus, all light sources are modelled inherently as having area. Examples of these techniques are shown in Holloway (*this volume*), Lucet (*this volume*), Pope and Chalmers (*this volume*) and De Nicola et al. (*this volume*).

Nevertheless, the goal is not to obtain "well illuminated models", but to explain spatial relationships using lighting and shadow models. The goal of the visual model should not be "realism" alone, for the sake of imitation, but in order to contribute to understanding of non-existing objects. We should remember that a "virtual" model is a model of something that does not exist, that cannot be seen. Consequently, the quest for realism among non-existing material is an impossible task. However, taking into account global models of illumination for understanding *position* and *relative location*, or including texture information into the geometrical model, can help us to understand geometrical properties which are too abstract to be easily understood. It is the ability to view from all angles and distances, under a variety of lighting conditions and with as many colour controls as possible which brings about real information (Fletcher and Spicer 1992, Forte 1997). The surfaces that are visible from the light source are not in shadow; those that are not visible from the light source are in shadow. Changing illumination and shadowing, we can get shaded relief, slope and aspect maps, which give clues to investigate surface and morphological differences, expressed as discontinuities in topography, in slope and in relief. The shaded relief map is useful to portray relief differences in hilly and mountainous areas. Its principle is based on a model of what the terrain might look like, as illuminated from a lighting source, seated at any position above the horizon. Parmegiani and Poscolieri show a shaded relief map of Lake Sevan (Armenia) during the Urartian Period. Perspectives and other geographical information is presented changing the colour-hue of the original image (Parmegiani and Poscolieri 1999)

The "interpretative" use of light is very clear in Lucet's paper (*this volume*). It is well known how meso-American architecture made use of special illumination effects in specific days of the year, as a way to control the calendar or as an homage to a God or to the cosmos. Such impressive knowledge of astronomical time was expressed in architectural masterpieces that survive until present days. For these reasons, illumination conditions are one of the characteristics that give to each construction its own personality, and changing illumination conditions of a building deeply affect the way we perceive it. In Frischer et al. (*this volume*), in their computer model of Santa Maria Maggiore, the reconstructed interior with the original fenestration in place revealed that the upper section of the interior was originally bathed in a golden light which enhanced the impact of the mosaics; conversely, the dark semidome of the apse floated above windows at a lower level. Comparable studies visualizing the interior of a church to see just how spectacular its illumination would have been, and how it is related with cult and ritual, are the Hera II model (Aucher and Gallardo 1998) and the Rievaulx Abbey project, where the goal was to determine whether the final result would have justified a dramatic break with tradition in its unusual orientation. The monks of the Cistercian Order regarded sunlight as a manifestation of the Holy Spirit. Is it possible that the desire of one group of 12th-century monks to have sunlight illuminating the daily business of monastic life was strong enough to rotate Rievaulx Abbey ninety degrees from the conventional and ecclesiastical east-west orientation (Kemp 1993)?

A very interesting example from Maltese Bronze Age monuments, shows how different ritual scenarios have been correlated with different lighting scenarios. The intervisibility and spatial interaction of the participating audience and various priests can only be assessed through alternative reconstructions of the contemporary architecture, ritual furniture and liturgical artefacts. Consequently, changing the illumination and shadow model parameters allows the investigation of alternative hypotheses on the ritual function of the site (Chalmers et al. 1995, Chalmers and Stoddart 1996, Chalmers et al. 1997). Pope and Chalmers (*this volume)* give a further enhancement to this approach. They argue how the process of rendering the sound field can provide the information missing from the visual display. By considering the interaction between the sound waves generated by the source and the surfaces present within the environment, we can generate a much more accurate approximation to the sound field than by spatialization alone. It is precisely the time delay associated with audible echoes that enables us to gain some indication of the room's geometry and materials.

Light also contributes to the analysis of activity areas inside a pithouse. In the Keatley Creek site in British Columbia, Peterson et al. could determine which parts of the structure would have been lit by sunlight at various times of the day. Data on artefact frequencies and feature location were then layered onto the floor of the structure and then compared with the information on illumination. This helped the researchers to determine usage areas in the structure. For example, they discovered that heavily retouched scrapers appeared most frequently in parts of the structure that were lit by midday sun (Peterson et al. 1995).

Another approach is used by Pásztor et al. (*this volume*), and by Goodrick and Harding (*this volume*), who evaluate whether prehistoric megalithic sites were orientated towards the sun or stellar constellations, many of which are known to have been so important to other cultures (see also Burton et al. 1999). This could only be achieved with the use of virtual reality or related visualization techniques. A representation of the contemporary night sky or sunrise could then be draped over the model. Another useful feature of these models is the ability to consider the colour and brightness of a surface inclined to a light source, in this case the sun. Different stones were selected by prehistoric megalith builders, because of their colour and brightness effects.

Points and areas connected by the same plane or surface do not have the same values. This variation is called *texture*, and it is used to understand those geometric properties based on local features. There are different approaches to generating these variations and integrating them into a geometrical model. The easier approach is called *texture mapping* and consists of fitting a digital image to a geometrical model (Weinhaus and Devarajan 1997). Combining computer generated models with scanned photographic material is particularly useful when reconstructing paintings or frescoes (see an example in Bloomfield and Schofield 1996). Here, the geometrical model provides shape information only, and the superposed image, all texture information. Hixon et al. *(this volume*), De Nicola et al. (*this volume*), Gurri and Gurri (*this volume*) and Pollefeys et al. (*this volume*) explain how they have used scanned textures to give realism to their monument reconstructions.

B. Britton has further developed this approach to create a virtual model of the Lascaux paintings. Photographs of the paintings have been included on a geometrical model of the cave, in such a way that there is a unique two-dimensional point in the picture associated with each 3D point in the geometric model (Britton 1998).

M. Forte (1992, 1993) reports an example of realistic territory texturing, using image synchronisation (digital aerial photographs or satellite images synchronised with the DTM). Practically, the texture mapping consists of the original image overlaid point by point on the DTM: the result is a realistic and significant landscape 3D image. This kind of simulation is especially useful to enhance the geomorphologic characteristics of the landscape in connection with its evolution and the ancient settlements. At this point we can simulate the exploitation of the landscape in a virtual space in which it is possible to process and study every single area. Ruiz Rodriguez et al. (*this volume*) offer an application of this technique.

From the earliest days of texture mapping, a variety of researchers used synthetic texture models to generate texture images, instead of scanning and painting them. That is, texture data can be *synthesised* or generated from a program or model, rather than from a digitized or painted image. This approach is used for the texture of landscapes. The key idea here is to index a colour look-up table by altitude, and to perturb that altitude-index with a fractal function (fractional Brownian motion). The geological analogues to this are soft-sediment deformation, in which layers of sediment are distorted before lithification, and the distortion generated by the orogenic (mountain-building) forces which raised the sedimentary rock into mountains (Musgrave 1994b). The most interesting "procedural" approaches are the statistical texture models that analyse the properties of natural textures and then reproduce the textures from the statistical data (Sonka et al. 1994, Ebert et al. 1994). In some cases, these statistical models are based on biochemical models, for instance, that produce (among other effects) pigmentation patterns in the skins of animals. There are not yet archaeological applications in this domain. The only procedural texture models proposed in archaeology come from use-wear analysis, in lithics or pottery. However, in most cases, those studies are limited to qualitative description. A preliminary investigation in statistical texture model for use-wear purposes is given in (Pijoan et al. *in press).*

Dynamic Models

A dynamic model is a model that changes in position, size, material properties, lighting and viewing specification (Burdea and Coiffet 1994, Thalman and Thalman 1994a, MacEachern 1994, Foley et al. 1996, Gröller et al., 1999). If those changes are not static but respond to user input, we enter into the proper world of Virtual Reality, whose key feature is real-time *interaction.* Here real-time means that the computer is able to detect input and modify the virtual world "instantaneously". Interactivity and its captivating power contributes to the feeling of "immersion", of being part of the action on the screen, that the user experiences (Burdea and Coiffet 1994). Let us examine some examples.

Paul Reilly has produced a computer animated simulation to illustrate an archaeological excavation. Briefly, the animation shows a flat green open space, perhaps a field, which gradually falls downward leaving a block of ground, which represents the simulated excavation volume, floating in space. The simulated formation is spun on its axis to show the different shapes of the major layers exposed in the profiles. Next, slices are cut away from one side, and later from the top, showing sections through the various pits and post holes cut into the layers within the formation. In another sequence, each of the major layers is removed to reveal the buried contexts cut into the surface of the next major layer below. Each new layer surface is exposed in the order an archaeologist would meet them. After this, the major layers are then ignored and only the cut features are visualised. At one point in the animation, these contexts are built up in reverse order (Reilly 1990). In this case, animation of solids and polygons is directed towards the understanding of the formation process of the site.

Another example of a computer animated model of archaeological dynamics could be to generate a world with objects and characteristics that may be easily changed according some hypothesis. This allows, for example, the number of arches to be increased or reduced, or the building height to be changed. The values may be altered by a control panel that is encoded and sent with the virtual model. Portions of the world may be relocated, resized, or otherwise altered. This would allow the user to both alter and affect the virtual world and to generate a complete new instance of that world. Ryan and Roberts (1997) have built a "user configurable" dynamic reconstruction model of the Canterbury Roman theatre. The user may adjust the building height, seat number or dimensions, or add a walkway between the seats to examine a range of possible appearances.

Geometric models may be "animated" to incorporate interactivity. In those contexts, the notion of animation is generalised to any changes occurring on the screen during viewing time (Thalmann 1990,Gershon 1994). If a series of projections of the same object, each from a slightly different viewpoint around the object, is displayed in rapid succession, then the object appears to rotate. By integrating information across the views, the viewer creates an object hypothesis. A perspective projection of a rotating pottery vase, for instance, provides several types of information. The maximum linear velocity of points near the centre of rotation is lower than that of points distant from the centre of rotation. This difference can help to clarify the relative distance of a point from the centre of rotation. Also the changing sizes of different parts of the cube as they change distance under perspective projection provide additional cues about the depth relationships. Motion becomes even more powerful when it is under the interactive control of the viewer. By selectively transforming an object, that is, by interpolating shape transformations, viewers may be able to form an object hypothesis more quickly.

Computer animation can be also used to model the object dynamics, and not only the user dynamics (Burdea & Coiffet 1994, Beardon and Ye 1995). Animation enhances the visibility of features embedded in the data by creating changes in the display data during the time of viewing rather than by moving the data relative to the observer. We can model virtual objects by specifying their physical properties, and not only their geometry and/or texture. Among those physical properties there are: mass, weight, inertia, surface texture (smooth or rough), compliance (hard or soft), deformation mode (elastic or plastic). An animated sequence can be produced by specifying how these properties change from frame to frame. These features are merged with geometrical modelling and behaviour laws to form a more realistic virtual model. Object behaviour may be modelled to follow simple Newtonian laws or more complex reflexes (so-called "intelligent agents").

The most usual examples of archaeological virtual animation are single or directed walks through a virtual environment, also called "fly-throughs" or interactive navigation inside the reconstructed model. The user can move in a city or landscape, and the model responds to his/her movement. Objects change their position and view perspective when the user changes his/her position and view angle. To simulate walking through the site, the camera, or point of view, is the only thing that will be moving. To animate the camera, you can use seven control variables: *x, y, z* location, pan and tilt angles, focal length and time. This allows the user to place the camera at a specific time and place, pointed at a specific object. Each of the points defined by the seven variables will be joined by a B-spline curve. The time parameter is used by the system to generate an interpolative curve to access the remaining six variables. Using this control sequence it will be possible to specify the camera location and view in a natural method and then have the computer generate a smooth path through the points required (Cornforth et al. 1991, Ozawa 1996, Hendrik et al., 1998, Ruiz Rodriguez et al. *this volume*).

An alternative approach is that of "Panoramic Virtual Reality". In essence, it consists of a series of sequential photographs, shot either outward from a central point or inward toward a central object, which are presented so that the view of the surrounding world or the object can be controlled. In truth, these representations are not truly 3-D, because the viewer is restricted to a single point from which the image is manipulated. Because a single landscape or object panorama is a very limited segment of reality, multiple panoramas are often linked together to form a semicontinuous spatial experience. The viewer can jump from one panorama, or "node", to the next, giving either the effect of travelling through space or of examining objects. In addition, still photographs or video clips can be linked to panoramas and displayed by clicking on specific points (usually called "hot spots"), allowing greater detail of subjects (Rick & Hart 1997, see also Forte and Borra *this volume*, Krasniewicz, *this volume*).

The purpose of "virtual" navigation or "flying" across the territory is to be able to explore a 3D model of that territory in all its perspectives, verifying the settlement conditions in different archaeological areas, and recreating exploration conditions that cannot be developed in another way. However, an animation is not necessarily a representation of the model dynamics. Using virtual environment control techniques, the researcher can rapidly change what and where data is displayed, allowing the exploration of complex environments (Reilly 1990, Forte and Guidazzoli 1996, Ruiz Rodriguez et al. *this volume*)). There are plenty of animated computer models of archaeological data (see Forte 1997, Mudur et al. 1999, among many others), but most of them are nothing more than pretty movies providing no information about the dynamics of the model.

The goal of all these interactive panoramas is to "imitate the processes" of actual reality: standing in one place and looking around to see everything that is visible from that spot as well as moving to another spot that provides an alternative view. The hope is that the viewer will "perceive patterns" in VR's multisensory representations more readily than in maps, drawings or simple photographs. This enhanced perception is directed towards data contexts that can enhance the interpretative process. But used alone, without contextualizing the objects presented, could make the object movie little more than a dramatic gesture. The problem arises when we give the same importance to virtual browsing (Krasniewicz, *this volume*) and to camera flying (Ruiz Rodriguez et al., this volume), using the second to give an impression of the first.

Virtual browsing in a physical model like the landscape suggests to the user the study of space from infinite perspectives, which cannot be done in a real scale. The facility to "get inside and walk around" the reconstructed buildings would give a greater feeling of enclosed space and volume and enhance the sense of being there. Since the computer contains a three-dimensional representation of the structure, perspective drawings from any point in space either outside the building or within it can be rendered automatically by choosing co-ordinates for that specific viewpoint. This is very important in understanding the way in which a building may function. Some authors have suggested that these dynamic models of landscape and built environments might focus attention on the act of perception as a means of more properly explaining the ways in which people interact with their social space (Wheatley 1992, Llobera 1996, Gillings and Goodrick 1996, Leusen 1999, Hendrik et al., 1999). Some built elements (barrows or hillforts, for example) act as a kind of landmark and therefore would have to be positioned in a location such that they would be intervisible. We can model the landscape in terms of which points on the landscape are the most visible from all landmarks. Changing interactively the point of view (from landmark to landmark) we can visualize the landscape as did the people who once lived in it.

Maurizio Forte (1995) has studied how to link GIS archaeological data with virtual flights, and the possibilities of this approach. Full processing and simulation are especially useful to discover and enhance the geomorphologic and archaeological features of the landscape in connection with its evolution and its ancient settlements (Forte 1998, Forte and Guidazzoli 1996a, Gilman and Tolba 1994, McCullugh et al., 1999). The same approach has also been used in archaeology for visibility studies. Based on a single or multiple line-of-sight calculations, the viewshed operation takes as its input the 3D surface and determines all points that are visible from one or more specified view points over the given surface, it is possible to take into account obstructions such as trees and buildings and the height of the observer/feature at a specific view point. The major shortcoming of viewshed analysis is the accuracy of the results. There may be errors in the digital terrain model used to calculate the viewshed, in the rounding up of elevations, and the failure of algorithms to take account of break points in the landscape, such as ridges. Those analyses have been mostly developed using 2D GIS models (Ruggles et al. 1992, Ozawa et al. 1994, Wheatley 1995, Sansoni 1996, Bell 1999, Loots et al. 1999, Leusen 1999), but they are better performed on a true 3D basis, using virtual navigation across the landscape (Forte and Guidazzoli 1996a, Ruiz Rodriguez et al. *this volume*).

Nevertheless, adopting viewshed- and cost-based techniques alone, these studies run the risk of making the same reductionist and ultimately "technique-led" mistakes that characterized the first block of archaeological GIS applications. In doing so these applications critically confuse the concept of "vision" with that of "perception". This direct equation of vision with perception appears to be implicit in almost all of the interactive navigation virtual models.

M. Gillings (1999) offers a way to solve this problem. The Tower at Peel Gap comprises a small, rectangular structure which was added to the back face of Hadrian's Wall shortly after its construction in the early second century AD. In its size and ground plan, the structure resembles most closely the regular series of turrets that characterise the length of the wall. These turret features have traditionally been interpreted as observation posts. A detailed micro-topographical survey of the immediate landscape of the tower was undertaken to generate input data for a 3D geometrical model of the footprint of the wall and related features. The resulting viewshed served to confirm earlier reservations as to the strategic significance of locating an observation post in this position, as the identified zone of visible ground was heavily restricted, focusing not upon the lands beyond the frontier but instead upon the immediate surroundings of the pass itself and the area to the rear of the wall. Although undoubtedly highly useful, the viewshed as generated had a number of shortcomings, particularly given the overall aims of the research exercise. The analysis failed to incorporate the notion of the observer as mobile and situated; instead the viewshed was static, serving to abstract a dynamic and uncertain perceptual act into a simple, well-defined projected zone, located unambiguously upon a flat projected map. Taking the GIS-based viewshed not as an end-product but as a first step, attempts were then made to enhance and complement it through the application of visualization and virtual-reality-based approaches. In practice, the line of the wall and tower foundations were used as a template from which a basic structural re-construction was undertaken in CAD. This was simply rendered and a number of animation sequences were generated. These served to re-create the view yielded by a gentle 360 degree rotation by a hypothetical observer located atop the reconstructed tower. As well as exploring the 'view from', the effects of 'viewing to' were explored by moving an observer past the structure along the course of the Military Way. The results were fascinating. In the former case, although the view out to the area beyond Hadrian's Wall was indeed seen to be blocked, as indicated by the GIS-based study, what was not at all obvious was the way in which the course of the Military Way dominated the view to the rear, often tracking the visible sky-line. In the case of the 'view to' what was most striking was the suddenness with which the tower first appeared out from behind the looming bulk of the crags. These re-constructions and animation sequences served to situate the observer and incorporated a degree of mobility, but they were still prescriptive. The final, and critical stage was to generate a representation whereby the observer was able to freely engage with the re-creation, choosing their own paths through, and their own viewing points within, the landscape. In addition, an important proviso was that observers should not only be able to freely engage with the representation, but they also had to be able to obtain, view, modify and alter it, treating it not as a definitive end-product but as a manipulable medium that could be incorporated into their own analytical environments. This would enable our tendered interpretation to be scrutinized and new interpretations to be formulated. As a result the decision was taken to implement the re-creation using virtual-reality-based techniques, specifically VRML, with the resulting model being freely distributed via the World Wide Web. The landscape could now be viewed from anywhere within it. Observers could explore the views from the tower or approach the wall from within the landscape actively seeking a position on the crags where you could see over the wall to the mysteries beyond. Functional factors such as the possibility of a wall-top walkway could be assessed and the effects of altering the reconstructed tower height explored dynamically.

A similar example is the dynamic model of the temple precinct of Roman Bath (Reilly 1992). The archaeologist approached the model from a number of different viewpoints, by means of 'view statements' which acted as a 'synthetic camera'. Placing the viewer at the entrance of the reconstructed precinct suggest that a person standing in this part of the precinct would have been immediately impressed by the aspect of the temple of Sulis Minerva. In stark contrast, viewed from the top of the steps of the temple towards the entrance, the attendant structures seem to shrink away. One response to this revelation is to ask whether feelings of superiority or inferiority were felt depending upon where in the precinct one happened to be standing? The model apparently can help sustain arguments relating to the precinct architect's conception of the relationships between power and space. A similar example is proposed by Martens et al. (*this volume*), and Frischer et al. (*this volume*). In this case, authors give strong emphasis to the findings regarding the urban impact of the virtually reconstructed building (Santa Maria Maggiore in Rome). Resituated in the topography of late antique Rome, the basilica was seen to have been oriented for maximum visibility along major thoroughfares and from other hills in the city following ancient theories of view-planning.

Graham Earl (1999) examines the Danebury Iron Age hillfort via spatial modelling in an attempt to answer explicit theoretical questions surrounding the function of altered spaces. In this study, models were produced which could be navigated around, in an attempt to identify the role both of defining features such as banks and ditches at different stages in their use, and the areas thus defined. "Space" is examined interactively via models rather than assessed in plan or in surviving states. Some kind of symbolic emphasis is suggested by a continuity in arrangement and interconnectivity of space which is clearly visible in the models of different phases of the entrance, and much less obviously in plan. The spaces do not appear to offer any defensive benefits in their early stages and it may be hypothesised that their later embellishment and continuity were similarly a product of symbolic as opposed to defensive requirements. This hypothesis fits with a body of research limiting the bellicose nature of Iron Age societies and with other spatial arrangements noted elsewhere at Danebury and at other 'hillfort' sites. Movement through the spaces, perhaps mediated by social circumscription, leads to the opening of new vistas with access to views of the hypothesized central shrine area closely defined by the earthworks.

On the other hand, computer animation methods may help us to understand social dynamics by adding motion control to data in order to show their evolution over time. Just as an architect might wish to give users access to both before and after views of a new development, archaeologists need a way of presenting alternative interpretations and changes through time. The problem to solve is how to express time-dependence in the scene, and how to make it evolve over time (Castleford 1991). Although we can now represent time with time, we may achieve only modest gains by so doing. Conceptualizing time only as an attribute limits the potential of dynamic displays. This is done by operating within a 2D spatial frame of reference and using the third axis to represent a time line. The location or feature is represented as a column that varies in width according to the probability of that location (Daly & Lock 1999).

Time can also be conceived as a variable to be manipulated, much as we manipulate size, colour, hue and space itself. Animation of dynamic objects involves a spatially linked sequence of scenes that are temporally dependent. MacEachern (1994) has identified four fundamental dynamic variables to study time: duration, rate of change, order and phase. We can animate an otherwise static map by explicitly controlling duration. A sequence of frames is a scene. Because duration is a quantity which can be precisely controlled with most animation software, duration of a scene or of a frame can be used to depict ordinal or quantitative data. Animation is applied to a static situation, short duration scenes within events might correspond to insignificant features and long duration scenes to significant features. Applied to dynamic processes, short duration scenes throughout an event imply smooth movement while long duration scenes suggest abrupt movement. The duration of individual frames of an event, or number of frames per unit time, determines the animation's temporal texture. Change in duration of frames in an event can suggest increasing or decreasing importance, or can imply accelerating or decelerating location or attribute change. When attribute or location change is depicted between frames, relative duration of frames can interact with the magnitude of this change. For example, many constant but short duration frames per unit time, with a constantly decreasing change in position will give the impression of a smoothly slowing movement. Frames of geometrically decreasing duration with constant changes in position, on the other hand, will produce an impression of slow abrupt movement gradually giving way to accelerated, explosive, continuous movement. Matching animation frame order with temporal order of the phenomenon depicted is the most obvious way that order can be used as a dynamic variable. With dynamic maps, however, we can use time order to represent, in a symbolic way, any order. Phase is a "rhythmic repetition of certain events". Map animation tools allow the length of time between repetitions to be controlled. From one frame to the next, any of the static visual variables can change, as can the dynamic variable of duration. Change in the location variable results in apparent motion and change in any other static variable draws attention to a location and, if change continues throughout an event, can suggest that an attribute at a location is changing.

In most VR archaeological movies, the user sees changes, but time is not used or modified as a parameter, and therefore temporal models are static. What we need is the more complex approach, that is, an analysis of time transformations in the structure of position, texture and colour, which implies a 4D processing (3D+time) (Forte and Guidazzoli 1996b). Bonfigli and Guidazzoli (*this volume*) and Kadobayashi et al. (*this volume*) explore this possibility. I. Johnson (1999) simulates the dynamics of temporal changes using the snapshot-transition model. In this model, the history of features is modelled as a series of snapshots at known points in time, and a series of transitions between these snapshots. Snapshots may consist of 2D vector objects (points, lines or polygons representing features on the surface of the landscape), 2D raster objects (geographically registered images, DEMs or other topographic and environmental data), or 3D models of structures. The strength of the snapshot-transition model is that it parallels our knowledge of the past. An alternative approach is the model temporal evolution using modular maps (Gagalowicz 1990, Françon and Lienhardt 1994). The method is as follows: the topology of surface S at tuime h is modelled as a modular map C_h defined as a set of vertices, edges and faces. One vertex is distinguished in each modular map and called the initial vertex. The modular map C_0, defining the topology of S at h=0 is particularly reduced to the initial vertex. The evolution of the topology of S between times h=0 and h=n is modelled by a sequence of modular maps ($C_0,..., C_n$). This approach is also very characteristic in complex systems research ("rugged landscapes", see Kaufmann 1995).

Another possibility for the visualization of dynamic processes is *phenomena modelling* (Bryson 1996). It is performed through computed simulation on theories which are specific to the discipline. Since these phenomena are usually defined not by geometric shape, but through a set of parameters, visualization requires a further step. To achieve a simulation, the animator has two principal techniques available. The first is to use a model that creates the desired effect. A good example is the building of a house, or the growth of a green plant. Here changes are the different steps of construction or growing. Typically, motion is defined in terms of co-ordinates, angles and other shape characteristics. It can be obtained by *dynamic equations of motion*. An archaeological example has been provided by Gröller et al. (the rise and fall of Chinese dynasties), but it is too reduced (only three parameters) to be considered a real example (Gröller et al., 1999, Feichtinger et al. 1996, see also van der Leeuw and McGlade 1997)

In the next generation of animated systems, motion is planned at a task level and computed using physical laws. This means that research will tend to find theoretical and physical models to improve the animation. The main purpose is not a validation of the theoretical models, but to obtain a graphic simulation of the motion that is as realistic as possible (Thalman and Thalman 1994a). Another approach is the possibility to link animation to an expert-system, where theoretical knowledge has been represented in form of production rules. This provide the opportunity to use archaeological, historical or anthropological knowledge to simulate the behaviour of objects (for instance temporal dynamics of landscape social use) within a modelled environment (Beardon and Ye 1995, Fishwick 1995, Noser and Thalmann 1994).

Toward Augmented Reality

Just as the desktop metaphor allows users to interact easily with computer's file structure, useful interaction metaphors are needed for virtual environment systems (Brogni et al. *this volume*). This fact has led to the concept of "enhanced" or "augmented" reality (AR). Augmented reality has been defined as the simultaneous acquisition of supplemental virtual data about the real world while navigating around a physical reality (Durlach and Mavor 1995). It is different from the concept of "immersive reality", where the eyes and ears or other body senses are isolated from the real environment and fed only information from the computer, providing a first-person interaction with the computer-generated world (see examples of both approaches in Sanders *this volume*, Kadobayashi et al. *this volume* Bonfligli and Gudazzoli, *this volume*, Frischer et al. *this volume*). For information pertaining to complicated 3D objects, augmented reality is an effective means for utilizing and exploiting the potential of computer based-information and databases (Sanders *this volume*). In an augmented reality system, the computer provides additional information that enhances or augments the real world, rather than replacing it with a completely virtual environment. In AR the computer contains models of significant aspects of the user's environment. AR provides a natural interface for processing data requests about the environment and presenting the results of requests. With 3D tracking devices a user may conduct normal tasks in his/her environment and the computer is capable of acquiring and interpreting his/her movements, actions and gestures. The user can then interact with objects in the real world, generate queries, and the computer provides information and assistance. Merging graphical representations of augmenting information with the view of the real object clearly presents the relationship between the data and the object. Using AR, the user can easily perceive and comprehend the spatial component of the queried data (Rose et al. 1995). Simulation embodies the principle of "learning by doing": to learn about the past we must first build a model of the past and make it run. To understand reality and all of its complexity, we must build artificial objects and dynamically act out roles with them.

Not every interactive system is an augmented reality environment. The CAVE interactive approach, for instance, is an immersive virtual environment, typically 3 x 3 meters in size or larger, in which the computer model is projected onto the walls, floor, and ceiling. In a CAVE, a guide can take visitors on a live, interactive tour of the 3D computer model, answering questions and giving views of the site that even the ancient visitor could not see or see so well. A teacher whose expertise pertains more to the use or history of the site than to its construction might use a videotape with a virtual tour of a site given by an archaeologist or architectural historian. The same videotape can be used in the auditorium of a museum or archaeological site to provide an orientation for visitors. Frischer et al. (*this volume*) offer an introduction to this kind of systems.

Kadobayashi et al. *this volume* offers another excellent example of integration between "immersive" virtual reality and "augmented" virtual reality. In their Vista-walk system, the interface between the user and the virtual world is provided by two different viewers. The first viewer, called the "Walk Viewer", gives a perspective scene from a human model and as such is the "user's viewpoint." The second viewer, called the "Auxiliary Viewer (Aux Viewer)" provides a scene from "another person's viewpoint." The height of the viewpoint can be changed to an arbitrary altitude so that the user can get a bird's eye view of the scene. In the "Aux Viewer", a human model (i.e., the avatar of the user) is also shown if the height is low. This avatar is used as the reference of the current position and the size of the site or building.

In the Bonfigli and Guidazzoli (*this volume)* virtual model of ancient Bologna, the user begins with the virtual reconstruction of the city as it is nowadays and travels backward in time using the time-bar, which consists of a text field showing the year, on a display and a bar with a cursor, on a time line. By selecting a year it is possible to visit the reconstruction of the city in that year. Each time a year is entered in the text field or the cursor is moved, the VRML scenario is dynamically updated on the basis of the information in a database; a sound environment has been introduced into the virtual world to enhance user orientation in temporal navigation. Each century is associated with a different sound-track. This allows visitors to identify, on an intuitive and perceptive level, the period they are visiting. Moreover to make sure that the visitor understands that he is seeing only as much as the historical sources can justify, each building is accompanied by an HTML document compiled by a historian. These hypertexts contain references to the historical resources and can be consulted at any time during the visit. Upon selecting a building of major importance, a new browser window visualizes both the HTML description file and an isolated high resolution VRML model of the building.

This way of "visiting" historic towns is increasingly popular. In the *Virtual Tübingen* system (see Hendrik et al. 1998) the authors have built a highly realistic virtual model of the historic centre of Tübingen. This is a fully interactive model, and the user can moves in real time in this virtual scenario. By comparing navigation and orientation behaviour in the real city and its digital counterpart, authors try to establish the relationship between space perception and human action.

Maybe future trends of augmented reality will be directed to systems like the Virtual Polis (Loeffler 1994b, Odegard 1994). It is a virtual reality application of a three-dimensional, computer generated city, inhabited by a multitude of participants joined by means of telecommunications. This city functions because of programming options:

- it is a distributed, three-dimensional inhabitable environment;
- it can support a potentially unlimited number of participants;
- it has private spaces and personal and public property;
- participants use tools to alter the environment while inhabiting it.

This inhabited city allows for investigation of Tele-existence in a distributed virtual construct. There are two kinds of inhabitants in this virtual city: real users, and computer-generated agents with a low-level artificial intelligence. At first sight the agents cannot be distinguished from the virtual humans. The agents have social behaviour imitating human beings in cities. In this kind of virtual environments the social space can be a physical experience. For instance, to have meaningful social interaction it is necessary for the participants to share a few social and cultural symbols and values; in networked interaction, too, the participants use shared symbols. Together, users create social space while using the media.

Examples of Tele-existence are the Gorilla Exhibit at the Zoo Atlanta (Allison et al. 1997), and the Singapore HistoryCity project (http://www.historycity.org.sg/). In the first case, students assume the role of an adolescent gorilla, and enter into one of the gorilla habitats at Zoo Atlanta, and interact as a part of a gorilla family unit. The virtual environment combines a model of the gorilla habitat at the zoo with computer generated gorillas whose movements and interactions are modelled as accurate representations of gorilla behaviours. The Singapore's HistoryCity project, modelled on 1870s Singapore, is an environment for children to "make history" by collecting and trading period items - and using them to create unique interactive dioramas. The goal of HistoryCity is to function as a historically-based virtual community. By working and playing with historical elements users learn the history of their culture with their own words and images. When children first join HistoryCity, they select avatars as their representations, and these become their representations in the world, and the way other users see them. There are over 200 different avatars to choose from. Children can collect objects from the environment and from other users, and create interactivet heatre pieces with them in their own personal rooms. Theatre elements are animated objects with associated sound-effects, and small groups of users can interact in each Personal Room, dynamically modifying these elements by adding, removing, rearranging, or activating them. Participants can also interact with each other using point-to-point speech or traditional text-chat. HistoryCity has several different types of agents: story-tellers, newspapermen, poets, jokers, writers, pawn-brokers, mailmen, and a governor. The story-teller, for example, allows users to read stories, many of which are based on the history, legends, fables,and folk tales of Singapore. Many of the key elements in these stories are collectible objects in the world, which allows users to create interactive theatre-pieces that recreate historical events. Similarly, the poet tells poems, the newspaperman provides HistoryCity news (a mix of historical and user-created), and the joker presents jokes. Users submit stories, poems, jokes, and news items of their own through writer. These are collected each day, and then made available as part of the different agents' repertoires the following day. Pawn-brokers allow players to trade objects with the system. The mailmen allow users to locate each other; by sending a messenger to locate another user. Individuals can determine where their friends are in HistoryCity. The governor provides users with a set of guidelines for appropriate behaviour in HistoryCity. At present, there are 21 communities in HistoryCity, and each of them has several clubhouses. When users become club members, they are given a Personal Room (with a Personal Theatre) and a Personal Page. Every Personal Room is different, with exciting patterns and unique shapes, and owners can even lock them. Personal Pages function as the Web of HistoryCity, allowing players to describe themselves and their interests. Residents explore, and live in, a virtual Singapore of 1870 complete with historical buildings, costumes, and objects. Players will have access to many different parts of old Singapore, from Chinatown to Pulau Brani to Commercial Square to Little India.

Mitchell and Economou (*this volume*) present another application of a virtual archaeological world populated with virtual actors. The particular medium that is being explored in the project is the Collaborative Virtual Environment (CVE). A CVE is a Virtual Environment in which more than one user can be present at the same time. Each user is represented as a Virtual Actor (or Avatar). So when a user enters the environment he/she can detect the presence of other users by seeing their avatars and in turn they will be represented by their own avatar. A Virtual Actor may also be used to represent not a person but a software agent. By populating the CVE with Virtual Actors a social element can be introduced. The CVE medium is thus ideally suited to supporting collaborative learning. Work in the Kahun project is focused on investigating the role of Virtual Actors in CVEs for learning . The environment consists of the Egyptian town of Kahun and various artefacts recovered from the site. Virtual Actors will be used to represent children, teachers, museum staff, and possible software agents.

T.A. Kohler and G.J. Gumerman (1996) have created a virtual "prehistoric" world populated with "artificial" agents. Agents simulate the economic behaviour of households scattered randomly on a virtual environment or placed where they actually existed. The parameters of the virtual environment may be left as they were originally reconstructed or adjusted to enhance or reduce maize production. Movement rules for agents are triggered when a new household is created or when a household can't produce enough maize to maintain the household.. Here "dynamics" refer to changes on household characteristics (quantity and quality of farmland, location of residential site, etc.). Doran has also proposed agent-based simulations, were "agents" are surrogates of people looking for food in the Palaeolithic and changing interaction ways and social relations as a result of joint tasks and planning (Doran et al. 1994). These models, however, are hardly visual, because computer power is directed to the processing of "virtual" behaviour.

Why this emphasis on "virtual humans" or actors? According to programmers, for the modeling of behaviors, the ultimate objective is to build intelligent autonomous virtual humans with adaptation, perception and memory. These virtual humans should be able to act freely and even emotionally. They should be conscious and unpredictable. The should reinforce the concept of presence (Thalman and Thalman 1994b). In other words, if we want to study unpredictability, then we should create virtual beings that simulate how humans interact. Most virtual actor systems as those described here should be considered along this lines. Instead of the fixed and linear nature of current simulation techniques, virtual interaction of real humans (the user) and virtual actors allows the understanding of the complex rules governing what seems unpredictable.

The current fashion towards "virtual museums" (Shaw 1994, Loeffler 1994a, Gottarelli 1996, Gordon 1999, Refsland 1998) is developing along these lines. They are virtual theatres where it is possible to dive into a number of cultural visits through ancient monuments and their most important historic monuments (see Kadobayashi et al. *this volume*, Bonfigli and Guidazzoli *this volume*, Frischer et al. *this volume*). A key element of a virtual environment is the ability to "really" move in three dimensions, and it should help us to bridge the gap between the "outside" material world and the conceptual worlds of archaeological and historical explanation. For instance, visitors to the University of Southern California Interactive Art Museum at the Fischer Art Gallery are able to view two-dimensional images and utilize remote telerobotic devices equipped with video cameras to view three-dimensional works and participate interactively, in real time, in art performances and installations. New techniques in 3D modelling, haptic interfacing, and augmented reality will permit onsite and remote inspection and manipulation of three-dimensional museum objects (http://digimuse.usc.edu/museum.html).

A similar approach may be imagined for the simulation of archaeological excavation, offering the alternatives between a complete animated excavation simulator comparable to a flight simulator, and a database-expert system engine for understanding user actions in the simulated environment. However, published essays up to now (Wheatley 1991, Molyneaux 1992) have a very poor 3D graphic interface, and this idea has not yet fully explored. They are more a "cognitive" emulation, than a virtual reality excavation. Forte and Borra (*this volume* fig. 16) give some insights about how to create a visually rich 3D excavation flight simulator. Kantner (*this volume*) also presents some examples.

Current Techniques Are More Complex Than Actual Questions

In most cases the use of virtual reality in archaeology seems more an artistic task than an inferential process. Virtual reality is the modern version of the artist that gave a "possible" reconstruction using water-colours. Computer scientists take the drawings of this "imaginative" reconstructions, and transform them into computer language. The computer gives 3D, colour and texture to archaeologists' (or architects') imaginations. As a direct result of this uncritical acceptance, fundamental questions relating to issues such as what we actually mean by virtual reality, and what our expensively assembled models truly represent have been left largely unexplored. Simply put, the better and more optimized the data used in a computer model, the more faithful the virtual model seems to be, and the closer it seems to come to the reality it seeks, or purports, to represent. In addition, as a result of this notion of the virtual-reality model as a painstakingly sophisticated surrogate, the reconstructions run the risk of being reified, becoming in effect end-products, finished, completed, free-standing and there to be visually devoured. The point here is that any given virtual representation can never be authentic. The considerable efforts currently being expended in incorporating ever more detail into models, whether through the use of individual bricks and stones rather than simplified blocks, or the application of highly complex textures, achieve little more than the generation of an even more fastidious investigative attitude on the part of the observer (Miller and Richards 1994, Gillings 1999). A computer model is an *analogy* (Goldstein 1996), and consequently there is not any *identity* between the archaeological record and its computer model. The visual model is an "interpretation" of archaeological data, and it is not readily apparent how one gets from the dig to the interpretation (Reilly 1990, 1992, Goodchild et al. 1994). According to Benjamin Wooley, increasingly complex, artificial environments can diminish our sense of reality (Wooley 1992). From this point we could affirm that virtual models are substituting real data, and consequently, soft images are substituting hard reasoning. V. Lull (1999) suspects that the virtual models we incorporate into archaeological research are the product of and, at the same time, the producers of the new style of life, in which rigorous, scientific observation takes second place to the accurate, graphic transfer of images, or the precision or definition, with which they are processed. There is a danger that our public face will become a mere simulacrum, behind which is hidden our own technocratic image, consisting of drawings, photography, animation, or three-dimensional images, and which will gradually become the identity card of all those who forget that it is merely a club-membership card..

To avoid these problems, archaeologists and visualization designers must determine what phenomena need to be "visualized", and the form of the representation, so that explicit communication objectives will be achieved. One taxonomy dimension which may facilitate this process is the following list (Tuk 1994: 29-30):

- Phenomena visualization: depiction of man-made phenomena recorded in terms of either point, local or global variables. An archaeological example is human settlement in a territory
- Meta-phenomena visualization: Display of the content/coverage, quality accuracy, etc. of a particular phenomenon. An example is the accuracy of human settlement evidences at different locations (probability values based on artefacts dispersion)
- Phenomena change visualization. Depiction of phenomena change over some specific time period, or the rate of change of a phenomenon or one of its attributes.
- Visualizations of relationships between phenomena. Display of specific, spatially based, relationships between phenomena of interest. An example is the pattern of correlations between the built environment (houses) and the volume of rubbish accumulated in each room for a set of occasions in a study area
- Causal visualization. Depiction of cause-effect relationships, known or inferred, involving the phenomena, for example the relationship between intensification of production (quantity of tools and means of production) and the architectonic complexity of houses and buildings.
- Meta-causal visualization. Displays of the reliability, validity, etc. of inferred causal relations.
- Information systems structure visualization. Depiction of the information system analysis/display functionality, for example the software modules needed to compare two different datasets.
- Analysis process visualization: Graphic depiction of the process of analysis used to generate a particular visualisation, for example the surface interpolation algorithm used.
- Motivational visualization. Graphic displays designed to catch and hold the viewer's attention.

Most of applications presented in this volume are examples of phenomena visualizations and phenomena change visualization. Archaeologists are asking computer scientists to build dynamic models of archaeological phenomena. There is also a lot of motivational visualization procedures, but very few causal reasoning. In the early days of visualization, it was rather difficult for the researcher to produce visualizations beyond conventional drawings and plots. Still nowadays, familiarity with computer graphics programming is required to do more sophisticated archaeological visualization, a need that seems addressed through the creation of "visualization shops", in which a visualization is produced to order. An archaeologist provides data to a visualization programmer, who then produces a high quality image or animation. Thus, there is a significant investment involved in the production of visualization. As a result, severe limits have been placed on the number of ways in which a dataset can be explored. That is, an explorer does not know a priori what images are unimportant, but when the effort to produce a visualization is large, there will understandably be a hesitation to produce a picture that is likely to be discarded. This serves the purpose of visualization as a presentation medium, but it hinders the use of visualization as an exploratory medium or as a computational theory.

For the moment, we are restricted to the creation of virtual environments, whose purpose is to sense, manipulate, and transform the state of the human operator or to modify the state of the information stored in a computer. Future advancement of virtual reality techniques in archaeology should not be restricted to "presentation" techniques, but to explanatory tools. Description is not explaination; it is only a part of the explanatory process, and archaeology is not a discipline involved in the presentation of past remains. Archaeology is history, it is anthropology, it is geography, ... Archaeology is a science for understanding our society through the analysis of its formative process. We suggest to use VR techniques not only for description, but for expressing all the explanatory process. An explanation can be presented as a visual model, that is as a virtual dynamic environment, where the user ask questions in the same way a scientist use a theory to understand the empirical world. A virtual world should be, then a *model*, a set of concepts, laws, tested hypotheses and hypotheses waiting for testing. If in standard theories, concepts are expressed linguistically or mathematically, in virtual environments, theories are expressed computationally, by using images and rendering effects. Nothing should be wrong or "imaginary" in a virtual reconstruction, but should follow what we know, be dynamical, and be interactively modifiable. A virtual experience is then a way of studying a geometrical model—a scientific theory expressed with a geometric language—instead of studying empirical reality. As such it should be related with work on the empirical reality (excavation, laboratory analysis). As a result we can act virtually with inaccesible artifacts, buildings and landscapes *through* their models (Colonna 1994).

"Manipulation" is then the key word for virtual reality. Any reasoning operation is, in a sense, a manipulation, that is, a transformation of input data. When we speak about something, we are manipulating this thing. When we measure archaeological objects, when we take photographs, when we produce interpretations,... all of these are logical transformations,linguistic changes, etc. A virtual world should be considered as another way of modification. We have seen in this paper how the visual manipulation proceeds. One advantage is that by using a computer and geometrical algorithms we know what we have done, and know the specific relationship between input (empirical data) and output (the virtual model). But why manipulate? Because *explanation* is always explicitly different from empirical information. If we need to explain, then we should transform data, that is, the thing to be explained. A vase cannot be explained with the same vase, but with a literary, geometrical, physical, description of the vase. VR techniques provides us with the best description language. The limitation is that we need to ask the proper questions to make this translation operation profitable. If archaeological questions cannot be presented in a geometrical language, the use of computational theories will have no future. We are still anchored in the old literary tradition. We all know that using words is not the best way to understand the dynamics of the past, but it seems very difficult to learn a new language, to change centuries of errors, to recognize the failure of the old way of doing things. Designing archaeological virtual worlds can be the solution, but we are still waiting for the question that should be answered with this solution.

Aknowledgments

P. Báscones, J. Gurri, L. Mameli, P. G. Pelfer, N. Ryan and D. H. Sanders contributed valuable ideas and suggestions. However they are not responsible for my interpretation of their comments or for opinions which may be contained in the text.

References Cited

ALGORRI,M.E., SCHMITT,F., 1996, "Surface Reconstruction from Unstructured 3D data". *Computer Graphics Forum* 15 (1): 47-60.

ALLISON,D., WILLS,B., BOWMAN, WINEMAN,J., HODGES,L.F., 1997, "The Virtual Reality Gorilla Exhibit" *IEEE Computer Graphics* 17 (6), pp. 30-38.

ASTHEIMER,P., DAI,F., GÖBEL,M., KRUSE,R., MÜLLER,S., ZACHMANN,G., 1994, "Realiosm in Virtual Reality". In *Artificial Life and Virtual Reality.* Edited by N.M. Thalmann and D. Thalmann. New York: John Wiley Publ.

ASTORQUI, A. 1999, "Studying the archaeological record from Photogrametry". In *New Techniques for Old Times. Computer Applications and Quantitative Methods in Archaeology.* Edited by J.A. Barceló, I. Briz and A. Vila. Oxford: British archaeological Reports (S757) .

AUCHER,L., GALLARDO, A., 1998, "Attempt to rebuild the Temple of Hera II" http://perso.wanadoo.fr/pixelle/paestum-eng.htm

BAJAJ,C.L., BERNARDINI,F., XU,G., 1995, "Automatic reconstruction of surfaces and scalar fields from 3D scans". *SIGGRAPH95 Conference Proceedings.* Pp. 109-118.

BARIBEAU,R., GODIN,G., COURNOYER,L., RIOUX,M., 1996, "Colour Three-Dimensional Modelling of Museum Objects". In *Imaging the Past. Electronic Imaging and Computer Graphics in museums and archaeology.* Edited by T. Higgins, p. Main and J. Lang. British Museum Occasional Paper, num. 114, pp. 199-209.

BARCELO,J.A., 1993, "Seriación de datos incompletos o ambiguos: una aplicación arqueológica de las redes neuronales". In *Aplicaciones Informáticas en Arqueología: Teorías y Sistemas.* Vol. 2, Edited by L.Valdés, I. Arenal and I. Pujana. Bilbao: Denboraren Argia.

BARCELO, J.A. 1996a, *Arqueología Automática. Inteligencia Artificial en Arqueología.* Sabadell: Ed. Ausa (Cuadernos de Arqueología Mediterránea, No. 2)

BARCELO, J.A., 1996b, "Heuristic classification and fuzzy sets. New tools for archaeological typologies". *Analecta Praehistorica Leidensia,* N. 28, pp. 155-164.

BARCELO, J.A., PALLARES,M. 1996, "From visual seduction to spatial analysis. A critique of GIS in Archaeology". *Archeologia e Calcolatori,* N. 7, pp. 327-335.

BARCELO, J.A., PALLARES,M. 1998, "Beyond GIS: The Archaeology of Social Spaces1". *Archeologia e Calcolatori,* No. 9, pp. 47-80.

BARRATT,G., BULLAS, S., DOYLE,S., 1999, "Digital Mapping and Remote Sensing at Merv (Digital Data Integration in a Field Context)". In *Archaeology in the age of the Internet.CAA 1997.* Edited by L.Dingwall, S.Exon, V. Gaffney, S. Laflin, M. Van Leusen. Oxford: British Archaeological Reports (Int. Series, S750).

BAUR,C., BEER,S., 1990, "Graphics Visualization and artificial Vision". In *Scientific Visualization and Graphics Simulation.* Edited by D. Thalmann. New York: John Wiley Publ.

BEARDAH,C.C., BAXTER,M.J., 1999, "Three-Dimensional data display using Kernel Density Estimates" In *New Techniques for Old Times. Computer Applications and Quantitative Methods in Archaeology.* Edited by J.A. Barceló, I. Briz and A. Vila. Oxford: British archaeological Reports (S757) .

BEARDON,C., YE,V., 1995, "Using Behavioural Rules in Animation". In *Computer Graphics. Developments in Virtual*

Environments. Edited by R.A.Earnshaw & J.A. Vince. London: Academic Press.

BEEX, W., 1993, "From Excavation drawing to archaeological playground: CAD applications for excavations". In *Computer Applications in Archaeology 1993.,* Edited by J.Wilcock and K.Lockyear. Oxford: BAR International Series No. 598,Pp. 101-108

BELL, T., 1999, "Reconstructing Archaeology from the Landscape: GIS. CAD and the Roman Signal Station at Whitby". In *Archaeology in the age of the Internet.CAA 1997.* Edited by L.Dingwall, S.Exon, V. Gaffney, S. Laflin, M. Van Leusen. Oxford: British Archaeological Reports (Int. Series, S750).

BERGER,B., KLEINBERG, LEIGHTON,t., 1999, "Reconstructing a Three-Dimensional Model with arbitrary erors". *Journal of the Association of Computer Machinery* 46 (2), pp. 212-235.

BERRY,J., BUCKLEY, D.J., ULBRICHT,C., 1998, "Visualize Realistic Landscapes" *GeoWorld* 11 (8): 42-47

BERTOL,D., FOELL,D., 1996, *Designing Digital Space. An architect's Guide to Virtual Reality.* New York. John Wiley.

BINNEY,C., BROWN,J., ELY,S., QUARTERMAINE,J., WOOD,J., 1993, "Survey data enhancement and interpretive works for the recording and conservation of Pendragonm Castle". In *Computer Applications in Archaeology 1993.,* Edited by J.Wilcock and K.Lockyear. Oxford: BAR International Series No. 598,Pp. 237-244

BISHOP, i., 1994, "Visual realism in Communicating Spatial change". In *Visualisation in geographical Information Systems.* Edited by H.M. Hearnshaw & D.J. Unwin. New York: John Wiley.

BLAKE, V.S., 1993, "Remote sensing in under-water archaeology: simulation of side scan sonar images using ray tracing techniques". In *Computer Applications in Archaeology 1993.,* Edited by J.Wilcock and K.Lockyear. Oxford: BAR International Series No. 598, pp. 39-44

BLOOMFIELD,M., SCHOFIELD,L., 1996, "Reconstructing the Treasury of Atreus at mycenae". In *Imaging the Past. Electronic Imaging and Computer Graphics in museums and archaeology.* Edited by T. Higgins, p. Main and J. Lang. British Museum Occasional Paper, num. 114, pp. 235-243.

BOAST,R., CHAPMAN,D., 1991, "SQL and hypertext generation of stratigraphic adjacency matrices". *Computer Applications in Archaeology 1990.* Edited by K.Lockyear and S. Rahtz. Oxford: Tempur Reparatum (British Archaeological Reports, S565). Pp. 43-51

BOLAND,P., JOHNSON, C., 1996, "Archaeology as Computer Visualisation: 'Virtual Tours' of Dudley Castle c. 1550". In *Imaging the Past. Electronic Imaging and Computer Graphics in museums and archaeology.* Edited by T. Higgins, p. Main and J. Lang. British Museum Occasional Paper, num. 114, pp. 227-234.

BORGHESE,N.A., FERRIGNO,G., PEDOTTI,A., FERRARI,S., SAVARÈ,R., 1998, "AutoScan: a flexible and portable 3D scanner" *IEEE Compter Graphics* 18 (3), pp. 38-41.

BRADLEY,J., FLETCHER,M., 1996, "Extraction and visualisation of Information from ground penetrating radar surveys". *Analecta Praehistorica leidensia* No. 28 (1), pp. 104-110

BRAUN,C., KULBE,T.H., LANG,F., SCHICKLER,W., STEINHAGE,V., CREMERS,A.B., FÖRSTNER,W., PLÜMER,L., 1995, "Models for photogrametric building reconstruction". *Computers & Graphics* 19 (1), pp. 109-118.

BRYSON,S., 1994, "Real-time exploratory scientific visualisation and virtual reality". In *Scientific Visualisation. Advances and Challenges.* Edited by L.Rosenblum et al. New York, Academic Press, pp. 65-85.

BRYSON,S., 1996, "Virtual Reality in Scientific Visualisation". *Communications of the ACM* 39 (5): 62-71.

BURDEA,G., COIFFET,P., 1994, *Virtual Reality Technology.* New York: John Wiley.

BURTON, N.R. HITCHEN, M.E. BRYAN, P.G., 1999, "Virtual Stonehenge: a Fall from Disgrace?" In *Archaeology in the Age of the Internet.CAA 1997.* Edited by L.Dingwall, S.Exon, V. Gaffney, S. Laflin, M. Van Leusen. Oxford: British Archaeological Reports (Int. Series, S750).

BUSER,P., RADIC,B., SEMMLER,K.D., 1990, "Surface Visualization". In *Scientific Visualization and Graphics Simulation.* Edited by D. Thalmann. New York: John Wiley Publ.

CASTLEFORD,J., 1991, "Archaeology, GIS, and the time dimension: an overview". In *Computer Applications in Archaeology 1991.* Edited by G. Lock and J. Moffett. Oxford: British Archaeological Reports (Int. Series S577), pp. 95-106

CHALMERS,A., STODDART,S., TIDMUS,J., MILES,R., 1995, "INSITE: an interactive visualisation system for archaeological sites". In *Computer Applications in Archaeology 1994.* Edited by Jeremy Huggett & Nick Ryan. Oxford: British Archaeological Reports (Int. Series, 600).pp.225-228

CHALMERS A G & STODDART, S K F 1996 Photo-realistic graphics for visualising archaeological site reconstructions" in *Imaging the past.* Edited by Higgins T, Main, P, & Lang, J British Museum Occasional Papers no. 114, 85-94,

CHALMERS, A.G., STODDART, S., BELCHER,M., DAY,M, 1997, *An Interactive Photo-Realistic Visualisation System for Archaeological Sites* (http://www.cs.bris.ac.uk/~alan/Arch/INSITE/research/comvis/insite2.htm)

CHAPMAN,G., 1991, "Do-it.yourself reconstruction modelling". In *Computer Applications in Archaeology 1991.* Edited by G.Lock & J. Moffet. Oxford: BAR International Series No. 577, pp. 213-218

CHAPMAN,P., WILLS,D., BROOKES, D., STEVENS, P., 1999, "Visualising underwater environments using multifrequency sonar". *IEEE Computer Graphics* 19 (5), pp. 61-65.

CHEN,C., 1999, *Information Visualization and Virtual Environments.* New York: Springer Verlag

COLLINS, B. 1993 'From Ruins to Reality: the Dresden Frauenkirche' *in IEEE Computer Graphics and Applications* vol. 13. (6), pp. 13 - 15.

COLLINS,B., WILIAMS,D., HAAK,R., TRUX,M., HERZ,H., GENEVRIEZ,L., NICOT,P., BRAULT,P., COYERE,X., KRAUSE,B., KLUCKOW,B., PAFFENHOLZ,A., 1993, "The Desden Frauenkirche-rebuilding the Past". In *Computer Applications in Archaeology 1993.,* Edited by J.Wilcock and K.Lockyear. Oxford: BAR International Series No. 598, pp.19-24

COLONNA, J.F., 1994, *Images du Virtuel* Addison-Wesley France

CORNFORTH,J., DAVIDSON,C., DALLAS, C.J., LOCK, G.R., 1991 "Visualising ancient Greece: computer graphics in the Sacred Way project". In *Computer Applications in Archaeology 1991.* Edited by G.Lock & J. Moffet. Oxford: BAR International Series No. 577, pp.219-225

CSÁKI,G., REDÓ,F., 196, "Documentation and modelling of a Roman imperial villa in Central Italy". *Analecta Praehistorica Leidensia* No. 28 (2), pp. 433-438

DALY, P.T., LOCK, G., 1999, "Timing is everything: Commentary on Managing Temporal Variables in Geographic Information Systems". " In *New Techniques for Old Times. Computer Applications and Quantitative Methods in Archaeology.* Edited by J.A. Barceló, I. Briz and A. Vila. Oxford: British archaeological Reports (S757) .

DANIEL,R., 1997, "The need for the solid modelling of structure in the archaeology of buildings", Internet Archaeology, 2, 2.3 (http://intarch.ac.uk/journal/issue2/daniels_index.html

De JONG, E.M., 1994, "Solay system visualisation: global science maps". *Scientific Visualisation. Advances and Challenges.* Edited by L. Rosenblum et al. Academic press. London, pp. 407-418

DELOOZE,K., WOOD,J 1991, "Furness Anney survey project - The application of computer graphics and data visualisation to reconstruction modelling of an historical monument". *Computer Applications in Archaeology 1990,* Edited by K.Lockyear and S.Rahtz. Oxford: British Archaeological reports (Int. Series 565), pp. 141-148.

DEW, P.M., FERNANDO, L.T.P., HOLLIMAN, N.S., LAWLER, M., MALHI,R., PARKIN, D., 1990, "Illuminating Chapters in History: Computer Aided Visualisation for Archaeological Reconstruction". In *Communication in Archaeology: a global view of the impact of information technology.* Edited by P. Reilly and S. Rahtz. Second World Archaeological Congress. Barquisimeto: Venezuela., pp. 15-25

DJINDJIAN,F., IAKOVLEVA,L., PIROT,F., 1996, "Résultats préliminaires d'un projet de reconstitution 2D et 3D de structures d'habitats préhistoriques". *Archeologia e Calcolatori* No. 7, pp. 215-222.

DOBSON,G.T., WAGGENSPACK,W.N., LAMOUSIN,H.J., 1995, "Feature based models for anatomical data fitting". *Computer aided design* 27 (2), pp. 139-145.

DORAN,J., PALMER,M., GILBERT,N., MELLARS,P., 1994, "The EOS Project: Modelling Upper Paleolithic Social Change". In *Simulating Societies. The Computer Simulation of Social Phenomena.* Edited by N. Gilbert and J. Doran, pp. 195-221. London, UCL Press.

DURHAM, P., LEWIS,P., SHENNAN,S., 1993, "Artefact matching and retrieval using the Generalised Hough Transform". In *Computer Applications in Archaeology 1993.,* Edited by J.Wilcock and K.Lockyear. Oxford: BAR International Series No. 598, pp. 25-30

DURLACH,N.I., MAVOR,A.S., (eds.), 1994, *Virtual Reality. Scientific and Technological Challenges.* Washington, National Academy Press.

EARL, G.P., 1999, "Visualising Danebury: Modelled Approaches to Spatial Theory" In *Archaeology in the age of the Internet.CAA 1997.* Edited by L.Dingwall, S.Exon, V. Gaffney, S. Laflin, M. Van Leusen. Oxford: British Archaeological Reports (Int. Series, S750).

EBERT, D.S., MUSGRAVE, F.K., PEACHEY,D., PERLIN,K., WORLEY,S., 1994, *Texturing and Modelling. A Procedural approach.* Boston: Academic Press Professional.

EDER-HINTERLEITNER,A., NEUBAEUER,W., MELICHAR,P., 1996, "Reconstruction of archaeological structures using magnetic prospection". *Analecta praehistorica leidensia* No. 28 (1), pp. 131-137.

EGGLI,L., HSU,C., BRÜDERLIN,B.D., ELBER,G., 1996, "Inferring 3D models from free hand sketches and constraints". *Computer aided design* 29 (2): 101-112.

EISLER,J., PEJSA,J., PREUSS,K., 1988, "A digital model of archaeological excavations as the starting point of a database of primary information in Egyptology:method-procedure-experience". In *Computer Applications in Archaeology 1988.* Edited by S.P.Q.Rahtz. Oxford: British archaeological Reports (Int. Series S446), pp. 109-132

ERICSON, J.E., STICKEL, E.G., 1973, "A proposed classification system for ceramics". *World Archaeology* 4, pp. 357-367.

EXON,S., GAFFNEY,V., 1999, "From Wroxeter to the Web: The British Telecom Access to Archaeology Project". In *New Techniques for Old Times. Computer Applications and Quantitative Methods in Archaeology.* Edited by J.A. Barceló, I. Briz and A. Vila. Oxford: British archaeological Reports (S757) .

FEICHTINGER,G., PRSKAWETZ,A., GÖLLER,E., FISCHER,G., 1996, "Despotism and anarchy in ancient China: visualising the dynastic cycle" *Jahrbuch der Wirtschaftswissenschaften* Band 47 (heft 1), pp. 1-13.

FISHWICK, P.A., 1995, *Simulation and Model Design and Execution. Building Digital Worlds.* Englewood Cliffs. Prentice Hall.

FLETCHER,M., SPICER,D., 1988, "Clonehenge: an experiment with gridded and non-gridded survey of data". *Computer Applications in Archaeology1988.* Edited by S.P.Q.Rahtz. Oxford: British archaeological Reports (Int. Series, No. 446), pp. 309-324

FLETCHER,M., SPICER,D., 1992, "The display and analysis of ridge-and-furrow from topographically surveyed data". In *Archaeology and the Information Age.* Edited by P. Reilly and S.Rahtz. London: Routledge, pp. 97-122.

FLORENZANO, M.J., , BLAISE, J.Y., DRAP.P., 1999 "PAROS. Close range photogrametry and architectural models". In *Archaeology in the age of the Internet.CAA 1997.* Edited by L.Dingwall, S.Exon, V. Gaffney, S. Laflin, M. Van Leusen. Oxford: British Archaeological Reports (Int. Series, S750).

FOLEY,J., RIBARSKY,B., 1994, "Next-generation data visualisation tools". In *Scientific Visualisation. Advances and Challenges.* Edited by L.Rosenblum et al. New York, Academic Press, pp.103-127

FOLEY,J., van DAM, A., FEINER, S.K., HUGHES, J.F., 1996, *Computer Graphics. Principles and Practice* (2. ed.). Reading (MA): Addison-Wesley

FORTE,M., 1992, "Image processing applications in archaeology: classification systems of archaeological sites in the landscape". In *Computing the Past.* Edited by J.Andresen, T. Madsen & I.Scollar. Aarhus (DK): Aarhus University Press, pp. 53-61

FORTE,M., 1993, "Un esperimento di visualizzazione scientifica per l'archeologia del paesaggio: la navigazione nel paesaggio virtuale". *Archeologia e Calcolatori* No. 4, pp. 137-152.

FORTE, M (ed),1997 *Virtual Archaeology: Great Discoveries Brought to Life Through Virtual Reality,* Thames and Hudson, London

FORTE,M., 1996, "Il Progetto ARCTOS. Verso un GI Multimediale". *Archeologia e Calcolatori* 7, (1), pp. 179-192.

FORTE,M., MOZZI,P., ZOCCHI, M., 1998, "Immagini satellitari e modelli virtuali: interpretazioni geoarchaeologiche della regione del Sistan meridionale". *Archeologia e Calcolatori* No. 9, pp. 271-290

FORTE,M., GUIDAZZOLI,A., 1996a, "Archaeology, GIS and desktop virtual reality: The ARCTOS project". *Analecta Preaehistorica Leidensia* 28 (2), pp. 443-456

FORTE,M., GUIDAZZOLI,A., 1996b, "Shape from motion: Dalle sequenze filmate alla modellazione tridimensionale. Progetto per l'elaborazione 3D Di immagini video archeologiche". *Archeologia e Calcolatori* 7, pp. 223-232.

FRANÇON,J., LIENHARDT,P., 1994, "Basic Principles of Topology-based Methods for Simulating metamorphoses of Natural Objects". In *Artificial Life and Virtual Reality.* Edited by N.M. Thalmann and D. Thalmann. New York: John Wiley Publ.

FRIEDHOFF, R.M., BENZON, W., 1989, *The second computer revolution: Visualisation.* New York: Abrams Publ.

FRY,C., 1998, "Navigating the Past and the Future" *GisEurope* 7 (5): 24-26.

GAFFNEY,V., OSTIR,K., PODOBNIKAR,T., STANČIČ,Z., 1996, "Spatial Analysis, field survey, territories and mental maps on the island of Brač". *Archeologia e calcolatori* No. 7, pp. 27-41

GAGALOWICZ,A., 1990, "Special Models for Natural Objects". In *Scientific Visualization and Graphics Simulation.* Edited by D. Thalmann. New York: John Wiley Publ.

GERSHON,N., 1994, "From perception to visualisation". In *Scientific Visualisation. Advances and Challenges.* Edited by L.Rosenblum et al. New York, Academic Press, pp. 129-139.

GILLINGS,M., 1996, "Not Drawing but Waving? Re-Humanising GIS. The Tisza flood plain revisited". In *The Present State of G.I.S. Applications and Analogous Systems in Praehistoric Archaeology.* Edited by A. Bietti, I. Johnson and A. Voorrips. The Colloquia of the XIII International Congress of Prehistoric and Protohistoric Sciences. Section I: Theoretical And Methodological Problems (Colloquium II). Forli: A.B.A.C.O. Edizioni.

GILLINGS,M., 1999, Engaging Place: a Framework for the Integration and Realisation of Virtual-Reality Approaches in Archaeology" In *Archaeology in the age of the Internet.CAA 1997.* Edited by L.Dingwall, S.Exon, V. Gaffney, S. Laflin, M. Van Leusen. Oxford: British Archaeological Reports (Int. Series, S750).

GILLINGS, M, AND GOODRICK, G T, 1996 "Sensuous and Reflexive GIS: exploring visualisation and VRML", *Internet Archaeology,* 1, (http://intarch.ac.uk/journal/issue1/gillings_index.html)

GILMAN ROMANO, D., TOLBA,O., 1994, "Remote Sensing, GIS and electronic surveying: reconstructing the city plan and landscape of Roman Corinth". In *Computer Applications in Archaeology 1994.* Edited by J. Huggett and Nick Ryan. Oxford, British Archaeological Reports (Int. Series No. 600). Pp. 163-174.

GISIGER,A., COOPER,E.S., YUAN,Y.LIMP,F., 1996, *Development and Implementation of a low cost Photogrammetric Data Archival System for artifact and osteological inventory.* Center for Advanced Spatial Technologies, University of Arkansas.

Technical report NPS MT0424-4-NC-22 (http://www.cast.uark.edu/cast/projects/arch/photogram/)

GOLDSTEIN, L., 1996, "Representation and geometrical methods of problem-solving". In *Forms of Representation* Edited by D. Peterson. Exeter. Intellect Books

GOODCHILD,M., BUTTENFIELD,B., WOOD,J., 1994, "Visualising Data Validity". In *Visualisation in geographical Information Systems.* Edited by H.M. Hearnshaw & D.J. Unwin. New York: John Wiley.

GOODRICK,G.T., 1999, "VRML, Virtual Reality and Visualisation: The best tool for the job?" In *Archaeology in the age of the Internet.CAA 1997.* Edited by L.Dingwall, S.Exon, V. Gaffney, S. Laflin, M. Van Leusen. Oxford: British Archaeological Reports (Int. Series, S750).

GORDON,S., 1999," The Virtual Museum - who needs it?" In *Archaeology in the age of the Internet.CAA 1997.* Edited by L.Dingwall, S.Exon, V. Gaffney, S. Laflin, M. Van Leusen. Oxford: British Archaeological Reports (Int. Series, S750).

GOTTARELLI,A., 1995, "La modellazione tridimensionale del documento archeologico: livelli descrittivi e procesamento digitale" *Archeologia e Calcolatori*, 5, pp. 75-103.

GOTTARELLI, A., 1996, "Museografia e Informatica. La riconstruzione virtuale della tomba menfita del generale Horemheb". *Archeologia e Calcolatori* 7 (2), pp. 1091-1099.

GRÖLLER,E., LÖFFELMAN,H., WEGENKITLL,R., 1999, "Visualisation of dynamical systems" *Future Generation systems* 15 (1), pp. 75-86.

GU,P., YAN,X., 1995, "Neural network approach to the reconstruction of freeform surfaces for reverse engineering" *Computer aided design* 27 (1), pp. 59-64.

GUIDAZZOLI, A., 1992, "Computer graphics videotaping in un ambiente di visualizzazione scientifica". *VII Convegno internazionale sulla applicszioni della computer graphics nella produzione, progettazione e gestione, Milano, 4-7 febbraio 1992*, pp. 347-354.

HAIGH, J.G.B., 1992, "Practical experience in creating digital terrain models". In *Computing the Past.* Edited by J.Andresen, T. Madsen & I.Scollar. Aarhus (DK): Aarhus University Press, pp. 67-74

HAGEN, H., 1994, "Visualisation of large data sets". In *Scientific Visualisation. Advances and Challenges.* Edited by L.Rosenblum et al. New York, Academic Press, pp. 187-198

HARRIS, T.M. LOCK,G., 1996, "Multi-dimensional GIS: exploratory approaches to spatial and temporal relationships within archaeological stratigraphy". *Analecta Praehistorica leidensia* No. 28 (2), pp. 207-316

HENDRIK A.H.C. HARTWIG, V.v., BRAUN,S.J. BÜLTHOFF,H.H., 1998 "Navigating through a virtual city. Using virtual reality technology to study human action and perception", *FutureGeneration Computer Systems* (14)3-4 (1998) pp. 231-242

HIGGINS,T., 1996, "Electronic reconstruction of a Digitised Aztecan Turquoise mosaic". In *Imaging the Past. Electronic Imaging and Computer Graphics in museums and archaeology.* Edited by T. Higgins, p. Main and J. Lang. British Museum Occasional Paper, num. 114, pp. 49-56

HOALA,N., BRENNER,C., 1999, "Unwrapping the detailed surface models Generation of Virtual City models using Laser Altrimetry, 2D Gis and CAD". *GIM International* 13 (3): 6-9

HOFFMAN C & ROSSIGNAC, J, 1996 'A Road Map to Solid Modelling' *IEEE Transactions on Visualisation and Computer Graphics* vol .2, pp. 3 - 10.

HOULDING, S.W., 1994, *3D Geoscience Modelling. Computer Techniques for Geological Characterization.* New York: Springer—Verlag.

HSIA,J.S., NEWTON,I., 1999, "A method for the automated production of Digital Terrain Models using a combination of Feature points, grid points and filling back points". *Photogrammetric Engineering and Remote Sensing* 65 (6): 713-719.

HUGHES,S.W., 1996, "Three-dimensional reconstruction of an ancient Egyptian mummy". In *Imaging the Past. Electronic Imaging and Computer Graphics in museums and archaeology.* Edited by T. Higgins, p. Main and J. Lang. British Museum Occasional Paper, num. 114, pp. 211-225

ISHIDA,J., 1997, "The general B-spline method and its application to the modification of curves and surfaces". *Computer aided design* 29, pp. 779-790

JAQUEL, D., *The 3D Modelling Web page* (http://www.mech.ed.ac.uk/~dom/3d/3d.html)

JOHNSON, I., 1999 "Mapping the fourth dimension: a methodology for recording and visualising cultural features through time". In *Archaeology in the age of the Internet.CAA 1997.* Edited by L.Dingwall, S.Exon, V. Gaffney, S. Laflin, M. Van Leusen. Oxford: British Archaeological Reports (Int. Series, S750).

JONES,Q., 1997, "Virtual-Communities, Virtual Settlements & Cyber-Archaeology: A Theoretical Outline" *Journal of Computer-Mediated Communication* No. 3 (3). (http://www.ascusc.org/jcmc/vol3/issue3/jones.html)

JUHL,K., 1995, *The relationship between vessel form and vessel function. A Methodological Study.* AmS-Skrifter 14. Arkeologisk museum i Stavanger.(Norway)

KADOBAYASHI, R., NEETER, E., MASE, K., NAKATSU, R., 1999, "VisTA: An Interactive Visualisation Tool for Archaeological Data". ". In *Archaeology in the age of the Internet.CAA 1997.* Edited by L.Dingwall, S.Exon, V. Gaffney, S. Laflin, M. Van Leusen. Oxford: British Archaeological Reports (Int. Series, S750).

KALVIN,A., REMY,A., ARDITO,O., ORLA,K., NOLAZCO,E., PRADO, J., FRANCO,R., MURGA,A., WIESE, G., 1999, Using Visualisation in the Archaeological Excavations of a Pre-Inca Temple in Peru" ". In *Archaeology in the age of the Internet.CAA 1997.* Edited by L.Dingwall, S.Exon, V. Gaffney, S. Laflin, M. Van Leusen. Oxford: British Archaeological Reports (Int. Series, S750).

KAMPFFMEYER, U., ZAMPERONI,P., TEEGEN, W.R., GRAÇA,L., 1987, *Untersuchungen zur rechnergestützten Klassifikation der Form von Keramik.* Arbeiten zur Urgeschichte des Menschen. No. 11. Frankfurt am Main, Verlag Peter Lang

KAUFMAN,A., 1990, *Volume Visualisation.* IEEE Computer Society Press Tutorial. Los Alamitos, CA

KAUFMAN,A., 1994, "Trends in volume visualisation and volume graphics". In *Scientific Visualisation. Advances and Challenges.* Edited by L. Rosenblum et al. Academic press. London, pp.3-19.

KAUFMANN,S., 1995, *At home in the Universe. The search for laws of self-organization and complexity.* Oxford University Press.

KEMP,D., 1993, "Personal computer based three-dimensional reconstruction modelling of standing buildings". In *Computer Applications in Archaeology 1993.,* Edited by J.Wilcock and K.Lockyear. Oxford: BAR International Series No. 598, pp. 249-254

KIM,T., MULLER,J.P., 1998, "A Technique for 3D Building Reconstruction" *Photogrammetric Engineering and Remote Sensing.* 64 (9): 923-930.

KOHLER, T.A., GUMERMAN,G.J., 1996, "Beyond GIS: Populating worlds with agents". In *The Present State of G.I.S. Applications and Analogous Systems in Praehistoric Archaeology.* Edited by A. Bietti, I. Johnson and A. Voorrips. The Colloquia of the XIII International Congress of Prehistoric and Protohistoric Sciences. Section I: Theoretical And Methodological Problems (Colloquium II). Forlì: A.B.A.C.O. Edizioni.

KOTSAKIS,K., ANDREOU,S., VARGAS,A., PAPOUDAS,A., 1994, "Reconstructing a Bronze Age site with CAD". In *Computer Applications in Archaeology 1994.* Edited by J.Huggett and Nick Ryan. Oxford: British Archaeological Reports S600, pp. 181-187

KVAMME,K.L., 1991, "Terrain Form Analysis of archaeological location through Geographic Information Systems. In *Computer Applications in Archaeology 1991.* Edited by G.Lock and J.Moffett. Oxford: British Archaeological Reports (Int. Series S557), pp. 127-136

LANG, S.A., 1992, *An investigation of image processing techniques at Pincevent Habitation No. 1, a Late Magdalenian site in*

Northern France. Arizona State University. Anthropological Research papers No. 43.

LAVENDER,D., WALLIS,A.,BOWYER,A.,DAVENPORT,P., 1990, "Solid modelling of Roman Bath". In *Communication in Archaeology: a global view of the impact of information technology.* Edited by P. Reilly and S. Rahtz. Second World Archaeological Congress. Barquisimeto: Venezuela., pp. 7-14

LEEUW, S van der., McGLADE,J., 1997, (eds.) *Time, process and Structures Transformation in Archaeology* London, Routledge.

LEUSEN, M., 1999, "Viewshed and Cost Surface Analysis Using GIS". In *New Techniques for Old Times. Computer Applications and Quantitative Methods in Archaeology.* Edited by J.A. Barceló, I. Briz and A. Vila. Oxford: British archaeological Reports (S757).

LEWIS,R., SÉGUIN,C., 1998, "Generation of 3D building models from 2D architectural plans" *Computer aided Design* 30 (10), pp. 765-769.

LLOBERA,M., 1996, "Exploring the topography of mind: GIS, Social Space and archaeology"*Antiquity* 70, 612-22.

LLORET, T., 1999, "Arqueología Virtual y audiovisual. Una nueva propuesta en la difusión del conocimiento arqueológico". *Revista de Arqueología* XX, 213, pp. 13-19.

LOCK,G., DALY,P., 1999, "Looking at Change, continuity and Time in GIS: an example from the Sangro Valley, Italy". In *New Techniques for Old Times. Computer Applications and Quantitative Methods in Archaeology.* Edited by J.A. Barceló, I. Briz and A. Vila. Oxford: British archaeological Reports (S757).

LOEFFLER, C.E., 1994a, "The Networked Virtual Art Museum and other projects". In *The Virtual Reality Casebook.* Edited by C.E. Loeffler and T. Anderson. New York: Van Nostrand Reinhold. pp., 31-37

LOEFFLER, C.E.., 1994B, "Virtual Polis: A Networked Virtual Reality Application". In *The Virtual Reality Casebook.* Edited by C.E. Loeffler and T. Anderson. New York: Van Nostrand Reinhold. pp.,60-77

LOOTS,L., NACKAERTS,K., WALKENS,M., 1999, "Fuzzy viewshwed analysis of the Hellenistic City Defence System at Sagalassos. Turkey". In *Archaeology in the age of the Internet.CAA 1997.* Edited by L.Dingwall, S.Exon, V. Gaffney, S. Laflin, M. Van Leusen. Oxford: British Archaeological Reports (Int. Series, S750).

LULL, V., 1999, "The new technologies and designer archaeology". In *New Techniques for Old Times. Computer Applications and Quantitative Methods in Archaeology.* Edited by J.A. Barceló, I. Briz and A. Vila. Oxford: British archaeological Reports (S757).

LUKESH,S.S., 1996, "Expanding the archaeologist's Toolkit: Scientific Visualisation of Archaeological data". In *Imaging the Past. Electronic Imaging and Computer Graphics in museums and archaeology.* Edited by T. Higgins, p. Main and J. Lang. British Museum Occasional Paper, num. 114, pp.245-256.

MA,W., HE,P., 1998, "B-spline surface local updating with unorganized points". *Computer aided Design*, 30, pp. 853-862.

MacEACHREN,A., 1994, "Time as a cartographic variable". In *Visualisation in geographical Information Systems.* Edited by H.M. Hearnshaw & D.J. Unwin. New York: John Wiley.

MCCULLAGH, M. MAGGI, R., PEARCE,M., RATCLIFFE, J., 1999, "From The Ground Up: Visualising Ligurian Archaeological Sites" In *Archaeology in the age of the Internet.CAA 1997.* Edited by L.Dingwall, S.Exon, V. Gaffney, S. Laflin, M. Van Leusen. Oxford: British Archaeological Reports (Int. Series, S750).

McCORMICK, B-H., DeFANTI, T., BROWN, M.D., 1987, "Visualisation in Scientific Computing". *Computer Graphics* 21(6):1-14.

MAIN, P., HIGGINS,T., WALTER,A., ROBERTS,A., LEESE,M., 1993, "Using a three-dimensional digitser and CAD software to record and reconstruct a Bronze-Age fissure burial". In *Computer Applications in Archaeology 1993.,* Edited by J.Wilcock and K.Lockyear. Oxford: BAR International Series No. 598, pp. 133-141

MAIN,P.L., SPENCE, A.J., HIGGINS,T., 1995, "Computer-aided design techniques for the graphical modelling of data from the prehistoric site of Runnymede, Berkshire". In *Computer Applications in Archaeology 1994.* Edited by Jeremy Huggett & Nick Ryan. Oxford: British Archaeological Reports (Int. Series, 600).pp. 235-243.

MARGALIOT,M., GOTSMAN,C., 1995 "Approximation of Smooth Surfaces and Adaptive Sampling by Picewise-linear Interpolants". In *Computer Graphics. Developments in Virtual Environments.* Edited by R.A. Arnshaw and J.A. Vince. London: Academic Press, pp. 17-27

MARR, D.C., 1982, *Vision* San Francisco: W.H.Freeman and Co.

MENARD,Ch. SABLATNIG,R., 1996, "Pictorial, Three-dimensional acquisition of archaeological finds as basis for an automatic classification". *Analecta Praehistorica leidensia* No. 28 (2), pp.415-428

MESSIKA,N., 1999, "Real Time, *in situ*; Computerized Graphic Documentation in Archaeological Excavation". In *New Techniques for Old Times. Computer Applications and Quantitative Methods in Archaeology.* Edited by J.A. Barceló, I. Briz and A. Vila. Oxford: British archaeological Reports (S757).

MEUCCI,C., BUZZANCA, G., 1996, "Simulazione e/o Seduzione. La Representazione mediante modeli di reperti, relitti, oggetti de altro". *Archaeologia e Calcolatori* 7 (2), pp. 973-982.

MILLER,P., RICHARDS,J., 1995, "The good, the bad, and the downright misleading: archaeological adoption of computer visualisation". In *Computer Applications in Archaeology 1994.* Edited by Jeremy Huggett & Nick Ryan. Oxford: British Archaeological Reports (Int. Series, 600).pp. 19-22.

MOLINEAUX,B., 1992, "From virtuality to actuality: the archaeological site simulation environment". In *Archaeology and the Information Age.* Edited by P. Reilly and S.Rahtz. London: Routledge, pp.312-322

MORTENSON, M.E., 1985, *Geometric Modelling.* New York: John Wiley & Sons.

MUDUR,S.P., GPOPALSAMY,S., SHIKANE,D., DIXIT,D.S., PATWARDHAN,B.S., NAYAK,N.S. SHANBHAG,S.V., 1999, "Graphics research at National Center for Software Technology in India. *Computer Graphics* 33(1): 21-25.

MUSGRAVE, F.K., 1994, "A Brief introduction to fractals". In *Texturing and Modelling. A Procedural approach.* Edited by Ebert, D.S., Musgrave, F.K., Peachey,D., Perlin,K., Worley,S.. Boston: Academic Press Professional.

MUSGRAVE, F.K., 1994b, "Procedural Fractal Terrains". In *Texturing and Modelling. A Procedural approach.* Edited by Ebert, D.S., Musgrave, F.K., Peachey,D., Perlin,K., Worley,S.. Boston: Academic Press Professional.

NELSON,T.H., 1987, *Literary machines.* Swathmore: T.H.Nelson

NEUBAUER,W., MELICHAR,P., EDER-HINTERLEITNER,A., 1996, "Collection, visualisation and simulation of magnetic prospection data". *Analecta Praehistorica leidensia* No. 28 (1), pp. 123-129

NIELSON, G.M., 1994, "Research issues in modelling for the analysis and visualisation of large data sets". *Scientific Visualisation. Advances and Challenges.* Edited by L. Rosenblum et al. Academic press. London, pp. 143-155.

NOSER,H., THALMANN,D., 1994, "Simulating the life of Virtual Plants, Fishes and Butterflies". In *Artificial Life and Virtual Reality.* Edited by N.M. Thalmann and D. Thalmann. New York: John Wiley Publ.

NOVAK, M.N., 1994, "Fractal geometry and its applications in visualisation". In *Scientific Visualisation. Advances and Challenges.* Edited by L. Rosenblum et al. Academic press. London, pp.232-335

ODEGARD, O., 1994, "To live in Virtual Polis". In *The Virtual Reality Casebook.* Edited by C.E. Loeffler and T. Anderson. New York: Van Nostrand Reinhold. pp.,78-83.

OZAWA, K., 1992, "Reconstruction of Japanese ancient tombs and villages". *Computing the Past.* Edited by J.Andresen, T. Madsen & I.Scollar. Aarhus (DK): Aarhus University Press, pp.415-423

OZAWA,K., 1996, "ASM: An Ancient Scenery Modeller". In *Electronic Imaging and Computer Graphics in museums and archaeology.* Edited by T. Higgins, p. Main and J. Lang. British Museum Occasional Paper, num. 114, pp.

OZAWA,K., KATO,T., TSUDE,H., 1994, "Detection of beacon networks between ancient hill-forts using a difital terrain model based GIS". In *Compyter Applications in Archaeology 1994.* Edited by J.Huggett and Nick Ryan. Oxford, British archaeological reports (Int. Series, No. 600), pp. 157-161

PAQUETTE,S., 1996, "3D Scanning in design and Human Engineering" *IEEE Computer Graphics* 16 (5), pp. 11-15.

PARK,H., KIM,K., 1995, "An adaptive method for smooth surface approximation to scattered 3D points" *Computer aided design* 27 (12), pp. 929-939.

PARMEGIANI,N., POSCOLIERI,M., 1999, "The Landscape of lake Sevan (Armenia) during the Urartian Period". In *New Techniques for Old Times. Computer Applications and Quantitative Methods in Archaeology.* Edited by J.A. Barceló, I. Briz and A. Vila. Oxford: British archaeological Reports (S757) .

PETERSON, PHILIP, F. D. FRACCHIA, B. HAYDEN, 1995 A virtual computer imaging technique for archaeological research. *Society for American Archaeology Bulletin* 13(4):30–33.

PETROV,M., TALAPOV,A., ROBERTSON,T., LEBEDEV,A., ZHILYAEV,A., POLONSKIY,L., 1998, "Optical 3D digitizers: bringing life to the virtual world" *IEEE Computer Graphics* 18 (3), pp. 28-37.

PIEGL.L.A., TILLER,W., 1999, "Computing offsets of NURBS curves and surfaces" *Computer Aided Design* 31, pp. 147-156.

PIJOAN,J., BARCELO, J.A., BRIZ,I., VILA,A., 1999, "Image Quantification in use-wear analysis". *Computer Applications in Archaeology '99.* Dublin. (in press).

POST, F.H., van WIJK, I.J., 1994, "Visual representation of vector fields: recent developments and research directions". *Scientific Visualisation. Advances and Challenges.* Edited by L. Rosenblum et al. Academic press. London, pp. 367-390

RATTENBURY, B., 1991, "The Hadrianic baths at Leptis Magna. A Reconstruction of the Buildings" (http://archpropplan.auckland.ac.nz/virtualtour/hadrians_bath/hadrians_bath.html)

REELER, C., 1999, "An analysis of the Structure and Function of Prehistoric maori *Pa* sites". In *Archaeology in the age of the Internet.CAA 1997.* Edited by L.Dingwall, S.Exon, V. Gaffney, S. Laflin, M. Van Leusen. Oxford: British Archaeological Reports (Int. Series, S750).

REFSLAND,S.T., 1998, "Finding the Virtual in our World Heritage History". *Computer Graphics* 32 (4): 16-19.

REILLY,P., 1990, "Towards a virtual archaeology". *Computer Applications in Archaeology 1990*, Edited by K.Lockyear and S.Rahtz. Oxford: British Archaeological reports (Int. Series 565), pp., 133-139.

REILLY, P., 1992, "Three-Dimensional modelling and primary archaeological data". In *Archaeology and the Information Age.* Edited by P. Reilly and S.Rahtz. London: Routledge, pp. 147-173

REILLY,P., THOMPSON,N., 1992, "Experiments with user-friendly volume visualisation and iconographic display methods to explore core data". In *Computing the Past.* Edited by J.Andresen, T. Madsen and I. Scollar. Aarhus University Press., pp.429-439

REILLY,P., SHENAN,S., 1989, "Applying solid modelling and animated three-dimensional graphics to Archaeological problems". *Computer Applications in Archaeology 1989,* Edited by S. Rahtz and J.Richards. Oxford: British Archaeological Reports (Int. Series 548), pp. 157-166.

RICK, J.W., HART, D, 1997, "Panoramic Virtual Reality and Archaeology" *Society for American Archaeology Bulletin* 15(5)

ROMANO, D.G., TOLBA, O., 1995, "Remote sensing, GIS and electronic surveying: reconstructing the city plan and landscape of Roman Corinth". In *Computer Applications in Archaeology 1994.* Edited by Jeremy Huggett & Nick Ryan. Oxford: British Archaeological Reports (Int. Series, 600).pp.163-174

ROSE, E., BREEN, D., AHLERS, K.H., CRAMPTON, C., TUCERYAN,M., WHITAKER, R., GREER, D., 1995, "Annotating Real-World Objects Using Augmented Reality". In *Computer Graphics. Developments in Virtual Environments.* Edited by R.A.Earnshaw & J.A. Vince. London: Academic Press.pp. 357-370

ROSENBLUM, L.J., KAMGAR-PARSI, B., 1994, "Progress and problems in ocean visualisation". *Scientific Visualisation. Advances and Challenges.* Edited by L. Rosenblum et al. Academic press. London, pp. 435-454

ROSSIGNAC, J.R., 1994, "Representing and visualising complex continuous geometric models". *Scientific Visualisation. Advances and Challenges.* Edited by L. Rosenblum et al. Academic press. London, pp.337-348

ROWNER, I., 1993 "Complex measurements made easy: morphometric analysis of artefacts using Expert Vision Systems". In *Computer Applications in Archaeology 1993.,* Edited by J.Wilcock and K.Lockyear. Oxford: BAR International Series No. 598, pp. 31-37

RUGGLES, C.L.N., MEDYCKYJ-SCOTT, D.J., GRUFFYDD, A., 1992, "Multiple viewshed analysis using GIS and its archaeological application: a case study in nortyhern Mull. In *Computing the Past.* Edited by J.Andresen, T. Madsen and I. Scollar. Aarhus University Press., pp. 125-132.

RYAN,N., 1996, "Computer-based visualisation of the Past: Technical 'realism' and Historical credibility". In *Electronic Imaging and Computer Graphics in museums and archaeology.* Edited by T. Higgins, p. Main and J. Lang. British Museum Occasional Paper, num. 114, pp.95-108.

RYAN,N., 1997, "Visualising Roman Canterbury: Computer Graphics in Archaeology" (http://www.cs.ukc.ac.uk/people/staff/nsr/arch/visrcant/visrcant.html)

RYAN,N., ROBERTS, J., 1997, "Alternative Archaeological Representations within Virtual Worlds" *Paper presented at the UK Virtual Reality Special Interest Group* (http://www.cs.ukc.ac.uk/people/staff/nsr/arch/vrsig97/)

SABLATNIG,R., MENARD,Ch., 1996, "Computer based acquisition of archaeological finds: the first step towards automatic classification". *Archeologia e Calcolatori* No. 7, pp. 429-446.

SANSONI,C., 1996, "Visual Analysis: a new probabilistic technique to determine landscape visibility". *Computer aided design* 28 (4), pp. 289-299.

SANDERS, D.H., 1999, "Virtual Worlds for Archaeological Research and Education" In *Archaeology in the age of the Internet.CAA 1997.* Edited by L.Dingwall, S.Exon, V. Gaffney, S. Laflin, M. Van Leusen. Oxford: British Archaeological Reports (Int. Series, S750).

SHAW, J., 1994, "The Virtual museum" In *The Virtual Reality Casebook.* Edited by C.E. Loeffler and T. Anderson. New York: Van Nostrand Reinhold. Pp., 27-30.

SHEPPARD, J.R.J., 1989, *Visual Simulation. A's guide for architects, engineers and planners.* Van Nostrand Reinhold. New York.

SIMS,D., 1997, "Archaeological Models: Pretty Pictures or Research Tools? *IEEE Computer Graphics* 17 (1), pp. 13-15.

SMALL, C.G., 1996, *The Statistical Theory of Shape.* Springer-Verlag. New York.

SMITH,M., 1983, *The study of ceramic function from artifact size and shape.* Ph.Dissertation. University of Oregon.

SONKA,M., HLAVAC,V., BOYLE,R., 1994, *Image processing, Analysis and Machine Vision.* London: Chapman and Hall

STECKNER,C., 1993, "Quantitative methods with Qualitative results in Expert System. Physical Qualities in Historical Shape design". En *AplicacionesInformáticas en Arqueología: Teorías y Sistemas vol. 2.* Edited by L. Valdés, I. Arenal and I. Pujana. Bilbao: Denboraren Argia, pp. 486-499

STECKNER,C., 1996, "Archaeological building reconstruction and the physical analysis of excavation documents". *Archeologia e Calcolatori* 7 (2), pp. 923-938.

STECKNER,C., STECKNER,C., 1987, "SAMOS. Statistical Analysis of mathematical Object Structure". *Bolletino d'Informazioni* No. 8 (1), pp. 79-99.

STEWART,N.F., 1990, "Solid Modelling". In *Scientific Visualization and Graphics Simulation.* Edited by D. Thalmann. New York: John Wiley Publ.

STEWART,W.K., 1991 "Multisensor visualisation for underwater archaeology". *IEEE Computer Graphics and Applications* 11 (2), pp. 13-18.

THALMAN, N.M., 1990, "Computer Animation: a tool that gives life to visualization". In *Scientific Visualization and Graphics Simulation.* Edited by D. Thalmann. New York: John Wiley Publ.

THALMAN, N.M., THALMAN,D., 1994a, "Computer animation: a key issue for time visualisation". *Scientific Visualisation. Advances and Challenges.* Edited by L. Rosenblum et al. Academic press. London, pp. 201-222.

THALMAN, N.M., THALMAN,D., 1994b, "Creating Artificial Life in Virtual Reality". In *Artificial Life and Virtual Reality.* Edited by N.M. Thalmann and D. Thalmann. New York: John Wiley Publ.

THALMAN, N.M., PANDZIC, I.S., MOUSSALY, J.C., THALMANN,D., HUANG,Z., SHEN,J., 1995, "The Making of the Xian Terra-cotta Soldiers". In *Computer Graphics. Developments in Virtual Environments.* Edited by R.A.Earnshaw & J.A. Vince. London: Academic Press. Pp. 281-295.

TSAI,V.J.D., 1993, "Delaunay triangulation in TIN Creation: An Overview and a linear-time Algorithm. *International Journal of Geographical Information Systems* 7(6):501-524.

TSINGOS,N., BITTAR,E., GASCUEL, M.P., 1995, "Implicit surfaces for Semi-automatic medical Organ Reconstruction". In *Computer Graphics. Developments in Virtual Environments.* Edited by R.A.Earnshaw & J.A. Vince. London: Academic Press.

TUK,A., 1994, "Cogent GIS visualisations". In *Visualisation in geographical Information Systems.* Edited by H.M. Hearnshaw & D.J. Unwin. New York: John Wiley.

VARADY,T., MARTIN,R.R., COX,J., 1997, "Reverse engineering of geometric models. An introduction". *Computer aided Design* 29 (4), pp. 255-268.

WANDELL, B.A., 1995, *Foundations of Vison.* Sunderland (MA): Sinauer Ass., Inc.

WATSON,D.F., 1992, *Contouring. A guide to the analysis and display of spatial data.* London: Pergamon Press.

WATT, R., 1988, *Visual processing: Computational, Psychophysical and Cognitive Research".* Hillsdale (NJ): Lawrence Erlbaum Ass.

WEINHAUS,F.M., DEVARAJAN,V., 1997, "Texture Mapping 3D Models of Real-World Scenes" *ACM Computing Surveys* 29 (4): 324-365.

WEISHAR,P., 1998, *Digital Space. Designing Virtual Environments* McGraw Hill.

WERGHI,N., FISHER,R., ROBERTSON,C., ASHBROOK,A., 1999, "Object reconstruction by incorporating geometric constraints in reverse engineering" *Computer Aided Design* 31, pp. 363-399.

WHEATLEY,D., 1991, "SyGraf-resource based teaching with graphics". In *Computer Applications in Archaeology 1990*, Edited by K.Lockyear and S.Rahtz. Oxford: British Archaeological reports (Int. Series 565), pp.,9-14

WHEATLEY,D., 1992, "Going over old ground: GIS, archaeological theory and the act of perception". In *Computing the Past.* Edited by J.Andresen, T. Madsen and I. Scollar. Aarhus University Press., pp.133-138.

WHEATLEY, D 1995" Cumulative viewshed analysis: a GIS-based method for investigating intervisibility, and its archaeological application", In *Archaeology and Geographical Information Systems*, Edited by in Lock, G and Stančič, Z., Taylor & Francis, London , pp. 171-186

WHITE, R., 1996, "Building an Urban Image". *Archeologia e Calcolatori* No. 7,Pp. 137-147

WHOLERS,T., 1995, "3D Digitizing for engineering". *Computer Graphics,* pp. 1-3.

WILHELMS,J., 1990, "Visualizing sampled volume data". In *Scientific Visualization and Graphics Simulation.* Edited by D. Thalmann. New York: John Wiley Publ.

WOOD,J., 1994, "Visualising contour interpolation accuracy in Digital Elevation Models". In *Visualisation in geographical Information Systems.* Edited by H.M. Hearnshaw & D.J. Unwin. New York: John Wiley.

WOOD,J., CHAPMAN,G (with the contributions by K.Delooze and M.Trueman), 1992, "Three-Dimensional computer visualisation of historic buildings -with particular reference to reconstruction modelling". In *Archaeology and the Information Age.* Edited by P. Reilly and S.Rahtz. London: Routledge, pp. 122-146.

WUNSCH,G., 1999, "Debating about the Graphic epresentation of the Spoatial distributions of points: 3-D vs. 2-D. In *New Techniques for Old Times. Computer Applications and Quantitative Methods in Archaeology.* Edited by J.A. Barceló, I. Briz and A. Vila. Oxford: British archaeological Reports (S757) .

ZACK, J.A., 1999, "'See' Possible Landscape Changes Through Visualisation". *GeoWorld,* 12 (3): 40.

ZAMPI,G., 1999, *Virtual Architecture* Batsford press.

ZHANG,R., TSAI,P-S., CRYER,J.E., SHAH,M., 1999, "Shape from shading. A survey". *IEEE Transactions on Pattern Analysis and Machine Intelligence* 21 (8), pp. 690-706.

ZHENG,J.Y., 1999, "Virtual Recovery of excavated Relics" *IEEE Computer Graphics* 19 (3), pp. 6-11

ARCHAEOLOGICAL PUBLICATIONS USING VIRTUAL REALITY: CASE STUDIES AND CAVEATS

Donald H. Sanders

Learning Sites, Inc., USA
dsanders@learningsites.com

Introduction

Virtual reality—the term brings to mind images of exploring imaginary places, spectacular arcade games, weird body suits, motion platforms, goggles, and recently, archaeological sites. Around the world, nearly 70 projects actively model ancient sites for viewing in virtual reality (VR).

This chapter will review some of the drawbacks of traditional methods of publishing archaeological data, counter with alternatives based on the use of virtual reality, touch on some complications of new media technologies, and conclude with some innovations that may usher in virtual archaeology of the new millennium. The focus of this chapter will be: "How we can best use virtual reality for the dissemination of archaeological material via excavation reports, teaching materials, and research resources." These three different types of publications will be illustrated using three different virtual worlds developed by Learning Sites, Inc. (http://www.learningsites.com).

Learning Sites designs and develops educational and research software using interactive three-dimensional digital models that are based on actual archaeological evidence and that are reconstructed to the highest standards of scholarship. We integrate archaeological data with advanced computer graphics to further education, data analysis, and the preservation of cultural heritage information. Learning Sites aims to create a globally integrated and interactive network of linked virtual worlds that can be used for teaching, research, archaeological fieldwork, museum exhibitions, and on-site interpretation centers.

Our software becomes a dynamic medium for promoting awareness of past civilizations, understanding of different cultures, and appreciation of different places, peoples, and their cultural heritage. Learning Sites is committed to producing serious educational and research tools as we work toward virtual reality-based schooling aids and digital archaeology for the 21st century.

To establish a background to our discussions, we must first ask, "Why are archaeologically based virtual worlds being built at all?" Generally, current uses fall into one of three categories:

(1) backgrounds for games;

(2) demonstrations of computing or modeling prowess; or

(3) visualizations for localized research or presentation, either in-house (such as at universities) or for special conferences and exhibitions.

But VR is not just about stunning texture maps, cool interactive worlds, or high-end rendering engines. Are we really taking advantage of new media technologies to advance the discipline of archaeology? Particularly, for publication purposes, paper prevails. Yet, virtual ancient environments can become tools for public education, discipline-wide research, and the sharing of excavation results. Our challenge is to use this, now not-so-leading-edge technology in ways that do not merely replace existing visualization techniques, but that take advantage of the medium to innovate, to educate, and to elucidate.

Traditional Limitations

We can use some famous precedents to discover what happens when a new technology is introduced into a well-established profession. When the architect, Imhotep, introduced ashlar masonry (for the pyramid complex of King Djoser, at Saqqara, around 2800 BCE), he designed stone *imitations* of reeds and other plants, the traditional Egyptian building materials. His innovation relied upon visual forms rooted, so to speak, in the plant-based construction of his predecessors.

As a second example, when the new plastic laminating material Formica™ was introduced in the 1930s, the textures first applied to its surfaces were imitation wood color or wood graining patterns. The first locations onto which the material was placed were furniture, countertops, and car detailing; that is, its location and visual vocabulary imitated wood—the previous technology. Again, as with Imhotep's use of plant motifs, there is no inherent reason why this should be so, since both cut stone and Formica have qualities suitable for many applications and patterns totally unique to themselves. Further, in each case, it took years before some alternative uses and motifs were explored.

Both technological visions became cloaked in the visual vocabulary of the previous technology. This is not to criticize; it just happens. Likewise, the interactive graphics created by archaeologists today often present data in ways that reproduce the look, the presentation mode, and even the graphic style of our predecessor's visualization techniques. Once archaeologists recognize this, we'll have more freedom to apply VR in ways that are not just digital replacements for traditional paper-based image types (fig. 1).

Our dependence on paper excavation reports and 2D images has been basic to our field since our profession's inception. We have all read them, maybe even bought a few. (fig. 2) They typically contain long descriptions of the excavation and its finds, and only as many pictures as printing costs or book length permits (or alternatively, as few illustrations—usually only black and white—as the publisher can get away with). Illustrations usually include pottery profiles, isolated views of a few artifacts or trenches, and token line drawings of key features of the excavation. Architectural drawings unquestionably repeat the plans, sections, and elevation reconstructions in use since our discipline's 18th-century origins (Sanders 1988). However, I do not think a publication with long descriptions, a few greyscale illustrations, and a couple of line drawings is really sufficient for truly understanding a site's stratigraphic or cultural complexity.

Even the most comprehensive reports necessarily present only selected portions of the whole story, and only single static views of artifacts, buildings, or trenches.

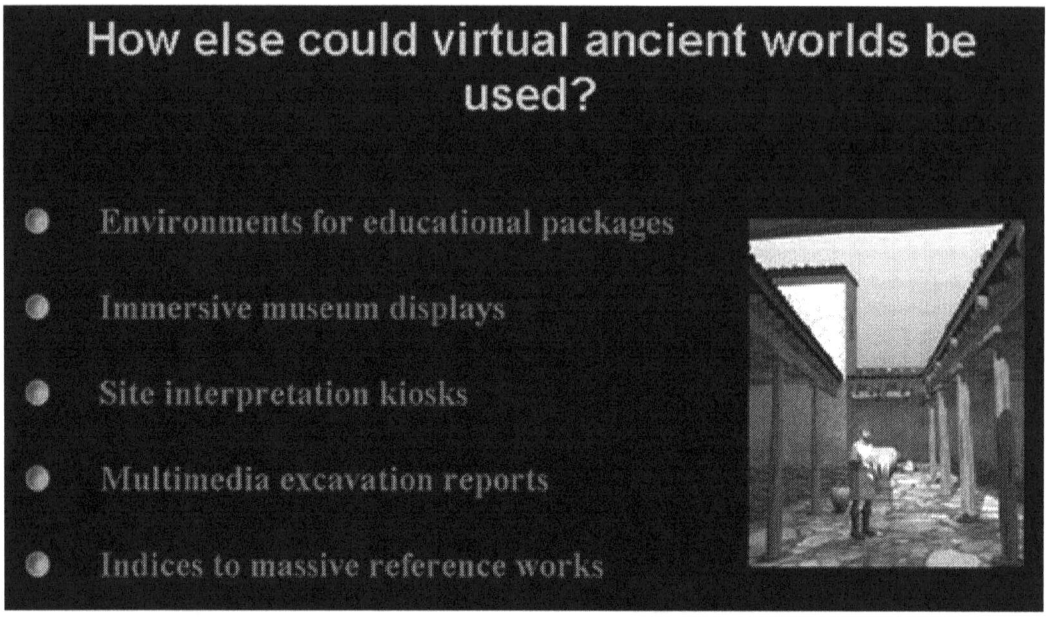

Figure 1. How else could virtual ancient worlds be used?

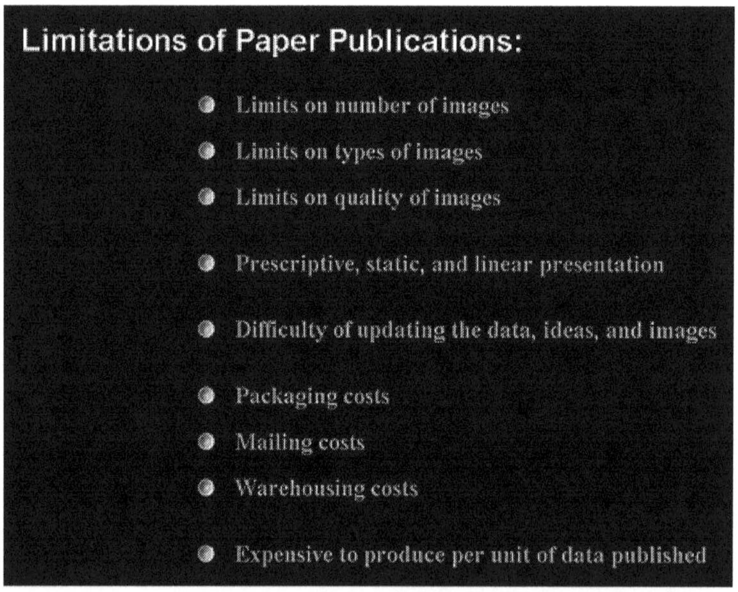

Figure 2. Limits to traditional publications

And what about updates? Ideas presented in paper publications cannot be expanded upon when new data become available, when alternative interpretations are offered, and when new visualizations are created. Articles are published and conference papers delivered, but the original publication remains a static document; synthesizing the very latest material with previously published information is a continuing chore.

Today's emphasis on quantitative methods of interpretation and on explanations of cultural totality demand more information. But not just more data without interpretation, not just more without innovative methods of assimilating and displaying the extra material. Just access to more stuff will not suffice; just look at the Internet. I believe VR and associated technologies can eliminate many difficulties with the traditional excavation report (fig. 3):

- the long time lag between uncovering the data and placing it between two covers;
- the limited audience who will get to own or read the final report;
- the severely limited amount of data that is published, compared to the amount actually retrieved;
- the singularly limited visual presentation methods; and
- the linear layout of most reports.

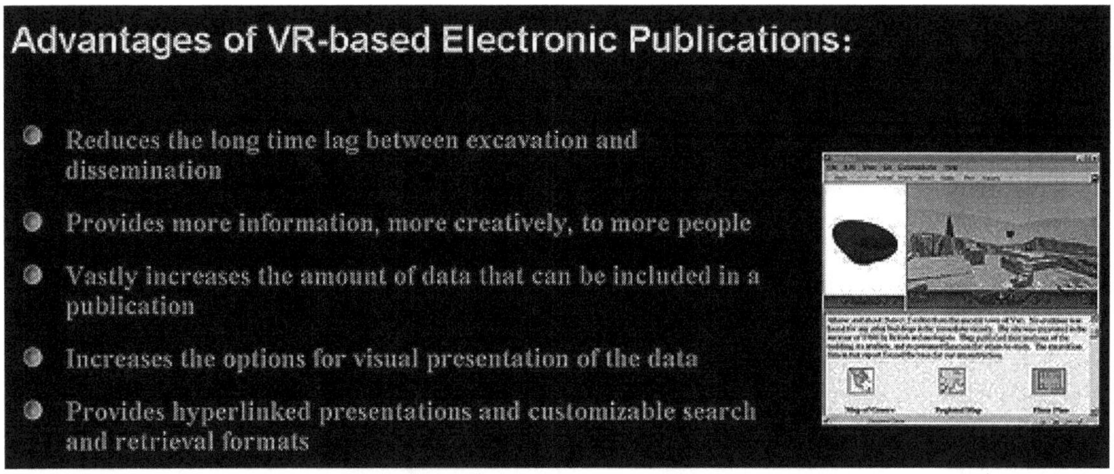

Figure 3. Advantages of VR-based publications

VR-Based Alternative Publications

We can help the site report overcome these limitations, creating greatly enhanced publications and offering them to a wider audience, more quickly, more efficiently, and more cost-effectively than ever before.

The benefits of using VR-based archaeological publications, that is, of breaking free of traditional plans and sections (the wood-grained or papyrus-shaped veneer that still linger in our professional reporting) can be demonstrated by three different types of electronic publications being developed by Learning Sites (fig. 4). Each will illustrate some of the approaches we are adopting in our attempts to redefine the encyclopedic research resource, the visual aid for teaching, and the excavation report. Please put on your digital hard hats—each virtual world package is still under construction.

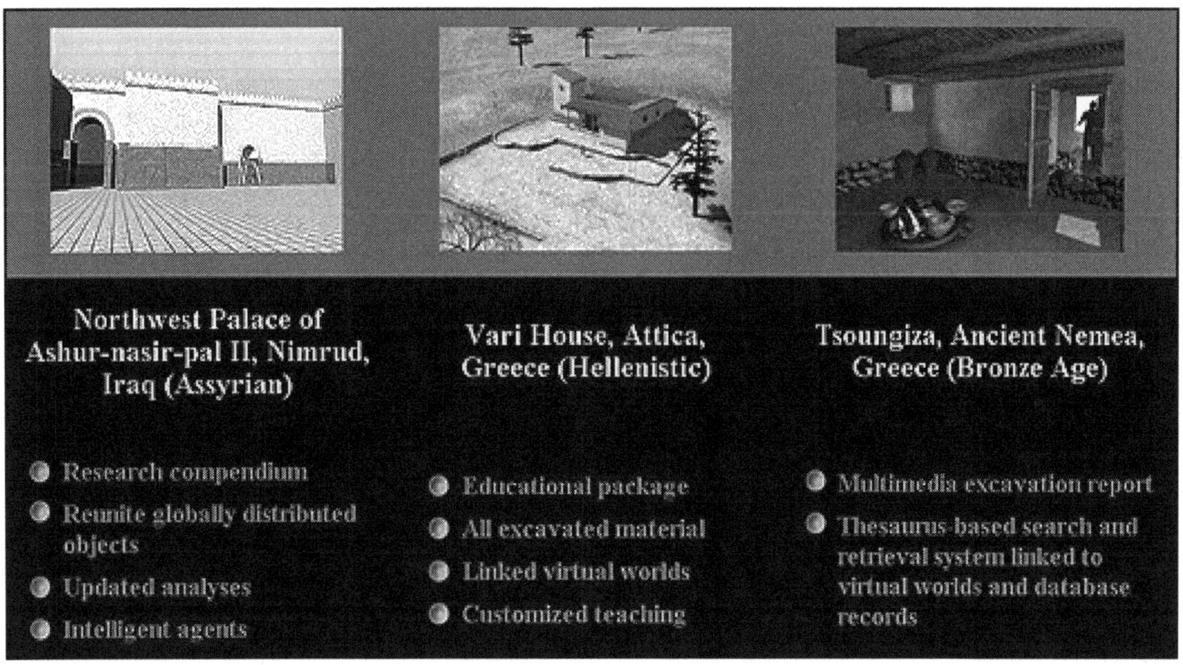

Figure 4. Sites list and images

THE MASSIVE RESEARCH RESOURCE

Since the days of its initial excavation by Austen Henry Layard in the 1840s, relief decoration from the immense Northwest Palace of Ashur-nasir-pal II (9th century BCE), at Nimrud (fig. 5), has been systematically removed from its context, cut up, and shipped to major museums and private collections around the world. The material is becoming even more globally distributed through secondary selling and looting, which continues today. This is a tremendous loss for scholars, since the original Assyrian sculptural program and ritual inscriptions can no longer be viewed or studied in their complex entirety. Further, the public, whether visiting the site or seeing pieces in museums can no longer appreciate the grandeur and scale of the monument.

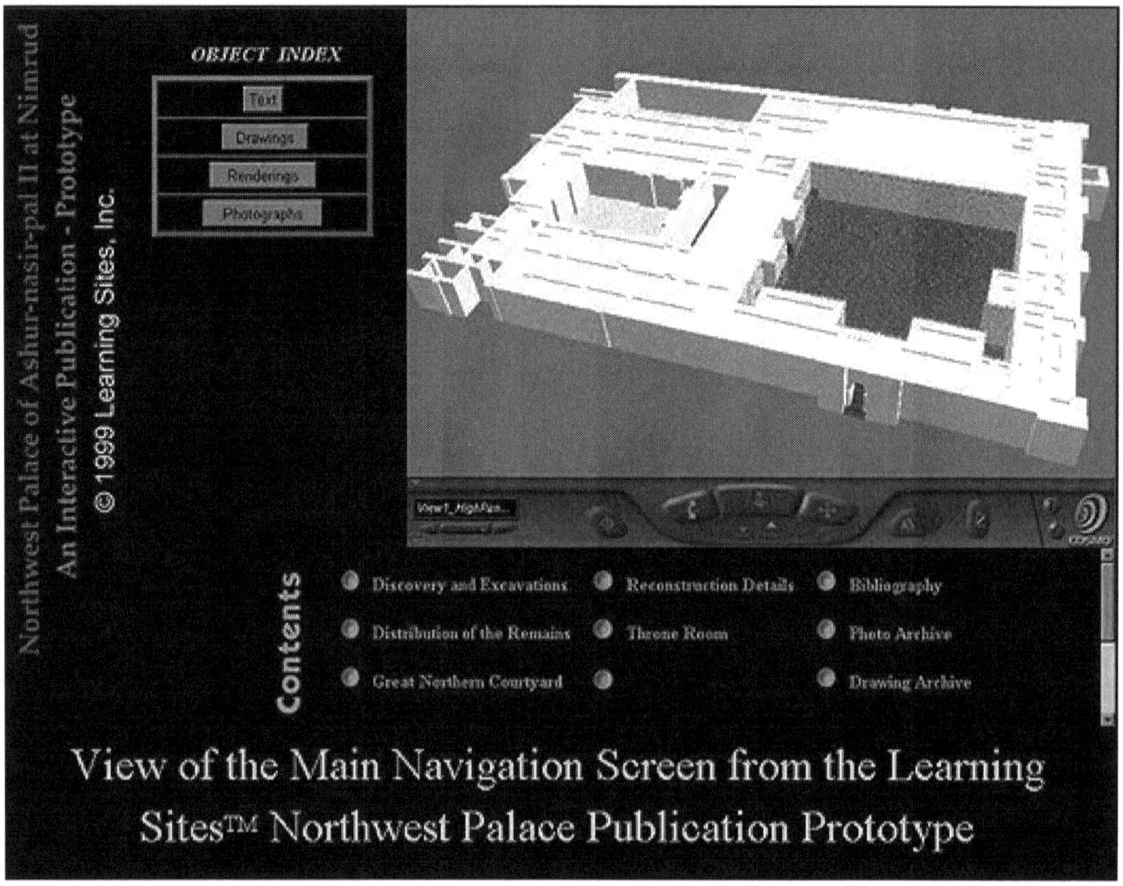

Figure 5. Northwest Palace overhead view from virtual world

It is a scenario begging for virtual reality (fig. 6). Re-building the Palace as a 3D computer model and re-positioning therein visual surrogates of the reliefs based on surviving evidence from collections all over the world and from reconstruction drawings suits new media technologies ideally (fig. 7). Learning Sites, with archaeologists and architects from the United States and from the Polish team that last excavated at Nimrud, aims to publish a massive research and educational resource partly on DVD and partly on the Internet.

Figure 6. Northwest Palace virtual world, view of Entry D

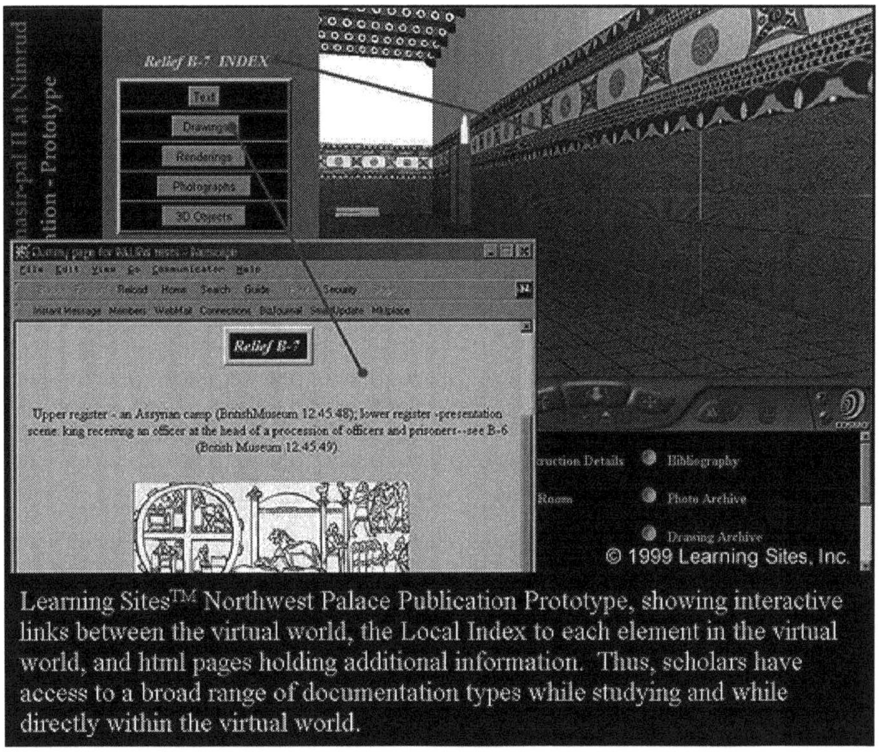

Figure 7. Northwest Palace virtual world, links to documentation (Relief D2)

Figure 8. Vari House virtual world, overview of the site.

Virtual reality allows us to collocate vast amounts of visual data, analyses, and background information—more than any paper format would allow—and present that material in ways unthinkable before VR. The result will be a virtual re-creation of the architectural design and sculptural program of the Palace. New interpretations, new reconstructions, and updated links to bibliography will be added as they emerge. Each museum with holdings from the excavations will be able to retrieve information on the original context of its sculpture. In final innovative aspect of the publication, virtual visitors using the product will be able either to explore independently or to accept the assistance of intelligent agents, special virtual Assyrians throughout the model who will be programmed to act as site interpreters.

THE EDUCATIONAL PACKAGE

The Hellenistic farmhouse at Vari (fig.8), about 18km southeast of Athens, was excavated by the British School at Athens in 1966. This small isolated building is important because it was home to a family of beekeepers. Excavated evidence thus documented for the first time that ancient writers' claims were accurate when they wrote that the best honey came from the slopes of Mt. Hymettus in Greece, precisely where the Vari house is located.

As a single-period, thoroughly excavated site (fig.9), the farmhouse offers a unique glimpse into rural life around 300 BCE and makes an ideal backdrop for a public school education package providing real-life content for teaching about ancient Greek history, economics, and religion, as well as excavation methods and ancient construction techniques.

Figure 9. Vari House virtual world, view of the kitchen (room 1)

Using the entire Vari excavation archive we developed this educational package to meet curriculum guidelines mandated in the United States for teaching social studies, ancient history, and geography (fig. 10). We also incorporated the Archaeological Institute of America's and the Society for American Archaeology's guidelines for teaching archaeology in public schools; and the guidelines set by the Virtual Reality in Education Laboratory at East Carolina University in North Carolina for using VR in the classroom. We are currently completing the final version which expands the theme to encompass a comparison between life in the ancient Greek farmhouse at Vari with that of life in an ancient Greek townhouse (specifically, the House of Many Colors, Olynthus). The updated package will incorporate more linked virtual worlds, animated characters, interactive artifacts, and databases linking text, excavation drawings and photographs, field notebook pages, and sounds to provide an engaging, participatory, VR-based learning experience that gives teachers real historical situations as the basis for education. This is the site report as interactive teaching aid.

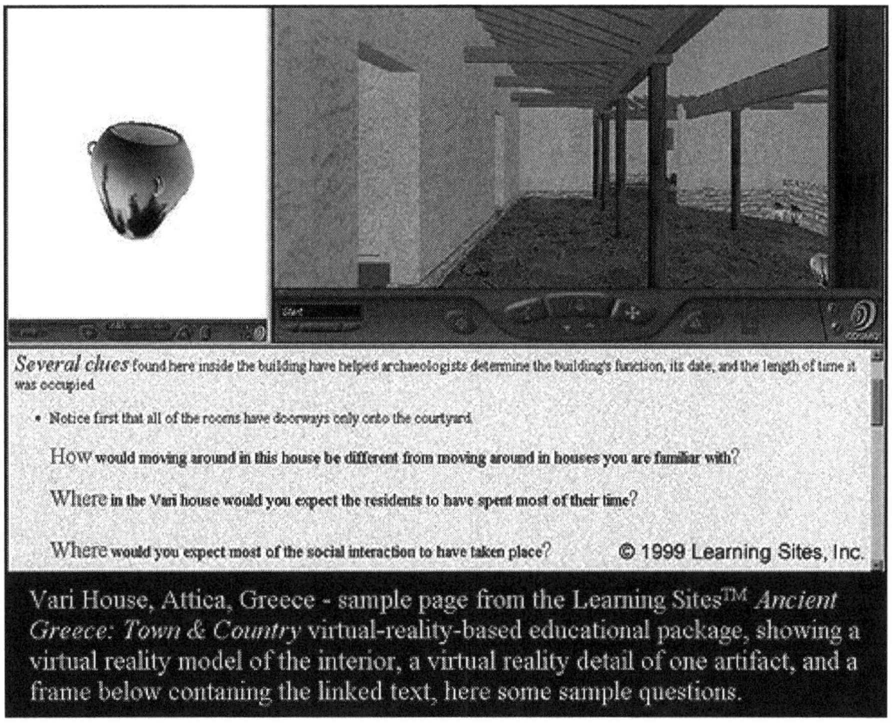

Figure 10. Vari House virtual world, educational curriculum links

THE EXCAVATION REPORT

The Bronze Age settlement of Tsoungiza, Ancient Nemea, Greece, was excavated during the 1980s, under the direction of a team from Bryn Mawr College. Our multimedia publication will include VR, video, animation, and sound synthesizing all information retrieved during excavation—all the artifacts, database records, architecture, photographs, drawings, and analyses (fig. 11). The entire product will be interactive, and present the data in three levels of depth—for the general public, for students, and for professionals. The result will be published on DVD and the Internet, allowing links to more background information, future updates, and new analyses.

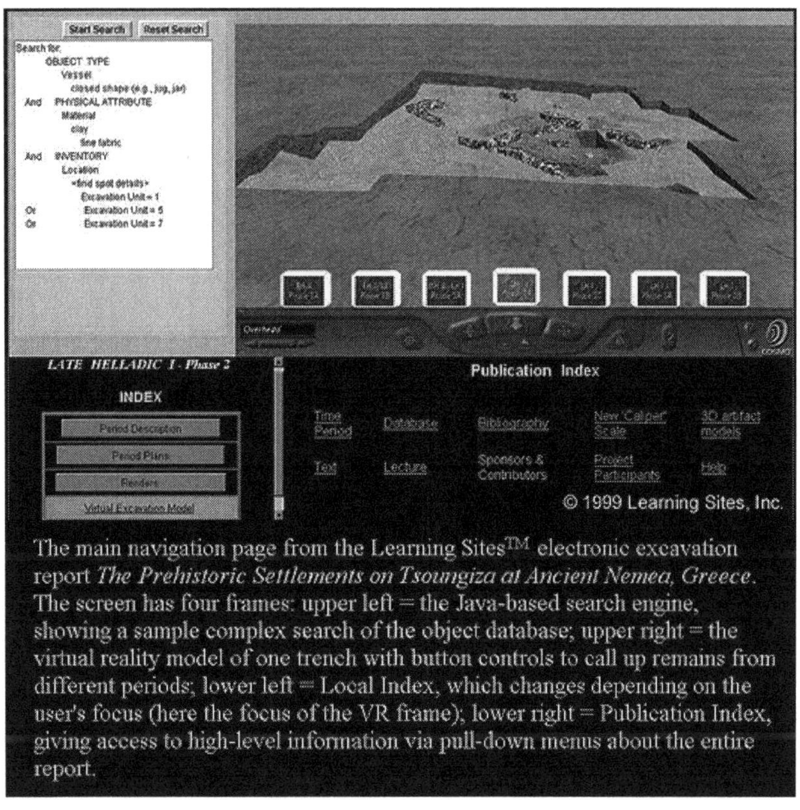

Figure 11. Tsoungiza digital excavation report, main index page

To take advantage of the new media (fig. 12), we developed a few features that have been beneficial to the archaeologists for their interim studies, teaching, and fundraising. For example, we have enhanced the traditional hand-drawn trench plan by overlaying it with excavation photos to provide a check on the accuracy of the drawings, to show settlement development more easily than possible with traditional site plans, and to use the view as a temporary hook to access their photo archive.

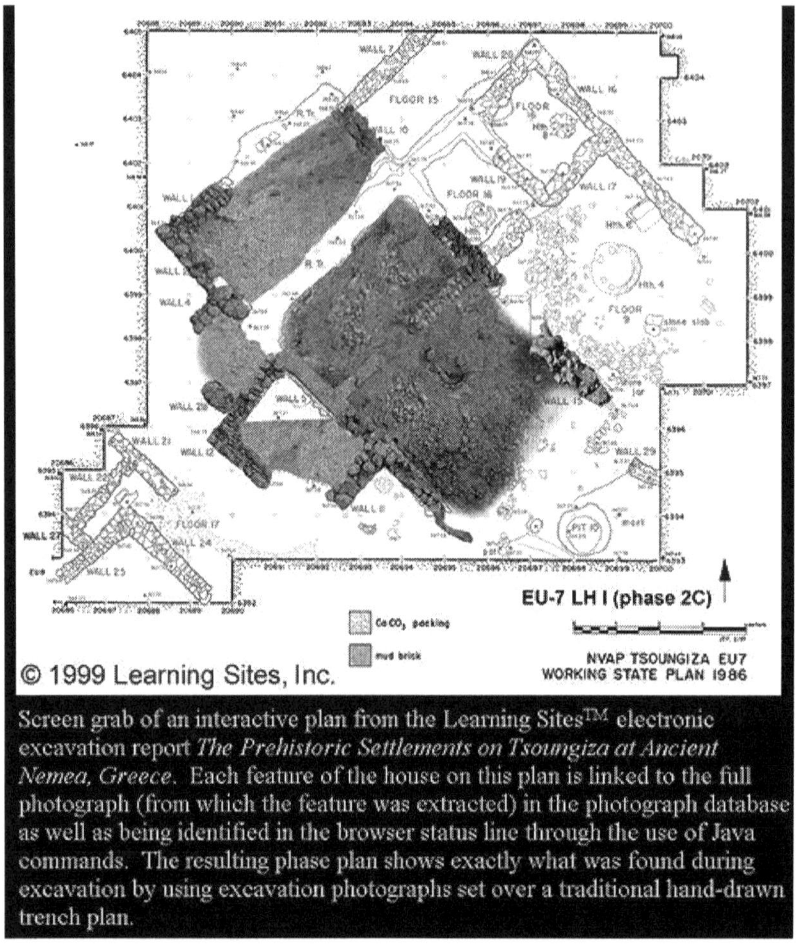

Figure 12. Tsoungiza digital excavation report, interactive plans

Another feature will make this publication a truly nonlinear, personalized, and customizable research tool (fig. 13). We have designed a Java-driven searchable database that links artifact records to virtual artifacts accurately located in their virtual contexts, and vice versa, objects in the virtual worlds will be linked back to their database records, photographs, drawings, and analyses. The virtual worlds thus become visual indexes to all the data about Tsoungiza. This will be the first all-digital, virtual reality-based excavation report.

Caveats

I do not want to leave the impression that our solutions are the only ones or that we have resolved all the problems with regard to VR-based publications. For example:

- While all VRML viewers meet the minimum requirements of the VRML 2.0 specifications, some add extensions that may not be supported by other players. This problem may be resolved by simply allowing some noncompliant sources to fail, rendering them not useful to world-builders. There has been talk of creating VRML 3.0, but the next wave may belong to the MPEG 4, which makes it possible to include in VRML worlds streaming video, morphing, and multimedia input and output.
- Converting files to and from VRML is not smooth, because some translators do not pass along all of the attributes. Further, many modeling and rendering packages can output to VRML but only a few can import a VRML file. Software companies are resolving this as VRML is no longer seen as fringe technology.
- Until recently VRML could not be displayed on Apple computers. Although the Macromedia Director™ plug-in VR Xtra™ claims to be available for Macs, we've had no confirmation of its reliable operation. Silicon Graphics Inc. demonstrated its Cosmo™ VRML viewer for Macs at the VRML98 Conference in California, but beta versions are still buggy and given the uncertainty over the Cosmo suite, things may not be resolved until the all-new Apple operating system appears.
- Digital archaeological data will need to be maintained so that they are readable by future generations of scholars and their computers. Digital libraries and Internet sites must ensure that their data are converted to the next generation of storage devices and file formats. There are several

initiatives and projects, inside and beyond the archaeological community, studying this problem.

- Colors do not display consistently across different computer monitors, programs, or Web browsers. This makes our rendering life really difficult, because at Learning Sites we build our worlds to exacting specifications. Yet what we build is not necessarily what other people see; and they let us know about it, too. We use both color calibration software allowing us to set our system colors properly in conjunction with external standards, and monitors with built-in color calibration controls that can be set to match external standards, like a Pantone™ chart, a greyscale card, or Munsell™ colors.

- With the ability to publish now literally at every person's desktop, the scholarly community can only retain some sort of quality assurance by sharpening our critical thinking skills; creating specialized e-journals and digital libraries with gate keepers; and retaining a peer-review jury system for publications.

Despite these words of caution—regarding mainly technical, not intellectual, obstacles—the advantages of virtual reality-based publications are many, and include: interactive self-guided research or teaching, access to the full range of excavated material, ability to virtually hold and investigate closely each artifact, and availability of data to a wider audience more quickly, more efficiently, and probably more cost effectively than ever before.

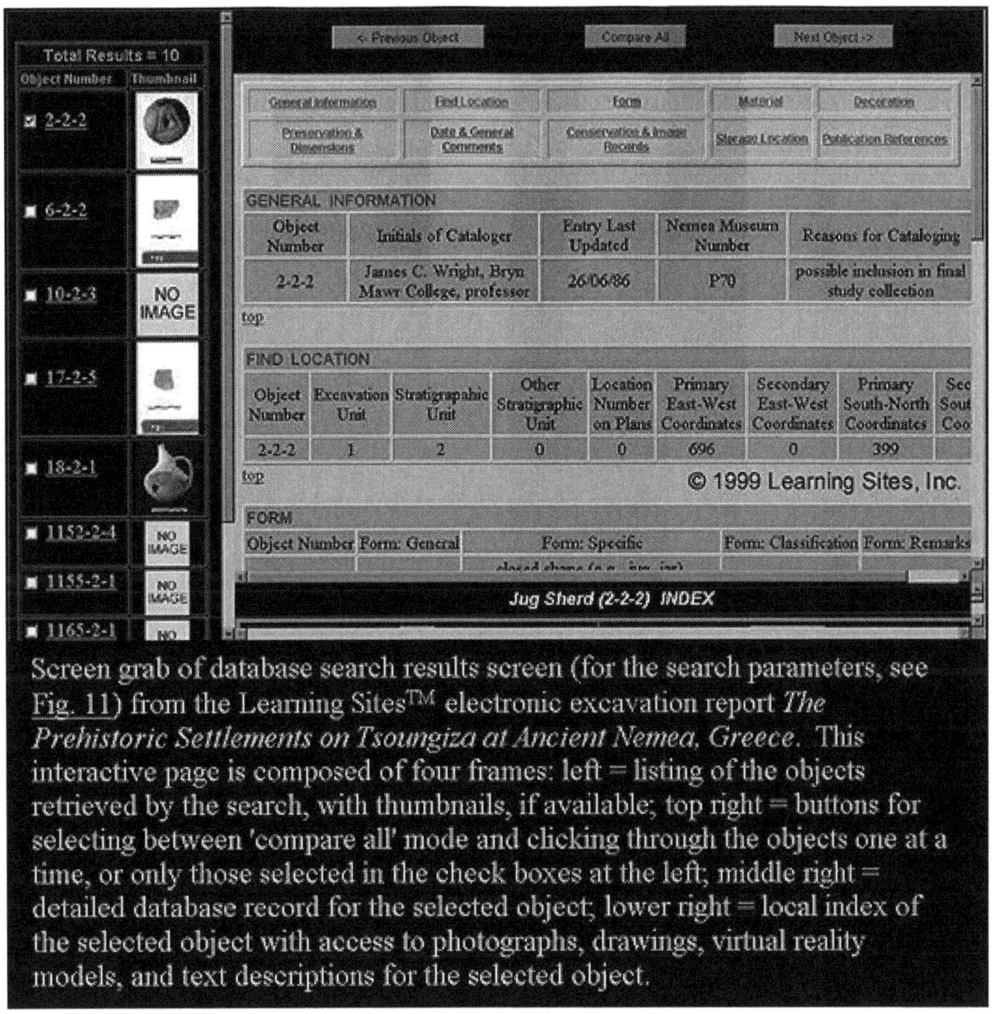

Figure 13. Tsoungiza digital excavation report, Java search engine and database example

Conclusion

Much innovation is still to come (fig. 14), judging from what has been demonstrated at recent trade shows, such as the incorporation of projection holographs to simulate full-scale spatial experiences. Multi-user virtual worlds, made possible by the merging of VRML and Java 3D, will permit several scholars to visit and study computer-generated ancient sites together; MPEG 4 will allow multimedia presentations to take place within virtual worlds permitting real-time distance education and video-conferencing. User interfaces won't depend on data gloves, spaceballs, or mice; instead body movements will be tracked in 3D space and translated into virtual world coordinates. Voice recognition systems will enhance input. More spectacular will be the ability to modify virtual worlds while moving through them to test hypotheses about the archaeological record against virtual simulations of the real events. 3D scanners now allow us to replicate the ancient world with millimeter accuracy, so we can study the intricacies of construction methods and artifact styles as if standing in front of the real thing. Some of these features will be standard by next year's CAA.

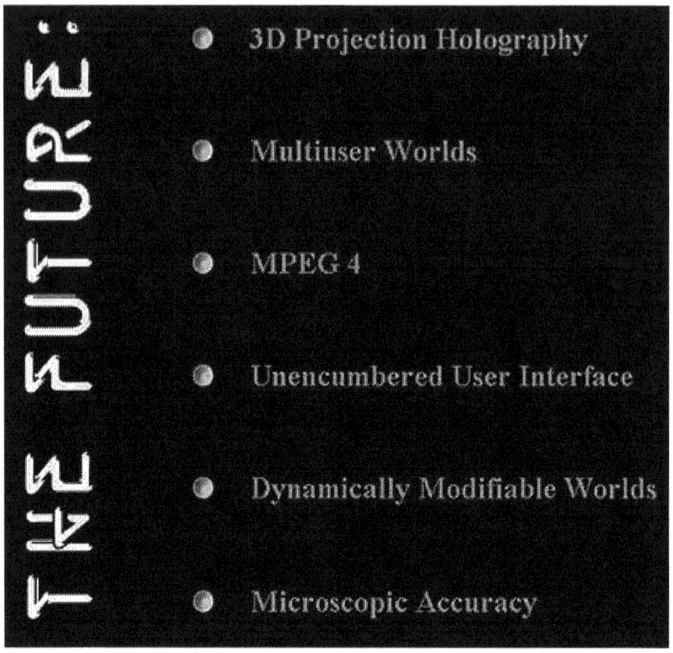

Figure 14. The Future

Despite these rapid and mind-bending advances, we at Learning Sites are concerned about the fact that the 3D data and visualizations from the important work occurring right now might be lost when current goals are met and projects or their funding cease. Especially in light of the enormous benefits to our discipline of using these virtual ancient worlds right now. We offer this solution to salvaging the efforts of all involved: We have sponsored the creation of the *Virtual Worlds in Archaeology Initiative* to preserve, catalogue, and actively use virtual ancient worlds. Toward this end, Learning Sites is willing to host a listserv to keep all of us ancient world builders aware of each other's endeavors; we have already built a Web site with links to the worlds currently online; and we will offer our expertise in developing data standards for the sharing of these worlds. These efforts can produce digital libraries of virtual ancient sites and linked databases enabling distance education, global research, and continual access to the latest interactive visualizations, which can only benefit our discipline's analysis and teaching of the ancient world.

And so, this is a very exciting time for us. Remember, our study of the past need not rely on methods of the past. New media technologies can be brought to bear on all aspects of data recovery, analysis, and publication, and our questions about the past can only benefit from these new means of visualizing the answers.

References cited

SANDERS, Donald H. 1988. 'Architecture: The Neglected Artifact,' in French, E. B. & Wardle, K. A. (eds.). *Problems in Prehistory*, Bristol Classical Press: Bristol, England, 489-498.

REALISM VS. REALITY: CREATING VIRTUAL RECONSTRUCTIONS OF PREHISTORIC ARCHITECTURE

John Kantner

Department of Anthropology and Geography
Georgia State University
kantner@gsu.edu

The reconstruction of prehistoric architecture using three-dimensional (3D) modeling software involves a series of compromises concerning what should or should not be portrayed in a 3D model. In the majority of cases, the data recovered from prehistoric architectural features are inadequate for the complete virtual reconstruction of a structure and its contents. The underlying issue is therefore focused on how "real" we should make our models, especially since the realism inherent in 3D modeling is easy to construe as the past reality when in fact a large proportion of what the viewer sees is heavily dependent on numerous inferences made by the modeler in the absence of relevant data.

This chapter discusses the many issues surrounding the process of creating virtual prehistoric architecture. In addition to the central concern of how to balance realism vs. reality, the discussion considers how decisions in the creation of virtual architecture are further constrained by the goals of the project and the intended audience, the desired product, the quality of archaeological information, and technological capabilities. The chapter ends by examining how these issues have been addressed in 3D reconstructions that I have made of prehistoric architecture from the southwestern United States.

Reality and Realism in 3D Architectural Reconstructions

Archaeologists have been involved in 3D reconstructions of prehistoric architectural features for as long as the discipline has existed. Sketches showing intact structures embellished with complete artifacts and surrounded by human figures have often accompanied both popular summaries of prehistoric societies and technical site reports. The intent of these sketches has always clearly been to portray how the architecture might have looked in the past when it was in active use by prehistoric groups. Such depictions have never been so realistic that they were confused with a past reality; in other words, viewers of these sketches have always been able to tell that their creators employed a considerable amount of artistic license to "bring the past alive." If, for example, roofing material was not recovered from the archaeological site, the sketch could simply show a dirt roof without having to consider details of how this roof might have been constructed or what the interior ceiling looked like. Alternatively, the sketch artist could have angled the reconstruction or carefully placed scenery such that the roof was not even visible.

In the past decade, however, the accessibility of sophisticated 3D modeling and rendering technology has blurred the distinction between what archaeologists actually know about the architecture they are reconstructing and the realism that the model necessarily conveys. It is much more difficult to gloss over missing information when one is creating a 3D model of a prehistoric structure (Figure 1).

Figure 1: The archaeological remains of the structure known as Chimney Rock, located in southwestern Colorado, do not provide many details on how the structure was roofed. For example, although this model includes "firewalls" that extend above the roof, their presence is not indicated archaeologically. They are included based on analogy with similar structures built by the Hopi and Zuni, the probable descendents of the prehistoric groups that occupied Chimney Rock.

If the archaeologist was unable to identify the roofing material, then what should the modeler do about a roof on the virtual reconstruction? Should the modelers leave a roof off, or should they put a "dirt-colored" square in its place? And if they do the latter, how thick should it be? With 3D models, unknown aspects of the prehistoric architecture cannot be as easily avoided.

The reason that this issue is important is that the ability to generate photorealistic renderings using actual materials and textures that archaeologists have recovered from actual prehistoric contexts can make it difficult for the end user to distinguish between the model's realism and the archaeological reality. The exceptional quality of 3D architectural renderings has made it substantially more difficult for viewers of visual reconstructions to determine which features were actually identified by the archaeologists and which represent more tenuous interpretations that the modelers were forced to make as part of the modeling process. In essence, the process of 3D modeling has made virtual reconstructions appear realistic whether or not they accurately reflect how the architecture really appeared in the past.

The importance of realism vs. reality in 3D modeling depends to a large degree on the goals of the reconstruction and on the constraints that affect the modeling process. The following sections explore these issues and how they can affect how virtual reconstructions are created and presented. This discussion is intended primarily to introduce important issues and is not intended to represent a rigorous program for guiding 3D reconstructions, for the specific criteria and constraints facing any given reconstruction will be unique to every project.

Goals and Audiences of 3D Architectural Reconstructions

Many of us who have been creating 3D reconstructions of prehistoric architecture began our modeling with no clear vision as to the function of our models. Certainly, in my case, 3D modeling began with little vision beyond surmising "wouldn't it be cool if I could do this." Only later did I realize the potential that 3D visualization held for achieving both research and pedagogical goals. As will be described later, my first models suffered greatly by not having clearly identified goals. Now, before I begin a 3D model of a prehistoric architectural feature, I carefully consider the purpose of the reconstruction and try to design the model accordingly. Particularly important is reaching compromises among three possible goals that may place competing demands on the modeling process: research, pedagogy, and public consumption.

RESEARCH

The virtual reconstruction of architectural features has yet to play a substantial role in archaeological research. An excellent example of the use of 3D modeling for addressing research questions is provided by the work of Philip Peterson, David Fracchia, and Brian Hayden on pithouses at the Keatley Creek site in British Columbia (1995). These researchers began with the identified floor area of an approximately 2,000-year-old pithouse and attempted to determine how the superstructure might have been constructed. Based on this reconstruction, the researchers could determine which parts of the structure would have been illuminated by sunlight at various times of the day. Data on artifact frequencies and feature location were then layered onto the floor of the structure and then compared with the information on illumination. This helped the researchers to determine usage areas in the structure. For example, they discovered that heavily retouched scrapers appeared most frequently in parts of the structure that were lit by midday sun (Peterson et al. 1995:33).

While this example shows the potential for using 3D reconstructions to address research questions, few other archaeologists have pursued this kind of study. Virtual reconstructions could be used to determine how much material would be required to construct walls of an architectural feature, or different theories of how a roof might have been built could be evaluated. A potentially promising area of investigation is the use of 3D models to evaluate architectural features that are hypothesized to have served as markers of astronomical events such as solstices or equinoxes. At the very least, the process of creating architectural models can identify inconsistencies in the actual archaeological data and rectify incorrect assumptions about the appearance of prehistoric features. For example, through their 3D reconstructions of habitations in the Central American community of Ceren, researchers determined that previous assumptions that interiors were dark and gloomy were incorrect (Novitski 1998:35). Other archaeologists have used 3D modeling in research directed towards preservation and management of archaeological resources on public land (e.g., Goodpasture 1997).

The modeling of prehistoric architecture to address research questions is obviously concerned with the faithful replication of the archaeological record. Since the goal is to address questions about the past reality, achieving a completely realistic view of the architecture is not important. It may not be important for the walls to be covered with realistic textures or for artifacts to be placed on the floor. Exactly what is modeled will be determined more by the research agenda than by the goal of creating a detailed representation of the past.

PEDAGOGY

Virtual reality reconstructions are especially useful for teaching students about prehistory. For example, at the University of California at Santa Barbara, Brian Fagan and George Michaels have developed software for an introductory course to archaeology that provides multimedia learning experiences for students (Fagan and Michaels 1992). Included are fly-throughs of prehistoric architecture from Sumerian Ur and Maya Tikal. The software for this course has recently been made available to select campuses over the Internet, allowing many more undergraduates to experience virtual architecture as an integrated part of their learning experience. A somewhat different project by John Rick at Stanford University presents a 3D model of architecture from Chavín de Huántar in Peru and then uses this as a "virtual fieldsite" through which students can make observations, form hypotheses about the site, and then test them with their explorations of the site model. Similar pedagogical uses of 3D models are becoming increasingly common (e.g., Flanagan 1998).

A potential problem is that, unlike models created to address research problems, those created for pedagogical purposes are expected to be complete representations of the architecture. This in turn usually requires a number of interpretations that may not be readily supportable with the actual archaeological evidence recovered from the structure's remains (Figure 2). For example, if no organic remains were identified during excavations, should baskets or wooden bowls be put in the 3D reconstruction? If they are not there, then students may be led to believe that such objects were never used by the prehistoric society in question. The essential problem is that if the model is a perfect recreation of the archaeological record, the result may be an austere representation that can mislead students into thinking that the structure was devoid of household goods. A similar but perhaps even more important problem is whether or not people should be included in a model, for their absence dehumanizes the representation of prehistory.

On the other hand, by providing a fully detailed image of the past, we run the risk of undermining students' imagination and interpretive skills for bridging between the archaeological data and a vision of what the past was like. One possible solution to this dilemma is to use the actual creation of 3D models as a learning experience for more advanced students. By directly involving students in creating a representation of the past from static archaeological data, not only will they gain a better understanding of prehistory but they will also be exposed to the interpretive challenges inherent in such an undertaking. At the same time that they are learning the subject matter, they are able to draw upon a generational interest in digital technology and develop their own computer skills. This is perhaps the 21st-century equivalent of having grade-school students build architectural models out of tongue depressors and papier-mâché, but the advantage with digital models is that the students can create the models using accurate measurements and actual "materials" that were used in the original structure.

Figure 2: The 3D model of the prehistoric structure of Kin Tl'iish, which is located in northwestern New Mexico, features rooms complete with pottery and blankets hung over poles. Because this model was created for teaching students about the prehistory of the Southwest, I took considerable liberty in populating the interior with artifacts to increase the realism of the experience. However, the structure itself has never been excavated, and therefore there is no information to suggest exactly what features were found in each room.

PUBLIC CONSUMPTION

Probably the most common goal for producing virtual reconstructions of prehistoric architecture has been for consumption by the general public. And undoubtedly the most widespread products in which 3D models have appeared are in computer games. From fanciful representations such as those found in *Tomb Raider* to the more complete models presented in *Qin: Tomb of the Middle Kingdom,* most young people today are likely to first experience prehistoric architecture in the context of digital entertainment. Of course, these experiences usually provide a bizarre perspective on both prehistory and archaeology, often combining features from disparate cultures and time periods. But at the same time many people become intrigued by these representations and often pursue this interest through more traditional channels to learn about the past. Computer games therefore cannot be disregarded as completely irrelevant to the discipline and to the goal of exposing people to prehistory.

Virtual models of prehistoric architecture created for public consumption are always fully realistic representations, and, especially in the case of computer games, they may even be populated with human figures. The production of these models therefore requires the greatest number of interpretive leaps between what is known archaeologically and the realism that they convey. In some cases, and particularly in computer games, the models are completely made up. In others, however, such as the game of *Qin: Tomb of the Middle Kingdom,* the models actually do have some basis in archaeological reality (Novitski 1998:26–27). In *Qin,* although the model is of an actual tomb and its surrounding structures, the tomb that is represented has not yet been excavated by archaeologists. However, in order to be as accurate as possible, the modelers turned to archaeological records from similar discoveries and used actual objects and textures recovered from other sites to complete their representation of the tomb.

Public consumption of virtual reconstructions also occurs widely on the Internet. For the most part, these representations appear to have been created to achieve either research or pedagogical goals and then placed on the Internet. In other cases, architects or digital artists with an interest in modeling prehistoric structures have created websites presenting their recreations. Either way, the wide availability of these models to people all over the world makes this an important arena for the representation of prehistoric architecture. Most people visiting these sites are formal or avocational students of archaeology and prehistory, and as such the interpretive problems associated with such models are similar to those discussed in the previous section. Care should be taken by the model's creators both to demonstrate the purpose of the 3D model and its accuracy in representing what is actually known about the architectural features it purports to recreate. Architectural reconstructions presented on the Internet have the most potential to be both misrepresented and misinterpreted since so many people with a wide variety of backgrounds both produce the online materials and view the resulting models.

Constraints on the Creation of 3D Architectural Reconstructions

The goals of a virtual reconstruction and the intended audience are not the only factors that structure how the modeler moves between the reality of the archaeological record and the realism represented by the 3D model. Also important are the quality of the available archaeological information from which to draw interpretations as well as the technological capabilities available to the modeler.

QUALITY OF ARCHAEOLOGICAL INFORMATION

The ability to create accurate 3D reconstructions of prehistoric architecture is clearly dependent on the degree of preservation of the prehistoric material and the quality of the archaeological research (Figure 3). Many of the largest and best-known prehistoric structures all over the world were either looted long ago or they were excavated in the 19th or early 20th century when modern techniques of data recovery were not available. While structural information is likely to have been preserved and identified in these early investigations, critical archaeological data on the contents of these structures were often discarded and not sufficiently recorded, and now we can only surmise what the interiors might have looked like. In other cases, such as in the pithouses digitally reconstructed by Peterson et al. (1995), much of the structure was organic and has long since decomposed, leading the modelers to rely on ethnohistoric information on how similar pithouses might have looked.

In contrast, contemporary archaeological projects have access to modern techniques of data recovery that can provide modelers with detailed information about the architecture and its contents. In special cases, such as the University of Colorado investigations at Ceren in El Salvador, the structures were buried by ash from a volcanic eruption and the degree of preservation is therefore extremely high. Both the archaeologists and the modelers in these situations do not have to make as many interpretive leaps as do those investigators working on material from older and less well-preserved excavations. Because 3D models convey a strong sense of realism no matter how complete the data on which they are based, scholars working with and presenting these virtual reconstructions should include descriptions of the underlying archaeology and the interpretive leaps that had to be made to build the model.

Figure 3: Kin Tl'iish, a prehistoric structure found in northwestern New Mexico, has not been excavated and the exact configuration of rooms is unknown. Although the remaining mound suggests that some portions of the original structure were multi-storied, this too cannot be ascertained without further excavation. The 3D model, therefore, provides an interpretation that may in fact be wrong. Providing a description of the interpretive leaps required to produce the model is important to mitigate against the reconstruction being interpreted as a completely factual snapshot of the past.

TECHNOLOGICAL CAPABILITIES

Access to appropriate technology and skills can play a major role in determining the scope and quality of a 3D model of prehistoric architecture. If the archaeologist is attempting to construct the model alone, he or she might not be expected to have either the modeling skills or the access to powerful hardware and software needed to produce a superior model. Accordingly, the most successful examples of high-quality reconstructions involve collaborations between archaeologists and either architects or computer artists specializing in architectural visualization, in which case the degree of communication between those with the archaeological knowledge and those with the modeling skills becomes critical. The increasing desire to create 3D models of prehistoric architecture is also beginning to sustain a small private industry of professionals with both the tools and experience to create superior 3D reconstructions. Many of these professionals have been trained both in archaeology and in computer graphics, making them perfect for bridging between the prehistoric reality and a model's realism.

Of course, access to professionals requires funding that has not traditionally been available to most archaeologists. Although many examples of the successful visualization of prehistoric architecture involve collaborations between academic departments or other in-house arrangements, archaeologists should consider seeking funding from extramural sources (e.g., Flanagan 1998). Money both to develop "digital labs" as well as funds earmarked for pedagogical purposes and public outreach might be obtained from large public-funded organizations such as the National Science Foundation and the National Endowment for the Humanities. For example, Education Development and Demonstration grants from the National Endowment for the Humanities are directed towards new electronic technologies that enhance students' understanding of humanities subjects.

Examples of Architectural Reconstruction in the Prehistoric American Southwest

The various factors described in this chapter provide often conflicting influences on the creation of 3D models of prehistoric architecture. Projects will therefore greatly benefit by a full consideration of these issues and how they might determine what is or is not feasible. In this section, I consider the lessons that I have learned in the production of 3D models of prehistoric Anasazi architectural features from the northern part of the American Southwest. This discussion will particularly focus on my reconstruction of a *great kiva,* a ceremonial structure that appeared in Anasazi communities between approximately A.D. 800 and 1150.

The reconstruction of the great kiva was structured by two major goals. The original impetus for pursuing the visualization of one of these structures was pedagogical. Although in my courses I was able to show slides of the ruins of great kivas, these images never adequately portrayed what one of these structures would have been like when it was in use (Figure 4). Great kivas were built mostly below the ground-level and then completely roofed, and they would have been dark and smoky places that clearly conveyed a mysterious and sacred atmosphere. The current ruins, on the other hand, are roofless and bright and accordingly appear much more open and accessible than the original structures really were. Therefore, the primary goal of modeling a great kiva was to better convey to students what it really would have been like to have been inside one of these structures. My intention was to produce a detailed reconstruction complete with artifacts, a fire in the firebox, and perhaps even background music, with the product available both over the World Wide Web and on a CD-ROM that I could use in the classroom.

A secondary goal for the project was to pursue research questions during the production of the model. In particular, I was interested in determining how great kivas would have been roofed, a question that has been pursued in other contexts (e.g., Lightfoot

1988; Snygg and Windes 1998), but which has never been addressed using 3D modeling. My intention was to evaluate a number of hypothesized methods for roofing such a structure based on both the known size of the structure and knowledge about available timbers in the area.

Figure 4: Chetro Ketl, a ceremonial *kiva* found in Chaco Canyon in northwestern New Mexico, is now a completely exposed archaeological site whose features, including the once-concealed niches along the interior wall, are easily visible. This, however, is not at all what this structure would have been like when it was in use by prehistoric people living in the canyon, for it would have been plastered and completely roofed.

Unfortunately, the production of the great kiva model ran into three interrelated problems. First, a major problem that I faced in achieving the desired detail was the relatively incomplete state of the archaeological data. A number of great kivas have been investigated, but almost all of the full excavations occurred earlier in the 20th century; most current projects only test portions of the structure. Because I needed a complete excavation in order to build a full 3D model, I chose the great kiva at a site named Chetro Ketl in Chaco Canyon in northwestern New Mexico. This structure was intermittently excavated over a period of 12 years beginning in 1920. The excavations were first conducted by the Museum of New Mexico and then continued both by the Museum and the School of American Research. My source of archaeological data came from Vivian and Reiter (1960), but this report contains very little information on artifacts recovered during excavations and few architectural details beyond descriptions of masonry features that were identified (Figure 5). For example, both because of poor preservation and incomplete reporting of the work, no information was available on the kinds of intact vessels found in the structure, the nature of the plaster covering the walls, or the roofing material that may have been used.

The creation of a complete 3D model therefore involved a number of interpretive leaps that relied on my knowledge of Anasazi prehistory and on excavations of other similar structures (Figure 6). For example, the plaster and pictographs that appear in the model were derived from investigations at other, much smaller kivas; no investigation of a great kiva that I know of has ever identified intact plaster with artwork on it. Particularly challenging was determining the function of the "vaults" located in the floor of the structure. The archaeologists who excavated the kiva felt that perhaps the vaults functioned exclusively as repositories of ceremonial goods. Other archaeologists have argued that these features were used as huge firepits, but no evidence of burning was found in the vaults. My interpretation of the function of these features was derived from ethnographic examples of Hopi kivas, which exhibit similar vault-like features that were covered with planks or leather and used as drums. A variety of such interpretations had to be made and are outlined in text that accompanies the great kiva presentations. These descriptions of the inferential process have actually been very useful for illustrating to students how archaeologists derive conclusions from archaeological data. For several of the features, I actually involved advanced students in the interpretive process, assigning them small research projects to determine how best to reconstruct and model specific features within the great kiva.

Figure 5: The excavation of Chetro Ketl occurred in a number of stages earlier in the 20th century. Very little information is readily available regarding the artifacts that were found within the structure. In order to create a realistic, if not real, 3D model of the interior space complete with portable artifacts, excavation records from other similar structures were examined.

Figure 6: No artwork was identified on the remaining plaster found in Chetro Ketl, but for pedagogical purposes, prehistoric imagery was placed on the model's walls, supported by analogy with similar structures in which artwork was identified. Similarly, the function of the mysterious vaults seen at the base of two of the posts has been debated by archaeologists. Based on ethnographic analogy, we interpreted these features as large foot drums. The ambivalence surrounding their function, however, cannot be easily conveyed in a realistic 3D model.

Figure 7: One of the research questions that guided the reconstruction of the Chetro Ketl kiva was to determine how such a large structure could have been roofed given the relative paucity of wood in Chaco Canyon. After investigating some of the ideas for roofing a kiva that have been proposed in the archaeological literature, a roof consisting of a minimum number of rare large beams and a multitude of smaller pieces of wood was designed for the 3D model. Unfortunately, the resulting 1,000-piece roof became very difficult to render.

A second problem that was encountered during the creation of the great kiva 3D model was how best to both accommodate the goal of providing sufficient realism for pedagogical purposes while also pursuing research questions. Because of my interest in determining how a great kiva would have been roofed, the majority of effort in the modeling process was focused on reconstructing the roof (Figure 7). While this research agenda was, in my opinion, sufficiently addressed, the result was a 3D model of the roof that included almost 1,000 objects and that consumed both my effort and computer power to create and to render. Although I can now calculate how much timber would have been required to roof the Chetro Ketl great kiva and how this roof was likely designed, the subsequent detail in the roof far exceeds the needs of the model for pedagogical purposes.

This brings us to the final and perhaps most difficult problem that I faced in creating the 3D model. Because I was trying to achieve realism for pedagogical purposes while also trying to make the roof as realistic as possible to answer my research questions, the resulting model became very complex and unwieldy. With well over 1,000 objects, each draped with high-quality textures, as well as a rotoscoped movie of a fire in the firebox, by the time the model was complete it was nearly impossible to render. Because I had no funding for this project, the software (Specular [now Metacreations] Infini-D) and the hardware (Apple Quadra 800) available to me were not powerful enough to achieve both my pedagogical and research goals at the same time. The result was that I was actually unable to fully render the model until over a year after it was first created, when I had access to more powerful equipment.

My latest projects in architectural visualization have endeavored to accommodate the lessons learned during the creation of the great kiva 3D model. I am currently attempting to reconstruct prehistoric *great houses,* quasi-ceremonial structures that were often found in the company of one or more great kivas within many Anasazi communities. This attempt is purely for pedagogical uses, and I have accordingly simplified many aspects of the model. For example, instead of a fully detailed roof, I am using a single flat object on which is mapped a photograph of a well-preserved interior ceiling from an actual great house, drastically reducing the processing power needed to render the structure. For this model, I also have access to comparatively complete archaeological records, facilitating the inferences needed to bridge from the archaeological reality to the realism allowed by the visualization process.

Concluding Thoughts

The production of 3D reconstructions of nonextant prehistoric architecture requires a careful consideration of the amount of realism conveyed and the faithfulness of the model to archaeological reality. At the basic level, these two objectives will never be commensurate simply because the archaeological record is necessarily an incomplete reflection of prehistoric reality. Further complicating the modeling process are the goals of the model, the intended audience, the quality of archaeological information, and the access to sufficient technology and skills. As the examples in this chapter have demonstrated, these factors can often work against each other, substantially complicating the production of the 3D model. Reconstructions will therefore benefit from a careful consideration of all potential constraints prior to the actual modeling process. Perhaps most importantly, the presentation of the final model should be accompanied by a description of the original archaeological material and the inferences that were made to build a complete model. As 3D modeling software and hardware become more sophisticated, the amount of realism that can be created can mislead end users into believing that the model represents true prehistoric reality. While the power of these models to advance our pedagogical and research goals is undisputed, we need to be aware of the dangers of misrepresenting the past.

References Cited

FAGAN, B. M. AND G. H. MICHAELS, 1992, "Anthropology 3: an experiment in the multimedia teaching of introductory archaeology" *American Antiquity* vol. 57(3), pp. 458–466.

FLANAGAN, J., 1998, "Imagining Lowry" *Common Ground* vol. 3(1), pp. 34–37.

GOODPASTURE, A. V., 1997, "Digitizing digs: archeologists use imaging to preserve Native American history" *PEI* vol. 40(4), pp. 24–26.

LIGHTFOOT, R. R., 1988, "Roofing an early Anasazi great kiva: analysis of an architectural model" *The Kiva* vol. 53(3), pp. 253–272.

NOVISKI, B. J., 1998, *Rendering Real and Imagined Buildings: The Art of Computer Modeling.* Rockport Publishers, Gloucester, Massachusetts.

PETERSON, P., F. D. FRACCHIA, AND B. HAYDEN, 1995, "A virtual computer imaging technique for archaeological research" *Society for American Archaeology Bulletin* vol. 13(4), pp. 30–33.

SNYGG, J. AND T. WINDES, 1998, "Long, wide roads and great kiva roofs" *Kiva* vol. 64(1), pp. 7–25.

VIVIAN, G. AND P. REITER, 1960, *The Great Kivas of Chaco Canyon and their Relationships.* Monograph No. 22. The School of American Research, Santa Fe, New Mexico.

NATIVE AMERICAN VIRTUAL REALITY ARCHAEOLOGY: AN ARCHITECT'S PERSPECTIVE

Dennis R. Holloway

Architect, Rio Rancho, New Mexico, USA
Archvr@roadrunner.com,

Pre-Columbian Native American architecture of the Southwest United States, specifically that of the so-called "Anasazi People," has always fascinated me. When my architecture practice brought me to work in New Mexico in 1990, I was amazed to find the extent of the presence of this native architecture in the high desert landscape. Ceramics, lithics, and mounds of collapsed village and compound walls can be seen on terraces wherever there is nearby flowing water and bottom land. While most visible traces of prehistoric native architecture have been destroyed in the rest of the U.S., due primarily to Eurocentric agricultural practices and urbanization, the American Southwest still displays an extraordinarily large number of sites, many of which have yet to be studied in depth by archaeologists.

My own architectural education and training had not fully prepared me for what I would re-discover in these ancient sites. When I was a student, history of architecture was one of my favorite subjects, but the architecture of Pre-Columbian America was only briefly touched upon by the professors. The study of European temples, cathedrals and "modernism" was the main emphasis. What I found during my casual explorations of the New Mexico landscape was a profoundly unique kind of vernacular architecture and a class of "great" architecture distinct from those in all other parts of the world. As I shared my enthusiasm for rediscovering this architecture with my New Mexican Hispano, Anglo, and Pueblo Indian friends, I was surprised to find that most of them did not know much about these ancient places. What most surprised me was the fact that Pueblo Indians, who worship their ancestors who built these places, had (seemingly) forgotten about them. A Pueblo Indian friend told me he had never visited the Great House ruins of Chaco Canyon nor the Cliff Dwelling ruins of Mesa Verde, which are among the most touristed places in the Southwest.

In architecture and anthropology libraries and collections, there is a great quantity of accumulated archaeological data and photography on this architecture, but very little information on theoretical visual reconstructions. Classical perspective or axonometric drawing in American archaeology seems to be a forgotten or yet-to-be-discovered art. Many sites have never been imaged or modeled in any way, other than measured plans, elevations, and cross-sections. Serious reconstruction pictures, perspective views or study models are rare. American archaeology seems to have overlooked the importance of architecture, in favor of other artifacts such as pottery and lithics. This has severely limited understanding of important world architecture. Surely architecture offers us an equally important, if not more important, access to the anthropology of prehistoric America.

In my spare time I began to study the collections of archaeological data on the Anasazi sites. Each site I studied was an architectural gem, which, because I am an architect, I could clearly imagine in my mind's eye; I could imagine these places inside and out, but there was no communicable image. I was struck with the diversity of space-planning and architectonic appearances of the various sites. There is a visual continuum in the various contemporaneous regional idioms of architecture of the Anasazi--in terms of construction materials, and geometrical and structural systems. Yet the conceptual design framework of each individual place is unique, different from all the rest in a ratio not unrelated to the ambient environmental variants.

I realized that something had to be done about the shortage of visual images of reconstructions of specific places. I wanted to show and share this beautifully unique and diverse indigenous architectural phenomenon with both the Native people and the American "newcomers." But to draw a classical static one-, two-, or three-point perspective or an axonometric view of each of the thousands of documented American sites, with the traditional pencils, ink, and paper could require the work of many people over a long period of time.

At about this time, I was beginning to learn to use new 3D CAD/Virtual Reality software on the Macintosh computer, introduced to me by my client and friend, artist Ronald Davis. I was astonished at how rapidly, clearly, and vibrantly a virtual reality model of a project design could be imaged on a computer and presented to the client. It was gratifying how positively my clients responded and how practice with this new technology brought in more referrals and commissions. The visual communication technology in the field of architecture is in revolution. One day it dawned upon me that with the advent of cybernetic virtual reality, rapid modeling of heretofore arcane Southwest archaeological information is possible. A person using a computer, now or in the future, could "virtually" walk into the pre-Columbian Native American architectural world. Thus I began a "hobby" of VR modeling of Anasazi places.

As a starting point, the research and writing of American archaeologist Stephen H. Lekson provided me with good information about Anasazi architecture. His *Great Pueblo Architecture of Chaco Canyon, New Mexico*, contains plan drawings, story numbers and heights, construction details, and construction sequence chronologies of the Great Houses of the Canyon. By scanning Lekson's drawings into my Macintosh, I had enough scaled three-dimensional and temporal information to build VR models of Pueblo Bonito and Pueblo del Arroyo in animated construction sequences. I was astonished at the speed at which the computer allowed me to do this. The success of these early reconstructions encouraged me to continue my hobby.

When I first exhibited printed still "ray-traced" color images of these VR models at the Bareiss Gallery in Taos, New Mexico, USA, in 1991, the reaction from local Hispanic Taoseos, Native Americans, and descendants of Chaco Canyon Anasazi was positive and encouraging. For the first time they could see something that they had only heard about. As well, they were initiated into some mysteries of the so-called "Chaco Phenomenon," known previously only by the archaeological community. One normally reticent Pueblo artist friend became ecstatic upon seeing for the first time in 3D the large number of kivas (round ceremonial chambers) of Pueblo Bonito, and began to expound his interpretation of what that meant.

Figure 1: "Ray tracing" is the most realistic way to visually represent a 3D object on a computer screen. It is more advanced than simple rendering in that the final image can have reflective, refractive, and texture qualities with shading and shadowing automatically calculated, given the source, color and intensity of light as well as the observer's viewpoint. Shown here is a reconstruction of the pre-Columbian Great House, "Pueblo Bonito," in Chaco Canyon National Historic Park, New Mexico, USA.

When I put my VR Anasazi work on-line on my web site, I was shocked at the world response. Currently the site is averaging about 60,000 hits per month, and I get voluminous e-mail from visitors worldwide. The gist of the feedback is that VR reconstruction of the past is vitally important. Subsequently, I continued this work to include, at this writing, about sixty models of "great" Southwest architecture. This work and future updates may be viewed on the Internet at http://www.taosnet.com/architectVRe/.

Figure 2: Ray-traced image of VR reconstruction model of the pre-Columbian Great House, "Chetro Ketl," Chaco Canyon National Historic Park, New Mexico, USA. With archaeological data supplied by Stephen H. Lekson, the model is constructed to show only what is known as a result of excavations.

Work on these VR models has been a profound personal education for me. Because the VR modeler becomes intimately acquainted with the archaeological data, the experience of building a VR model can be an intense one--perhaps the most intense and complex form of study possible. While building the VR model from the data, the modeler may begin to get intuitive flashes of how architecture or a place looked during its existence. Sometimes working late at night, I had a comforting sense that the original "architects" of these places were standing over my shoulder, teaching me while guiding my hand through the many mouse-clicks and key-strokes required for each model. In building these models I learned an entirely new idiom of world architecture and village planning, the environmental principles of which seem, in my opinion, more relevant to the American milieu than the transplanted architectural and planning principles of the so-called "modern movement" of the Industrial Revolution. This experience has influenced my New Mexico architecture practice in the way I think about design and materials of construction, and I have been honored by several New Mexico Indian Tribes, who have commissioned me to design "culturally relevant" buildings as alternatives to main-stream architecture.

Virtual reality models are dynamic processes--not static pictures as with previous Western presentation media. VR models allow us to put all of our contemporary knowledge and thought about an object into a user-interactive presentation or encounter. VR models may be modified with the passage of time or as new information becomes available. Thus, a VR model can be a repository for all new knowledge about the past, present, and theoretical future of an object. When I work on a VR model, as with my work in architecture, I try to be aware that my product is going to be experienced or revised by other people long after I am gone. Because VR models are likely to exist into the future, they may be refined in the future by others as new archaeological data becomes available. They should be constructed with that in mind--in a way that facilitates future corrections, expanded detailing or changes in scale. Processes like grouping elements, labeling and dating of all the parts, phases, and subcategorizes, and showing scale and orientation can facilitate the VR model's future enhancement. I think of the VR model as a complete known specification for a site that should be capable of accepting new information as it becomes available. Because VR is the daughter of the computer, like the computer, it must be future oriented--even while expanding knowledge of the past.

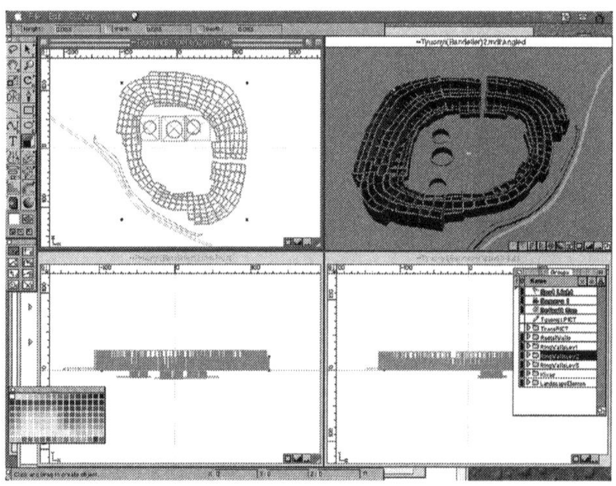

Figure 3: Screen capture of VIDI Presenter Pro (recently renamed 3D Joy) software; shown here in process of reconstruction is the Great House of Tyuonyi, prehistoric Rio Grande Anasazi site, Bandelier National Monument, New Mexico, USA. The working environment includes top view, front view, right view, interactive perspective view, tools and color palettes, and hierarchical groups window. VIDI web site may be found at http://www.VIDI.com.

Useful information to acquire in preparing for construction of a VR architectural archeology model could include measured or surveyed floor plans, sections, and elevations. This data should contain a graphical scale and a "true" north arrow that has been corrected from magnetic variance. Topographical data of the surrounding site or site context including proximity to water courses, aerial photographs and other site photos, adjacent structures or natural formations, and underground or other "hidden" data. Dating of the parts of the object/buildings/compound to be modeled is essential for construction-sequence or metamorphic modeling. Construction details for outer walls, inner walls, floors, and roofs, specified materials used for construction, and their color and texture can all be built into the VR model. Once this information has been acquired for a given site, the images can be scanned into the computer and referred to as the model is constructed using VR software. In the future, we should see dramatic developments in software that allows the archaeological team to construct the VR model directly as surveying, surface scanning or excavation proceed.

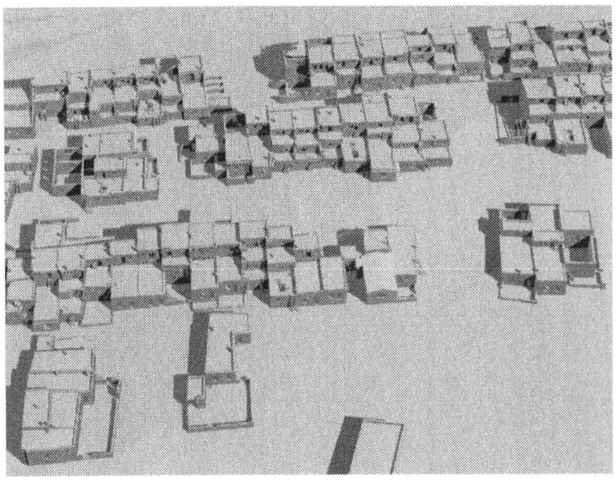

Figure 4: Ray-traced VR model image of Acoma Pueblo considered to be the oldest continuously inhabited place in North America. Data for this model is from the 1934 Historic American Building Survey of the architecture of the Pueblo. All measured exterior elevations and plans were scanned, and used as model templates. The window frames and doors have not yet been modeled in this work-in-process.

Figure 5: Electronic photo-montage showing "Kwastiyukwa," ancestral village of Jemez Pueblo and largest of the known pre-Columbian Indian Pueblos. The model and sun angle were manipulated "by eye" to match the angles of Paul Logsdon's aerial photograph of the ruin site. Using Photoshop the image of the model was "pasted into" a selected area of the scanned site photo. The composite image was then retouched to create the "treeless" area surrounding the Pueblo.

Figure 6: Electronic photo-montage showing the interior of the "Great Kiva" (with roof covering removed), Aztec National Monument, New Mexico, USA. The VR model was first ray traced, and then a scanned image of the sky was pasted into the background to give a more realistic effect.

This new freedom to interactively animate a model in VR space, look at it at will in real time, photo-realistically from any angle, inside or outside, and at different points in its temporal existence, is the most radical new way of looking at objects in space since the early European Renaissance. It has enormous implications for the advancement of all fields using visual 3D information.

Virtual reality can be a very powerful medium for presenting new ideas about the past. The potential societal impact of new archaeological knowledge gained from VR experience should be taken very seriously by the VR model builder. In the nineteenth century, John Ruskin declared that architecture is the most permanent collective cultural memory of an age--a "lamp" that all future generations will see. Today, at the dawn of the cyber age, and with the new VR technology, the past can be remembered as never before. By refreshing cultural memory, archaeology has been a powerful influence in the development of emerging world ideas and politics. Utilizing the tool of virtual reality, archaeology will continue to gain in importance.

When European architects (the first "archaeologists") studied and became conscious of the architectural ruins of ancient Greece and Rome, a European Renaissance resulted, which influenced all the world arts and sciences down to the present time. With the new VR study of ancient Native American architecture, can a similar phenomenon be underway in the Americas? Certainly the culture of Native Americans will be empowered. Can the general shift towards world-wide VR archaeology herald a New World Renaissance in which all the people of the world become re-awakened to the wonders of a forgotten past? Certainly we will all better understand our human inter-connectedness, and that can contribute to the search for world peace.

With the advent of VR, society has taken a quantum leap in visual imagery and visual literacy. To meet the future needs of this new VR-savvy audience, the disciplines of archaeology and architecture must collaborate much more integrally than in the past. VR architects can work alongside VR archaeologists to create the most virtually real images and experiences of forgotten buildings and places. Archaeology and architecture schools need to encourage reciprocal cross-disciplinary studies, so that this necessary teamwork will be less daunting. Indeed the emergence of VR may propound a new field of study; perhaps we should call it "archaeotecture" --from ancient + building.

As we VR-image places that heretofore have existed in esoteric library collections, those places become more integrated into the public consciousness about the planetary past. This consciousness-raising is a logical extension and augmentation of the green or environmental movement. Virtual reality is important, because it brings us closer to an understanding of the illusion in which we exist--from VR we get a broader understanding of our place and time in the cosmos, and we are sensitized to the significance and meaning of living in our own time. By knowing where mankind has been, we may better understand where we should go.

Through the experience of VR, the relativity of Space and Time has become palpable--not just theoretical. Today, while sitting in front of a computer console, it is possible to experience the VR flythrough of ancient Egypt and simultaneously be in web cam ICQ chat with someone in the Netherlands. In the future there is no telling to what new perceptual thresholds VR technology will take us.

References Cited

Peter Nabokov and Robert Easton, 1989, *Native American Architecture*, Oxford University Press, New York and Oxford.

Stephen Lekson, William B. Gillespie, and Thomas C. Winde, 1984, *Great Pueblo Architecture of Chaco Canyon, New Mexico*, University of New Mexico Press, Albuquerque, New Mexico, USA.

Stephen Lekson (Editor), Jeffrey S. Dean, Peter J. McKenna, Richard L. Warren, and Thomas C. Winde, foreword by Florence Hawley Ellis, 1983, *The Architecture and Dendrochronology of Chetro Ketl, Chaco Canyon, New Mexico*, Division of Cultural Research, National Park Service, U.S. Department of Interior, Albuquerque, New Mexico, USA.

Peter Nabokov, 1986, *Architecture of Acoma Pueblo: The 1934 Historic American Building Survey Project*, Ancient City Press, Santa Fe, New Mexico, USA.

William Morgan, 1994, *Ancient Architecture of the Southwest* [U.S.], University of Texas Press, Austin, Texas, USA.

William C. Sturtevant (General Editor) and Alfonso Ortiz (Volume Editor), 1979, *Handbook of North American Indians*, Volume 9, Southwest, Smithsonian Institution, Washington D.C., USA.

Michael A. Adler (Editor) 1996, *The Prehistoric Pueblo World A.D. 1150-1350*, The University of Arizona Press, Tucson, Arizona, USA.

Technical Papers

PLANS, ELEVATIONS AND VIRTUAL WORLDS: THE DEVELOPMENT OF TECHNIQUES FOR THE ROUTINE CONSTRUCTION OF HYPERREAL SIMULATIONS

Mark Gillings

School of Archaeological Studies
University of Leicester, UK
mg41@leicester.ac.uk

Introduction

I would like to begin by suggesting that for developments in Virtual Reality to be truly useful to archaeology, they must be firmly grounded in archaeological theory and accessible and applicable at all levels of archaeological practice[1]. To realise such an aim, a number of important areas of research have to be investigated:

- Firstly, archaeologists must take a critical look at the ontological and epistemological foundations of mainstream archaeological applications of VR.
- Secondly, the notion of VR models as comprising little more than ingenious 'end-products' needs to be challenged. Techniques must be embedded at all levels of archaeological investigation, serving not only as sophisticated visual summaries, but also as primary recording methods, heuristic devices, and display and communication mechanisms.
- Finally, and intimately linked to the above, is the need to develop and adapt a number of routine field and laboratory based methodologies that can be integrated into current archaeological practice. As long as VR is perceived as both specialist and resource intensive, its impact will be at best muted—an avenue of research regarded as desirable but ultimately esoteric and inaccessible.

To date, research into archaeological VR has been characterised by a continual drive towards methodological refinement. A relentless questing for the elusive grails of photo-realism and ever more painstaking and faithful simulation. Sophisticated virtual models are generated largely because it can be done. Only after models have been generated does attention turn to the uses to which they can be put. When it comes to sophistication and ingenuity, it is fair to say that these eventual uses show considerably less ingenuity and innovation than was expended in the creation of the models. A good example can be seen in the case of the increasingly sophisticated approaches being developed for the solid modelling of complex architectural structures. Here, rather than creating models using simple surfaces, for example a single, flat plane to represent the wall of a building, the construction of a virtual simulation is based upon a virtual re-building on a simulated stone-by-stone basis (for a detailed discussion of such approaches, see Daniel 1997). The levels of technical detail and sophistication that go into the creation of such a virtual building are breathtaking. What are the benefits of such a painstaking and technologically intensive approach?

- Questions can be answered about the physical structure itself, such as its volume, mass and centre of gravity.
- Factors relating to the economics of construction can be determined, such as quantities of material and labour cost per cubic metre.

The object of analysis becomes the building itself as a sterile architectural shell, stripped of people and the bricolage of everyday social practice. You do not need to know or understand the mass or centre of gravity of a building to dwell within it and imbue it with meaning. Questions concerning the economics of construction, whilst no doubt interesting, run the risk of privileging the question *how* over that of *why*, achieving little more than a hollow echo of earlier, limiting debates as to the person-hours involved in the construction of various monuments (for a classic example, see Renfrew 1973). What is clear is that the application leads the study, its uses to archaeology are retrospectively assigned.

The current discussion aims to make a positive contribution to the process of re-evaluation and exploration that I am arguing is essential if archaeology is to maximise the enormous potential VR has to offer. In attempting to characterise the beneficial role VR can play in archaeological research I intend to concentrate upon two of the key issues mentioned above:

1. The incorporation of VR into everyday archaeological study.
2. The development of routine practical methodologies.

Aspects of the first of these categories will be examined through a brief discussion as to how VR-based techniques are being woven into the fabric of an ongoing programme of research—the *Negotiating Avebury* project, focusing upon the late Neolithic henge complex of Avebury located in the southwest of England.

The bulk of the discussion is directed towards the final category, the design of a range of routine and accessible techniques. Techniques that are essential if we are to create a series of developmental pathways down which innovative VR-based approaches can percolate through to all levels of archaeological study. An intrinsic element of the *Negotiating Avebury* project is the development and refinement of more readily accessible (and inherently egalitarian) VR methodologies. Working within a broad theoretical framework, emphasising the fluidity and contingency of VR models as fully mimetic modes of representation (Gillings, *in press*), the goal has been to integrate VR techniques into the generation of primary archaeological records. In this way the idea that VR simulations could, and should, be seen as a natural and complimentary adjunct to the familiar maps, plans and elevation drawings of traditional archaeological research, is strengthened and reinforced.

[1] In such a formulation the term 'Virtual reality' is being used to refer to the diverse set of visualisation, rendering and solid-modelling applications currently finding a growing place within archaeological research.

Theoretical Considerations

Regarding the question of epistemology, and the theoretical issues raised by any attempt to fully exploit VR for archaeology, a number of discussions have been published which explore in detail the ways in which this diverse set of approaches can be realised and incorporated within archaeology (Gillings and Goodrick, 1996; Gillings 1999; Gillings, *in press*; Goodrick and Gillings, *in press*). Although it is not my intention to repeat these debates in full here, it is useful to summarise the main points.

In much the same way as GIS, VR has gained widespread acceptance within archaeology despite having no critical history of its own production and few detailed investigations into its ontological and epistemological foundations (Pickles 1995:1-2)[2]. At present, developments in archaeological VR appear to have fallen into a teleological trap structured around a desire to create 'realistic' virtual models of the artefacts and sites under study. This discourse is characterised by the exploitation of increasingly sophisticated hardware and software resources in the quest to create wholly realistic representations of some unproblematic past reality [3]. If left unchallenged, such an emphasis runs the risk of limiting and marginalising VR and ultimately reifying the resultant models. Archaeological VR becomes all about the creation of pictures—ingenious pictures—but pictures nevertheless. The interpretative uses to which such models can be put are relegated to a secondary consideration, when they are considered at all. Far too often, rather than taking on the mantle of flexible and dynamic heuristic devices, the enormous potential such simulations have to contribute to new ways of thinking about and approaching the past are not realised.

In actively seeking to develop a more flexible and useful framework for the incorporation of VR into mainstream archaeological research, issues such as the relationship between 'model', 'reality' and 'authenticity' have been examined in an attempt to answer the question *what does it mean to describe something as virtually real?* (Gillings, *in press*). Building upon the work of critical theorists, such as Jean Baudrillard (Baudrillard 1983) , and philosophers, such as Walter Benjamin (Snyder 1989), an enriched notion of mimetic representation has been offered as a constructive framework for future developments. This is a framework which simultaneously incorporates and emphasises the two characteristics of the process of archaeological interpretation: the empirical commitment to the material remains of the past we carefully recover, curate and study; and the degree of speculation and creativity inherent in the process engendered by the fragmentary nature of the archaeological record.

[2] In this, VR applications share similarities with early applications of GIS in archaeology. What is encouraging is the way in which the latter has been quick to respond. For rare critical discussion of the underlying rationales of archaeological VR, see Gillings and Goodrick (1996); Pringle and Moulding (1997); Gillings (1999).

[3] For "realistic", read photo-realistic, i.e. the resemblance of a model to a photograph of an original. As a number of authors have pointed out photographs themselves by no means present an unproblematic and objective representation of the world (for a recent discussion within archaeology see Shanks 1996). To quote the Geographer Duncan "A camera is a machine constructed to produce an image based upon artificial perspective. Only if one accepts the claims of the naturalness of renaissance artificial perspective can we accept photography as a mimetic representation of the world" (Duncan 1993: 43). This is expressed forcibly by Ihde when he points out that "*The photograph, more than merely representing, 'teaches' a way of seeing*"(Ihde 1993: 48, italics in original).

The incorporation into everyday archaeological practice : The primacy of the problem and development of a context

As discussed above, this programme of research into the theory and practice of VR is currently embedded in a major programme of study centred upon the late Neolithic henge monument of Avebury, located in the county of Wiltshire in Southern England. The monument at Avebury comprises a complex arrangement of standing stones held within a substantial circuit of ditch and bank. It lies within a culturally 'thick' landscape of stone settings, enclosures, burial monuments and earthworks (Whittle 1993; 1997). Following the work of archaeologists such as Barrett and Thomas and the social anthropologist Ingold, a number of research threads have been identified. Central to these is a concern with how the texture, colour, physicality and architecture of stone, ditch and bank served to choreograph and structure social practice
within the monument during the later Neolithic and Bronze Age (Barrett 1994; Thomas 1993; Ingold 1992). Linked closely to this is a meta-archaeological investigation into the ways in which the fabric of a working village within and around the monument served to fuel and shape the antiquarian imagination during the seventeenth and eighteenth centuries (Pollard and Gillings, 1998).

To be able to approach the study of the monument in such a way, based as it is upon notions of bulk and physicality, a detailed record of the surviving morphology is required. Although extensively studied over the last three hundred or so years, the techniques used for the recording of the site have concentrated upon the production of abstracted 2-dimensional representations: hachure plans for the earthworks and both quantitative and qualitative elevation drawings for the extant stones. These have been supported by a number of reconstruction drawings rendered from what the phenomenologist Ihde has referred to as the *reading perspective* — i.e. the downward looking attitude adopted when reading a book (Ihde 1993: 82). In the context of Avebury, examples of such depictions can be seen in sources as diverse as Pollard's recent reconstruction of the Avebury environs (Whittle 1997: 165) and Crocker's 1812 plan of the site, reproduced here as Figure 1.

Figure 1: Crocker's plan of Avebury (reproduced from Burl 1979: 55).

More recently, the recording of the monument has been dominated by a prodigious portfolio of photographs (for example, see Burl 1979).

In the context of the current research such representational schema proved unsatisfactory for a number of reasons:

- They privileged an holistic understanding of the monument at the expense of the more partial and fragmented appreciation gained from actually walking over, around and through it.
- They served to remove and isolate the archaeological observer from the frame of study.
- They presented the monument as a series of distinct components, laid out as if upon a dissecting table, uniformly lit and stripped of bulk and texture.

That such representations, despite their claims to clinical objectivity, conceal as much as they reveal has been commented upon by a number of researchers (e.g. Harley 1988; Pickles 1992; Gregory 1994: 15-69). That they also yield a very different understanding of the monument to that derived from being situated within and moving around it has also been highlighted (Barrett 1994: 9-19). In the context of the Avebury research programme, such limitations become major problems, as in attempting to interpret the monument through a more situated and embodied perspective, it is precisely this latter type of understanding we are trying to access and explore.

In our work at Avebury it rapidly became clear that we needed to move beyond existing representations of the monument rendered as sterile two-dimensional plans, sections and elevations, or frozen within the frame of the photograph. Instead we needed to represent and study the monument as a complex three-dimensional entity. As intimated above, the first problem encountered was the lack of suitable data. Hachure plans and simple stone elevations are of little use in the construction of fully three-dimensional simulations. Existing attempts to produce three-dimensional models of such monuments have relied upon a battery of highly sophisticated, time-consuming, specialised, and costly techniques, well beyond the range of most field archaeologists. The textbook illustration is English Heritage's 'Virtual Stonehenge' (Burton *et al* 1999). Such models have also been geared around the production of a comprehensive and highly 'realistic' end-product. In the case of 'Virtual Stonehenge' this extended down to the visitors car-park, ticket office turnstile and the site post-box. In the Avebury research, VR models are first and foremost seen as primary records, linked directly to specific archaeological problems. For example, to what extent does the bulk of the stones constrain vision within and across the monument? Rather than the creation of a single monolithic 'Virtual Avebury' the aim is to create a large number of highly contingent 'Virtual Aveburys' through which it will be possible to examine particular questions and problem areas. Photo-realism is a secondary consideration when it is considered at all (Pollard and Gillings, 1998).

If VR-based approaches in general are to have wider and more routine application, what are needed are a set of effective methodologies for the three-dimensional recording of both the earthworks and the megalithic stone settings. With the earthworks a methodology was already in place. This was based upon the use of a total-station survey instrument to record three-dimensional co-ordinate locations on the ground surface. From this data vector-based Triangulated Irregular Networks (TIN's) and GIS-based Digital Elevation Models (DEM's) could be constructed and interfaced with fractal visualisation and VR-world-building utilities (Gillings and Goodrick 1996). As the costs of digital survey instrumentation and computer hardware have fallen, such methodologies have become a commonplace in archaeological fieldwork and research, being recently enhanced through the introduction of advanced data-logging facilities and relatively low-cost kinematic Global Positioning Systems (GPS).

With the recording of the stones at Avebury we faced a much greater problem. As intimated above, two-dimensional footprints and elevation drawings, whilst conforming to the sterile, objectifying ideals of the neutral scientific record, were of no use as raw materials in the construction of fully three-dimensional representations. What was needed was a reliable fieldwork methodology that would yield data suitable for the construction of VR simulations. To ensure that the methodology would find a place in routine archaeological practice the following considerations were foregrounded:

- The techniques should be cost-effective, in terms of both time and resources
- They should be simple in execution
- They should not involve any reliance upon access to highly specialised staff or equipment.

The Development of Routine Methodologies

PHOTOMODELER

The solution adopted at Avebury has been based around 35mm photography and the commercial software package Photomodeler [4]. The latter is a low-cost computer programme which has been designed specifically to transform multiple photographs into accurately scaled, three-dimensional models. Over the last three years it has found increasing application within archaeology for the recording of standing buildings and other built structures, and had already been successfully applied by members of the project in the context of early research into the archaeological potential of the Virtual Reality Modelling Language (VRML) capabilities of the World Wide Web (WWW) (Gillings and Goodrick 1996).

Photomodeler creates fully three-dimensional models on the basis of shared points that can be identified upon multiple photographs. Photographs taken of a single object from a variety of different viewing angles. Before any photographs are taken, the camera is calibrated within Photomodeler to establish the relationship between the focal node of the camera lens, and the film plane. To aid in this calibration process Photomodeller supports the use of fiducials. These are physical points in the camera that are imaged on the film at the same time as the image coming through the lens (EOS Systems Inc. 1996: 257-8). By including fiducial marks on the image you ensure that a constant frame of reference is included on each photograph that links the image to the camera. The process of adapting a camera to use fiducials involves the simple addition of a small plastic insert into the film plane [5]. The fiducials can be seen as characteristic triangular marks in the left hand corners of each image (for example see Figure 3b). To ensure the highest accuracy a non-zoom lens is recommended, as the focal length on certain zoom lenses is liable to change as the level of zoom is adjusted. All of the photographs in the current project have been taken using a standard 50mm lens.

Once the camera has been described, Photomodeler is able to examine a photograph taken with the camera and project straight lines (rays) from any recorded point on the surface of the image, through the focal node of the lens and out into space (Figure 2). Provided you have identified the same point on ideally three or more photographs, Photomodeler is able to project and intersect

[4] Full details of the Photomodeler software can be obtained directly from EOS systems Inc. at http://www.photomodeler.com

[5] Although not directly used by the LX version of the software used in the surveys described here, all of the photographs taken at Avebury have incorporated fiducial inserts. This has been to ensure that the photographic archive comprises a flexible data set that can be used to generate models with increased accuracy with the full release of the Photomodeler software.

these rays to locate the point accurately in three-dimensional space.

In practice, photographs are taken, and the approximate location of the camera position relative to the object is recorded for each. Photographs are then processed either directly onto CD, using the Kodak PhotoCD format, or to slides/prints can be scanned using either a film or print scanner. The resultant images are imported into Photomodeler as graphics files. Once all of the required photographs have been imported, an interactive procedure is initiated whereby the approximate position of the camera relative to the object at the time the photograph was taken, is described for each image. These locations are referred to as Camera Stations [6]. When the camera stations have been approximately defined, you then go on to mark the locations of distinctive points on the surface topography of the object as recorded on each of the component photographs. A typical example of points you may want to record are diagnostic features such as the corners of a building and window and door frames. Where points are linked by lines or faces, such as the frame of a window or edge of a wall, this information can also be entered at this stage.

Once all of the necessary points have been marked, the next stage is to identify which points are the same on multiple photographs, in effect cross-referencing specific points between photographs. When all of the points you wish to use in a given model have been marked and referenced, a point audit is performed to enable you to examine the relative quality of each of the component points in the project. For example, points appearing in only one or two photographs are highlighted and points prone to measurement error, such as those where angle between the photographs used to reference them is very small, are clearly flagged. This stage is critical for identifying and editing specific problem points before any detailed processing of the data is undertaken. Following any edits made as a result of the audit, Photomodeler can be instructed to process the points marked and cross-referenced, to generate a final three-dimensional model. Through the application of an iterative algorithm, the positions and angles of camera stations and marked points are adjusted until a satisfactory model is generated. Histograms and a quoted total error statistic enable the accuracy and quality of the resultant model to be evaluated.

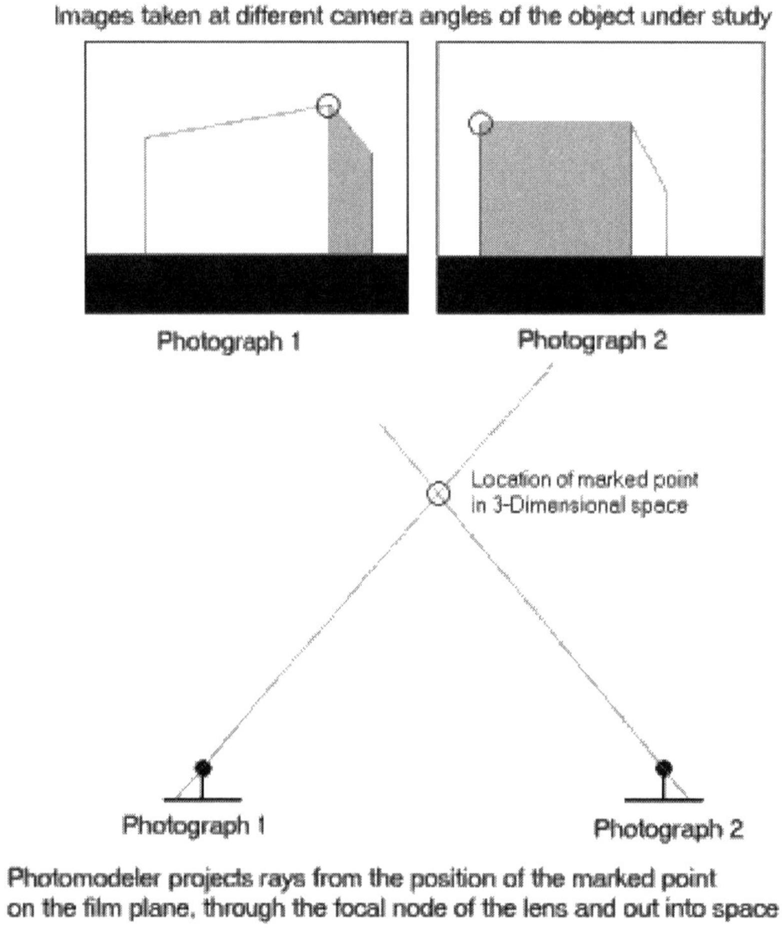

Figure 2: How Photomodeler locates points in three-dimensional space.

[6] In practice the location of each camera station does not have to be defined with any great precision. The greater the number of points involved in a given project the more approximate the camera stations can be located. In the latest version of the software (Photomodeler Pro 3.0) camera station orientation has been made a fully automatic process.

The model comprises a cloud of points located in three-dimensional space, linked by lines or faces as indicated during the marking stage. Once the point-cloud has been generated, lines and faces can be also be added through an interactive process to link up the component points where necessary. The final stage is to scale and rotate the models to place them within the appropriate project co-ordinate system. These stages are summarised in Table 1.

Table 1

Stage	Description
Take photographs	Take a series of photographs around the object. Try to ensure that there is a good angle between the photographs, i.e. as near to 90 degrees as possible. In addition make sure that any clearly diagnostic points, for example corners of a building, are visible on at least 3 images. Record the distance from the camera to the object and approximate angle.
Process and import photographs	Negatives can be scanned or processed directly onto PhotoCD ready to be imported into Photomodeler. Digital images can be imported directly.
Describe Camera Stations	Use the distance and angle information recorded in the first stage to inform Photomodeler as to the approximate position of the camera relative to the object for each photograph.
Mark fiducials	If utilised mark the occurrence of any camera calibration marks, such as frame edges or film plane inserts to improve the accuracy of the resultant model.
Mark points	Interactively mark the occurrence of diagnostic points on each of the component photographs.
Reference	Cross-reference the occurrence of diagnostic points between photographs.
Process	Process the 3D model
Mark lines and faces	Link up diagnostic points from discrete lines and planar faces. This stage can also be undertaken interactively whilst marking points.
Scale and orient	Interactively scale and orient the resultant model using measured points on the photographs.
Export	Export the resultant model for use in 3D modelling and VR software.

The level of accuracy of any Photomodeler model depends upon a number of factors, principally:

- Having sufficient clearly identifiable reference points
- The presence of such points on ideally three or more photographs
- Ensuring that there is a good angle between component photographs, ideally as close to ninety degrees as possible
- Having a well-calibrated and described camera

The quoted accuracy varies between 1:200 and 1:10000 depending upon the quality of the camera definition and reference points. Using a calibrated camera, a good spread of clearly identified points, and the LX release of the software, as we have at Avebury, a typical accuracy of the order of 1:1000 is to be expected. In a recent study undertaken by the Department of Geomatics, of the University of Newcastle upon Tyne, the accuracy of a number of methods for the creation of three-dimensional models of a structure were examined, in this case a four-storey town house. The techniques considered comprised: Theodolite angle intersection; Multiple Oblique photographs (Photomodeler Pro 2.1); and Single Oblique image (using the Phoenix algorithm developed at Newcastle). The three-dimensional models generated by these techniques were compared to a control model derived from a process of metric photogrammetry where the Photomodeler-derived models showed a very high level of correlation and accuracy (Bottrill *et al* 1998).

The real strengths of the method for archaeology are that it is cost effective and relies exclusively upon techniques and expertise already well developed within the discipline, i.e. the ability to take photographs. In terms of fieldwork no specialised equipment beyond a basic 35mm camera (we use a Praktica MTL 5B 35mm SLR) is involved and the fieldwork procedure involves little more than the taking of a set of photographs around the structure of interest.

RECORDING THE STONES: A TALE OF TIDDLYWINKS AND PLASTIC PUTTY

In the context of the Avebury project, the challenge came in applying the Photomodeler methodology to objects other than the regular and relatively simple shapes typical of buildings. Shapes with easily identifiable corners and features, in effect a finite number of potentially diagnostic points. Instead we were faced with natural, unmodified blocks of rough sarsen stone that often lacked even a clear distinction between back, front and sides let alone a set of unambiguous points of reference. In effect we were presented with a series of infinitely complex entities. To overcome this we relied upon the concept of 'targets', small highly visible markers that can be affixed to the object to indicate nodal points in its changing surface topography. In practice each stone was sketched and multi-coloured plastic markers — tiddlywinks purchased from a local toy shop — were affixed to the stone surface using small balls of blu-tack [7]. In this way points of change on the surfaces of the stones could be clearly flagged and marked. Through a careful process of interpretation and simplification, the net result of this process was to break the surface up into a series of discrete planar facets.

The more complex the stone the greater the number of individual targets needed to capture its shape. This process of interpretation directly influences the degree of simplification-reduction inherent in the resultant model and it was felt particularly important that this was undertaken whilst in the field, and in direct contact with the stone, rather than at a later date far removed from the object under study.

Once the stone had been marked, a north-south line two metres in length was carefully marked out on the ground surface adjacent to it, using a metal tape and surveying arrows. This served to provide important scaling and orientation information and also gave us a reference line that could be used to locate the stone model within the total-station based earthwork survey being undertaken at the same time. With the targets and calibration line in place a series of overlapping photographs were taken around the stone. The actual number of photographs taken varied between four and nine depending upon the size and bulk of a given stone, with six being typical. As will be discussed shortly, this proved to be inadequate and in more recent fieldwork the number of photographs has been in the order of typically twelve. In practice each stone could be fully marked and photographically recorded by a team of two in the space of approximately one hour, depending upon its size and complexity.

On completion of the photographic recording the 35mm films were developed directly onto Kodak PhotoCD to provide an instant source of high resolution digital images ready to be imported into Photomodeler. All of the processing was undertaken using a very modest Pentium 150Mhz Wintel machine, with 48MB of RAM, a 1.7GB hard disk, and running the NT 4.0 operating system. The various stages in the processing procedure are illustrated in Figure 3.

Figure 3a: The set of photographs taken around Stone 206.

[7] Tiddlywinks are small, flat plastic counters used to play the game of the same name. In practice one tiddlywink is used to apply pressure to another to cause it to flick up into a cup or other container. Not only are tiddlywinks cheap to purchase, they also provide an enjoyable means of unwinding after a hard day in the field.

Figure 3b: Marking the target points in Photomodeler.

Figure 3c: The complete set of marked photographs

Figure 3d: Referencing target points between photographs.

Figure 3e: The 3D cloud of target points generated after processing the marked and referenced photographs.

Figure 3f: Linking target points to form planar faces.

THE RESULTS OF THE EVALUATION

The results of the methodological evaluation were a number of fully scaled three-dimensional simulations of individual sarsen stones. These can be viewed and examined within Photomodeler, or exported as three-dimensional CAD models which can be input into advanced three-dimensional rendering and animation packages such as 3D Studio. Most interestingly in the context of our stated aim of egalitarianism, is the support for VRML formats. The latter models can be exported directly into VRML using simple faceted surfaces. They can also be texture mapped, using images extracted from the source photographs that were used to generate the model. If photographic texture mapping is desired, then it may be the case that the highly visible targets, essential to the construction of the model, are not wanted in the final texture maps. This is easily prevented by retaining a set of copies of the photographic images used to generate the models, and painting out the targets using a simple graphics programme (in practice Paint Shop Pro). When constructing the texture map in Photomodeler these images can be directly substituted for the originals, leading to a target free mapping. This procedure is also useful for filtering the images to emphasise and enhance very subtle shadow effects or highlight zones of changing surface texture. The VRML simulations generated of Stone 206 can be seen in Figures 4 and 5, as viewed using a standard WWW browser and VRML plug-in (Netscape 4.03 and Cosmo 2) [8].

It is important to emphasise that the stones are not simply end-products, though there is nothing to stop them being viewed as such. The aim is to create truly flexible representations that through the creative use of colours, artificial textures and context, can be used to stimulate new ways of thinking about the physicality of the monument. Acting first and foremost as a primary record of the morphology of each stone, they can be treated as little more than complex three-dimensional shapes, or used as templates upon which factors as diverse as lichen spread, working indicators (such as prehistoric axe polishing zones), and surface colour trends can be recorded. Linked to this latter set of objectives, work is currently underway to develop a library of visual metaphors that can be used to signify textural, colour and

[8] The quoted stone numbers at Avebury follow the scheme proposed by Smith (Smith 1965).

perceptual associations. Where photographic texture mapping is utilised, it is to stress very subtle surface trends, too small to be captured using the tiddlywink method. These are often recorded within changing patterns of light and shadow across the surface of the stone and, as mentioned above, can be enhanced in the photographic texture maps.

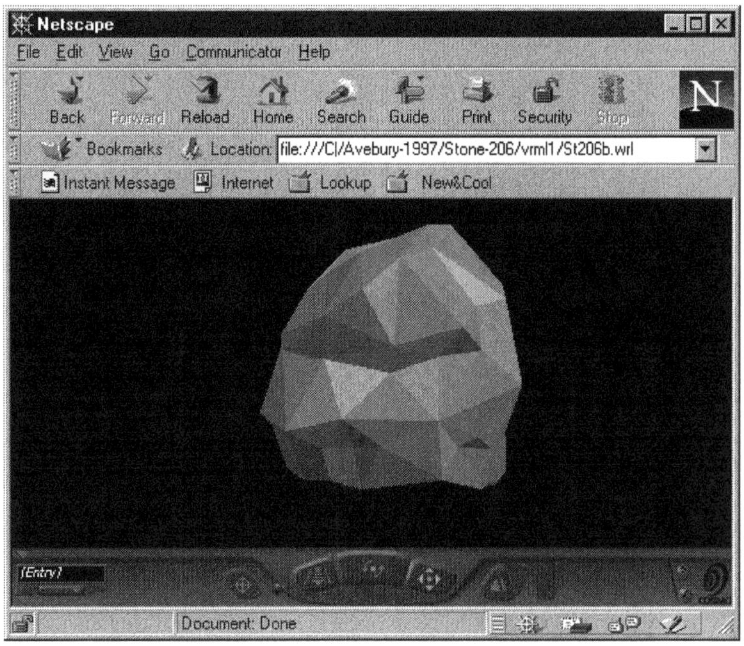

Figure 4: The resultant VRML model of Stone 206.

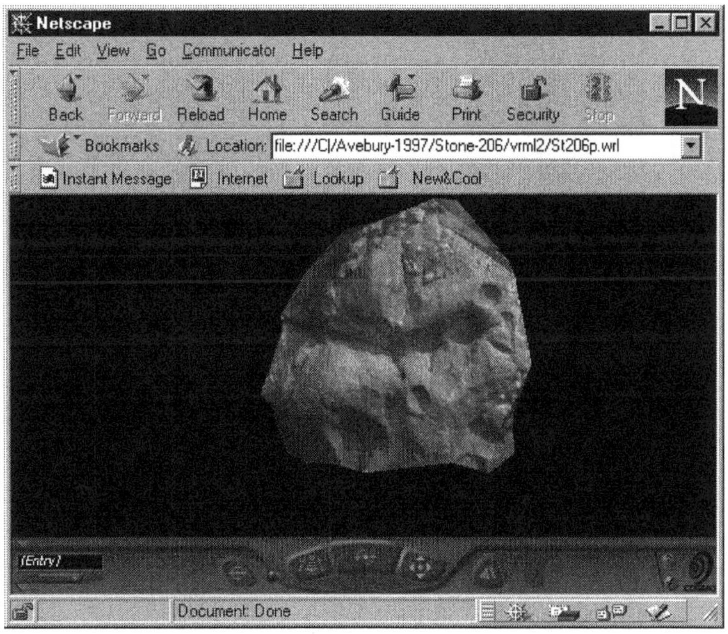

Figure 5: The VRML model with the photographic texture map applied.

It is important to realise that the stone simulations also function as individual components in a much larger exploratory environment. An environment which is being generated to enable archaeologists to explore issues related to movement, bodily access and the choreographies of social practice engendered by the evolving structural composition of the monument. It is critical to emphasise that the virtual-simulations represent a flexible heuristic device. They can be examined in splendid isolation, floating in the inky blackness of a browser window, or fixed into the topographical survey context through the provision and integration of geo-referencing information. The point to reiterate is that in the context of the Avebury research, the application of VR is not directed towards the creation of a sophisticated, monolithic 'Virtual Avebury', but is ongoing and exploratory.

As an exercise in the development of routine tools for the collection of VR data the methodology developed has been highly successful. It is relatively rapid, makes no excessive demands upon human or technical resources, and produces flexible models. Despite this a number of shortcomings have been identified. Some are related to the field methodology employed and some to the introductory version of the Photomodeler software that was utilised in the evaluation. These factors have been summarised in Table 2.

Table 2

Problem:	**Solution:**
An input limit of 6 photographs and 200 reference points built into the LX version of the software, whilst reasonable for the recording of simple geometric structures, made it impossible to adequately model the more complex stones.	Upgrade to Photomodeler Pro 3.0 which has no input limit on the number of photographs or reference points
Lack of photographic detail of the top of the stones has resulted in a failure to close the stone tops in certain simulations.	Take more photographs!
Some stones lacked enough photographs to generate sufficient reliable 3D points	Take more photographs!
On some photographs the shiny plastic markers were too small to be clearly visible and were prone to reflections which obscured their colour	Use larger, matt finished markers
Bright sunlight introduced deep shadows on certain photographs which were carried through into the texture mapping	If texture mapping is required, use a graphics package to balance the brightness of the source photographs before generation of the model or enhance those textural features of specific interest

What is most encouraging is the fact that all of the limitations, for example those built into the LX version of the software, and the failure to secure an adequate number of photographs with sufficient unambiguously identifiable target points, are easily remedied. In more recent work at Avebury we have rectified these limitations by upgrading the software; improved target visibility by fixing the tiddlywinks to multi-coloured fluorescent backing cards; used hand-annotated Polaroid photographs to guide the face creation process; and ensured that at least twelve photographs are taken of each stone to provide a comprehensive coverage pool from which images can be selected.

In conclusion, the basic Photomodeler method was cost-effective, rapid and involved a set of procedures well within the capabilities of most research and commercial archaeological units. Ideally the next stage would be to work with a high resolution digital camera, enabling the process of model creation, evaluation and updating to be undertaken on-site (and such an evaluation is currently underway). As it is, it is hoped that this work has shown that VR techniques are within the reach of the majority of archaeologists and that Virtual simulations have the potential to be as routine an element of on-site recording as the section, plan and elevation.

Conclusions

Over the last five years the term "virtual reality" has become ubiquitous within all aspects of contemporary Western society, synonymous with a developing generation of photo-realistic and fully interactive computer-generated environments. As a discipline, archaeology has been quick to embrace the enormous potential such developments have to offer.

It has been argued here that the agenda for this rapid adoption has been dictated by technological considerations and a preoccupation with photo-realism. This has come at the expense of a number of pressing conceptual problems within archaeological research and a failure to realise the full implications of the technology within archaeological practice.

If VR is to achieve, and perhaps even exceed, its undoubted potential, it must be realised that the generation of ever more photo-realistic models is but one application amongst many. Although the dominant approach taken at present, in the final analysis it may prove to be the least useful to archaeology. In the present discussion an attempt has been made to re-negotiate the role of VR within archaeological study. Through the development of accessible, routine methodologies, it is hoped that the first, admittedly small, step has been taken towards more fully integrating VR-based approaches within archaeology.

It is clear that this represents the very first stages in a complex process, and that applications of VR within archaeology will change and develop as both archaeology and the techniques at its disposal develop. Through the development of routinised methodologies embedded and implicated within a clear body of theory, it is hoped that such innovation and change can be embraced.

Acknowledgements

I would like to take this opportunity to thank Chris Gingell and Ros Cleal of the National Trust, Andrew David of the Ancient Monuments Laboratory, and Nick Burton of English Heritage for their enthusiastic support of the project and their granting of permission to undertake the fieldwork at Avebury. I would also like to thank the Universities of Leicester and Southampton for providing funding and both McCarthy Taylor Systems and EOS Systems Inc. for software sponsorship.

Extra special thanks go to the following individuals for helping to refine and develop the methodologies and undertake the evaluative fieldwork: Patty Baker, Dave Gibson, Glyn Goodrick, Josh Pollard, Dave Salisbury, Tim Sly and Dave Wheatley.

References Cited

BARRETT, J., 1994. *Fragments from Antiquity: An Archaeology of Social Life in Britain, 2900-1200 BC*. Oxford: Blackwell.

BAUDRILLARD, J., 1983. *Simulations*. New York: Semiotext(e)

BOTTRILL, A., PEIRSON, G., TAYLOR, G., PARSLEY, S. and THOMAS, P., 1998. "3D modelling of structures - new versus traditional methods" *Surveying World vol.* 6 (5), pp. 22-25.

BURL, A., 1979. *Prehistoric Avebury*. New Haven: Yale University Press.

BURTON, N. R., HITCHEN, M. E., and BRYAN, P. G., 1999. "Virtual Stonehenge: a fall from disgrace?" In L. Dingwall, S. Exon, V. Gaffney and M. van Leusen (eds). *Archaeology in the Age of the Internet - CAA 97 - Computer Applications and Quantitative Methods in Archaeology Proceedings of the 25th Anniversary Conference, University of Birmingham, April 1997*. Oxford: British Archaeological Reports International Series 750.

DANIEL, R., 1997. "The need for the solid modelling of structure in the archaeology of buildings" *Internet Archaeology* 2, 2.3 (http://intarch.ac.uk/journal/issue2/daniels_index.html)

DUNCAN, J., 1993. "Sites of representation: place, time and the discourse of the other" In J. Duncan and D. Ley (eds), *Place/Culture/Representation*, pp. 39-56. London: Routledge.

EOS SYSTEMS INC., 1996. *Photomodeler LX 3.0 user manual*. Vancouver: EOS Systems Inc.

GILLINGS, M. 1999., "Engaging place: exploring the potential of VR in experiential landscape studies" In L. Dingwall, S. Exon, V. Gaffney and M. van Leusen (eds). *Archaeology in the Age of the Internet - CAA 97 - Computer Applications and Quantitative Methods in Archaeology Proceedings of the 25th Anniversary Conference, University of Birmingham, April 1997*. Oxford: British Archaeological Reports International Series 750.

GILLINGS, M., (in press b) "Virtual archaeologies and the hyperreal (or, what does it mean to describe something as *virtually*-real?)" In P. Fisher and D. Unwin (eds). *VR and Geography*. New York: Taylor & Francis.

GILLINGS, M. and GOODRICK, G.T., 1996. "Sensuous and Reflexive GIS: exploring visualisation and VRML" *Internet Archaeology* 1, (http://intarch.ac.uk/).

GREGORY, D., 1994. *Geographical Imaginations*. London: Blackwells.

HARLEY, J.B., 1988. "Maps, knowledge, and power" In D. Cosgrove and S. Daniels (eds), *The iconography of Landscape: essays on the symbolic representation, design and use of past environments*, pp. 277-312. Cambridge: Cambridge University Press.

IHDE, D., 1993. *Postphenomenology*. Illinois: Northwestern University Press.

INGOLD, T., 1992. "Culture and the perception of the environment" In E. Croll. & D. Parkin (eds), *Bush Base: Forest Farm*, pp. 39-56. London: Routledge.

PICKLES, J., 1992. "Texts, Hermeneutics and Propaganda Maps" In T.J. Barnes and J.S. Duncan (eds), *Writing Worlds: Discourse, text and metaphor in the representation of landscape*, pp. 193-230. London: Routledge.

PICKLES, J., 1995. "Representations in an Electronic Age: Geography, GIS, and Democracy" In J. Pickles (ed.). *Ground Truth: the social implications of Geographic Information Systems*, pp. 1-30. New York: The Guilford Press.

POLLARD, J., and GILLINGS, M., 1998. "Romancing the Stones: towards an elemental and virtual Avebury" *Archaeological Dialogues* vol. 5 (2), pp. 143-164.

PRINGLE, M.J., and MOULDING, M.R., 1997. "Applications for Virtual Reality, and associated Information technology, in the illustration of archaeological material" *Graphic Archaeology: the Journal of the AAIS*.

RENFREW, C., 1973. "Monuments, mobilisation and social organisation in Neolithic Wessex" In C. Renfrew (ed.), *The Explanation of Culture Change*, pp. 539-58. London: Duckworth.

SHANKS, M., 1996. "Photography and Archaeology" In Molyneaux, B. L. (ed.). *The Cultural Life of Images*, pp. 73-107. London: Routledge.

SMITH, I.F., 1965. *Windmill Hill and Avebury: Excavations by Alexander Keiller, 1925-1939*. Oxford: Clarendon Press.

SNYDER, J., 1989. "Benjamin on reproducibility and aura: a reading of 'The Work of Art in the Age of its Technical Reproducibility' " In G. Smith (ed.). *Benjamin: Philosophy, Aesthetics, History*, pp. 158-174. Chicago: University of Chicago Press.

THOMAS, J., 1993. "The Politics of Vision and the Archaeologies of Landscape" In B. Bender (ed.), *Landscape; Politics and Perspectives*, pp. 19-48. Oxford: Berg.

WHITTLE, A., 1993. "The Neolithic of the Avebury area: sequence, environment, settlement and monuments" *Oxford Journal of Archaeology* vol. 12 (1), pp. 29-53.

WHITTLE, A., 1997. *Sacred Mound, Holy Rings - Silbury Hill and the West Kennet palisade enclosures: a Later Neolithic complex in north Wiltshire*. Oxford: Oxbow

ACQUISITION OF DETAILED MODELS FOR VIRTUAL REALITY

M. Pollefeys*, M. Proesmans, R. Koch, M. Vergauwen and L. Van Gool

ESAT-PSI, K.U.Leuven, Belgium
Marc.Pollefeys@esat.kuleuven.ac.be

More and more archaeological sites are being reconstructed in virtual reality. The problem remains the huge effort that has to be made to obtain realistic models. Besides taking on-site measurements, much time is often spent in manually rebuilding the whole site with a CAD package or a 3D-modelling tool. This limits the tractable complexity. In this paper two flexible automatic 3D surface acquisition systems are used to "virtualise" archaeological sites. The Roman site of Sagalassos (Southwest Turkey) is used as a test case to illustrate the potential of these new approaches. Besides the construction of a virtual site consisting of different levels of detail, some other applications to archaeology and conservation of heritage sites are presented.

Introduction

Virtual reality is a technology that offers promising perspectives for archaeologists. It can help in many ways: new insights can be gained by immersion in ancient worlds, inaccessible sites can be made available to a global public, courses can be given "on-site" and different periods or building phases can coexist.

One of the main problems is, however, the generation of these virtual worlds. They require a huge number of on-site measurements. In addition, the whole site has to be reproduced manually with a CAD- or 3D modelling system. This requires a lot of time. In addition, it is difficult to model complex shapes and to take all the details into account. Obtaining realistic surface texture is also a critical issue. As a result walls are often approximated by planar surfaces, stones often all get the same texture, statues are only crudely modelled, small details are left out, etc.

An alternative approach consists of using images of the site. Some software tools exist, but require a lot of human interaction (PhotoModeler) or preliminary models (Debevec, 1996). In this contribution some tools are presented which allow generating dense surface models of statues, monuments, buildings or archaeological sites using only consumer products such as photographic or video cameras. With these techniques the complexity of the acquisition is moved from hardware to software. This involves many advantages. A camera can work in demanding circumstances. It is cheap, easy to transport and can be handled by a non-specialist. The on-site acquisition time of the presented technique is short (i.e. it only involves taking relatively few images). These models that are immediately extracted from images contain much more detail than models which are built from a restricted number of measured points. In addition the images themselves are also used to generate the texture. These are important advantages for generating realistic VR walk-throughs. These detailed models open the way to new applications of VR in archaeology. Once it is easy to obtain detailed 3D models of almost any part of a building, it becomes possible to build "Virtual Reconstructions". It is much easier to test building hypotheses on a graphics workstation than on the site itself. Broken pillars can be reassembled using VR tools or even using automatic registration software to find corresponding parts.

Another promising application is the full 3D recording of the excavations for every stratigraphic layer. Therefore the archaeologists would not only dispose of a 3D model of the excavation, but of its evolution over time. An associated VR tool would not only allow travelling in space, but also in time.

All the examples in this contribution were taken at the archaeological site of Sagalassos in Southwest Turkey. The images were obtained with a consumer photo camera (digitised on photo-CD) and with a consumer digital video camera.

High-quality Surface Reconstruction with Single-shot Range Sensor

The technique presented in this section is an active technique (Proesmans et al., 1996; Proesmans and Van Gool, 1998). It is very flexible and only requires a minor calibration step. A pattern is projected with a standard slide projector onto an object. A single image of the illuminated object is then sufficient to obtain a very accurate textured 3D reconstruction of that object. This technique was used to generate models of statues and masks found at Sagalassos. These can be found on the companion CD-ROM.

The advantage of this technique is the fast delivery of accurate 3D models of objects at a fraction of the price of a laser range scanner. This is due to the use of off-the-shelf components – slide projector and camera— complemented with software.

Overview of the method

Starting from an image that contains the projected grid the first step consists of extracting horizontal and vertical lines. From this an initial grid is constructed. In general this grid still contains some inconsistencies. These are detected and corrected. Then the grid is refined to obtain subpixel accuracy. From the deformation of this final grid the shape is computed. At the same time the lines are filtered away to obtain the texture. In Figure 1 an overview of the different steps of the method is given.

* Postdoctoral fellow of the Fund for Scientific Research Flanders (Belgium) (F.W.O. Vlaanderen)

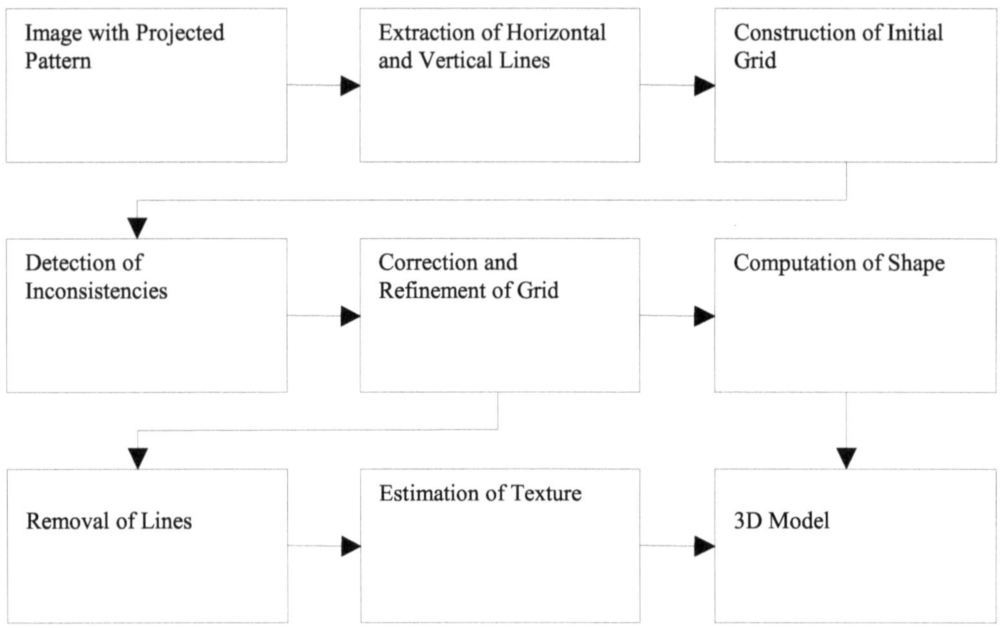

Figure 1 Overview of the single-shot range sensor method

System Calibration

Given the restriction of pseudo-orthographic projection, one can verify (Proesmans et al. 1996) that the shape can be recovered up to a scale, if the angle between the directions of projection and viewing is known. In order to find this angle, the system is initialized or "calibrated". For calibration it suffices to show two planar patches and to give their subtended angle. In practice, showing a box or corner of a room and specifying the angle is all it takes to perform this calibration. The system will extract the grid as explained below, look for the two largest planar regions within that grid and using the knowledge about their orientation (typically 90 degrees) give the angle between directions of viewing and projection.

Extraction of the grid

Once the system is calibrated, the object to be modeled in 3D can be shown. The system first extracts the grid lines in the image, through a set of horizontally and vertically aligned line detectors. The different edge segments are then linked to two sets of crossing contours. The crossings are used to generate a complete grid representation of the pattern. Each grid point or "node" has at most 4 neighbors which are labeled *N*, *E*, *S* and *W*. Note that nodes that are vertices of quadrangles are of special interest, since they indicate how the square pattern is deformed under projection. In order to determine the lines with sub-pixel precision, a snake-like process is introduced. The problem is stated as the minimization of the energy functional that relates both the intensity along the grid connections as well as its smoothness. This makes sure that the grid will move towards the darker parts of the image and let it more closely follow the pattern lines.

Correction of the extracted grid

Ideally, we would now have a complete set of all the line intersections or nodes, together with their connections. Of course, the extracted grid will not be perfect yet. Nodes or their connections may have gone undetected, and similarly spurious nodes and connections may have been found. Furthermore, in order to arrive at a 3D reconstruction the connectivity of the lines has to be known. The important difference with classical techniques lies in the fact that no absolute correspondences between the lines in the grid and the lines in the image are (nor can be) derived. Finding the correct connectivity between lines is the crux of the matter (see Proesmans et al. 1996). To that end, iterative procedures mend the initially extracted grid. Two principles underlie this mending. First, the grid should look square when viewed from the direction of the projector. Secondly, the mending should lead to a consistent numbering for the two sets of grid: whatever path is taken between two nodes, the grid based city block distance should be the same. Based on these principles, connections are broken and created. These procedures allow the system to work its way around local discontinuities in the grid, e.g. discontinuities due to sudden changes in depth. A limitation of the system as described is that the grid patches should be connected somewhere in the image to be reconstructed as a single surface.

Extraction of 3D shape

As soon as the grid has been extracted and the connectivity has been established, the extraction of the 3D shape is quite straightforward. The grid in the image plane can be modeled as the cross-section of two sets of planes with the object's surface. To each node a depth value can be assigned (see Proesmans et al. 1996). Note that the reconstruction is up to a scale factor. The knowledge of a single distance between two points fixes the scale.

As mentioned, the ability to deal with discontinuities is restricted to connected sets of data. If two or more separated objects are present in the scene, they will be reconstructed independently in the sense that their relative positions are not extracted. For many applications in visualisation, this is not necessarily a problem, because objects are either shown separately or the scene is synthesized starting from individual object models.

Discontinuities by self-occlusion need not be a problem, however. The system recovers from self-occlusions. Of course, there are gaps in the reconstructions for those parts not visible to the camera.

It is noteworthy that the system yields a genuine surface description, not a mere cloud of points. The connections found between the nodes are used in the description, which consists of small bilinear patches (the little squares of the pattern). Thus, problems with retrieving the correct topology are largely eliminated.

Extraction of surface texture

With the given setup, shape and texture extraction could in principle be very simple by just alternating between images with and without the grid. The former would yield shape and the latter texture. Alignment would be perfect as the same, fixed camera takes both images. However, the need for switching the pattern on and off would complicate system operation. For one thing, it would require additional provisions to block the pattern. Moreover, if the alternations should follow each other quickly and automatically, this would require the synchronisation of this blocking with the image acquisition by the camera. All this much to the detriment of the simplicity gained by using nothing but a simple camera and slide projector.

Therefore, a method was developed (and patented as the rest of the system) that extracts surface texture with the pattern on. It does away with the need to alternate between shape and texture frames altogether. The underlying principle literally is to read between the lines. This might seem a weird approach at first, but actually the human visual system solves a similar problem. The blood vessels on our retina are positioned in front of the photoreceptors. As with the blind spot, we are hardly aware of these obstacles because they are filtered out.

Figure 2 shows an example of an image of an object with the grid pattern projected onto it. Figure 3 shows a view of the reconstructed 3D model.

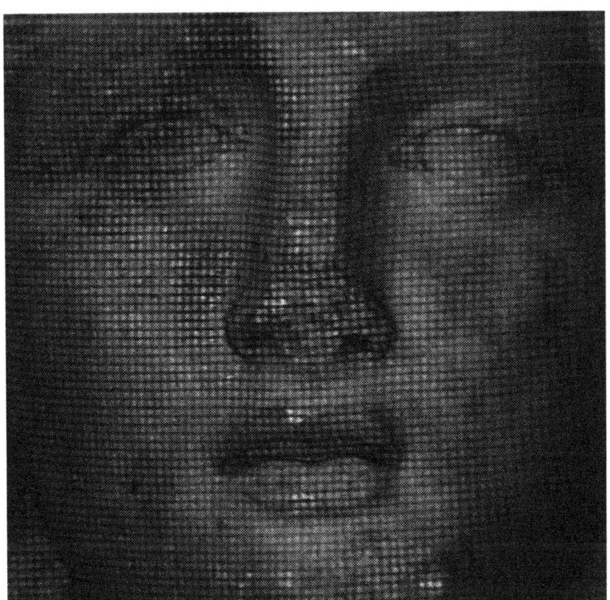

Figure 2 Grid projection on 3D object

Figure 3 Reconstructed 3D model of Dionysos

3D Reconstruction from Uncalibrated Image Sequences

The second technique (Pollefeys et al. 1998; Koch et al. 1998) starts from an uncalibrated image sequence of a scene. Using nothing other than the images, a textured 3D reconstruction of the recorded scene is obtained in an automated way. The sequence can be taken with a simple hand-held video or photo camera. The camera need not be calibrated and zoom and focus can be used freely. The motion is unconstrained and we do not make use of any reference points. In addition the method is just as easy to use for small objects as for complete sites. Our method therefore offers a lot of flexibility and is easy to use. We have, for example, obtained not olny a global reconstruction of the whole site of Sagalassos (Turkey), but also of separate monuments. Some examples can also be found on the companion CD-ROM.

This technique could therefore be an alternative for a wide variety of measurement techniques used nowadays by archeologists, which range from drawings and measurements done manually, over traditional photogrammetry to the computation of a DTM (digital terrain map) from aerial photographs.

Overview of 3D-model acquisition from multiple views

Starting from the images, the knowledge about the scene and the cameras is gradually increased. At first a partial camera calibration is obtained together with a sparse reconstruction of the scene. This is all done using robust algorithms to insure that the algorithms can work on real images. The next step consists of upgrading the calibration of the cameras, imposing some constraints that are in general valid for standard cameras. The next step consists of determining the complete surface (i.e. not only a few feature points). This is done through dense correspondence algorithms. Finally a 3D-model is built that contains the geometric (i.e. the shape) and photometric (i.e. the color and the texture) information of the scene. These models can then be used for visualization or measurement purposes.

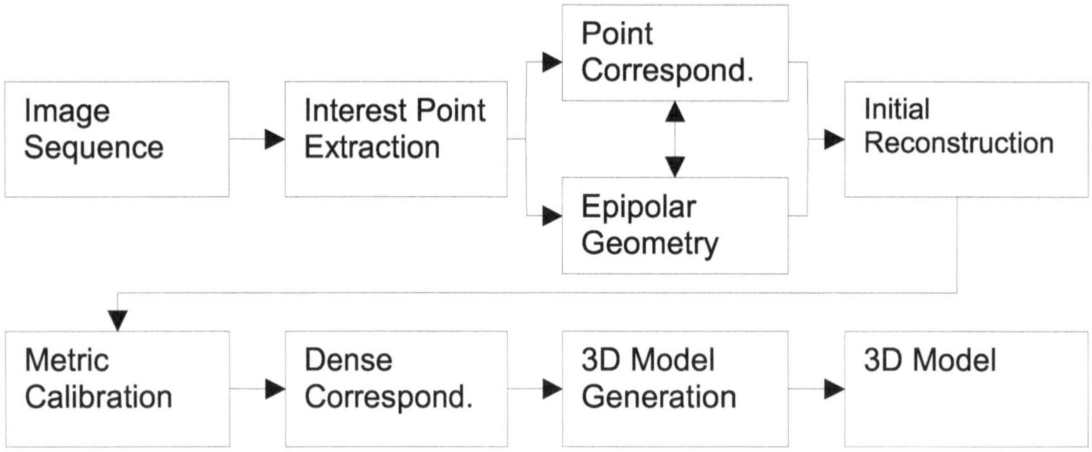

Figure 4 Overview of 3D-model acquisition from multiple views

The acquisition of the image sequence
The first step is to take the images from which the 3D model of the scene will be generated. It is important to take some restrictions of our method into consideration at this point. Since the images are to be matched automatically, consecutive images of the sequence should not be too different. Consecutive viewpoints should be targeted at more or less the same point and should not be separated by more than 5 to 10 degrees. Illumination conditions are also important. If shadows are present at the time of the image acquisition, these will be found in the final model. Additionally the reconstruction of parts that are in the shadow will be more complicated due to the restricted range of the intensity values in these parts of the images. Therefore the ideal circumstance for image acquisition is an overcast sky, although quite good results can also be obtained in other circumstances.

The images can be taken with different types of cameras. We have already used video cameras, digital still cameras and standard photo cameras. In this last case the images can either be scanned in or put on photo-CD. Typically images of 700x500 pixels were used. When a higher resolution was available it was used to get a better texture map for the final model. An example of an image sequence can be seen in Figure 5.

Figure 5 Image sequence of a part of the Roman baths in Sagalassos

Relating the images
A first step in the reconstruction procedure is to relate the different images to each other. Therefore it is necessary to put points from different images into correspondence (i.e. finding the points which originate from the same 3D point). When the images are not too different the neighborhood of these points will have the same appearance and they can therefore be matched through normalized intensity correlation.

To avoid a complication of the problem, only a restricted amount of so-called interest points will be considered at this stage. These are extracted through a special filter which selects corner-like features from the images (Harris, 1988). In fact these features are often not real corners, but this filter tends to extract the same points in consecutive images (i.e. points corresponding to the same 3D points).

An important concept to simplify the matching process between two images is the epipolar geometry. This expresses the fact that a point which is situated on a specific plane through the two camera centers is bound to be projected on the intersection lines between that plane and the respective image planes. These lines are therefore in so-called epipolar correspondence (i.e. the corresponding point of every point on an epipolar line in one image should be found back on the corresponding epipolar line in the other image). All these epipolar lines pass through the epipole. This point is the intersection of the image plane with the line through the two camera positions.

If this geometry is known, the matching complexity is reduced from a 2D (whole image) to a 1D search (epipolar line). In uncalibrated circumstances the only way to obtain this epipolar geometry is by computing it from a number of matches. We are therefore confronted with a chicken and egg problem. The approach that is followed first obtains a set of initial matches, then computes some candidate epipolar geometry from a minimal subset of matches. If this epipolar geometry receives enough support from the rest of the matches, it is accepted, else another subset is selected and the procedure is repeated. Once some satisfactory epipolar geometry has been obtained it can be used to generate more matches who in turn allow refining the epipolar geometry (see Torr (1995)).

A first reconstruction

Once the epipolar geometry and a set of corresponding points are known it is possible to generate a first reconstruction. This reconstruction is only determined up to a projective ambiguity. This means that besides not knowing the absolute position, orientation and scale of the scene some additional parameters are missing. In fact parallelism and orthogonality can not be verified at this stage and metric properties like relative distances and angles can not yet be measured.

This initial reconstruction is only based on the two first images of a sequence and is therefore far from complete. For additional images the epipolar geometry (with the previous image) is determined as described earlier. Then the relative position and orientation of the camera in the frame determined from the first two views is determined in a similar way through the already reconstructed points. At this point the reconstruction is refined, extended and corrected. A technical description of this approach can be found in Beardsley et al. (1996).

Obtaining metric information

The projective reconstruction obtained in the previous paragraph is clearly not satisfactory for our purposes since both visualisation and measurement applications require at least a metric reconstruction. Luckily algorithms have been developed which can upgrade projective reconstruction to metric reconstructions. The approach presented here is based on the work described in Pollefeys et al. (1998).

It is always possible to factorise the cameras in intrinsic (e.g. focal length) and extrinsic parameters (i.e. position and orientation of the camera). In the case of a projective reconstruction the obtained parameters do not have a physical interpretation. In the metric case however they correspond to actual physical entities that are subject to some constraints. Self-calibration therefore consists of finding the projective transformation that transforms the initial reconstruction into a reconstruction for which all these constraints are satisfied.

The most successful methods to achieve this are based on abstract geometric concepts. When a camera is moved through space, its relative position to the *plane at infinity* and the *absolute conic* does not change. This property allows identifying both entities in projective space. These entities encode the metric properties of space and are therefore equivalent to a metric calibration. Once the metric calibration is retrieved, the initial reconstruction can be transformed to a metric reconstruction. This reconstruction is now a true scale model of the initial scene that was recorded. The absolute scale can be determined through a single measurement in the scene.

Dense correspondences

At first, only the correspondences for specific feature points were extracted, but in fact the correspondences can be determined for almost all the points of the images. In this way a full surface model of the recorded scene can be reconstructed. This is not only important for visualisation, but also for measurements, since not all the interesting points are always retrieved as feature points in our sparse reconstruction.

The epipolar geometry greatly simplifies the matching problem. As described previously, corresponding points have to be found on each other's epipolar lines. The matching problem can therefore be solved line by line. To obtain efficient algorithms the images are first warped so that corresponding image rows are also corresponding epipolar lines. This procedure is called rectification. The matching proceeds row by row over both images. Not only the correlation score is taken into account, but a cost is also included for discontinuities in the surface. Some other constraints are also taken into account (e.g. uniqueness, ordering). An optimal solution can then be obtained through dynamic programming. The result is a disparity map, which is an image were the value associated with each pixel indicates the position of the corresponding pixel in the other. Since at this point the cameras are calibrated, this can immediately be translated to a depth map, which is an image that contains the distance from the camera center to each pixel in the scene. This is often called a 2.5D representation.

To obtain more accurate and more complete depth information, more than two images should be used. We have implemented an approach, which is described in detail in Koch et al. (1998). At first the depth maps are computed pair-wise for the whole sequence. Then, to compute accurate depths for a specific image, the disparities are used to create a correspondence chain that goes over multiple images. Taking into account the other correspondences of the chain using an extended Kalman filter refines the initial depth. The chain is interrupted once the back-projected ray falls outside the 95% probability bounds. An important advantage of this approach is that one can go both backward and forward in the sequence. This allows avoiding most of the occlusion problems one typically encounters with stereo. In addition the inaccuracy of small baseline and the difficulty of matching for wide baseline stereo are both solved through this technique. Additionally this multi-viewpoint stereo also allows improving the quality of the texture. One 3D point is observed in many images and the texture can therefore be robustly estimated. Highlights and other artifacts can easily be removed.

Building the model

The 3D-model surface is constructed of triangular surface patches with the vertices storing the surface geometry and the faces holding the projected image color in texture maps. The texture maps add very much to the visual appearance of the models and augment missing surface detail. The model building process is at present restricted to partial models computed from a single viewpoint and work remains to be done to fuse different viewpoints. Since all the views are registered into one metric framework, it is possible to fuse the depth estimate into one consistent model surface.

As an example, a few views of the reconstruction of a part of the Roman baths are shown in Figure 6.

Figure 6 **Reconstruction of a part of the Roman baths in Sagalassos**

Constructing VR Models of Archaeological Sites

In the previous sections it was explained how textured 3D surface models could be extracted from one or more images. In this section this will be applied to the construction of VR models of archaeological sites.

A first approach to obtaining a virtual reality model for a whole site consists of taking a few overview photographs from the distance. Since our technique is independent of scale this yields an overview model of the whole site. The only difference is the distance needed between two camera poses. An example of the results obtained for Sagalassos are shown on the companion CD-ROM. The model was created from nine images taken from a hillside near the excavation site. Note that it is straightforward to extract a digital terrain map or orthophotos from the global reconstruction of the site. The problem is that this kind of overview model is too coarse to be used for a realistic walk-through around the site or for looking at specific monuments. Therefore it is necessary to integrate more detailed models into this overview model by taking additional image sequences for all the interesting areas on the site. These are used to generate reconstructions of the site at different scales, going from a global reconstruction of the whole site to a detailed reconstruction for every monument. These reconstructions thus naturally fill in the different levels of detail that should be provided for optimal rendering. On the CD-ROM the reconstructions of the Roman baths are given for three different levels of detail (site overview, complete Roman bathhouse and detail of right corner).

An interesting possibility is the combination of these models with other type of models. In the case of Sagalassos some building hypotheses were translated to CAD models, and these were integrated with our models, as illustrated in Figure 7. Also other models obtained with different 3D acquisition techniques could easily be integrated.

The models delivered by the different techniques presented in this paper are thus well suited for generating VR models for virtual exhibitions. The models have a high visual quality since they are immediately generated from real images. Complex shapes like statues, masks or pottery can accurately be modeled. An important advantage of these virtual exhibitions is that it allows placing the object back in its natural environment. In this respect the method based on multiple views offers the advantage that the environment can also be "virtualised" without too much effort.

Figure 7 Combination of 3D model of Sagalassos with CAD models

Other Applications

Since these 3D models are almost completely automatic and the on-site acquisition time is very short, several new applications come to mind. In this section a few possible applications of the presented techniques are described.

3D Measurements

Once a 3D surface model of an object is obtained, the model can be used to obtain 3D measurements. Our models are up to scale and can therefore immediately be used to obtain relative length measurements. Carrying out a single length measurement in the real scene allows getting absolute lengths from the model. Measuring lengths on the 3D model is much simpler than in the real scene. It is sufficient to click on two points on the model surface and the computer immediately computes the distance between the two points. When the model coordinates are aligned with the world coordinates a simple click on the model surface results in the absolute coordinates of the indicated point. It is clear that these procedures result in an important gain of efficiency for generating plans of the archeological sites.

Testing building hypotheses through VR

The presented techniques do not only allow acquiring the 3D-model of the remains of a building, but also of the broken down parts which are retrieved on the site. It becomes possible to carry out a "virtual reconstruction", reassembling the different parts of a monument on the screen of a computer.

This offers a flexible method to test building hypotheses without the problems of manipulating the real building blocks. Additional tools could be developed to simplify reconstruction even more; for example broken parts of pillars could automatically be matched using standard registration software (see e.g. Chen and Medioni, 1991).

3D stratigraphy

Since much evidence is destroyed during excavation, it is very important for archaeologists to annotate all the findings. Traditionally a lot of pictures are taken, many plans and notes are made, and the stratigraphic structure of slices of the terrain is drawn. An alternative would be to do a 3D recording of a location after the removal of each stratigraphic layer. In this 3D reconstruction specific models of pieces of interest could be inserted at the exact location were they were discovered. The whole could then be assembled to a complete annotation model where a slider would allow to travel through time by adding or removing stratigraphic layers at will. Some of these concepts are also illustrated through examples on the CD-ROM.

Conclusion

The two techniques for 3D acquisition presented in this paper both heavily rely on state-of-the-art computer vision and image processing algorithms. Compared to traditional acquisition techniques the complexity of the acquisition has been moved from hardware to software. Additionally, geometric insights have been used to avoid complicated calibration procedures and provide a maximal flexibility in acquisition. These different factors make the presented techniques especially suited for use in archaeology where often non-technical people have to carry out 3D acquisition in difficult circumstances.

Additionally the presented techniques offer the possibility to develop new applications or to improve existing approaches. A few examples of these applications were given in this paper.

Acknowledgements

We would like to thank Prof. Dr. Marc Waelkens and his team for making it possible for us to do experiments on the archeological site of Sagalassos (Turkey). We would also like to thank Dr. Andrew Zisserman and his team in Oxford for providing us with robust projective reconstruction algorithms. The financial support of the Belgian IUAP project IMechS is gratefully acknowledged.

References Cited

BEARDSLEY, P., TORR, P. AND ZISSERMAN, A., 1996, "3D Model Acquisition from Extended Image Sequences", *Computer Vision - ECCV'96*, Buxton, B. and Cipolla, R. (eds.), Lecture Notes in Computer Science, Vol.1065, pp. 683-695. Springer-Verlag.

CHEN, Y. AND MEDIONI, G., 1992, "Object Modeling by Registration of Multiple Range Images", *Image and Vision Computing,* No.3, pp.145-155.

DEBEVEC, P., TAYLOR, C. AND MALIK, J., 1996, "Modeling and rendering architecture from photographs: A hybrid geometry- and image-based approach", *Proceedings of SIGGRAPH'96,* pp.11-20, ACM.

HARRIS, C. AND STEPHENS, M., 1988. "A combined corner and edge detector", *Proceedings Fourth Alvey Vision Conference,* pp.147-151.

KOCH, R., POLLEFEYS, M. AND VAN GOOL, L., 1998, "Multi Viewpoint Stereo from Uncalibrated Video Sequences", *Computer Vision - ECCV98*, Burkhardt, H. and Neumann, B. (eds.), Lecture Notes in Computer Science, Vol.1406, Springer-Verlag.

KOCH, R., POLLEFEYS, M. AND VAN GOOL, L., 1998, Automatic 3D Model Acquisition from Uncalibrated Image Sequences, proceedings CGI'98 (Computer Graphics International)

MARTENS, F., LEGRAND, P., LEGRAND, J., LOOTS, L. AND WAELKENS, M., "Computer aided design and archaeology at sagalassos: methodology and possibilities of 3D computer reconstructions of archaeological sites", *this book.*

PHOTOMODELER, by Eos Systems Inc., (for more information: http://www.photomodeler.com).

POLLEFEYS, M., KOCH, R., VERGAUWEN, M. AND VAN GOOL, L., 1998, "Metric 3D Surface Reconstruction from Uncalibrated Image Sequences", *3D Structure from Multiple Images of Large-Scale Environments*, Koch, R. and Van Gool, L. (eds.), Lecture Notes in Computer Science, Vol. 1506, Springer-Verlag.

POLLEFEYS, M., KOCH, R. AND VAN GOOL, L., 1999, "Self-Calibration and Metric Reconstruction in Spite of Varying and Unknown Internal Camera Parameters", *International Journal of Computer Vision,* 32(1), pp.7-25.

PROESMANS, M., VAN GOOL, L. AND OOSTERLINCK, A., 1996, "One-shot active range acquisition", *Proceedings International Conference on Pattern Recognition,* Vol. C, pp.336-340, IEEE Computer Society Press.

PROESMANS, M., AND VAN GOOL, L., 1998, "Reading between the lines—a method for extracting dynamic 3D with texture", *Proceedings International Conference on Computer Vision,* pp.1081-1086.

TORR, P., 1995, *Motion Segmentation and Outlier Detection,* Ph.D. Thesis, Dept. of Engineering Science, University of Oxford.

3D FACIAL RECONSTRUCTION AND VISUALIZATION OF ANCIENT EGYPTIAN MUMMIES USING SPIRAL CT DATA SOFT TISSUE RECONSTRUCTION AND TEXTURE APPLICATION

Giuseppe Attardi
Dipartimento di Informatica, Università di Pisa, Italy

Marilina Betrò
Dipartimento di Scienze Storiche del Mondo Antico - Egittologia, Università di Pisa, Italy
betro@sta.unipi.it

Maurizio Forte
CNR (National Research Council) ITABC (Institute of Technologies Applied to Cultural Heritage, Italy)
forte@mlib.cnr.it

Roberto Gori
CINECA-VISIT (Centro Interuniversitario di Supercalcolo - Laboratorio di Visualizzazione scientifica) Casalecchio sul Reno, Bologna, Italy

Silvano Imboden
Dipartimento di Informatica, Università di Pisa, Italy

Francesco Mallegni
Dipartimento di Scienze Archeologiche - Antropologia, Università di Pisa, Italy

Hail to you, you who are on the head of the Great One, you mistress of brow and neck, at whom Re' is joyful when he sees her on the road which is in the Sacred Land... who folds her arms on account of the Inert One... May you place for me my head upon my neck when you gather together life for the throat. May you make me into a spirit, may you enfold my members, ***may you knit on my face****. . . .*
(Coffin Texts, spell 229; ca. 2000 B.C.)

Introduction

The problem of rebuilding a face from human remains has been, until now, especially relevant in the field of forensic science, where the obvious orientation moves toward the identification of otherwise unrecognizable corpses; but its potential interest to archaeologists and anthropologists is not negligible. We present here the preliminary results of a joint research between the University of Pisa, the University Supercomputing Center of CINECA (Bologna), and the CNR-ITABC (Institute of Technology Applied to Cultural Heritage, National Research Council, Rome) whose aim is reconstructing, through Spiral Computed Tomography data and virtual modeling techniques (in our case with VTK software), 3D models of the possible physiognomy of ancient Egyptian mummies. This work is carried out through a multidisciplinary approach, involving different competences: image processing, anthropology, Egyptology and computing archaeology.

State of the Art Technology

Since 1898 (Petrie 1898), radiology techniques were increasingly used and appreciated throughout the 20th century, as a non-invasive means of investigation. As a result, Egyptological, anthropological and paleo-pathological information could be obtained without disturbing the mummy's wrappings. The coming of Computed Tomography in the 1970s marked a further milestone in the history of mummy investigation. CT numbers allowed a very fine discrimination between materials with different densities, providing an enormous amount of information not only about the mummy and its skeleton, but also about the artefacts buried with the mummy in its coffin (Notman 1986). Compared to traditional, x-ray techniques, multiple axial images displayed in a clearer way different details of cartonnage, wrappings, amulets and internal organs of a mummy, allowing easy measurements of exact distances between objects inside or outside the mummy (Foster et al. 1997). Since the mid 1980s, new developments in computer technology enabled the three-dimensional displaying of axial CT images. The use of this new technique has widened the range and quality of possible investigations on Egyptian mummies (David 1986, D'Auria 1988, Drenkhahn et al. 1991, Baldock et al. 1994).

The Research Project

Previous works were not specifically interested in the problem of physiognomic reconstruction. However, when the interest then existed and plastic models of the mummy's head were produced, the final molding of soft tissues was essentially a "human matter", the joint result of the anthropologist's expertise and the artist's sensibility, thanks to the use of manual stereo-lithography (Pommert 1991; Wisseman 1994). A similar method was already experimented for the reconstruction of a model of the head of the prince Wadje (about 2000 B.C.) (Mallegni 1996).

In our case study, focusing on the problem of facial reconstruction, we chose a mummified head in good condition, from the Egyptian Section of the Archaeological Museum in Florence (inv. N. 8643). The date of its acquisition is 1893, and we lack any other reliable information about its origin. Carbon-14 calibrated dating of a sample of the hair gave a probability distribution between 339 and 201 BC. The exceptional condition of the head, reflecting the quality of an ancient embalming process, makes us prefer the more ancient date.

Figure 1 The mummified head in Florence (inv. N .8643) (Soprintendenza Archeologica della Toscana)

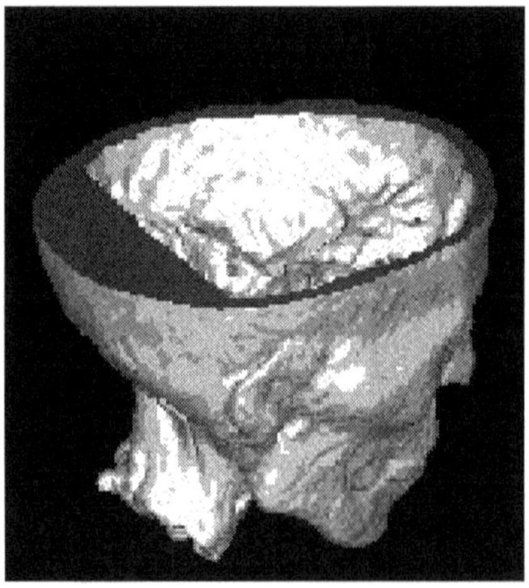

Figure 2 CT scanning of the head demonstrated the post-mortem transnasal ethmoid fracture created by the embalmers to extract the brain tissue; the cranial cavity was filled with hot melted resin, later solidified, introduced with the mummy resting on its back, as the model reconstructed from the CT images clearly displays.

Project Planning

The project involved these main steps:

1. Anthropological and Egyptological analysis of the head;
2. Spiral CT of the head;
3. Reconstruction of a 3D model of the skull generated from CT data processing;
4. Reconstruction of soft tissues;
5. Application of textures fitting the somatic features.

Different stages are not strictly sequential. As we shall see, the spiral CT scannings and their subsequent 3D reconstructions provide new interesting data to the anthropological and Egyptological analyses.

First two phases of research: Preliminary anthropological results

1. The anthropological study of the mummified cranial remains allowed us to identify a male subject who died at the age of about 40 years. The general appearance of the subject, especially regarding the face, the shape, and the structure of his hair, lead us to exclude Negroid influences, however finding resemblance to present and past Berber ethnic characteristics. The exceptional conservation of the head indicates an individual high in the social hierarchy, able to grant himself an effective (and expensive) embalming process.

2. With the collaboration of the Radiology Department of the Careggi Hospital (Florence), the mummy was scanned on 18 April 1997, using a Siemens Somatom Plus 4 Spiral Computer Tomographer scanner. Sections taken throughout the skull were at 0.5 mm of thickness. CT scanning of the head demonstrated the post-mortem *transnasal ethmoid* fracture created by the embalmers to extract the brain tissue; the cranial cavity was filled with hot melted resin, later solidified, introduced into the mummy resting on its back, as clearly exposed by the model reconstructed from the CT images. Embalming *ex-cerebration* through the *ethmoid* was very common in the Late Period, practised until the Ptolemaic age. During this period, there also existed the practice of filling the cranial cavity with resin (Strouhal 1986, 1992; Macke 1993).

The spiral CT images were later electronically transferred to the Onyx2 workstation (Silicon Graphics) at CINECA for post-processing.

3. Reconstruction of a 3D model of the skull

In the methodology used for 3D reconstructions generated by spiral CT data sets, CT slices must be stacked up and interpolated in order to build a volume. After creating a volume, it is possible, by means of suitable algorithms, to generate surfaces whose points have the same function value (*isosurfaces*) (Lorensen et al. 1987). The same elements were used in the 3D reconstruction of our mummy's skull. The principle underlying the application of this algorithm to the kind of problem here described is that similar materials have the same radio-opacity and are, consequently, represented in a CT scan by the same, *densitometric level*. It is therefore possible to process the CT scan sequence so as to obtain a 3D grid where each "knot" (control point) is associated with the densitometric value measured by the CT scans. The result is a 3D 256-grey-levels image.

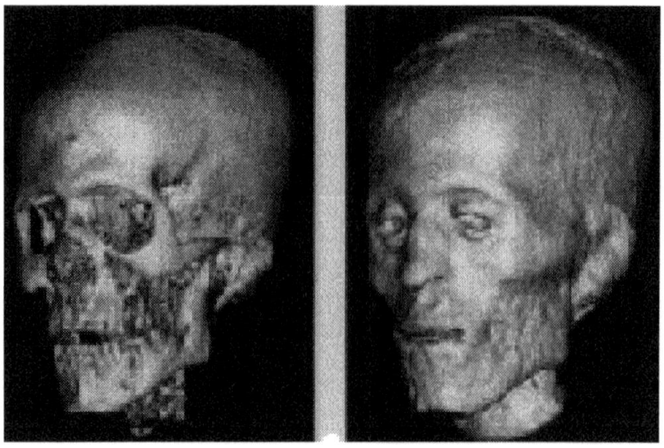

Figure 3 a) hard tissues b) external surface

This phase of the work was particularly interesting from the anthropological perspective. The use of this technique allowed us to visually exclude the mummified soft tissues and directly observe the cranial bones with an extremely high image resolution. This method offered also the chance of a morphological and morphometric check of the anthropologist's observations on the specimen (covered by the soft tissue later dissected): these two methods of investigation led to the same diagnosis of Berber group typology.

The image of the skull gave us the chance to observe, directly on the cranial vault, a bone pathology (a visible wound) and a biological answer to the pathogenic factor, showing that wound cicatrised and the subject lived long after receiving the wound. X-ray examination of the mummified skull showed in more detail the reactions of the man's organism to this kind of pathology, so that we were able to perform a global analysis of the sample.

4. Reconstruction of soft tissues

This stage of our work is still in a preliminary phase. Among the possible methodologies to deal with this complex problem, we focused on two different promising methods:
A. Implementation of the anthropologists' protocols developed to reconstruct soft tissues on the skull;
B. The use of warping techniques.

A. An anthropological method borrowed from Forensic Sciences was used to reconstruct soft tissues on the skull. As is well known, the thickness of the soft tissues is reconstructed on the bones through the use of pegs at marked points. All the pegs are joined by Plasticine strips of fixed thickness. The empty spaces between these pegs are then slowly filled becoming moldable material. Warping techniques allow enhancement of the mummy model with information coming from another complete CT scanned head of the same ethnic group with the correct characteristics. The indications that aid the reconstruction are based on anthropology and forensic studies of people varying in ages and populations (Ubelhaker 1989, Rhine et al. 1984). Though this method has a certain degree of subjectivity, nevertheless it is sufficiently reliable. A software implementation of the above mentioned protocols could assist the operator in locating the markers on the 3D model of the skull by a graphic interface, so as to choose the correct set of anthropological parameters. Subsequently, interpolation methodologies could carry out automatically the growing of the soft tissues.
B. A different method consists in the distortion (warping) of the 3D model of a reference scanned head, until its hard tissues match those of the mummy. The subsequent stage is the construction of the hybrid model composed by the hard tissues of the mummy plus the soft ones of the reference head (Beier et al. 1992, Bergeron 1994, Kaufmann et al. 1993, Litwinowicz 1994, Van den Elsen et al. 1993, Wolberg 1990, Michael et al. 1996). We believe that very good results could come through a semiautomated interactive procedure, integrating the two methodologies here described.

5. The application of textures

While hard and soft tissues give morphological information, textures provide colors and aesthetical features. They are "pasted" over the 3D models by means of mapping procedures.

Development of the Project: Soft-Tissue Reconstruction Using VTK

Having generated a 3D digital model from CT scans of the mummified cranial remains, our task is to reconstruct the lacking elements. As we have described above, we work with a hybrid approach. Our aim is to obtain a perfect match among hard tissues so that the soft tissues of the reference model can be used to represent those of the mummy with a good approximation. Moreover we are developing a tool in order to apply to the model cylindrical textures obtained by multiple views of a well-suited individual or from other sources such as ancient Egyptian sculptures. Software implementation has been designed using VTK (The Visualization ToolKit), a public domain library for scientific visualization, in order to guarantee performance and portability (Schroeder et al.).

For the subsequent steps to work correctly, CT scan data representing our model and the mummy should have the same placing, orientation, dimensions and resolution. This is generally not true, especially when dealing with data coming from different machines, so the first step is to perform a manual registration, that is a rigid transformation among volumes in order to work in the same system of coordinates. As further requirement, greyscales of hard tissues must be similar, in spite of different methodologies of acquisition, though the mummy's tissues may be deteriorated. We prefer to transform the reference model to preserve the original data of the mummy. For volume resampling, smoothing (to remove aliasing phenomena) and surface generation, VTK internal facilities are used. We usually take into account isotropic volumes with squared voxels of 1 mm as a trade-off between performance and image quality.

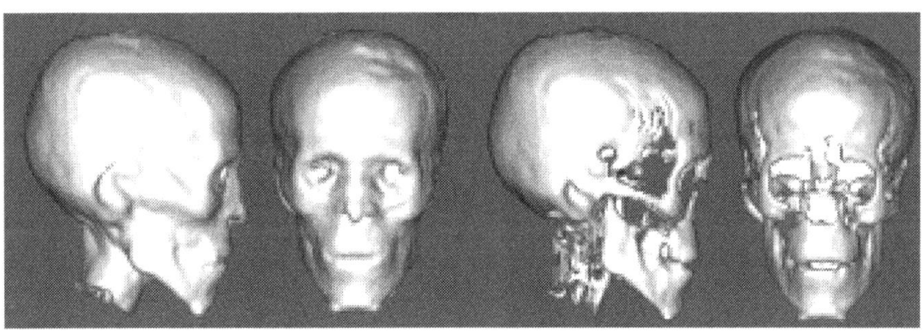

Figure 4. Digital model of the mummy: surfaces corresponding to soft (left) and hard tissues (right)

At this point we proceed with the setup of landmarks ("Manchester pegs": Prag et al. 1995) onto the surface of the hard tissues of the mummy, while for the reference model it can be predetermined. The aim here is to fix some constraints for the resulting physiognomy and to provide a first guess for the following step, which is *features tracking*. Pegs are mapped onto a spherical surface of parametric ratio, so that the user can place quickly the whole set and adjust single pegs. Calculating vector displacement among couples of corresponding points, we obtain a scattered field to drive a first warp phase. In the next stage, we proceed to a warp driven by a features tracking. Features tracking consists in determining a correspondence between sets of characteristic points pertaining to the volumes in order to obtain a scattered motion field with more details. Initially this set of points is chosen as a subset of points that are vertices of hard tissue surfaces of the mummy; some of these points, with particular characteristics, are identified as features. If, after a test, a feature is retained as reliable, we search the corresponding position in the reference volume . If the result is good, the resulting motion field is defined among subsets of bone surfaces, from the reference model to the mummy volume.

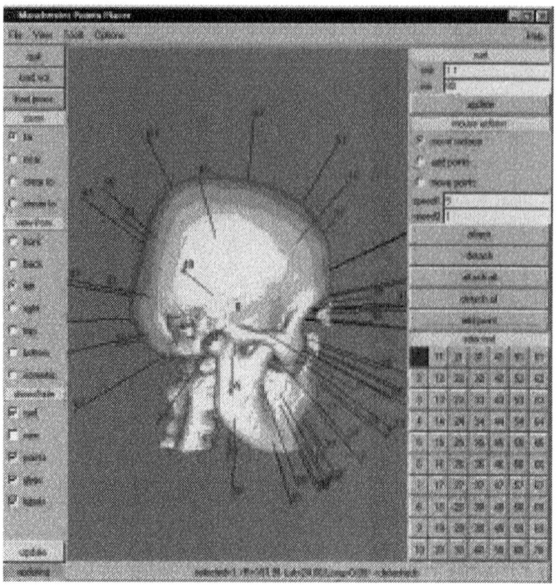

Figure 5. Bringing the points over the model

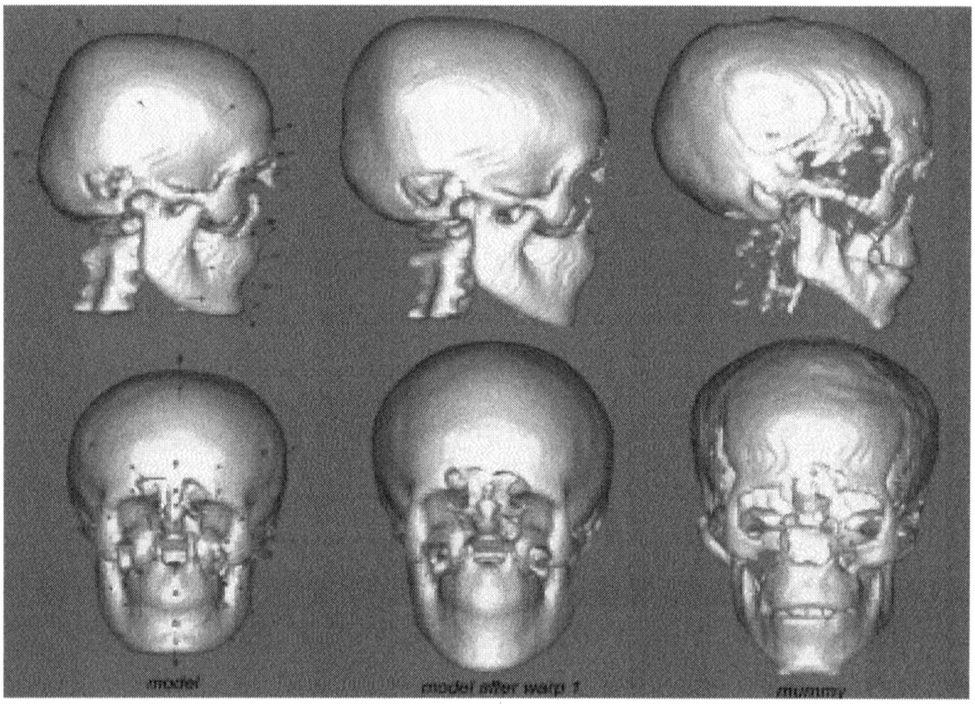

Figure 6. Warp driven by Manchester points

Once generated, a scattered motion field must be diffused within the whole reference volume. This is performed using the Shepard method (Wixom et al. 1978) available in VTK. The diffused motion field can be used to warp (again using VTK facilities) every structure pertaining to the reference model correspondingly with the mummy model; therefore we reconstruct mummy soft tissues warping those of reference model. The theory of this algorithm (we will go through a brief explanation) is taken from a rework of the Lukas-Kanade algorithm (Lucas et al. 1981). We have adapted this algorithm to our requirements and built a VTK filter. We consider the relation between hard tissue surfaces of the reference model and hard tissue surfaces of the mummy as a continuous deformation in time. As the final stage of soft tissue reconstruction we present warp driven soft tissues.

Figure 7 Points on isosurface of bone are used as feature points. Grey levels represent the reliability values

For each landmark we find its corresponding point on the skin surface; in this way we can measure the actual soft tissue thickness. By consulting the thickness table we find the corresponding desired thickness measure. Saying that the actual thickness must become the desired thickness, we generate another scattered field that will drive this third warp. This last step is performed just on the skin surface.

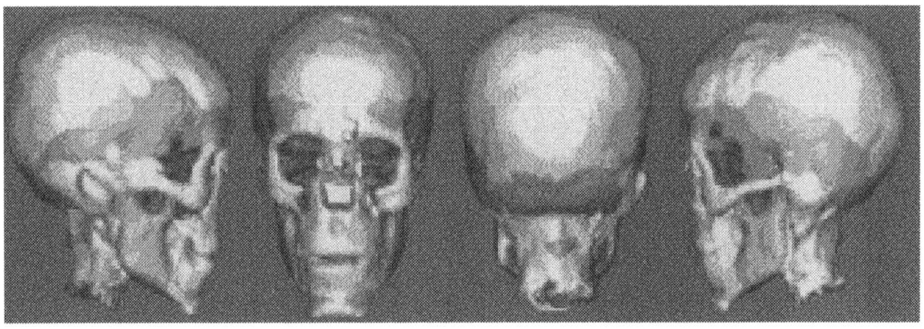

Figure 8 Model skin (grey) and mummy skull (white)

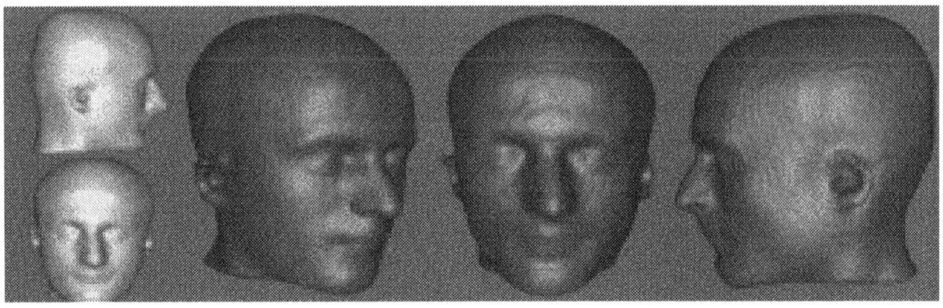

Figure 9 Face generated

For texture application, starting from at least three views we generate a cylindrical texture (Morten 1996). Each point P on the cylindrical texture will be projected on the cylindrical axes, intersecting a point q on the surface; watching the angle between the normal in q and the normal of the view, we can determine which of the views q can see. The color for the point P is given by a weighted sum of the colors taken from the visible views, and the weights depend again on the angle among the normals. Before the extraction from the views, colors have to be modified to match the corresponding projection of the whole mode. We can realize this morph implicitly after fixing a way to map projections in the desired points of the view. This mapping could be achieved by projecting the landmarks ("Manchester points") over the views and letting a user move them in the right place.

Figure 10. Texturized model of recontructed soft tissues of the mummy

Conclusions: The Virtual Model

Finally: who is he ? How we can identify a person ? The facial identification depends on many factors: mainly physical characteristics such as cranial and soft tissue volumes, face features. Also to be considered are practices in fashion and culture. On the other hand, in archaeology we can suggest different models of anthropological identification, also considering physical and cultural anthropology.

In our project, for obtaining better performances through the virtual 3D visualization of the reconstruction we have used the powerful workstation Onyx2 (Silicon Graphics at VISIT, CINECA). In fact the main problem, processing a large amount of data, was to process the volume of data and visualize it in real time and in 3D. The interactive way to explore and show the whole model gives the possibility of understanding deep features of the data: in our case, our interdisciplinary team was able to discuss in real time problems and characteristics of the data, comparing in detail hypotheses and interpretations about the Egyptian head, anthropometric data and computer/image information. We can describe the processing as a cognitive model of the find.

Finally, next developments of the project could concern:

- Integration of CT scan data and reconstruction with Egyptian iconography (i.e. ancient sculptures of the same period).
- New graphic and software interface for reconstructing step-by-step volume rendering, soft tissues and the final aspect of the face.
- Images databases and graphic library on line on the Internet for organizing a world-wide collection of this type of data.
- Project integration with other sciences with the same aims, such as forensic sciences, virtual surgery, biology, criminology.

References Cited

BALDOCK C., HUGHES S.W., WHITTAKER D.K. et al., 3-D reconstruction of an ancient Egyptian mummy using x-ray computer tomography, *Journal of the Royal Society of Medicine* 87 (12), 1994 Dec., 806-808

BEIER, T. and NEELY, S., Feature-based image metamorphosis, Computer Graphics, vol. 26(2), 35-42, New York, NY, July 1992. *Proceedings of SIGGRAPH '92*

BERGERON, P., Morphing as a means of generating variation in visual medical teaching materials. *Computer in Biology and Medicine*, 24 (1).11-18, Jan. 1994

DAVID A.R. (ed.), *Proceedings of the "Science in Egyptology Symposia", Part I: Selected papers, 1979. Part II: papers presented 1984,* Manchester 1986

DRENKHAHN R. and GERMER R. (eds.), *Mumie und Computer. Ein multidisziplinäres Forschungsprojektin Hannover*, Sonderausstellung des Kestner-Museums Hannover, 1991

FOSTER, G, CONNOLL, J.E., WANG, J.Z., TEETER, E., MENGONI, P.M., Evaluation of an ancient Egyptian Mummy using spiral CT and 3-D Reconstructions: interactive display using the World Wibe Web, *Radiology* 205(P), 734-35, 1997

HILL B., MACLEOD I., WATSON L., Facial reconstruction of a 3500 year old Egyptian mummy using axial computed tomography, *Journal of Audiovisual Media in Medicine* 16 (1), 1993, 11-13

KAUFMAN, A., COHEN, D., YAGEL, R., Volume graphics, *Computer*, 26(7):51-64, July 1993

LEWIN P.K., TROGADIS J.E., STEVENS J.K., Three-dimensional reconstruction from serial X-ray tomography of an Egyptian mummified head, *Clin. Anat.*, 3, 1990, 215-218

LITWINOWICZ, P., Efficient techniques for interactive texture placement, Computer Graphics Proceedings, Annual Conference Series, 119-22, New York, NY, July 1994. *Conference Proceedings of SIGGRAPH '94*

LUCAS, B. and KANADE, T., Performance of optical flow techniques, proc. DARPA IU Workshop 1981

MACKE A., Les orifices d'viscérations endocraniennes aux Basses Epoques, *Annales du Service des Antiquités Egyptiennes* 72 (1993), 135-147.

MAGID D., BRYAN B.M., DREBIN R.A., NEY D., FISHMAN E.K., Three-dimensional imaging of an Egyptian mummy, *Clinical Imaging* 13 (3), 1989, 239-240

MALLEGNI, F., Un volto di gioventù per il principe Uage, in: M. Forte (ed.), *Archeologia. Percorsi virtuali nelle civiltà scomparse*, Milano 1996, 50.

MARX M., D'AURIA S.H., Three-dimensional CT reconstructions of an ancient human Egyptian mummy, *Amer. J. Roent.* 150, 1988, 147-149

MICHAEL, S.D., and CHEN, M., The 3D Reconstruction of Facial Features Using Volume Distortion, *Preceedings of Eurographics (UK Chapter)* (eds. H. Jones, R. Raby and D. Vicars), 5 1 (vol. 2) (1996), 297-305

MORTEN Bro-Nielsen, *Medical image registration and surgery simulation*, Ph.D. Thesis at the Technical University of Denmark, 1996

NOTMAN, D., Ancient Scannings: Computed Tomography of Egyptian Mummies, in: *Science in Egyptology. Proceedings of the 'Science in Egyptology Symposia* (ed. R.A. David)", Manchester, 251-320, 1986

PETRIE W.M.F., DESHASHEH, 1897. Fifteenth Memoir of the Egypt Exploration Fund. London 1898

PICKERING R.B., CONCES D.J Jr., BRAUNSTEIN E.M., YURCO F., Three-dimensional computed tomography of the mummy Wenuhotep, *American Journal of Physical Anthropology* 83 (1), 1990, 49-55

POMMERT, A., KLIEGIS, U., in: DRENKHAHN R., GERMER R. (eds.), *Mumie und Computer. Ein multidisziplinäres Forschungsprojektin Hannover*, Sonderausstellung des Kestner-Museums Hannover, 1991

PRAG, J. and NEAVE, R., 1997, *Making Faces: using forensic and archaeological evidence,* London, British Museum Press

RHINE, J.S.and MOORE, C.E., *Forensic Anthropology*, Maxwell Museum Technical Series I, 1984

SCHROEDER, W., MARTIN, K., LORENSEN, B., *The Visualization Toolkit*, 2nd edition Prentice Hall PTR http://www.kitware.com

STROUHAL E., Embalming Excerebration in the Middle Kingdom, in: R. David (ed.), *Science in Egyptology*, Manchester 1986, 141-154

STROUHAL E., Secular Changes of Embalming Methods in Ancient Egypt, in: *Actas del I Congreso Internacional des estudios sobre momias*, Tenerife 1992, 862-63

UBELHAKER, D.H., Human Skeleton Remains, Washington 1989, tabella 122-123.

VAN den ELSEN, P.A., POL, E.-J.D., VIERGEVER, M.A., Medical image matching --- a review with classification, IEEE Engineering in Medicine and Biology Magazine, 12(1):26-39, Mar. 1993

W.E. LORENSEN and H.E. CLINE, Marching Cubes: A high resolution 3D surface construction algorithm, in: *Proc. SIGGRAPH '87* (Anaheim, Calif., July 27-31, 1987), vol. 21(4), pp. 163-169. ACM SIGGRAPH, New York July 1987.

WIXOM, J. And GORDON, W.J., On Shepard's Method of Metric Interpolation to Scattered Bivariate and Multivariate Data, *Math. Comp.* 32:253-264, 1978

WOLBERG, G., *Digital Image Warping*, IEEE Computer Society P., Los Alamitos, CA 1990

YASUDA T., SHIGEKI Y., OHSHITA H., TORIWAKI, *3-D visualisation of an ancient Egyptian mummy,* IEEE Comp. Graph. App., May 1992

PUBLICATIONS ON THE WEB

BALDOCK C., HUGHES S.W., WHITTAKER D.K. et al., 3-D reconstruction of an ancient Egyptian mummy using x-ray computer tomography, www-ipg.umds.ac.uk/MEDPHYS/projects/jen

FOSTER, G., CONNOLL, J.E., WANG, J.Z., TEETER, E., MENGONI, P.M., Evaluation of an ancient Egyptian Mummy using spiral CT and 3-D Reconstructions: interactive display using the World Wibe Web, www.rad.rpslmc.edu/rsnamumie/rsnamumie.html

POMMERT, A., Dreidimensionale Darstellung altägyptischer Mumien aus computertomographischen Bildfolgen http://www.uke.uni-hamburg.de/institute/imdm/idv/publikationen/mc91/katalog.de.html

SCHROEDER, W., MARTIN, K., LORENSEN, B., The Visualization Toolkit, 2nd edition Prentice Hall PTR http://www.kitware.com

EVISON, M.P., Computerised 3D facial reconstruction, http://www.shef.ac.uk/~assem/1/evison.htm

EVISON, M.P., FINEGAN, O.M., BLYTHE, T.C., Computerised Facial Reconstruction: Research Update, http://www.shef.ac.uk/~assem/4/4evison.htm

WISSEMAN, S. et al., Imaging the Past..., in: Ancient Technologies and Archaeological Materials, 1994, 217-23, www.grad.uiuc.edu/departments/ATAM/imaging.html

VISUALISATION OF VIRTUAL ENVIRONMENTS OF ANCIENT ARCHITECTURE: THE PROBLEM OF ILLUMINATION

Geneviève Lucet

Dirección General de Servicios de Cómputo Académico (DGSCA), Universidad Nacional Autónoma de México
lucet@servidor.unam.mx

Light is an essential aspect of architecture. That is the reason why accurate simulation of illumination is a sine qua non condition to create images which show the spaces created by human beings, without falling into falsification of history. Visualisation in the study of ancient architecture needs to go beyond the mere attempt to describe the structural elements and their finish, offering the precise reproduction of other elements involved in the definition of architectural space. This would improve our understanding of the relationship between society and the environment built around it.

Results obtained from various software packages that implement different algorithms are compared in this paper. It is shown how a precise modelling of the behaviour of light is important to obtain realistic illumination, and how a precise description of original light source is necessary.

Therefore, the preference for using lighting visualisation systems in archaeology, rather than the typical software directed to the movie-making industry, can be understood.

Also, while the theoretical characteristics of the illumination model can explain the different results obtained, other factors are important for their practical implications, such as the impact of the technique of image production, the visual quality of images, the adherence to natural illumination, and furthermore, the interactive possibilities.

Previous Work

When the visualisation work of the virtual reconstruction of the meso-American site of Cacaxtla (AD 1-1000) was performed, problems concerned with the achievement of realism arose. Consideration of the way in which the inhabitants thought and designed their living space and resolved their needs appears to be fundamental.

The first images of the site were produced with the usual light sources (ambient, distant, spot and point lights), the only definitions available into the software used. We were working with local illumination algorithms enhanced with shadow mapping. Initially, we though that realism, limited here to its visual components, was obtained, as we had a precise geometric modelling of the structural elements and nice textures, and the illumination tried to show the different elements using classic lighting design tips, such as contrast, equilibrium and sense of depth (Feldman, 1996).

The production of images required long and tedious work of turning on and off the light sources and changing their characteristics. However, it was erroneous to think that the intuitive way we were defining lights and giving them their characteristics could be close to a simulation of natural illumination. We were reproducing a theatrical method for atmosphere creation, nothing else. When we used only one light with the orientation corresponding to the sun, most of the model remained in the dark as local illumination is not designed to support reflected light. With the inclusion of several lights, results looked better but were not reliable. Thus we decided to move to software having the capability to simulate physical behaviour of light.

Virtual Reality in Archaeology

In archaeology the production of images--including animation and virtual reality systems--representing ancient architecture does not find its justification in achieving "beautiful, funny or spectacular" images, but rather aims to extract new information to contribute to the understanding of cultural expression and historical phenomena. Were the objectives based only on image consumption, then the task should be left to Hollywood, a proficient image creator for non-academic purposes.

Images are based on virtual reconstruction. Virtual reconstruction is much more complicated and interesting than simply the geometric modelling of an old construction. It is based on scientific data, and carried out with a strict rigour (Lucet, 1997). Thus, images are a result of a laborious task that renders a contribution on its own. As demonstrated in the project about Cacaxtla's digital reconstruction, multiple benefits can be obtained from this methodology, even before the visualisation.

During all the virtual reconstruction process, a continuous feedback analysis of archaeological data was an essential condition. The analysis of the constructive sequence demanded the assignment of a hierarchy to each structural element in order to establish their relative location in time and space. Additionally, a deep understanding of the function of elements in defining the architectural space was necessary.

Following these rules, we were able to extract some of the design and composition norms followed by the builders. By inference, that allowed us to propose global configurations of the studied site.

Furthermore, digital rebuilding of Cacaxtla leads to a better understanding of how it was planned and designed by its creators. This stage, before the production of images, contributed to a better knowledge about the culture of the place.

Images are a result of a precise calculation. The genesis of images created by computer and the followed methodology are fundamental in the potential of computer graphics applied to archaeology. We introduce precise data, therefore the image is a result of calculations and the consequence of a sequence of instructions.

If we manage to model in a precise and complete way every component that defines architecture, such as geometry, materials, colours, atmospheric conditions and illumination, we are better equipped to obtain images closer to the reality, *i.e.* images that do not lie about the building and about the history. If we compare the whole process of image creation, from the traditional drawing to a complete computerised one, the new technological trends may lead to the loss of the artistic and creative human side while providing the bonus of a more precise and neutral visualisation. This is indeed the best justification for resorting to computer visualisation as a tool of research in archaeology.

Images are tools for the visualisation of architecture. Visualisation tools will find their justification for archaeology due to the way they calculate and show the architectural space and simulate with precision physical phenomenon such as lighting effects. In this way, they are the most complete way to understand the architectural space and are very important for both: the study of architecture and the diffusion of the results of such analytical process. On the other hand, the future looks very promising. We can foresee an important extension of realism that will permit the complete experience of architecture with participation of the full sensorial spectrum. This total immersion in the virtual world will occur with inclusion of sounds, smell, temperature, humidity, sense of touch and a natural exploration interface. In the case of destroyed architecture, as at Cacaxtla, the opportunity to live it virtually will be in our reach.

Even if the perception spectra offered by virtual reality is quite distant from the real world one, as we are working on destroyed architecture there is no way to obtain a perception from the past. Ruins are as far away from original buildings as digital worlds are from the real one. In Cacaxtla, it is possible to observe nowadays reduced walls which correspond to different phases of occupation in the site and talus built only to hold the upper constructive layers which were never part of the spatial conformation. We can also find unevenness of soil fill which allows the preservation of structures situated at different levels. In addition, a huge roof of 50 x 100 m, which drastically changes the illumination, covers the site. So, visualisation through digital reconstruction will allow the architecture to live, virtually, as it may have been built. For example, the scale relation between person and space, and the relationship between constructive space and mural paintings, which are mostly very deteriorated, are both visualisation cases that help explain the way the people conceived their surrounding world and that cannot be appreciated without visual data.

If we exercise care in fulfilling conditions to obtain scientific visualisation from archaeological facts, the virtual reconstruction may become a new tool that will offer possibilities surpassing every traditional tool.

Since the seventeenth century, scientific method, with the purpose of producing objective knowledge, established rigorous rules about data and analysis methodology. Later, techniques were developed to describe, classify and quantify these data, such as databases and statistics; and that was assumed as the only way to produce a "scientific" understanding of the world, the only acceptable one. In order to understand that huge quantities of information, graphics and sometimes images are produced. Nevertheless, there is still information that cannot be found without visualisation, and that is the case with human visual perception of architectural space. Furthermore, this cannot be discarded, as it is part of the general problem of the understanding of the architectural production of the past.

Architecture does not exist without light. The architect, *i.e.* the builder, creates spaces using elements such as walls, columns, floors and roofs that acquire presence thanks to light. According to their nature, materials respond to the light impact in a way determined by their reflective characteristics, roughness or colours.

For many architects, light is a major factor when design decisions must be made. The illumination that applies to a church is quite different from that of an office. The criteria used can vary from functional, emotional, aesthetic and even religious aspects.

The functional use of light is understood by calculating illumination in quantitative terms, which are in many cases related to the activities developed in a room. In a given case, it is important to distinguish if the room was full of light, if it was dark, if there were big contrasts between light and dark areas, or if the illumination was even. Due to the fact that the light in a space can be related to the uses of the space, visualising the illumination can participate in the study of functional use of the space.

The use of light for aesthetic purposes is widespread in modern architecture. It resorts to rhythms and special locations from natural and artificial sources, so that, with the combination of materials, beautiful space is created. It can deeply change the perception of built elements. For example, it can allow a facade to be even or with contrast. The movement of the sun is used also to animate those environments.

Of particular interest in archaeology is the finding of the use of light to create religious phenomena. For example, it is well known how meso-American architecture used special illumination effects on specific days of the year, as a way to control the calendar or as homage to a God or to the cosmos. Such impressive knowledge of astronomical time was expressed in architectural masterpieces that survive until present days. For example, in Chichén Itza, on the 21 of March the stairs of a pyramid become a snake sliding down the facade at a specific time of the day. Similar phenomena observed in existing buildings has been reported in many places, from Egypt to Gothic architecture. However, with constructions that are in ruins, it is only possible to reproduce their lighting with the capture of precise data and computer simulation. In the same manner, we can imagine spaces where the light bounces on a red surface, which at certain times of the day fills the room with red light, allowing us to give it an esoteric meaning. The interpretation towards scientific, stationary or magical contents will nevertheless require the use of complementary data beyond the simple observation of the phenomenon.

Finally, light can be used to create atmospheres, and it then becomes an instrument that works over the perception of space and the induction of an emotional state. Thanks to it, a place can become intimate, comfortable, cold, introverted, extroverted, give us a sense of security, etc.

Even when the architect does not give importance to the illumination as a fundamental tool for design, or if his use of light corresponds to other intentions, the perception of a building is completely linked to it and vision is the sense that receives the most important information. The study of perception is complex because it is related to the culture and the memory of a population and each individual. It is very difficult to deduce these components as they existed in ancient times, as they are so subjective. Nevertheless, the visualisation of past environments can allow us a personal and present perception of the space created by other cultures.

Natural illumination from the sun changes, providing ambient characteristics that modulate the light, and the outcome is very different when moving from one place to another. Impressionist painters for example, were particularly aware of this richness of nature. For these reasons, lighting is one of the characteristics that give to each construction its own personality and they deeply affect the way we perceive them.

In consequence, if one of the purposes of a virtual reconstruction of archaeological sites is to approximate the original building as it was conceived and constructed by its builders, and if we want to experiment and live such ancient space, it becomes clear why the precise modelling and simulation of light is a key aspect of realistic reconstruction. It is for these reasons that we should assign to the reproduction of illumination the same importance we give to geometric modelling.

Digital Lighting Systems Comparison

We believe that the comparison of the different illumination effects using different algorithms is an extremely useful process. Furthermore, a constant evaluation of the tools employed is necessary to keep awareness of the potential and limitations of each one and, in turn, to know when they are responding to our needs.

METHODOLOGY

Software. We produced several proofs with different software packages that use distinct models of illumination:

- RenderMan ®, which uses a local illumination model
- Alias ™, a high-end ray tracing based software
- BlueMoon©, by Larry Gritz, a ray tracing based program with the capability to include radiosity calculation
- Lightscape ™, a radiosity based software that may include ray tracing for still images. Lightscape is aimed to visualisation of illumination, with simulation of real light sources both artificial and natural

Materials. Since the aim of the comparison is mainly related to exploring the effect of using distinct illumination models upon the resulting quality and realism of illumination of a scene, and not to benchmark each software, we reduced the materials to their simplest. They are matte, with no bumps simulated, and no techniques used to make dirty surfaces. Colours are close to the ones of the site of Cacaxtla.

Illumination source. As part of the purpose of the work was to develop the virtual reality of a meso-American archaeological site, only the simulation of natural lighting was considered as a solution for the illumination. Pre-Hispanic architecture is mostly an outdoor architecture with in-between spaces like porticoes. There is no use of window systems and the only entrance of light into the inner rooms is through the access doors or an opening in the roof. Even if there are some fireplaces, these constructions have a completely sun-oriented lighting design.

Image creation. The first images were created using RenderMan, Alias and BlueMoon. Then, we compared the results with those obtained using Lightscape, which is designed to emulate the physical work of the light. Table 1 shows computer time needed in order to produce the 1200 x 800 pixel images shown in this paper. Because of the use of distinct computers, absolute comparisons are avoided. Nevertheless it can be appreciated that a substantially long calculation time is needed for radiosity. In general, it is with algorithms of radiosity where variables introduced by the user can affect more drastically the quality of the results as well as time and memory involved for the calculation. During the process, geometric entities are divided into a coarse mesh, and subdivisions are done with progressive refinement iterations. This goes on until few contrasts are obtained in the illumination values across the mesh element, or elements are too small for further subdivision. Contrast and minimum size of the elements are variables provided as input by the user, therefore some experience is needed in order to obtain satisfactory results without increasing either the database or the calculation time.

Table 1

Software	Equipment	Duration
Alias	Onyx	10 min.
BlueMoon	Octane	2 hours
Lightscape	Indigo 2 Ex	3 hours for radiosity 4 additional hours for ray tracing
RenderMan	Indigo 2 Ex	45 min.

THEORETICAL BACKGROUND

In computer graphics, the results of illumination depend on characteristics of the material, calculation of the shading of a surface, the model of illumination implemented and lighting source definition. Special effects that affect propagation of light such as motion blur, depth cue and fog may be included too, in order to improve the feeling of movement, distance and atmospheric components. As stated above, for this work, material definition was limited to simple matte, opaque, colour surfaces. Shading corresponds to the calculation of the illumination of one polygon, independently of surrounding context, and is an intrinsic part of the illumination model; however, only model of illumination algorithms and lighting source definition will be studied.

Models of Illumination

Illumination models can be divided into two categories: the local illumination model and the global one. The first one, with shading such as Gouraud or Phong, works only on the relation "light source – object" in order to calculate the illumination, while the second one, based on ray tracing and radiosity, includes context such as the presence of other objects which modify the behaviour of the emitted light or become light sources by themselves.

Local illumination

Local illumination algorithms were the first ones developed. They are very primitive and their original definition does not offer much realism, since they reduce the illumination problem to the relation between an object and the light sources, which is very far from the reproduction of the complex behaviour of the light. They do not consider transparency (when light passes through a surface and makes it possible to see objects behind), reflectivity (mirror effect and reflection of light toward other surfaces) and the casting of shadows over other surfaces. Complementary procedures were developed in order to improve the quality of the results. For example, mapping techniques were used to reproduce shadows and reflection. Despite their limitations, these algorithms are still very useful since the simplicity of the involved calculation allows for quick results and makes this kind of algorithm very suitable for real time animation such as in virtual reality.

Global illumination

Ray tracing techniques calculate an image pixel by pixel, tracing rays from the observer's position through each pixel of the image and simulating backward the travel of light. If the ray does not intersect anything, the resulting pixel has no value. If an object is reached, rays bounce from the surface of the object in the directions of the light sources. If nothing intersects them, this part of the object is directly illuminated and resulting colour is calculated. When some object appears between the surface and the light source, or if the surface is transparent or shiny, as a result of ray tracing calculation, then shadows, back objects and reflections appear.

The calculation time of images varies in relation to the transparency and reflection characteristics of the material, and grows accordingly, reaching often high levels of complexity. The resulting images, though, may be very attractive for the quality of shadows, transparencies and reflections.

Nevertheless, diffuse interreflection does not consider the indirect lighting produced by neighbouring illuminated surfaces. This is generally compensated for by an abstract ambient light, a general value that affects every surface and has no correlation with physical behaviour of light. Furthermore, as the algorithm is logically based on the user position, any change in the camera parameters implies an overall recalculation. That is the reason why it is impossible to consider ray tracing as a feasible tool in real time animation, such as a walkthrough with total immersion in a virtual reality system. The quality of ray tracing images, though, makes it a favourite for calculated animations such as those used in the cinema.

Radiosity models of illumination follow a completely distinct logic. Instead of calculating image pixels, they calculate the complete tridimensional illumination of the objects, independently of the camera position. Geometric entities are converted to a mesh that is subdivided regarding illumination factors. Illumination is calculated considering original illumination sources and the light reaching the object after bouncing from other object surfaces. Such light is generally called *secondary light* or *indirect light*, and the process corresponds to the modelling of diffuse light reflection between objects. The colour of a wall and its illumination intensity influence the colour and illumination of neighbouring surfaces. Once the calculation is terminated, the corresponding view from the camera is shown on the screen.

Modifying camera parameters only involves the calculation of the view and does not imply the calculation of the complete illumination. Thus, the initial calculation is large, but since it is view-independent, an important benefit of this algorithm comes from the fact that it allows the modification of the camera parameters without making all the calculations again. For animations, savings in time have considerable importance. Theoretically, it permits walkthrough in real time, however a fast computer is highly recommended. Illumination results can be saved as a texture that is used as mapping in other programs for animation effects.

For the production of still images, the importance given to objects that do not appear in the frame may seem unnecessary, but their inclusion is important since they may influence the final results. Some works have been made in order to compute radiosity solutions in respect to predefined views, reducing calculating time by giving to the surfaces a proportional contribution regarding their importance in the scene (Smits et al., 1993).

In opposition to ray tracing, radiosity does not include specular reflection nor transparency. However in the case where the entities are only defined with opaque and matte materials, this is not such a serious problem.

Radiosity plus Ray tracing

Radiosity and ray tracing, have complementary qualities and characteristics that should be joined. As a result, images worked in this way represent a better choice resulting in an increase in realism. They show both diffuse and specular light reflection. Calculation time increases too, as can be seen in Table 1. Additionally, because of the use of ray tracing, it is impossible to preserve the advantage of real time animation obtained with radiosity, and this technique is thus useful only when dealing with still images.

Definition of Light Sources

Usually, light sources included in rendering software are designed with the purpose of giving tools for entertainment animation, cinema or games. They resolve the problem of a completed control lighting for scenographic purposes. Therefore, they have nothing to do with real life light sources. The definition of real lights should include the modelling aspect with sufficient factors to give it real geometry and parameters, as well as behaviour, *i.e.* the distribution and capability to simulate the physical action of the produced light as it travels from the source to the object and to the observer.

Abstract light sources. The most usual lights found in graphics package are ambient, distant, spot and point light. Other light source definitions are generally derivatives from these. They are characterised by existence or non-existence of an origin and a direction.

The ambient light has neither origin nor direction. It is the light that allows the seeing of objects that do not receive direct illumination.

The distant light, sometimes called parallel light, has no origin but has a direction. This light is generally used to simulate the sun.

The spotlight has both origin and direction. Light intensity may decay over distance, with user-controlled parameters.

Finally, point light has an origin but no direction, as it spreads all around its position.

Furthermore, lights have attributes such as intensity (usually into the range 0-1) and colour.

Real light source simulation. Most of the usual real-life lighting sources are produced by the sun (sometimes a fire or candles) and electric light. Thus, none of the four lighting sources just described above fits real illumination systems, not in size, shape, nor in the distribution of emitted light, and even less, in the way of defining their intensity.

In order to aid decision-making in building design, lighting prediction software has been designed. Among them, Radiance, by Greg Ward of the Lawrence Berkeley Laboratory, has been used since 1987 by the Architecture Department at the University of California, at Berkeley. Radiance is a freeware software, running in Unix operating system, and its lack of graphic interface has limited its exploitation by computer experts.

Electric light is senseless in virtual archaeological visualisation, therefore we will focus our attention on natural illumination. Simulation of sunlight is quite complex and still under investigation, although approximate and quite precise models are available for computer graphics.

Forgetting complicated equations that describe sunlight, it can be seen as a direct light, rays coming directly from the sun, and indirect light from the sky. Skylight is an extended light source that produces an illumination resulting from the scattering of light from the Earth's atmosphere because of the presence of small particles and molecules in the air and clouds (Nishita, 1993; Mardaljevic, 1995). For the software user, elements that could influence natural illumination should be: orientation of the construction regarding north; geographic location (latitude and longitude); date and time. This information will have a direct relation with the sun position. Regarding intensity, variation from sunny to cloudy should be available although more sophisticated systems should include atmospheric conditions such as humidity level, temperature and transparency of air.

Results

Results are divided into two parts: the first deals with the working process in order to prepare the objects and the scene to obtain images with each of the described packages, and the second one examines the resulting images, their visual quality and accuracy.

LIGHTING DESIGN OF A 3D SCENE

With a local illumination program such as RenderMan, in order to simulate solar illumination, it is necessary to define a distant light within the 3D world. Distant light has parallel rays of light with no decay of the intensity as the distance increases. Surfaces that are not directly illuminated remain in darkness, as there is no calculation of the diffuse and specular reflections, missing the simulation of the fact that illuminated surfaces should become also sources of illumination (Figure 1). The use of global and ambient parameters for materials and lights only serve the purpose of obtaining greyish surfaces instead of black ones, and has nothing to do with a real behaviour of light (Figure 2). Then, it is necessary to include complementary lights to compensate the lack of interreflection. This process is not easy. When you turn on new lights, several surfaces get over-illuminated or you lose contrast. To obtain acceptable results it is necessary to try a large number of combinations, see the results and accordingly change the different parameters such as type of light, intensity, location, colour, etc. This takes a lot of time. In the case of the "Red Temple", two entrances of natural light into the room could be distinguished, *i.e.* from the front and from the top of the stair. With RenderMan and Alias, it was very hard to design an illumination to simulate such an effect and still manage to show the volume of the stairs. For this case we had to include four lights (Figure 2).

Figure 1. Illumination of the "Red Temple" with RenderMan. Left: image obtained with only one distant light and a global light. Right: complementary lights.

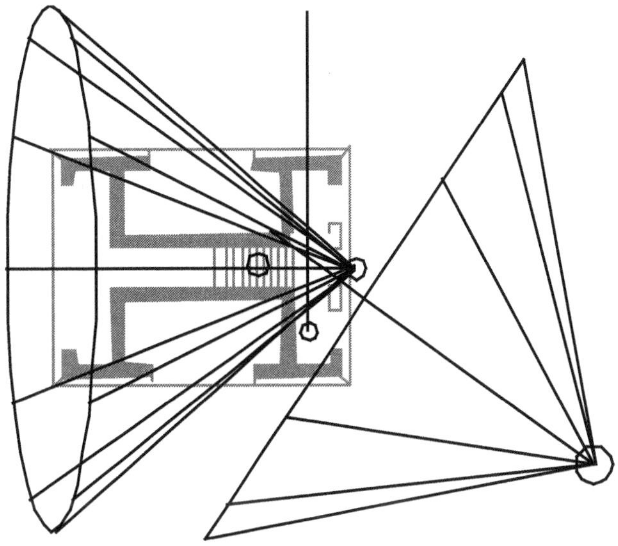

Figure 2. Lighting map of the "Red Temple"

With a ray-tracing program such as Alias, the process is similar. The presence of just one light does not permit a complete visualisation of the whole geometry, especially when materials are opaque and dull. In fact, comparing images obtained with RenderMan and with Alias (Figures 3 and 4), results are very similar and the advantages of ray tracing are especially evident from the quality of shadows.

With radiosity, the illumination design of a scene is much easier. With one light, it is possible to obtain a general perception of the geometry without the necessity to add complementary lights (Figure 5). This is due to the multiplication of light sources as diffuse light reflections are considered. As a result, illumination becomes much more complex, a large variety of shadows are included, colour range and tonal variation increase to reproduce the complicated real illumination phenomena. Actually, one of the most common uses of radiosity is found in the simulation of architectural ambience. It is where radiosity finds its more appealing application. As Lightscape works with sunlight simulation, the illumination of the scene was still easier. You define the orientation, latitude and longitude of the site, date and time, sunny-cloudy sky. There is nothing more to do, as this information is enough in order to have the package calculate the sun position and intensity.

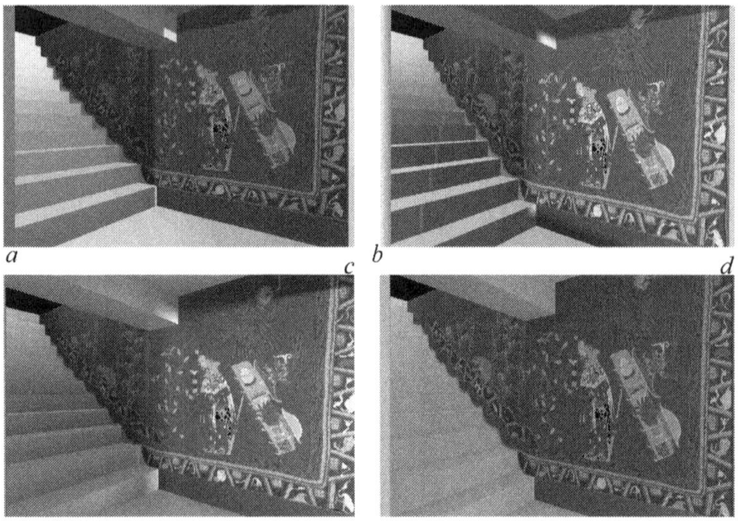

Figure 3. Red Temple. RenderMan (a), Alias (b), BlueMoon (c) and Lightscape (d)

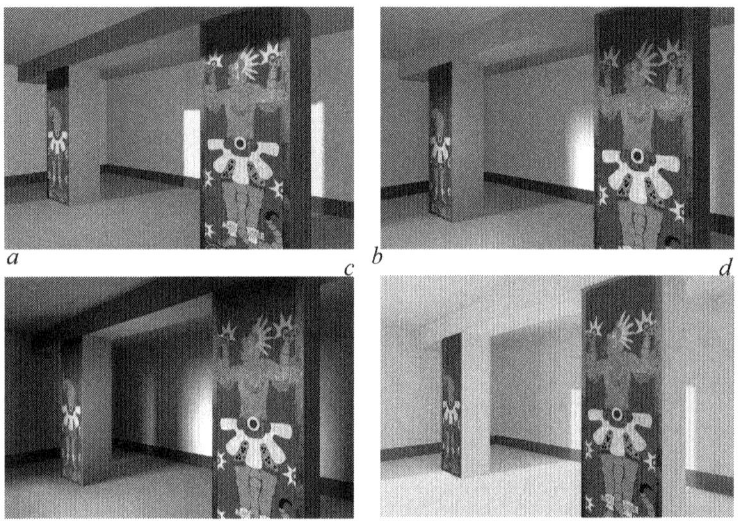

Figure 4. Venus Temple. RenderMan (a), Alias (b), BlueMoon (c) and Lightscape (d)

Figure 5. Results of radiosity with only one light source simulating the sun's behaviour.

PREPARATION OF THE GEOMETRIC MODEL

While radiosity saves substantial time in designing the lighting solution, this is lost because of the demand to improve the geometry for correct results with this illumination model. Thus, when the polygons are overlapped, even by a small fraction of their coordinates, undesired shadowing effects known as "shadow leaks" appear because shading calculation of the vertex of the back polygon is black, influencing the result obtained by the extrapolation of values across the mesh subdivision. This is really a problem as, in order to simplify the modelling, it is a common practice to have floors and roofs uninterrupted by walls or columns. When using ray tracing or local illumination, this simplification of the modelling did not produce these visual artefacts. This was not the case for radiosity where illumination is affected (see the intersection between the wall and the roof in figure 5), and it became necessary to model a floor that contours the different vertical elements. Another solution is to reduce the minimum size of mesh elements, but a dense mesh results into severe constraints in calculation time and memory demands. Local illumination or ray-tracing, however, are not so dependent on the precision of the model.

In addition, the radiosity process transforms the geometric entities into a mesh. If the model includes complicate volumes such as moulding, in order to show all the curvatures and lighting changes, the size of the mesh elements has to be small. Large number of coordinates will be necessary to obtain enough accuracy. In consequence, memory needs and calculation time will result very high. For this kind of geometry, ray tracing is more efficient since it does not require the use of a mesh division and admits more optimised geometric definitions such as bicubic surfaces.

COMPARISON OF RESULTS: VISUAL QUALITY

As mentioned previously, the simulation carried out by radiosity is based upon diffuse light reflection and the fact that illuminated surfaces become by themselves sources of lighting. Thus, light sources are multiplied and illumination acquires further variations affording richer quality and colour closer to the visual quality of the real world. As light arrives directly or indirectly, with distinct intensity and colour, the probability that two surfaces receive the same illumination is very low. That is not the case when local illumination is used, as only primary light sources are considered.

With local illumination models, if distant light is used to represent the sun light, the fact that it has no decay over distance implies that parallel surfaces receive the same intensity of light even if they are located at different distances. If they have the same material, they will have the same response to the light impact. Only shadows or perspective effects will allow the recreation in the observer's mind of the sense of volume and the perception of depth. It can be seen that the latter may become a drawback for realistic visualisation.

Some remarks are possible at this point, after comparing results of calculation of the same scene using different algorithms.

- With radiosity, the surfaces present an important **colour variation** corresponding to interference of neighbouring surfaces.
- In consequence, the extent of the **chromatic palette** increases after reflecting all the subtleties, producing images that are in general more appealing and realistic.
- Additionally, with the use of radiosity there is a **spatial coloration**. Neighbouring surfaces receive a tint from each other, as seen with the colours of some of the surfaces close to the mural paintings.
- The change of planes is less abrupt in radiosity than in ray tracing or local illumination, resulting in less acute, though more **realistic edges** (compare the edges of stairs in figure 3).
- In radiosity, though, there exists a general **loss of contrast**, which sometimes leads to weaker images without personality. In figures 3 and 4, the contrast between shadowed and illuminated parts of the mural paintings disappears. So far we can not attribute this to defects in radiosity or the software itself.

About shadows:

- The **quality of shadows** establishes a strong distinction between RenderMan and Alias. In the first one, the shadows do not always match the geometry because they are generated through mapping as can be appreciated in the corners of the buildings in figure 6. On the other hand, shadows in Alias are a direct result from the ray tracing process and remain totally linked to the structures.

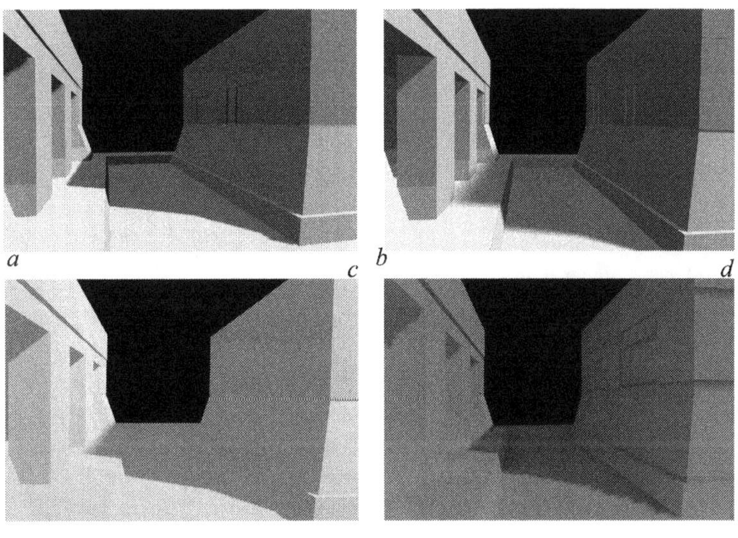

Figure 6. Radiosity in exterior views. RenderMan (a), Alias (b), BlueMoon (c) and Lightscape (d).

- We can distinguish between two kinds of shadows, the umbra and the penumbra. In the former there is no direct lighting, while the latter corresponds to the transition between an illuminated zone and a dark one.

Penumbra, as a physical phenomenon, widens as the projection gets farther away (Minnaert, M., 1993). For example, the penumbra of a table leg almost vanishes at the region close to the floor and widens as the shadow comes from the higher parts. Alias handles penumbra correctly, although it is under user control by means of a variable, leaving its effects to intuition.

- Radiosity by itself does not resolve the problem of the **boundaries of shadows**. Thus, instead of penumbra, we obtain a stair-like zone that follows the radiosity mesh and corresponds to the interpolation of the mesh vertex (Figure 7). This problem vanishes when adding the effects of ray tracing to the radiosity algorithm.

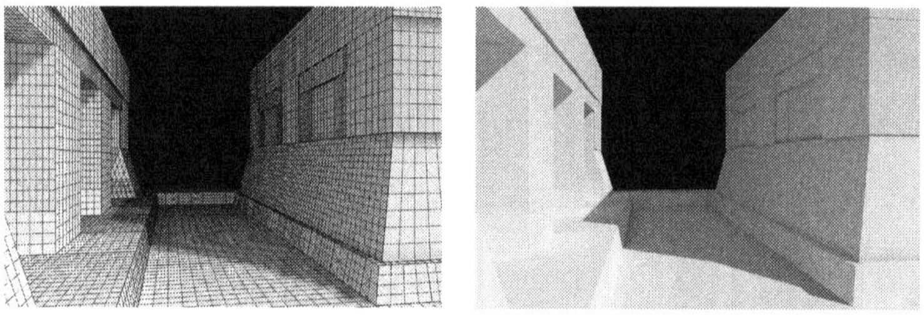

Figure 7. Lightscape. Left: radiosity mesh. Right: radiosity plus ray tracing.

- Radiosity allows various **levels of shadows**; it reproduces shadows inside the shadow, as can be seen in figure 4. The reproduction of secondary shades makes the whole illumination more complex, subtle and interesting.

As a result, we can observe that some scenes are substantially different when generated with different software packages.

Comparison of results: Realism of images

As mentioned before, archaeological visualisation not only needs the objects to look real and the images to be beautiful, but it requires that it allows a valid perception of the built ambience. This is achieved by the simulation of elements that participate in space definition. Therefore, it is important to observe which of the used programs fulfill this demand.

Radiosity in exterior views

In rendering of outside views (Figure 6), the results of radiosity were barely realistic although an excellent definition of the relief in the shadows was observed. The simulation of the way in which sunlight is scattered by air and atmospheric conditions is a highly complicated calculation indeed, and radiosity in open environments is still an important field of research. Apparently, newer versions of the software should improve these algorithms.

Comparison of results: Accuracy

In interiors, particularly in figure 4, the empirically designed illumination produces very different ambiences with respect to the solution calculated from natural light simulation. Although the darker images are perhaps more appealing, the solution given by Lightscape is more exact, since the illumination of white materials from the floor and walls produces a higher illumination of the whole room.

Actually, in the reconstruction of meso-American ambience, we have no precise reference about how the real illumination was, because we do not have buildings of that period in good condition, only with reduced walls and deteriorated finishes. Therefore, for illuminating scenes with RenderMan and Alias, the use of several lights was completely conditioned by human creativity and was very subjective. Generally, we tried to obtain an illumination that allowed a complete appreciation of geometry, good contrast and an appealing atmosphere. The search for realism then is converted into a construction of a scenography process. Although, it is possible to reproduce a natural ambience with these tools, at the same time it is also very easy to make a mistake.

Radiosity and physical simulation of light

The use of radiosity does not imply that the physical work of light has been properly simulated. For example, in the two cases of radiosity of figures 3 and 4, figures at the bottom right corner simulate physical conditions while figures at the bottom left corner use abstract lights such as point or distant. Very important differences result from these approaches.

In addition to the advantages that an illumination algorithm can offer over another one, it is very important to consider the weight given to the real simulation of the physical light phenomena. While Lightscape uses radiosity, Radiance uses ray tracing and integrates additional methods to calculate diffuse inter-reflection, in order to visualise lighting. Unfortunately, we were not able to carry out such testing with Radiance at this point.

A comparative analysis was carried out (Khodulev et al., 1996) regarding "physically accurate global lighting simulation" found in different software. In this detailed and scientific work, Radiance, Lightscape and Specter are studied mainly from the aspect of accuracy. Even though they are all designed for the same purpose, important differences may be found in the results. This shows that even if we have to rely on software capabilities, there is still some work to be done by developers.

Problems of perception

In addition to the mentioned problems, the one dealing with perception persists.

While sunlight is part of the physical world, what reaches our eyes is information relative to the colour. In the reproduction of ambience, even when software as Lightscape uses the full light spectrum for calculations and not just the RGB scheme, a limitation is found in hardware. Important differences can be observed in monitors. They have gamut restrictions and different gamma output. So, the way they present images varies substantially.

The ambient condition of the observer is equally decisive for perception. Virtual images of a dark room seen through the monitor in a well illuminated office will seem darker than they actually are. In this context, a complete immersion inside the virtual world isolates the observer from its ambience and gives him a better perception.

Conclusion

As we have seen, the result of illumination with different software varies considerably. This has direct consequences in the perception of the architectural ambience, and in the evaluation of the historical space. In a first period of virtual reconstructions of archaeological sites, it was satisfying to visualise the structures. Nowadays it is very important that we enter a more demanding period regarding the exactness of the created images. The precision of the geometrical models has existed for a long time, but we can hardly begin to find tools in the market that can allow us a good simulation of natural illumination. While scenographic illumination allows artistic exploration, it is not appropriate for archaeological reconstructions. These demand exactness and accurate visualisation of architecture, before its aesthetic presentation.

If we do not present a precise representation of archaeological ambiences, we will be forging history.

Acknowledgements

I would like to thank Victor Godoy for the calculation of the images produced with BlueMoon and Alias; and particularly to Araceli Casas for her collaboration in the project of "Virtual Reconstruction of the Archaeological Site of Cacaxtla", in the survey of the site, the modelling and the visualisation process.

References Cited

ASHDOWN, I., 1995, "Measuring and Modeling Complex 3-D Light Sources", *Realistic Input for Realistic Images*, Course Notes 1, Siggraph.

ASHDOWN, I., 1996, "Global Illumination and Lighting Design", *Global Illumination in Architecture and Entertainment*, Course Notes, Siggraph.

CORNFORTH, J., DAVIDSON, C., DALLAS, C.J., LOCK, G.R., 1992, "Visualising Ancient Greece: computer graphics in the sacred way project", *Computer Applications in Archaeology 1991*, Edited by G. Lock & J. Moffet, Oxford: BAR International Series No. 577, pp. 219-223.

FELDMAN, S., 1996, "Photorealism in Architecture and Entertainment", *Global Illumination in Architecture and Entertainment*, Course Notes, Siggraph.

FOLEY, J., VAN DAM, A., FEINER, S., HUGHES, J., 1991, *Computer Graphics, principles and practice*, Addison-Wesley, reprinted.

HALL, R., 1989, *Illumination and Color in Computer Generated Imagery*, Springer Verlag.

KHODULEV, A.B., KOPYLOV, E.A., 1996, *Physically Accurate Lighting Simulation in Computer Graphics Software*, http://rmp.kiam1.rssi.ru/articles/pals/introduction.htm

LUCET, G., 1997, "The Virtual Restitution of the Mesoamerican Site of Cacaxtla: a Methodological Point of View", *Archeologia e Calcolatori*, 8, pp. 129-138.

MARDALJEVIC, J., 1995, "Daylighting Models", *Realistic Input for Realistic Images*, Course Notes 1, Siggraph 95, 4, pp. 1-29.

MINNAERT, M., 1993, *Light and Colors in the Outdoors*, Springer-Verlag, second edition.

NISHITA, T., (1993), "Lighting Simulation for Extended Light Sources", *Global Illumination,* Sigrraph Course Notes, 42, 8, pp. 1-33.

SMITS, B.E., ARVO J.R., SALESIN, D.H., 1993, "An Importance-Driven Radiosity Algoritm", in *Global Illumination*, Course Notes 42, Siggraph '93.

WARD, G., 1992, "Tools for Lighting Design and Analysis", *Computer Graphics*, 26, 2, July 1992, pp. 273-282

RAY-TRACING TECHNIQUES IN A PARALLEL ENVIRONMENT: THE CASE STUDY OF A HORSE GRAVE

R. De Nicola, A. Giordano, S. Guarino
Istituto per la Ricerca sui Sistemi Informatici Paralleli (IRSIP) CNR Naples (Italy)
guarino.s@irsip.na.cnr.it

B. Genito, S. Laurenza
Dipartimento Studi Asiatici (DSA) Istituto Universitario Orientale (IUO) Naples (Italy)
archaeo@ irsip.na.cnr.it

Introduction

The reconstruction of monuments has both a cognitive and an educational function. It is obviously one thing to imagine what a monument looked like, another to actually see it. Today, the precision of computer-guided graphical reconstruction is total, thanks to the development of techniques capable of determining objective technical correspondences between the preserved and the lost parts. Reconstruction is very useful both in teaching and in research, as it allows monuments to be studied in their totality, even when they are only partially preserved. Thus, information technologies offer extremely promising perspectives in the art-historical and cultural fields.

In the course of its history, technological evolution produced a wealth of communication tools, but the basic content of communication was often little considered. Our artistic and cultural heritage could provide some of the most significant contents for the new media and become itself a stimulus for future technological development. The "lords of information technologies" have understood it, and are now out to buy copyrights on the reproduction of museum objects, archive documents and books.

In the framework of a collaboration started a few years ago between the IRSIP-CNR (the Institute for the Research on Parallel Computer Systems of the Italian National Research Center) and the Department of Asiatic Studies of the Naples Oriental Institute, a team of archaeologists and draftsmen of the IUO (Oriental Institute) of Naples and programmers and engineers of the IRSIP-CNR began to test and develop a new method for the reconstruction of archaeological sites and ancient landscapes by means of ray-tracing techniques. Since we were mainly interested in the technical computing aspects, we decided, initially, to limit our experiment to a single archaeological sample: an Avarian horse grave.

The grave was excavated during a joint archaeological expedition, begun in July 1996, directed by Dr. Laszlo Madaras of the Jasz-Nagy-Kun Szolnok County Museum of Szolnok (SE Hungary) (JANASZO) and Prof. Bruno Genito of the IUO of Naples. The focus of the expedition was the excavation of an Avarian-age cemetery (7th century AD) near the small town of Ocsod. The cemetery has yielded about 60 graves so far, including a very interesting grave of a man buried together with his horse. This burial ritual, typical of the Eurasian nomadic peoples of the Early Middle Ages, bears witness to the eminent role played by horses among the pastoral peoples that migrated from Central Asia to the Carpathian Basin.

Computer Graphics and Archaeology

During the last ten years, computer graphics have been applied especially to monumental archaeology. Initially, 3-D modelling was used to produce high-quality drawings of reconstructed monuments, and the costs were very high. Nowadays, as the cost of hardware and software equipment has fallen and solid modellers are integrated into easily available CAD packages such as AutoCAD R14, computer graphics and solid modelling have become more accessible.

In fact, today almost all the modellers used in archaeology are CAD software extensions, as archaeologists are mainly interested in the possibility offered by CAD systems to turn layers on and off and combine the different layers of a drawing with other drawings. However, we must keep in mind that archaeologists are interested in recording what was there, instead of what could have been there. Thus, archaeologists approach computer graphics and three-dimensional modelling in a very different way than other professionals, e.g., architects.

To reach a better understanding of how virtual reality or computer graphics are applied to archaeology, a good term of comparison is a movie production, which, like an archaeological undertaking, is characterised by an elaborate organization, a huge investment of energies, and a collaboration between different professional figures.

As is usually the case, in the beginning there is the idea, which arises from different needs. The purpose of a historical reconstruction is usually to make visible and evident something that is partially hidden or lost, by means of regenerative restorations. Once the project has been conceived, we must study its feasibility by analysing its costs and benefits. After the theoretical and technical needs have been established, the designing stage can begin. At this point, one can start to process the data in two parallel but related steps: computer graphics and programming.

The main difference between virtual reality and computer graphics is the rendering times. A virtual reality application renders images in real time (in order to obtain a good and fluid effect, we need at least 25 frames per second), while a video in computer graphics can take hours or days for the rendering of each scene. This is because the modellers usually employed in computer graphics use special effects requiring huge computing power, such as reflections, shadows and lights, and bump mapping, to increase the realism of the scene; hence, the modeller must necessarily compute off-line.

Normally, in the development of a computerised graphic reconstruction the programmer divides the graphic part of the application into two phases: solid modelling and texturing. First, one analyses the plans, views and photos of the monument to be reconstructed. Then the solid modelling process can start. This part of the work is mainly the task of the draftsmen and the archaeologists: the target here is to maintain the realism of the graphic model without exceeding the available computing power. The quality of the work depends on achieving the right balance between graphic detail and the quantity and quality of the textures. The amount of graphic detail is a function of the number of polygons employed: the more numerous the polygons, the higher the detail. The function of textures (2-D images superimposed on the faces of 3-D polygons) is to complete the overall appearance of the objects:.

Thus, there is a technical limit to the number of polygons and textures that can be manipulated by a computer in real time; hence, the ability of both the draftsmen and the programmers is crucial for the quality of the final result.

For the programmer the real challenge is the frame rate, i.e., the number of frames per second that the application can compute and display. In the case of virtual reality, these images are computed in real time, with a frame rate of 10-15 frames per second, i.e., using a longer computing time to increase the quality, instead of the 25-30 frames used in computer graphics. As one can imagine, there is a great difference in resolution between the two techniques.

Another problem posed by 3-D-computer graphics is the generation and management of shadows; the presence of shadows helps the end user to better understand the spatial relationships among objects. The most popular algorithm for the automatic generation of shadows, ray tracing, requires a huge amount of computing power, and it is hence still not possible today to obtain shadows in real time with these techniques.

Finally, for our purposes, namely the application of ray tracing to archaeology, there is another aspect that cannot be overlooked: the complexity of the solid modellers typically included in CAD packages, which can be forbidding for non-specialist users—in our case the archaeologists themselves and the draftsmen. Hence, one of our priorities was to find a way of dispensing with modellers. We also hoped to show that it is not necessary to have powerful special-purpose computers to reach better and faster results if one works with a simple but heterogeneous parallel computer architecture.

Parallel processing and PVM

Parallel processing is a method that allows large computing jobs to be carried out by subdividing them in several different small tasks. There are two main categories of parallel processing:

- Massive Parallel Processing (MPP): hundreds or thousands of CPUs, installed in the same cabinet, are connected to hundreds of gigabytes of memory. Each CPU is exactly the same as the others as regards resources, software, and communication speed;
- Distributed computing: a network of computers working together at the same large job.

With distributed computing, it is possible to equal and even exceed the computing power of a large MPP calculator by using many general-purpose workstations connected by a high-speed local area network. It is also possible to use different MPP computers for distributed computing; the computing power thus obtained is of course very high. Distributed computing is extremely cost-effective compared to MPP, as one can employ a network of pre-existing local heterogeneous computers without having to buy expensive MPP machines.

Distributed computing and MPP have in common the notion of "message passing": data must be exchanged by co-operative tasks. Message-passing systems for heterogeneous environments make sure that the exchanged data are understood by computers with different data formats. This can be achieved by using Parallel Virtual Machine (PVM), a software which allows a group of heterogeneous computers to function like one single virtual machine. PVM manages message routing, data conversion and task scheduling across a network of incompatible computer architectures in a transparent way. Furthermore, every PVM task can start or stop the other tasks or add computers to, or remove them from, the virtual machine. Considering that our main purpose was to develop a new methodology and not to create a new ray-tracing software toolkit, our choice fell on PVM because of the availability of a PVM version of the well known ray-tracing software POV-ray with a patch for the original code-sources of PVM.

Ray-tracing Algorithms and POV-Ray

Ray tracing is a rendering technique used to generate realistic images on a computer by "shooting rays" into a scene. The ray-tracing algorithm transforms the scene, which is composed of shapes, textures, light sources, and a camera, into image space. The viewpoint is assumed to be at infinity, on the positive Z-axis. Thus, all the light rays are parallel to the Z-axis (Fig. 1).

Each ray goes from the viewpoint through a pixel of the image and is tested for intersection with any of the objects in the scene. The path of each ray is traced to determine which objects in the scene are intersected by the ray. If a ray intersects an object, all possible intersections of the ray and the object are determined. This may yield multiple intersections for multiple objects. The intersections are sorted by depth. The intersection with the maximum Z-value represents the visible surface for that pixel.

The attributes of this object are used to determine the pixel's characteristics. Every time an object is hit by a ray, the colour of the surface at that point is calculated. The most important element of a visible surface ray-tracing algorithm is the intersection routine. Any object for which an intersection routine can be written can be included in a scene.

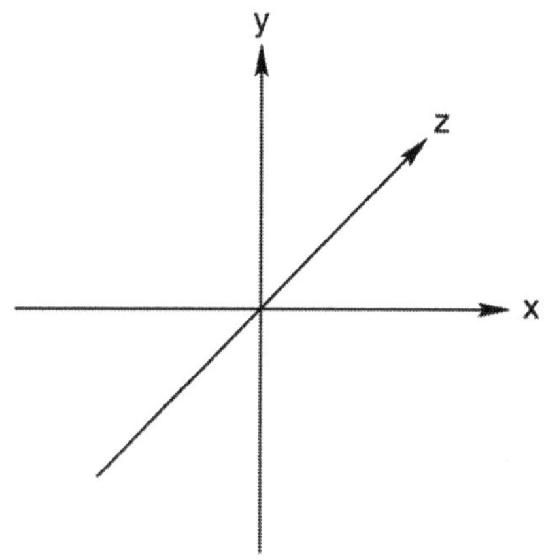

Figure 1. Co-ordinate system

Objects in a scene may be composed of a mixture of planar polygons, polyhedral volumes, or volumes defined or bounded by quadric, binomial or polynomial parametric surfaces. Since 75-95% of a ray-tracing algorithm is used to determine intersections, the efficiency of the intersection routine significantly affects the efficiency of the algorithm. Determining the intersections of an arbitrary line in space with a particular object can be computationally taxing.

Special effects like inter-diffuse reflection (radiance) and atmospheric effects require the shooting of a lot of additional rays into the scene for each pixel. All this mathematical simulation of light rays also requires considerable computing power, especially when the scene is complex.

For our application we decided to use a freeware ray-tracing tool, the Persistence of Vision(tm) Ray-Tracer (POV-Ray ver.3.0) developed in their spare time by the POV-Team(tm) (David K. Buck and Aaron A. Collins). The Persistence of Vision(tm) Ray-Tracer (POV-Ray) creates three-dimensional, photo-realistic images using a ray-tracing rendering technique. It reads from a text file containing information describing the objects and lighting in a scene, and generates an image of that scene from the viewpoint of a camera also described in the text file.

Ray tracing is not a fast process by any means, but it produces very high-quality images with realistic reflections, shadings, perspective and other effects.

POV-Ray's features include easy-to-use scene description language, very high quality output image files (up to 48-bit colour), 15 and 24-bit colour display on IBM-PCs using appropriate hardware, the creation of landscapes using smoothed height fields, Phong, specular highlighting for more realistic surfaces, and inter-diffuse reflection (radiance) for more realistic lighting.

POV-Ray supports unions, merges, intersections and differences, and assigns to the objects materials called textures (defining the colouring and surface properties of a shape). Thus, users can create their own textures or use pre-defined textures such as Copper, Gold, Silver, Stone, and Wood.

In conclusion, we chose POV-Ray not only because it is an excellent all-around package and works with PVM, but because it stands out above the rest for two reasons: first, it is freeware; secondly, it is distributed with its code sources, so that users can compile it on any platform.

Reconstructing the Horse Grave

As we said, we set out to test a new methodology based on a ray-tracing technique in a parallel environment for two main reasons: first, we wanted to find a method allowing us to create 3-D photo-realistic images directly from hand drawings or photos of excavations, without needing to master the complexities of the solid modellers found in CAD packages; secondly, we wanted to verify whether a heterogeneous parallel environment made up of different computers (PC, Workstations, etc.) could offer the high computing potential required by ray-tracing processing (Fig. 2).

We used a heterogeneous parallel architecture of the IRSIP-CNR of Naples equipped with eight elaboration nodes consisting of an IBM Risc System/6000 Scalable Power Parallel Systems (IBM SP2) with six elaboration nodes, an IBM Risc 6000 with one elaboration node, and a Sun Sparc 10, also with one elaboration node. The operative system employed was Unix. The software was PVM and POV-Ray ver. 3 freeware.

The graphic documentation of the horse grave was originally drawn up for the simple purpose of recording the excavation, since there was no plan at the time to develop a 3-D reconstruction of the grave. The idea to apply our methodology to the horse grave came to us only several months after the end of the excavation.

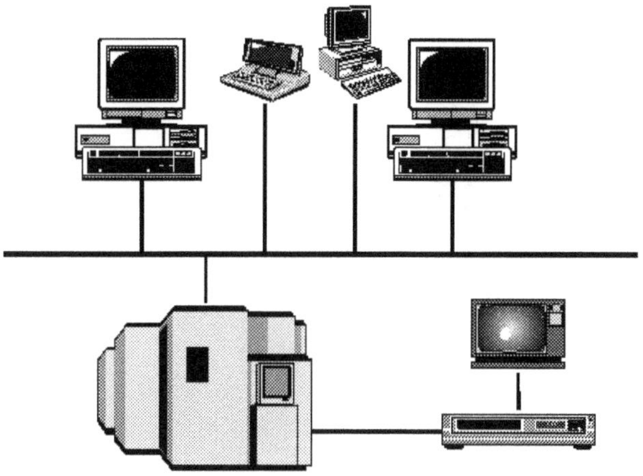

Figure 2. Computers arranged in a parallel architecture

Re-examining the graphic documentation, we immediately realised that there were no high-quality vertical photos of the grave and the only available documentation was the hand-drawn sections and plans of the grave. Since these were too full of "noise" to be suitable for computer processing (Fig. 3), we had to scan and clean them first.

Then we proceeded to identify the "objects", by which we mean all the elements in the plan: the grave, the horse, the man, and the grave goods. Finally, we positioned the objects on X-Z coordinates, using the "left-handed coordinate system" required by POV-Ray and inputting the data directly into POV-Ray's text file. The result was a multi-layer plan allowing us to proceed with the ray-tracing phase.

To determine elevation, we used a POV-Ray function called "Height-fields". A height-field is an object whose surface is determined by the colour value or palette-index number of a graphic image file (Fig.4). The maximum height corresponds to the maximum possible colour or palette-index value in the image file (on a scale of grays ranging from 0 to 255, where 0 is black and 255 is white). The resolution of the height-field is determined by two factors: the resolution of the image and the resolution of the colour/index values. The image size determines the resolution along X and Z. The resolution along Y is determined by the colour/index value.

To calculate the proper colour/index value, we used the following formula:

$$colour = h * H / COLOUR \qquad (1)$$

where:

colour is the unknown colour/index value;
h is the value of the height being processed;
H is the maximum height of the excavation;
COLOUR is the maximum possible colour or palette index.

For our purposes, 8-bit grey levels were sufficient to grant a high level of precision, since they allow 256 different height levels to be distinguished. For an H (Maximum height) value of 54 cm, which is the maximum depth of the grave, and a COLOUR value of 256, we obtain an approximation (H / COLOUR) of about 2 mm (Fig. 5).

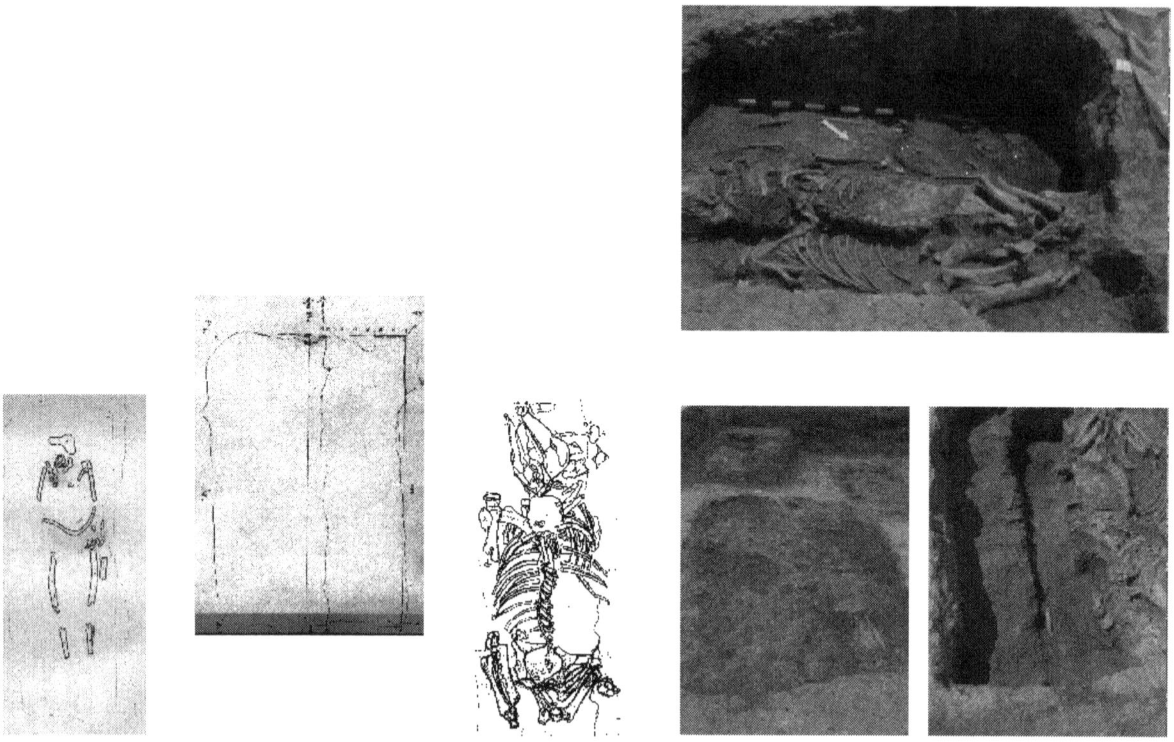

Figure 3. Graphic documentation

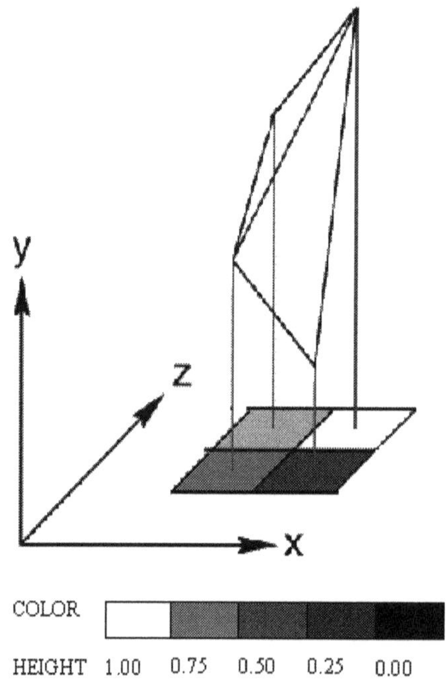

Figure 4. Heights and colours in height-field fusion

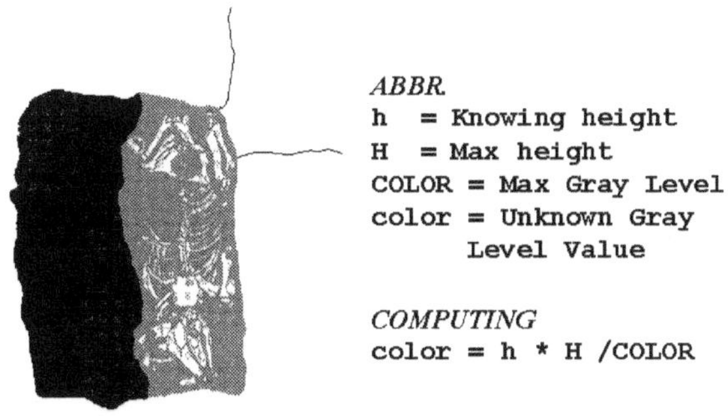

Figure 5. Formula to determine the colour value

In the following phase, we decided to apply the textures before instead of after the final ray-tracing process to prevent problems with camera zooming during the animation. Moreover, as we can see in Figure 6, which shows several of the textures employed, the levels are so shallow that they yield only slightly different shades of grey, and it is hence difficult to appreciate differences in depth. That is why we show alongside the image the textures that we used for each different object, each with a different grey-level value (Fig. 6).

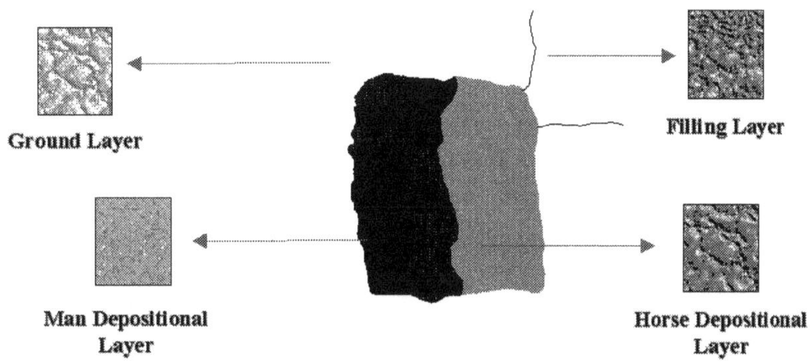

Figure 6. Texturing phase

Since we were dealing with rough surfaces, such as different types of terrain, we decided to apply the textures contemporaneously with the creation of the height-fields in order to solve the above-mentioned problem of camera zooming, smooth surfaces and unsatisfactory rough-texturing. Formula (1) proved capable of calculating not only the height of an object, but also the roughness of the texture applied to it.

All the objects of the excavation, initially arranged in several layers, were finally combined in a single height-field image to be processed by ray tracing and rendering (Fig. 7).

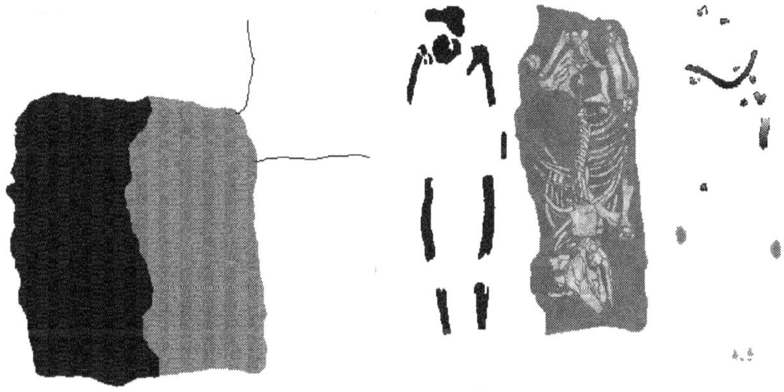

Figure 7. Object layering

Ray-tracing Phase

The virtual machine used to render each frame of movie was composed of 3 different main units: the Risc 6000, the Sun Sparc 10, and the IBM SP2.

The two first machines are workstations. The third is a parallel machine with six nodes, each regarded as a single computing node. As we said above, the purpose of combining different machines was to verify whether a heterogeneous environment would actually be able to rise to the occasion.

Figure 8 shows the computing times of each machine. The parsing time is shown in grey, the tracing time in black. Parsing time means the time that the ray-tracer needs to analyze the scene (textures, bitmaps, objects, camera position, lights, etc.). Tracing time means the computing time needed by ray tracer to compose the scene.

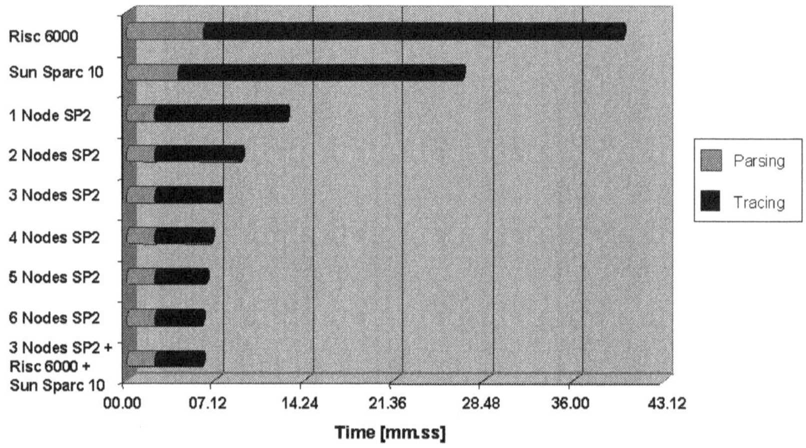

Figure 8. Performance evaluation

The diagram in Figure 8 shows that the parsing time is not split in parallel, but is different for each node which is analysing the scene file. The parsing time of this machine is longer than the total time required by the other nodes; in fact, the Risc6000 node will never begin the tracing phase. This behaviour is illustrated by the diagram bar relative to the Risc6000 node.

The diagram also shows that increasing the number of nodes diminishes tracing time. Starting with a virtual machine (VM) with a single SP2 node, one will remark that the addition of a node reduces the tracing time. The end of the diagram shows us the VM with all 8 of its nodes. It is interesting to note that the total time of this VM is slightly lower than that employed by the VM *without* the two workstations.

This behaviour contradicts the expected results, since in theory a higher number of nodes should yield more computing power. Instead, the Risc6000 node not only does not contribute at all to the job, its parsing time being longer than the total time of the other nodes it also slows down the other nodes, which must employ part of their own computing time to exchange information with it. The SunSparc10 manages to compensate for only part of the delay caused by the Risc6000.

A general rule can be deduced from this result: in order to exploit a heterogeneous environment at its best we need the parsing time to be reduced as much as possible. Several methods could be suggested to attain this objective, e.g., parallel parsing, the pipelining of frame rendering, optimising the parsing code, etc. At any rate, we regard the final result we obtained as satisfying. The time needed to render a scene was reduced from about 40, 26, 13 minutes respectively for Risc6000, Sun Sparc 10, 1 Node SP2, to about 6 minutes for the complete VM.

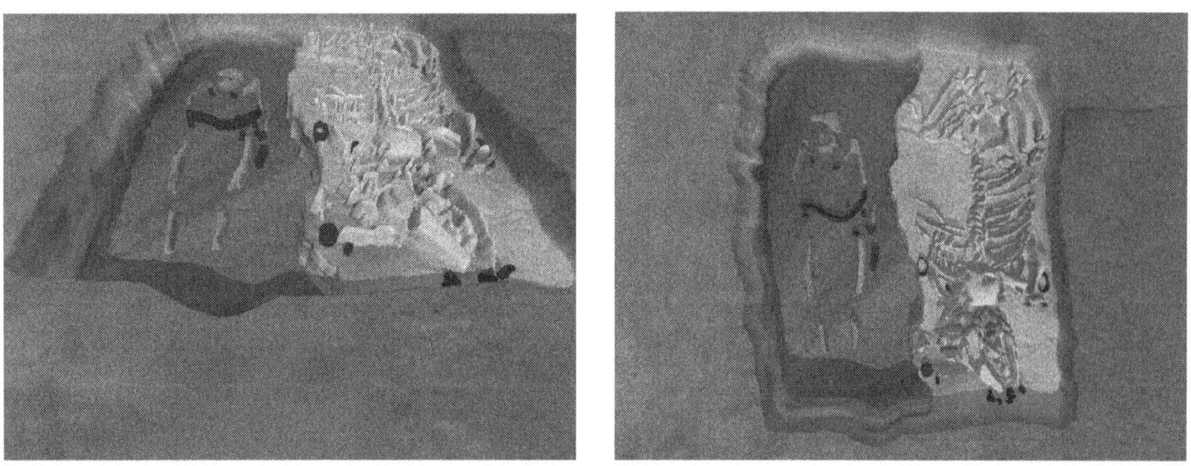

Figure 9. Final images

Final Results and Future Developments

Having verified the validity of our method, we proceeded to create a series of images that we assembled in a videotape in which a virtual camera moves over and inside the grave, showing it from several different angles without loss of detail (Fig. 9). The animation is in the TGA format. We used an Onyx2 to produce the movie on a Beta PAL videotape lasting 1 min. 19 sec. and rendered at 25 frames per second at 24 bits.

This case study has allowed the testing of a new approach to ray tracing in a parallel environment that may open the way to new interdisciplinary applications. In fact, we are presently studying the possibility of developing some new tools based on this technique (e.g., texture libraries, automatic pattern-recognition based on the grey-level palette) which could be applied to other aspects of archaeology, such as the reconstruction of ancient landscapes and stratigraphic sequences.

ACKNOWLEDGMENTS

The authors would like to thank Multimedia LAB of the IRSIP-CNR of Naples for their collaboration.

References Cited

ROGERS, D.F., "Procedural Elements for Computer Graphics" *McGraw-Hill Book Company.*

GUARINO, S., PLAITANO, A., 1994, "Strategie di Routing per Architetture Parallele" *Collana IRSIP, Pubblicazione n.24.*

HAEBERLI, P., SEGAL, M, 1993, "Texture Mapping as a Fundamental Drawing Primitive".

GEIST, A., BEGUELIN, A. et ali, "PVM: Parallel Virtual Machine, A User's Guide and Tutorial for Networked Parallel Computing", *MIT Press Cambridge, Massachussetts.*

FUSNER, C., "Tutorials for the POV-Ray User Guide".

AMUDSEN, C., "Tutorials for the POV-Ray User Guide".

CASON, C., "POV-Help".

REILLY, P., RAHTZ, S., 1992, "Archaeology and the Information Age" *Routledge, London.*

REILLY, P., Towards a Virtual Archaeology, 1990, "Computer Applications and Quantitative Methods in Archaeology" *BAR Intern. Series 565.*

PRE-RENDERING ACOUSTICS AND ILLUMINATION FOR ARCHAEOLOGICAL RECONSTRUCTIONS

Jackson Pope and Alan Chalmers

Department of Computer Science, University of Bristol, UK
pope@cs.bris.ac.uk

Virtual Reality (VR) can be used as a powerful tool for the reconstruction of archaeological sites. Accurate reconstructions of sites that are no longer intact can provide insights into the lives and civilisations of earlier cultures. However, as VR applications typically have to render the scene in real time providing many frames of animation and large quantities of sound information to the user every second, there is little processing power available to provide physically accurate sound and lighting information. In this paper we present a method for pre-rendering the lighting and sound information and then presenting these results to the user in real time. These results, generated using a physically accurate modelling technique, provide many extra visual and auditory cues to the user, improving their sense of presence within the environment and the realism with which they perceive the reconstruction.

Introduction

When experiencing real environments, our senses provide us with detailed information about the space we are present in. Our eyes collect information on the size, geometry and materials of the scene and our ears confirm those details using auditory cues (Shi et al. 1993). We also use touch to determine the materials used. Unfortunately, many archaeological sites are no longer intact; therefore in order for us to experience those sites undamaged they must be reconstructed. It is often unfeasible to repair the remains due to cost or preservation concerns, so computer reconstructions using VR applications provide a cheaper, more viable option.

The use of a computer for reconstructions has its drawbacks, as we are no longer able to touch the materials of the scene, and the use of a computer monitor for display hampers our visual experience. Computer monitors fill only a small portion of our peripheral vision and can display only a fraction of the luminance range of the human eye.

Although our visual system dominates our experience of environments, the auditory system provides valuable information which can both support the evidence provided by the visual cortex and provide information about parts of the scene that are not currently visible to the user. When the user is experiencing a VR reconstruction his/her visual system is limited in the information it can provide by the small fraction of peripheral vision filled by the monitor. Under these circumstances the information provided through sound cues becomes more important as it has the potential to fill in some of the missing visual details.

In addition to the intrinsic problems of computer reproduction, the real-time constraint of VR applications limits the amount of processing power available for accurately representing the geometry, lighting and sound of the environment. Recent advances in rendering hardware have enabled the majority of the graphics processing to be performed by dedicated hardware rather than the central processing unit (CPU). These hardware engines have the ability to render large volumes of triangles or other polygons at very high throughput rates, and also handle texture mapping and direct lighting. In most indoor environments the majority of surfaces reflect light diffusely--light is equally reflected in all directions, as shown in fig. 1--so highly reflective surfaces like white walls can act like light sources significantly contributing to the lighting of nearby objects. This diffuse inter-reflection between surfaces cannot currently be performed by 3D graphics hardware nor can the calculation of accurate soft shadows, but they should not be ignored, as their inclusion has a very noticeable effect, and greatly improves the realism of the VR experience.

Typically the sound field is also simplifed for VR applications, an approximation is chosen, in such a way to limit the amount of processing carried out in real-time. This ranges from the very simplistic 'ambient' sound where sounds are played in the environment with no directional information; through spatialised sound, where the distance and direction from the user are recreated using multiple loudspeakers or specialist Head-Related Transfer Functions (HRTF's) through headphones; to auralised sounds which describe the environment in which they are presented by means of echoes and reverberation.

It is the auralisation--the process of rendering the sound field--that can provide the information missing from the visual display. Spatialised sound by itself can allow us to place the sound source in the 3D virtual environment, but it does not convey any information about the geometry, size or materials of the environment. By considering the interaction between the sound waves generated by the source and the surfaces present within the environment we can generate a much more accurate approximation to the sound field than by spatialisation alone. The slow speed of travelling sound—relative to the speed of light—enables a user to detect subconsciously the delays associated with the echoes which have been reflected off the surfaces within the scene (Kleiner et al. 1993, Kuttruff 1979). From this information we can 'hear' the size of the room within which we stand and determine our position with respect to the surfaces in the environment (Borish 1984, Kleiner et al. 1993, Kuttruff 1979). Such knowledge is hard to discover from a graphical monitor as no information about the surfaces to the sides or behind the viewing frustum is shown.

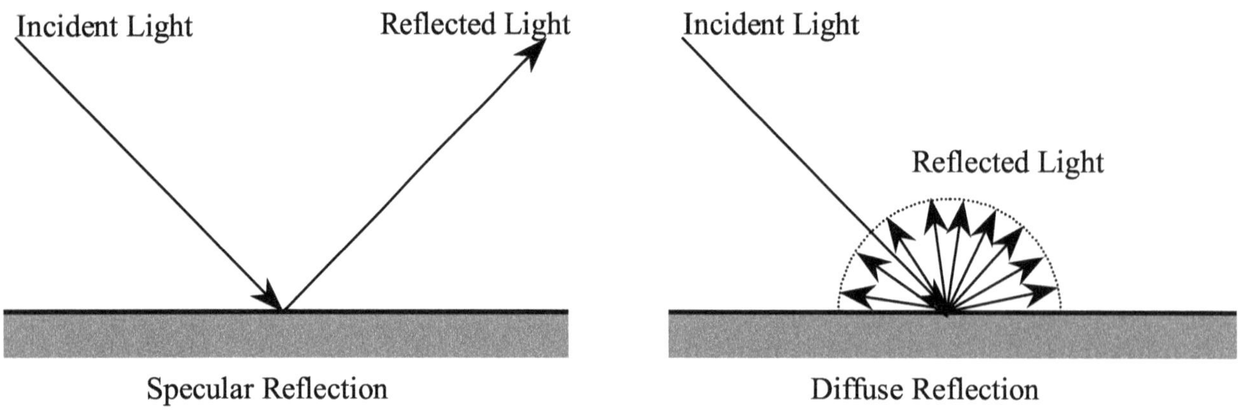

Figure 1 Specular and Diffuse Reflection

Previous Work

Despite the significant effect the sound field within the environment has on our perception of a scene, sound rendering has been studied less than rendering of the visible spectrum. Previous work on computer modelling of room acoustics has tended to cater to the design of theatres, concert halls and other auditoria, or on noise control in factories. Many tools have been developed to aid the design of such buildings, improving the acoustics by removing dead spots and other effects caused by the geometry of the room (Kleiner et al. 1993, Kuttruff 1979). Such acoustic tools model the propagation of sound waves through the environment in a very similar manner to the ray tracing technique (Whitted 1980) used in computer graphics. They calculate impulse responses which describe the sound field at a particular point within the environment in terms of the time of arrival and amplitude or energy of echoes generated within the scene. Separate impulse responses may be constructed for multiple reference points.

In the past, simplified techniques have been used to give some indication of the sounds within an environment, but these, while describing the sound and its position relative to the observer, provided no information concerning the geometry of the room. This can lead to confusion in the perception of the virtual environment. One such technique is the 'ambient' sound method, where sound is treated as global. The only calculation done is to decrease the intensity of the sound relative to the distance from the source. This is the technique used in Virtual Reality Modelling Language (VRML) worlds (Ames et al. 1997). Another method is 'spatialised' sound in which sound is computed according to distance from the sound source and the direction of the source, thus making use of the brain's ability to position a sound according to slight differences in intensity, phase, and time delays between left and right channels (Kleiner et al. 1993, Lehnert et al. 1992, Møller. 1992). Both the ambient and spatial sound methods only deal inherently with direct sound—that is, sound that has reached the receiver without having been reflected off any surfaces. However, it is precisely the reflected sounds that allow us to perceive the geometry and size of the room. We subconsciously process the echoes that are reflected off surfaces that delimit of the environment we are in (Borish 1984, Kleiner et al. 1993, Kuttruff 1979).

Other techniques have been used to render both direct and reflected information. The ray tracing technique, where sound rays are traced from a sound source through the environment until the energy they carry is sufficiently small to be negligible is one such method (Krokstad 1968). The ray tracing technique works in a very similar way to graphical ray tracing, but with the inclusion of time dependence. It has been used to model both specular and diffuse reflection and remains one of the most popular methods in use. Another method, the mirror image source technique, accurately generates the reflections rather than relying on a stochastic process to determine the reflections (Borish 1984). In the mirror image source method the sound source is mirrored in the surfaces of the environment to provide a reflected source. Reflecting sources that have already been reflected by other surfaces generates higher order reflections. This method does not scale well for very high order reflections or scenes with complex furnishings although image source culling methods exist. The image source method does not take into account diffuse reflection, and cannot model non-planar surfaces. Radiosity methods have been adapted by Greenburg et al. from heat transfer to model the diffuse inter-reflection of light (Greenburg et al. 1986). Shi et al. and others have used the radiosity model to calculate the diffuse reflection of acoustic energy (Shi et al. 1993). However, due to the far greater wavelengths concerned when modelling sound waves, sound reflection is more specular than when modelling light, hence surfaces cannot be treated as perfectly diffuse. Beam tracing has also been used to model sound fields; Funkhouser et al. used beam tracing to generate a tree of valid mirror image sources in an off-line stage to enable real-time rendering of the sound field for small numbers of reflections (Funkhouser et al. 1998).

Audio Visual Pre-Rendering

We present in this paper combined audio-visual rendering using an augmented particle tracer (Pattanaik et al. 1992). Particle tracing models the emission of light particles from a source and tracks them as they are reflected around the environment, until they are finally absorbed. The surfaces within the scene are subdivided, and as particles are reflected from a surface patch the brightness of that surface patch is incremented, which leads to the calculation of the global illumination within the scene. This technique is extended to trace the expanding sound wavefront as it emanates from the source and interacts with the surfaces within the environment. We consider only scenes with static surfaces and one static sound source—although the method does not preclude multiple sound sources—and generate the sound field results at a set of receivers distributed evenly throughout the environment. This gives rise to two adjustments that must be made for rendering sound: the treatment of the time taken to traverse the environment—light is considered instantaneous—and the collection and correlation of the results at the receivers as opposed to the surfaces. When rendering light information we assume that the light distribution within the environment has reached equilibrium, so time can be ignored, but it is precisely the time delay associated with audible echoes that enables us to gain some indication of the room's geometry and materials.

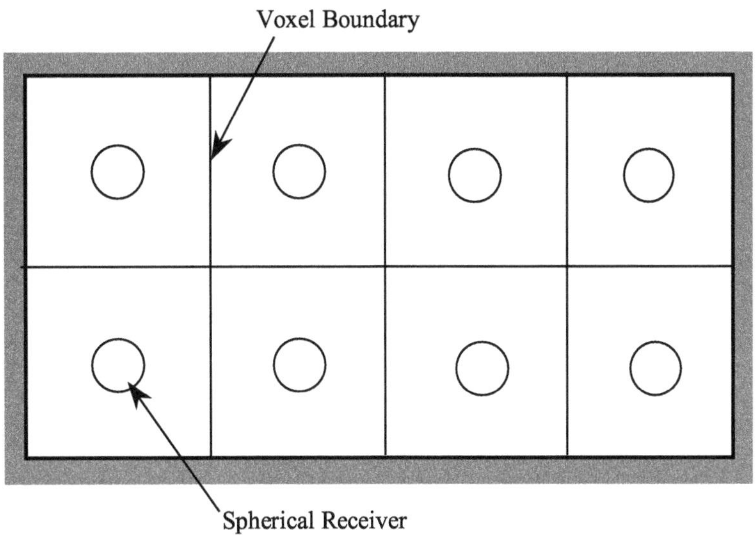

Figure 2 – Plan view of a scene showing receiver positions

The scene is partitioned into a grid of cubic elements (voxels) for the purpose of optimising the object intersection tests, these voxels can be used in sound rendering for housing sound receivers, as shown in fig. 2. The sound field is then calculated at the centre of each voxel in a manner similar to the generation of irradiance volumes done by Greger et al. (Greger et al. 1998). By positioning the cells adjacent to each other, in a regular grid, the perceived sound field may be calculated evenly throughout the environment. This will enable us to explore the results in real time by assuming that the sound field at the user's location is equivalent to that at the centre of the voxel within which the user is positioned. By decreasing the size of the voxels the accuracy of the assumption improves, but there is a trade-off with memory required. The advantage of this method as opposed to conventional ray tracing methods—where only one receiver is considered—is the independence from listener position that is achieved by generating multiple approximations of the sound field.

RENDERING LIGHT AND SOUND

The modelling of light as particles that are emitted from light sources and reflected between the surfaces of the environment is intuitive, as light is comprised of photons emitted from light sources with different frequencies. Modelling sound in this fashion is less intuitive, but the approximation still holds. Sound is the result of displaced air molecules, which cause small air pressure changes that the ear can detect. Unlike light, sound waves are longitudinal, each molecule vibrating back and forth along the wave causing compression and rarefaction and displacing the next molecule in line. If we consider a molecule as it moves away from the sound source, then, as it starts to return towards the sound source, we consider the next molecule that it has displaced, then we have a series of particles moving with the wavefront which we can treat as one continuous particle trajectory.

The sound we model within the environment is a Dirac impulse, an infinitely short sound comprised equally of all frequencies. The advantage to modelling an impulse as opposed to a real sound is that the room impulse response describes how the echoes are generated for a single sample; these impulse responses can then be read as a graph, and can be applied to any input signal by the process of convolution. We model the impulse as a single sample of unit amplitude in each frequency being modelled. Although our method can model multiple sound frequencies, thus giving improved results as the spectral behaviour of sound is considered, memory usage is linear with the number of frequencies rendered, so typically only one is considered. In a similar way to light rendering, a large number of particles are traced, and these particles are distributed stochastically over either a full spherical wavefront or a conical section of a spherical wavefront.

The directions of the modelled sound rays are chosen stochastically over either a sphere for isotropic sources or a cone for directional sources. If (for now) we ignore the effects of diffraction in the air, then the sound rays may be assumed to travel in straight lines. Each ray is traced until there is a 60dB drop in its energy (a factor of 1×10^6). The sound wavefronts arriving at a receiver fall into two categories: early and late reflections. Early reflections are distinct enough for the brain to distinguish them individually, while late reflections, on the other hand, appear as one long audible blur giving some indication of the size of the room. Most current systems model these two separately, using beam tracing, ray tracing or the image source method to calculate the early reflections, and use a function to calculate an approximation of the late reflection. Using particle tracing to model all the reflections results in a more accurate model for both.

Particles are traced until they intersect either a surface (such as a wall or chair) or until a sound particle intersects a receiver. When a particle collides with a surface, it is first attenuated by the collision, losing energy according to the surface material properties, sound particles are also attenuated by air over the distance they have travelled since their last collision. If the particle retains enough energy, it is then retraced in a new direction. The direction is chosen to be either specular reflection, as from a mirror; diffuse reflection, in a direction chosen uniformly over a hemisphere centred on the surface at the intersection point; or transmission, where the particle is refracted through the surface as light passes through glass.

RECEIVERS

Sound particles also must intersect with the receivers stored in the voxels throughout the environment to generate the impulse responses we need for the real-time stage. As we treat the sound source as a point in the environment, we need to model the receivers as objects with a volume, to enable particles to hit them. For the purposes of this research we model the receivers as head-sized spheres, with a diameter of 20 centimetres. The collisions with receiving cells are considerably simpler to compute since there is no need to calculate a reflection. The distance from the last intersection point is calculated and the air attenuation effect is subtracted. The resultant energy is stored at the receiver together with the time delay and a three-dimensional vector describing the incident angle of the particle on the receiver and the particle continues on its path.

As the results arrive at the receiving cells an impulse response is constructed describing the sound field as the centre of the receiver sphere, and approximating the sound field throughout the receiver's voxel. The impulse responses are a time-delay filter through which the played sound is convolved. Each impulse response contains four channels of information: the first is an amplitude describing the sum of all the amplitudes of the echoes for each time step; the remaining three form a three dimensional vector describing the average direction of all the echoes arriving per time step. The impulse responses use the same sample rate as the input and output signal, and must store four floating point values per sample, so for long impulse responses at high sample rates very large quantities of memory and storage space are required. To limit the number receivers that have to be rendered to and stored we cull all the receivers that will not be used during the playback stage, this includes all receivers that are less than 1m off the floor or more than 2m above the floor.

PLAYBACK

After the pre-rendering has been completed, we have accurately calculated the lighting as it varies across the surfaces of the environment and modelled the sound field at a set of regularly spaced points throughout the environment. All that remains now is to present this information interactively, allowing the user to explore the environment and experience the more realistic results.

STORING THE RESULTS

The surfaces within the scene have a colour associated with each of the patches, which describes the light reflected from that patch. This can easily be converted into information that can quickly be displayed by today's graphics accelerator cards. By storing the vertices of each grid patch, and determining the colour at each vertex by blending the colours of the adjacent patches, we generate a list of planar polygons, with a colour associated with each polygon's vertices. This information is simple for the graphics hardware to display, as it is one of the main functions for which the hardware is optimised. We can also apply textures to the accurately lit surfaces by modulating the incident energy on the patch by the texture colour. The sound information is stored as it is, one four-channel impulse response filter per receiver is saved; the only operation performed on these filters is to compress them by storing only those time steps in which echoes arrived.

REAL-TIME EXPLORATION

The graphics display is now straightforward; once the user's position and orientation have been determined the graphics hardware will display the correct graphical information automatically. However, the sound presentation is not so simple. As the user traverses the scene, the cell within which the user is positioned is determined from his/her position. The impulse response for the cell in which the user resides is then convolved with the clean input signal. It is important that the input signal, which will be presented to the listener, is clean and has no echo information of its own, otherwise the two sets of echoes will provide conflicting information. Suitable input signals will have been recorded in a studio, anechoic chamber or have been computer generated. Once the correct impulse response has been chosen and convolved with the input signal the result is a four-channel signal containing: the input signal; the echoes it has generated within the environment; and the directional information describing where the sound is coming from. Before we can present the sound information to the user, the direction coefficients, which describe the direction from which each echo is arriving, must be rotated to account for the orientation of the user within the scene. We then use a technique called Ambisonics developed by Gerzon (Gerzon 1977, Gerzon 1980), to accurately spatialise those results using an array of loudspeakers. Ambisonics requires that all the loudspeakers are all identical, and arranged in diametrical opposite pairs.

Results

In this research we considered a model of the underground Hypogeum, at Hal Salfieni, Malta, shown in Figure 3. In Figure 4 we show the difference between a simple scene rendered using only the graphics hardware capabilities such as direct lighting and the pre-rendered scene. In the pre-rendered scene the lighting effects appear far more realistic, with soft shadows, a caustic formed by the transparent sphere. In addition, as can be seen in the colour images on the CD-ROM, the colour of the room significantly changes when the inter-reflection between the yellow ceiling and the other walls is accounted for.
The effects of the sound rendering are also very significant. Figure 5 shows the different impulse responses generated by: direct sound only; only the first eight reflections considered; and sound particle tracing. The simplified models throw away huge quantities of information, which provides our brains with cues about size, geometry and materials used in the environment. The simplified models, by discarding large amounts of information, can provide the user with information contrary to that provided by the visual display that will reduce the perceived realism of the scene.

Figure 3 A view of the Hypogeum at Hal Salfieni, Malta.

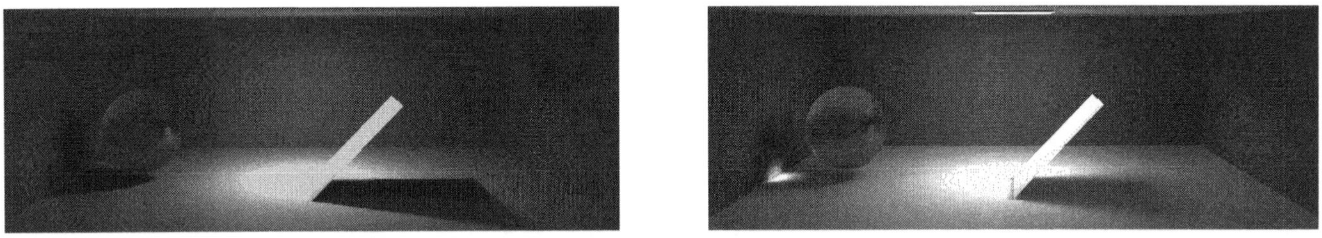

Figure 4 A comparison of direct lighting (l.) versus the pre-rendered solution (r.)

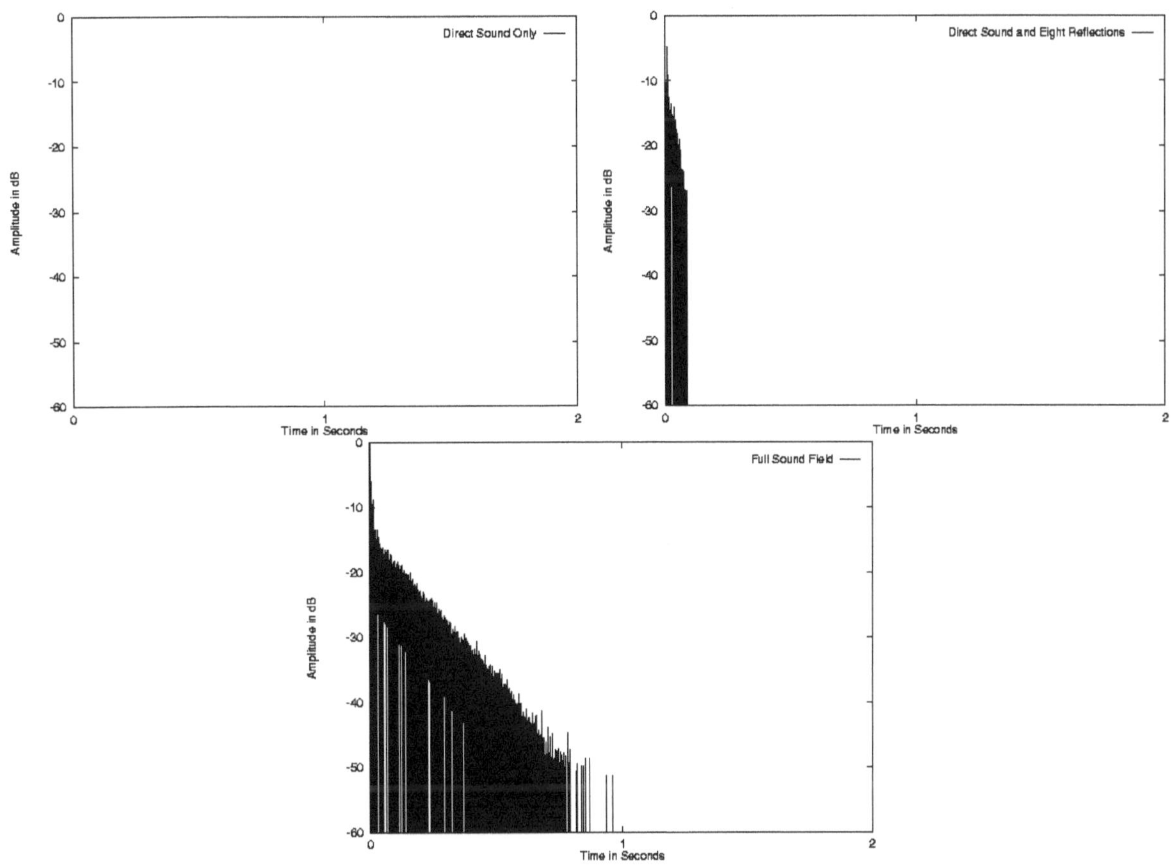

Figure 5 A comparison of direct sound, 8 reflections, and the full sound field

Hardware

The results we have presented were rendered on a Sun Ultra Sparc 1, with 160 megabytes of memory. Rendering took approximately 6 minutes per million rays traced from the sound source. The memory requirements for rendering were 1.4 megabytes per receiver, but these impulse responses were compressed to contain only non-zero samples for saving and during playback.

The playback section was performed on a Silicon Graphics Onyx, which drives an ADAT interface to the loudspeakers. Our loudspeaker array consisted of eight speakers arranged in a cubic configuration.

The results presented here have been first tested in a small acoustically damped environment, before being presented to multiple users in a larger, more realistic listening environment, which contains a large 120 degree conical section projection screen and no acoustic damping.

Conclusions

Realistic rendering is an important part of most virtual/augmented reality environments. While lighting simulations, such as the particle tracing method, can provide an acceptable approximation of the illumination within environments, the image they present to the user is restricted by the viewing frustum. We have presented a method for combining both graphics and sound in the display to provide multi-sensory feedback to the user. Sound information, in the form of impulse responses and speaker output, can improve the user's perception of the size and geometry of the whole environment.

Due to the high computational overheads of the accurate impulse response calculations we are unable to recalculate them in real time. This limits this approach to the accurate modelling of sound fields for static scenes where the geometry of the scene and the position of the sound source are unchanging. However, this does not exclude many archaeological reconstructions.

This research presents the advantages of using time-consuming physically accurate rendering techniques to model the complex behaviour of light and sound fields within a closed environment. The method presented here enables the results of a sound rendering to be stored in such a way that they can then be used during a real-time stage to provide a moving user with accurate sound information. By removing the rendering from the interactive stage, most of the advantages of physically accurate rendering are retained and the results can still be explored interactively.

Future work

The main disadvantage to the current sound modelling technique is the assumption made that the sound field remains constant throughout the voxel in which the receiver is centred. This assumption is true for very small voxels, but becomes increasingly inaccurate as the voxel size increases. Unfortunately due to the memory requirements for receivers we cannot make the voxels arbitrarily small. Research needs to be carried out into the effect on the listener of varying the size of the voxels.

The later reflections which arrive at the receiver after being reflected a large number of times are both quieter and less distinct from each other. This knowledge could be used to improve the realism without affecting the memory requirements by splitting the impulse responses into two sections, early and late. The early sections to which our ears are more sensitive could be modelled in small voxels to achieve a more accurate result, while the late reflections which vary less with position could be modelled on a larger grid—offsetting the memory increase required for the smaller early grid.

Acknowledgements

We would like to thank David Creasey for his valuable input to this project, and Erik Reinhard for his useful comments.

References Cited

AMES, A., NADEAU, D., MORELAND, J., 1997, "VRML 2.0 Sourcebook, Second Edition" New York: John Wiley & Sons.

BORISH, J., 1984, "Extension of the Image Model to Arbitrary Polyhedra" *Journal of the Acoustical Society of America,* vol. 75 (6), pp. 1827-1836.

DANCE, S., SHIELD, B., 1997, "The Complete Image-Source Method for the Prediction of Sound Distribution In Non-Diffuse Enclosed Spaces" *Journal of Sound and Vibration*, vol. 201 (4), pp. 473-489.

FUNKHOUSER, T., CARLBOM, I., ELKO, G., PINGALI, G., SONDHI, M., WEST, J., 1998, "A Beam Tracing Approach to Acoustic Modelling for Interactive Virtual Environments" *Computer Graphics (ACM SIGGRAPH '98 Proceedings),* pp. 21-32.

GERZON, M. A., 1977, "Design of Ambisonic Decoders for Multispeaker Surround Sound." *Audio Engineering Society 58th Convention*, NRDC/FCC 6.

GERZON, M. A., 1980, "Practical Periphony: The Reproduction of Full-Sphere Sound" *Audio Engineering Society 65th Convention*, Preprint No. 1571 (A6).

GREENBURG, D. P., COHEN, M. F., TORRANCE, K., 1986, "Radiosity: A Method For Computing Global Illumination.", *Visual Computer*, vol. 2 (5), pp. 291-297.

GREGER, G., SHIRLEY, P., HUBBARD, M., GREENBERG, D., 1998, "The Irradiance Volume" *IEEE Computer Graphics and Applications*, vol. 18 (2), pp. 32-43.

HEINZ, R., 1993, "Binaural Room Simulation Based on an Image Source Model with Addition of Statistical Methods to Include the Diffuse Sound Scattering of Walls and to Predict the Reverberant Tail", *Applied Acoustics* vol. 38, pp. 148-159.

KLEINER, M., DÄLENBACK, B.-I., SVENSSON, P., 1993, "Auralization - An Overview", *Journal of the Audio Engineering Society* vol. 41 (11), pp. 861-875.

KROKSTAD, A., STRØM, S., SØRSDAL, S., 1968, "Calculating the Acoustical Room Response by the Use of a Ray Tracing Technique", *Journal of Sound and Vibration*, vol. 8 (1), pp. 118-125.

KULOWSKI, A., 1985, "Algorithmic Representation of the Ray Tracing Technique", *Applied Acoustics*, vol. 18, pp. 449-469.

KUTTRUFF, H., 1979, "Room Acoustics, Second Edition", New York: Applied Science Publishers.

LEHNERT, H., BLAUERT, J., 1992, "Principles of Binaural Room Simulation", *Applied Acoustics* vol. 36, pp. 259-291.

MØLLER, H., 1992, "Fundamentals of Binaural Technology", *Applied Acoustics* vol. 36, pp. 171-218.

NAYLOR, G., 1992, " Treatment of Early and Late Reflections in a Hybrid Computer Model for Room Acoustics", *Proceedings of the 124th Acoustical Society of America meeting.*

PATTANAIK, S., MULDER, S., 1992, "Computation of Global Illumination by Monte-Carlo Simulation of the Particle Light", *Proceedings of 3rd Eurographics Workshop on Rendering*, pp. 71-83.

PATTANAIK, S., 1993, "Computational Methods for Global Illuminations and Visualisation of Complex 3D Environments", *PhD Thesis*, Birla Institute of Technology and Science, Pilami, India.

SHI, J., ZHANG, A., ENCARNAÇÃO, J., GÖBEL, M., 1993, "A Modified Radiosity Algorithm for Integrated Visual and Auditory Rendering", *Computers & Graphics*, vol. 17 (6), pp. 633-642.

WHITTED, T., 1980, "An improved illumination model for shaded display", *Communications of the ACM*, vol. 23 (6), pp. 343-349

COMPUTER SIMULATION OF STONEHENGE

Emília Pásztor
Dunaferr Humán Intézet, Dunaujvaros, Hungary
pasztor@altavista.net
Ákos Juhász
School of Architecture Technical University of Budapest, Budapest, Hungary
Miklós Dombi
Dpi Design, Budapest, Hungary
Curt Roslund
Department of Astronomy Gothenburg University, Gothenburg, Sweden

Virtual Reality

Architects are today served by large-capacity computers that can visualise complex building structures that otherwise would have been difficult to assess prior to construction. Programs for this purpose are called *Computer Aided Design,* or for short CAD, programs. They have revolutionised the work in the drawing office, as it is practically impossible to achieve the same result in a reasonably short time with traditional drawing methods.

Scientists have increasingly begun to exploit the possibilities that CAD programs offer. Archaeologists have, from established ground plans of buildings and from excavated artifacts found in them, built up whole settlements to be seen in three dimensions on the computer screen (Forte *et al.* 1977). Moreover, the passage of time can be incorporated to show how the settlements were transformed, how buildings decayed to be replaced by new ones and how the surroundings were affected by changing population levels and the adoption of new farming methods.

Such applications are well-suited for exhibitions and demonstrations at museums and for shows on film and television. At the same time, they might be highly informative as well as entertaining. For scientists, the greatest potential for CAD programs, however, lies not so much in their ability to simulate conceivable events as in the virtual reality they can produce. The strength of virtual tools is their efficiency in resolving scientific questions. New theories about buildings can swiftly and accurately be verified by CAD programs. This paper reports on such an investigation of the famous prehistoric monument Stonehenge, 120 kilometres west of London.

Light and Shadow Effects

The part of Stonehenge chosen for our study lends itself amiably to such a project. The geometry of the studied structure is very simple and straightforward. It consists of one set of huge blocks of stones standing along a circle and another set along a horseshoelike curve. Secondly, the whole structure seems to be orientated towards the point on the horizon where the summer solstice sun rises (Hawkins 1966, Hoyle 1972: 19-54), which gives it a certain prominence among megalithic monuments. Our question is whether the light of the rising sun on this particular occasion interacts with the building in a way that could have been used as an architectural element to enhance proceedings taking place inside it.

The use of sunlight to highlight the importance of a building has been both a natural and a self-evident choice for architects of all times. The Pantheon in Rome from the second century AD lets a beam of sunlight enter a central opening in the roof of its dome to travel along a symbolic path whose position on the inside of the rotunda varies with the seasons of the year (Licht 1968). Sunlight through windows in the basilica San Miniato al Monte in Florence from the eleventh century illuminates important symbols inside the church (Gettings 1987). The interaction of sunlight with the church interior is still a vital source of inspiration for contemporary artists like the Japanese architect Tadao Ando with his Church of the Light in Osaka in Japan (Jodidio 1977: 84-89) and the Finnish architect Juha Leiviskä with his Männistö Church in Kuopio in Finland (MacKeith 1944: 84-89), to mention only two famous examples.

Stonhenge: An Engineering Marvel

Stonehenge's history goes far back in time, and the complex has gone through several building stages. The structure that concerns us here emerged around 2500 BC (Allen *et al.* 1995: 8). Its ruined remains embody what we generally associate with Stonehenge today. It was during this building phase that thirty huge sandstone blocks of roughly identical size and shape were set up around a circle 31m wide. Each stone is about 4m tall, 2m wide, 1m thick and weighs around 25 tons. This kind of stone is called sarsen stone and must have been brought from its nearest source, Marlborough Downs, 30km to the north of Stonehenge. The stones were linked together by an unbroken ring of stone lintels, weighing 6 tons each 4.5m up in the air, creating a space architecturally cut off fom the surrounding world but open to the sky.

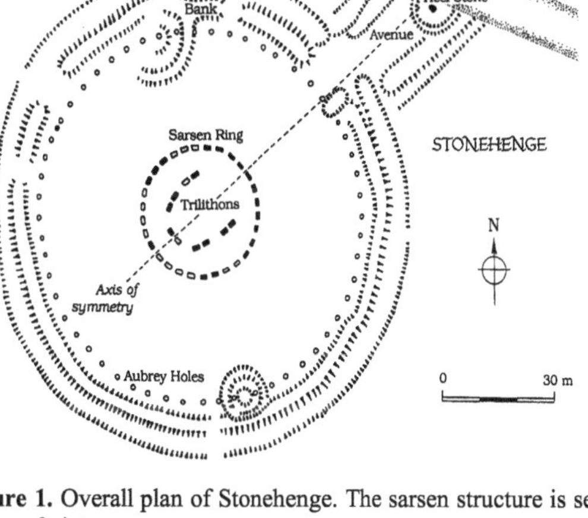

Figure 1. Overall plan of Stonehenge. The sarsen structure is seen in the centre of picture.

Inside this ring of stones, which is called the Sarsen Circle, five sarsen trilithons stand along a horseshoelike curve with its opening towards the northeast and the rising point of the summer solstice sun. A trilithon consists of two stones standing close together and crowned by a stone lintel. The central trilithon is the tallest with a height of 7.9m including its lintel and is called the Great Trilithon. The height of the other trilithons decreases towards the opening of the horseshoe, the outer pair measuring only 6m. The Trilithon Horseshoe is an enigmatic structure, breaking up the conformity of the Sarsen Circle and lessening its monotonous appearance.

In order to simplify the computer work in this study of shape and distribution of locations, the stones were assigned an ideal size based on published measurements of stones still standing. The stones were treated as square blocks, as their original shape is unknown and minor deviations in their outline are less important than the overall geometry of the monument.

Computer Simulations

ArchiCAD software was chosen for modelling Stonehenge from different directions and distances. This computer tool was developed by the Hungarian company Graphisoft Ltd. It is today one of the most popular CAD programs among architects all over the world.

In order to follow the light and shadow effects on Stonehenge, the ArchiCAD software was combined with the American-made 3DS MAX program which has a built-in sun engine. The latter is able to produce changes in the sun's altitude and azimuth during the day in accordance with the observer's geographical location and the season of the year. It also allows the speed of the sun in its daily path accross the sky to be adjusted to suit different goals. Another useful feature of 3DS MAX is that it can compute the colour and brightness of a surface inclined to a light source, which in this case is the sun.

An advantage of the 3DS MAX software is that any desired camera path can be chosen. Some extreme camera paths were used in this investigation in order to study the behaviour of the motion of the sun and its shadow on particular stones. The camera moves smoothly along its designated path and its speed can be adjusted at key positions. The focal length of the camera can be altered to suit different scenarios.

By recording a series of pictures on video tape, one gets a film sequence greatly facilitating the study of progress of particular light and shadow effects. In our case, a Beta tape was used. It has the benefit of being able to receive one picture after the other by inserting a special video card that transforms the computer signal to one that the video tape is able to accept.

Computer Results

Our computer studies dealt only with the light and shadow effects generated by the rising summer solstice sun. They showed that the first rays would have entered the Sarsen Circle by proceeding forward along the axis of symmetry of the Trilithon Horseshoe, penetrating the narrow confine between the uprights of the Great Trilithon and exiting the Sarsen Circle through an opening opposite its entrance. The passage of this first light would have been an exclusive spectacle with strong symbolic implications (Burl 1994: 91-92).

Figure 2. Computer results of the VR illuminated model

Our computer studies also revealed that the part of the Great Trilithon that reaches above the Sarsen Circle would have functioned like a gigantic reflector that cast the rays from the rising sun down into the space of the Trilithon Horsehoe. The sarsen stone is normally quite a dark stone, but lit from the front, it changes into a brightly reflective surface. The light that filled the Horseshoe alcove would have stood out in sharp contrast to the surrounding darkness inside the Sarsen Circle, although the openings between the stones in the Sarsen Circle that face the morning sun would have been flooded with light like the windows of a Gothic cathedral.

The light that falls on the lower parts of the trilithons comes from the same openings in the Sarsen Circle. The openings produce parallel vertical bands of light and shadows like the ribbons of light one sees behind a picket fence. This light pattern moves from the left to the right across the trilithons for an observer with his back towards the sun, illuminating one stone after the other. Light that falls on the stones in the middle pair of trilithons strikes their surfaces at a shallow angle that might temporarily have brought forth faint symbols carved into the stones. A bronze dagger and several flanged bronze axes can still be seen on the left-hand trilithon in appropriate light.

Further Prospects

Our study was in its first stage limited to the sunrise under clear skies at summer solstice, but a suitable computer program can in addition take into account effects of contrasting weather conditions on the appearance of Stonehenge. The study can also be extended to include other dates of astronomical interest.

By changing step-by-step the layout and the dimensions of Stonehenge, the number of stones, their shape and size, the computer can help us to evaluate how close the designers of Stonehenge came to the optimum effect of light and shadows. Stonehenge is unique as a stone structure, but the information gained from computer simulations of its interaction with light might assist us in making out the function and design of the timber roundhouses that once stood inside other henges like Durington Walls, Marden, Mount Pleasant, Woodhenge (Wainwright 1989) and Stanton Drew (Aveling 1997: 232-233) and whose existence we only know from circles of postholes in the ground. The ground plans of these buildings show a certain resemblance to that of Stonehenge, but the suggestion that the roundhouses might have had a conical roofs (Pigott 1939; Musson 1971) cannot be brought into accord with the light and shadow play observed at Stonehenge.

References Cited

ALLEN, M.J. and BAYLISS, A., 1995. "Radiocarbon dates", in R.M.J. CLEAL. K.E. WALKER, and R. MONTAGUE (eds.), *Stonehenge in its landscape*: 6-8. London: English Heritage.

AVELING, E., 1997. "Magnetic trace of a giant henge." *Nature* vol. 390, pp. 232-233.

BURL, A., 1994. "Stonehenge: Slaughter, Sacrifice and Sunshine." *Wiltshire Archaeological and Natural History Magazine* vol. 87, pp. 85-95.

FORTE, M. & SILIOTTI, A., 1997. *Virtual Archaeology*. London: Thames and Hudson.

GETTINGS, F., 1987. *The Secret Zodiac*. London: Routledge & Kegan Paul.

HAWKINS, G.S., 1966. *Sonehenge Decoded*. London: Souvenir Press.

HOYLE, F., 1972. *From Stonehenge to Modern Cosmology*. San Francisco: W.H. Freeman.

JODIDIO, P., 1997. *Tadao Ando*. Köln: Benedikt Taschen Verlag.

LICHT, K. de F., 1968. "The rotunda in Rome. A study of Hadrian's Pantheon" *Jutland Archaeological Society Publications* vol.8.

MACKEITH, P., 1994. "Instrument of Light." *Architectural Review* No. 1168.

MUSSON, C., 1971. "A study of possible building forms at Durrington Walls, Woodhenge and the Sanctuary", in G.J. WAINWRIGHT and I.H. LONGWORTH (eds.), *Durington Walls: Excavations, 1966-8*. London: Society of Antiquarries.

PIGOTT, S., 1939. "Timber circles: a re-examination." *Archaeological Journal* vol. 96. pp. 193-222.

WAINWRIGHT, G., 1989.*The Henge Monuments*. London: Thames and Hudson.

Virtual Reality at the Neolithic Monument Complex of Thornborough, North Yorkshire

Glyn Goodrick and Jan Harding
Department of Archaeology, University of Newcastle, UK
G.T.Goodrick@newcastle.ac.uk

Introduction

While virtual reality has been in use since the 1960s (Sutherland 1965), and employed within archaeology as a presentation tool since the early '90s, its acceptance as a mechanism for research is still little evident in current archaeological practice. This is despite the many distinct opportunities that such an approach can provide (Gillings & Goodrick 1996). Its limited impact on research practices can perhaps be attributed to two common misconceptions, which themselves are manifestations of the close link that has emerged between a public awareness of this tool and those larger virtual reality projects undertaken by computing companies: for it is assumed that the development of virtual reality models requires not only specialist skills but also large budgets. In presenting this paper, however, it will be demonstrated how a particular project, at the Neolithic monument complex of Thornborough in North Yorkshire, is employing virtual reality as an integrated part of its research programme. The VRML model presented here was developed primarily as a 'proof of concept' to illustrate that virtual reality techniques can be applied to specific archaeological questions with meaningful results, in this case to evaluate whether the site was orientated towards stellar constellations. This case study, which is itself only the starting point for further research based upon the monument complex, demonstrates how these techniques are not beyond the means of archaeologists, requiring neither specialist knowledge nor unlimited budgets.

An Archaeological Problem

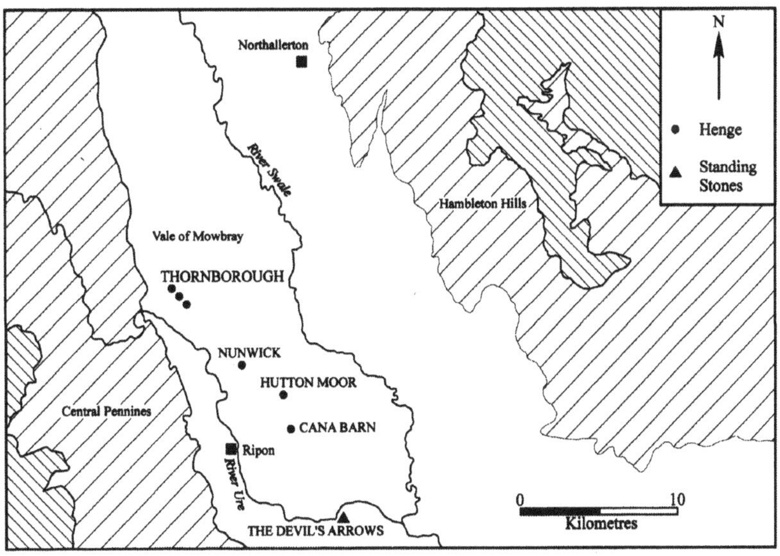

Figure 1. Location of Thornborough monument complex.

The Neolithic monument complex of Thornborough, located in the low-lying Vale of Mowbray near the eastern edge of the central Pennines (Fig. 1), presents a specific problem which can only be fully addressed by the use of virtual reality and related visualisation techniques. This remarkable collection of sites—which has recently been the focus for extensive excavation and surface collection (Harding 1998)—includes three massive, almost identical and equally spaced henge monuments, whose double entrances all share exactly the same north-west/south-east alignment (Fig. 2). The regularity of these sites, and their relationship with one another, appears to demonstrate that there was a unity of purpose or level of preconceived intention behind the development of the complex, an observation which is reiterated by the close spatial integration of other monuments: aerial photography indicates that the central henge is directly superimposed upon a cursus (Thomas 1955; Vatcher 1960), while a double pit alignment is located alongside the southern henge (St. Joseph 1977). There is, in other words, an apparently planned layout to much of the complex. The study of this ceremonial centre must therefore attempt to identify the criteria which determined the siting of these impressive monuments across the landscape.

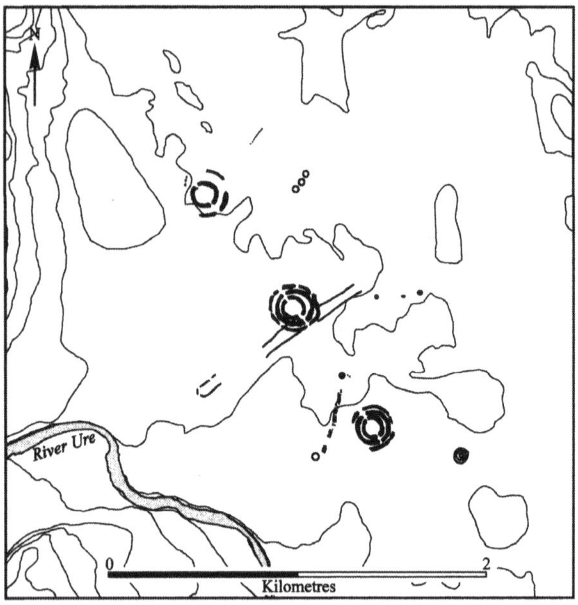

Figure 2. Thornborough monument complex

It has been widely documented that monumental complexes, which are usually dedicated to the celebration or commemoration of supernatural beliefs, generally possess meaningful orientations (Carmichael et al 1994). This element of spatial planning is part of the process by which cognitive structures, or the ideal concepts and codes by which society recognises itself, are materialised. It is often the case that these alignments are directed at significant and highly visible topographic features which form part of a society's symbolic universe, and a number of archaeological studies have explored the possible importance of this during the Neolithic (e.g., Tilley 1994). A preliminary examination of the Thornborough complex and its surrounding landscape did not suggest, however, that any of these monuments were orientated according to the surrounding topography (Harding *in press*; pace Richards 1996). It therefore seems likely that the layout of this complex was principally determined by other factors. Such a conclusion is of considerable interest for there is substantial evidence that many of the most complex and impressive monumental centres through the ages were orientated according to observed astronomical phenomena (Aveni 1997; Krupp 1997). The cyclical events which are so integral to this imposing and mystical domain often actually constitute the very essence of religious belief. The significance of astronomical alignments has certainly been demonstrated for the Neolithic (Ruggles 1984; 1996), but unlike well known examples such as Stonehenge or Newgrange, the complex at Thornborough does not appear to reify either solar or lunar events. Hence, it was necessary to evaluate whether this site was orientated towards stellar constellations, many of which are known to have been so important to other cultures. This could only be achieved with the use of virtual reality or related visualisation techniques.

The specific objective of the virtual reality element of the Thornborough project is to develop a model of the monument complex and the surrounding landscape. A representation of the contemporary night sky could then be draped over the model. It was decided that in order to best refine the necessary techniques, a specific site, other than the alignment of three henges, should be selected as a case study. The monument chosen was the impressive double pit alignment, next to the southern henge, which extends for 350m on a north-east/south-west orientation (St. Joseph 1977; Harding 1998, fig.4, 32 & 34). The site, which is visible on aerial photographs, is likely to have been a generally contemporary element of the monument complex. It was anticipated that a simplified model of this double row of pits, with its night sky drape, would allow the archaeologist to inhabit a virtual world, thereby enabling the interactive investigation of any possibly significant alignments between the monument, the surrounding landscape and stellar constellations in the night sky. The aim was not to produce a highly detailed photo-realistic model as this would contribute little to the archaeologist's understanding of the site, while adding considerably to the cost, construction time and hardware requirements of the virtual reality model. On the contrary, efforts were made to ensure that its hyper-real character were clearly exaggerated.

Creating the Model

The topographical data relating to the monument complex had already been collected for GIS analysis and was available within the ARC/INFO format for re-use in the virtual reality model. This data was exported as a 50m grid of elevation points and modified by hand within a text-editing package to produce a VRML ElevationGrid. This height field forms the basis for the virtual reality model. It recreates the gentle slope of the fluvio-glacial terraces across which the double pit alignment is located and the elevated ridge, immediately to the west of the monument, which is the most immediately striking topographic feature in a relatively flat landscape.

There had been small-scale excavation at the double pit alignment prior to the development of the model. This demonstrated that the pits originally held timber uprights (Harding 1998, 32 & 34). These posts were about 0.5m in diameter, and by employing the post hole depth/post height ratio of 1:3.5, it was calculated that they originally stood at least 1.8m above the ground surface. Additional information was provided by aerial photography which indicates noticeable variations along the length of the monument. The central and northern sections of the avenue included larger pits and it was assumed that these held larger timber uprights, which were estimated to be 0.7m in diameter and 2m in height above the ground surface. The aerial photographs clearly illustrate nine pairs of closely-set trenches at the northern terminal end of the monument, which are perhaps best interpreted as the settings for short fence lines. Comparisons with excavations elsewhere at Thornborough led to the supposition that these were 0.3m wide with an above ground height of 1.5m. Also evident on the aerial photographs was a pair of large pits, located quite some distance from the northern terminal of the alignment. It was decided to include these in the model. They were interpreted to have held uprights 0.7m in diameter and 2m high.

The evidence from excavation and aerial photography provided valuable but only limited data about the possible appearance of this monument. It was accordingly decided that the virtual reality model should be kept as simple as possible. The above calculations of post size, which were employed within the model, represent very conservative estimates for the dimensions of these timber uprights. As the precise nature of the various post settings along its entire length could not be fully postulated, it was decided that the virtual reality model should not represent any specific interpretation of these features but rather illustrate them as primitive archetypes or simple representations of timber uprights. The posts were therefore simplistic in shape and garishly coloured so as to emphasise their abstraction. The size variations noted above were distinguished by the use of different colours and the northern terminal feature is shown as a series of simple rectangular blocks. The location of each post was established by photo-rectification within AutoCAD. The pits themselves were clearly visible on the aerial photographs, and while the number of control points for rectification was limited, it was believed that the relatively flat landscape would limit the level of error. This was certainly borne out by corroborative evidence obtained during subsequent excavation.

The unique and most challenging component in the construction of the virtual reality model was the representation of the night sky during the Neolithic. A number of software packages exist which enable the production of prehistoric star maps. SkyMap Version 3.1 was chosen for the project on account of being widely regarded as the most accurate version available. In order to generate the overhead drape it was initially necessary to produce a single image within SkyMap which represents the night sky as seen from the specific location of the double pit alignment at a given time, date and year. Before this image could be incorporated within the virtual reality model it had to be flipped to represent the sky as viewed looking down from the heavens rather than up from the earth's surface. This corrects its east-west inversion. It was originally anticipated that this image could then be simply mapped on to the VRML model using the VRML background node. This proved, however, to be impossible.

The projection used to map the night sky by software packages such as SkyMap turned out to be incompatible with the projection used to map textures on to the VRML background node. This resulted in vertical deformation close to the horizon and the zenith. Stars that should have appeared close to the horizon were too high, and conversely, stars close to the zenith were too low. A quick fix was employed to correct this problem. The VRML background node was not used, and instead, it was necessary to construct a geo-dome, in the form of a vertically compressed hemisphere, over the landscape, onto which the star map was draped. Its precise shape was calculated to correct to the projection used (Fig.3). To minimise perspective errors it was important that the scale of the geo-dome was many magnitudes greater than that of the landscape, and that movement within the virtual environment is limited to an area at the very centre of the geo-dome. As the size of the dome relative to the landscape is limited by the capability of VRML browsers, this is not the ideal solution to the problem: perspective errors could still occur should it become necessary to explore a larger geographic area. A performance penalty is also paid for the utilisation of this technique. The geo-dome consists of only a limited number of polygons, the basic building unit of VRML models, and it may therefore be assumed to have had little effect on performance. Nevertheless, VRML browsers are inefficient at texture mapping very large objects, and the resulting VRML world runs noticeably slower than the original model utilising the background node.

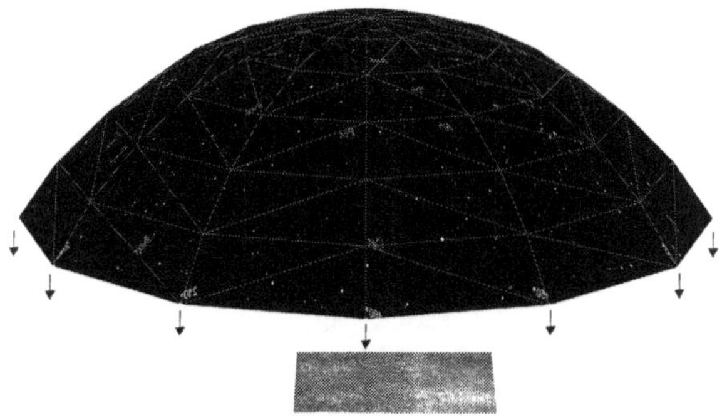

Figure 3. Draping the star map over the geo-dome enclosing the landscape model.

An additional element was added to the model. In order to provide a sense of scale it was felt that a human figure should be represented within the landscape. A 3D-Studio model of a human female was converted into a VRML format and placed within the scene (Fig.4). This figure consists of a large number of polygons and, as such, again slows down the VRML model. A simpler solution to this problem would have been to utilise an image of a figure on a single VRML billboard node. Unfortunately, at the time that the model was constructed the billboard node was implemented differently by various VRML browsers. This was not therefore considered to have been a valid alternative.

It was then finally necessary to combine these various elements within a single VRML model. This was undertaken manually within a text-editing package. However, any future projects of a similar nature could now probably be completed with one of the newer VRML editing packages or the improved export capabilities of conventional three-dimensional modelling packages such as 3D-Studio.

Interpreting the Model

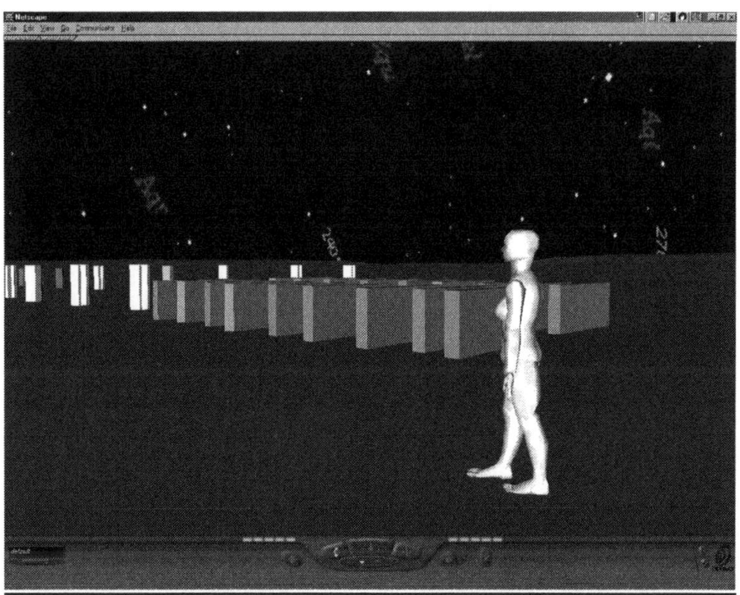

Figure 4. Exploring the virtual timber avenue

To determine if the double timber avenue was of astronomical significance it was necessary to identify whether it was orientated towards any noticeable stellar constellations or particularly bright stars. The VRML model demonstrated that the site did not actually possess a common axis, but rather, was characterised by some discernible shifts in its course. There were also significant variations in the width of the monument. The double row of posts did not therefore embody a single alignment which could be linked with a noticeable feature of the night sky. However, the model also demonstrated that the western line of timber uprights tapered markedly outwards at the northern end of the monument to create a wide opening next to the pair of nine closely-set fence lines. If what appears to be a formal entrance is taken to indicate the possible importance of these unusual settings then it is of some interest that the layout of the latter all shared the same orientation. Indeed, their very appearance suggests that they could have quite conceivably acted as 'sight-lines'. It should also be noted that the two posts, located some distance from the northern terminal, may also possess a significant alignment.

It was obviously insufficient to simply ascertain if these various features were orientated towards specific stars at any point in their nightly procession. Instead, it was essential to question whether there was any such correlation during a particular 'celestial event' in this evening cycle. Noticeable examples of such events would include the rising and setting of constellations above and below the horizon. Similarly, the procession of stars across the night sky varies enormously from year to year. It was therefore necessary to establish a chronological framework for investigating the possible astronomical alignment of this monument. While little dating evidence was produced by the small-scale excavation of the site, it could be reasonably concluded that the double timber avenue, as an integral part of the monument complex, dated to between the end of the early Neolithic and the beginning of the early Bronze Age (3100-2100 BC).

It was discovered that the northern terminal fence lines and the two outlying posts were both aligned towards the rising of the same stellar constellation at the beginning and end of the established chronological framework for this site. The pair of posts to the north of the avenue would, at around 3000 BC, be orientated towards the three stars of Orion's Belt, one of the most distinguishable of constellations, as it rose above the horizon and began its nightly track across the southern hemisphere sky. An identical correlation, dating to around 2200 BC, was identified for the closely set fence lines. It may obviously be argued that both associations are meaningless given that it is highly unlikely that the monument was in use for the 800 years which separate these dates. It should be remembered, however, that there is no reason to assume that the two outlying posts were actually contemporary with the avenue. Their siting some 87m to the north, near to the shared axis of the three henges, suggest that they were not indeed integral to this site. It is therefore possible that early in the development of the monument complex these two uprights were erected to signpost the rising of Orion's Belt above the horizon. That this should be considered a deliberate and meaningful act is certainly reiterated by a triple-ditched round barrow which occurs on a slight ridge to the south-east of these timber uprights (Fig. 2). This monument lies on exactly the same orientation, and surprisingly, its ploughed ditch fill has produced pottery which fits comfortably with a date of 3000 BC. In contrast, each end of the timber avenue is known to have been associated with a single-ditch round barrow and the excavation of the northernmost example produced early Bronze Age grave goods (Lukis 1870). It is therefore possible that this alignment was indeed constructed later in the development of the monument complex, but again the rising of Orion's Belt was sited upon as a particularly important celestial event.

The Limitations of the Model

It can be concluded that the VRML model achieved its specific objectives. It is now possible for the archaeologist to inhabit a virtual representation of the Thornborough landscape, to wander through and around the double post alignment, and observe the possible astronomical importance of some of its features. This process provides a new insight into the use and meaning of this monument. Yet, while the VRML model has proven extremely valuable as both an experiential and analytical tool it does possess a number of important limitations:

- The archaeological interpretation of the double timber avenue's original appearance was based on limited evidence. The size of the uprights in the present model were determined from the results of small-scale excavation, while their location was fixed according to the digitised aerial photographs. The coarseness of this data could mask significant variations along the length of the monument.
- It is evident that the geo-dome is an inefficient way to represent the night sky.
- No tree line is represented within the current model although this would clearly affect the perceived horizon.
- To enhance the topographical value of the model a far larger area of landscape will need to be incorporated, possibly at a lower resolution so as to illustrate the true horizon.
- At present the model is non-interactive. In order to change the time, day, date or year represented by the night sky it is necessary to render a new image within SkyMap, to flip this image within an image editing package, to edit the VRML file to reference this new image, and finally to reload the VRML file within the browser. This cannot be undertaken without losing the observer's position within the model.

Further Work on the Model

These limitations obviously render the application of the VRML model less effective than is desirable. As a result, these problems will constitute the focus for future work on the model:

- A programme of excavation, along the entire length of the double timber avenue, has now begun. This will result in detailed evidence as to the location and estimated size of each individual upright. The data will be employed to recreate the virtual reality model of the monument.
- These improvements will involve the technological development of a simple software package to re-map the images produced in the astronomical mapping programme so as to enable them to be used directly within the VRML background node. This will result in the enhanced performance of the VRML model and its greater accuracy as the size of the landscape model increases.
- The representation of tree lines will be undertaken by the development of a simple script, based on parameters such as altitude and slope, which will generate random billboard nodes as trees. This will enable the model to be investigated with various degrees of tree cover, and their species or stages of development could also be altered. As an interim measure billboard nodes can be placed manually within the model. While this achieves the desired results, it is labour-intensive to both construct and adapt.
- Three different approaches will be employed to overcome

the need for a larger landscape model. The United States Geographic Survey Data has been modified to provide a very large-scale backdrop to the study area. But with a single data point every kilometre this can only provide a crude representation of the distant landscape. It will therefore be necessary to fill in the near-distant landscape by acquiring additional information, either in the form of pre-existing digital data or by digitised analogue data. A simplified horizon will in the meanwhile be provided by the use of panoramic photographic techniques. This will consist of photographs taken from locations within the site which are then pasted together to form a single panoramic image. By using a methodology similar to that employed for the night sky, the panorama will be wrapped around the cylinder encompassing the landscape but within the geo-dome. The sky in these photographs will be rendered transparent, thereby making the background image of the night sky visible. This will provide a quick fix to the problem but will not enable the accurate modification of tree lines.

- The problem of interactivity is far harder to resolve. Two possible alternatives have been identified. Firstly, a Java/Java Script interface could be developed to enable the linking of the virtual environment directly to a suitable astronomical mapping programme. This would add a level of interactivity by which it would be possible to automatically update the night sky from within the VRML browser. This solution would inevitably only run on a machine specifically set-up for this purpose, and therefore be unsuitable for other projects which involved a number of individuals. A second and far more ambitious option would be to write at Java programme to map the night sky, and implement this programme as a *proto* within the VRML model. This would remove the requirement for all users of the VRML model to have standard software set-up on their viewing platform, and could be run under most operating systems. If such an approach were implemented the controls for time and date could be provided as a head-up display (HUD) within the VRML model. The user would be able to simply type the relevant information into text fields, which would be constantly available on the screen, resulting in the night sky either updating instantly or possibly animating between the previous and selected settings. The great advantage of this approach is that once such a proto has been developed it could be quickly and simply implemented within any VRML model.
- The structural elements of the model will also be made interactive by the addition of a further head-up display. This will enable the viewer to modify the size or colour of various structural elements in the model, such as the timber posts of the alignment, without actually leaving the virtual environment.

These improvements will significantly enhance the accuracy and usefulness of the model. It is believed that collectively these developments will enable archaeologists with little or no training in virtual reality to modify and interact with what they can see on the screen. This could be of enormous benefit as it would allow more spontaneous 'what if' investigations to be made of the model.

The Archaeological Implications of the Model

The technology of virtual reality has often appeared marginal to research agendas within archaeology. Its impact beyond being widely accepted as an effective presentational tool has unfortunately been limited. Yet, the possibilities of virtual reality should be seen to complement those recent developments within theoretical archaeology which have emphasised the need for a phenomenological approach to the evidence of the past (eg. Thomas 1996; Tilley 1994). Part of the problem with the latter has been the difficulty of equating the archaeological perception of sites—consisting of denuded earthworks, aerial photographs, two-dimensional plots and excavation records—with the comprehension of those who originally congregated at these sites. However, the virtual world, by integrating these data-sets into a three-dimensional reality, actually provides an ideal framework for exploring the human body's experience of particular spatial configurations, and as this paper demonstrates, to go even further and investigate the symbolic or cognitive universe within which agency is embedded. Such an agenda was certainly integral to the development of this particular VRML model, and it is believed that the model provided an insight which was hitherto simply not possible. But if the results highlight the significance of Orion's Belt—both as a determining factor in the unusual layout of the monument complex at Thornborough and as a set of codes or concepts which characterised ritual activity at these sites—then these are observations which will be more fully explored by the future expansion of the virtual reality model to include the alignment of three henges. In such a way, the programme of research for the Thornborough complex enjoys a reciprocal and productive relationship between more conventional means of archaeological investigation and this relatively new technology.

References Cited

AVENI, A 1997 *Stairways to the Stars: skywatching in three great ancient cultures*, Cassell Publishers Ltd: London.

CARMICHAEL, D L et al (eds) 1994 *Sacred Sites, Sacred Places*, Routledge (One World Archaeology 23): London, 89-98.

GILLINGS, M AND GOODRICK, G.T 1996 Sensuous and reflexive GIS: exploring visualisation and VRML *Internet Archaeology* 1 (http://intarch.ac.uk/journal/issue1/gillings_index.html).

HARDING, J 1998 'Recent fieldwork at the Neolithic monument complex of Thornborough, North Yorkshire', *Northern Archaeology* 15/16, 27-38.

HARDING, J in press 'Ceremonial centres, cosmology and pilgrimage: the monument complex of Thornborough, North Yorkshire', In Ritchie, A (ed) *Neolithic Orkney in its European Context,* McDonald Institute Monograph Series: Cambridge.

KRUPP, E C 1997 *Skywatchers, Shamans and Kings: astronomy and the archaeology of power*, John Wiley & Sons: New York.

LUKIS, W C 1870 'On the flint implements and tumuli of the neighbourhood of Wath', *The Yorkshire Archaeological Journal* 1, 116-21.

RICHARDS, C 1996 'Henges and water: towards an elemental understanding of monumentality and landscape in late Neolithic Britain', *Journal of Material Culture* 1(3), 313-36.

RUGGLES, C L N 1984 *Megalithic Astronomy*, British Archaeological Reports (British Series) 123: Oxford.

RUGGLES, C L N 1996 'Archaeoastronomy in Europe', In Walker, C (ed) *Astronomy before the telescope*, British Museum Press: London, 15-27.

ST. JOSEPH, J K 1977 'Aerial reconnaissance: recent results, 43', *Antiquity* 51, 143-5.

SUTHERLAND, I 1965 The Ultimate Display Information Processing, Proceedings of the IFIP Congress 65, 2, New York

THOMAS, J 1966 *Time, Culture and Identity: an interpretive archaeology*, Routledge: London.

THOMAS, N 1955 'The Thornborough Circles, near Ripon, North Riding', *Yorkshire Archaeological Journal* 38, 425-45.

TILLEY, C 1994 *A Phenomenology of Landscape: Places, Paths and Monuments*, Berg: Oxford.

VATCHER, F 1960 'Thornborough cursus, Yorks', *Yorkshire Archaeological Journal* 40(158), 169-82.

FORM AND FABRIC, THE REAL AND THE VIRTUAL: ROMAN ECONOMY-RELATED GEOMETRICAL MASS CONSTRAINTS IN DRESSEL'S TABLE OF AMPHORA FORMS

Cornelius Steckner

Römisch-Germanisch Zentral Museum, Köln, Germany
101.59215@germanynet.de

"fingatur autem libra..." (Archimedes)

Gravity Piloting in Virtual Data Spaces

A virtual reality need not necessarily represent a world-like environment; it also may be an information space by real-world means. Such conceptual information spaces are based on parametric algorithms of visual cognition. Accordingly the conceptual understanding of form and order is one of the main goals of a variety of sciences to improve man-machine interfaces and also machine vision. In general these are cybernetic mapping processes. Their purpose is to read information from natural spaces to predict forthcoming physical positions. Or they generate multi-dimensional conceptual spaces with object-like representations to guide possible actions by content visualization and data taxonomy. In these worlds the conceptual information is represented by spatial distances, order, clusters, directions, colors, surfaces and lights. Some of these worlds are Cartesian spaces like the Information Cube (University of Alberta) or the free Unix mSQL-based InfoViz document-finder to generate spatial VRML-worlds for content visualization (url: http://fabdo.fh-potsdam.de/infoviz.html; Daessler, 1998). A further concept to plot information into virtual worlds is the use of more or less immersive virtual Cartesian space cubes to scale down conceptual multidimensional data spaces. One of these elaborated data mining systems is mapping multi-causality into a gravity-space in a box. This space looks Cartesian but is multi-dimensional using the gravity paradigm of clustering. This is possible because the original data represent physical world dimensions. The objects stored in the database are in original size and state. This is the data base of all following conceptual analysis and visualization the multi-causal space inclusive.

Such space refers to a physical world and is explored by a kind of space flight through constellations of colored and named primary data objects which here are cubes to show the central gravity gradient by their spatial orientation (screen-shot, fig. 1). The data exploration in this virtual space is like piloting a spacecraft through gravity constellations. The gravity-model does not only relate the exploring pilot to the gravity center within the information cube. The clusters of the small data cubes have their positional message as well as they have their conceptual gravity message of their own as referenced primary bodies.

Archaeology is a science, based on the conceptual understanding of form and the spatial and layered distribution of finds. These mainly are pottery. To understand the concept of ancient economy, the fundamental information is represented by amphorae and related commercial ware, described by their shape and measure, plus the related epigraphic material. What we see in fig. 1 is part of a conceptual world different from our Cartesian minds. The gravity clusters and the definite position of every single cube according to dimensional gradients represent the physical properties following amphora shape to fit the Roman economy. Each of the cubes represents a specific shape from Heinrich Dressel's table of amphora forms (CIL XV, fig. 2) mainly representing finds with commercial inscriptions from the Monte Testaccio and the Castro Pretorio in the city of Rome. It is visible that the gravity constellations form "pearl necklaces". The members of these constellations we find as groups in the order of the table, where they represent specific amphora forms which are related to the physical density of the substance, the container was designed to hold and to transport. To understand the involved constraints of shape related to the Greek and Roman economy, measurable virtual and thus virtual physical objects have to be reconstructed. The basic information in this respect is the digitized shape scaled to the original physical size. The automatic measurement of the virtual objects like height, diameter, volume, capacity, tare, surface, silhouette etc. (fig. 3) has numerical results which best are analyzed by an object orientated statistical multi-causal data mining system. The chosen system (data analysis system D.A.S, by g.d.p) also helps to generate the content visualization and data taxonomy. The generated conceptual clusters, like physically bound constellations, fall into the quality of gravity.

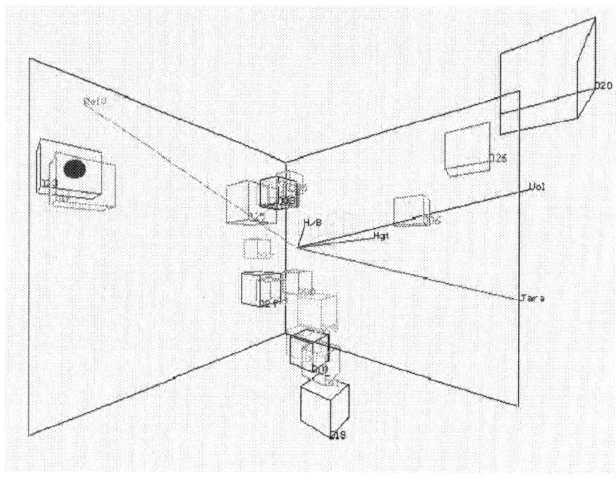

Figure 1. Fly-through in a generated conceptual multi-dimensional space (animation screen-shot). The cubes form constellation-like clusters. These show shape-mass dependencies related to the measure and weight standards of the Greek and Roman economies. Technically they represent the geometrical mass constraints of shapes found in the table of amphora forms of CIL XV, 1899. Top left U1FK61 (fig. 3) is marked in relation to Dressel 23 (fig. 2).

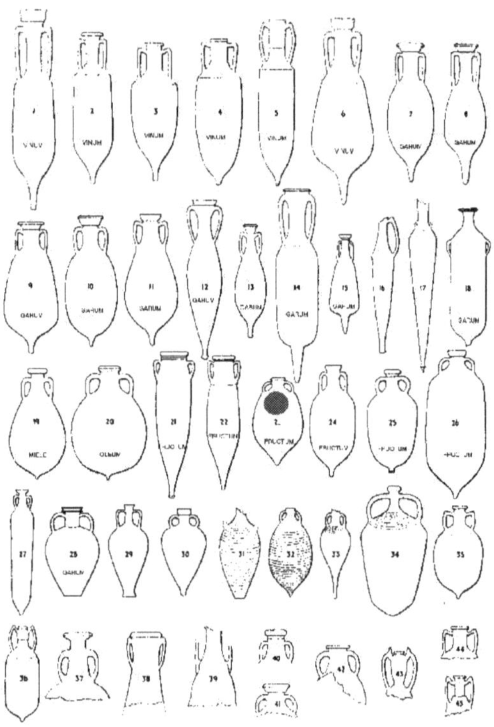

Figure 2. Table of Amphora Forms from CIL XV (1899). The order does not represent chronology, but shape physically related to the content.

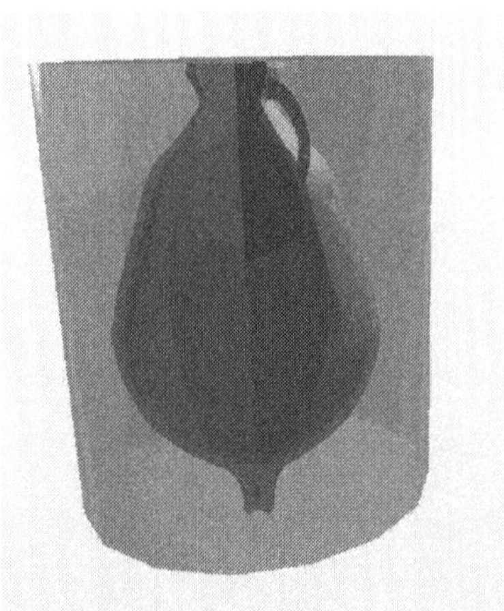

Figure 3. Rotating lines generate cylindrical closed surfaces to give measurable form to objects. This is the concept of the potter`s wheel and the generalized cylinders. The amphora is shape-generated from the measurable objects stored in physical size in the data base (U1FK21 from the Samos Gymnasium excavation, Greece). The shape generated is an information space, where the general measurements are: BODY HEIGHT: 42 cm, BODY DIAMETER MAX. 26.94 cm, H/D: 155.92 %, SILHOUETTE: 618.22 square-cm, NECK LENGTH: 2.89 cm, NECK DIAMETER: 6.37 cm FOOT DIAMETER: 3 cm, MAXIMUM VOLUME: 9.5 l, CAPACITY AND MASS: 9.4 l, BODY: 18.27 %, BODY VOLUME AND MASS (TARE): 2.12 l, RELATIVE VOLUME: 82.14 %

Obviously the physical constraints of shape represented by the constellation-like clusters following the dimensional axes are the same concepts which are seen in the order of the table of amphora forms which will be discussed in detail later (table 2, column 4). The page-like order of the table (fig. 2) also represents the order of entries with the metrology-related epigraphic material in the related volume of the corpus of Latin inscriptions which is not a chronological order, but a general order by kind which is caused by form (CIL XV,2.1, 1899: 560). So both visualizations show in general the same causality in the amphora forms. The comparability of the multi-causal order and the order of the table lead to a closer look at the shape-generated physical qualities of the container classes as conceptual artifacts. The table has to be considered as an early example of content visualization and data taxonomy. Its purpose is to understand Greek and Roman economy surviving in the concept of form and fabrication. This is the closed-surface generated by shape to fit the system (fig. 3). Of course also there are physical constraints in shape visually guiding a variety of other behaviors than commerce. But even the kitchen is linked to the economical standards. We may understand the pan in its purpose of frying, but the precondition is found in the standardized quantities and substances. Such shape-related and shape-generated qualities, their variation and distribution, are in the view of the Statistical Analysis of Mathematical Object Structures (SAMOS). The study of macro-symbolic language in the parametric constraints of shape is derived from the SAMOS-project.

The outline of the SAMOS-project first was published together with Clemens Steckner. The original data used to explore the interrelation of shape and physical data by multi-causal data analysis were from the Samos Gymnasium (Martini & Steckner, 1993). Recent research focuses include:

- fitting ancient commercial pottery to the Greek and Roman economy and commercial supply system by shape, measure and weight down to kiln and villa rustica.
- showing the function of the pottery of every-day life by distribution (e.g. a set of pottery for kitchen use) and functional form (e.g. a pan is for frying)
- the aspects of visually guided behavior. This is the way three-dimensional shape predicts function and handling in visual-driven behavior. The experimental bio-cybernetic approach is handled by the FOCAS-project (Formative Cognitive Anticipatory Systems) (Steckner, 1999). This project explores the predictive mapping processes in cognition which allow the mentioned self-reference of things which look like what they are.

General Concepts in Shape

The SAMOS-project relates measurable virtual objects as measurable data spaces to multi-causal information spaces of more than just three or four dimensions. The single shaped object is seen as a conceptual pattern related to the visible and accessible stream of information which makes economy possible. A good example in this respect is the CATO-project (Morris & Walsh, 1981). The specific data-types needed suggest that this kind of geometry, gravity, standard, time and value-related material is best handled by statistical relational data analysis systems. Relational databases by definition have a structure comparable with statistical contingency tables. The information units scaled there are the quantities measured in pounds and the units of volume, the qualities of kind, their value and the related taxes. Every commercial object is designed to fit into this frame, and the better the fit is visualized, the better the visual driven behavior may be organized. So shape has to be understood as the frozen path of the process to fit the three-dimensional form in the system. At this point the concept of generalized cylinders meets the potter's wheel (fig. 3). Originally the generalized cylinder is an AI concept to improve machine vision (Hollerbach, 1975), recently adapted as a VRML node to visualize virtual objects. There in fact we find again the relation in form and fabric. The frozen path is responsible for the physical properties of the object which by its shape represents a conceptual and communicative pattern.

Today the interrelation of geometry and gravity is not transparent. Modern commercial measures and weights are conceptual cubes because the liter is thought to be a cube of water. The ancient economy instead followed the idea of the generalized cylinder and the resultant constraints according to kind. All refined shapes of Greek and Roman pottery, by this approach of Archimedes, was directly linked by measure, quality of kind and weight to economy and domestic life. The generalized cylinders are a general concept to understand visual-driven behavior (Humphreys & Bruce, 1995), with a conceptual geometry of their own (Winston, 1979: 227-234). Hollerbach picked the idea from the conventional archaeological description of Greek and Roman shape. So this view has much to do with common archaeological methods, as the gravity model has, showing causality by distribution of archaeological finds. There the functions remain visible in the pattern of distributed objects and the time series in the distinct succession of layers.

In this respect the archaeological finds mainly are pottery. Vice versa the fragment and the single object indicate by their specific shape their relative position in time and related geographic distribution. Recent CD-ROM editions of Roman pottery (Archaeologische Materialkompendien I: Roemische Gefaesskeramik, Scriptorium: Muenster 1997) help to indicate specific shapes visually by classified bit-mapped pictures. But this kind of data representation has no direct access to the shape as information. For retrieval, you have to keep your pottery shape in mind to find something resembling it. A more intelligent approach would use shape itself as a pattern of information retrieval. This is realized by the automatic retrieval concepts of the SAMOS-project. But as the precondition, there remains the parametric and physical research and the understanding of shape as communicative quality with its historical background.

The refined shape of pottery in Roman and Greek economy and domestic life visualized qualitative information: "For example, the amphorae used in antiquity had a variety of forms. The particular shapes of amphorae were guides to the nature of the contents" (Small, 1996: 3). Thus the visual appearance has to be seen as a guide to physical qualities and quantities, standardized weight and volume (Small, 1996: 129). This aspect in context of the Roman Economy and the related standards is the focus here, not the time sequence of shapes or the practical qualities, when form follows function. Technically, quality analysis and time series have the same data basis. Thus shaped objects may be understood as three-dimensional data-spaces visualizing their qualities by self-reference. And these things which look like what they are, address cognition and communication. Here virtual space becomes the communicative front end of content visualization and data taxonomy to guide the visual-driven behavior.

The Dressel Table of Amphora Forms Revisited

Taxonomy not only addresses complete objects, aids in classifying and completing fragments. But only these complete things will unveil by their properties the intended constraints of their shape. To obtain the measurements, the methods implemented in the SAMOS-project extrapolate fragments to the statistical most likely complete object. For that predictive purpose there must be a good understanding of the parametric properties of the single object related to the variation and distribution of its class. The empirical basis are surviving complete objects, or *holons*, which represent the structure of their classes. In the case of the SAMOS-project this empirical basis consisted of: the completely surviving Dressel 23 amphora U1FK61 from the Samos Gymnasium (both in the left top corner of fig. 1); the measurable virtual real amphora restored from CIL XV (fig. 2); and the conceptual preconditions which will be discussed in detail later.

The first such holon-based approach in content visualization and data taxonomy in the archaeological field of amphora forms was published in the Corpus of Latin Inscriptions by the table of amphora forms (CIL XV, 2.1), compiled by Heinrich Dressel (1845-1920), a man who was trained in biological methods of classification. This table of 1899 was revised by D.P.S. Peacock and D.F. Williams following their new economy-related classification "Amphorae and the Roman economy": "It will be clear that our arrangement of the material owes much to previous writers, particularly Dressel". (1986: 9). They reprinted the table of amphora forms as their figure 1 (our fig. 2), illustrating some difficulties in using Dressel's original scheme: "Firstly, the drawings are small and lack detail so that in many cases it can be difficult to assign, and secondly a majority of the types illustrated date to the middle of the first century A.D., with poor representation of later Roman amphorae." Because in 1899 the fabric of the vessels had found scant attention, now form and fabric were cataloged to improve visual object identification by detectable shape characteristics as well as by visible surface and petrological characteristics of fabric, at least to identify the potteries and kilns where they were made, but not the economical standards they were produced for. This new view therefore unfortunately did not discuss the original concept of object measurement and the resultant content visualization by the table. The fundamental definition of class was the holotype. This is a type definition by an object of reference. The empirical data of this first container measurable by weight and capacity according to physical SI-standards is related to the Roman or Greek standard measures and other information stamped or written on it, to have total experimental access to the qualities that follow the specific shape—including the lost contents.

This economic object of reference definition (which the SAMOS-project by measurable virtual objects has sampled from the original table, which will be discussed later on) was abolished by the new 1986 approach. To give order to the entries, both form and fabric now became classes of efficiency. This economy of efficiency is not related to ancient standards and practice. It is a simple arithmetic mean of the content capacity of the containers of a given shape-class.

Efficiency as a Measure of Form and Fabric

Efficiency as the measure of form and fabric is a qualitative quotient. It is the average volume of a group of containers. This is related to the average weight of fired clay as the factor of the fabric of form. The economy of form therefore is measured in l/kg: "Obviously, the higher the number the more efficient the amphora" (1986, p. 52). In the following ranking the increasing efficiency apparently is the conceptual frame of all form-classes.

CLASS	EFFICENCY	REFERENCE
Class 4	0.88 l/kg	1
Class 10	1.68 l/kg	3
Class 15	1.67 l/kg	2
Class 25	2.21 l/kg	9
Class 34	3.52 l/kg	3
Class 36	3.56 l/kg	13
Class 37	3.56 l/kg	

For Class 4 only a single measured Dressel 1B reference was available; 3 examples of Dressel 2 - 4 gave the average for Class 10; 2 examples of Haltern 70 for Class 15; 9 examples of Dressel 20 for Class 25; 5 references of Africana Grande for Class 34; and 13 examples of Tripolitanian for Class 36 and 37 (Peacock & Williams, 1986: 52). This is a minimal empirical basis, but methods like SAMOS uses, measuring volume and weight from a variety of fragmented visual and physical sources, were not at hand.

The new arrangement of form erased the original structure of the table of amphora forms, which also was a structured guide to the "tituli picti in amphoris reliquis" of CIL (fig. 2 and table 2). The table was designed to give the visual appearance as a guide to the nature of the contents and the order of the inscriptions. The table of Dressel was not at all morphological, but empirical. The table was based on a variety of measured unbroken containers and it related weight and volume to the Roman commercial inscriptions on these forms (table 2, column 5). To detect the nature of the content related to the particular shapes Dressel had a different idea of the average. This he clearly expressed in his earlier publications after 1874, and especially in 1879, where he published an early scaled version of the table of amphora forms based on amphora finds from the Castro Pretorio (Dressel, 1879, tables).

The Holotype and the Concept of Form and Content

Dressel did not define a class of forms by the average of a set of surviving containers, though his form 20 in CIL XV has four measured objects of reference. His empirical reference was the first entire container described, the *holotype*, defined as the single specimen selected by the original describer of a species. This has been mentioned above, but now the virtual restoration of real-world dimensions to the lost objects of reference will be discussed. Therefore it has to be remembered that it was stated that holotype specimens should be in secure collections that are open to inspection over long terms. The chosen object became and remained the reference for the physical properties and detected variation in objects found later found always refers to the first. So for Dressel 20 on the table of forms the amphora of CIL XV 3637 should be shown. This vessel in 1879 was # 99, while the ordinal numbers of the following complete vessels were 104 and 110 (table 2, column 1 and 3). Such exemplary first objects became the empirical basis of Dressel's product identification. The first set of these is reproduced in scale on his 1879 table of amphora forms. And because these objects with their inscriptions and measurements were published again in the table of forms in CIL XV, together with later found vessels, these also become measurable by picture analysis and statistical interpolation. The primary heights are listed here in table 2, col. 2. In the original printed table of amphora forms of 1899, 6 cm therefore equals 100 cm in reality.

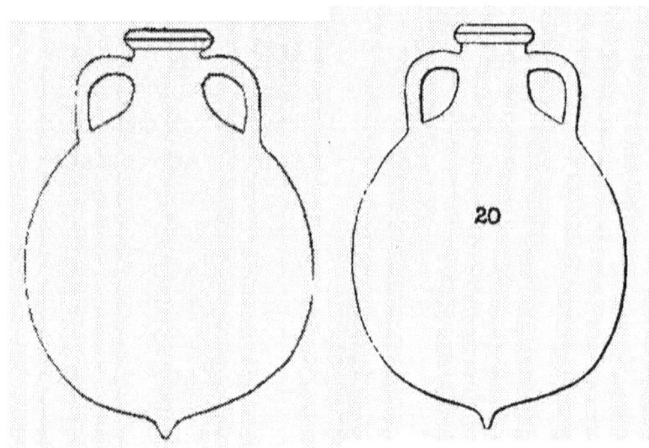

Figure 4a Forma 11 in 1879 (h 73 cm). **Figure 4b** Dressel 20 in 1899 (h 73 - 75 cm)

The Table of Forms as a Table of Form and Content

Though in 1899 "the drawings are small and lack detail" (Peacock & Williams, 1986: 7), as entire objects they are representative of the properties of the related objects and, as it is demonstrated here, represent sufficient information even to restore them to original size as virtual whole objects (or in clay, if desired). Dressel did not use the widely adapted "pars pro toto method" of G. Morelli (1816-1891). He had in mind the properties of the whole form and its content according to the inscriptions, which also were related to the whole amphora to trade. From the properties of his surviving entire vessels he understood the particular shapes of amphorae as guides to the nature of the contents, to the wine, the oil, the garum and liquamen fish-sauce and other substances. This aspect of empirical product identification in the context of Roman trade measures is lacking in the new view of 1986—though the book is entitled "Amphorae and the Roman Economy". Much important economic material is compiled there (Peacock & Williams, 1986: 55-60). Much is based on Dressel, but not his fundamental idea of linking the shape and the measurements of the amphorae with the standards of the Roman economy. This is not even discussed. And so the 1879 # 106 amphora (Dressel, 1879: 150-152) is listed in 1986 a bit hidden among the nine Dressel 20 forming the arithmetic average (Peacock & Williams, 1986: 52). Surprisingly there is no reference to CIL XV, 3647 (fig. 2), where with new measurements the container clearly is identified as form 19 (fig. 5). This form 19 has no Class equivalent, though also CIL XIII, 10008: 43 a, 54, 55, 56 and 58 deal with honey and the related specific trade pound of kind (Steckner, 1985).

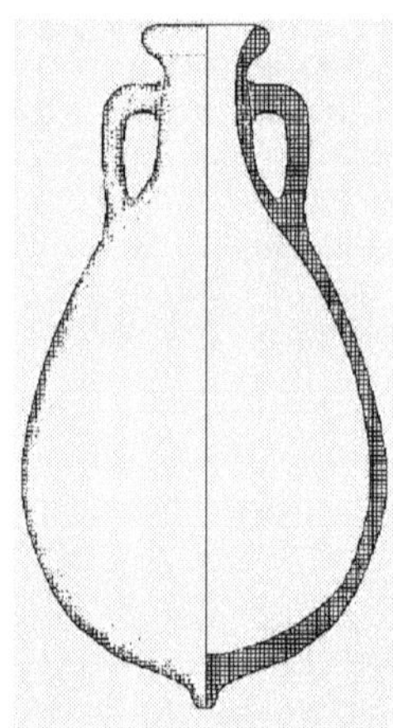

Figure 5: 2D plot of Dressel 19 (CIL XV, 3647) regained from the scaled tables of amphora forms of 1879 and 1899 (table 2). It is a container designed to transport and store honey. Apparently this was done by a specific standard.

The content-related qualities of the forms (table 2) organize the table of amphora forms in CIL XV 2.1. Because these qualities fit the shape properties related to volumetric content, it is possible to recalculate the volumetric properties of the objects of reference from these drawings. Also the table of amphora forms is related to the arrangement of the inscriptions:

BullCom 7, 1879	Size from the 1879 table	objects measured in 1879	CIL XV 1899 table of forms	CIL XV Inscription	Content f	Peacock/ Williams, 1986
Forma 19	130 cm		Dressel 1	4537	vinum	Class 1
Forma 13	97 cm		Dressel 2	4532	vinum	Class 10
Forma 14	86 cm		Dressel 3	4530	vinum	Class 10
Forma 17	97 cm		Dressel 4	4558	vinum	Class 10
Forma 18	108 cm		Dressel 5	4652	vinum	
Forma 12	121 cm		Dressel 6	4551	vinum	Class 8
Forma 2	90 cm		Dressel 7	4732	garum	Class 16
Forma 3	93 cm		Dressel 8	4734	garum	Class 16
Forma 4	86 cm		Dressel 9	4570	garum	Class 16
Forma 6	83 cm		Dressel 10	4533	garum	Class 16
Forma 5	88 cm	# 76	Dressel 11	4726	garum	Class 16
			Dressel 12	4724	garum	Class 14
			Dressel 13	4695	muria	
			Dressel 14	4714	garum	
			Dressel 15	4777	garum	
			Dressel 16	4712	garum	
			Dressel 17	4762	garum	
Forma 1	91 cm		Dressel 18	4730	garum	
Forma 10	72 cm	# 106	Dressel 19	3647	garum	
Forma 11	73 cm	# 99	Dressel 20	3637	oleum	Class 25
Forma 15	95 cm	# 126	Dressel 21	4790	fructum	Class 7
Forma 16	87 cm		Dressel 22	4799	fructum	Class 7
U1FK61	42 cm	*	Dressel 23	4803	fructum	Class 26

Table 2

Following table 2:

- Dressel 1 - 6 were identified, by experience and inscriptions, as designed for wine trade, and these were in context of the inscriptions # 4529 to 4686;
- the forms 7 - 16 and 18 (of which some have no Class equivalents) were identified as designed for garum and liquamen (# 4687 to 4731) and other kind of fish-sauce like muria and liquamen and garum as well (# 4732 to 4782);
- form 19 (CIL XV 3647) was identified by measure and inscription to be a container for honey trade (fig. 2).
- Dressel 20 was identified first by its measurements in relation to the inscription CIL XV 3637 as a globular container for olive oil.
- Dressel 23 (object of reference: U1FK61 from the Samos Gymnasium, Greece) were for olives imported from Greece.

The remaining forms Dressel 24 to 45 Dressel were arranged according to a further variety of content inscriptions, among these Dressel 28 with a measured reference (CIL XV 4700). About these forms and their properties in 1986 we only read: "It is striking to note that Dressel 20 is appreciably more efficient than other contemporary and earlier types" (Peacock & Williams, 1986: 53). From that point the whole of Dressel's table was reorganized: by the structural efficiency of Dressel 20 (Class 25).

Fired clay will not only have specific petrological characteristics, but also specific gravity to sum up in the total weight of the form as tare. This is related to the capacity and the specific gravity of a content as net weight. When the weight in kilograms of the fired clay is related only to liters of the volume, by definition this makes any content become distilled water:

1 l * 1 kg/l [distilled water] = 1 kg by weight.

Any quotient of liters per kilograms implicitly includes the specific gravity of distilled water, and unfortunately in the context of Roman commercial amphorae this concept of efficiency implies the Roman economy to be optimized to transport and trade distilled water. To avoid that misleading concept Dressel had emphasized in CIL XV 2.1 p. 560 and in his earlier publications that it was not water to define the detected physical and economical properties of the Roman amphora shape, but the specific gravity of the content. The inscriptions were commercial inscriptions. There was inscribed the tare by weight on the neck (alpha) and the net weight on the belly (gamma), both in relation to form shown by the container itself and of content according to some other type of stamp or inscription directly or indirectly (CIL XV, 560). The efficiency therefore as a factor of form, and following fabric and content, results in the gross weight to trade and transport.

Figure 6: A Dressel 20 container (h 76 cm) published by H. Dressel in 1878. "Alpha" (tare) is inscribed on the neck: xxcvs; and "gamma" below: cxcvis.

This aspect of content is not neglected in 1986. There E. Rodrigues-Almeida (1972) and his explanation of the dipinti is summarized (1986: 13): "incidentally it is also possible to demonstrate that the contents were olive oil, for multiplication of the empty volume by the specific gravity of olive oil produced the number 'gamma'". Rodrigues-Almeida followed Dressel. Since 1878, and then in CIL XV 2.1, 560 and the related entries, always the specific gravity of wine, garum, honey and oil is seen as bound to form and its following physical properties: according to the Roman measures and weights and their volumetric definition Dressel had referred to (Hultsch, 1888: 114). None of these standard and product-related calculations are found in "Amphorae and the Roman Economy.

The Geometrical Constraint of Physical Properties

"It is striking to note that Dressel 20 is appreciably more efficient than other contemporary and earlier types", wrote Peacock & Williams (1986: 52). This is not striking but addresses the fundamental knowledge of Greek and Roman the physical geometry applied to transporting the lightweight oil: The geometrical constraint that for a body to have minimum surface area for a given volume requires a spherical shape. In other words: The more global a shape, the less the weight of the fired clay and the more the content in relation to the total weight to be transported. This is specific physical constraint of shape and may be measured from virtual reality objects, but hardly from physical ones. In fig. 1 it is the Relative Volume. This globularity best fits to the lightest of the products: To the specific gravity of oil. The container is designed to be efficient in relation to the product. The kg/l-efficiency without the aspect of shape will not realize the given physical constraint of globularity. Furthermore the relationship suggests oil to have been handled as one basic class of products in commerce.

Numerical Shape Analysis and Cognition Research

The "efficiency" in volume and weight is the numerical expression of the geometrical constraint of globularity (fig. 1 top left vector). Here the statistics of shape meets the geometry of AI and Virtual Realty, the one focusing the average object, the other the exemplary shape construction. For both, shape is a guide to the nature of the contents: "This relationship continues down to the present day: nobody need confuse the contents of a bottle of white wine with the contents of a bottle of whiskey, as shape tells all" (Small, 1995: 3). In this respect AI research focused the general geometrical concept of ancient pottery (Hollerbach, 1975).

The neuronal linguistic approach of W. Labov has to be seen in this context (Schwarz, 1992: 86). Also neuronal cognition research followed this view which was mentioned above, but will be discussed now in detail (Marr & Nishihara, 1978: 269-294; Humphreys & Bruce, 1995: 69).

Generalized Cylinders and Geometrical Constraints

Consequently the cylinder generalization recently was adapted in VRML, following the OpenGL specification. There are nodes to describe lights, and others describe the surface properties of the objects, such as their textures and materials. To describe the objects, there are nodes for shapes like spheres, cubes, cones and cylinders. All of these also may be described as surfaces of revolution and extrusion. So since VRML specification 1.1 there is the extreme generalizing node "GeneralCylinder", to produce surfaces by extruding a circle along a path through space. Among these extruded surfaces are sweeps and poly-cylinders and, by variation of the circle's radius along the path, this generalization even produces cubes. The cross-section then appears as a square, and the path as a straight line. By this general construction all the Platonic geometries (sphere, cylinder, cube) as well as all the variation in pottery shape may be represented: because these are all surfaces of revolution, defined by a 2D line known as profile or contour. Vice versa any such 3D volume with its physical properties may be regained from such a contour. The geometrical constraint both is defined by physical properties and if defining these properties, which may be expressed by numbers, like the globularity. Therefore the statistics of shape may use geometrical 2D or 3D virtual representation as a front end of numerical calculation.

The constraint of best numerical efficiency in weight and volume is the globular shape, for the single object as well as for the class of objects. And if in this case the shapes of quantities of containers are calculated, the representation of the mean is something which never existed before except as a concept. The reason is, as mentioned, that both the physical measurements of existing things and of a prototype-based fabrication has Gaussian or normal distribution. The following emphasis on statistical numerical calculation makes it even possible to use fragmented information of single shapes or larger groups of objects. The numerical calculation may be the interpolation of fragmented contour information according to their physical properties, or the physical recovery of the pottery shown in Dressel's table of amphora forms with all its real world physical properties just on the basis of these outlines. In related research, the statistics of shape meets generalized geometry as a constraint of a variety of physical properties (Steckner, 1992: 241-251) related to the economy and its standards. The simulation of the Roman agricultural production and economy becomes possible by the analysis of the geometrical mass constraints. This was realized by Johannes Kepler when he tried to bring order to the confusing system of commercial measures and weights. For that purpose he revived the related methods of Archimedes (Steckner, 1999). Also the seasonal simulation of agricultural processes in its architectural frame, the product transport by land and sea and the related trade and economy may be examined (Steckner, 1996). There again the numerical constraint analysis meets the geometrical construction of spatial representation.

With the recent attempts to present things with visual realism, also the physical individualization beyond the geometrical generalization appeared. Individualization is just one of many aspects in the new interest in the physics of light and the physics of shape with respect to behavior. One of these behavior fundamentals is the physical gravity of matter. In this respect the geometry of form becomes a physical geometry, to determine, on one hand, physical light behavior, but on the other the gravity related behavior of the object itself: the physical density and elasticity of a quantity of material by weight, determining the portability of a generalized cylinder which may look like a ball or a cube, a cone or a cylinder, or like the variety of ancient pottery, as Hollerbach had demonstrated in 1975 in his AI approach.

With the need to individualize object representation, increasingly geometry becomes a physical constraint. The related allometric research of Julian Huxley is available again since 1972. The main concepts in the study of shape spaces are found in Small, 1995: 5. 81. 112.

Ponderated Form

This view of shape-dependent physical object properties is not a modern view of things. The geometrical constraint of physics by generalizing cylinders was studied by Archimedes of Syracuse. A generalized cylinder not only has surface and transparency to refract light in dusty air, also the closed surface also envelops qualities of radiance and of gravity, either to deal with the energy of light or the energy of an impact. To detect the interrelation of geometry and gravity, Archimedes ponderated any of his generalized cylindrical constructions on a thought balance:

“fingatur autem libra...” On one side of the balance was a suggested weight, on the other side the cylindrical construction as an envelop of substance substance: An extrusion along a path or a rotated contour (fig. 3).

Shape Space in the Contract of AD 243

Ponderated geometry is addressed in a contract from AD 243 from the Middle Egypt town of Oxyrhinchus (Cockle, 1981) . The surviving papyrus contract specifically outlines by which definitions such an individual container became a member of its class. According to the contract, three different containers were to be produced in the kiln: 15,000 jars, 150 double amphorae (ceramia) and 150 two-chouse jars. It is clear that in 15,000 jars, though they are intended to be alike, not only will the measurements show normal Gaussian variation, but also some physical variation will occur: by the specific potter, or the specific material, or the specific technical process of manufacturing on the potter’s wheel. Thus it is of interest how much the terms of the contract limited the variation.

The mentioned jars and ceramia in the contract first were materially defined by a specific composition of clay to be fired, made by three components which are listed as friable earth, sandy and black earth. So far this is according to the view of form and fabric, where the fired clay is a precondition of form. To define the form classes in general the vessels in the contract were called by name: wine jar and ceramion (amphora). So far the 1986 concept of fabric and form-classes of efficiency seems to be proved in the source. But apparently the qualitative terms found in the contract also determined capacity and measure and thus visibly had volumetrically interrelated shapes. A form-class like the double amphora, the Oxyrhynchite two-chous and the four-chous thus were both a quality of shape and a volumetric definition. So the expression defines the “jar” by a specific shaped fired clay to become the Oxyrhynchite four-chous container. The given geometry linked the jar to the standards of its agricultural and commercial background. Following Archimedes such a container was balanced by a counterweight: “each four-chous jar holding up to the rim 20 Maximinan cotylae” (Cockle, 1981: 90). This is a gravity equivalent measure, which meant that the four-chous as mass M1 had to be equal to the 20 Maximinain cotylae as mass M2 by weight. These measures had to be taken in account while shaping the clay on the potter’s wheel, foreseeing the percentage of shrinkage following the firing of the material.

In practice it was almost impossible in the real world to check the volumetric properties of all the fired pottery. This could happen by filling up their shape space, though the contract defined a watertight pitching of each of the vessels. But the volume could easily be estimated visually by correct shape and measured by correct weight. The precise definition of the clay also defined the specific gravity of the fired material, so the weight of a fitting shape as tare also gave the volume of the vessel. This practice follows Archimedes. The main related theoretical examples are found in his “Eratosthenem methodus” (fig. 7). There geometrical form has a mass M1, which is controlled by an independent mass M2. Following these volumetric principles of Archimedes, in the contract of AD 243 three aspects came in balance defining fabric, form and shape space:

1) the defined material quality with its specific density as the precondition not only of the transportability but of the commercial weight of the vessel (tare),
2) the form-class outlining the visible spatial properties of the empty container as the precondition of capacity, and
3) the counterweight, to control these spatial properties in relation to the kind of content by weight.

In shape constraints, the physics of spatial construction meets the developments in virtual space construction by the concept of generalized cylinders (fig. 3). The statistics of shape detects spatial as well as physical properties on numerical basis, while the generalized cylinders simulate the physical properties of form according to fabric, gravity and light refraction. Gravity visualization in the information cube (fig. 1) remains to be developed as an instrument of conceptual research.

Figure 7: “fingatur autem libra ...” are the first words by Archimedes to prove by mass-relation the volume of a sphere to fit its cylinder box by 2 : 3.

References Cited

COCKLE, H., Pottery Manufacture in Roman Egypt. A New Papyrus, Journal of Roman Studies, vol. 71, 1981, pp. 87-97.

CURTIS, R.I., 1987, "Product identification and Advertising on Roman Commercial Amphorae", Ancient Society, vol. 15-17, 1984/87, pp. 209-228

DRESSEL, H., 1879, "Di un grande deposito di anfore rinovento nel nuovo quartiere de Castro Pretorio", Bullettino della commissione archeologica communale di Roma, vol. 7, pp. 36-112, pp. 143-195.

DRESSEL, H., "Instrumentum Domescticum", Corpus Insciptionum Latinorum XV, Berlin (= CIL XV).

DAESSLER, R. & PALM, H., 1998, Virtuelle Informationsraeume mit VRML, dpunkt Verlag: Heidelberg.

HOLLERBACH, J.M., 1975, "Hierarchical Shape Description of Objects by Selection and Modification", MIT Artificial Intelligence Laboratory Technical Report 346.

HULTSCH, H., 1888, "Griechische und roemische Metrologie", 2. ed., Berlin.

HUMPHREYS, G.W. & BRUCE, V., 1995, "Visual Cognition. Computational, Experimental and Neuropsychological Persepctives", Lawrence Erlbaum Associates: Hove, London and Hillsdale.

HUXLEY, J., 1972, Problems of Relative Growth, 2nd. ed. Dover: New York.

MARR, D. & NISHIHARA, H.K., 1978, "Representation and recognition of the spatial organization of three-dimensional shapes." Proceedings of the Royal Society of London, Series B, 200, London, pp. 269-294.

MARTINI, W. & STECKNER, C., 1993, "Das Gymnasium von Samos", Rudolf Habelt: Bonn (= SAMOS XVII).

PATERSON, J., 1982, "Salvation from the sea: Amphorae and trade in the Roman West", Journal of Roman Studies, vol. 72, pp. 146 - 157.

MORRIS, HOLLY J. & WALSH, VICKY A, 1981, "CATO: A Computer Simulation of a Roman Wine and Oil Plantation", Patton, P.C. & Holoien, R.A., Computing in the Humanities, Gower: Aldershot, pp. 181-195.

PEACOCK, D.P.S. & WILLIAMS, D.F., 1986, "Amphorae and the Roman economy", Longman: London & New York.

RODRIGEZ-ALMEIDA, E., 1972, "Novedades de epigrafia anforaria del Monte Testaccio", Collection de L`Ecole Francaise de Rome, vol. 10, pp. 102-242.

RUF, Th., 1997, "Scientific & Statistical Databases", Vieweg: Braunschweig.

SCHWARZ, M., 1992, "Einfuehrung in die kognitive Linguistik", Francke: Tuebingen.

SMALL, C.G., 1996, "The Statistical Theory of Shape", Springer.

STECKNER, C., 1985, "Arabische Reformen und Hansische Handelsnorm", Miscellanea Mediaevalia, vol. 17, pp. 421-428.

STECKNER, C., 1992, "Designanalyse und Packungsoptimierung", in: Goebl, H. & Schader, M. (ed.), Datenanalyse, Klassifikation und Informationsverarbeitung, Physica: Heidelberg, pp. 241-251.

STECKNER, C., 1993, "Quantitative Methods with Qualitative Results in Expert System". Physical Qualities in Historical Shape Design", in: L. Valdes et.at.,Aplicationes Informaticas en Arquelogia: Teorias y sistemas, Gastiburo: Bilbao, pp. 486 - 499.

STECKNER, C., 1995, "SAMOS: Automatic Classfication of Ancient Greek Pottery according to Shape", Nissan, E. & Schmidt, K.M. (ed.), From Informationto Knowledge, Intellect Books: Exeter, pp. 126-150.

STECKNER, C., 1996, "Archaeological building reconstruction and the physical analysis of excavation documents", P. Moscati (ed.), IIIrd International Symposium on Computing and Archaeology, Roma, pp. 923-938.

STECKNER, C., 1999, "Anticipatorial Maps", in: CASYS. International Journal of Computing Anticipatory Systems, vol. 4, pp. 101 - 124.

STECKNER, C., 1999, "Cross-modal visual transfer and the forming of haptic anticipatory phantom objects", Buelthoff, H.H. & Fahle, M. & Gegenfurtner, K.R. & Mallot, H.A., Beitraege zur 2. Tuebinger Wahrnehmungskonferenz, Max-Planck Institut fuer biologische Kybernetk, Tuebingen, p. 100.

STECKNER, C., 1999, "Keplers Kessel -Keplers Gesetze", in: ORDO ET MENSURA IV/V, Scripta Mercaturae: St. Katharinen, pp. 255 - 266.

STECKNER, C., 1999, "Ponderierte Form. Metrologisch-systematische Folgerungen aus der empirischen Analyse mathematischer Strukturen", in: Witthoeft, H., Acta Metrologicae Historicae V, Scripta Mercaturae: St. Katharinen, pp. 122 - 131.

WINSTON, P.H., 1979, "Artificial Intelligence", Addison-Wesley.

AN INTERACTIVE SYSTEM FOR THE PRESENTATION OF A VIRTUAL EGYPTIAN FLUTE IN A REAL MUSEUM

A. Brogni, E. Bresciani, M. Bergamasco, F. Silvano

PERCRO Laboratory, University of Pisa, Scuola Superiore S.Anna, Egyptology
Pisa – Italy
Bresciani@sta.unipi.it

This paper addresses a new paradigm of virtual interaction with virtual reconstruction of archaeological artefacts. At present the use of synthetic images for the presentation of archaeological works is performed by the use of computer screens, projectors or retroprojectors capable of providing immersive experiences in the virtual reconstruction scenery. More sophisticated systems exploit the so called CAVE, in order to allow a deeper sense of immersion in the reconstructed site.

The new paradigm of visual interaction we have considered is related to the representation of virtual archaeological artefacts on a portable flat screen; this is held by the human observer and pointed along the line of sight to the spatial real position where the object would be located in the museum. It is assumed that the virtual artefact occupies a physical position in the real three-dimensional space and that the observer acquires its 3D images through a graphical window located on the screen. The real-time representation of the exact perspective and dimensions of the virtual object on the video screen is controlled by monitoring the position and orientation of the screen itself by a tracking sensor.During the exploration of the virtual space, the observer can also obtain historical and archaeological information about the artefact and its production phases, by touching the screen on graphic buttons located at the side of the window.

The system includes a SiliconGraphics Indigo2 R10000 High Impact workstation, connected with a commercial flat screen (weight 3.5 Kg, width 55 mm), with touch-screen incorporated. The tracking sensor is a Fastrak Polhemus, which can detect electromagnetic fields emitted from a source, and describes position and orientation giving analog signals; this sensor is physically attached to the portable screen.

The software application comprehends the following modules:

- graphical interface for the consultation and exploration system; this module was realised by programming with the Xforms library and C++ language;

- 3D model of the artefact, created by the PowerAnimator of Alias| Wavefront graphical software;

- sensor driver, for the communication of the position and orientation data;

- the OpenGL library in C++ language has been used.

Experimental results were obtained by utilising the above system for the representation of an Egyptian blown glass flute, decorated with cut gold leaf and coloured paints; this flûte dates back to the III sec. A.D. and it was discovered in a tomb of the necropolis of Sedeinga, Sudan, in the 1970. The 3D shape of the flute has been reconstructed from a series of photographs and measurements. The decorations describe four human figures and some animals, which have been painted on the glass, warping the pictures on the model, after some deformation to correct the optical distortions from the cylindrical chalice to planar photography.

Introduction

In the last few years we have witnessed a constant evolution in the relationship between the technical and the archaeological sciences, which started from simple data recording and is developing in a closer relation.

The work described here intends to develop a new system for a fuller enjoyment of works of art by trying to make the most of the new interactive technology. We have developed and carried out the plan, on a new paradigm of visual interaction between the user and the virtual artefact, and we have used a portable flat screen like a real window on the virtual world.

The O_x.y.z system reference frame is connected to the window, and therefore to the observer and his point of view. The position and orientation of the screen are monitored by a 3D tracker and we can reproduce them in the virtual environment. The screen is held by the user and pointed along the line of sight to the real position, where the artefact would be located, so that the user is immediately informed about the physical dimension of the artefact.

The system also allows total access to the information about the archaeological artefact by means of an environment with text-windows and buttons (Graphic User Interface), which allows us to interact with the application and guide the consultation, requesting more information as needed.

At present this application is used for the representation of an Egyptian glass flute, but it is a suitable platform for every artefact, and the virtual environment could even be a tomb, or an ancient palace.

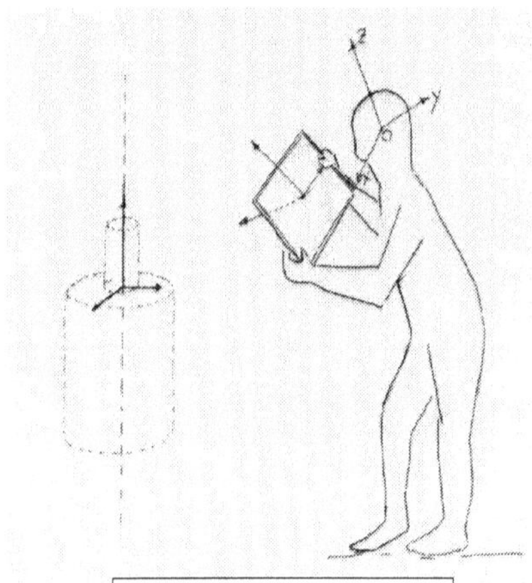

A real window on the virtual world

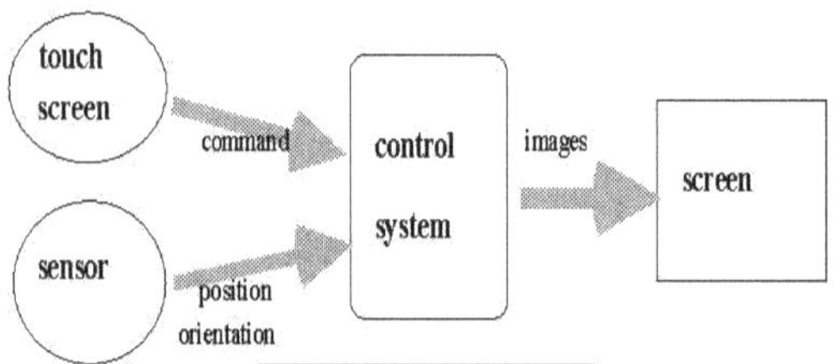

The interaction system

The visitor gives his orders by touching the screen on graphic buttons, located on the side of the screen, which are easy to hit with the same fingers that hold the screen. At the same time, the tracking sensor gives all the information about the movement in real space relative to the central system, which can prepare the new image for the screen according to the new point of view.

Unlike the traditional 3D browser, where the user chooses what to look at and the browser moves the virtual camera, in this system the user actually walks in the real space, and the point of view of the camera follows his/her movements.

The Blue Glass Flute from the Schiff Giorgini Collection

The subject of our virtual reconstruction is a blue glass flute from the Schiff Giorgini Collection, now in the Egyptological Museum of the University of Pisa, Italy.

The flute is 20.1 cm high, and it consists of a base, a stem and a cup.

The flute was discovered in 1970, along with an identical object of the same origin and form currently preserved in the Museum of Khartoum.

The flute was retrieved from a tomb in the Sedeinga necropolis, situated between the second and third Nile cataracts, and subsequently donated to the University of Pisa by its discoverer, Michela Schiff Giorgini.

Tomb WT8, where the flute was located, belongs to the final period of the necropolis, i.e. the second half of the 3rd century BC, and hosts the remains of an individual whose rank, judging from the richness and quality of the funerary apparel, was rather high.

The burial place did in fact contain some 3000 glass fragments, from about 30 very differently shaped vessels. Both the flutes were found broken into a large number (about 70) of fragments; they were probably purposely shattered during the funerary rites celebrated in the tomb during the burial of the dead.

The Greek inscription along the rim of the chalice and the peculiar workmanship, suggesting the work of very skilled craftsmen, emphasise a strong Alexandrine influence, albeit supplemented by undeniable indigenous motifs and themes of a genuine Pharaonic tradition.

3D Shape Reconstruction

We have used the Alias|Wavefront PowerAnimator 8.5 and StudioPaint3D 4.0 software to model the flute. We decided to build the model as a composition of many meshes in order to obtain a good level of realism and high visualisation performance.

The flute is irregularly shaped: the base, as well as the stem, are uneven and not symmetrical. The artefact shows the traces of having been reassembled from many fragments and it leans to one side. The modelling of the artefact was piecemeal and we achieved a satisfactory degree of accuracy by correcting every little detail. We divided the flute in eight parts: base, stem, bottom, low decoration, middle decoration, high decoration, top and inside. This subdivision allowed us to work textures better, by working on the decoration in detail and using just the material colour for the other parts.

The top was separated because it presents a surface with acute angles and a very sharp circular relief. We deemed it more convenient to model it alone because the final model would be a polygonal model, and it is important to limit the large numbers of polygons to just where we need them to keep the total number low enough for a good application performance in real time.

Our solution for a real-time rendering was the use of the VRLib graphic library, developed in our laboratory, based on the OpenGL library. To save the final model we chose the RTG format, a typical format used in 3D commercial game animations, because it allows us to save an ASCII text with information about the vertices and the material colour and to connect texture files to the objects.

The measurements of the flute, for reconstruction, were taken from many photographs, three for every 45 degree angle, and one each for the top, the middle and the bottom, respectively. In this way we could adjust the right images and obtain the model of the flute, by working with the advance functions for the surface manipulation of PowerAnimator.

We built the base like a revolution shape and we completed it by moving the single vertices of the mesh, to obtain a good reproduction.[ALIAS1_98]

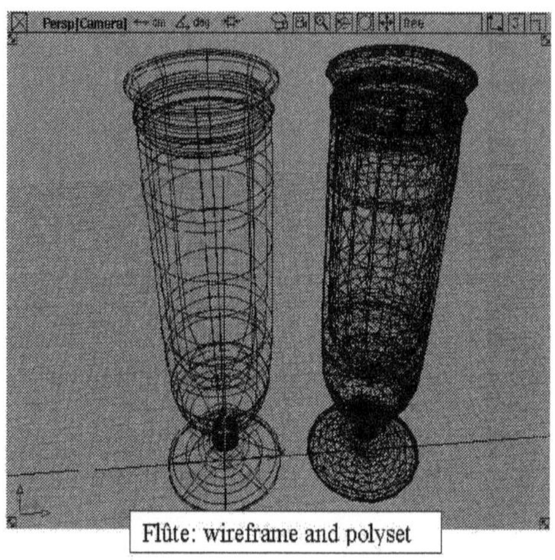

Flûte: wireframe and polyset

The stem is uneven, so we preferred to model it with a different technique: we built many circles, on different heights, with different radii, following the geometric data from the pictures, then we linked them together with only one surface; we therefore obtained a strange cylinder, unsymmetrical and irregular, as in the real flute.

All the other parts are built like revolution solids, from convenient curves, and fitted together to look like a single object. From the NURBS mesh, we converted it in a polyset and saved it in the RTG format.[ALIAS4_98]

Since we work with real-time applications, and we need to keep the total number of polygons displayed on the screen at minimum, we used the division to dedicate more polygons to the complex parts, like the top or the base, and less to the regular parts, like the middle, which is almost a cylinder.

We obtained the final number of polygons after many framerate tests with different polysets; we opened an OpenGL window 800x600 pixels on the screen, like the final window on the application, and we displayed moving objects. For the test we used a SiliconGraphics Indigo2 R10000 HighImpact workstation with 64 Mbytes RAM.

The speed parameters are the following:

No. of polygons	geometric definition	framerate
1106	very poor	86 (frame/sec)
2078	poor	72
3997	good	36.5
6284	very good	18.1
8248	excellent	10.5

The final mesh consists of 3997 polygons:

base	912
stem	304
bottom	336
low decoration	224
middle decoration	192
high decoration	192
top	1316
inside	521

Besides the flute, we also built other models: a pedestal for the flute and a little slab for the planar vision of the decoration. The pedestal consists of 240 polygons, just enough for a good definition but not too numerous to slow down the system .

We attached the decoration textures on a slab, consisting of 304 polygons, to give the user a complete view of the scene represented.

Texture Mapping of the Flute

The first step was fixing the right value for the material colour and the transparency; by loading the photographs on the computer with a scanner, we could measure the chromatic RGB value (Red Green Blue) for the ground colour. We matched these values with the light in the virtual environment to define the final RGB value.

We fixed the transparency value by putting a little rod inside the flute and changing the value and choosing the best condition. We can control the transparency value by a fourth number, called alpha, to add onto RGB, with a range from 0 (completely opaque) to 1 (transparent).

We used a different technique for the decorations because in this instance transparency is needed just where the flute is unpainted. We therefore built a transparency map, on a grey scale, to fix the value in detail; we saved the map as a file and we linked it to the RGB file of the model.

We had to reconstruct the picture of the decorations, and we did so by manipulating the photographs. By taking a photograph of a cylinder we obtained a distorted image and we used just the little central strip; with a technique called *warp,* we cut the strip and stretched it in detail to offset the distortion.

When reconstructing the decorations, we kept in mind their real production phases, and we obtained many textures for each phase, by following the published studies on them.

A big problem was mapping the texture on the polyset. On a NURBS model we can project the texture around the mesh and obtain a good mapping. When we change the model, we transform it into a polyset, losing every connection. For this reason we need to build a new map associating the right coordinates of the texture to the single vertices.[ALIAS3_98]

We removed the old texture coordinates, and by using a cylindrical projection we created the UV coordinate on the polyset too. Then we mapped the texture; to limit the break effect of the texture rolled up on a cylinder, we normalised the coordinates, with values from (0,0) to (1,1).

The textures of the decorations

Rendering of the Flute

Since we needed to work in real-time, we chose the RTG format, and the rendering of the scene depended just on the OpenGL platform and on the hardware we used.

Regarding the texture, we chose to save them on the ppm format because it allows a good image definition with reasonably small files.

Rendering of the flûte model

Hardware Description

The workstation is a SiliconGraphics Indigo2 with IP28-195 MHz audio processor, MIPS R10000 CPU and MIPS R10010 floating point FPU; it has a parallel pipeline structure, with 32 Kbytes data cache, 32 Kbytes instruction cache, 1 Mbyte secondary unified instruction/data cache and a 64 Mbytes RAM. The graphics card is a High Impact with 1 Mbyte texture memory and 8 Mbytes DRAM and it has 1280 x 1024 as max resolution and a 32 bit double buffer with a 24 bit Z-buffer for a resolution of 1024 x 768.

The system interacts with the user through two different inputs: the tracking sensor and the touch screen. The sensor (an electromagnetic Polhemus Fastrack sensor) provides information about the user's position in real space and the perspective from which he/she is looking at the virtual object.

With a C++ driver we read the value from the sensor on the serial port of the workstation and we process the data with an appropriate software. With another driver we read the data from the touch screen.

The output is displayed on an LCD flat screen, with low energy cost (slightly less than 15 Watt) and without geometric distortion for a wide angle of vision.

Software Description

The application works on the UNIX platform, a SiliconGraphics IRIX 6.2 system; the whole programming has been performed on this platform. The application was realised by programming with C++ language, and by using many libraries, Xforms, OpenGL, GLUT and VRLib. The main building block of the system is the graphical interface, which shows every window or button and regulates the interaction with the sensor and calculates the correct image for the animation. For this we used the Xforms library, programming in XWindow environment.[ZHAO_97]

The management of every high level graphic function is controlled by the VRLib library developed in our laboratory (PERCRO Lab - Scuola S.Anna - Pisa - Italy) to achieve a very high performance in virtual reality applications. This library allows us to visualise in a simple manner a complex scene with many objects present, and at the same time to manipulate the models; it thus becomes possible to move the camera in the virtual environment in real time.

We connect the VRLib to the graphical hardware by means of the OpenGL library, by exclusively managing the several objects, with the exception of their visualization. The images rendering management is in fact peculiar to each hardware platform, and for this reason each individual operator should use his particular system. In our case, this was the GLUT library, for the sole purpose of open an OpenGL window into the screen.[DAVIS_97] The GLUT (OpenGL Utility Toolkit) is a low level GUI, purposely developed for the OpenGL.[KILGARD_97]

Our application had to be very easy to use and with a large diffusion potential. For this purpose we decided to use a library compatible with every platform, UNIX or otherwise. The VRLib works on any platform, while it is possible to download from the Net the free version of the suitable library for every platform.

Porting on PC platform

To reduce the cost of the system, we developed the final application to be totally compatible for a WindowsNT platform. We installed the same libraries on the PC, an X-server, a free Xwindow emulator for the Xforms, and we used a commercial 3D graphics card: the performances are good enough for a fluent animation on the screen. At present the application works on both platforms, UNIX and WindowsNT.

The Application

The system needs a very user-friendly interface, so that anybody can easily use it in a museum exhibition. We decided to use a few, large buttons on each window, with very clear functions.

The application includes the possibility of changing the consultation language (English and Italian are currently available). The user can choose the language at the start of the exploration and can change it at any time: changing the language means translating every information text and every label on the buttons.

It was also important to give a lot of historical and archaeological information about the artefact, as well as some photographs and maps; we placed the appropriate buttons for obtaining this information. It is possible to obtain information about the production phases also, with text and images: the images are obtained by rendering the models with the appropriate textures for each phase.

There is a main menu, which the user uses between the consultations; the buttons are on the sides of the screen. On the left are the buttons to modify the system, as well as the language choice, the help, the quit and the bibliography information buttons; on the right are the interaction buttons for the virtual exploration or the production steps. In consultation with the archaeologists, we divided the production steps into five phases, as described in the published research on it.[LECLANT_73]

Virtual exploration is possible through a full screen window and the user can choose to look at the model of the flute or at the model of the planar slab. This second possibility is important because it allows the user to see another aspect of the artefact. To complete the visual information on the flute, which is almost a cylinder, we decided to "unwrap" the decorations. For different objects, for example a sarcophagus, it is possible to use this exploration to have a closer look at the mummy or other artefacts found in the same tomb.

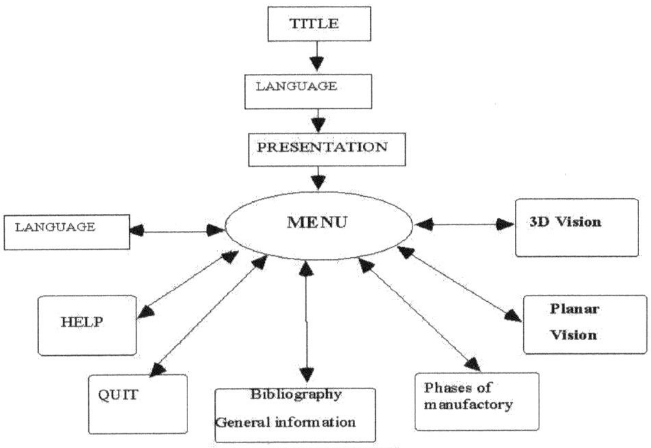

The application

Software Development

We developed the whole application with C++ language to ensure good real-time performance. The code consists of many files with different functions. The files for the description of the GUI (Graphic User Interface) are kept together, and there is a static part of the code, which is loaded for the sole purpose of building the interface, at the start. Some files contain the operative functions, for the movement (sensor), the graphic rendering (VRLib, OpenGL and GLUT) and the internal functions. There are also data files with English and Italian texts, photographs and 3D models, from which some functions load the necessary data, and many of these callback functions are linked to the buttons. Three functions manipulate the sensor: by activating it, by reading its position and orientation, and by deactivating it before closing the application.

The loading phase of the 3D models is very slow, therefore we prefered to do it before everything else to have it ready when starting the application, allowing the user to immediately explore the virtual environment. There are many windows which the application uses just once, like the title, the presentation and the first language choice. We thus decided to clear this window from the memory after its use, in order to achieve better performance.

To open and manipulate an OpenGL window we used the GLUT, the VRLib and the Xforms together; at the beginning the system is controlled by an Xforms function (fl_do_forms), but during the virtual exploration the control passes to the GLUT with its control function. A function called idle function, which is present in both libraries, works autonomously every time the system is not performing other operations. We used this function to read the sensor data and check the buttons; when it can, the idle function reads the sensor, checks the buttons with an Xforms function (fl_check_forms) and decides the right image to send to the screen.

A very delicate module is the control of the sensor; to limit the problem we designed it to activate on the first exploration by the user and to deactivate when the user closes the application. During the idle function operation, the position and the orientation of the sensor are controlled, and we can assign the six global variables (XPOS, YPOS, ZPOS, YAW, PITCH, ROLL) for the visualisation module. The electromagnetic sensor, like the Polhemus Fastrak, is often distorted and inaccurate; the errors were extremely sensitive to the distance between the source and the receiver (beyond 1.5 meters the scatter becomes macroscopic) and to the environment electromagnetic environment.[BRYSON_92] Therefore we had to control the working conditions: the short range of action around the virtual artefact and the use of a LCD monitor, with low emission, allow use of the value directly from the control driver. The control system of the Polhemus has an EPROM memory, with a low pass filter programmable for the position and orientation values; we used those filters with the default settings. We added a linear filter to take the average of the last three values: the sensor framerate is 120 frame/sec.: thus our filter did not present a delay of the image, nor any sliding effect.

During the virtual exploration, it is possible to retrieve particular information about the figures in the decoration of the flute. When a button is touched, the virtual exploration stops and a window opens with a photograph and an explanation text. We defined a function that calculates the point of view of the user and chooses the right explanation. This function uses the data sensor, the position of the camera and the laying vector of the virtual camera in the virtual environment; it calculates the intersection point from the camera and the bounding box of the model by choosing one of the four explanations of the figures.

Conclusions and Project Development

In this paper we have presented a global system for a new visual interaction between the virtual artefact and the user.

We have proposed a system that allows the enjoymentn of works of art by using the new technology and giving visual and textual information about the artefact. The application results are very easy to use: the user can walk in the real space and look at the virtual object, holding only the screen.

The future technical development of this system will aim at bringing the costs down, with a perfect porting on a PC platform, and at improving the conditions for a consultation site in a real museum.

We are also planning to realise a multi-user system, in which many people will be able to move freely, unencumbered by cables, with a radio connection, and they will be able to use the application and the models together.

References Cited

[ALIAS[1]_98] AA.VV. - *NURBS modelling in Alias* - Alias|Wavefront Silicon Graphics 1998

[ALIAS[2]_98] AA.VV. - *Rendering in Alias* - Alias|Wavefront - Silicon Graphics - 1998

[ALIAS[3]_98] AA.VV. - *Polygonal modelling in Alias* - Alias|Wavefront Silicon Graphics – 1998

[ALIAS[4]_98] AA.VV. - *Games Data Transfer* - Alias|Wavefront - Silicon Graphics - 1998

[BRESCIANI_92] E. Bresciani, F. Silvano - *La collezione Schiff Giorgini* - Ed. Giardini – 1992

[BRILL_91] R.H. Brill - *Scientific investigations of some glasses from Sedeinga* JGS 33 - 1991

[BRYSON_92] S. Bryson - *Measurement and calibration of static distortion of position data from 3D trackers* - RNR Tecnical Report - 1992

[BURDEA_94] G. Burdea - P. Coiffet - *Virtual Reality Technology* Wiley - Interscience - 1994

[DAVIS_97] T. Davis - *The GLUT Library* - Innovation[3] - summer 1997

[DELORENZO_96] A. De Lorenzo - *Toy Story Dossier* - Computer Grafica - giu./sett. 1996

[FORSBERG_97] A.S. Forsberg, J.J. LaViola, L. Markosian, R.C. Zeleznik "Seamless interaction in virtual reality" *Computer Graphics and Application – IEEE* - nov./dec. 1997

[FORTE_96] M. Forte - A. Siliotti (eds.) *Archeologia: percorsi virtuali nelle civiltà scomparse* - Mondadori - 1996

[KILGARD_97] M.J. Kilgard - *The OpenGL Utility Toolkit (GLUT) Programming Interface* API Version 3 - Silicon Graphics, Inc. - 1997

[KING_97] C.F. King - *Medical Volume Visualization* - Innovation[3] -

summer 1997
[LECLANT_73] J. Leclant - *Glass from the Meroitic necropolis of Sedeinga* - JGS - 1973
[MATTHIAE_95] P. Matthiae - *Ebla - Un impero ritrovato* - Einaudi - 1995
[MAZZEO_97] F. Mazzeo - *Architettura al calcolatore* - Computer Grafica - ott./nov. 1997
[ROEHL_97] B. Roehl - *Virtual Archaeology* - Innovation³ - summer 1997
[SHERIDAN_92] T.B. Sheridan - *Telerobotics, Automation and human supervisory control* The MIT Press - 1992
[SIMS_97] D. Sims – "Archaeological Models: pretty pictures or research tools ?"*Computer Graphics and Application - IEEE* - jan./feb. 1997
[WALTZ_97] M. Waltz – "New immersive display heat up high-end visualization" *Innovation³* - summer 1997
[ZHAO_97] T.C. Zhao - *Forms Library - A Graphical User Interface Toolkit for X* Department of Physics, University of Wisconsin-Milwaukee 1997.

IMMERSIVE WALK-THROUGH EXPERIENCE OF JAPANESE ANCIENT VILLAGES WITH THE VISTA-WALK SYSTEM

Rieko Kadobayashi, Kazushi Nishimoto, and Kenji Mase

ATR Media Integration & Communications Research Laboratories
Seika-cho, Soraku-gun, Kyoto, Japan
rieko@mic.atr.co.jp
knishi@mic.atr.co.jp
mase@mic.atr.co.jp

Introduction

META-MUSEUM

Museums are popular places for the general public to see, enjoy, and study the results of archaeological research. For archaeologists, museums are also popular and are almost the only place to show their research results to the general public. These research results are usually open to museum visitors as museum exhibitions. However, museum exhibitions are generally designed for a single type of visitor, e.g., a high school student with average knowledge of the theme of an exhibition. However, museum visitors often have wide diversity in their personal backgrounds, age, nationality, knowledge level, interests, etc. This is the biggest problem that prevents museum visitors from understanding a museum exhibition and prevents experts (curators, museum staff, researchers) from accurately conveying an their expert knowledge. In order to solve this problem, we have proposed Meta-Museum as a new concept for museums (Kadobayashi 1995, Mase 1996).

The aim of Meta-Museum is to provide a new environment where experts and novices can easily communicate with each other so that they can share broad knowledge related to all aspects of humans and nature. A practical formation of Meta-Museum would be a combination of traditional museums that have physical objects and virtual museums that have digital information.

What traditional museums have lacked, and a Meta-Museum has a great deal of, are interactivity and personalization. Interactive systems and methods for personalizing museum exhibitions help visitors understand the exhibitions based on their own interests, even though the exhibitions are totally the same physically, i.e., in the arrangement of showcases and rooms, displayed artifacts, posters hung on the walls, etc. In that sense, computer graphics and virtual reality are promising technologies for museums as a new knowledge-sharing environment, since they can add new interactivity to traditional exhibitions.

We think interactivity should exist not only between visitors and exhibitions but also between visitors and experts, since the real understanding of exhibitions cannot be accomplished without experts' help. It is also true that experts need feedback from visitors to improve the exhibitions so that some of their highly organized knowledge is well conveyed to the visitors. This observation led us to the notion that a Meta-Museum should provide three types of tools for helping experts to study, represent, and convey their research results, and tools for helping visitors understand exhibitions based on their personal backgrounds. Moreover, it is preferable that these three types of tools have continuity, or even that these tools be the same, since it is easier for experts and visitors to communicate if they use the same tools.

VISTA AND VISTA-WALK

We have developed the VisTA (Visualization Tool for Archaeological data; Kadobayashi 1997) and VisTA-walk (Kadobayashi 1998) systems based on the Meta-Museum concept. These systems simulate the transition process of an ancient village. As we discuss in detail later, the expected users of VisTA will be archaeologists, and the users of VisTA-walk will be museum visitors, although this is not a strict definition. Users (here it may refer to experts) can visualize the transition process through real-time three-dimensional computer graphics (3D CG) after they interactively set the value of each building's lifetime. Users intuitively learn the ancient landscape of the site because they can walk through the reconstructed 3D CG village. The systems provide intuitive information access through the selection of objects such as buildings in the 3D CG scene. Hence, VisTA will serve the users as a tool for aiding their research and for easily making good presentations.

The VisTA-walk system is based on the VisTA system but is especially developed for museum use. The essential difference between the two is the user interface. VisTA-walk has a gesture-based user interface as well as a traditional mouse and keyboard interface. The gesture-based user interface gives museum visitors more pleasure by letting them use natural physical actions and relieves their anxieties about using a delicate computer system.

This paper discusses both systems and also shows an evaluation of the user interface adopted in VisTA-walk to give users immersive sensations. First, a detailed description of the VisTA systems mainly developed for research use is given in Section 2. Section 3 reports our experiment on exhibiting the VisTA system at a museum and the problem of using the research-use-oriented system in a museum exhibition. Section 4 discusses the VisTA-walk system that exploits a new user interface tailored to museum use and describes the usability experiments of its user interfaces. Section 5 concludes this paper.

The VisTA System for Experts

GOAL OF VISTA

VisTA is basically designed to help researchers study. Generally, study activity is modeled as the iteration of the following steps. First, the target data is selected from databases that contain the primary data, such as excavation data. Second, the hypothesis is set up to explain the relation among patterns commonly owned by the data. Finally, the hypothesis is tested. If the hypothesis is not perfect, this process is repeated again and again until successful results are obtained by modifying the hypothesis or finding other patterns among the data.

The VisTA system can interactively simulate the transition process of an ancient village over time. Archaeological data is multi-dimensional data and a huge amount of data can be obtained from an excavation of one historical site. It is very hard to study the spatio-temporal transition process of a whole site in detail using the data, and hence there has been no research. Researchers can check the transition process of the site by real-time visualization using 3D computer graphics after adding the attribute values; for example, they add types of buildings and existing time to the geographical model data of the site and the position and size of each remaining excavated building. Researchers can use this capability to visualize their hypotheses of changes over time and increase the consistency of the spatio-temporal aspects of the hypothesis. Researchers can also walk through the reconstructed village and this helps them intuitively understand the landscape of ancient times.

Overall use of VisTA

VisTA consists of: a module for managing a historical site database, a space-time simulation module, a Web browser and documents in HTML format, and viewers. With the database management module, a user can store 3D land models, locations of excavated buildings, and 3D building models as basic data, and can input and/or modify hypotheses on space-time transitions from an editing window. The space-time simulation module allows users to walk through the visualized ancient village in 3D CG by using two viewers that provide scenes from different viewpoints as well as set the simulated year. The simulation and visualization module is implemented in C++ using the Open Inventor library. The Web browser is connected to the main object in the viewers, and if this object is selected it shows the relevant HTML documents. A part of Figure 1 shows the internal structure of VisTA.

When initiating the VisTA system, the user selects a site database that contains geographical data of the site and the position data of formerly existing buildings. The floor marks, which have a rectangular or circle shape corresponding to the floor shape of the former building, indicate the position of the buildings. The user selects these floor marks one by one and inputs the type, duration, and name of the building. After setting the value for a part or the whole floor marks in the village, the user can simulate the transition over time and view the process with 3D computer graphics. If the user does not agree with the result, the user can modify the value and repeat the process until the user reaches the desired result. Thus, the user can set up and test a hypothesis of the transition process of ancient villages and can obtain new knowledge.

The user can walk through the village while simulating time transition or stopping at specific year. The user can walk into a house and see the architectural structure and artifacts excavated from the house. This function provides the opportunity to study the view from a certain point in the village.

User interface

The selection and control of these functions are provided by a Graphical User Interface (GUI) using windows. There are two types of windows. The first one controls the simulation over time (top right in Figure 2) and the second one, the "viewer window," displays the visualized village (bottom left and middle right in Figure 2). The simulation control window has an interface like a VTR control panel and has functions to play, pause, and stop the simulated village's images. An interface that handles the data of buildings is also given (top left in Figure 2) so that the user can modify the value of each building.

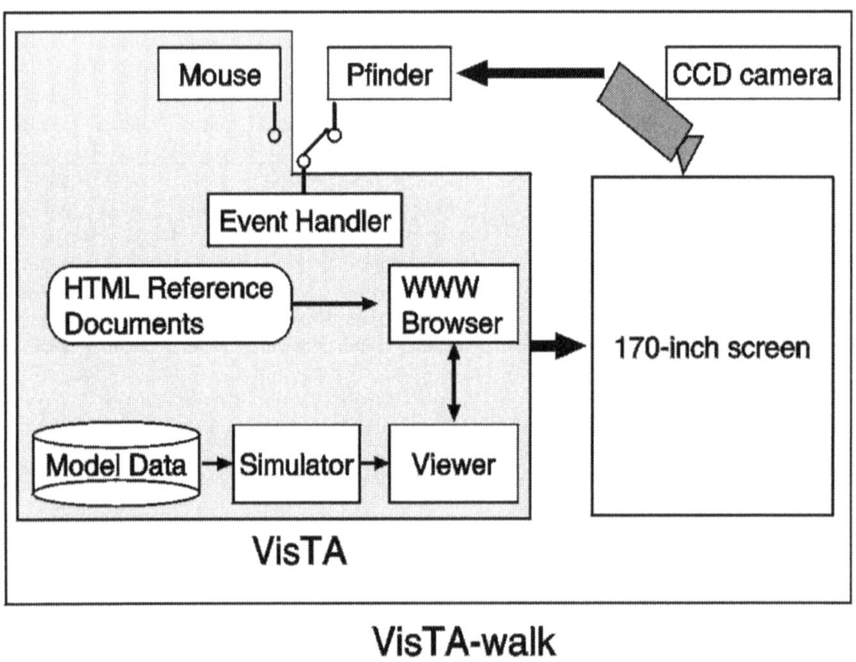

Figure 1. Block diagram of VisTA and VisTA-walk

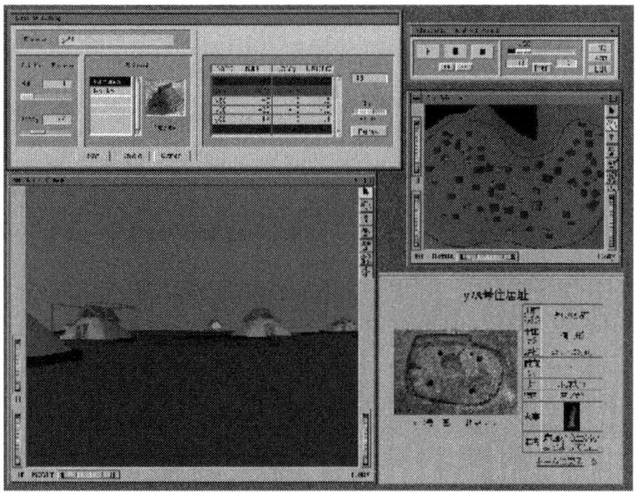

Figure 2 . User interface of VisTA

The viewer windows provide images of the village from particular positions at particular times. The viewer windows are interfaces for "walking-through" the village. The primary behaviors in the windows are to go forward or backward, and turn left or right.

The interface between the user and the virtual world is provided by two different viewers. The first viewer, called the "Walk Viewer" (Figure 2, bottom left), gives a perspective scene from a human model and as such is the "user's viewpoint." The second viewer, called the "Auxiliary Viewer (Aux Viewer)" (Figure 2, middle right) provides a scene from "another person's viewpoint." The height of the viewpoint can be changed to an arbitrary altitude so that the user can get a bird's eye view of the scene. In the "Aux Viewer", a human model (i.e., the avatar of the user) is also shown if the height is low. This avatar that is designed as a human model with a height of 170 centimeters is used as the reference of the current position and the size of the site or building. A scene is generated in the Walk Viewer using the coordinates of the avatar's eyes.

THE OTSUKA SITE

We used the Otsuka site (Otsuka 1991, Otsuka 1994) located in Yokohama city, which is a typical village from the Yayoi era, as an example for VisTA. There were several reasons why we chose this site. First, the Yayoi era continued for about 600 years from 2300 years ago and is a very interesting period for archaeologists because ancient Japanese villages are thought to have begun forming into cities at this time. Otsuka is surrounded by a ditch about 2 meters deep with a barrier approximately 1.5 meters high. Second, the site is a rare case where the whole area was excavated. Third, there were many cases where the remains of houses overlapped with each other. (Archaeologists found 86 houses and 10 warehouses.) Some of the houses were repeatedly reconstructed during the existence of the village, which makes it especially difficult for archaeologists to determine the spatio-temporal transition of the village. Therefore, we expected VisTA to be a powerful tool for analyzing such a complicated site. Finally, we can easily obtain a contour map of the site because the excavation reports have been published. In addition, each floor has been clearly recorded and the data on position, size, and shape of each floor is also easily accessible.

3D MODELS

We created five types of 3D models: land, floor marks, buildings, earthenware, and humans. These models, excluding the human model, were created based on archaeological data included in various reports. Note that only the land model depends on the Otsuka site, and the rest can be used for studying other sites in the Yayoi era.

The land model consists of the site terrain and the sky above the virtual village. We input contour data obtained from a contour map and make a 3D contour map. This 3D contour map is then complemented with a surface to create a real terrain model. The sky is modeled as a texture-mapped cylinder object with a cone top, which is independent of the archaeological data but is used to provide an environmental scene. Floor marks, each of which has a rectangular shape, are put on the land model to indicate the position, direction, and size of the building's floor. At this point, the 3D modeling of the surveyed area is accomplished and the fundamental database of the site is ready for archaeologists to apply their hypotheses.

Two different kinds of structures—houses and warehouses—are modeled as buildings. Both have three different levels of detail models in order to achieve quick responses in interactions with the viewers. The system automatically chooses an appropriate detailed model based on the apparent size of the building in the viewer. The closer the user gets to a house, the more detailed the model becomes.

Each kind of building needs its own kind of floor mark, so two different floor models are incorporated. The buildings are set on the floor marks and automatically scaled to proper sizes according to the sizes of the floor marks. We applied the same floor marks to all of the houses or all of the warehouses, although there is little difference between them. This is because the main purpose of the VisTA system is to help the study from a spatio-temporal and macroscopic point of view.

The models of earthenware placed in the houses are not complete 3D models. Each has a thickness or depth of zero, and a 2D image of earthenware is put on it as texture. These models are put in the houses where they were originally found.

STUDY ASSISTANCE

In addition to the simulation and visualization functions, VisTA has another important capability. It helps users easily set up a hypothesis. For example, the right half of the window shown in the top left in Figure 2 shows the distance between the selected building and the other buildings. Archaeologists have knowledge about this type of village, and they know that many houses burned down in such villages (the fire animation in the web browser shown in Figure 2 shows this house was burned down). This knowledge leads to the hypothesis that people in the village built the houses and separated them from each other to prevent the spread of fire. This function provided through the window supports the test of such a hypothesis and was implemented based on the comments of an archaeologist who used the VisTA system. As future work, we are planning to implement such functions to set up and test the hypothesis of each researcher in an easy way.

Exhibiting the VisTA System

VisTA can be used as a tool to show research to the general public as well as a tool to help the researchers' studies. This is because the visualization of data and hypotheses using 3D computer graphics benefits both researchers and novices with the same representation. The system effectively introduces the representation that is intuitive for experts in research support and opens the research to novices as exhibitions. In addition, such visualizations provide an opportunity to the general public to examine the study process of experts. However, as we will discuss later, the mouse and keyboard operation is not easy for those who do not use computers daily.

Experiment at an exhibition

We displayed the VisTA system at the Ori-Amu Museum in Osaka in a museum exhibition from November 4 to December 3, 1996. The main theme of the exhibition was the typical villages of the Yayoi era. As we mentioned before, the Otsuka site is an example of such villages. Therefore, the museum staff thought the VisTA system would fit well in the overall exhibition. For us, this was a good occasion to evaluate the effectiveness of the system for non-experts.

The expected users were the general public, who may not have had archaeological knowledge, as well as children. For non-experts, we arranged another version that differed from VisTA in the functions and user interfaces. The clear distinction was the hiding of set up and evaluation functions for different hypotheses since this version would be used to easily understand archaeological results. In other words, users could not set and/or modify the value of each building, but they could simulate the temporal transition, walk through the village, and get data about the Otsuka site. For this purpose, this version provided only a mouse for the user interface to let users concentrate on experiencing the contents.

Information on selected buildings is provided via a web browser as shown in Figure 2 (bottom right). This method makes it easy to get other detailed information such as the description of the Otsuka site, and wider access to a variety of information related to the site through the Internet.

User evaluation

We handed out questionnaires on the VisTA system and obtained eighty-seven replies during the exhibition. The questionnaires contained twelve questions, each of which had five grades, e.g., the user's interest in archaeology, his/her familiarity with PCs, the usability of the system, and a free description of the system.

More than 90% of the visitors who answered said that they had an interest in archaeology. The number of PC users was almost equal to the number of non-users. About 75% of these visitors answered that they were interested in the VisTA system. For the system's usability, the percentages of visitors who answered 'easy', 'moderate' and 'difficult' were 33%, 26%, and 41%, respectively. More than 80% answered that the VisTA system was useful for obtaining a better understanding, and more than 90% answered that they wanted to try to use systems like VisTA in other exhibitions.

We obtained a significant correlation on the ease of use between visitors familiar with PCs and visitors not familiar with them. That is, the percentage of visitors who answered VisTA was easy to use was high in the former group while the percentage of visitors who answered VisTA was difficult to use was high in the latter group. However, there was no significant difference between these two groups concerning the question of whether they wanted to use VisTA again. We concluded that the user interface is especially difficult for those unfamiliar with PCs and should be improved, yet it still greatly helped visitors understand the contents of the exhibition.

The VisTA-walk System for Museum Visitors

Overview of VisTA-walk

We learned in the VisTA exhibition that it is necessary to develop a new interface that takes less time for users to get used to if VisTA is to be used in museum exhibitions.

What kind of interface is appropriate for museum visitors ? If the goal of VisTA and other systems using virtual reality technology is to just provide realistic sensation for the visitors, devices commonly used in virtual reality applications such as head-mount displays and/or data gloves may be enough for the user interface. However, if the goal is also to help visitors understand the exhibition content, such user interfaces are not preferable. This is because these interface devices are still under development and are burdensome for visitors, in particular young children and aged people.

Therefore, we have proposed a new interface, a full-body and non-contact gesture interface, for exploring cyberspace that does not require visitors to wear extra devices. At the same, time it is easy to use and can provide an immersive walk-through and information accessing capabilities. We named the system with the new interface "VisTA-walk."

VisTA-walk uses a large projection screen for immersive cyberspace presentation and allows the user to walk through "virtual villages" by taking physical steps and to retrieve information on objects displayed in the scene by pointing at them. It has a gesture interface for input and a 170-inch screen as its output interface, in addition to the original mouse and keyboard interfaces of VisTA. One ccd camera that captures the user's image is also added to the system. The block diagram of the system is shown in Figure 1.

The camera installed on top of the screen captures the image of the user standing in front of the screen. This image is sent to the Pfinder program (Wren 1997a), which detects the gestures and position of the user. Pfinder first extracts the area of the user from the captured image and recognizes the user's head, hands, body, and feet. It then recognizes gestures like standing, sitting, and raising hand(s) and the user's position.

Gesture commands

Gestures recognized through the process are interpreted as commands to either walk through the virtual village displayed on the screen, change viewpoints, or select a building and get information (Kadobayashi 1998). Table 1 lists the gesture commands.

Table 1: List of gesture commands

Gesture	Command
stand in the neutral position	stop
step forward	move forward
step backward	move backward
step right	rotate right
step left	rotate left
raise a hand	select a building
raise both hands	look up
Crouch	lower viewpoint

Gestures for walk-through

How can we assign a standing position to the control events of the walk-through system? There are at least three choices for control schemes: mouse, joystick (Wren 1997b), or steering wheel and accelerator. The positioning action of a mouse is that of a locator-type device, while a joystick and a steering wheel are valuator-type devices. According to the terminology proposed in (Zhai 1993), a valuator-type device is classified as an "Isotonic Rate" control scheme. We employ a steering wheel-like control scheme for gesture interaction in the VisTA-walk system.

Stepping away from the neutral region is used to guide the direction of walking. This is somewhat similar to the movement of a steering wheel. Stepping forward or backward is assigned to an accelerator with which a user moves the viewing position forward or backward in the virtual environment. A user must return to the neutral region in order to stop at a desired point in a scene.

The speed of steering and walking is proportional to the stepping distance from the neutral region, and the ratio of speed to distance affects the usability assessment. If the speed is too fast, a user can quickly arrive within the proximity of a destination point, but it is difficult to stop at the exact desired point. On the other hand, if the speed is too slow, a user may have to step far from the neutral region to quickly arrive at a point; stopping at the desired point necessitates moving back by several steps, and this causes inaccuracy.

The reason we chose not to use the mouse control scheme is that the area in which the user can move is limited; furthermore, the user cannot warp over the position without creating sensor events, which is often desirable in a mouse control scheme. In a joystick control scheme, the position is used for the velocity vector. This would be a good scheme if we had another way to change the orientation, for example, by using a horizontal body rotation recognition algorithm. In any case, it would require a much larger vocabulary of recognized gestures or require more dimensions in the recognized space. The steering wheel control scheme makes it possible to come face to face with the target building by only using walking gestures.

Gestures for pointing at objects

The current interpretation of pointing gestures are a "left one" or a "right one". The VisTA-Walk gesture interpreter uses the output recognition results of Pfinder, e.g., "stretch left/right hand" or "raise left/right hand". The interpreter chooses an object on the left (right) side when it detects a "left (right) one" request from Pfinder outputs. Figure 3 depicts how a user uses VisTA-walk. In this case, the user raises her/his left hand to select the house and get information about it in the right top window, that is, raising the hand is interpreted as an object selection command.

Figure 3 Snapshot of user in VisTA-walk

The pointing actions recognized by Pfinder are insufficient to locate a particular object among many objects, and this is due to the camera position. Pointing and stretching a hand toward the screen is hard to detect because the camera is on top of the screen. A stereoscopic multiple camera arrangement is necessary to get complete 3D information about hand and body gestures (Fukumoto 1994), and such an arrangement is presently impractical because many cameras would be necessary to completely cover the area of a user in motion.

Gestures for changing viewpoint

The gestures of raising both hands and crouching are interpreted as commands to change a viewpoint. A user raises both hands to look up and crouches to lower the viewing position. These changes in the viewing elevation and the viewing position facilitate a user's immersive sensations.

These two gesture commands are closely related to the content of the system. At present, the system has one database of the Otsuka site. As houses in a typical village in the Yayoi era in Japan, they had floors lower than the outside. Nevertheless, the VisTA-walk system cannot change the floor level. However, the system allows the visitor to look outside just as if the visitor is in a real ancient house by the crouching gesture.

We created the model of a house as accurately as possible from an architectural point of view. These ancient houses, unlike modern houses, did not have ceilings, which is one of the important highlights in the reconstructed Otsuka site. The visitor can see the roof and the beams supporting it by raising both hands when she/he is in a house. Note that this somewhat unnatural gesture is due to the installation of only one camera in the VisTA-walk system. The Pfinder program processes the silhouette of a visitor captured by the camera and hence the system cannot detect whether the visitor is looking up or not. Although adding more cameras may provide more natural gesture commands, it increases the management and processing costs as well as the complexity of the system.

Functions not controlled by gestures

As mentioned earlier, VisTA-walk is an extension of VisTA. Hence, VisTA-walk uses the functions of VisTA, such as temporal simulations that can be carried out through the simulation control window. At present, VisTA-walk does not provide gesture commands to control these functions because of the limitation of recognition accuracy. Contact devices such as data gloves increase the recognition accuracy while decreasing the easiness and burden of use. In the same way, more cameras increase the recognition accuracy while increasing the complexity of the system. Introducing unnatural but distinguishable gestures may provide enough gesture commands but the visitors must learn more. Considering these trade-offs, we decided that gesture commands were better in order for visitors to enjoy the experience of a virtual walk-through.

EXPERIMENT OF USABILITY

In order to evaluate whether the gesture interface is effective as a user interface for systems used in museum exhibits, we executed subjective experiments on VisTA, VisTA-walk, and VisTA170 prepared for the experiment as shown in Figure 4. VisTA170 uses a mouse as its input device, which on the stand located in front of the screen, and a 170-inch screen as its output device.

Figure 4 . Experimental systems: from left to right, VisTA, VisTA170 and VisTA-walk

The subjects were five researchers, six secretaries, five undergraduate students, and four expert users of VisTA and VisTA-walk. The researchers were experienced in operating a PC and a mouse; the secretaries were somewhat experienced; and the students were not so good at handling a mouse. Except for the expert users, none of the subjects had ever used VisTA, VisTA-walk, or VisTA170 before.

The learning effect of these three kinds of systems was compensated by execution in different orders for different subjects. We tested five different speeds for VisTA-walk in order to observe the change in operability according to the change in mapping between the distance of the user's movement and the speed in the virtual space. The slowest VisTA-walk is called VisTA-walk-1 (V-w-1), and the fastest VisTA-walk is called VisTA-walk-5 (V-w-5). The movement speed v_i of VisTA-walk-i is given by the following equations:

$$v_i = a_i(d\text{-}38) \qquad (d >= 38\text{cm})$$
$$v_i = 0 \qquad (d < 38\text{cm})$$

where, d is the distance from the center of the neutral region (the neutral region is a circle of 38cm radius) and a_i is the coefficient of speed. v_1 is 1.25 (m/s) where d is 80(cm) (i.e., $a_1 = 0.03$) and the ratios a_i / a_1 (i=2~5) are 2, 4, 8 and 12, respectively. The mappings of rotational movement are done in a similar way.

The task for the subjects was to walk through the course from the start to the goal as quickly as possible while passing three houses. We ordered subjects to stop at the center of each house to check if they passed the specified houses in the correct order. This task was repeated three times for each subject for VisTA, at each of the five different VisTA-walk speeds, and VisTA170, i.e., seven systems in total. We measured time and distance. In addition, we asked subjects to fill out a questionnaire consisting of a five-grade evaluation and a space for free comments after they finished one experiment. The results of the subjective evaluations and measured values of time and distance are shown in Figures 5 and 6, respectively.

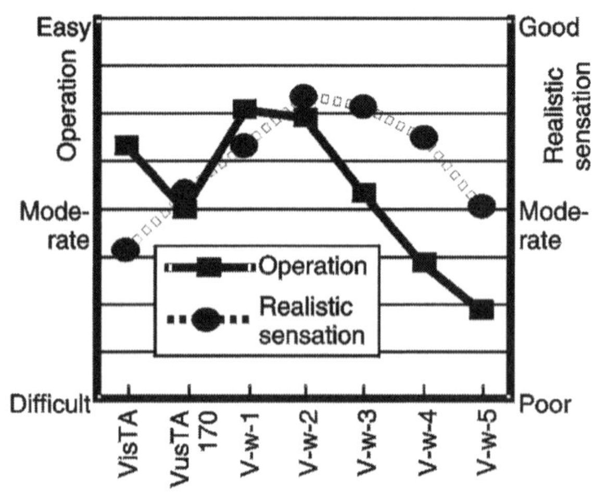

Figure 5 Subjective rating of the seven systems (average of all subjects; V-w-n denotes VisTA-walk-n)

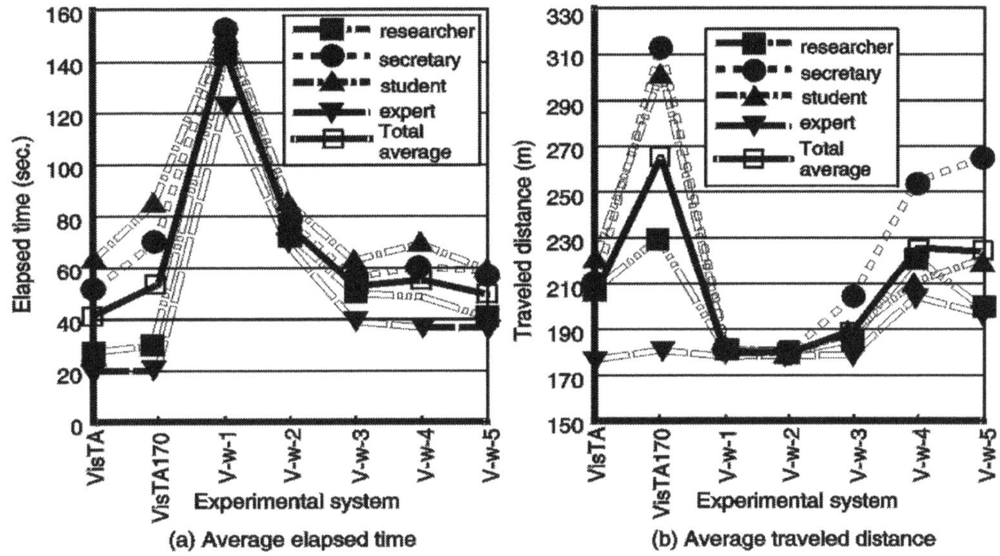

Figure 6 Average elapsed time and average traveled distance

Evaluation 1: Realistic sensation and operational ease

From Figure 5, we can see that VisTA has a less realistic sensation than VisTA170 and the five different VisTA-walk speeds. However, compared with VisTA170, VisTA is easier to operate. This is supported by the fact that the average time and distance of VisTA170 are longer than those of VisTA (Figure 6(a)). In particular, the difference of distance is significant by the t-test. Accordingly, we can say that a large screen can give a more realistic sensation while it decreases operational ease when it is used with a traditional mouse interface. There is no significant difference between VisTA and V-w-3 or V-w-4 in terms of the average elapsed time. This suggests that the gesture interface is equal to a mouse in operational efficiency.

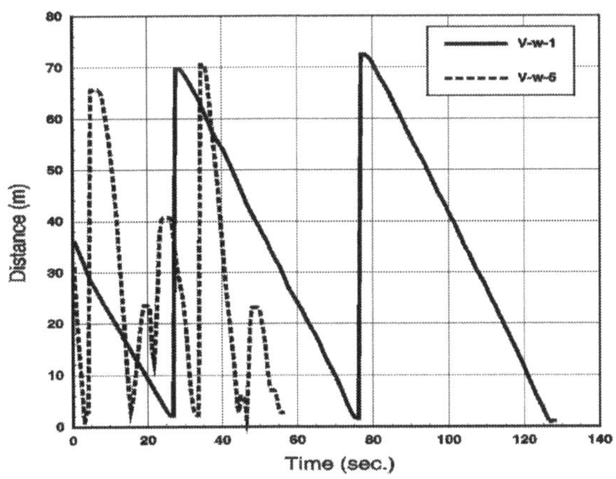

Figure 7. Typical example of movement

Consequently, it is not sufficient to simply enlarge the screen, but it is necessary to apply a suitable interface to provide both a realistic sensation and an easy-to-use interface. Our results also indicated that a gesture interface can provide an operational efficiency equal to that of VisTA while providing a more realistic sensation than VisTA. We can thus conclude that a gesture interface is suitable for systems that use a large screen for immersive presentations in museum exhibits.

Evaluation 2: Speed and operational ease

What is the appropriate mapping between the amount of movement in real space and the speed in virtual space when a gesture interface is used for walking through the virtual space? The time needed to travel the course can be theoretically reduced to 50%, 25%, 12.5%, and 8.3% in the V-w-n (n = 2,3,4,5) systems compared with V-w-1. However, the experimental results are different. Even though travel time is reduced to approximately 52% in V-w-2, it is reduced at most to approximately 36%, 38%, and 35% in V-w-3, V-w-4, and V-w-5, respectively. The migration distance is almost equal to the theoretical distance of the course in V-w-1 and V-w-2. The migration distance is longer than the theoretical distance in V-w-3, V-w-4, and V-w-5 (Figure 6(b)).

To explain this situation, we show an example of a subject's typical movements in Figure 7. The horizontal axis indicates the elapsed time from start to goal, and the vertical axis indicates the distance in a straight line to the target house. Since there are three target houses in the experimental course, there are three points where the distance is almost equal to zero meters. (The condition to clear each target is to stop within a three-meter radius from the center of the house.) The distance to each target linearly decreases in V-w-1. In contrast, an increase and decrease in distance is frequent in V-w-5. This is because stopping gets more difficult, and at that point users pass back and forth across the target if the speed increases.

From these observations, we can see that if the speed moderately increases it takes less time to reach the goal, while it takes more time and more distance if the speed excessively increases. In the subjective evaluation, V-w-1 and V-w-2 received good results for ease of operation, while some subjects answered that they become irritated at the slow speed in V-w-1. Therefore, we decided that a mapping between V-w-2 and V-w-3 would be appropriate to shorten the migration time and reduce useless movement.

Conclusion

This paper described VisTA and VisTA-walk, which were developed as a part of the Meta-Museum project. VisTA, which seeks to assist experts in their studies, allows the experts to easily set up and test hypotheses on the spatio-temporal transition of ancient villages by visualizing simulated transition processes of the villages with 3D CG. VisTA-walk is a tool for experts to convey the knowledge acquired with VisTA to the general public. VisTA-walk has a gesture-based user interface that is different from VisTA and suitable for use in museum exhibits. We evaluated the effectiveness of the user interface by subjective experiments. The results show that the user interface is suitable for museum exhibits because it is easy to use and can give a very realistic sensation without the need for burdensome external devices.

VisTA-walk is displayed in a state-of-the-art technology gallery, which we regard as a predecessor to the museum of the future. We hope to observe how visitors interact with VisTA-walk and then propose better user interfaces based on the results.

Acknowledgments

The authors would like to thank Yasuyoshi Sakai, Ryohei Nakatsu, and the members of the ATR Media Integration & Communications Research Laboratories for the research opportunity and helpful advice. The authors would also like to thank Mr. Eduardo Neeter and Mr. Tadashi Takumi for their cooperation in developing VisTA and VisTA-walk, and the Perceptual Computing Section of the MIT Media Lab. for providing the Pfinder program.

References Cited

FUKUMOTO 1994

M. Fukumoto, K. Mase, and Y. Suenaga, "Finger-pointer: Pointing interface by image processing," *Computer & Graphics*, Vol. 18, No. 5, pp. 633-642, 1994.

KADOBAYASHI 1995

R. Kadobayashi and K. Mase, "MetaMuseum as A New Communication Environment," *Proceedings of Multimedia Communication and Distributed Processing System Workshop*, pp. 71-78, 1995 (in Japanese).

KADOBAYASHI 1997

R. Kadobayashi, E. Neeter, K. Mase, and R. Nakatsu, "VisTA: An Interactive Visualization Tool for Archaeological Data," *Archaeology in the Age of the Internet - CAA97 - Computer Applications and Quantitative Methods in Archaeology: Proceedings of the 25th Anniversary Conference*, University of Birmingham, BAR Publishing Publishers of British Archaeological Reports, p.266, 1999. (Full paper is included in the attached CD-ROM of this book.)

KADOBAYASHI 1998

R. Kadobayashi, K. Nishimoto, and K. Mase, "Design and Evaluation of Gesture Interface for an Immersive Virtual Walk-through Application for Exploring Cyberspace," *Proceedings of The Second International Conference on Automatic Face and Gesture Recognition (FG98)*, pp. 534-539, 1998.

MASE 1996

K. Mase, R. Kadobayashi, and R. Nakatsu, "Meta-museum: A supportive augmented reality environment for knowledge sharing," *Proceedings of International Conference on Virtual Systems and Multimedia '96*, pp. 107-110, 1996.

WREN 1997a

C. R. Wren, A. Azarbayejani, T. Darrell, and A. Pentland, "Pfinder: Real-Time Tracking of the Human Body," *IEEE Transactions on Pattern Analysis and Machine Intelligence*, Vol. 19, No. 7, pp. 780-785, 1997.

WREN 1997b

C. R. Wren, F. Sparacino, et. al. "Perceptive Spaces for Performance and Entertainment: Untethered Interaction using Computer Vision and Audition," *Applied Artificial Intelligence*, Vol. 11, No. 4, pp. 267-284, 1997.

OTSUKA 1991

Yokohama City Treasure Trove Research Center, Otsuka Site: *Kouhoku New Town Excavation Report XII*, 1991.

OTSUKA 1994

Yokohama City Hometown History Foundation, Otsuka Site II: *Kouhoku New Town Excavation Report XV*, 1994.

ZHAI 1993

S. Zhai, P. Milgram and D. Drascic, "An evaluation of four 6-degree-of-freedom input techniques," *Adjunct Proceedings of INTERCHI'93: ACM Conference on Human Factors in Computing Systems*, 1993.

A WWW VIRTUAL MUSEUM FOR IMPROVING THE KNOWLEDGE OF THE HISTORY OF A CITY

Maria Elena Bonfigli
Università degli Studi di Bologna, Italy

Antonella Guidazzoli
CINECA, InterUniversity SuperComputing Center - VisIT Lab, Casalecchio di Reno (Bologna)
guidazzoli@cineca.it

Nuovo Museo Elettronico della Cittá di Bologna: the Virtual Historic Museum of the City of Bologna

Nu.M.E. (Nuovo Museo Elettronico della Cittá di Bologna), the WWW Virtual Historic Museum of the City of Bologna, is a "four-dimensional" web environment that realizes a link between the concepts of "culture" and "technological innovation" (Veltman 1997) by the creation of a venue being a cultural, scientific and technological meeting point that is both a WWW application and a place in which the city can reclaim its collective identity. On the one hand there is the traditional concept of the museum as a physical venue; on the other hand, there is also the opportunity to expose information we have about the historic and urban development of the central area of the city, to visualize it by means of virtual reality, and to distribute it with the use of the Internet (Bocchi 1997).

Interacting with the Nu.M.E. interface the user begins with the virtual reconstruction of the city as it is nowadays and travels backward in time using the time-bar. As the user travels back in time, recent buildings disappear into the ground and ancient buildings that no longer exist pop up.

Figure 1. The Nu.M.E. Interface

Interface navigation (shown in figure 1) includes integrating:

- Web visualization of real VRML scenarios: the city of Bologna as it is today; VRML artificial scenarios: the city recreated as it was in the past centuries; and their integration. It is necessary to consider a balance between an accumulation of details to achieve maximum realism and simple drawing models to insure maximum interactivity (Guidazzoli and Bonfigli 1999). In fact a detailed reproduction of all the geometric, 3D models which constitute a building results in a slow viewing process of the global, virtual world. In order to improve performance in terms of download time or of frames per second, we use photos as texture applied to simplified 3D, single, architectonic elements; for example roofs, porticoes, columns, and buildings. Moreover, each element or building is created in multiple versions, with a level of detail that increases with the proximity to the building: the closer the visitor approaches to the building, the more detailed the 3D reproduction becomes (Guidazzoli and Bonfigli 1999).

- Specific 4D Navigation Tools such as the 2D Orientation Map the Time Bar and the *CosmoPlayer Console* (Bocchi, Bonfigli and al. 1999, Bonfigli 1999). The 2D Orientation Map of the area of Bologna reproduced in Nu.M.E allows visitors to visualize their position in the virtual world with a red rectangle and the direction of observation of the city with a green rectangle. The Time Bar consists of a text field showing the year, on a display and a bar with a cursor, on a time line. By selecting a year it is possible to visit the reconstruction of the city in that year. Each time a year is entered in the text field or the cursor is moved, the VRML scenario is dynamically updated on the basis of the information in a database. Finally, the *CosmoPlayer Console* includes 3D Navigation tools for interacting with objects and for moving around in the visualized VRML scenario, and Viewpoints that are interesting views of the virtual world.
- Multimedia solutions: sounds, images, voice, text, etc.A sound environment has been introduced into the virtual world to enhance user orientation in temporal navigation. Each century is associated with a different sound-track (Bocchi, Bonfigli and alt 1999, Bonfigli 1999). This allows visitors to identify, on an intuitive and perceptive level, the period they are visiting. Moreover to make sure that the visitor understands that he is seeing only as much as the historical sources can justify, each building is accompanied by an HTML document compiled by a historian. These hypertexts contain references to the historical resources and can be consulted at any time during the visit. Upon selecting a building of major importance, a new browser window visualizes both the HTML description file and an isolated high resolution VRML model of the building. This isolated model can be enhanced with additional lights and viewpoints. For example, the isolated model of the Garisenda Tower figure includes the Dante's point of view of the tower itself as described in *The Divine Comedy* (Inferno XXXI, 136-141).

How Virtual Reality Can Improve Knowledge of the History of a City

Nu.M.E. was born as a tool for historians in order to experiment with and test different hypotheses regarding historical development of the city of Bologna. It is worth noting that research in the field of urban history will greatly benefit from the application of this type of four-dimensional model. In fact this complete representation of the city will allow historians to explore areas of the history of the city not yet considered.

In reconstructing a building graphically, it is necessary to include the following information in order to consider as many details as possible: the height of the building, the number of columns, the apertures in the walls, and materials of construction. It is also necessary to include information about: the morphology of the roofs, the interior courtyard spaces, the height of porches, or portici, and the morphology of vaults. The need to collect this data requires and stimulates continuous historic research in more detail so as to identify new resources and compare them to existing data already collected. This type of research and especially its particular graphic representation of historic material obliges the historian to assume a different work methodology. Aside from this new role in Nu.M.E. development, the historian also assumes a point of intellectual impulse that stimulates the development of hypotheses concerning the city (Bocchi, Bonfigli and al. 1999).

Nu.M.E. is also a powerful interface tool to improve cultural knowledge about the city for general virtual tourists. It can be useful for a virtual tourist in at least three different ways:

1. to witness the evolution of the city from the end of the first millennium to today;
2. to understand the history of the city of Bologna better;
3. to improve his/her knowledge of the great amount of miniatures, written documents, paintings, frescos, etc. about the city of Bologna that are collected in Museums and Record Offices in Italy and in the rest of the world.

In order to explain better these three aims, we can show three different examples described in the following three sections.

URBAN CHANGES IN PIAZZA DI PORTA RAVEGNANA

Using Nu.M.E. the visitor can witness the urban changes in a specific area of the reconstructed city of Bologna by simply travelling backwards in time using. For example, in the case of *Piazza di Porta Ravegnana*, the visitor can see the changes about the buildings placed all around the *Two Towers*, which have been standing for at least 900 years. In particular we can consider four different time steps (Bocchi 1999), shown in Figure 2 below.

1. The virtual visit begins in present-day Bologna, and the visitor can navigate around the area, to see the Asinelli and Garisenda towers from each side, to go up above ground level, to count the scaffolding apertures, to see the windows, and to examine the "castellations" and the roofs. He can explore the western part of a building that dates back to the beginning of this century, then going on to the church of S. Bartolomeo, coming round the two towers and ending up at the fifteenth-century Palazzo degli Strazzaroli.
2. The following main chronological step, working backwards, consists of the great clearance scheme at the beginning of the present century, when it was thought desirable to destroy an entire block of the central part of the city, to bring it into line with what at that time were considered to be the needs of the modern age. The result is the destruction of a large number of buildings and also of the Artenisi, Riccadonna and Guidozagni towers. We are able to reconstruct them electronically in a very precise manner thanks to some photos taken in 1918 just before their demolition (see figure 3.a below), and after the demolition of the surroundings buildings.
3. The next step is to go back to the general situation before the year 1798, when the Chapel of the Cross, one of the most significant urban landmarks of the city, was demolished. Even in this case the virtual reconstruction is not based on hypothesis, because we still have the measurements that were taken at the time of the demolition, when the Romanesque marble of the chapel was taken away, the structure of which has been identified, complete with marble columns, gryphons and lions, dating back to the thirteenth century.
4. The last step is to illustrate the period preceding the construction of the present-day church of S. Bartolomeo. Here the images are less detailed and more essential, since the source presents the complex of the city as a whole. However, there is sufficient detail to provide the visitor with hypotheses that do not

contradict the sources and are clearly stated as such, in a continual interaction between historical data and reconstructional hypothesis. We think that it will be quite a faithful scenario that will enable us to include the data obtained from the miniature of the market contained in the Drapers' Standard of 1411(see figure 3.b). This is full of details, not just architectural—the Chapel of the Cross may be clearly seen—but also showing the market itself with its characters, that are to be studied in order to be reproduced electronically. The resulting model includes also data extrapolated from the *Liber Terminorum(1294)*. It is a form of census where the measurements of all street facades and any constructions built past a system of pavement signs, called *termini*, that indicated the boundary between the public square and private property. This document specifically displays dimensions, structural characteristics of the buildings, and whether there existed benches lined against city walls for use in trading when the market was in session. It established the layout of the area and, by accepting those parts of houses that jutted out onto public property, acted at the same time as a sort of official "pardon", in that the irregularity was recorded but was not punished because it did not create particular difficulties (Bocchi 1995-98). Note that in this model the visitor cannot see the *rocchetta* (the castellated portico at the base of the Asinelli tower) that was not built until the fifteenth-century.

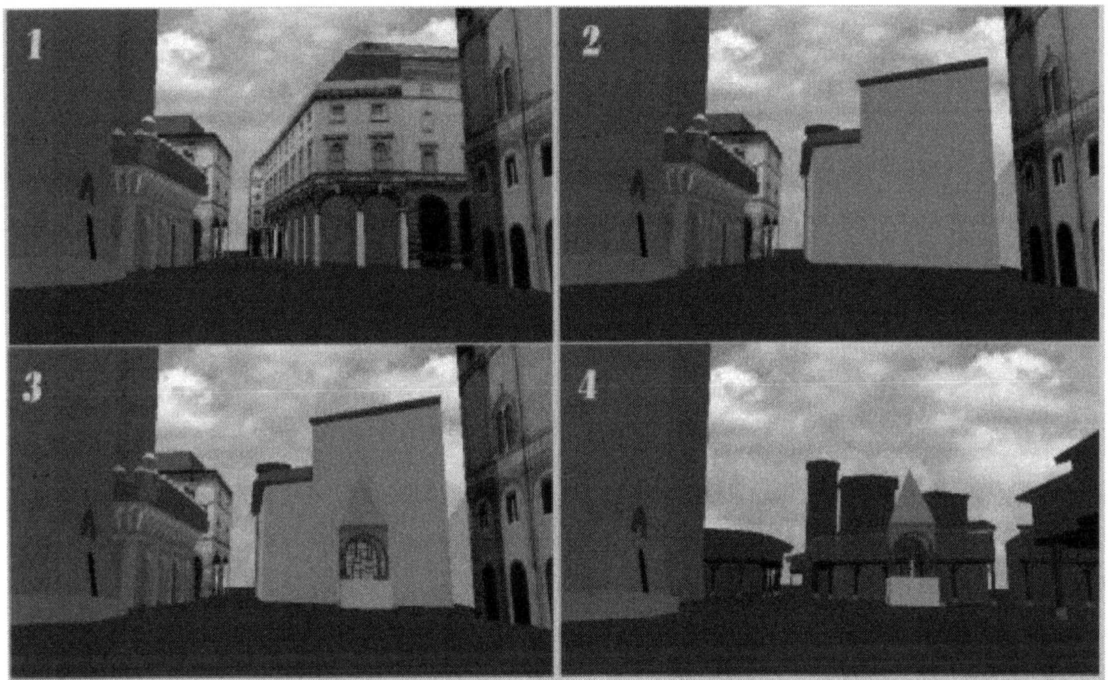

Figure 2. Time Steps: 1. Piazza di Porta Ravegnana in the 20th century - 2. Piazza di Porta Ravegnana in the 19th century 3. Piazza di Porta Ravegnana in the 18th century - 4. Piazza di Porta Ravegnana in the 13th century

a. b.

Figure 3. Historic resources: a. The three towers Artemisi, Riccadonna and Guidozagni in 1918; b. the Drapers' Standard of 1411

FROM VIA MERCATO DI MEZZO TO VIA RIZZOLI

With the Urban Development Plan of 1889, for the first time the city administration, together with the bourgeois classes of the city who were increasingly keen on property investment, displayed an intention to guide and plan a long-term process of urban development. A major element in the projects provided by the Urban Development Plan in the city center was the construction of a new Roman road, that was to be implemented by widening Via Rizzoli, along with the demolition of the buildings that closed in the northern side of Palazzo Re Enzo and the access to Piazza Maggiore on the side of the Pavaglione, the demolition of the Artemisi, Guidozagni and Riccadonna towers and the medieval Reggiani houses in order to construct a rectangular square between the Asinelli tower and Piazza della Mercanzia. The question of the widening of the ancient Via Emilia met a number of requirements: improving the circulation of both public and private traffic (Via Rizzoli was just seven meters wide and was used by a number of tram routes); providing a view of the two great towers and of the restored part of Palazzo Re Enzo; improving the old quarters by demolishing them since they no longer fitted into the modern 1880s scheme of geometric blocks; meeting the needs of the existing landlords and new speculative investors. The Via Rizzoli clearance scheme was the most complex and controversial operation of its kind among those in the history of Bologna in the nineteenth and twentieth centuries. It was postponed for a long time due to its high cost and to much debate and discussion, and was begun only in 1912 and completed in 1928 (Bocchi 1995-98).

Teaching this (and other) historical concepts can be facilitated by the use of Nu.M.E. showing to the students who can understand better this portion of the history of the city of Bologna. In particular the virtual reconstruction can be a tool to involve the students in the debate about the advantages of the widening of Via Rizzoli versus the change of nature of the city-center (Scannavini 1990):

- From a social point of view: the citizens are used to taking a walk in this area during the evening or before lunch time. These walks are considered as a sort of appointment to meet people, talk, etc.
- From an economic point of view: in the new Via Rizzoli offices, industrial enterprises and insurance companies replace hundreds of retail shops and commercial activities that have constituted the market-area for centuries.
- From an historical/cultural point of view: several attempts to defend the medieval houses and the towers facing Piazza della Mercanzia were made with well-documented critical arguments and counterproposals by Alfonso Rubbiani and then by the Committee for Bologna's historical and artistic heritage. They succeeded in saving only the Reggiani houses. This failure was partly due to the uncertain position of the inspector of ancient buildings, the Consiglio Superiore delle Antichità e delle Belle Arti, and in spite of the defense of the towers in 1917 by Gabriele D'Annunzio.

Figure 4. The widening of Via Rizzoli

THE CAMPIONE DEI BENI DELL'HOSPITALE DI S. MARIA DELLA VITA

Finally Nu.M.E. can be also used in order to promote cultural tourism in the city of Bologna, helping not only tourists, but also citizens, to discover miniatures, paintings, written documents, etc. that are collected in Record Offices and Museums. We offer the example of the virtual reconstruction of Via Pescherie in the 17th century, shown in figure 6 below.

Figure 5. Via Pescherie in the 17th century

We chose to take the textures for the virtual model directly from the miniatures of the Campione dei beni dell'Hospitale di S. Maria della Vita—a beautiful document collected in the Bologna Record Office, shown in figure 7 below. They were painted between 1585 and 1601 in order to list the properties of the Hospital. A great many of them illustrate the buildings of the block between Via Pescherie Vecchie and Via Clavature where the hospital itself and the S.Maria della Vita Church were placed (Bocchi 1990).

Figure 6. The miniatures of the Campione dei beni dell'Hospitale di S. Maria della Vita (1601) used for reconstructing Via Pescherie

In spite of the fact that the Campione dei beni is a work of art very appreciated by historians, it is not well known by common people. This is one specific example that demonstrates how Nu.M.E. can enable us to collect all the historical resources relevant for Bologna in a Virtual Museum, accessible through the Internet.

Acknowledgments

The authors wish to thank the Scientific Director and Coordinator of the Nu.M.E. Project Prof. Francesca Bocchi (University of Bologna); the Technical Director Prof. Pierugo Calzolari (University of Bologna); Manuela Ghizzoni, Sofia Pescarin and Rosa Smurra (University of Bologna) for their historical research; Vittorio Valenti and Esteban Cruz (Centro Ricerche Carpi) for CAD modeling; Luigi Calori, Federico Fraticelli, Moris Mariani and Filippo Baldassari (CINECA) for the implementation of the virtual city.

References Cited

F.BOCCHI, 1990, *L'edilizia civile bolognese fra Medioevo e Rinascimento*, Grafis Edizioni, Bologna.

F. BOCCHI (ed.), 1995-98, *Atlante Storico della città di Bologna*, Grafis Edizioni, Bologna.

F.BOCCHI, L.CALORI, F.FRATICELLI, A.GUIDAZZOLI AND M.MARIANI, 1997, "The 4 Dimensional City", *Science and Supercomputing at CINECA*, 1997 Rep., 408-414.

F. BOCCHI, M.E. BONFIGLI, M. GHIZZONI, R. SMURRA AND F.LUGLI, 1999, "The 4D Virtual Museum of the City of Bologna – Italy", *ACM SIGGRAPH99 Conference abstracts and applications*, Los Angeles (USA), pp. 8-11..

F. BOCCHI, 1999, "New Methodologies. The four dimensional city", in *Medieval Metropolises Proceedings of the Congress of Atlas Working Group International Commission for the History of Towns*, F. Bocchi (ed.), Grafis Edizioni, Bologna, pp. 29-33.

M.E. BONFIGLI, 1999, "The implementation of the Nu.M.E. project: the New Electronic Museum of Bologna town in *Medieval Metropolises Proceedings of the Congress of Atlas Working Group International Commission for the History of Towns*, F. Bocchi (ed.), Grafis Edizioni, Bologna, pp.142-150.

A. GUIDAZZOLI, M.E. BONFIGLI, 1999, "The Creation of the Nu.M.E. Project", *ACM SIGGRAPH99 Conference abstracts and applications*, Los Angeles (USA), pp. 31-32.

R. SCANNAVINI (ed.), 1993, *Piazze e Mercati nel centro antico di Bologna*, Grafis Edizioni, Bologna.

K.H. VELTMAN, "Frontiers in Electronic Media", *Interactions - New Visions of Human-Computer Interaction* IV, 4 (July 1997), pp. 32-64.

THE INTERNET AND VIRTUAL ENVIRONMENTS IN HERITAGE EDUCATION: MORE THAN JUST A TECHNICAL PROBLEM

William L. Mitchell and Daphne Economou

Department of Computing & Mathematics,
Manchester Metropolitan University,
B.Mitchell@doc.mmu.ac.uk
D.Economou@doc.mmu.ac.uk

The rise of new media such as the Internet and Virtual Environments has provided new opportunities for archaeology. Unfortunately, the problems of reconstructing artefacts and sites are often seen as being of merely a technical nature. The error in this approach is most apparent when considering archaeological resources intended for use in education. The paper argues that the problem is rather one of how to ensure rigour in the development of these new media resources. Possible solutions can be found in the fields of Computing and Information Systems. The solution proposed is the use of a methodology that would take account of three key issues:

- *how to obtain requirements for the resource*
- *what guidelines the designer can follow to make best use of the particular properties of these new media*
- *what techniques can be used to evaluate these resources*

The research findings have been derived from work on two educational resources for museums based on ancient Egypt: the Tomb of Menna and the town of Kahun.

Introduction

New media such as the Internet, Multimedia, and Virtual Environments (VEs) provide new opportunities for archaeology. Hypermedia (e.g. the World Wide Web [WWW]) allows information to be structured in a non-sequential, networked manner. This allows material to be structured in various ways to reflect different narratives or means of interpretation. The Internet allows users remote access to materials and opens up lines of communication between the general public and subject experts. Virtual Environments provide the means of putting artefacts into context and allowing users to interact with them.

There is increasing demand for museums and other heritage organisations to have a presence on the World Wide Web. In the UK the main impetus has come from the Government's proposed National Grid for Learning (NGfL) (DfEE 1997), (DfEE 1998). One element of the NGfL is providing access to a set of WWW-based resources for use across the educational sector. The museum sector is seen as one of the key content providers for the NGfL.

Archaeologists are in a good position to ensure that the content of the resources developed are of a certain level of quality. One difficulty is having adequate technology skills to develop these resources. However, archaeologists face two further problems. Firstly, the resources must balance a range of user requirements. It is no longer sufficient to develop reconstructions of sites and artefacts that are good in terms of content and technical quality. The resources must also be suitable for a range of user needs. In particular, pedagogical needs must also be taken into account.

Secondly, there is lack of rigour in development of the resources. Many of the resources created by archaeologists have relied on a craft-based approach to development. The success of these systems has relied on the personal touch that comes from being developed by someone from within the subject area or institution. However, the rapid changes in technology and the pressures of the National Grid for Learning mean that more rigorous approaches for developing systems need to be adopted.

A possible solution is the use of a design methodology for the development of these resources. The field of Computing and Information Systems often deals with the problem of developing systems for a wide range of subject domains. The need for design methodologies to ensure rigorous development of such systems is well recognised. In addition, the field of Human-Computer Interaction has focused on developing systems that are centred on a range of user needs (Newman 1995).

The first issue for a methodology is the gathering of requirements. Without correct requirements, useful resources cannot be developed. The requirements gathering process needs to ensure that the needs of archaeologists are correctly reflected and balanced with the needs of others. This is particularly so for resources centred around artefacts that may be used in a wide variety of ways by a range of users (e.g. scholars, general public, education, or commercial).

The second issue that needs to be addressed by a methodology is the provision of guidelines that can be followed in the design of the system. Such guidelines can be used to guide decisions at the high-level conceptual phase as well as the more detailed design phase.

The problem is that subject experts (and educational staff) are often not aware of the potential of the new media. The UK Museum Documentation Association (MDA) recognises this itself in its call for curators and other staff to be more involved with the technologies. However, this is still focusing on the technological problems surrounding the media. What should be focused on is gaining an understanding of each of the media in turn and identifying its particular properties that make it suitable for use in particular situations and applications. This understanding can then be formulated as a set of guidelines to help make design decisions.

The final issue for a methodology is the use of appropriate evaluation techniques. Several issues need to be addressed. Is the evaluation meant to be summative (providing a summary of the effectiveness of the system) or formative (providing information that will go into forming design decisions)? Is the information gathered mainly quantitative or qualitative?

The issues in design methodologies are illustrated by two case studies: the Tomb of Menna and the town of Kahun.

The Tomb of Menna Project

The Tomb of Menna project was set up to investigate how the Internet could be used to provide access to archival material from the Griffith Institute at the Ashmolean Museum, Oxford (Mitchell 1999). A web site was constructed based on the Egyptian noble Menna. The site included a 3D walk-through of the tomb as well as supporting pages containing text and photographs. The site went live in April 1996.

The issues that arose from the project were the use of the media and the problems of evaluation.

A VIRTUAL WALK-THROUGH

Two main objectives were identified at the start of the project:

- to investigate the process of creating a virtual artefact from existing information sources
- to provide alternative ways for visitors to access the virtual artefact

One of the main criteria used in deciding on a possible artefact was that the information should require as little interpretation as possible to be turned into an artefact. This would provide a means of demonstrating how existing information sources can be quickly and simply used. At a more practical level, as this was a pilot project the subject experts were unable to commit time and resources to interpreting the information into a form suitable for use by the resource developers.

An Egyptian tomb was chosen due to its simple geometry. This would help to simplify the design and construction process. In order to model a tomb accurately, it is necessary to have information about the plan of the tomb to base the geometry of the artefact upon. In addition photographic data is needed for every surface of the tomb. Unfortunately, very few Egyptian tombs have been completely documented.

The tomb that was chosen was the Tomb of Menna (TT. 69), which is located at Sheikh Abd el-Qurna, the most central area of the Theban necropolis and where most of the tombs of officials are located. Menna lived in the 18th Dynasty either during the reign of Tuthmosis IV or that of his successor, Amenophis III. His title (Scribe of the fields of the Lord of the Two Lands) suggests that his official duties were connected with agriculture, and this is reflected in one of the best known scenes from his tomb. He had a wife called Henuttawi, two sons, and four daughters, all of whom are pictured in his tomb.

It was decided to use the Tomb of Menna because of the completeness and ready availability of data about it. The data was gathered in a survey conducted by Robert Mond between 1914 and 1916 (Malek). Mond measured and created a plan of the tomb (see Figure 1). He also photographed the interior ceiling, wall and floor coverings, covering 90% of the tomb's surfaces.

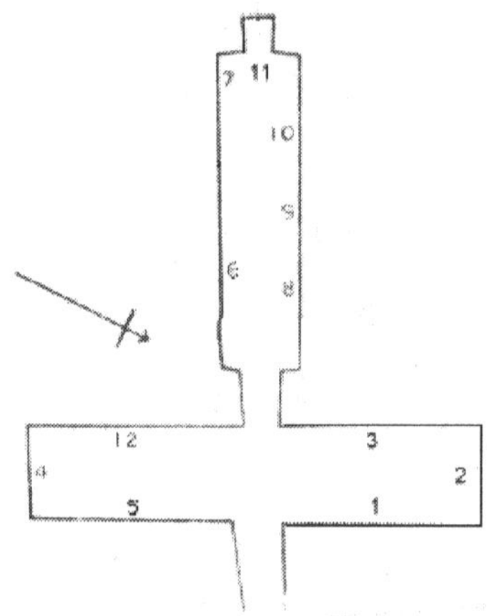

Figure 1. Mond's plan of the Tomb of Menna

Mond used a sophisticated set of photographic techniques that have parallels with those used today to capture images for 3D modelling purposes (Mond 1933). He created a framework mounted on rails around the interior of the tomb. To this he attached a simple camera and lighting equipment. He then photographed each surface by taking a sequence of overlapping photographs from a distance of 18-20 inches away. These photographs were then developed and the prints were cut and arranged (like a mosaic) onto cardboard. The resulting mosaic was then retouched by hand to hide the joins between the prints and then photographed again. Mond himself realised the problems of displaying this information to the general public. His solution was to enlarge the photographs and paste these onto a cardboard reconstruction of the Tomb (see Figure 2). The reconstructed environment created by Mond thus is parallel to the virtual reality walk-through produced by the current project 80 years later.

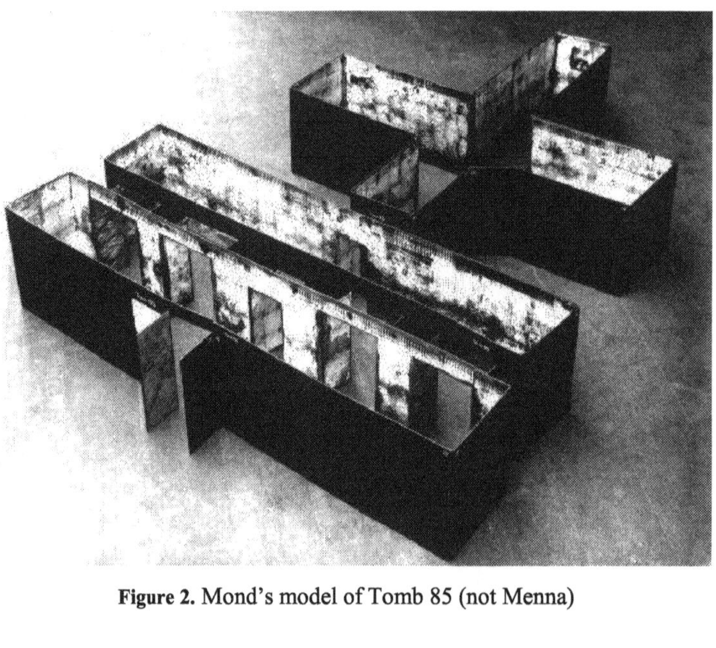

Figure 2. Mond's model of Tomb 85 (not Menna)

The present Tomb of Menna project was targeted initially at the general Internet user. Thus the level of background information could be kept reasonably simple and allow the project to concentrate on issues surrounding the virtual walk-through. The project built the walk-through using Virtual Reality Modelling Language (VRML) (see Figure 3). A VRML model consists of a file describing the geometry of the world along with texture files that are "pasted" onto the geometry in order to create the complete world. The higher the level of detail the larger the files that are required. This has implications for the processor that has to regenerate the scene presented to the user as they move through the world. It also has implications for the speed and capacity of communications link being used. A particular problem at the time of the project was the mismatch between the VRML models being created and placed on the web and the low-performance platforms available to most users.

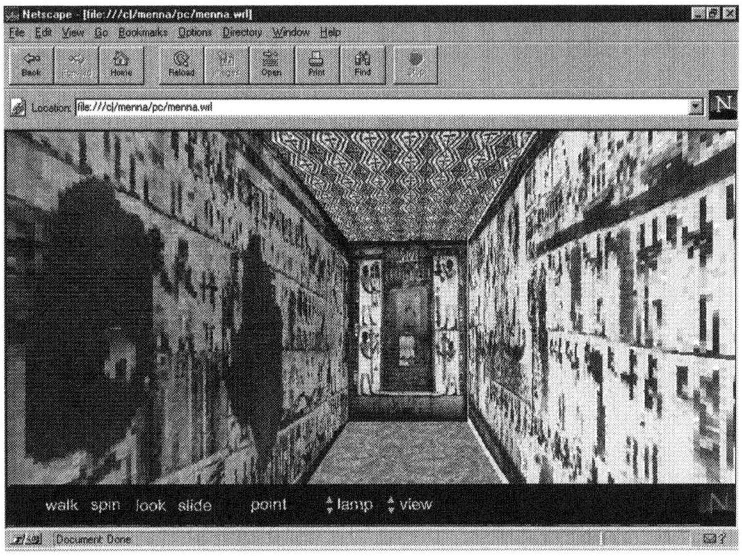

Figure 3. Virtual walk-through of the Tomb of Menna

The project showed that models could be provided for low-cost platforms. The solution adopted was to compromise the resolution of the VRML model and provide much higher-resolution still images for in-depth study of the wall coverings.

COMMUNICATING VIA THE INTERNET

The Internet did not merely provide a means for distributing material about the tomb cheaply and quickly. The most important property of the Internet is its capability for providing new channels of communication. Visitors to the web site have taken advantage of the email link to the developers. This set of queries, which has grown over the two years of the site's existence, provides a useful set of data that can be analysed in order to evaluate usage.

Each query can be classified according to the system stakeholder best able to deal with it. Queries directed at the subject experts (Egyptologists) can be subdivided into queries relating to Egypt in general (e.g. what did the Egyptians eat) and queries relating to the Tomb of Menna in particular (e.g. who painted the walls). Other queries relate to the developers of the web site. These include queries concerning platform problems, how the models were created and wider questions about the research project. A third category of queries was directed at the museum/institute itself. These concerned issues of copyright involving the reuse of the tomb pictures. As with most query situations some defy categorisation (such as queries about archaeological courses offered at university). Into the latter category could be put one of the most interesting queries received so far, which came from the great-nephew of Robert Mond, the surveyor of the tomb.

It has only been possible to deal with some of these queries. The nature of queries to Egyptologists can vary widely and there are limits on their time. This is a particular problem for the Griffith Institute which is mainly a scholarly institution rather than one aimed at the general public. This means that Egyptologists are not available to deal with on-going queries. The maintainers of the web site (in this case the developers) are not subject experts but are the only direct email contact. The solution taken is to refer more general queries to other Egyptology web sites linked to from the Tomb of Menna site. Institutional queries are referred to the Griffith Institute itself.

EVALUATING THE TOMB OF MENNA RESOURCE

Evaluation of the success or usability of the Tomb of Menna resource was a problem as it was Internet based. Analysis of email queries made by users provided some useful results (see below). An on-line feedback form was also provided. However, the accuracy of responses could not be guaranteed due to the anonymous nature of the technique. In addition, what was lacking was some of the detailed information about the resource in use. In order to obtain a more detailed summative evaluation it was thought that it would be useful to observe users.

Observation would prove difficult as the users of an Internet-based system are usually physically distributed and access the site at a time of their own choosing. The solution adopted was to evaluate the resource in use during Manchester Museum's activity week. This ensured a good sample of subjects (children on half-term break) who could be observed using the system in a realistic context. It was thought that such a situated evaluation (Twidale 1994) might yield better results.

Evaluation took place via observation and interview (Mitchell 1999). This took place during four 2-hour periods spread over 3 days. Approximately 8 children per period were observed. Children ranged in age from 5 to10 years old. Children were asked to explain a tomb scene and walk-through to the far wall of the VRML model. Children were also asked to carry out various exercises using a hieroglyphics writing section of the site that was developed specifically for the evaluation.

The evaluation proved useful in obtaining feedback from real users and identifying problems with the interface. For example, it raised particular issues over the granularity of web pages. Younger children sometimes found it difficult to scroll down text pages or pan across images to find objects in a scene. However, the evaluation also raised wider issues about the ways in which such a system could be used as a learning resource. From this point of view the evaluation was more formative or exploratory rather than strictly summative.

The Kahun project

The initial aim of the Kahun project was to investigate how an Internet-based resource could be used to support the work of the Education Service at Manchester Museum (Mitchell 1999). (The Museum possesses numerous objects recovered from the site of Kahun, a pyramid builders' town near the entrance to the Faiyum.)

Requirements gathering

Requirements gathering was a major problem in the Kahun project. The education staff were all part-time, having little time to reflect on current practices. Coupled with this was their unfamiliarity with the new media and their potential.

The problem can be seen as not just that of requirements gathering (what should the system do) but one of opportunity identification (where is a system needed). The solution adopted was to use as a starting point Soft Systems Methodology (Checkland 1990). The initial stages of system design can be seen as:

- developing a rich picture of the problem area
- identifying opportunities
- deriving requirements

Manchester Museum contains galleries ranging from Botany, Mammals and Ethnology to Egyptology. The Education Service caters mainly to primary school visits. Egyptology is seen as one of the particular strengths of the Museum and is one of the main attractions both for the general public and school groups. This provided an initial focus for the subject area of the resource.

The first step in developing a rich picture of the requirements was to identify the various stakeholders in the resource:

- educationalists
- Egyptologists
- the Museum
- technologists
- children

This involved identifying the agenda of each of the stakeholders. Involvement of the stakeholders in the design results in benefits for the stakeholder as well as a better resource. It was also important to be aware of political issues with the Museum and also wider issues effecting the Education and Museum sector.

In order to identify agendas, existing documentation was consulted. For educationalists the National Curriculum for History identifies clear learning targets (Purkis 1992). This helps in identifying various attainment targets:

- knowledge and understanding of history, e.g. familiarity with the concepts and terminology of history
- interpretations of history, e.g. treating history as about a set of interpretation not facts
- use of historical sources, deducing information from sources

As for the Egyptology collection itself, it is contained in two main galleries: Funerary Beliefs and Customs (the mummies) and Daily Life. Artefacts are displayed in glass cases with accompanying information panels. There are no interactive exhibits available in either gallery.

A task analysis was also carried out of a typical school visit. This involved examining materials used in the visit (e.g. work sheets) as well as a series of observations of visits. Interviews were conducted with children and teachers during visits.

The rich picture of the problem area was then analysed to identify areas of opportunity for introducing an educational resource. Three areas in particular were identified. Firstly, the major constraint on the school visit was that of time. This encompasses not only the time each student has in the gallery but also the time available for each student with the teacher or Education staff.

Secondly, children were capable of performing the tasks on the work sheets such as finding objects in the cases, or naming or drawing them. However, interviewing often exposed a lack of deep understanding. For example, children were often baffled when asked what the brick mould was (see Figure 4).

Thirdly, for many children Egypt was equated with pyramids and death. They were very interested in the contents of the Funerary Beliefs and Customs gallery. This is not surprising bearing in mind the gory nature of the mummification process (organs were removed and stored in canopic jars, brains were removed through the nose of the corpse). In comparison the objects from the Daily Life gallery were understandably less interesting.

Figure 4. The brick mould

This suggested a set of requirements for the resource:

- support for pre/post visit

  This would allow children to make the most of their time in the museum and allow follow-up work after the visit.

- focus on Daily Life

  This is of less interest to children and thus poses a greater challenge for a resource.

- provide context for objects

  The children found it difficult to relate to objects that had been removed from their original context and placed in glass cases.

- show how objects were used

  Demonstrate how objects were used and perhaps allow children to handle the objects and use them in a task

Conceptual design of the Kahun resource

An initial concept for the resource was suggested by the latter two requirements identified above (to show objects in context and to show them in use). The Virtual Environment (VE) medium is particularly strong in providing contextualisation and animation. A VE allows a 3D space or world to be created. The user can navigate around this world and interact with the objects in it. Thus an initial conceptual design is a VE for everyday life in which objects can be placed. Children could then either see animations of an object in use or manipulate the object themselves to learn about how it worked.

One opportunity provided in the Kahun project came about through a study of the museum's collection. Many of the objects were recovered from one site—Kahun, a pyramid builders' town (David 1986). This provides two advantages. Many of the objects are from everyday life and not as select as those that have been recovered from sites such as tombs. Secondly, as the objects were found on one site it provides a historically accurate context in which they can be relocated.

The particular medium that is being explored in the project is the Collaborative Virtual Environment (CVE). A CVE is a Virtual Environment in which more than one user can be present at the same time. Each user is represented as a Virtual Actor (or Avatar) (Granieri 1995). So when a user enters the environment they can detect the presence of other users by seeing their avatars and in turn they will be represented by their own avatar. A Virtual Actor may also be used to represent not a person but a software agent. By populating the CVE with Virtual Actors a social element can be introduced. The CVE medium is thus ideally suited to supporting collaborative learning. Work in the Kahun project is focused on investigating the role of Virtual Actors in CVEs for learning (Economou 1998).

The environment consists of the town of Kahun (see Figure 5) and various artefacts recovered from the site. Virtual Actors will be used to represent children, teachers, museum staff, and possible software agents.

Figure 5. Reconstruction of Kahun

The choice of artefacts from the collection was a balance of stakeholders' interests. The Keeper of Egyptology suggested the fire stick as it was unique to the Museum. The needs of educationalists were reflected in guidelines issued by English Heritage for learning from objects (Durbin 1990). From a research perspective the artefacts had to encourage collaboration between users.

The five artefacts selected for inclusion in the VE are: senet (a board game for two players); shaduf (a device used for raising water from the river (see Figure 6)); the brick mould; weights and measures (cubit); and the mirror.

Figure 6. The shaduf: a device for raising water form the river

KAHUN EVALUATION

As explained earlier, the aim of the Kahun project is to investigate the role of virtual actors in CVEs for learning. The process being followed is to construct prototype systems, observe them in use, and so identify requirements of the system (Economou 1998). Evaluation of the success and usability of the system is thus used in a very formative way in this project.

A prototype senet environment has been constructed using 2D multimedia technology (Macromedia Director) (see Figure 7). This allows two users to move pieces on the board and access instructions on how to play the game. The prototype has been observed in use in two different situations.

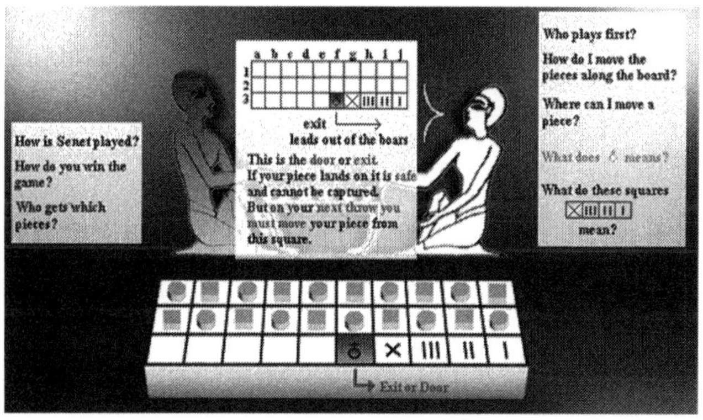

Figure 7. Senet game environment

The first of these was another activity week at Manchester Museum. Pairs of users were observed using the game. This gave a good mix of pairs. In some cases the pairs were class mates. However, a pair would often comprise a parent and a child or a pair of siblings. The latter, while not "typical" of the classroom situation, is quite typical of learning in the home. Observations were focused on the patterns of communication between the players and the communication between players and guides (in some cases the parent, in others an experimenter).

In an attempt to have more controlled conditions, the next set of observations was carried out on school parties visiting MMU for an open day. In each session 3 pairs of children were observed using the system over 25 minutes. Five sessions in all were conducted. The idea was that the observer could look at each of the pairs and then concentrate on the "best" or "most typical" pair. In this way an unresponsive pair would not result in a wasted observation.

However, despite the efforts made to control the situation, other communication patterns were observed. In several of the sessions there was communication between all three pairs. These types of behaviours are precisely those that do need to be taken into account when designing a system. The inter-group communication is actually a pattern of communication that is very likely to arise in, and would need to be supported by, a collaborative virtual learning environment.

Conclusions

The most significant outcome from the two research projects is the need for requirements to be reflected throughout the development of the resource. The distinction between requirements gathering and evaluation can be seen as somewhat artificial. Evaluation can thus be seen not as something that occurs after the resource has been built but as enveloping all aspects of system design (Randall 1996).

The rapid expansion of the World Wide Web has increased opportunities for disseminating information. Unfortunately, there are a plethora of web sites created by enthusiastic members of the general web community which are well presented but flawed in content. This was the main motivation for the Griffith Institute to have a presence on the web. They recognised the large number of sites related to Egyptology that were of poor quality. They saw the Tomb of Menna site as a way of reclaiming their subject and defending its academic respectability.

It is important that archaeology professionals empower themselves by becoming familiar with the technologies behind the new media. However, this paper argues that the field should go further and recognise the ways in which a design methodology can ensure rigour and also ensure that requirements are correctly identified and incorporated. These methodologies can then be applied by archaeologists developing systems "in-house" or by using outside software companies. Only in this way will resources be developed which are of true educational merit and not simply technological showcases.

Examples of work from the Tomb of Menna and Kahun projects can be accessed at the MMU Virtual Museum web site:

http://www.doc.mmu.ac.uk/RESEARCH/virtual-museum/

References Cited

CHECKLAND, P. and J. SCHOLES, J., 1990, *Soft Systems Methodology in Action*, John Wiley, Chichester.

DAVID, A.R., 1986, *The Pyramid Builders of Ancient Egypt*, Routledge & Kegan Paul, London.

DFEE, 1997, Connecting the Learning Society: The Government's Consultation Paper on the National Grid for Learning, Department of Education and Employment, U.K., October 1997.

DFEE, 1998, *Open for Learning, Open for Business: The Government's National Grid for Learning Challenge*, Department of Education and Employment, U.K..

DURBIN, G., MORRIS, S. and WILKINSON, S., 1990, *A Teacher's Guide to Learning from Objects*, English Heritage, 1990.

ECONOMOU, D., MITCHELL, W.L., and BOYLE, T., 1998, "A Phased Approach to Developing a Set of Requirements for the Use of Virtual Actors in Shared Virtual Learning Environments", *Proceedings of ED-MEDIA & ED-TELECOM'98: 10th World Conference on Educational Multimedia and Hypermedia & World Conference on Educational Telecommunications*, T. Ottmann and I. Tomek (eds.), Freiburg, Germany, Association for the Advancement of Computing in Education (AACE), pp.1620-1621.

GRANIERI, J.P. and BADLER, N.I., 1995, "Simulating humans in Virtual Reality", in *Virtual Reality Applications*, R.A. Earnshaw, J.A. Vince and H. Jones (eds.), Academic Press, pp.253-269.

MALEK, J., *The Private Tombs of Thebes, The Photographic Survey by Sir Robert Mond 1914-1916*, Griffith Institute, Ashmolean Museum, Oxford.

MITCHELL, W. L., 1999, "Moving the museum onto the Internet: The use of virtual environments in education about ancient Egypt", in J.A. Vince and R.A. Earnshaw, *Virtual Worlds on the Internet,*. IEEE Computer Society Press, pp. 263-278.

MOND, R., 1933, "A method of photographing mural decorations", *The Photographic Journal*, January 1933.

NEWMAN, W.M. and LAMMING, M.G., 1995, *Interactive System Design*, Addison-Wesley, 468p.

PURKIS, S., 1992, *A Sense of History, Key Stage 2 Ancient Egypt Teachers' Handbook*, Longman.

RANDALL, D., TWIDALE, M. and BENTLEY, R., 1996, "Dealing with Uncertainty - Perspectives on the Evaluation Process", in *CSCW Requirements and Evaluation*, P. Thomas (eds.), Springer-Verlag, London.

TWIDALE, M., RANDALL D., and BENTLEY R., 1994, "Situated Evaluation for Co-operative Systems", in *Transcending Boundaries: Proceedings of CSCW'94*, ACM Press, Chapel Hill, North Carolina.

VIRTUAL REALITY AND ANCIENT ROME: THE UCLA CULTURAL VR LAB'S SANTA MARIA MAGGIORE PROJECT

Bernard Frischer
University of California at Los Angeles (UCLA), USA, Department of Classics; Director, UCLA Cultural VR Lab
frischer@ucla.edu,
Diane Favro
UCLA Department of Architecture and Urban Design
Paolo Liverani
Vatican Museums, Department of Classical Antiquities, Vatican
Sible De Blaauw
Istituto Olandese di Roma, Italy
Dean Abernathy
Architect and Doctoral Student (UCLA Department of Architecture and Urban Design)

Introduction

Since the fall of 1995, professors of Classics, Architecture, Education, and Information Science at UCLA, in conjunction with colleagues in the United States, Britain, and Italy, have been developing virtual reality (VR) models of buildings and monuments in ancient Rome. This collaborative research effort is called the Rome Reborn Project in honor of the first systematic study of Roman topography, Flavio Biondo's mid-fifteenth century *Roma Instaurata* (de Grummond 1996: 160-61). Since January 1998 the project has been housed in the UCLA Cultural VR Lab, which was created with support from Intel, the Creative Kids Education Foundation, and the UCLA Division of Humanities and College of Letters and Science.

The Lab's mission is to provide technology support for projects like Rome Reborn that strive to recreate three-dimensional computer models of sites of great historic and cultural interest around the world. The Lab was founded on the assumption that in the next few years it will be as usual for archaeologists to commission highly accurate 3D computer models of their sites as it is for them to order radiocarbon dating of their organic finds or other tests. Just as there are several laboratories commonly used for radiocarbon dating, it is logical to expect that there will be a handful of 3D modeling facilities known for providing this new kind of archaeological service. The UCLA Cultural VR Lab hopes to be one such service provider.

Research and planning to date strongly suggest that the vision of Rome Reborn which a few short years ago would have been a utopian dream is practicable today. The 1990s have seen a fortuitous convergence of scholarly and technical advances that make a high-fidelity VR model of Rome feasible and affordable. For example, several comprehensive reference works on the building and topography of ancient Rome have been recently published (see Richardson 1992; Steinby 1993--99). Those responsible have become collaborators on the project, and their success in synthesizing previously published material has greatly simplified for us the task of data collection. New technologies available today are especially well-suited for a study and recreation of lost worlds like ancient Rome. For example, realtime VR--which even three years ago was possible only on a supercomputer costing hundreds of thousands of dollars--is now available on a personal computer. Thus, today the challenge is not so much to gather the data needed for a virtual reality model or to create exotic new technology to run the model, as to integrate the information and computer resources already available in a scientifically accurate and coherent way.

Rome Reborn is producing its model of the ancient city in reverse chronological order, starting with Late Antiquity; and in concentric circles starting from two centers: the old civic center in the Roman Forum, and the new Christian quarter of the city in the southeast sector of the city, between S. Giovanni in Laterano and Santa Maria Maggiore (see Krautheimer 1980: 54-58). The project's short-term goal is to connect the individual sites modeled and to recreate an itinerary from the pagan civic center to the Christian religious center. In 1998-2000, the Basilica of S. Maria Maggiore and buildings in the Roman Forum are being modeled. As with all models produced by the Cultural VR Lab, the basilica has been created in MultiGen^{TM}, a software package that supports highly detailed 3D modeling run in realtime.

In the long-term, the Lab's goal is to work with other interested parties in developing open standards for cultural VR so that a chronologically and geographically full model of ancient Rome (or, indeed, of any other archaeological site) can be created by hundreds of individual scholars or scholarly teams publishing their work in a compatible digital, scientific, and aesthetic format through dozens of electronic publishers. That is to say, UCLA researchers are acutely aware of the fact that a single team or laboratory is unlikely to have the manpower and resources to complete the entire model of ancient Rome from its beginnings in the Iron Age until Late Antiquity. Moreover, in a certain sense the task of modeling the ancient city will never be complete. As long as the field of Roman Topography is kept alive by new discoveries and new scholarly interpretations and controversies, it will be necessary and indeed desirable to update old models and to create new ones. Furthermore, it is important for scholars and modelers to maximize the value of their efforts by utilizing compatible technologies to allow for the exchange of building models.

In this article, the project to model the Early Christian Basilica of S. Maria Maggiore is discussed. This model has been chosen because it exemplifies the values and methodologies of the entire Rome Reborn project. These include close cooperation with cultural authorities responsible for management of the site; collaboration between the 3D modelers, on one hand, and the archaeologists and architectural historians, on the other; the use of VR to help illustrate, detect, and resolve archaeological controversies; and the use of VR to facilitate visualization of the past by students and the public.

Introduction to the Site and Early History of Santa Maria Maggiore

Among the Early Christian basilicas of Rome, S. Maria Maggiore is the one which best preserves its structure and an essential part of its original decoration. As a manifesto of the rebirth of Classicism expressed in a new Christian idiom, the building looks backwards toward the monumental civic architecture of the high Roman Empire and forwards toward the religious architecture of the Christian Middle Ages (cf. Krautheimer 1980: 49). Despite its historical importance and good state of preservation, many points remain to be clarified about the oldest phases of the church.

Several recent publications on S. Maria Maggiore have explored the building's history, early use, and decorative program. Nevertheless, a three-dimensional understanding of its original architectural form has remained somewhat elusive. Reconstruction drawings of S. Maria Maggiore's Early Christian form by Spencer Corbett were published in the third volume of Richard Krautheimer's corpus on basilicas in Rome (1971). Updated reconstructions appeared in later publications, yet these tended to be small in scale, and to focus on specific aspects of the building (De Blaauw 1994). Since no comprehensive 3D reconstruction of the basilica have incorporated all the new findings and interpretations postdating the efforts of Corbett and De Blaauw, the Basilica of S. Maria Maggiore is an ideal subject for VR modeling. In particular, the model created by the Cultural VR Lab is heavily dependent on the concepts of De Blaauw, who, as a member of the Scientific Committee, has further developed the ideas he published several years ago.

The main problem of the reconstruction of the fifth-century basilica by Krautheimer and Corbett was that it contradicted a ninth-century text in the Liber Pontificalis. This description of the liturgy in S. Maria Maggiore under Pope Paschal I (817¬824) suggests strongly that the apse had openings to a space lying behind it, where women were standing during the mass. According to the text, the women annoyed the pope, who was sitting on the cathedra in the apex of the apse. Krautheimer could not accept an open apse with a deambulatory because it did not correspond to the conventional typology of urban basilicas. Nevertheless, Geertman had already established in 1976 that the layout of the thirteenth century apse and transept was fully coherent with the modular system of the original design of the church. At the same time, liturgical sources did not allow the presumption of the papal cathedra of S. Maria Maggiore standing in any other position than the traditional one: in the apex of the apsidal hemicycle. These considerations, taken together, already tended toward a correction of the reconstruction by Krautheimer and Corbett. But the suspicion of a deambulatory behind the original apse was entirely confirmed by the discovery of a fifth-century foundation wall by De Blaauw in 1986. It exhibits the same building technique as the other foundation walls of the basilica; is concentric with the original apse and an integral part of the original modular system; and it was partially reused as a foundation of the thirteenth-century rebuilding of the apse.

New important pieces of evidence emerged from the excavation conducted at the beginning of the 1970s. These excavations under the side aisles of the basilica were undertaken in order to eliminate the source of humidity that was damaging the fabric of the building. On that occasion there came to light remains of an impressive Roman house which occupied the northwest half of the area on which the church stands (Magi 1972; Liverani 1988), as well as ample stretches of the foundations of the fifth-century basilica (fig. 1). The house was built around the middle of the first century A.D. and was transformed and redecorated many times in the four centuries of its existence. Its richness and its position in one of the best quarters of the ancient city indicate that its owners were part of the Roman elite who occupied this high point of the city. Part of the house's large peristyle was excavated, as were several rooms on the northwest (the side of the basilica's apse); but the principal part of the house still remains buried to the northeast of the basilica where there are also traces of a small bath complex. In the last quarter of the second century A.D., the peristyle of the house was painted with the fresco of a calendar illustrating country scenes. Each month had a painting showing the work appropriate to the season of the year. It is probable that this decoration alluded to the rural properties of the owner. According to a recent hypothesis (De Spirito 1995) the last occupant of the house may have been Flavius Anicius Auchenius Bassus, the consul of 431, whose family was known to have owned property in this part of Rome. New observations made during research which is still in progress make this hypothesis appear less likely; instead it seems that there was a period in which the house was abandoned between the end of the fourth century A.D. and the time when the new basilica was built. A conflicting theory, however, associates the initiation of the project with Pope Celestine (422-432). Other remains found during the excavations include the foundations of the nave and side aisles and of the original apse. In 1295, under Pope Nicolaus IV, the fifth-century apse was demolished and rebuilt in a new position behind the old one.

Figure 1. Cutaway view of the Basilica of S. Maria Maggiore showing Roman domus at lower level

Construction of the Early Christian basilica required the partial destruction of the earlier Roman house. The southwest wall of the house was pushed into service as both a retaining wall and the foundation for the church. The remainder of the house was buried under six meters of earth to create a level platform atop which the new church could be built. The new ground level conformed to the high point of the hill, where the facade of the basilica was built. Extending 86 meters in length and 35 meters in width, the new basilica subsumed several properties atop the Cispian Hill. New information that came to light in the excavations have solved an old problem. According to the biography of Sixtus III, this Pope supposedly built the Basilica of S. Maria Maggiore "which the ancients called the Basilica of Liberius" (Lib. Pont., I, 46 c.3). If correct, Sixtus' basilica will have been the rebuilding of a basilica originally constructed a century earlier by Pope Liberius (352-356). This notice in the biography has caused numerous difficulties, and it has been suggested that it grew out of an erroneous identification made by the redactor of the sixth-century biography (Krautheimer, Corbett, Frankl 1967: 56-57). Recently, an attempt has been made to defend the notice in the Liber Pontificalis by proposing to limit the building of Liberius to the area of the nave of the Basilica of Sixtus III (Cecchelli 1988). Such a solution is, however, not convincing. The excavations have shown that there is no evidence of a basilica older than the fifth century; furthermore, the foundations brought to light by the excavations are all part of a single project which is coherent both with regard to its building technique and its architectonic modules (Geertman 1986: 286-287; De Blaauw 1994: 346). We must therefore search for the Basilica of Pope Liberius in another area nearby.

The Santa Maria Maggiore Scientific Committee: Procedures and Issues

The Scientific Committee for the Basilica of S. Maria Maggiore Project was composed of distinguished international scholars in the area of ancient and Early Christian art, architectural history, and archaeology. Dr. Diane Favro, Professor, Architecture and Urban Design, UCLA served as chair. Other Committee members were Dr. Paolo Liverani, Curator of Classical Antiquities of the Vatican Museums; Prof. Sible de Blaauw, Art Historian, Istituto Olandese; and Prof. Arnold Nesselrath, Curator of Byzantine, Medieval and Modern Art of the Vatican Museums. The Principal Investigator of the project, Dr. Bernard Frischer, Professor, Department of Classics, UCLA, charged the Scientific Committee with ensuring the highest possible scientific and historic accuracy for the reconstructed VR model by carefully evaluating the data used, identifying specific issues for examination, and periodically reviewing the model during construction. The complex technical, architectural, and historical issues involved in researching, modeling, and archiving require modelers with special expertise. The Scientific Committee worked closely with the modeling team headed by Dean Abernathy, a registered architect with a great deal of archaeological experience as well as a professional 3D computer modeler. Helping Mr. Abernathy were advanced graduate students at UCLA with training in architecture, architectural history, and archaeology.

IDENTIFICATION AND EVALUATION OF SOURCES

At the initial meeting of the Scientific Committee, the members first discussed and agreed upon a date for the building reconstruction of approximately A.D. 440, just after the full mosaic program was installed in the basilica. The creation of 3D computer models requires almost the same range and type of information needed to actually build a structure, including accurate topographical plans, and complete "working drawings" (reconstruction elevations; floor, ceiling, and roof plans; sections; details; structural analyses; and identification of materials). To start, the Committee used the modeling subject questionnaire developed for the Rome reborn project. This questionnaire asks for both information sources, including scholarly publications, archaeological archives, photographic resources, secondary representations (e.g. paintings showing the early basilica), and for the names of individuals with specific expertise relating to the building (e.g. archaeologists, archivists, historians, photographers). The Committee discussed the merits of each source and debated various reconstructions and interpretations, selecting those to be used for the VR model. Since no one reconstruction satisfied the Committee, the group analyzed various components and compiled a variety of sources to create the model. For building parts lacking documentation, the Scientific Committee identified extant buildings of approximately the same date to provide analogues. For example, reconstructions of the fifth-century atrium at the nearby church of S. Prassede were used to create a hypothetical plan for an atrium at S. Maria Maggiore (fig. 2); the pavement inside the basilica was derived from the contemporary floor of S. Giovanni in Laterano. As a further aid for the model-makers, the Scientific Committee also identified general information on the architecture of the era, such as surface treatment of materials, favored proportional systems, and construction techniques. In addition to an initial meeting regarding research sources, the Scientific Committee along with the primary modeler, Dean Abernathy, made several site visits to examine the extant building and the preserved archaeological remains. Such hands-on examination was vital for a comprehensive understanding of the building's form, materials, and construction.

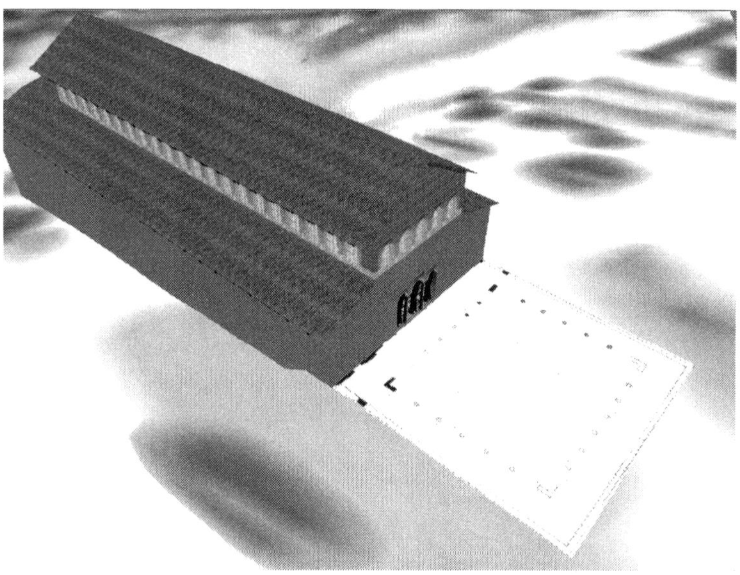

Figure 2. Bird's-eye view of the Basilica of S. Maria Maggiore with hypothetical plan of atrium.

Data collection

Thanks to the cooperation of the cultural authorities responsible for the Basilica, the Committee was able to provide the modeling team with highly accurate data. These included the latest state plan, elevation, and section of the building as well as a selection of color transparencies showing the recently restored nave mosaics. For the final version of the model, the modeling team was able to include digital versions of even more detailed large-format transparencies of the mosaics (18 x 25 cm.), which were licensed for the project. On his several visits to the Basilica, Dean Abernathy was able to take high-resolution digital photographs of such surface materials and architectonic elements as columns, brickwork, trusswork, and marbles. Thus, the model achieves a high degree of photorealism as well as architectural accuracy.

Identification of historical and archaeological research issues

VR models have many uses, from educational applications to didactic aids for heritage diffusion. Equally important, they help scholars to address research issues. The experts on the Scientific Committee carefully discussed various ways in which the VR model of the Basilica of S. Maria Maggiore in the early fifth century could be used to further research agendas. They identified several specific topics of scholarly concern, including the interrelationship between the pre-existing Roman building on the site and the new Christian basilica, the existence of an atrium, the topographical impact of the fifth-century structure, the interior lighting, the ceiling configuration, and the treatment of the original apse, especially as it related to Early Christian ritual. By specifically highlighting these topics at the beginning of the modeling process, all concerned (from the data-gatherer to the modeler) were able to give them special attention. The Scientific Committee also discussed various ways to maximize the model's usefulness, evaluating the scholarly value of creating alternative reconstructions and of conducting various analyses using diverse computer programs, e.g. a lighting study using Form Z™.

As the modeling progressed, the data-gatherers, primary modeler, and head of the Scientific Committee conferred on a regular basis, with periodic consultation with the rest of the Committee members and the Principal Investigator in person, and via e-mail; ways were explored to allow the Committee to view the models interactively on a password-protected web site. At periodic station points during the development, the experts on the Committee were all shown the same version of the model either in the UCLA Cultural VR Lab, or as a fly-through on video, or as printed images. In addition to the Scientific Committee, outside consultants were consulted regarding specific questions. For example, Professor Philip Jacks of George Washington University reviewed the open truss system of the ceiling used in an early version of the model and evaluated the proposed scheme for coffering, which was used in the final version; Professor Fikret Yegül of UC Santa Barbara assessed the construction techniques. Notably, the type of media presentation had a significant impact on the issues addressed by the experts. When the interactive, kinetic model was viewed, they focused on broad questions of form, structure, and experiential impact; with 2D prints they gave greater emphasis to materials, textures, colors, and individual details. The ideal interaction was between the modeler, scientific expert, and head of the Scientific Committee examining the model on the computer together.

Traditionally, reconstructions of historic buildings have been executed as 2D drawings of selected views or as simplified three-dimensional models. Both are static forms which can be altered only with great difficulty. With VR technology, the recreated building is constructed in 3D but is also 4-dimensional, since it can be experienced temporally. Viewers can move through the structure in real time, or see a modeled building evolve over time. A VR model is not static, allowing for several simultaneous versions and repeated updates. This flexibility allowed the Rome Reborn team to model new or conflicting interpretations, layer different building phases and test various hypotheses. For example, since scholars do not agree about the treatment of the entry into the nave, the team modeled the building entry with both a trabeated door and an arcuated, curtained opening (fig. 3).

Figure 3. Alternative reconstructions of the front entrance of the Basilica of S. Maria Maggiore.

To demonstrate the close connection between the earlier Roman house and the Early Christian building, the team modeled the Roman archaeological layer beneath the basilica (fig. 1). VR models also allow the restoration process to be more transparent. In traditional models, the evolutionary phases passed through during construction of the physical model or of the drawn reconstruction are generally lost, along with an understanding of how and why reconstruction decisions were made. With VR models, various iterations can be preserved through archiving, thereby documenting the creation process and simultaneously preserving progressive versions for reuse. In addition to documenting phases of the model, the Rome Reborn team also archived modeled and scanned data on individual building components and materials. These digital libraries are supported by written files recording the research sources, analogues, and experts consulted for each modeling decision, and for each visual and material source. Since the VR reconstruction model can be continuously updated in response to new discoveries and interpretations, it is never "completed." However, once a version satisfies the criteria of the Scientific Committee it is described as "certified." Future updates are possible, though always in consultation with the Committee.

Technical aspects of modeling

The goal of the modeling process is to create a high-fidelity, multiple dimension database integrating the research and expertise of the Scientific Committee. Initial modeling efforts focus on the physical data and descriptions of the early basilica. Scaled plans and sections were drawn prior to modeling to assist in making the 3D reconstruction. The sources for the model varied in quality and quantity, requiring a synthesis of information vetted by the Scientific Committee. The reconstruction then progressed from the general building form, commonly known as a massing model, to the specific details. This transition required an initial survey of all the building components. The component types were built, then customized and inserted into the model. The reconstruction thus tends to proceed in an uneven manner, with large improvements during the development of the massing model and almost imperceptible changes after the model components have been customized since the early changes are executed globally through undifferentiated building components, while later changes must be repeated on each custom component. The modeling process lingers in the undifferentiated stage as long as possible, so that changes and improvements can be enacted over all the components of the same type before they are differentiated. As the model matures all components are refined, updated and archived, resulting in the "certified" database in the final version of the model.

The VR database is created by combining two types of information. First is the geometric model created using 3D modeling software like Form Z™, Autocad™, 3D Studio Max™ and MultiGen™, the primary choice of the UCLA Cultural VR Lab because of its support of many realtime applications. The graphics, or surface textures form the second component. These are manipulated in software like Photoshop™, or any other similarly suited software package. The integration and management of the geometry and the textures is a difficult task. More sophisticated modeling softwares like MultiGen™ or 3D Studio Max™ facilitate the process with specific tools. MultiGen™, because of its development as a virtual reality world-building software, also provides a scene graph view of the data. This allows the simulation designer to program interactivity into the model and to optimize the data for real time simulations like virtual set technology. The MultiGen™ flight file format can also be translated into other formats allowing the database to be used with other to test lighting, structures, or materials.

Model creation

The four-dimensional form of VR models compels a holistic approach to historic architectural reconstruction which, in turn, shaped the ideas of the Scientific Committee. First and most obvious was the visual impact of decisions regarding materials, architectural decoration, and art. Reconstructions of components which seemed logical when seen in isolation or in black and white frequently had a decidedly different visual impact when viewed in the full context of the entire building. For example, the original brickwork of the basilica was photographed and digitized for the reconstruction of the structure's entire exterior surface. When faced with the huge scale of the reconstructed brick walls the Scientific Committee immediately requested this rough surface be plastered. Similarly, the uniform interior columns in an initial phase seemed too regular when seen within the great expanse of the basilica's interior; they were subsequently made more irregular in form and alignment following the example of other Early Christian buildings with *spolia*. Building elements which seemed minor or inconsequential during abstract discussions took on greater importance when seen in the 3D context of the model. Thus, at first the Scientific Committee was not overly concerned with the interior pavement, yet the powerful visual impact of the floor on the perception of the entire basilica soon demonstrated the significance of this feature (fig. 4). Several different pavements were tested and the impact of the colors, textures, and pattern size on the overall visual experience carefully evaluated. The final choice was based on a roughly contemporary floor pattern from the Basilica of San Giovanni in Laterano (see fig. 5). In a few instances, visual intensity became an issue.

Figure 4. View of the interior of the Basilica, with early version of floor and mosaic in semidome

Viewing the interior of the model the Scientific Committee felt the aediculae surrounding the mosaics above the side aisles lacked sufficient visual impact and asked the modelers to enhance their form and shadows. Similarly, the initial color scheme for the interior plaster walls appeared too dominant when seen in context and was subsequently muted. The appearance of the model also called to question some aspects of the building structure. In particular, the visual weight of the apse semidome compelled consultants to question whether there was adequate structural support.

Viewers can examine the VR model from any angle. Such multiple viewpoints immediately compelled an interest in the building's overall urban setting and topography. The Scientific Committee believed the form of the building could not be understood without recreating the surroundings. Unfortunately, information about the topography of Rome in the fifth century is limited. Drawing upon nineteenth-century excavation data, the team located spot points and analyzed the current state of the hill to recreate a topographic map of the area in late antiquity (see fig. 6). The model of the Cispian Hill's northwest slope, along with the appearance of the basilica model, compelled the Scientific Committee members to rethink the reconstruction of the apse end of the building; in response, they recommended the removal of the buttresses originally modeled around the exterior of the deambulatory of the apse in emulation of the church of S. Agnese in Rome.

Figure 5. View of the final version of the semidome of the apse and of the floor.

Especially troublesome were building components for which documentation was limited. While most scholars agree the Basilica of S. Maria Maggiore would have had an atrium court in front, no archaeological, pictorial, or written evidence exists. The team experimented with various versions of an atrium based on contemporary analogues. When seen in the context of the entire model, however, these speculative reconstructions garnered too much attention. As a result, the team decided to show the atrium in plan, in contrast to the three-dimensional representation of the basilica itself (fig. 2). This representational convention is an effective compromise, allowing viewers to understand the placement and form of the atrium, without being distracted by a hypothetical structure. Another convention was developed for the apse decoration on the interior. Scholars believe decorations embellished the original semidome of the apse, though no specifics have been preserved regarding their appearance. Rather than show the eye-catching mosaic currently in place which dates to a later period (cf. fig. 4), the modelers decided to mute the shapes and colors to evoke the existence of a decorative program without emphasizing the specifics (fig. 5).

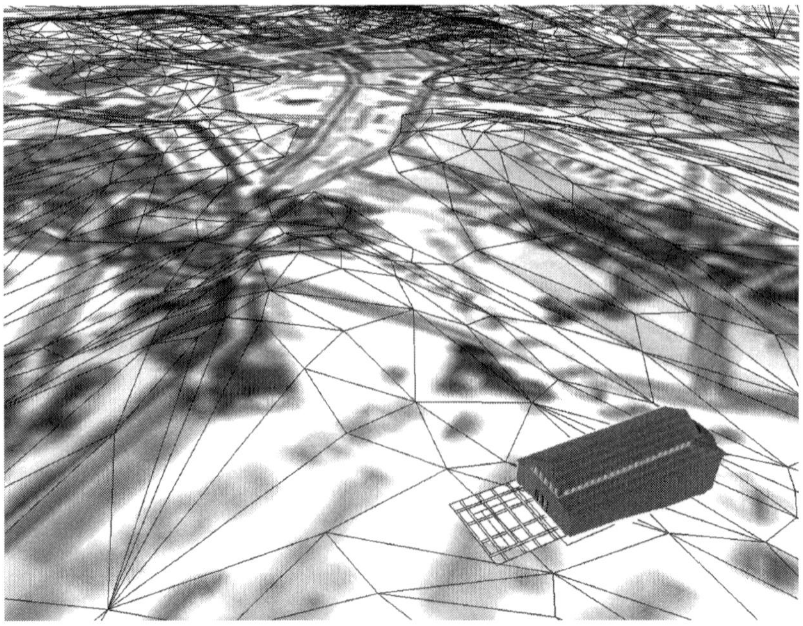

Figure 6. The topographic context of the Basilica of S. Maria Maggiore.

INSIGHTS

Every new tool has an impact on research. In the case of VR modeling, the unique requirements for creating a model compelled the acquisition and integration of complex construction data very different from that required for other types of research or reconstructions. The 4D capabilities of the modeling system also impact our understanding of past buildings. Four significant new insights resulted from the creation of the S. Maria Maggiore model. First, the temporal layering of the basilica over the earlier Roman building underscored the close integration of the two projects and the significant topographic alterations to the site. Second, the reconstructed interior with the original fenestration in place revealed that the upper section of the interior was originally bathed in a golden light which enhanced the impact of the mosaics; conversely, the dark semidome of the apse floated above windows at a lower level. Third, the reconstruction of the apse based on liturgical sources raised significant structural concerns. Fourth, and perhaps most dramatic, were the findings regarding the urban impact of the building. Resituated in the topography of Late Antique Rome, the basilica was seen to have been oriented for maximum visibility along major thoroughfares and from other hills in the city following ancient theories of view-planning. The creation of the model also highlighted areas for further research. These include questions about the translucency of the windows, the types and placement of furniture and embellishments; the exterior wall treatments; and the junctions between building parts, especially between the atrium and facade, and between the apse, ambulatory and side aisles. At the current stage, the model has greatly expanded our understanding of the construction and visual impact of the basilica's form. The next step is to investigate the building's original use through the integration of ritual furniture and live actors or avatars reenacting the ceremonial use of this magnificent structure.

Dissemination and Uses of the Santa Maria Maggiore Model

Models can be used for a variety of purposes, including architectural walk-throughs and urban simulations; historical reconstruction; architectural analysis; nondestructive conservation and restoration; recontextualization of works of art that have been moved from their original location; and virtual sets in documentaries or in works of fiction.

Models are computer files consisting of 3D geometry and textures applied to the surfaces of the geometry. They may be viewed on the computer either in realtime or in prerendered, pre-encoded video clips. Models may also be used as assets in educational videos for delivery on videocassettes or over broadcast and cable television.

The advantage of realtime is flexibility: the user can explore the model along an infinite number of paths chosen spontaneously by the user himself. Since persistence of vision in realtime ideally requires the computer to render at least 30 frames per second, the price the user pays for this flexibility is a loss of detail: geometry and textures may have to be simplified to permit the computer to create frames at a fast enough speed. Effects such as reflections, translucency, shadows, or perspective correction may have to be sacrificed. The advantage of prerendered video is that it supports a high level of visual detail and effects. The disadvantage is that, as the term prerendered implies, the user is limited to precisely those paths through the model that have been selected in advance.

Both realtime and video applications can be enhanced with animations and hot spots linked to other files or World Wide Web sites. Through animations and hot spots models can be linked to information that can help the user to understand the history, cultural significance, and archaeological evidence of a model. Interactivity in varying degrees and through differing tools thus characterizes the use of a model on the computer.

Contrasted to this, a model utilized as an asset on an educational video is linear. Fly-throughs of a model can be outputted to a video recorder. Files of models can be used in a virtual set system to create the illusion that live actors (e.g., an archaeologist or architectural historian) have been transported into the virtual world. When combined in postproduction, fly-throughs and virtual set shots can enable the archaeologist or other expert to give a tour of the site as reconstructed on the computer. Since the medium is video, the same high degree of realism is possible (lighting effects, shadows, translucency, etc.) that characterizes prerendered video delivered on the computer. And since video cassette recorders are commonplace in homes and schools, and since streaming video can now be delivered over the World Wide Web, the educational video offers a combination of low cost and high visual quality that more than compensates for its lack of interactivity.

Each of these delivery modes has its appropriate use. For example, a scholar might use a realtime model during a lecture in order to present his own analysis of a site. It could also be used in a VR theater with a screen wrapping around the audience or in a CAVE environment installed in a museum or on the archaeological site. A CAVE (literally, a "computer-assisted virtual environment") is an immersive virtual environment, typically 3 x 3 meters in size or larger, in which the computer model is projected onto the walls, floor, and ceiling while viewers stand in the middle of the space. CAVEs are thus typically more immersive than are VR theaters (which typically contain projections on just three walls), but VR theaters have the advantage of more readily accommodating a large number of viewers, who, moreover, can be seated during the VR experience. In a CAVE or VR theater, a guide can take visitors on a live, interactive tour of the 3D computer model, answering questions and giving views of the site that even the ancient visitor could not see or see so well.. A teacher whose expertise pertains more to the use or history of the site than to its construction might use a videotape with a virtual tour of a site given by an archaeologist or architectural historian. The same videotape can be used in the auditorium of a museum or archaeological site to provide an orientation for visitors.

The UCLA Cultural VR Lab has been actively experimenting with ways of combining the strengths of all the approaches just mentioned into an integrated archaeological information system that is scalable to the needs and interests of users ranging from high school students to advanced scholars. Thus, on the Rome Reborn Web site (URL: http: //www.humnet.ucla.edu/rome-reborn) can be found pre-rendered video models, realtime models as well as videoclips of fly-throughs and virtual set shots. Users can simultaneously watch a videoclip while reading the script in a text window. Technical terms in the script are themselves linked to a glossary window. Although the videoclip is linear with respect to the world it depicts, it is presented in a viewing window that permits interactivity in the form of starting, stopping, and reversing the clip itself. Thus the user is empowered to learn at his own pace.

The Office of Academic Computing, the central computing facility on the UCLA campus, is building a virtual theater, which is scheduled to open in January, 2000. The theater, which will be known as the Visualization Portal (URL: http://www.oac.ucla.edu/portal/), is a unique facility at an American university. It will provide seating for over twenty viewers to sit in a space surrounded by an 8 meter x 3 meter highly luminous screen, onto which models and related information can be projected in realtime. The facility will be available to the researchers of the Cultural VR Lab as well as to students in the classes they teach. When it opens, a new era in the Lab's history will begin as it changes its emphasis from model creation to the use of 3D models in teaching and research. It will be a splendid resource to use for immersive viewing of the Basilica.

Aknowledgments

We thank the following institutions and individuals who have sponsored the Rome Reborn Project: Alitalia; Canyon Video; Creative Kids Education Foundation; Design Visualization Partners; Digital Media Interactive; Intel; KPMG Peat Marwick ICE; Jeff Klein Productions; Mr. Kirk Mathews; The Production Group; Pamela Robinson; Daniel and Joanna Rose; Giuseppe Santulli Sanzo; Stream; Tecnark Italia; UCLA College of Letters and Science; UCLA School of the Arts and Architecture, UCLA Humanities Computing Facility; UCLA Office of the Vice Chancellor for Research. We also wish to express our deep gratitude for the help given to this project by Monsignor John D. Lewis, Amministratore Pontificio dell'Arcipatriarcale Basilica Liberiana di S. Maria Maggiore.

For further information about the Rome Reborn Project (www.humnet.ucla.edu/rome-reborn) or about access to the model of the Basilica of S. Maria Maggiore, please contact Prof. Bernard Frischer (frischer@ucla.edu).

References Cited

CECCHELLI, M., 1988, "Dalla Basilica Liberiana al complesso paleocristiano e altomedievale," in *Santa Maria Maggiore a Roma* (Nardini: Florence) pp. 71-84.

DE BLAAUW, S., 1994, *Cultus et decor: Liturgia e architettura nella Roma tardoantica e medievale* (Biblioteca Apostolica Vaticana: Vatican City).

DE GRUMMOND, N. T., ed., 1996, *An Encyclopedia of the History of Classical Archaeology,* vol. 1 (Greenwood Press: Westport CT) pp. 160-61.

DE SPIRITO, G. , 1994, "Contra pelagianos o delle cause storiche e teologiche che presiedettero alla edificazione della basilica di Santa Maria Maggiore in Roma," *Romanobarbarica*, forthcoming.

GEERTMAN, H., 1976, "The Builders of the Basilica Maior in Rome," in*: Festoen. Opgedragen aan A.N. Zadoks Josephus Jitta bij haar zeventigste verjaardag* (Groningen-Bussum), 277-295.

GEERTMAN, H., 1986-87, "Forze centrifughe e centripete nella Roma cristiana: Il Laterano, la basilica Iulia e la basilica Liberiana," *Rendiconti della Pontificia Accademia Romana di Archeologia* 59, pp. 63-91.

KRAUTHEIMER, R., CORBETT, S., FRANKL, W., 1971, *Corpus basilicarum christianarum Romae,* vol. III (Pontificio Istituto di Archeologia Cristiana: Vatican City) 1-60.

KRAUTHEIMER, R., 1980, *Rome. Profile of a City, 312-1308* (Princeton University Press: Princeton NJ).

LIVERANI, P., 1988, "L'ambiente nell'antichità," in *Santa Maria Maggiore a Roma* (Nardini: Florence) pp. 45-53.

MAGI, F., 1972, "Il calendario dipinto sotto S. Maria Maggiore," *Memorie della Pontifica Accademia di Archeologia* 11.1, pp. 3-48.

RICHARDSON, Jr., L., 1992, A *New Topographical Dictionary of Ancient Rome* (Johns Hopkins University Press: Baltimore).

STEINBY, E.M., ed., 1993--99, *Lexicon Topographicum Urbis Romae,* 5 volumes (Edizioni Quazar: Rome)

IMMERSIVE IMAGING TECHNOLOGIES FOR ARCHAEOLOGICAL RESEARCH

Louise Krasniewicz

Digital Archaeology Lab, Cotsen Institute of Archaeology at University of California at Los Angeles, USA
kraz@ucla.edu

Introduction: Representing Research

So much of the data archaeologists collect is visual and four-dimensional (three spatial dimensions and time). Maps, drawings, photographs, texts, charts, tables, databases and sketched profiles have long been the standard forms for presenting the visual components of archaeological research. Is this because they are the best way to represent the data or is it that until recently there have not been any accurate, accessible and easy to use alternatives?

The translation of archaeological information into text, charts or graphs for presentations and publications has meant an inevitable loss of not only most of the visual elements but also of some of the richness, accuracy and immediacy of the data. While maps, drawings, photographs, and profiles can supplement these presentations, these depictions of the material remains of past cultures also suffer from what Tufte (1990: 15) has called "the difficulties of dimensional compression." Such flattened, compressed and static images decrease not only the dimensions represented but also the density of data that is usually available about the "multivariate worlds" that humans occupy and imagine (ibid.: 12). This multivariate world allows one to look around and see things from different angles and distances and to imagine them across time, an absolute necessity for archaeologists.

It is easy to understand, then, why computer imaging techniques, especially the various forms of virtual reality and 3D simulations, are appealing to archaeologists. 3D models, virtual reconstructions, distribution map graphics, computer-based drawings, or immersive imaging all promise an accessible, highly visual, and interactive experience of difficult-to-see data placed back in at least some aspects of its original context. Virtual reality of all forms seems to promise a more vivid and multisensory representation of the material evidence of past cultures, opening up new ways of presenting research and interpreting results. And as computer processing power in desktop computing increases, researchers are more easily moving into three- and four-dimensional representations of their data and are exploring technologies that can immerse their reader/viewer into an archaeological project.

It is not always the case, however, that virtual reality immerses the viewer in the *context* of archaeological data as they were collected and interpreted; often the immersion is into an idealized 3D model of only select and dramatic elements of a project, usually architecture on a grand scale. This paper will examine the potential connections between virtual reality and archaeology that exist beyond the modeling of large-scale architecture in 3D simulation programs. It will argue that for archaeological researchers, it is more important to find ways to use virtual reality as a way to immerse readers into the context of the primary archaeological data rather than into a final reconstruction of an archaeological site.

Virtual Reality and the Contextual Goals of Archaeology

It is, of course, difficult to discuss archaeology as a cohesive and uniform discipline except on the most general levels. This paper favors archaeology as a social science that is concerned with studying and understanding the human past and its relation to the present. Sharer and Ashmore (1979: 12) define (for undergraduates first encountering the discipline) the goals of archaeology as the study of the form, function and processes of the past: describing and classifying the recovered material remains; determining the uses of these materials in order to reconstruct "ancient customs, behaviors and beliefs" of past peoples and the important events in their lives; and understanding and explaining how and why cultures changed. This is consistent with Fagan's description of archaeology, in his introductory text on the subject, as a social science with the goal of understanding "how people have dealt with the world around them from the earliest times" (Fagan 1988: 12).

It is in this social science approach that archaeology, the study of "the social and cultural past through material remains" (Sharer and Ashmore 1979: 11), has these three basic goals (Fagan 1988: 12):

1. describing the cultural histories of a particular place across time
2. reconstructing past lifeways and cultural practices
3. studying cultural processes and cultural change

There is no mandate in anthropological archaeology to literally reconstruct cultures, that is, make visual representations of the physical environs and elements of the ancient life. Rather, the "reconstruction" called for here is more behavioral, a matter of being able to explain how people made a living, solved their problems, dealt with change, engaged the environment, performed rituals, developed religions and created meaning. This information is teased out of the data and its related contexts.

There are many theoretical approaches to archaeology and many particulars of methodology, but whether archaeology is approached as a science, an art, or a social science, it does have some consistent aspects. Archaeology usually involves the collection of data in a systematic way through fieldwork. The data are then analyzed in relation to their contexts in order to provide an image of a past way of life.

Without context, archaeological material, like looted treasures, is all but useless for the researcher. "Context is the interpretation of the significance of an artifact's deposition in terms of its matrix, provenience, and association—that is, where it is and how it got there" (Sharer and Ashmore 1979: 84). The matrix, or material the artifacts were found in, provides information on the deposition of the artifacts. The provenience pinpoints the location and the association tells what other artifacts or features were nearby. This focus on recovering and then interpreting material remains in their context is the heart of archaeological analysis. This is why looted material, with its compete lack of context, is such an unacceptable source of data for most archaeologists.

The importance of publishing research results is recognized by every scientific discipline, but for archaeologists there is the added responsibility of making primary data, collected in the field along with its contexts, available to the archaeological community. This is because the destruction of the context of that data is inherent in the archaeological method. The process of excavating an archaeological site, whether a humble house mound or a glorious temple, removes not only artifacts from the ground, but also the contextual information which tells how, when and where that material was deposited. This contextual evidence can only be encountered one time, in its pristine state; an original archaeological excavation cannot be replicated but through virtual reality it can be simulated.

Virtual reality is usually described as the computer-based technology that presents the illusion of entering a world that is artificial and exists only in the computer (Coyne 1995: 179; Rheingold 1991). Limiting the definition of virtual reality to artificial worlds that have no reference back to things on solid ground certainly limits our thoughts about what virtual reality can and should do; for archaeology, adhering to this definition of virtual reality would limit its usefulness for research.

Virtual reality researcher and multi-media producer Brenda Laurel (1993: 199n) provides a richer definition of virtual reality as:

> A medium in which the human sensorium is surrounded by (or immersed in) stimuli that are partially or wholly generated or represented by artificial means, and in which all imagery is displayed from the point of view of an individual participant, even as he or she moves around.

The virtual reality experience in archaeology should be designed to simulate the experience that is specific to archaeology, not the experience of thrill rides, motion pictures, or video games. This is precisely what Laurel describes: the experience of a particular point of view that processes various forms of information as the archaeologist moves through the material remains of a culture. Research-oriented archaeological virtual reality might be thought of as an experience that simulates being in a location that provides the context for a collection of archaeological data. This data can be explored through computer technologies which help represent the multi-sensory contexts found in archaeological sites. As Barcelo and Bascones explain in this volume, "a virtual model is not knowledge in itself, but a means to acquire knowledge."

Virtual reality tools can help restore some of the archaeological context so that other archaeologists can see where and how the data were found. This does not mean creating idealized models of a site, but rather using the technology to immerse other researchers into the origins of the data. In the past this was done through textual descriptions, maps, photographs, and drawings. Now this can be done through computer-generated 3D models or through interactive photographic panoramas and other forms of virtual reality.

Virtual Reconstructions

The use of computer visualization in archaeology has almost become synonymous with 3D computer-generated reconstructions. Forte points out that such models are important because, "above and beyond its strong popular impact, computer reconstruction allows the presentation of complex information in a visual way that enables it to be used to test and refine the image or model that has been created" (Forte 1997: 12-13). For example, the work on the analysis and restoration of the Tomb of Bakenrenef in Egypt, which used 3D reconstructions, shows how these technologies can aid in the research process. Computer-generated models aided in the complex task or organizing thousands of wall and ceiling fragments, found in the tomb, into coherent pictures. But more significantly, the many other pieces of this complex puzzle, which will always be held in museums or private collections, could be added to the computer models to create a more complete picture of the tomb. The 3D virtual reality models "elegantly avoids some of the problems that would be posed by permanent in situ restoration," most notably allowing for the virtual removal of obstructing materials and identifying actual remains from inferred reconstructions (Betro 1997: 40-41).

3D computer-generated reconstructions do not always, however, encourage a view of archaeological sites as consisting of data and their contexts. Rather, it often makes buildings and structures the dominant form of information and makes the movement through structures the most meaningful activity. The promotion of rapid movements through large structures and spaces (fly-throughs or walk-throughs) that are usually cleared of debris and artifacts and the other material remains of a past human presence is a hallmark of the 3D reconstruction but not of actual archaeological practices. Fly-throughs provide a nice understanding of a space, which requires the ability to move from one location to another (Tuan 1977: 12). However, few archaeologists really "fly" through an archaeological site; instead they spend long amounts of time looking intently at sometimes obscure features, at the relationships between artifacts and their specific, often unglamorous, contexts. A form of virtual reality that enhances this sense of being in the place where data was collected and which represents the condition of that place at the time of data acquisition could be very useful for archaeological research.

Navigable Spaces with Interactive Panoramas

The Digital Archaeology Lab was established in the Cotsen Institute of Archaeology at UCLA in order to explore the uses of digital media for archaeological publications. This state-of-the-arts digital production facility, staffed by both archaeologists and professionals in multimedia and computer-based production, is committed to finding the most practical, useful and affordable methods for presenting primary archaeological data to both general and professional audiences. The goal is to create digital media that can be useful at every stage of research and that are practical, easy and inexpensive to produce. The Lab creates media not for high-end work stations but for the desktop machines commonly found in academic settings.

The UCLA Digital Archaeology Lab is exploring virtual reality technologies that can provide immediate and practical access to the contexts of archaeological data. This means that we are not primarily seeking to create reconstructions, but rather we want to exploit one of the other features of virtual reality—its ability to provide a sense of immersion in a specific place and time. Our primary goal is to enable archaeologists to revisit an archaeological site at any point in the interpretive or analytical process. This visitation enables *imagining* the data back in the actual context from which it had been removed. This is quite different from *imaging* the site at an ideal point in its past life or in a conclusive form after research is complete.

To achieve these goals, the UCLA Digital Archaeology Lab is utilizing a form of virtual reality that consists not of rendered models but of multiple photographic views of an archaeological site blended together to form an interactive and immersive 360 degree panorama (see Figure 1).

Figure 1. 360° QuickTime VR panorama of Xunantunich, a Maya city in Belize

The panoramas are interactive without being burdened by excessive technology: without using any special gloves, helmets or high-end computer work stations, the viewer can use the mouse and keyboard to rotate the view horizontally 360 degrees, giving the illusion of standing in one place and looking at the scene in every direction (see Figure 2).

Figure 2. Panoramas provide 360° immersive view

Most panoramas also allow a limited vertical movement, tilting the view up or down. A user can also zoom in for a closer look or zoom out for a wider perspective, all with a simple keystroke.

This type of panoramic immersive virtual reality has commonly been called QuickTime VR (QTVR) after the technology developed by Apple Computer in the early 1990s. QTVR is a component of QuickTime, Apple's "industry-standard, software architecture that makes it possible to create, integrate, and publish all types of digital media" (Apple Computer 1997: 2). QuickTime plays not just sound and video but also text, still images, animations, 3D models and virtual reality. QuickTime is the multi-platform foundation for dynamic media that can be produced and played on Macintoshes, Windows PCs, and Silicon Graphics machines, the three most common platforms in academic research. QuickTime VR is the component of QuickTime which enables interacting with images, giving the sense of either standing at a point and looking out at a scene (a panorama) or looking in at an object that can be "picked up" and rotated to be viewed at all angles (an object movie).

QTVR has been the general term for these interactive panoramas and object movies but recently there has been a move to change the name to something more general. This reflects the introduction of new software and media formats beyond those on the Macintosh for authoring and playing the panoramic interactive movies as well as variations in the photographic VR format. The International QuickTime VR Association (IQTVRA), a group of professional panorama and object movie producers and equipment manufacturers, has already been struggling to develop a new name, arguing in its communications to members that the phrase "QTVR" promotes just one manufacturer and does not reflect the unique interactive quality of this medium (IQTVRA web site 1998). The membership did not approve a name change in 1998 but other versions of the Panoramic VR like those from IPIX and Live Picture continue to confuse the name issue. Kaidan, one of the major producers of specialized equipment for producing QTVR, has recently shifted its advertising materials to the term "immersive imaging" which, as one IQTVRA member argued, is technology neutral and distinctive from VR that requires headsets or utilizes VRML (Virtual Reality Modeling Language, a currently popular web-ready low resolution interactive 3D imaging protocol). eVox, a company that creates panoramas and object movies commercially, also uses the term "immersive imaging."

In the rest of this paper, the term "panoramic VR" will be used to refer generally to these photographic interactive movies that look outward from a fixed spot, usually 360° around. "QTVR" will be used when referring to the actual Apple technology. "Object movies" will refer to the interactive movies that simulate looking inward at an object. Live Picture's and VRWorx's approaches to panoramic VR are essentially the same as Apple's. The IPIX bubble technology (360 above and below as well as horizontal) will not be addressed directly because the licensing and per-use payment requirements do not make it a practical choice for academic use. Other versions of panoramic VR are in development.

The effect of these interactive photographic panoramas is to "imitate the processes" of actual reality: standing in one place and looking around to see everything that is visible from that spot as well as moving to another spot that provides an alternative view (see Kitchen 1998: 4). Panoramic VR offers "the viewer the same viewing choices she would have if she were actually there" (ibid.: 5), providing an experience of space and context. Virtual reality, Brenda Laurel says, "reminds us of what we are good at; namely, perceiving the world from a located and situated vantage point" (Laurel 1993: 205). The hope is that the viewer will "perceive patterns" in VR's multisensory representations (ibid.: 206) more readily than in maps, drawings or simple photographs alone.

This enhanced perception is directed towards data contexts that can enhance the interpretive process. It is of course notoriously difficult to measure or quantify this enhancement. Productivity studies may measure the efficiency or convenience of accessing data but they cannot explain how the data was used better or how it improved understanding or insights by a researcher (see Bennett 1999: 73). Nevertheless, if archaeologists rely on contextualization for all their interpretations, then technology that promotes context will doubtless provide a useful service.

The Panorama and Virtual Realities

If virtual reality, even that seen in the immersive photographic panorama, depends on illusion for its effects, how can it help us grasp the facts of archaeological data? Relying on photographic realism is not an automatic solution. As Rheingold suggests, more and more realism in VR does not necessarily lead to more "truthfulness" (Rheingold 1991: 45). What does the photographic panorama offer beyond its ease of use and sense of immersion? The answer may lie in the history of the panorama.

Panoramas are images that surround the viewer, wrapping around so the viewer can look to all sides to see the panorama without being distracted by the viewing environment. Panorama is a term "created for a specific form of landscape painting which reproduced a 360-degree view and was invented independently around 1787 by several different European painters" (Oettermann 1997: 6). The large painted panoramas of the 18th and 19th centuries, displayed in special cylindrical buildings, were the first mass medium that enabled audiences to step into or immerse themselves into a simulated environment. These panoramas, Oettermann says, "imitated the experience of travel to a great variety of exotic locales," transporting spectators "to distant places 'in the twinkling of an eye' and 'as if in a dream.' And the trips they could take in panoramas were not only faster and more comfortable, but above all cheaper" (ibid.: 21). Popular panoramas depicted great battles, the interior of famous buildings, or famous cities. The basic purpose of these panoramas was to "reproduce the real world so skillfully that spectators could believe what they were seeing was genuine" (ibid.: 49). They were immensely popular and the exhibition of painted or photographic panoramas in special buildings lasted for 100 years.

Tracing the history of these panoramas, Oettermann points out that the development of the panorama coincided with some significant shifts in how humans were instructed by their culture to view the world. The panorama developed as part of the push in the sciences, in travel, in literature and other areas to see beyond the limits of the horizon, see things from a new angle, and have a broad overview of a situation or scene (Oettermann 1997: 20). "'Panoramic' vision is primarily a way of 'getting a grip' on things, a grip that leaves what is observed undamaged, but surrounds and seizes the whole" (ibid.: 22); it also provides multiple perspectives as opposed to the unique perspective required for proper viewing of a painting presented on a two dimensional surface. The panorama acts as a sort of "visual encyclopedia, a reference work for a portion of the visible world" because it took in the view from so many different directions (ibid.: 121). One reviewer of a panorama exhibit called it a "concentrated history" (ibid.: 137) superior to maps, drawings and descriptions because it condensed multiple experiences into a single event.

During this same time, archaeology was developing as an academic discipline. As Willey and Sabloff explain, the long-standing antiquarian interests in the Old World developed into professional archaeological practices as a consequence of many shifts in intellectual thought and practices. Included among these are "a general rise and appreciation of science in general;" "the rising industrialism in western Europe and America;" explorations of and expansions into remote parts of the world; the introduction of Darwinian evolution; geological concepts of strata and dating; and ideas of progress in human societies as being linear and progressive (1974: 2-4). Archaeology, then, was part of the intellectual climate that was incorporating a "panoramic" view of the world and of the relation between scientific disciplines.

The panorama and the beginnings of scientific archaeology came together in the person of Frederick Catherwood. An artist and architect, Catherwood first began sketching ruins in Italy in the 1820s and eventually found his way to Egypt, Greece and the Near East. He is perhaps best known for his collaborations with John Lloyd Stephens on the reporting and recording of Maya ruins in Mexico and Central America beginning in 1839, just as academic archaeology was beginning to take form. Some of the sketches Catherwood brought back of ruins in the Near East were transformed into painted panoramas that were exhibited in London in the 1830s. In 1838 he opened his own panorama house in New York after spending years struggling to finance and complete it. This round building featured many painted 360° views of archaeological ruins and ancient cities. Catherwood's biographer, Victor Wolfgang Von Hagen, reports that panoramas drew "immense numbers of curious people" (1950: 38). Despite his financial success and fulfilling his ambition to open a panorama house, Catherwood returned to exploring archaeological ruins.

What Catherwood discovered with his use of panoramas to depict ancient cities and civilizations was more than just an experience, as one guidebook described them, "where the eye was pleased without the brain being duly exerted" (Hagen 1950: 38). The panoramas were able to transport people to these ancient places in a way no single-view painting could. Combined with Catherwood's lectures, they created a multi-media approach to immersing the audience in a different world. Oettermann reports that panoramas were more successful in Europe than the United States because they served this function well for a society that was expanding its curiosity about other worlds: "For Europeans, the 360° vista of the panorama reflected this curiosity and represented an enormous expansion of perspective. Americans, on the other hand, were dealing with dimensions in their own country that could not be grasped or conquered" simply with circular paintings (Oettermann 1997:323).

CREATING PANORAMIC VR AND OBJECT MOVIES

The panorama, then, creates an automatic interactive experience, requiring the viewer to choose a viewpoint and movement through the image. There are clearly continuities between these past experiences of archaeological sites viewed through panoramas and the present use of computers to create a similar immersive experience. But like the panorama houses of old, much of the current archaeological virtual reality requires inordinate amounts of money, resources and expertise to create and sustain. Highly trained and expensive 3D modelers and animators produce the 3D reconstructions on high-end, expensive graphics work stations with software that can cost tens of thousands of dollars and salaries that can range even higher.

In order to be useful for a wider array of archaeological researchers, virtual reality that is designed to reach a wider audience needs to take the form of panoramic VR which can be easily produced by researchers themselves while they are in the middle of fieldwork and interpretations. For example, archeologists in the Cotsen Institute of Archaeology at UCLA have taken panoramic rigs to China, Easter Island, the Farallon Islands off the coast of California, Peru, and Belize in the past year with minimal training and experience with the equipment and technology. Some were at the late stages of research and were recording final excavations but others used the rig to record early surveys of potential sites. In each case they produced very valuable and high quality panoramas for their ongoing research.

The features of immersive photographic panoramic VR suggest that besides these historical and theoretical continuities with panoramas of the past, there are more practical reasons for choosing photographic immersive imaging to enhance archaeological research.

Panoramic VR has the following advantages for archaeological researchers:

1. it can be authored cross-platform
2. it is playable across platforms
3. it is playable on low-end computers
4. it is deliverable on disk, CD-ROM, web, or email
5. it can be created with existing or inexpensive photographic equipment
6. it can be highly interactive
7. it is able to provide a sense of immersion in a photographic rather than3D modeled environment
8. it can be created by anyone with minimal training
9. it is non-linear
10. it can be produced from many different types of source materials including

    digital camera images
    film camera images
    video camera still images
    computer rendered images

Looking at how a panorama is made will demonstrate some of these capabilities. The panorama is photographed with a digital or film camera set on a tripod and a panorama rig (see Figure 3). The rig is required in order to rotate the camera around a fixed point so that the images can be seamlessly combined and parallax eliminated (in a parallax error, "close objects will appear to move in relation to far objects as the camera is rotated" (Kitchens 1998: 43)).

Figure 3: Panoramic rig on Easter Island

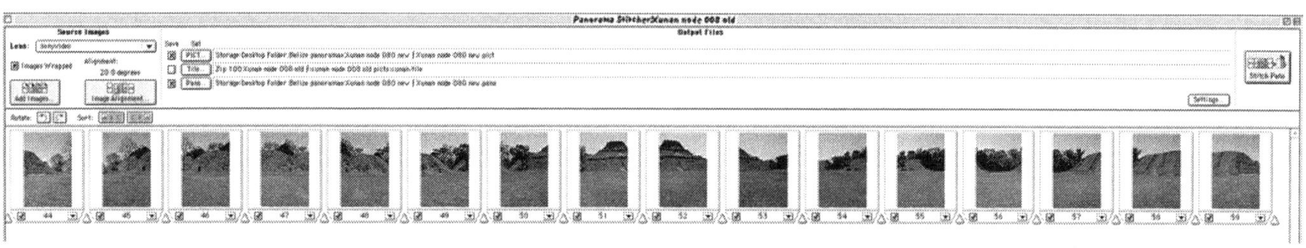

Figure 4. Sixteen images that will be blended into a panorama; software interface from Apple's QTVR Authoring Studio.

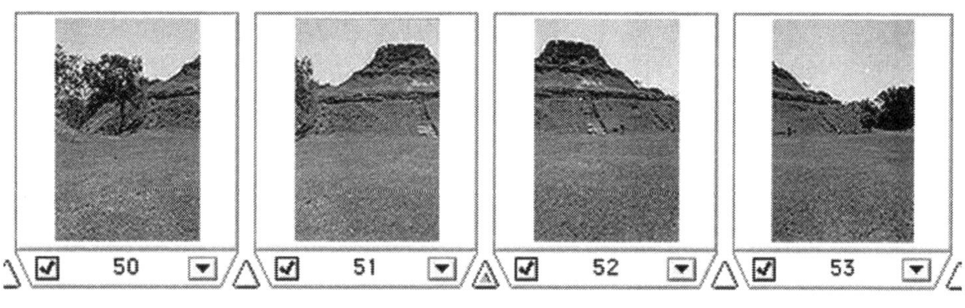

Figure 5. Detail of four adjacent images.

Depending on the lens used, each panorama requires between 12 and 24 images (see Figures 4 and 5) shot vertically to maximize the vertical panning range.

If the images are captured into a digital camera, they can be downloaded immediately into an authoring program such as Apple's QuickTime VR Authoring Studio, Live Picture or VRWorx. Images shot with a regular camera can be processed and scanned professionally as a photo CD which can hold 100 images at multiple resolutions.

The images are overlapped and blended together in an authoring program to make a complete 360° panorama. The stitched panoramas are wrapped inside a virtual cylinder and the image is warped so that no matter what direction the viewer looks, the image holds the correct perspective. The point from which the viewer surveys the scene is called a node. Several panoramas can be linked together into a scene which enables movement through the space by moving from one node to another. Locations in a panorama can be marked for interactivity; clicking on such a "hotspot" could lead to another node in the scene, to a still image, a sound, a web site or another movie.

There is another form of photographic VR that is useful for archaeologists. "Object movies" are interactive photographic movies that look inward at an object that can be rotated on all axes. Object movies can have one horizontal view (or row) with 36 images to create a smooth transition from one image to another, giving the sense of turning the object in either horizontal direction (see Figure 6). More complicated object movies can be created with a rig that moves the camera in an arc around the object, enabling multiple vertical views of the object. The result is a simulation of holding the object and looking at it from all angles. In a sense the object movie reverses the process of the panorama, looking inward instead of outward. Used alone, without contextualization of the objects, the object movie may provide little more than a dramatic gesture. But combined with panoramic VR and more traditional methods of contextualization (maps, photographs, feature drawings), the object movie can represent the artifacts of an archaeological project better than most other methods.

Figure 6. Images from single row object movie (Maya figurine, Belize National Collection).

Conclusions

Can virtual reality really promote the goals of archaeological research and publishing? The choice of how technology is used to present the data is more than just an aesthetic one. The difference is really on whether the virtual reality is used to aid ongoing research, contextualization of data, and interpretations, or is primarily used as a medium at the completion stage where virtual reality models present a visual enactment of the final research results.

The virtual reconstruction of an archaeological site through computer-generated 3D models is an activity that usually takes place in the last phases of research (Forte 1997: 10), a final product of years of analysis, study and design (Forte and Siliotti 1997: 37). As Forte and Siliotti dramatically demonstrate in their book *Virtual Archaeology: Re-creating Ancient Worlds,* accurately representing ancient buildings and settings requires a complicated, multidisciplinary approach that "extrapolates" a 3D visual representation from large quantities of already interpreted data. This process usually requires specialists in computer science, graphics and scientific visualization who translate archaeological data into computer forms.

This paper explored the alternative to computer-generated 3D architectural models and considered one other tool available to the archeological researcher seeking to emphasize and represent the context of archaeological data. Panoramic VR and object movies can provide one accessible and easy to use method for recontextualizing data.

Archaeologists assume that the "correct" and expected sequence of archaeological work is: excavation, post-excavation analysis, interpretation, and writing with often a large gap between the beginning and ending activities (Richards 1995: 218). A technology that closes the circle and enables the archaeologist to virtually return to the point of data collection during the post-excavation period would be valuable. The goal of enhancing the understanding of the context from which the data have been extracted will be met by virtual reality experiences that provide a sense of revisiting the site while the archaeologist is conducting analysis and interpretation.

It is the concern over the loss of irreplaceable archaeological data and their contexts that should compel archaeologists to make representing the context of their data a top priority. Archaeologists have the responsibility of making the contexts of their primary data available to the archaeological community. The inability of most archaeological projects to report fully and share their primary data is a significant problem in a discipline where the destruction of the context of that data is inherent in the archaeological method. anoramic VR is one tool for achieving these goals of sharing primary data and its contexts.

References Cited

APPLE COMPUTER, 1997 *Using the Quicktime VR Authoring Tools*. Apple Computer, Inc. Cupertino, CA.

BENNETT, SCOTT, 1999, "Information-Based Productivity" in *Technology and Scholarly Communication,* R. Ekman and R. Quandt, eds. Berkeley: University of California Press, pp. 73-94.

BETRO, MARIA CARMELA, 1997, "Saqqara: From the Past to the Future," in *Virtual Archaeology: Re-Creating Ancient Worlds*, Maurizio Forte and Alberto Siliotti, eds., Harry N. Abrams, Inc., Publishers. New York, pp. 26- 41.

COYNE, RICHARD, 1995, *Designing InformationTtechnology in the Postmodern Age: From Method to Metaphor.* Cambridge: MIT Press.

DARK, K.R., 1995, *Theoretical Archaeology.* Ithaca: Cornell University Press.

FAGAN, BRIAN, 1988, *Archaeology: A Brief Introduction.* New York: Addison-Wesley-Longman.

FORTE, MAURIZIO, 1997, "Introduction," in *Virtual Archaeology: Re-Creating Ancient Worlds*, Maurizio Forte and Alberto Siliotti, eds., Harry N. Abrams, Inc., Publishers. New York, pp. 8-13.

FORTE, MAURIZIO AND ALBERTO SILIOTTI, EDS., 1997, *Virtual Archaeology: Re-Creating Ancient World.* New York: Harry N. Abrams, Inc., Publishers.

KITCHEN, SUSAN A., 1998, *The QTVR Book: Creating Immersive Imaging on Your Desktop.* Berkeley: Peachpit Press.

LAUREL, BRENDA, 1993, *Computers as Theatres.* New York: Addison-Wesley Publishing Co., Inc.

OETTERMANN, STEPHAN, 1997, *The Panorama,* translated by Deborah Lucas Schneider, Urzone, Inc. New York

RHEINGOLD, HOWARD, 1991, *Virtual Reality.* New York: Summit Books.

RICHARDS, COLIN, 1995, "Knowing about the Past," in *Interpreting Archaeology: Finding Meaning in the Past*, Hodder, et al., eds. New York: Routledge.

SHARER, ROBERT AND WENDY ASHMORE, 1979 *Archaeology: Discovering Our Past.* Mountain View, CA: Mayfield Publishing Co.

TUAN, YI-FU, 1997, *Space and Place: The Perspective of Experience.* Minneapolis: University of Minnesota Press.

TUFTE, EDWARD R, 1990, *Envisioning Information.* Cheshire, CT: Graphics Press.

VON HAGEN, VICTOR WOLFGANG, 1950, *Frederick Catherwood, Archt.* New York: Oxford University Press.

WILLEY, GORDEN AND JEREMY SABLOFF, 1974, *A History of American Archaeology.* London: Thames and Hudson.

Archaeological Applications

TRAVEL TO THE TIME OF THE IBERIANS

Arturo Ruiz Rodríguez, Manuel Molinos Molinos, Luis María Gutiérrez Soler (lmsoler@ujaen.es), ***María Ángeles Royo Encarnación***
Centro Andaluz de Arqueología Ibérica, Universidad de Jaén, Spain

Antonella Guidazzoli (Guidazzoli@cineca.it), ***Luigi Calori***
CINECA (Consorzio Interuniversitario per la gestione del Centro di Calcolo Elettronico dell'Italia Nord-Orientale), Italy

Introduction

Over the last few years we have presented several projects related to the archaeological research and analysis of Iberian settlements. The working methods have benefitted from the use of new software and successive generations of more and more powerful and efficient graphic workstations.

Archaeological landscape navigation forms the basis of our research. As a part of this type of computer graphics we have included a different type of computer resource, from digital image processing to graphic design (Gutiérrez & Alcázar, 1995), without rejecting the possibility of including databases which convert a model into a completely interactive module visually accessible via the Internet. Combination of different techniques and scales of procedures allows a wide variety of views and approaches. It also permits a global understanding of the landscape and centres upon increasingly specific aspects related to the definition of archaeological sites and even activity areas.

Continuation of the introduction of global information networks and the creation of a Net Virtual Museum will be followed by efforts to integrate these applications as a part of the same multimedia process of territorial reconstruction. Our experience to this effect has allowed us not only to advance in our research but also to protect and make known our national heritage, which in our case was focused on the documentation concerning the Iberian culture in the province of Jaén.

Archaeological Landscape Navigations

Since 1994 several navigations have been carried out, first in the city of Jaén, and secondly in the *oppida* of Giribaile and Puente Tablas. These are computer animations with a photorealistic aspect that allow a fly-over of the territory. This territory is considered as a 3D space that is the basis of a historical hypothesis based on the interpretation of the archaeological documentation, in this case the Iberian population patterns in the Upper Guadalquivir basinThe technical aspects of this work revolve about image synthesis whose basis is a digital terrain model (DTM). The DTM is constructed from the altimetric data within a system of known coordinates, and, for texture, an aerial photograph or a satellite image. The synthesis of both images, a raster type, is made by a process of rectification and synchronisation. Finally we overlay the vector information, and then the virtual navigation inside the model is carried out. This allows us to start the reconstruction of historical hypotheses on the landscape. This method is based on a series of established steps into which changes of various kinds can be introduced—such as changes related to the quality of the images used, their possible digital processing, use of graphic design techniques—giving a wide range of possibilities.

We focus now on the practical analysis of some of the advantages and disadvantages of this method based on our own experience. The plan, aimed at producing a navigation of the features here developed, could be summed up as follows:

1) Acquisition of altimetric data in UTM coordinates.

As a reference cartographic support we have used the 1:10.000 maps of the Regional Council (*Junta de Andalucía*); although specific topographical surveys of higher quality are also available, this is the most exact and uniform scale available to the whole territory under study.

The contour lines of these maps are transformed into vectors by AutoCAD, which has the advantage of creating files with the extension .dxf, compatible with most software packages presently available.

2) Transformation of the altimetric values into a DTM.

This allows representation of the territory in a 3D form as a precise mathematical model viewed as a polygonal grid worked out starting from an interpolation surface created from the value of the height given to each point of the ground. (This was done using software such as Idrisi, or, the one we found most useful, Grass, a public domain software that we used for the construction of the DTM, the rectification of the aerial photograph or satellite image and their synchronisation.) The DTM can be generated from the altimetric data taken directly from cartographic maps, from the computerised tachometric relief carried out on the ground.

The fact that there is varying number of points for each contour line may result in an inaccurate estimation of slopes, especially in rough terrain. Therefore we tend, as far as possible, to distribute regularly the points used in the digitalisation.

3) Acquisition in digital format of aerial photographs of the area of interest or of satellite images.

Up to now we have used black and white aerial photographs (1:25.000) taken during recent flights in the autumn of 1991, as well as colour aerial photographs taken from commercial flights in a lower scale. We have also used one satellite image in the navigation made in the *oppidum* of Puente Tablas; this is a SPOT PAN scene from December 1988. The definition of the image will depend therefore on the spatial resolution of the *pixel* in the image and the size of the digitalised area.

In the near future the actual view of the landscape shown by aerial photographs or satellite images that we have used so far will be completed with the restoration of the ancient landscape taken from the historical interpretation of the territory. Up to now, the most usual information has been archaeological documentation related to agricultural use of different types of soil, to geology, and to the slope of the land.

From these criteria and from the results of all the paleoecological analysis and the symbolical interpretations of the landscape, we can understand the life of the inhabitants of a certain territory in a specific period, in our case the Iberian culture.

While the surface of the terrain is represented by altimetric information, the user can also choose other data to show the vertical dimension. Most continuous data can be represented and accordingly viewed as measurable landscape features.

4) Digital image processing.

One of the main contributions to this field has been the programming of a specific computer process capable of giving a real colour to each value of the shades of greys in the spectrum. This technique has been used to colour artificially the black and white photographic mosaic used for the navigation in the territory historically bound to the *oppidum* of Giribaile. This has allowed us to generate a virtual geographic palette that is quite close to the real colours typical of the area under study.

Other more usual applications are linked to the digital image processing with the intention of emphasising certain kinds of useful information to be viewed scientifically afterwards. We often use some applications provided by software specifically designed to carry out these tasks such as Erdass or Ermapper. The possible interpretations offered by the automatic classification of certain images and the use of filters are especially useful for the archaeologist.

We should also include here the use of remote sensing in satellite images, allowing us to build predictive models which will help us to find archaeological sites from the interpretation of significant evidence on the surface of the ground.

5) Rectification of the aerial photograph or satellite image and synchronisation with the DTM.

Such a long and sometimes tedious process can be carried out using ground control points, which are easy to recognise in the image. These points must be always distributed in a uniform way, taking special care in including corners and spreading enough regularly distributed points all over the scene.

It is often useful to carry out the rectification using a vectorial layer which includes all the places (houses, roads, etc.) chosen as ground control points in the aerial photograph or in the satellite image. A practical aspect to take into account when carrying out this process is the need for both the digitalised area and the overlay image to show a bigger surface area than that desired, thus compensating for the loss of detail of the image during the rectification.

6) Texture mapping of the aerial photograph or satellite image.

During the synchronisation process the aerial photograph or the satellite image act in practice as an overlay texture on the DTM.

7) Acquisition in a vectorial format of all types of information useful for subsequent elaborations on layers.

After the synthesis of images placing the aerial photograph or satellite image on the DTM has been completed, vectorial information overlaying is the starting point for the reconstruction of the historical hypotheses of the landscape.

The type of information we have used most is that in the archaeological documentation concerning settlement dispersion and other aspects related to the environment, such as hydrographical networks.

8) Interactive navigation inside the reconstructed model.

The long process of reconstruction over, one can feel the sensation of flying over the territory inside the computer, the territory being understood as a historical reconstruction originating from interpretation of archaeological documents. This research methodology is the result of years of work, as the software and hardware equipment have continually changed and improved.

As mentioned above, our main software have always been AutoCAD (for reconstruction of vectorial models) and Grass (for the basic operations of the process, such as the construction of the DTM, the rectification of the aerial photograph or satellite image and their synchronisation). The Grass SG3d module also allows interactive navigation inside the model reconstructed on a Silicon Graphics platform. Although this kind of work can be done with other software packages, we chose AutoCAD and Grass for being widely available and involving low cost.

9) Publication on the Internet.

The final product of this kind of simulation has been the elaboration of slides, using the focus device, videotapes in a Pal Betacam system and publication on Internet, on a demonstrative level, of VRML and VRML2 models.

The models generated from computer processes, especially the ones related to the development of such specific scientific display techniques as we have used, are particularly suitable for publication in cd-rom.

This type of medium, especially videotape, has been widely used in recent exhibitions (Amiens, Roveretto, Barcelona, for example) where the latest productions were shown to large audiences.

Although publication of archaeological works in these media is popular, our next challenge has already been planned thanks to the Mosaic Project: a Net Virtual Museum. Some of our experiences can be visited through the web sites of the CINECA or the University of Jaén.

The Territory of Giribaile

The *oppidum* of Giribaile is one of the most emblematic settlements of the Iberian period in the province of Jaén in terms of its size and its monumental character. From the study of this territory we have obtained documentation of great interest, especially with regard to the Romanisation process in the innermost areas of the Upper Guadalquivir (Gutiérrez, 1998a; 1998b). Starting from these data of the survey of the surface we determined the evolution of population patterns from the foundation of Giribaile in the early 4thcentury BC until the introduction of manor houses in the Flavian period.

The analysis of population patterns allowed us to establish 3 archaeological horizons:

1.The scattered pattern: the valley settlement

The latest surveys in the *oppidum* of Giribaile have brought to light the existence of a dense population pattern made up of almost a hundred sites distributed along the river meadow.

These settlements lie on the terraces close to the river Guadalimar, in the confluence of the tributary streams, following their course until visual contact with Giribaile is lost.

The compendium of material culture that they offer is very limited, represented predominantly by amphorae. Although it is difficult to estimate accurately the chronology of these materials, the comparative analysis with a sample from the *oppidum* and with another from the latest excavations carried out in the sanctuary of Altos del Sotillo in Santisteban allows us to date them to after the 3rd century BC, setting a later Iberian horizon that was little known until now and that appears immediately after the end of the Second Punic War.

The most probable historical hypothesis is that this was a stipendary community dependent on the *oppidum* which was not abandoned until the beginning of the 1st century BC.

This process came to an end when the objective conditions of the relationship between Rome and the local authorities in the Upper Guadalquivir changed. This caused a general crisis that, in this case, resulted in the *oppidum* of Giribaile being replaced by La Monaria, a fortified settlement lying on a flat area.

2. The village of Monaria: a centralised pattern

The analysis of the space planning in the settlement of La Monaria allowed us to identify the existence of a module consisting of a house with a court. This module maintains many of the uses and customs of the traditional buildings found in Giribaile, as late as the first half of the 1st century BC.

It is evident that Giribaile is of great importance in the understanding of the Iberian and Roman historical evolution. Through the territory of one specific *oppidum*, lying in the province of Jaén, we can for the first time understand the complex historical evolution that took place in a transitional period difficult to identify in the archaeological record.

3. The horizon of the manor houses

The last period studied in the evolution of the old territory dependent on the *oppidum* of Giribaile allows us to define a new archaeological horizon made up of a framework of high imperial houses that were in the hands of private owners. This horizon is not related to the old guiding principles of aristocratic condition which had been used for centuries as cohesion factors for the Iberian society.

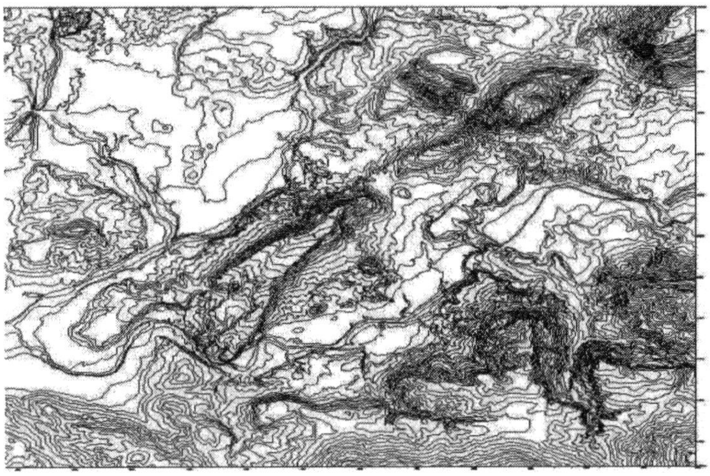

Figure 1. Contour map

THE TECHNICAL PROCEDURE

In the model of Giribaile we have used as a referential cartographic base the 1:10.000 scale maps issued by the Regional Council (*Junta de Andalucía*). The digitalised area spreads over a surface of 144 km^2, that is to say, a square with sides of 12 km. The construction of the DTM has been caused by the transformation of this vectorial file into raster in Grass.

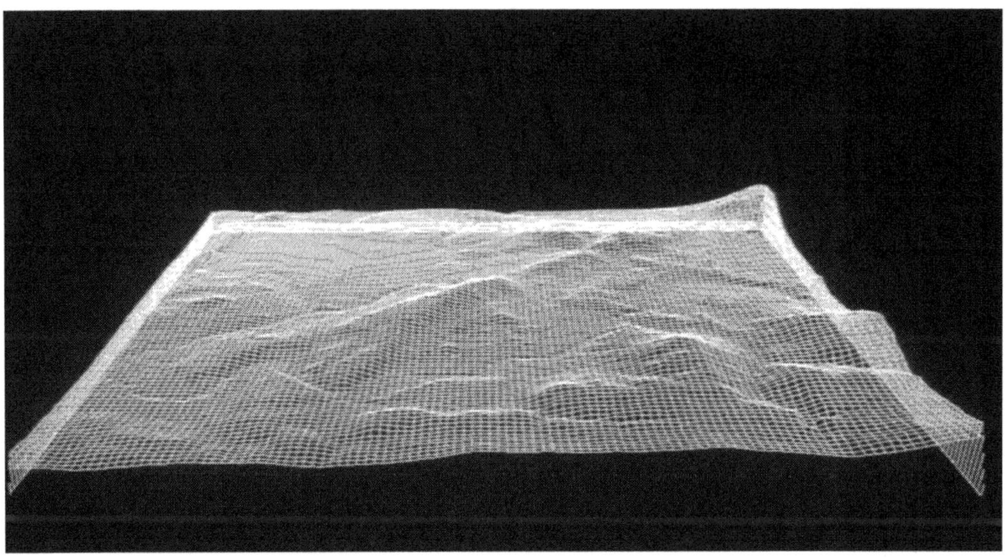

Figure 2. A DTM representation of altimetric values

As texture we have used a 1:25.000 scale black and white photographic mosaic, reproducing artificially the palette of colours of the valley, where the reddish shade predominates in a triassic landscape. The *oppidum* of Giribaile is in the centre, showing its central position in the population model.

Figure 3. Satellite image mosaic as texture

After rectification and synchronisation of both images, several vectorial layers were mapped, each of them with the spatial distribution of the places for each cultural horizon identified in the survey. Another layer showed the fluvial network.

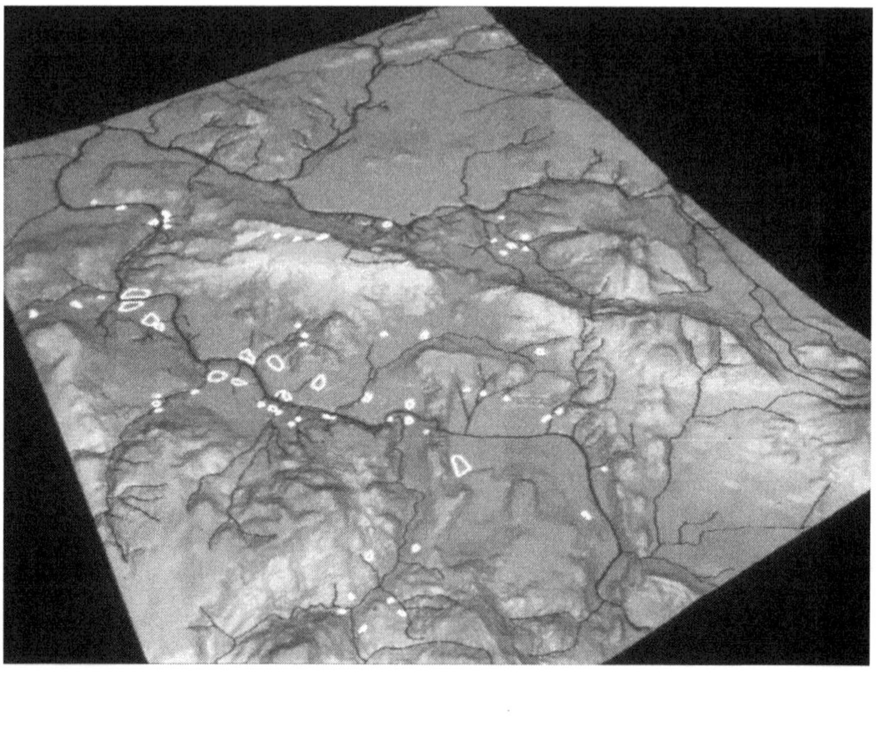

Figure 4. A multilayer model of the territory

The output in this case is a videotape over 17 minutes long in which real image mixes with computer animation and graphic design. The latter have focused on La Monaria, a fortified settlement lying on a flat area dating back to the first half of the 1st century BC.

We here propose an immersion navigation over the territory, to show the evolution of population patterns over history. Based on the thesis obtained from survey of the *oppidum* of Giribaile we show the evolution of territory in the Iberian age from the beginning of the 4th century to the 1st century BC. Here we can separate three historical periods using several vectorial layers where the sites are represented. These three periods result from different proposals of routes across the valley, observing the changes in population. Other vectorial layers have different types of information useful for successive elaborations of the landscape.

The *oppidum* of Puente Tablas

The first archaeological navigation of the territory, focused on the city of Jaén and produced in the CINECA in 1994, showed the closeness and dependent relationship established between two of the *oppida* in the countryside of Jaén, 5 km away from each other. One of them is on the hill of Santa Catalina, at present the high part of the city and partially known through urban excavations, and the other lies in the tableau of Puente Tablas, in the valley of the river Guadalbullón. This is very well known thanks to systematic excavations.

This general approach to the *oppidum* of Puente Tablas reveals some of the features that allow us to define the characteristic site of the *oppida* in the countryside of Jaén, on tableaus near watercourses.

The limits set by the vectors mapped to the navigable model spread beyond the real extension of the *oppidum*, including a bigger area which was predetermined by criteria related to management and preservation of historic heritage. This area, expropiated and delimited by a fence by the provincial authority in charge of cultural activities, was thus protected from urban development. This was years later completed with a second navigation inside the settlement.

The basis of the model was a 1:5.000 scale photorestitution on which we mapped a colour aerial photograph. The photo was centred on the tableau of the Guadalbullón where the *oppidum* is situated.

The object of the project was the visualisation of a navigable model to show some significant aspects of the urban nature of the settlement, using data from systematic excavations carried out between 1985 and 1990, and from the geophysical survey carried out in 1994. A first approach to the settlement shows the fortified nature of the tableau and an important wall which follows the topography of the terrain. The part of the face of the wall which has been discovered can be seen in some detail. We mapped a vectorial layer on the settlement showing the results of the geophysical survey. This showed the urban planning of the settlement, with several blocks separated by streets crossing at right-angles. Navigation also shows the excavated area and several houses, using the data from the excavations. This is a graphic design constructed in 3dStudio incorporated into the navigation by a process similar to the one described in the settlement of La Monaria which belongs in the navigation of the territory of Giribaile.

THE TECHNICAL PROCEDURE

The image used is part of a SPOT pan satellite image and therefore can only be viewed in a scale of shades of grey with a spatial resolution of 20 m per pixel. The image was spatially and radiometrically rectified and its contrast was improved digitally to make it clearer and easier to read.

Figure 5. Pan satellite image of Puente Tablas

The majority of the computer processes (construction of the digital model, rectification of the satellite image and synchronisation of both raster files) used for the sequence have been carried out with Grass. The 3D viewing of the model used the SG3d module on an Indigo SGI platform.

The improved animation was filmed on Betacam video, modifying the SG3d module for improved quality and increase in the number of frames per second. The Indigo platform has the advantage of having a video card which allows the use of a video. We added peripheral devices to the post-editing of the video sequence and combined scientific visualisation techniques with graphic post-editing techniques.

In the most recent elaboration on the model of Puente Tablas we incorporated an SGI platform of the Onyx2 type with an infinite reality graphic accelerator. The increase in the power of geometrical processors, now capable of calculating several million polygons per second, allowed us to build a more complex 3D model and to elaborate the overlaying of the texture on the three-dimensional model in real time, and also to view the model with extraordinary fidelity in relation to the geometrical model.

Videoregistration was also carried out in real time, including the results of the geophysical survey and the 3D reconstruction of several houses in Puente Tablas. This model, generated in 3dStudio, was processed with the help of Cosmo Worlds and included in an intrasite navigation. This model, a VRML2 application, can be viewed on our web site.

The Sanctuary on the Hill "El Pajarillo"

The excavation campaigns carried out on the hill called El Pajarillo revealed a large heroic sanctuary in the eastern part of the province of Jaén, on the course of the river Jandulilla. The importance of this monument lies in that an Iberian sculptural group from here has been documented with archaeological methodology for the first time. It is an area with a central tower where the sculptures were found broken on the ground.

The excavation has allowed the sculptures to be placed in their original positions inside the monument, giving a view of how the monument must have looked originally, and also yielding a ground plan for the construction of a digital model built with a graphic design program. This model will serve as the basis of the reconstruction of the monument's sculptural group.

THE TECHNICAL PROCEDURE

The first view of the territory was possible thanks to a navigation that, taking the sanctuary as the centre of the model, allows navigation of its near surroundings. The view has been built starting from a vectorial file made with AutoCAD, which has been the reference for overlay of the DTM. A 1:25.000 scale black and white aerial photograph has been synchronised onto this model following the same method used for the visualisation of the *oppidum* of Puente Tablas. The development of the process on an SGI platform of the Onyx2 type with Cosmo Worlds and its videoregistration in real time gives better quality and saves time in comparison with previous elaborations.

The next planned stage is to place each sculpture on its original platform according to the archaeological excavation. The reconstruction of the bulk of the sculptures will be based on a complete photographic file compiled on the occasion of the publication of the monograph of the excavation of the monument.

The project is not limited to the reconstruction of the monument in isolation, but is also intended to set it in the context of the surrounding territory. In this way, one of our main aims is the inclusion of this reconstruction inside a wider 3D navigation model. This will allow us to cross the valley of the river Jandulilla from the entry to the valley, the hill El Pajarillo, to Úbeda la Vieja, an old *oppidum* later developed into a Roman town.

The most important aim of this navigation is to understand the way in which this new political and economical territory appeared at the Iberian time. This was a general process from the 4th century BC in the most important valleys of the eastern part of the province of Jaén.

Travel to the Time of the Iberians

In the near future these works will be included in a project of a Net Virtual Museum of the territory called *Travel to the Time of the Iberians*. This project has been developed by the Andalusia Centre for Iberian Archaeology (Centro Andaluz de Arqueología Ibérica), funded by local authorities of the province of Jaén (Diputación Provincial de Jaén) and supported by three institutions: Diputación Provincial de Jaén, Office of Culture of the Regional Government (Consejería de Cultura de Andalucía) and the University of Jaén. *Travel to the Time of the Iberians* is a museum program whose main aim is to implement adequately the personal property and land of the Iberians based on documentation produced and interpreted by archaeological and historical research. This documentation assesses the historical heritage of the Iberian culture in the province of Jaén.

The Iberian archaeological research in the province of Jaén, started in the early 20th century, has given rise to a heritage of great importance in quality and quantity. Unfortunately, the subsequent treatment of this heritage has been careless or even non-existent. Among the archaeological excavations carried out until the 1980s in Iberian sites in Jaén, only the properties in the granary of Toya and in Cástulo have been preserved. In the other sites, including Castellar, Despeñaperros and Porcuna, preservation measures and protection were non-existent, as was the diffusion and assessment of this heritage. It is enough to say that there is nowadays no information centre or panel for visitors.

The treatment of the Iberian archaeological heritage began to change in the 1980s when the first preventive actions and strictly non-archaeological processing took place. But these are always concrete actions that in most cases have consisted only of burying remains again to avoid damage and await "better times", or action for consolidation at a specific site, such as that in Plaza de Armas of Puente Tablas in Jaén.

The personal archaeological heritage has been more fortunate in terms of its physical preservation, but its museum and scientific treatment has left a lot to be desired. With the exception of the latest actions carried out in the Monographic Museum of Cástulo, which tried to make personal heritage understandable by museographic contextualisation, the levels of exposure in the Provincial Museum are more important as a document of nineteenth-century treatment. The most striking sculptural group of all Iberian archaeology, Cerrillo Blanco in Porcuna, was not given suitable treatment until February 1999 (Chicharro, 1999).

What is most important, however, is the lack of a policy of diffusion, public use and consequent valuation of this heritage. Archaeology in Jaén has not been of additional value to the provincial economy. It has not even represented a cultural distinguishing mark or an element of self-esteem in a province which, apart from its condition as a poor province, has for historical reasons some of the most important elements in Iberian archaeology.

In 1997 a far-reaching event took place in the province: the international exhibition *The Iberians: Princes of the West* (VV.AA., 1998). This exhibition caused a significant change because it made institutions and citizens realise the unknown wealth that the museums and territories in Jaén possess. Although the project *Travel to the Time of the Iberians* started in 1996, it has now the necessary basis to develop.

THEORETICAL BASES OF THE PROJECT

The Iberian archaeological heritage in Jaén, apart from its unquestionable scientific value and its contribution to Iberian history, is intensely disjointed. Artefacts have been taken out of their contexts, which has produced, as usual in archaeology, a break in the possibilities of diffusion and has created a lack of solidarity in the province since all the museum heritage is concentrated in the two museums of the province. This is at present the only possibility that the people have to approach the Iberian archaeological heritage in Jaén. The heritage wealth, new research and the new dynamics that the cultural, institutional and civic movement have raised about the Iberian archaeology in Jaén allow for new work to be carried out, focused on developing integrated actions on the aspects of the heritage known today and any aspects which may come to light as a result of further research. This is the context in which *Travel to the Time of the Iberians* is set.

Artefacts, which are or can be at the same time objects of artistic and historical interest, should be shown in the sites in which they were found, their authentic scenario at the time of the Iberians. These sites therefore become at the same time objects of historical interest and, in turn, "containers" of other objects of historical interest. Sometimes, however, artefacts are taken from their original sites to be housed in new "containers": museums: although this is not the best solution, it is often the most practical one. However, this must not lead to breaking or forgetting the link between the artefacts and the sites in which they were discovered. This is the aim of this research program: moving the real material from its context to the museum while avoiding the loss of historic content that the separation can produce.

Travel to the Time of the Iberians must also act as a redistributor of the wealth that the Historic Heritage generates. It must provide a process of return of artefacts to their sites, both in economical aspects and in the ideological basis of social values. The creation of the International Museum of Iberian Culture is one of the most important aspects of the program. The program *Travel to the Time of the Iberians* has a double direction: first to move the artefact from the site to the new context taking into account its quality and its link to the territory and, on the other hand, after taking the artefact out of its context, to act as an adjuster of the social and economical failures created by museographic centralisation without calling into question its obvious positive values.

It is not, however, only a question of producing this dialectic relationship which allows an authentic pact of territorial solidarity in the province of Jaén. New technologies must also be adequately used so that the physical separation of the archaeological finds from the building property and the personal belongings are reintegrated by whatever means are necessary. The use of the Internet and virtual reality make an important contribution, together with *Travel to the Time of the Iberians*.

CONTENTS

The virtual journey that the program presents must cover all the key moments in the History of the Iberians, with four principal objectives:

- The Second Punic War with the submission of the Iberian people of the Upper Guadalquivir first to Carthage and then to Rome.
- The 4th century BC, when the first large territories ruled by princes appear.
- The 5th century BC, when the first territorial states ruled by princes are established and heroic power is taken as a Mediterranean aristocratic ideology model.
- The formation of the *oppidum* over the 7th and 6th centuries BC and the appearance of princes.

This work must show the audience the different functions of the culture they are interested in:

- Sanctuaries or centres of worship.
- Necropolis.
- *Oppida* or princely cities.
- Material culture (e.g., sculpture, pottery)

STRUCTURE OF THE PROJECT

The structure of the project consists of the following levels:

The proposal of a basic tour of the actual sites which at present meet the conditions necessary for becoming integrated into this project. Within this general scheme, and a part of the first stage of the project, an additional tour has been included to integrate visits to interpretation centres and Iberian halls in local museums such as the Monographic Museum of Cástulo in Linares and the Local Museums in Porcuna and in Castellar de Santisteban or the future International Museum of the Iberian Culture. It also includes the creation of open air museums in Plaza de Armas in Puente Tablas in Jaén, the heroic sanctuary El Pajarillo in Huelma, the funeral chamber of Toya in Peal de Becerro, Cerrillo Blanco in Porcuna, Cástulo, the rock sanctuary of Cueva de la Lobera in Castellar and of Despeñaperros in Santa Elena, or the *oppidum* of Maquiz in Mengíbar. These are basic milestones to understand the history of the Iberians, important references for research and knowledge and, hence, the basis of our work.

First stop

There are three options:

- The sanctuary of Collado de los Jardines in Santa Elena.
- The sanctuary of Altos del Sotillo in Castellar.
- The *oppidum* in Maquiz (Mengíbar).

The former two are ethnic sanctuaries (Prados, 1996; Nicolini *et al.*, 1990) of the 4th and 3rd centuries BC, and the latter is an Iberian *oppidum* that was converted into the city of Iliturgi by the Romans. Maquiz achieved great importance during the late Iberian period and during the process of romanisation in Upper Andalucía (Arteaga & Blech, 1987).

The historical contents of this stop are based on explaining the formation in the 3rd century BC of kingdoms of *oppida* associated with client princes or princes dependent on other prince. The Oretanos, with capital status in Cástulo, are the most important example of this. Both sanctuaries lie in this field, while Maquiz is within the limits of Oretanos and Túrdulos.

Second stop

The Monographic Museum of Cástulo (Linares).

This is the meeting point of all the travellers in time and the best place to arrange the journey due to the infrastructure of the museum and the excellent collections it possesses from the excavations carried out in Cástulo (Blázquez & García-Gelabert, 1994).

The historical contents of the stop are the Second Punic War, the struggle and causes of the confrontation between Roman and Carthage, and the role of the Iberians in the fight. Other important facts are the history of Cástulo and Iliturgi, the wedding of Hannibal and Himilce, the death of Publio Cneo Scipion, the revenge of Scipion the African on Iliturgi and the surrender of the city of Cástulo to Scipion by Cerdubeles in 206 BC.

Third stop

The chamber of Toya (Peal de Becerro).

The aim is basically functional: we try to show what a princely funeral chamber is and its meaning within an Iberian aristocratic society.

Historic content of the stop: the historical nature of the Iberian prince. It must allow us to study life beyond the grave and the features of Iberian architecture (materials, building systems...) (Cabré, 1920; Blánquez, 1999).

Fourth stop

The heroic sanctuary El Pajarillo (Huelma). The sculpture group was found in an important monumental context and the relationship between the context and the sculpture must be shown, especially given the excellent preservation conditions.

Historic content of the stop: it must show how a political model superior to the *oppidum* is formed and its historical conditions, the concept of the patronage system and the use of gift-giving to achieve power, and the hero's role, which is another variation of the power of a Mediterranean prince (Molinos *et al.*, 1998).

Fifth stop

The *oppidum* of Puente Tablas (Jaén).

Functional definition: Iberian *oppidum* dated between the 8th and 3rd centuries BC (Ruiz & Molinos, 1987; 1993).

Historical content of the stop: to show a village of the 5th century, and how the princes and their clients lived. The fortification will help us to explain the origin of the *oppidum*, and connect it with the origin of the Iberians.

Sixth stop

The International Museum of the Iberian Culture (Jaén).

Functional definition of the site: a museum displaying artefacts from Iberian villages in the province of Jaén. It includes the historical sequence of the formation and development of Iberian culture.

Historical content of the stop: to show the museum and the complete history of the Iberians. Here we can talk about the sculptural groups in Porcuna, Huelma, the bull in Porcuna, the wheel in Toya, the pottery collection, the urn in Villargordo.

Seventh stop

Cerrillo Blanco (Porcuna).

Functional definition: necropolis of the Tartessic inhumation, and ritual burial place of the sculptural group dated between the 8th and 5th centuries BC (Torrecillas, 1985; Negueruela, 1990).

Historical content of the stop: to show a necropolis and the funeral ritual in the origins of the Iberians in order to understand the origin of the aristocracy from the reconstruction of a burial mound. The end of this journey is the reconstruction of the context of one of the most emblematic discoveries of Iberian archaeology, that visitors have already seen in the International Museum of Iberian Archaeology.

Other journeys planned

We propose also secondary journeys capable of being incorporated into the basic journey in future. Some of these are more complex and are considered a consequence of the development of a second stage of the project.

Because of the cost and the possibility of implementing within a short time an action able to give good results, a shorter basic tour has been planned, to be later divided into other secondary tours. It can be extended in time adding other journeys where the seasonal or functional nature is the priority and where other actions can be included, not necessarily archaeological but related to the subject in some way. Some thematic journeys are included making up a route network distributed throughout the territory:

-Trip to the mining forts.

-Trip along Hannibal's path.

-Trip to the Iberian necropolis.

-Trip to the fortifications.

-Trip along the route of the Turdulos.

The navigation in the archaeological landscape of Giribaile, described above, relates to one of the thematic routes, the journey to the mining forts.

A PROPOSAL OF COMPLEMENTARY ACTIONS

Educational activities will be prepared at every stop. The procedures of scientific visualisation, especially archaeological navigation, will play an important role in the museum program. Therefore the traveller will have the opportunity to undertake these virtual journeys before doing so in real life.

Focusing on the cultural aspects of *Travel to the Time of the Iberians,* this program will be completed by the inclusion of information related to the artefacts and Internet sites using html web sites.

It is planned to show the documentation in a preliminary sketch of *Travel to the Time of the Iberians*, consisting of a collection of pictures of characters and a bestiary. This is a wide representation of the Iberian world, taken from bronzes, stone sculptures, and illustrations, which can be seen in the museums of the province of Jaén included in this project.

A comprehensive catalogue has been compiled which includes all the archaeological sites where the presence of the Iberians is evident. This archaeological documentation is full of data from both old and recent excavations surface surveys. It is a wide database that, together with the maps included, allows an exact study of the landed property that constitutes the rich archaeological Iberian heritage in the province of Jaén.

Conclusions

The main aim of this project, *Travel to the Time of the Iberians*, is the creation of a New Virtual Environment organised as a web site and, in the future, hopefully as an immersive virtual environment, that will allow the user to visualise and absorb the Iberian archaeological and cultural heritage. This new concept of dissemination of information is related to advanced virtual reality technology to enable visitors to look back over the archaeological landscape.

New technologies have frequently been used to solve traditional research problems (Veltman, 1997; Bocchi *et al.*, 1997). In particular, a virtual reality approach to the reconstruction of archaeological sites provides a powerful tool for tourists to activate various scenarios for visiting the landscape, for archaeological researchers to experiment with and test different hypotheses, and for urban planners to support the decision-making process relating to landscape development and management.

Two possible approaches for the use of archaeological data are: networking technologies, including the emerging features of 3D visualisation and integration of distributed archives and databases or using, in a realistic manner, physical access in individual booths in which visitors can experience the immersive perception of the recreated scenario.

Moreover, digitised museum contents related to the archaeological sites could also be effectively simulated and visualised using the available archaeological models as a powerful graphic user interface.

Travel to the Time of the Iberians is based on the design and the implementation of a New Virtual Environment of the landscape of Jaén (Spain) as a virtual multidimensional environment characterised by efficient and effective navigation and orientation tools, using virtual reality and interaction techniques to represent real scenarios (the landscape of archaeological areas of interest as it is nowadays), artificial scenarios (the recreated landscape of the past within 3D reconstruction) and their integration.

In particular, the multimedia navigation is based on the 3D reconstruction of the landscape, with the introduction of tools to show 3D reconstructed models interactively by addition or removal. *Travel to the Time of the Iberians* aims to integrate all the sources available in order to render them in the form of a *continuum* exploiting multimedia and virtual reality technologies to recreate the archaeological scenario. Metaphorically speaking, *Travel to the Time of the Iberians* methodology should enable us to collect the archaeological documents and decode them while travelling through the landscape.

The challenge of the project consists of merging virtual multimedia reality with the scientific approach of archaeological research. So the setting up of *Travel to the Time of the Iberians* is a highly multi-disciplinary activity requiring the cooperation of different professional competence for such tasks as digitising the documents, standardising the data, and constructing CAD models for the virtual environments. CINECA is responsible for implementing the New Virtual Environment in virtual reality and for the planning and development of instruments for viewing the archaeological landscape both on-line (via the Internet) and by immersion.

The aim of this paper is to show the present state of *Travel to the Time of the Iberians* in order to make concrete the idea of a *MultiDimensional Digital Archaeological Landscape*, which translates archaeological data derived from archaeological research into multimedia virtual reality scenarios.

The project is intended not simply to set up a virtual museum of the landscape of archaeological areas of interest, but also to make available a model that can be applied to any archaeological setting. This model, enabling the visualisation of data relating to the archaeological development of the landscape and its transformations, may be considered to be valid only if at the design stages (archaeological research, CAD modeling, database set up and graphic interface to all the collected information) a high degree of scientific rigor has been applied. Starting from this premise, it is possible to make use of the most advanced multimedia display techniques available.

Briefly, the implementation tasks, outlined in the following sections, can be described as follows:

1. Creation of archaeological areas of interest by 3D model in VRML format for networked distribution.
2. Setting up of the web site of the project including interactive tools for 3D navigation.
3. Creation of archaeological areas of interest in VR format for immersive navigation.

THE FUNDAMENTAL ROLE OF ARCHAEOLOGICAL RESEARCH

The markedly interdisciplinary nature of *Travel to the Time of the Iberians* is a fundamental and distinguishing characteristic, enabling it to make a justified claim to excellence. It is necessary to give some examples of what we mean by 3D electronic reconstruction and what can be done with it from the archaeological point of view.

The construction of a 3D vector model requires extremely detailed archaeological research. The need to provide all the elements, to put together an overall picture with every detail in place, including environmental ones, obliges the archaeologist to carry out research in all sectors, to bring to bear all the methodologies and cultural and human resources that are available, from architectural elements to reconstruction components, from information regarding meteorological conditions to earthquakes.

On the other hand, archaeological research will receive a great boost from this type of application. The need to graphically create a reconstruction or archaeological area that is no longer in existence provides a considerable incentive for archaeologists to carry out through research in order to try to fill in the gaps. In all honesty it will be necessary to specify which parts are based directly on scientific data and which parts are based on a hypothetical reconstruction.

THE IMPLEMENTATION PHASES

The idea of making the *Travel to the Time of the Iberians* accessible on the Internet arises from the necessity to facilitate interaction among archaeological researchers, to reach a great number of users and, of course, to publicise the project. For this reason, we chose to implement *Travel to the Time of the Iberians* with VRML and Java languages. Used together, they make it possible to develop dynamic and interactive 3D environments in a portable, standardised and platform-independent manner.

In general terms, at each stage of production the following problems will be considered: the quality and stability of the platform, the availability of internationally or generally recognised standards, both with regard to hardware and software, and the maintenance aspects and forward compatibility in relation to technological developments (future proofing).

Briefly the implementation process of the *Travel to the Time of the Iberians* consists of a progressive introduction and integration of 3D models of archaeological landscape and 3D reconstructions. This process can be subdivided into four phases:

-the creation of DTM

-the translation of CAD models of digital reconstruction into VRML models

-the collocation of CAD models in the digital landscape (3D world)

-the graphic processing of VRML models in order to render them photo-realistic

During the graphic processing phase, implemented with the software tool Cosmo Worlds, the VRML files are processed in order to render them realistic in photographic terms. A detailed reproduction of all the geometric 3D models which constitute a reconstruction allows a notable slowdown in the visualisation process of the global virtual world. In order to improve performance in terms either of download time or of frames per second, we adopted the strategy of matching a simplified construction of 3D single architectonic elements with the use of photos as texture to be applied to them and a different level of detail.

It is necessary to strike a balance between a lot of details for maximum realism and quick drawing for maximum interactivity. A technique that we adopted to control detail is the level-of-detail (LOD).

Only two of the stops of the basic journey have been started following the scientific visualisation procedures, currently being at different stages of completion. The most advanced one is the VRML2 model of Puente Tablas while the other, the reconstruction of the heroic sanctuary of El Pajarillo, is in its first phase.

THE INTERFACE SYSTEM

The interface is designed to allow the user to visit a virtual reconstruction of archaeological areas of interest that could be acceptable in terms of display speed for every type of user and to provide the user with a simple and efficient navigation mode to visit the landscape and to interact with reconstructions.

The high-resolution model and the light model

Travel to the Time of the Iberians has a great variety of potential users. Clearly, an archaeological researcher needs a more detailed 3D visualisation than the average virtual tourist. On the other hand a virtual tourist, who is connected to the Internet with standard PC and modem is likely to give preference to speed of access rather than to the careful reproduction of too much detail. So we provided two different ways of accessing this virtual environment: one using a LAN connection or a visualisation in a local virtual environment in VISIT lab of CINECA, and one using a remote connection to the Internet. In particular, we implemented two models respectively, the high-resolution model and the light model, with different level of details in which 3D models and multimedia data are stored with a different resolution. The data visualised in both models are equally validated by archaeological research.

In order to allow more complex behavior depending on outside data or user interaction, we used External Authoring Interface (EAI) to control the VRML world externally with a Java applet. The choice of VRML and Java guarantees equal conditions of access for all platforms (Brutzman, 1998).

Designing and implementing the immersive virtual environment

The term *virtual theatre* is used to denote a physical space where a group of people can navigate in a virtual reality environment. If necessary, the visitors may be provided with polarised eyeglasses for a stereophonic view of the projected image. From the technological point of view, three essential characteristics must be considered: immersion, interaction and high-quality graphics with photo-realistic characteristics. The virtual theatre could be the natural development of our high-resolution models.

The virtual reconstruction of archaeological areas provides a realistic simulation environment where every kind of visitor (landscape residents, researchers, public administrators, industrial technicians, designers) can receive data and information not otherwise available, e.g., from inaccessible viewpoints, or time travelling.

Travel to the Time of the Iberians is designed with a view to future developments, increasing access to various kinds of information about the landscape in order to improve our understanding of the processes that contribute to its development.

The project *Travel to the Time of the Iberians,* whose first part is expected to be available soon, is a good opportunity to develop new approaches in museology. These approaches will integrate scientific values, based on archaeological documentation, and new scientific visualisation procedures.

References Cited

ARTEAGA, O.; BLECH, M., 1987, "Excavaciones en el cerro de Maquiz (Mengíbar, Jaén). Campaña de 1985", *Anuario Arqueológico de Andalucía*, vol. II, pp. 169-172.

BLÁNQUEZ, J., 1999, "La necrópolis del Cerro de la Horca y la Cámara de Toya" *La Cultura Ibérica a través de la fotografía de principios de siglo*, pp. 127-134.

BLÁZQUEZ, J.M.; GARCÍA-GELABERT, M.P., 1994, *Cástulo, ciudad ibero-romana*, Madrid, Istmo.

BOCCHI, F.; CALORI, L.; FRATICELLI, F.; GUIDAZZOLI, A.; MARIANI, M., 1997, "The 4 dimensional city", *Science and Supercomputing at CINECA, 1997 Report*, pp. 408-414.

BRUTZMAN, D., 1998, *The virtual reality modeling language and Java*, Communication of a ACM.

CABRÉ, J., 1920, "Arquitectura hispánica: el sepulcro de Toya", *Archivo Español de Arte y Arqueología*, vol. I, pp. 73-101.

CHICHARRO, J.L., 1999, "Las esculturas de Porcuna, una nueva propuesta expositiva", *La cultura ibérica a través de la fotografía de principios de siglo*, pp. 321-330.

GUTIÉRREZ, L.M., 1998a, "Roma y el poder local en el territorio del *oppidum* de Giribaile", in *Actas del Congreso Internacional Los Iberos, Príncipes de Occidentes: estructuras de poder en la sociedad ibérica*, Fundación "La Caixa", Barcelona, pp. 405-412.

GUTIÉRREZ, L.M., 1998b, "Computational and scientific visualization applications to archaeological survey", *Science and Supercomputing at CINECA-1997 Report*, pp. 703-704.

GUTIÉRREZ, L.M.; ALCÁZAR, E.M., 1995, "Image processing for archeological uses", *Notizie dal CINECA*, vol. 22 (3), pp. 1-2.

MOLINOS, M.; CHAPA, T.; RUIZ, A.; PEREIRA, J.; RÍSQUEZ, C.; MADRIGAL, A.; ESTEBAN, A.; MAYORAL, V.; LLORENTE, M., 1998, *El santuario heroico de "El Pajarillo", Huelma (Jaén)*, Jaén, Servicio de Publicaciones de la Universidad de Jaén.

NEGUERUELA, I., 1990, *Los monumentos escultóricos ibéricos de Cerrillo Blanco de Porcuna (Jaén)*, Madrid, Ministerio de Cultura.

NICOLINI, G.; RUIZ, A.; ZAFRA, N., 1990, "Informe sobre la campaña de excavaciones arqueológicas en 1987 en Los Altos del Sotillo, Castellar de Santisteban (Jaén)", *Anuario Arqueológico de Andalucía de 1987*, vol. II, pp. 216-220.

PRADOS, L., 1996, Imagen, religión y sociedad en la toréutica ibérica, in R. Olmos (Ed.), *Al otro lado del Espejo: aproximación a la imagen ibérica*, Madrid, Lynx, pp. 131-143.

RUIZ, A.; MOLINOS, M., 1987, "Informe preliminar de la campaña de excavación sistemática de 1985 en el cerro de la Plaza de Armas (Puente Tablas, Jaén)", *Anuario Arqueológico de Andalucía de 1985*, vol. II, pp. 345-352.

RUIZ, A.; MOLINOS, M., 1993, *Los iberos. Análisis arqueológico de un proceso histórico*, Barcelona, Crítica.

TORRECILLAS, J.F., 1985, *La necrópolis de época tartésica del Cerrillo Blanco (Porcuna, Jaén)*, Jaén, Instituto de Estudios Giennenses.

VELTMAN, K.H., 1997, *Frontiers in electronic media, Interactions-new visions of human-computer interaction*, vol. IV (4), pp. 32-64.

VV.AA., 1998, *Los iberos. Príncipes de Occidente*, La Caixa, Barcelona.

MOSAIC PROJECT (Net Virtual Museum), funded by the European Union as part of the Tentelecom action-URL http://mosaic.cineca.it

THE BATHS OF BAETULO: FROM ARCHAEOLOGICAL TO VIRTUAL REALITY

Josep Gurri Costa, Esther Gurri Costa
(with the contribution of Montse Comas and Pepita Padrós)
Images: Quique Grases, Josep Gurri, Pako Bagur
Dortoka Disseny, Ltd.
Barcelona, Spain
dortoka@jet.es

A Little Bit of History

The Roman city of Baetulo, nowadays Badalona, is located in the coastal area of Laietània, in the region of el Barcelonès. Together with other cities along the Catalan coastline, such as Empúries and Mataró, Badalona was affected by the agricultural colonization that the Romans carried out after their landing in Hispania in 218 BC. Baetulo was built from scratch, settled in a spot where no previous settlements had been established. Surrounded by walls, it had around 2,000 inhabitants and occupied 11 hectares. Its streets intersected each other at right angles, and some of them stretched from the mountain to the sea, while others ran parallel to the coastline.

The baths of Baetulo, located beneath the Museum of the city of Badalona, were built around the 1st century BC (67-33). They have two different areas: the gym, in the open air, and the baths in themselves, located indoors. The Roman baths of Baetulo were found in the mid 1950s, during the urban developement works of el Clos de la Torre. In order to protect them, the city built the museum that is nowadays on top of them. The baths building takes up a total surface of 350 square meters and follows traditional Roman patterns. The baths were built in the second third of the 1st century BC (67-33) and they were rebuilt during the reign of the emperor Augustus: some rooms were enlarged, and the decoration and finishes were embellished by using different types of marble. There is another baths building in the city very close to this one, on the other side of Via Augusta, in a place called l'Hort de les Monges, which is not open to visitors at this time.

The Project

DORTOKA DISSENY had already dealt with projects of this kind. We had carried out other virtual reconstruction projects, such as the reconstruction of El Moré, a Roman village in Sant Pol de Mar (Maresme) known for its wine making, the reconstruction of the Palacio del Buen Retiro (Madrid), commissioned from us by the Museo del Prado, or the reconstruction of the Roman city of Iluro (Mataró). In all our previous projects, the final product of the work was a video, which made it necessary to have a linear script to explain what that place and its surroundings were like in ancient times, in a clear and understandable way. But working with video was a limitation, since the explanation unfolded as a sequence of correlative images, not allowing the user to have an active part.

However, in this present case, the project will be on a CD-rom, to be used as a didactic tool. This new format allows the use of multimedia techniques so that the user can interact with the program and can obtain additional information through texts, videos, images and narrations.

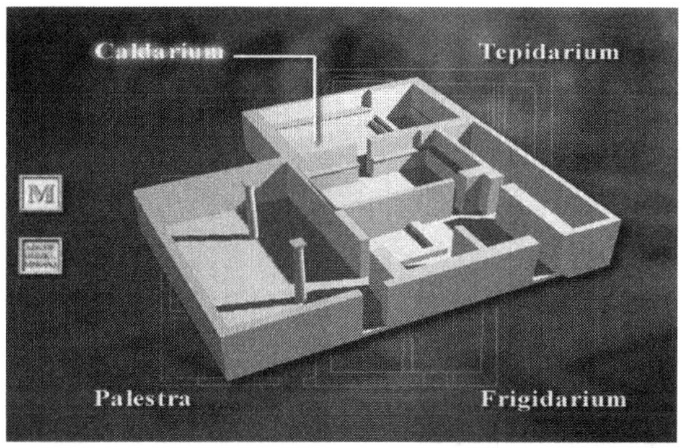

THE AIMS

The main goal of this multimedia project was to provide the general public with an idea of what the Roman baths were like, how people lived, how things were done and which objects and tools were used in that historical period—all in all, to reconstruct the different parts of the baths as accurately as possible.

THE SCRIPT

When it came to writing the script and defining the design and the way to stage the virtual images, we had to decide which sensations we wanted the user to perceive and how we wanted to create them, always bearing in mind the target of our product.

There is a main menu from which one can have direct access either to the baths or to an introduction about Baetulo. Once in the baths we can visit—virtually—the different rooms of the building: the *palestra*, the *frigidarium*, the *tepidarium* and the *caldarium*.

This virtual route takes as a starting point a real image of the baths, that is, the viewpoint of the visitors to the Museum of Badalona's basement. Then that image becomes a virtual one.

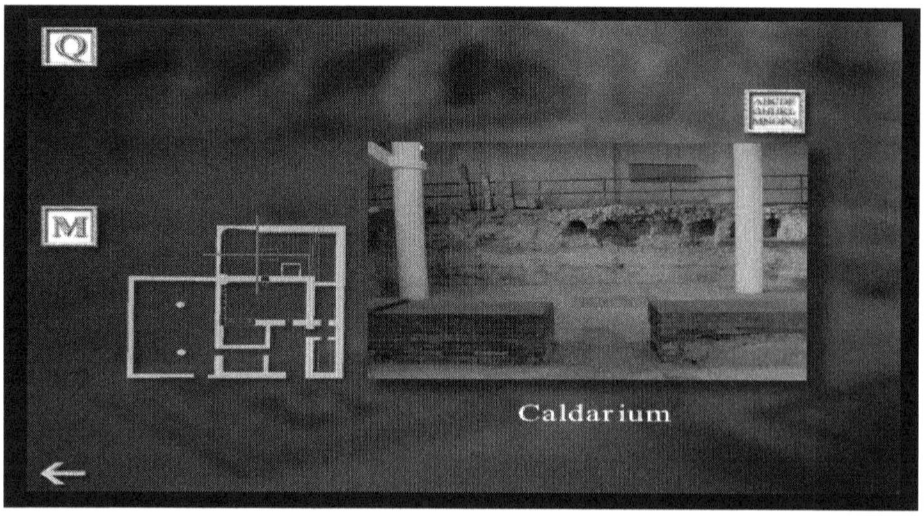

The graphic part is very important in all the screens, although there is also a narration that explains some details about each one of them. Moreover, there is the chance to have access to further information through an additional text or listening to another narration, for those who want to know more about it. The text contains hypertext links, which relate concepts to a series of images in order to make the text more easily understandable.

The basis: the initial files

Before starting to work with the infographic software, we needed to have the ground plans of the baths' archaeological remains digitally delineated (with CAD). Part of this process had already been done by the Museum of Badalona some years before. The two-dimensional delineation had been done with AutoCAD so that it would be as accurate as possible, and it had to accomplish certain standards to make it three-dimensional. The man in charge of the delineation, Antoni Fonollà, worked with polylined entities, *Splines* or views convertible into *raster* format.

The elevation of the walls that were still standing also had to be drawn, as well as the longitudinal and transverse sections of the building, which had to be delineated in order to draw the sections of the pools and the mouldings of the walls. In some cases, these drawings were already done in sketches on paper, and therefore we only had to digitize them. In some other cases, we had to draw them for this occasion.

The museum had drawings of all the mosaics of the baths made on polyester paper on a 1:1 scale. Taking those as a starting point, we digitized them so that they would be a part of the delineation of the ground plans.

Reconstruction criteria

The criteria used in the reconstruction of the parts of the baths' structure that were missing are based on two grounds. On the one hand, the interpretative works done by the archaeologists of the Museum of Badalona (Guitart, 1976; Guitar, Padrós, 1990). On the other hand, the structure of some other Roman sites, most of them in Italy, such as the baths in Pompeia (the ones in the Foro, the Stabian ones and the Centenario baths) as well as the suburban baths in Hercolano and especially the ones in Musarna (Viterbo) because of their similar structure and distribution. The baths in Buticosos or the ones in Rome were a point of reference in some other particular aspects.

The Building Process

Before starting to create the three-dimensional geometry inside the computer, we had to delineate two-dimensionally some parts of the baths that had never been drawn by computer before, such as the friezes, the mosaics and the mouldings.

Having the digital two-dimensional delineation as a starting point, we created the 3D geometry. The elevation of the walls and the roof were inferred from the remains of the building that had been preserved and by taking into account other parallels found. Through the infographic software, the bi-dimensional shapes were created following the Z parameters according to the archaeologists' hypotheses. Once that was done, we had a geometry made of faces. Each one of these faces contains a large amount of information, and that is why one of our premises when creating geometries was that the objects had to have as few faces as possible. This premise is basic in any virtual scene, because the amount of information with which we work determines the calculation time of the scene. The more information we work with, the more difficult it is to work in real time with the computer, since the regeneration of the drawing is slowed down. We also have to bear in mind that if we work with a lot of information, any modification will take much longer. These concepts have to be specially taken into account when we are dealing with animations, because for each second of animation we need 25 images (that is if we work in PAL format. If we used NTSC, we would need 30).

For this reason, we had to optimize the information, eliminating the vertices where they were not strictly necessary. The perfection of the vertices was carried out always taking into account the path of the animation, so that the definition of the object that had to be seen would not be affected.

Once the elevation of the walls was determined, it was time to define the shape of other parts of the building that had not been preserved, such as the roof, its openings and the mouldings.

As far as the openings were concerned, we followed the interpretations of J. Guitart (Guitart, 1976), who suggested a barrel vault. His hypotheses were based on the finding of some remains of joined bricks that supposedly supported the flat tiles that covered the semicircular vault. This archaeologist also based his hypotheses on the parallels of the Pomepeian baths, the roof of which still shows the openings through which light came into the different rooms. In these baths, as in many others where the roof has been preserved, there can be seen round openings. Due to the many coincidences between these Roman baths and the ones in Baetulo, we thought it appropriate to build them this way. Thus, the *caldarium* was lit from above the sink (*labrum*), whereas the *frigidarium* and the *tepidarium* where lit from the side of the room.

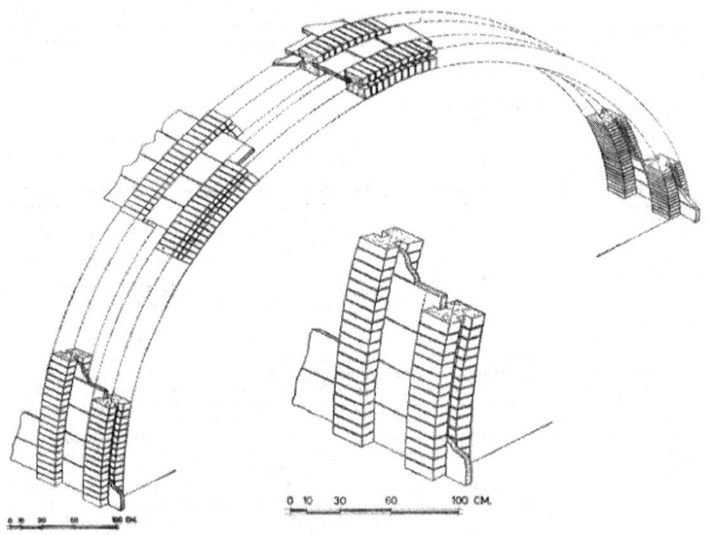

As for the perimeter mouldings (of which some sections in different rooms of the baths are preserved), we followed the same procedure. That is, the reconstruction was based both on the parallels of other Roman baths and on the archaeologists' hypotheses.

TEXTURIZATION AND CREATION OF AN ATMOSPHERE

When it came to texturizing the scene, we used the materials found during the excavation of the baths, mainly pavements (mosaics, *opus signinum*), paintings and marbles. The marbles that were found covered the walls up to a height of 1.5 m, which is a common characteristic of many Roman baths. In this case, the marble found was mainly whitish, and that is why we used this shade of colour. In order to create the virtual marble and to give the impression that all the pieces of the structure were different, we digitized many types of marble. Once we had all the digital images, they were modified with Adobe Photoshop and were mixed so that we would get many different patterns and each piece would be unique.

In the Roman baths of Baetulo there were two types of pavement: the mosaics and the *opus signinum*. As for the mosaics, most of them were quite well preserved, but some parts had to be rebuilt. In only one case did we have to do a geometrical investigation in order to infer the missing part of the mosaic. When it came to creating the virtual mosaics, we generated a material that simulated the different pieces of the mosaic, to give the impression that they were made of tesserae. For the *opus signinum* we created a material based on the photographs of different parts of the *frigidarium*'s floor, where the pavement is still preserved. After that, we treated the images digitally in order to disguise the tiling of the texture.

The paintings of the walls in the *palestra* were digitally restored taking as a starting point the paintings found in the same *palestra* and in other buildings of the city of Baetulo, such as the taverns of the Plaça Font i Cussó and the Rectoria de Santa Maria. These paintings were scanned and then were finished up using CorelDraw. These restored paintings wer then fitted to the walls where they were supposed to be placed.

The light and atmosphere effects where essential in trying to create a realistic impression of the baths. Thanks to the latest programming of special effects within the infographic programs, which can now have plug-ins incorporated, we have been able to create an atmosphere that was hardly possible to create up to now. As far as the lighting is concerned, it must be said that the rooms of the baths originally were quite dark, since the light came in only through the openings in the roof. Apart from this lighting, there were some standing lamps that lighted up the room a bit more. In order to simulate the light that came in through the openings in the roof we used volumetric lights, which gave the room a touch of dense atmosphere. As for the steam and the smoke from the braziers, we created plug-ins to simulate them. Finally, the movement of the water was created by using different systems of particles and plug-ins. We have to bear in mind that what helps create the right feeling is the appearance of a realistic material applied to all these elements.

In order to make the atmosphere of the different rooms more realistic, we looked for information about the objects used in the different activities that were carried out in each of the rooms, such as wooden sandals, unguent vases, togas, braziers, benches, lamps and so on. These objects gave the scene quite a realistic appearance.

A WALK AROUND THE BATHS

When it came to deciding what kind of virtual walk we wanted to provide, we considered two options. On the one hand, a virtual world, giving the user the chance to decide which way to go. On the other hand, an animation for each different area. In the first case, using QuickTime VR, the effect on the user had a greater impact, since there is a total interaction and the user can choose which way to go and can move closer to or farther from the objects that he or she comes across. However, since QuickTime uses a series of fixed images, the animation of the water and the atmospheric effects (such as the lighting and the steam) could not be shown. That is why we chose the second option which, despite not giving the user the chance to choose which way to go, is more true to life. Through the animations, regardless of which room one is in, we could work with the movement of the water, the creation of an atmosphere, and the burning of the braziers, thus giving the rooms a more realistic touch.

Giving a realistic feeling to the walk was one of our main goals, and this was the best method to achieve it. This animation work also required some a data compression research so that the animations could be seen with a normal computer without any cuts or leaps. The combination video images, narration and music during the virtual walk made it necessary for us to work with much more information, and that posed a difficult problem. We carried out some tests to determine the minimum number of frames per second we needed to get good quality. After experimenting with 10, 12, 15 and 18 fps, we decided that the best option was 15 fps. This, together with the colour compression done with the *codec*, made the amount of information considerably smaller.

Conclusions

In the first place, as far as learned investigation is concerned, by putting into practice the current theories about the typological and functional aspects of a building, the reconstruction allows archaeologists to propose hypotheses after seeing their constructive and atmospherical proposals volumetrically built. As has already happened in some other previous cases, the archaeologist gains new awareness of the building and can work further on his hypotheses, or even modify them, according to the result.

In the second place, our project contributes to the popularization of our cultural heritage, since it shows the archaeological remains to the general public in a clear and understandable way. People who are not professional in the field will presumably understand better the meaning of what they see, thanks to our project.

And last, our project demonstrates certain economical advantages. A virtual reconstruction is relatively inexpensive in comparison to the cost of a real one, and moreover it has the advantage that it can be more easily modified than a real reconstruction.

References Cited

ADAM, J.P, 1984, *La construction romaine. Materiaux et techniques.* Grands Manuels. Picard, 1984. Paris.

ARIZA, L.M, 1999, "La arqueología virtual reconstruye el pasado". *Revista Muy Interesante.* núm 204 Pp 16-26

BAGUR, P; GURRI, E; GURRI, J; MEDRANO, J, 1999, "El Moré (Sant Pol de Mar, el Maresme) Reconstrucció virtual d'un centre romà de producció de vi". *Digithum.* Revista Universitat Oberta de Catalunya.

COMAS, M; PADRÓS, P,1992, *Baetulo. Ciutat romana.* Museu de Badalona, 1992.

GUITART, J, 1976, *Baetulo topografia arqueológica, urbanismo e historia.* Museo de Badalona. Monografías Badalonesas, 1. Pp 61-88 Badalona, 1976.

GUITART, J; PADRÓS, P, 1990, "Baetulo, cronología y significación de sus monumentos". *Stadtbild und Ideologie. Die Monumentalisierung hispanischer Städte zwischen Republik und Kaiserzeit.* Munic. Pp. 165-177

GURRI, E.; GURRI, J; BAGUR, P; MEDRANO, J, 1998, "Un centre productor de vi laietà: El Moré (Sant Pol de Mar, el Maresme). De la realitat arqueològica a la virtual." *El vi a l'antiguitat. Economia, producció i comerç al Mediterrani Occidental.* Col·loqui Internacional d'arqueologia romana. Badalona.

GURRI, J ,1997, "Arquitectura virtual". *Revista del Centre d'Invstigació de la Construció.* núm 306 Pp 70-74

V.V.A.A. ,1987, *Terme Romane e vita quotidiana.* Edizioni Panini, 1987. Modena.

THE USE OF DIGITAL PHOTOGRAMMETRY AND GEOMETRIC MODELLING IN MEDIEVAL ARCHAEOLOGY

Olivier Feihl

ArcheoTech, S.A., Pully, Switzerland
archeotech@archidata-sa.com

The experiences we have accumulated for several years in Switzerland led us to develop an entire integrated system of data produced by the interdisciplinary work groups involved in restoration and in excavation at archaeological sites.

Without going into great detail regarding the techniques used, we shall examine here two fundamental aspects situated at the studies'documentary chain's opposite ends. We identify first the need to procure on site an image that is as close as possible to reality and to use advanced space acquisition techniques. Secondly, we discuss the restitution of space and the production of synthesis images that may be used to illustrate results of a study or restoration alternatives.

Spatial Information Acquisition (Site or Objects Survey)

In order to count upon consistent and coherent support from all the disciplines involved in the study of a monument, it is necessary to provide an objective representation of its surrounding space. To achieve this, we must resort to a variety of measuring techniques. Close-range photogrammetry covers most requirements but must be combined with laser telemetry methods to achieve the integration, with the same accuracy, of areas that cannot be viewed in proper perspective or tha are obstructed (Fig.1).

Figure 1

Besides, the use of orthophotography allows for the swift survey of areas dense with information or decorative elements. Information may thus be acquired and updated rapidly as work proceeds on site, at the same time providing a non-interpreted basis. It has proved useful in the study and documentation of painting and mosaic restoration, and in archaeological surveys of burials and stone-work.

The data produced by these different methods is then integrated into one restitution tool, Bentley's Microstation Software. This program of an exemplary modularity works in all computer environments (Unix, Windows, Mac Os) with the same interface. Most analytical or digital photogrammetry programs are created around or within Microstation.

Historical data include established facts and archaeological hypotheses, and are presented in the form of texts, iconographic/pictorial representations. Those data are structured into layers and linked to a descriptive database worked out within Oracle Power Objects.

In the example presented here, the church of Saint-François, built in the second half of the thirteenth century, the external photogrammetric pairs were taken from a gondola hanging at the end of a 60 meter arm fixed on a truck; in other cases a helicopter was required for taking the oblique shots necessary for the definition of geometry in plan as well as in elevation. The slides were taken with a Leica R4 S Elcovision metric chamber and a Pentax 6/7 Elcovision.

Timber roof structures, stairs and small spaces were measured with a reflectorless total laser station. All the adjustment and detail points were linked to a main polygon-line determined by a system of coordinates oriented according to the monument's main axis and then linked to national coordinates. The building interior was covered bay after bay from a scaffolding on wheels. Timber roof structures and small spaces were first drawn up traditionally so as to allow the transfer of topometric points and of conventionally measured quotes.

The data was restituted in Microstation in the Leica Elcovision and ISM DIAPS programs.

All the geometric data was distributed into different layers according to their constituent material nature (masonry, carpentry, tin-ware, etc.) (Fig. 2).

Links with archaeological and historical databases provide an unprecedented easy access to the above mentioned elements that may easily be found or sorted according to chronology or architectural typology. The resulting database allowed us to then record all the restoration project's information and data into new layers (techniques, new infrastructures, etc.) providing us at the same time with a structured basis for archiving the operation, and a memoir of the monument.

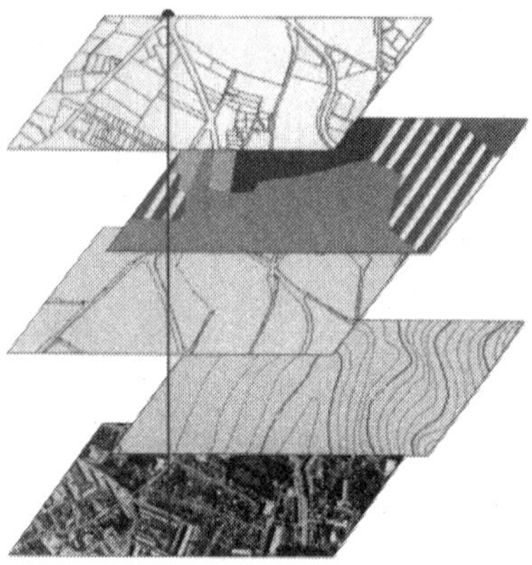

Figure 2

Figure 3

Geometric Modelling and Presentation of Construction Stages in Synthesis Images

Once site studies were completed, and the results were recorded into the database, they were interpreted: a stage code was alloted to each element so as to represent chronology in the traditional form of plans, sections and elevations, directly publishable into the postscript format (Fig. 3).

Then the computer modelling of the different stages could begin. We chose in our example (Fig.4) a complete surface modelling, avoiding the use of geometric primitives that would have been covered by digital images (image and texture mapping).

Figure 4

The option we chose for the modelling of each stage's set of structures forced us to come up with plausible architectural reconstructions, compelling us to frequently re-interpret the archaeological data. On the other hand the numeric data that arose from the survey hardly allowed for the use of regular geometric primitives (paralepipeds, cones, cylinders, etc.) without risking great losses in precision. The selected solution required a huge effort of surface modelling. Each element was classified according to which determined chronological stage it belonged to in the database (Fig. 5, Fig. 6)

Figure 5

Figure 6

The lost elements were, in some cases, reconstructed in accordance with pictorial or historical sources at hand. When these were not available, contemporary regional examples were used; for example the reconstruction of the 13th-century timber roof structure was copied from that of Romainmôtier's Cluniac abbey, of a slighly later time.

The process of building the model helped us to come up with solutions that integrate all the architectural and archaeological data, as well as to propose convincing structural solutions. The state of knowledge acquired up to then had been fixed into two-dimensional space (Fig.7)

Figure 7

After having created the model, we could verify our hypotheses and discuss improvements with an extraordinary demonstrative and communicative tool.

Once the geometrical foundations of each stage were modelled, the question arose whether the final images should be "photo-realist" or not. On the one hand realizing beautiful images was very tempting, on the other, the lack of information regarding surface finishes at different epochs kept us from choosing this solution for fear of being led into hardly justifiable reconstructions.

The data available led us to propose two solutions. In all the cases where sufficient evidence was not available, reconstructions were presented in the form of geometrical surface models made out of only one material. However in one of the stages we had an early 17th-century representation from which we could achieve a reconstruction of the appearance of most materials.

Nevertheless, this action proved very time-consuming and went far beyond the research assignment, in a financial framework that did not involve this type of committment. Yet, in order to communicate results, the development of this type of presentation proved necessary. Furthermore it helps towards a better understanding for a wider audience (Fig.8, Fig. 9).

Figure 8

Figure 9

Images were worked out with Bentley's Masterpiece program. Animation pieces and QuickTime VR sequences were both produced for the future realization of a CD-ROM on the history of the first Franciscan convent in Lausanne.

Toward Assisted Decision and Information Systems in Restoration of Monuments

Apart from the points mentioned above, 3D (three-dimensional) modelling provides many possibilities for simulating restoration alternatives, lighting shemes and the placing of heavy load-bearing structures, possibilities we shall illustrate with three other projects we took part in.

EXAMPLE N° 1

At the Abbey of Romainmôtier, the 3D modelling of the 14th-century timber roof structure was used for the study of how to integrate a metallic structure to reinforce lateral load-bearing walls and support the medieval timber roof structure. All the elements of the engineer's and architect's project were introduced into the numeric model by repeating the insertion maneuvers of the over-two-ton steel beams that had to be integrated in between the medieval pieces without damaging them (Fig. 10, Fig. 11)

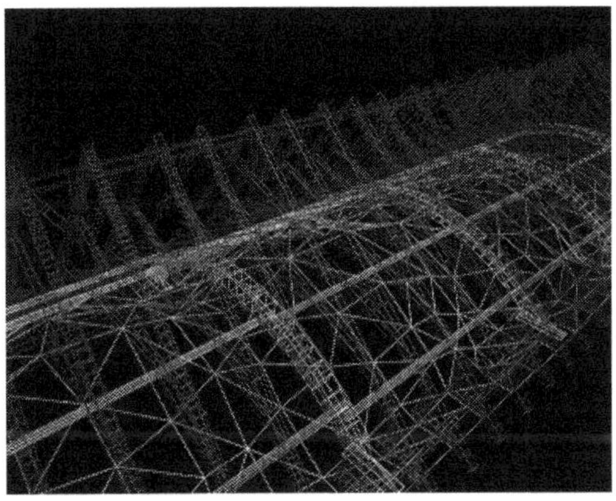

Figure 10

Figure 11

The required mounting precision only allowed for a site adjustment margin of 2 to 3 cm. The structure was mounted on site in two days without having to return a single steel element to the workshop.

EXAMPLE N° 2

The question of integration and filling the areas left void by the passage of time and man's brutality, arose on the occasion of the restoration of the early-14th-century paintings at Chillon Castle's chapel. In a colloquium on the restoration that went on at the chapel, the idea came up to fill in void areas with luminous projections, showing what the original paintings in those positions might have looked like.

From the photogrammetric wall survey and orthophotographs of walls (Fig. 12), an artist drew several alternatives providing the complementary elements indispensable to the understanding of the iconographic cycle. These different schemes were then integrated into a 3D model. After having convinced by this means the responsible authorities, the artist's paintings were then digitized in high resolution; their geometry was modified in Microstation with the IRASC program from Intergraph to compensate for the deformations resulting from the projector's centers that are out of axis and irregularities in the walls. The modified paintings were flashed to create slides from their digital image. These were projected against the walls in the void areas. Different settings in the colorimetric saturation balances were tested in order to harmonize the new paintings with the historical remains.

Figure 12

This solution helped us provide a relatively coherent vision to the visitors of the most visited Swiss monument. For specialists and art historians, the light may be switched off.

EXAMPLE N° 3

The survey and modelling of the great treasure reliquary of Sion is the last example presented here. This 11th-century piece was entrusted to the Museum of Art and History of Geneva, who commissioned us with its survey . The aim was to obtain all the useful information for the dismantling of the silver plates that covered its four faces, and then allow for restoration simulations (Fig. 13). These had to be able to provide a visualization of the filling-in of voids and the remodelling of highly deformed or sunken surfaces.

Figure 13

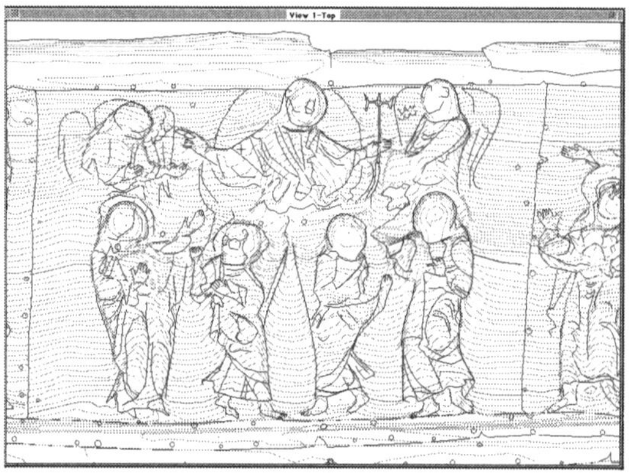

Figure 14

A digital model of the 4 walls and the lid was worked out from a photogrammetric survey reconstructed with 1 mm equidistant curves (Fig. 14). One million facets were generated in Microstation with the Intergraph Siteworks program. Different materials were assigned to the different facets in order to get a coherent representation of the object. Orthophotographs were subsequently calculated to assign restoration results into layers superimposed upon this support (Fig. 15).

Figure 15

The action of placing deformed parts back into their original position was simulated by manipulating the data of the digital model until the assumed original position was reached. The removal of the silver plates that covered the wooden trunk for treatment made us discover unknown previous paintings covering the four faces of the trunk. After mounting the trunk back together, the museographic presentation of this previous stage, the painted trunk, will be a virtual reality model giving the visitor the possibility to manipulate the object as desired, while seeing the object in all its facets. This presentation will also be available on the Internet.

Conclusion

As we have seen, digital information processing in archaeology and in the context of restoration of works of art allows for varied approaches and qualitatively tested solutions, bearing upon the ethical as much as on the financial fields. Setting up assited decision systems shall become more and more frequent in the practice of restoration and in the perspective of durable development. Constant evolution in the technological meansavailable will facilitate the generation of more and more projects analogous to those we have realized, often with heavy equipment and gropingly moving forward.

The spatial reference knowledge databases are meant to be useful for "territory managers" as much as for those in charge of historical heritage who, with this resource at hand, can meet and collaborate when their respective areas of responsibility intersect.

3D VISUALIZATIONS OF A FIRST-CENTURY GALILEAN TOWN

Charles Hixon *(1)*, ***Peter Richardson*** *(2)*, ***and Ann Spurling*** *(3)* *

(1) Cartesian-FX, Inc.
(2)University of Toronto
(3) ***WXXI-Television***
Hixon@bergmannpc.com
Prchrdsn@chass.utoronto.ca

More alarming even than the engines was their whirring drone, more frightful than the missiles the crash. Then there was the thud of the dead falling one after another from the wall. Fearful shrieks from the women within the town mingled with the moans of the dying victims without. The whole surrounding area in front of the fighting lines ran with blood, and the piles of corpses formed a path to the top of the hill.

[Flavius Josephus, Jewish War *3.247-49]*

Virtual Reality for Educational Television

In July of 1996, a crew of five from WXXI-TV (a PBS affiliate in Rochester, NY) arrived at the archaeological dig at Yodefat (Jotapata), Israel, to begin shooting a one-hour PBS network documentary called "Echoes from the Ancients." Flavius Josephus's eyewitness account of the "Siege of Jotapata" was no small factor in the station's decision to undertake the project. It is a vivid tale of courage, treachery and tragedy. And until the excavations had begun, Josephus's narrative had given the world the only known details of Yodefat's role in first-century history.

It is rare to have a full account of a Roman siege by the defeated general, but that is exactly the case at Yodefat. The author, Josephus, was sent to the Galilee in 66 CE to command the northern forces in the First Jewish Revolt against Roman counterattack. In 67 CE, the Roman general Vespasian and his son Titus—sent out by Nero—closed upon Yodefat, the first walled city that resisted. The hilltop community had been swelled by others fleeing Rome's forces, much beyond the 2000 or 3000 it could comfortably hold. Vespasian's siege, which ended on 20 July 67, lasted 47 days. Though Josephus's account may be exaggerated and politically colored, most of his description was borne out by the excavations.

Yodefat is a steep hill located about half way between the Mediterranean Sea and the Sea of Galilee. From the second century BCE to the first century CE it flourished as a small Jewish town. Its archaeological and historical importance lay in several factors: (1) the site had not been built over since 67 CE; (2) Josephus's account provides a literary context alongside which the excavations could be placed;[1] (3) the town offered the likelihood of a pristine Galilean Jewish town of the first century—the time of Jesus—thus anchoring all first-century studies; (4) it shed light on the transition from a small Hellenistic farmstead to a Jewish town following the Hasmonean resettlement of the Galilee. The last two factors give Yodefat international significance and affirmed WXXI's commitment to the project.

The excavations at Yodefat were carried out jointly by the Israel Antiquities Authority (IAA) and the University of Rochester, Rochester, New York (U of R) between 1992 and 1997.[2] The team assembled covered those disciplines ordinarily found in a modern archaeological excavation. For the students, the field work was reinforced with a series of trips, explanations of what they were finding at the site, and nightly classes in all related disciplines.

CHALLENGES

WXXI's goal for the documentary was to give viewers a new perspective of the evolution of two world religions through information revealed at the Yodefat site. Simply capturing images of those various activities would not result in an interesting television program. A general audience would not understand the significance of the history being discovered, and being made, at the Yodefat site. Archaeology is an imaginary science; experts called on years of experience and stores of multi-disciplinary knowledge to re-imagine the first century city. WXXI's responsibility was to do the same for a national audience, to bring the past alive in a readily accessible form.

The storytelling obstacles were daunting: (1) the siege of Yodefat had happened over 1900 years earlier, so there were no contemporary artistic depictions of the battle; (2) in 1996, the excavation was still in the discovery, not in the final analysis stage; (3) daily life in second-Temple Judaism—with its emphasis on ritual purity and the artifacts associated with that—are not familiar to the general public; (4) the more significant finds—aside from Roman *ballista* stones, catapult bolts, and arrowheads—were not self-explanatory.

* The authors extend their thanks to Mordechai Aviam of the Israel Antiquities Authority and to William Scott Green of the University of Rochester for their support of this early publication of some of the features of the excavation. Charles Hixon was the digital expert, Peter Richardson the architect in the archaeological excavations and expert in Christianity and Judaism, and Ann Spurling was the producer and script-writer for the television station WXXI that produced the resulting film.

[1] After Vespasian's ascension to the Imperial throne, Josephus settled in Rome where he wrote four major works: *Jewish War* (about 75CE), *Antiquities of the Jews*, *Life*, and *Against Apion* (all in the 90's CE). All were in one sense or another apologetic works presenting Judaism positively.

[2] The IAA's Mordechai Aviam, district archaeologist for the Western Galilee, was director and archaeological supervisor, the U of R's William Scott Green, specialist in Second-Temple Judaism and early Rabbinism, co-directed and supervised the educational and administrative aspects of the dig. The team they assembled consisted of experts in the disciplines of pottery, numismatics, mapping, surveying, Auto-CAD, architecture and history of religion, and were drawn from Israel, the USA and Canada. In the last several seasons of archaeological work, the dig's AutoCAD expert was Wolf Schleicher. The volunteer work was done by students from the U of R and other institutions, and non-students.

A central focus for the program gradually emerged in the compelling link between events in the life of the dig Director, Mordechai Aviam, and events involving Josephus and the first-century people of Yodefat. On this backbone, a mechanism had to be built that would allow viewers to "see" what ancient life in the Galilee was actually like.

Tools

WXXI decided on a series of virtual reality recreations of Yodefat based on three factors that ensured the end product's historic and archaeological integrity. (1) The Yodefat excavation was one of the first in Israel to employ AutoCAD technology, useful to archaeologists to store information in an easily retrievable form. At Yodefat, the dig's digital expert employed AutoCAD to store six seasons of excavation results, which could then be merged with the mountain's topography and known physical features, such as cisterns. Once stored, each artifact could be shown as it related to other discoveries in each excavated square, or expanded to show it in relation to the entire site. (2) WXXI found a digital partner in the USA capable of the using the stored AutoCAD information as a basis for three-dimensional recreations. CartesianFX, the digital animation arm of Bergmann Associates, a large national architectural firm, is expert in the art of transforming AutoCAD information into virtual reality reconstructions. (3) One of the experts employed during the 1996 excavation was Peter Richardson, a former architect and current New Testament scholar, who concentrated his efforts on understanding Yodefat's first century community in three-dimensional form.

Site Excavations and Small-Town Architecture

U of R / I.A.A. excavation at Yodefat

Josephus

The town of Jotapata is almost entirely built on precipitous cliffs, being surrounded on three sides by ravines so deep that sight fails in the attempt to fathom the abyss. On the north side alone, where the town has straggled sideways up a descending spur of the mountains, is it accessible. But this quarter, too, Josephus, when he fortified the city, had enclosed within his wall, in order to prevent the enemy from occupying the ridge which commanded it. [Josephus, *Jewish War* 3.158-59]

Josephus is more concerned in his descriptions to titillate his readers with the drama of the site and the events there than to give informed architectural descriptions. The architectural information in the account in Josephus, *Jewish War* 3.110-408, is slender, and can be summarized briefly. After describing with great enthusiasm the town's situation with the wadis around it (3.158), Josephus remarks that he built the wall around it (3.159; cf. also 3.111, adding that Yodefat was the strongest of all the fortified towns in Galilee); he claims to have increased the height of the walls during the siege itself to a total of twenty cubits (about 10 meters; 3.171-75); no excavated walls have survived high enough to substantiate this claim and it is probably an exaggeration. The defenders, he explains, had sufficient food but not enough water, because the town had no water source (3.181) and the siege took place in summer, when there was no rain; the Romans knew the Jewish plight, because sentries could see the townspeople running to a central spot to distribute the limited water supplies(3.184-85; the topography allowed Roman observers to see directly into the lower plateau from the higher hills to the east and west and to pin-point catapult fire). Josephus describes the progress of the Roman siege ramp, the effect of the battering ram on the defenders (3.213-21), and efforts to ameliorate its destructive effects (3.222-28). He does not describe, however, one important defensive stratagem that was seen in the dig, the filling in of rooms adjacent to the walls to increase the walls' resistance to the battering rams.

When the Romans entered the city at dawn on 20 July, they took "the citadel" (*akra*, implying that the hilltop had an inner fortress; 3.326). This put them "in the midst of the city," permitting them to "drive the people down the hill from the citadel, slaying them as they drove them down" (3.329), an accurate description of the relationship of the hilltop to the remainder of the city to the south. The defenders were hampered by narrow streets and the steepness of the hillside (3.330). Josephus describes the great number of cisterns distributed through the town (3.334); in the Roman underground search-and-destroy missions during the following days, he says they found 1200 persons hidden below ground in addition to the 40,000 who had already died in the siege (both figures exaggerated no doubt). The city was razed and burnt, as the excavations have vividly attested (3.336-39).

Josephus is the main actor in his final scene. He had gone to ground in a large cistern, which forty "leading persons" had stocked with provisions (3.340-42). After several days, the forty-one persons entered into a mutual death pact by drawing lots (3.390-91), as a result of which Josephus and a friend were fortuitously the last two alive. When Josephus surrendered and was brought to Vespasian, he predicted Vespasian's future rise to the Imperial purple, thus beginning a long friendship with the Flavian family (3.399-408).

EXCAVATION STRATEGY AND RESULTS

A three-pronged excavation approach was developed: (a) the whole site of just over 4 hectares (40dunams or 10 acres) was laid out, mapped, and surveyed; (b) extensive areas related to the defensive walls and to the Roman siege were investigated in detail; (c) selected areas of housing reflecting the character of the first-century Jewish town were explored. This permitted some general assessment, (d), of the urban layout of Yodefat.

(a) Mapping. The key-hole shaped town had a round bald hilltop at the north, with narrower, straight-sided extensions to the south occupying a plateau, some 30 meters below the top of the hill. While most of the main hill was incorporated into the walled town, on the south and southeast little of the hillsides down into the surrounding wadis were included, so that there were steeply raked housing areas on the main hill, but on the lower plateau the housing sloped more gently. Nothing north of the main hilltop was built up. The north face of the main hill sloped down to form a saddle that was the main line of approach to Yodefat, both normally and for Vespasian's siege. Vespasian's siege ramp ascended this less steep northern slope. Contrary to usual practice, he built no formal siege camp; presumably he believed that the siege would be concluded quickly. His main camp was on the hills north of and overlooking Yodefat, with subordinate observation points on the hills around; according to Josephus, Vespasian could see inside Yodefat from several posts. The survey traced the walls around the perimeter of the town and demonstrated that the whole area inside the walls was built up, though it was more intensely occupied on the hilly areas than on the southern plateau. A large number of rock-cut cisterns were concentrated in the area of the hill top, and a large open rectangular pool was located where the hill joined the plateau. There was extensive evidence of rock-cut architectural features, especially on the bare hilltop, the interpretation of which has not been concluded, though it is clear that the cuttings come from different periods of occupation, some going back to the earliest Hellenistic occupation of the site. There may also be evidence of a fortress. Since the town had no natural water supply, cisterns were absolutely crucial to town's existence. Yodefat survived entirely on what could be collected and stored during the winter rainfall, in private and public cisterns and in the large rectangular open pool. The cisterns were of several types, some very large for communal water supplies (or for a fortress, perhaps), but most were domestic. Some had rock-cut stairs (either circular or rectangular shafts), others were accessed by lowering a jug through an opening (both round horizontal openings and rectangular vertical openings).

(b) Walls. The defensive walls on the northwest were of special interest, for that was the location of the Roman siege ramp. Extensive excavations were conducted along those walls during each season. The walls were explored at a couple of other points on the east and south-east (and in 1999 on the southwest). Generally, the walls were simple, a couple of meters wide, in relatively straight runs, with towers interspersed for part of the perimeter, usually about 50 meters apart, projecting about two or three meters from the line of the wall. The construction of the walls was rough field stones, with hewn stones being usually limited to the projecting towers and more characteristic of the earlier periods. The walls have survived in some places to a height of 2 to 3 meters. At the northwest corner walls from five periods have been identified (Hellenistic, Hasmonean I, Hasmonean II, Early Roman I and Early Roman II).[3] The latest period of wall construction at the northwest corner was linked with the construction of additional fortification and the threat of Vespasian's attack, presumably Josephus's own activity. Around the southern plateau there seems only one period of wall-building. Much of the wall was built during the Revolt, for it intersects or parallels domestic walls (in some places casemate walls were constructed using existing house walls). Near the top of the Roman ramp on the northwest, an extremely complex stratigraphic record emerged, with parallel, superimposed, and bisecting walls, indicating that (1) the northwest corner was always the weakest point, (2) occupation had never expanded in this direction, and (3) additional defensive installations were hurriedly constructed because of Vespasian's threat. The earliest walls were Hellenistic, with subsequent impressive wall-building activity at two different points during the Hasmonean period, and less impressive building during the early-Roman period. Part of the northwest casemate wall had been filled with rubble and debris to strengthen them against the force of the Roman attack.. Deposits of stone chips formed a make-shift glacis outside the walls, in one square at two different levels, suggesting that the defenses had been improved at two different stages, once at the time of the Roman siege and earlier, probably in the late Hasmonean period. The town's main gate must have been in the northern wall, east of the Roman ramp; no subsidiary gates were located certainly, though there was likely one in the middle of the west wall and another on the east side near an olive press cave.

(c) Housing. Several promising locations to investigate the various kinds of first-century housing and evidence of daily life were identified: the areas just inside the complex walls on the northwest corner; an area of very steeply-terraced housing just inside the wall on the east side of the main hill; lower down the hill to the south, where the plateau meets the hill; still farther south, another area just inside the wall on the plateau; and an area in the middle of the southern plateau. Houses were relatively simple, with walls of one or two stories; higher walls were utilized in areas of terraced housing where the wall of the house below supported the wall of the house above. Walls were constructed in a rough masonry rubble, with relatively few stones finished even around the openings and almost no genuine ashlars. There was little indication of mortar, or of plaster or stucco wall finishes; the walls must have been bonded with a mud mortar and finished in a mud plaster, both of which have largely washed away. Because the town was burned, no evidence has survived of upper floors and roofs; they would have been constructed of small locally-cut wooden beams with sticks and branches and mud forming the finished floor and roof surfaces. No domestic stone beams or arches have been found, and no roof tiles. Floors were simple: most floors were either beaten earth or exposed and roughly-leveled bedrock; occasionally a rough flagstone floor was found, laid on a bed of mortar.

---

[3] In Palestinian terms, the Hellenistic period runs from 332 to about 37 BCE, the Early Roman period from 37 BCE to 70 CE, and the Middle Roman Period from 70 to about 180 CE. The Hasmonean period is usually identified as a sub-period, extending from about 167 or 140 BCE to either 63 or 40 BCE (Galilee was brought under Hasmonean control during the reign of Alexander Jannaeus [103-75 BCE] or his predecessor Aristobulus I [104-103 BCE]), when Herod took control. The occupation of the town thus covered about 300 years or so.

(d) *Urban Layout*. The lower plateau, representing just under a third of the total area of the town, may have been laid out on a Hippodamian plan between the two long parallel north-south walls. Though not fully investigated, sufficient evidence of this has been observed that this sensible solution seems probable for the layout in the southern portion of the city. No street plan could be traced on the hill, but a Hippodamian plan would have been quite inappropriate in the steeper areas; the streets on the hill would have been adapted to the hill's contours, with little or no effort to impose regularity.

Where excavated squares on the south included the walls, there was a narrow street two meters wide surfaced with stone chips immediately inside the wall. At other points (the steeply terraced housing on the east and just inside the wall at the Roman ramp), however, houses abutted the wall directly with no intervening street. These areas on the main hilltop reflect one or more of an earlier pattern of construction, adaptation to steeper terrain, or additional strengthening of the walls.

Most of the site was devoted to housing. There was no cemetery within the walls, no market area, no public buildings. Two main features that amend this view may be noted, and one question raised. In the southeast area a large open rectangular pool or cistern had access steps (partly rock cut, partly built) and waterproof plaster, with surface remains of a rock-cut balustrade at one corner near the steps. This communal water supply will have been used for such purposes as watering sheep or goats, laundry, and perhaps emergency water supplies, as Vespasian observed. The pool would have been filled by runoff water from streets and lanes, from roofs and courtyards. The second feature to be noted is the hilltop, the earliest section of the site to be settled and the location of the Hellenistic farmstead. This was undoubtedly the location of the fortress, if there was one at Yodefat. The rock-cuttings that crisscross the top may eventually yield a sensible reconstruction of the structures on the hilltop. It has been tentatively concluded that there was a roughly circular wall—whether only at one stage or until the end of occupation is not clear—around the hill top. Any major facilities or public buildings were likely on or near this now bare top. It is questionable whether Yodefat had public or communal buildings, a synagogue perhaps? None has been found, though architectural finds (out of context and from disparate locations) suggest the possibility of either a Hellenistic structure, perhaps destroyed during Hasmonean reoccupation of the site, or a Jewish public building, or both.

Architectural and Small Finds

There were numerous remains of the seven-week Roman siege of 67 CE (arrow heads, catapult bolts, *ballistae*, rolling stones, sandal nails), pottery that was typically Galilean (the majority local), sherds of earlier Galilean common ware, and some evidence of wine amphorae from the Greek islands. Two especially significant evidences of Jewish life were found. First, numerous stone-cut cups, bowls, and jugs, of a wide variety of shapes and sizes showed a strong concern for ritual purity and a common wish to avoid contamination in articles used in everyday activities. Evidence for the use of stoneware in Second-Temple Judaism has accumulated in recent years, and its importance is now generally acknowledged. Second, two plastered *mikvaoth* (Jewish ritual bathing pools) in adjacent houses in the southeastern area, reinforced the concern for ritual purity. Both types of evidence imply a strong domestic attention to ritual purity. Given the strong Second-Temple evidence of *mikvaoth* found in Jerusalem, the Yodefat *mikvaoth* underline the similarity between rural Galilean and urban Judean concerns for purity.

An almost complete olive press was found in a cave just outside the east wall. The crushing stone, weights, pressing pits, slots for beams in the walls of the cave, were all intact. There was evidence of the raising of sheep and goats for their wool, evidenced by numerous loom weights and some very fine decorated spindle whorls. There was also strong evidence of a pottery industry.

A very unusual inscribed stone was found in the last season, apparently a defender's carving during the siege. One side had a zodiac-like representation of a crab, the other a frontal view of a mausoleum with pyramidal cap, similar to those in Jerusalem. Aviam has interpreted the crab as the zodiac sign for July, when the town fell, and the mausoleum as a sign of death. The result: "I die in July." This is a unique object from antiquity.

Architectural fragments are important for reconstruction purposes. A surface find from the bottom of the hill outside the west wall and totally without context was one piece of architrave (a meter or so long, with three simple bands and associated moldings). Two column drums were found in the southeastern area, one inside one of the two *mikvaoth*, that had rolled down the hill at the time of the Roman destruction of the town. Another column drum was found in a balk at the northwest corner, again a result of Roman destruction. A large door jamb (over two meters tall, about a meter deep, half a meter wide) was found in secondary, though pre-67 CE, usage *in situ*. The jamb-stone had been removed from its original location and reused as a corner-post in a (first-century?) house. To the north of the site, in the saddle between Yodefat and the hill to the north, was a small, poor, Byzantine synagogue, where a number of column drums of varying diameters were found *in situ* along with several capitals, all in secondary usage, not as columns and capitals. This later synagogue was constructed partly from fragments found on the site of ancient Yodefat. All these fragments—column drums, capitals, and architrave—might provide evidence of a public building in the earlier period. Given the distribution of the find spots, the likeliest location for the public building was on the now-bare hilltop.

Architecture

The major architectural remains in Yodefat were housing; one significant result of the dig will be to increase substantially knowledge of first-century Galilean housing types (Hirschfeld 1995; Guijarro 1995:42-65). The following are preliminary comments on Yodefat's housing-types.

First century mikveh discovered at Yodefat

(a) *Eastern Hillside Terrace Housing*. An extensive housing area was excavated on the steep east slope of the main hill, just inside the town wall. It had a number of points in common with the housing from the same period at Gamla, likewise destroyed by the Romans in 67 CE: foundations and lower floors were rock cut; houses of one or two stories; higher-level houses built on the walls of houses below; buildings abutting the walls with no intervening street; roofs below being used by neighbors higher up as additional living areas. In Yodefat, the houses were densely packed and built up tight to the walls; there were no signs of wealth or of unusual facilities. Similar features occur at other nearby sites such as Cana.

(b) *Southeast Housing*. Lower down the hillside and a short distance inside the walls, where the slope was much less steep, the houses closely followed the contours, with floors at varying levels. The foundations were sometimes rock-cut, as were the floors, one of which was roughly plastered on the bedrock. The rooms were larger on average than the rooms in the terrace housing, and more artifacts illustrative of daily life were found in this area. Occasional lanes serviced the houses and provided access.

(c) *Mikveh Houses*. At the juncture of the main hill and the lower plateau, parts of three or four houses were uncovered. Two had private *mikvaoth*, indicative of religiously-observant occupants. These houses were somewhat more complex, and could be reconstructed in more detail. Most floors were rock cut, though one was roughly paved; rock-cut cisterns in the bedrock were filled from runoff water from the roofs above; the collecting pool and channel survived. An adjacent though collapsed cave formed part of one house, either for storage (perhaps olive oil or wool) or for animals. An oven (*tabun*) was found in one area, in another a small rock-cut olive crushing area. One *mikveh* was in a room of its own, the other was in a rock-cut cavity, immediately adjacent to a cistern and near rock-cut water channels that may have provided the *mikveh* with a source of running water. The houses were separated from the town wall by a narrow street, from which a dead-end lane branched to serve other houses whose plans were partially visible from rock-cut surface features. West of this complex was the large rectangular rock-cut open pool, which helped to give focus to this neighborhood. This area is informally laid out and less compact than the areas on the hill slopes.

Digital re-creation of the Mikveh House

(d) *Lower Plateau*. To test the occupation of the whole of the lower plateau, an area was excavated farther south; this demonstrated that the whole lower plateau was built up during the first century. The houses were simple one or two room houses, built on almost level ground, and more regularly laid out on orthogonal axes.

(e) *Rock-cut Courtyard House*. Everywhere on the site, but especially where the south slope of the main hill meets the plateau, there was surface evidence of rock-cuttings for houses still visible. One noteworthy house had rock-cut features that were half a meter to a meter high and seems to have been planned around a central courtyard; though the interior areas had collapsed into the cisterns below, the rock-cut front walls with front door, rear wall, and side walls were readily visible. This may have been one of the larger and better houses in town.

(f) *Fresco House*. In the 1997 season one unexpectedly different room was discovered on the east side of the town. Almost five meters of painted-plaster wall (fresco) was found, decorated in a geometric style reminiscent of Pompeii (a kind of simplified first style) with similar colors. The floor of the frescoed room was also plastered and painted. This was a major exception to the other housing in several respects: (1) it pointed to much more wealth than the other housing, which were characteristic of a small, rural, agrarian town reflecting peasant life in the Galilee; (2) its nearest Jewish analogies were in wealthy houses in Jerusalem and in Judean palaces built by Herod the Great (Jericho, Herodium, Masada, Machaerus, Caesarea Maritima); (3) the house's frescoed wall was the most vividly painted and intact found from first-century Israel; (4) no frescoed floor has been found dated to the first century in Galilee. Further excavations will be required to understand this 1997 evidence properly. Was the rest of the house consistent in style and decoration? Was it a peristyle house in a town that has little direct evidence of such styles? Were there any other houses in town sharing these features? What was the relationship between the owner of this house and his fellow townsmen? Should provision be made for a continuously differentiated social structure in town? Or is this one house set apart from all the others? No explanation for such a wealthy house in Yodefat is forthcoming. Nothing in the historical record suggests a purpose for a sophisticated house more characteristic of an urban setting than a small town, populated mainly by agrarian peasants.

(g) *Northwest Wall Houses*. At the northwest corner near the Roman ramp was a complex of houses giving crucial indications of the vigor of the Roman siege and destruction. The area was filled with housing up against the wall, and showed more evidence than other areas of sequential occupation and reconstruction from one period to another. Some evidence was Hellenistic, overlaid by first-century BCE and CE housing: blocked-up doorways, changes in plan, and, at the time of the siege, rooms adjacent to the wall being filled with debris. The most interesting room, full of pottery destroyed when the houses were demolished during the siege, was a kitchen area with a *tabun* (oven) and a piece of stone table top or kitchen "counter," all on a beaten earth floor with an adjacent higher-level rock cut floor.

RESULTING HISTORY OF THE SITE

The rough history of the site can be sketched. The earliest construction on the hilltop was a fortified Hellenistic fortlet or farmstead, perhaps owned by a citizen of Tyre. Following the success of the Hasmonean revolt and its extension into the Galilee, the hilltop was taken over and a small Jewish town, perhaps contained within the original fortifications, was built there. Its attraction to the new settlers would have been that, even without a natural water supply, there were sufficient facilities (walls, cisterns, buildings) to offer the basis of a town. Later, the town was expanded into a Jewish regional walled town, with extensions of the settlement down the southern slope and then, perhaps later, onto the lower plateau. These later developments may have begun under Herod the Great (40-4 BCE) and continued under Antipas and Agrippa (4 BCE-38 CE; 38-44 CE). If this surmise is correct, usual formulations of Galilean social history that emphasize the rapacity of the Herodian period and the tendency for land and wealth to become accumulated in relatively few hands with the consequent diminishing of the lower middle class may need correction, for this expansion of the town must represent a period of significant development, with contributory trade and commerce, and even wealth.

The 3D Reconstruction

Though the layout of Yodefat is still not fully understood (the percentage of the site that has been excavated is still small), the general shape could be communicated to the consulting architects preparing the virtual reality visualizations. Much of the work preliminary to the 3D reconstructions focused on the neighborhood that included the *mikvaoth* houses, an unexcavated but significant cave, the partially excavated rectangular open pool, two squares north of the open pool that exposed more housing, and rock-cut features visible on the surface in adjacent areas. This neighborhood included streets and lanes, a section of the town wall, and the almost intact olive press outside the wall. Much of the information passed on to the architects was a sustained analysis of this neighborhood, resulting in freehand sketches suggesting logical choices for the original form of these few houses and some of the likely elements in the urban layout.

Elements used as key indicators in the reconstruction included construction features such as width of walls, drainage indications, doors, and types of floors; and functional elements such as the tabun, olive crushing basin, cisterns and cave, mikvaoth. Decisions were made about the limits of each house, indoor versus outdoor space, existence of second floors, function of the cisterns, and so on. Though the sketches were very rough, they transmitted adequately information from one architect to another.

Little research has focused on first-century housing in rural Galilean villages and towns, so much of the reconstruction was developed from first principles. First-century houses have been excavated at Gamla, similar in certain respects to Yodefat's terrace housing, though the local building traditions in the Lower Galilee differ both in materials and methods of construction from those in the Golan Heights, where columnar basalt permits strong and lengthy stone beams and where arches and "window walls" are common. Capernaum, Magdala, Meron, Beth Yerah, Bethsaida, Sepphoris, and a few other locations may have comparable early-Roman housing. One of the benefits of the process in which the archaeological results were converted into an educational film was that it demanded close attention to the reconstruction of first-century housing in the Galilee.

Digital Animation and TV Production

DIGITAL ANIMATION AND VIRTUAL REALITY

In the world of architecture, digital animation and virtual reality have become key design and presentation tools, where their role is to convey and express the architect's vision clearly and compellingly. When Bergmann Associates was contacted to create animation for the Yodefat site, it seemed to them a natural progression beyond the more usual architectural responsibilities. Both architecture and archaeology disciplines utilize detailed record keeping to track a project; both also use the same elements needed to create digital animation. The main difference, as was pointed out in one of the interviews in "Echoes from the Ancients," is that architecture builds up while archaeology breaks down. In essence the two disciplines are the reverse of each other and have a very close intellectual connection.

Digital re-creation of a first century room with cistern

Digital animation provides four unique functions or tools for the architect. (1) It can be used as an interactive design review and *scientific analysis* tool. By visualizing the project clearly, design options can be assessed faster and at less expense. "Virtually" reviewing the design saves field changes at a late stage in the completion of a project, changes that cost the project both time and money. (2) Another key function is *interference detection*. Identifying design flaws or potential interferences is easier and better when they are viewed through digital animation. This becomes readily apparent when comparing the attempt to identify flaws through the use of stacks of plans and elevations with the opportunities inherent in an interactive three dimensional model provided digitally. (3) The third key function is *construction sequencing*. Part of the design and build process is the organization required for construction purposes. Coordinating the various disciplines necessary to construct a building or facility is very complex. Digital animation can improve many of these coordinating issues, and permits keeping the general and sub-contractors more clearly informed, with the result that projects are more likely to be completed on time and on budget. (4) Finally, another key function is *public review and approval*; digital animation can be a powerful tool used to sway public opinion or to educate the public better.

This last function (4) was the one clearly relevant to the challenge of interpreting the Yodefat site for a broad public. Instead of having the television viewer try to comprehend complicated CAD data or still renderings, digital animation would clearly convey a sense of the town as it might actually have looked. Animation could also help the viewer understand the beauty and design of a people that lived long ago. It would transport the viewer back to a time when the site was an active community, linking them to the past in a more direct way.

TEAM PROCESS

To achieve these goals, Bergmann Associates worked closely with a variety of people and organizations. The first task was to understand clearly the history of Yodefat and the vision of the town's recreation by the archaeologists and site architects. This was accomplished through in-depth interviews with the key people and by research in the period and location. It was critical to know as much as possible both about how the people of Yodefat lived and how they built the homes in which they lived. Since the digital artists had not been at the site, they had to rely heavily on those who had been directly involved. This understanding of the daily life of the people of Yodefat allowed those who created the animation to "see" the site accurately. Most importantly, they needed to know that they were following the vision of the archaeologists.

The most creative events were meetings between the digital artists, architects, the TV crew, and the excavators at the beginning of the development of the 3D-reconstruction process. Materials made available to the digital artists included videotapes of the site (aerials and various shots of the mountain and countryside), rocks brought from the site (providing color and texture for the visualizations), freehand sketches, site drawings, sketches, and CAD data in AutoCAD version 12 format. The discussion was evocative, as the excavators attempted to convey to the architects and digital artists the significance of the various finds. The digital artists prodded the excavators and the film team to clarify the basis on which the reconstructions were being proposed, and worked with the dynamic visual needs of a national television production.

This talking-through of the architects' problems when producing a virtual reality segment for the film began to create trust between the excavators and the architects. It happened quickly, and it survived the whole process. The digital artists quickly developed confidence in proceeding on the basis of what they understood, and the excavators were confident that the artists had heard and were capable of developing responsible animations. Thus, as draft virtual reality reconstructions were circulated to the excavators, living in three countries on two continents, critiques of those drafts could be developed and communicated to the architects with complete frankness and confidence. To make this possible, the use of e-mail, Internet WEB-based services and telecommunications was necessary. Over the course of six months there were actually only three face to face meetings with the entire project team. Everyone relied heavily on e-mail and file transfer protocols such as FTP to share information. This process saved significant amounts of money due to less travel and, more importantly, the project was kept on track due to the excellent lines of communication.

Several general features were deemed important to convey to the larger public audience that was anticipated. (1) The overall character of the town and its walled perimeter, set in an accurate reconstruction of the topography, had to be faithfully portrayed, together with an understanding of the process of recording, storing and utilizing the information about contours, squares, rock-cut features and finds. (2) The neighborhood about which the most was known would be used to provide insight into the domestic scale of the town, especially the character of one house with its cave, and the nearby open rectangular pool seemed especially important. (3) The needs of educating a large audience required visualizations of details that could be readily grasped and that would be particularly informative about Jewish life in antiquity. Issues such as the outdoor living arrangements, the mikveh in one room of the house, and the cistern in another room, all required much discussion and detail.

Once the digital artists had an understanding of the people and their customs, they needed to comprehend the architecture of the region and the period. The fundamental features of the site were contained within the excavation reports and the AutoCAD data compiled from the six-year excavations. Interviews with key personnel confirmed the interpretation of this site information, and the basis for the reconstructions emerged from the characteristic aspects of the homes at Yodefat and other first-century communities. The key elements at Yodefat were its simple one- and two-story buildings, the relative poverty of most of the dwellings (in general the people of Yodefat were not wealthy), the simplicity of the materials used, the modest size of the rooms, and their sparse furnishings.

Armed with those understandings, the digital artists worked closely with the producers at WXXI to determine more specifically what should be modeled and animated for the production. Since digital modeling and animation takes weeks to accomplish, changes in the scope of the project could not be permitted, once the modeling process had begun. To ensure that all parties understood what was being created, storyboards were prepared. Decisions such as scene settings, viewpoints, materials, colors, textures and animation paths were included in the storyboards, which had to match up with the television script that was already written. Several meetings were needed to discuss the storyboards and their revisions. Once all the parties involved gave final approvals, digital modeling began.

TECHNICAL PROCESS

The CAD data compiled at the site was the key factor in replicating the city and its buildings. To accomplish this, the site was surveyed. The survey points were in turn inputted into the AutoCAD (version 12) program and a digital terrain model (DTM) was created. A digital terrain model is a series of triangles, formed from the survey points, which create a 3-dimensional representation of the terrain. The DTM was the basis for all the digital modeling created. The DTM allowed the digital artists to place the buildings and walls of the city properly, and also to grasp the scale of the terrain's elevation. Photographs and sketches did not clearly represent the severity of the terrain. The DTM did. As detailed as the CAD data was for each individual excavation square, it would have been quite insufficient without the DTM.

With the DTM in place, the CAD data for each square could then be used intelligently. Since the data was in two dimensions, it was used as a template to extrude the forms into three dimensions. To add substance to the buildings, intense conversations were held between the digital artists, the site architect, and the archaeologists. Aesthetic elements such as window placements, flooring, and wall textures were discussed. For example, since only partial CAD data existed for the *mikveh*, the insights and reconstructions of the historians and archaeologists were invaluable in completing the digital model.

Once these issues were resolved, the creation of the digital model could begin. A total of four high-end Silicon Graphics workstations running Alias Power Animator 6.0 were used to recreate the city of Yodefat. Alias Power Animator was used because of its superior digital modeling tools and fast render times. CartesianFX (CFX) chose the Silicon Graphics product line based on its incredible capacity for handling complex graphics. Adding in elements such as water from the cisterns and local vegetation, for example, increased the complexity of the digital model, so that as the model of the city grew, it eventually exceeded 12 million polygons in size, whereas most digital models are in the range of 1-2 million polygons. The Yodefat model was thus twelve times this size, requiring the most advanced computing power available. CFX utilized a Silicon Graphics R4400 ONYX with 512MB of RAM to render out these images.

Digitally re-created aerial view of first century Yodefat

With the modeling finished, the next step for the digital artist was to complete the "texturing" of the digital models. In texturing, the digital artist assigns the model coloring, lighting, shading, and textures. To match accurately the textures of the houses, especially the walls and floors and ceilings of Yodefat, individual samples of stones and pottery were examined. Where possible, artifacts were scanned for accurate coloring and textures. These scanned images (24-bit color) were brought into the software program Adobe PhotoShop 5.0. PhotoShop allows the digital artist to "clean-up" scanned images. Anomalies such as poor image quality and/or lighting are corrected within PhotoShop. The software allows the digital artist to match the textures provided to him almost identically. This process was reflected in the final animation. Again, interviewing was needed to settle some issues authentically, such as lighting; the digital artists needed to know how intense first-century lighting was, for correct lighting values would bring the model to life. The digital artists also viewed WXXI's videotape footage and photographs of other first-century cities in the area. Such information was essential in helping the digital artists understand how walls were assembled and roughly mud-plastered. Clips from the WXXI video footage led to a better understanding of how ceilings and roofs were constructed.

Digital re-creation of the main gate to the city

With the modeling and texturing in place, animation could begin. CartesianFX worked closely with WXXI to obtain the proper video footage needed, for it was a goal of the group to match existing video footage with the digital model, where applicable. WXXI wanted the digital animation to blend with the actual footage of the site. The overall aim was to permit the viewer to understand not only what the site might have looked like in the first century but also what it looks like today. Footage was eventually selected for the aerial fly around of the city and for the *mikveh* scenes.

Once the video footage had been selected, the animation path could be laid out on the digital model. At this point, CartesianFX's Silicon Graphics Onyx supercomputer power was needed. To create one second of animation takes 30 frames or renderings. Each frame takes the supercomputer approximately 10 minutes to calculate. Thus, one second of animation could require up to 300 minutes of raw computing time. On a normal PC, rendering times were over 45 minutes per frame, much too long to produce effectively. In all, approximately 60 seconds of animation was completed. The CFX team had the difficult task of matching the camera angle and speed when laying out the animation path. To create a seamless blend, all viewing elements had to match perfectly. With the animation path defined, the computer can then begin the lengthy task of producing each individual frame needed for the animation. In total there were 1800 frames required for the animation. It took approximately 18,000 minutes (over 12 straight days) to render out all the frames. From these individual frames, several still renderings and graphics were used throughout the production. With the animation complete, all the electronic files were turned over to WXXI for post-production work.

To accomplish all these tasks takes a highly trained digital artist, with expert knowledge in computer systems and software. The high degree of artistry needed by the digital artist requires a background in art and photography, as well. Instead of ink, pencil, and paint, their medium is the computer. Even with all the high technology computer hardware and software, the most important requirement for this project was communication. Without it, the vision of the archaeologists and architects could not have been properly expressed.

Reactions and Benefits

In broadcast television, the success of a program is most often gauged by ratings; the size of the audience, where they live, their ages and incomes. "Echoes from the Ancients" was a feature presentation of the Public Broadcasting System in December of 1998 and again, in August of 1999. It was carried by affiliates in two-thirds of the United States, and seen by over 20 million people in the USA and in Canada. The program's companion international web site is currently being accessed by an additional eighteen to twenty thousand people each week. Perhaps the best gauge of impact is the personal feedback from viewers, which ranged from housewives to international scholars. The consensus was that the program enabled them to see history not just as texts, but as people. "Once I could see how they lived," remarked one viewer, "they were no longer esoteric. I saw where and how they lived, how they practiced their religion. Suddenly, first century Israel had meaning."

The centerpiece animation of a *mikveh* at Yodefat also achieved its goal. The evolution of Second-Temple Judaism into Rabbinic Judaism, the influence of the Hasmoneans, and the religious roots of Jesus of Nazareth are complex and controversial concepts to present to a general television audience. The animation, however, enabled people to see a central feature of first-century Judaism in the Galilee. A viewer told WXXI, "I understand Judaism and Christianity in a way I never thought possible. The influences of Judaism on early Christianity is not something I learned in the classroom. It was intriguing!"

The 3D animations contained in the WXXI documentary are testament to the effective combination of scholarly research, digital science and integrity of content. The goal was not to dazzle, but to place them in a programmatic setting that enhanced the content, and enlightened and informed the widest audience possible. Those who were intrigued by the program will no doubt pursue other journeys into the fields of history, science, and religion. Digital animation helped everyone from the archaeologist, to the architect, to the television viewers hear the faint "Echoes from the Ancients."

References Cited

JOSEPHUS, *Jewish War* (Loeb Classical Library; Cambridge MA: Harvard University Press, 1927 [Books I-III], 1928 [Books IV-VII), translated by H. St.J. Thackeray.

GUIJARRO, Santiago, 1997. "The Family in First-Century Galilee," in Halvor Moxnes, ed., *Constructing Early Christian Families* (London and New York: Routledge), pp. 42-65, with extensive bibliography.

HIRSCHFELD, Yizhar, 1995. *The Palestinian Dwelling in the Roman-Byazntine Period* (Jerusalem: Franciscan Printing Press/IES), with extensive bibliography.

COMPUTER-AIDED DESIGN AND ARCHAEOLOGY AT SAGALASSOS: METHODOLOGY AND POSSIBILITIES OF CAD RECONSTRUCTIONS OF ARCHAEOLOGICAL SITES

F. Martens, J. Legrand, P. Legrand, L. Loots, M. Waelkens

University of Leuven, Belgium
Femke.Martens@arts.kuleuven.ac.be

Introduction

The ancient town of Sagalassos is located in southwestern Turkey, about 100 kilometers north of the modern city of Antalya, ancient Attaleia. The town was first rediscovered near the beginning of the eighteenth century and was visited by several travellers (Waelkens 1993a: 40-41). In 1986 a systematic survey was begun as well as the drawing of a general plan of the town centre at a scale 1:1000 (Fig. 1) (Mitchell et al 1986: 37-43).

Large-scale excavations only started in 1990 under the direction of M. Waelkens of the Catholic University of Leuven, Belgium. Now, nearly 10 years and as many excavation campaigns later, a large number of buildings, monuments and other archaeological remains have been exposed, documenting the monumental aspect of the Hellenistic, Roman and early Byzantine history of this town (Waelkens 1993a ; Waelkens 1993b ; Waelkens et al 1995 ; Waelkens et al 1997).

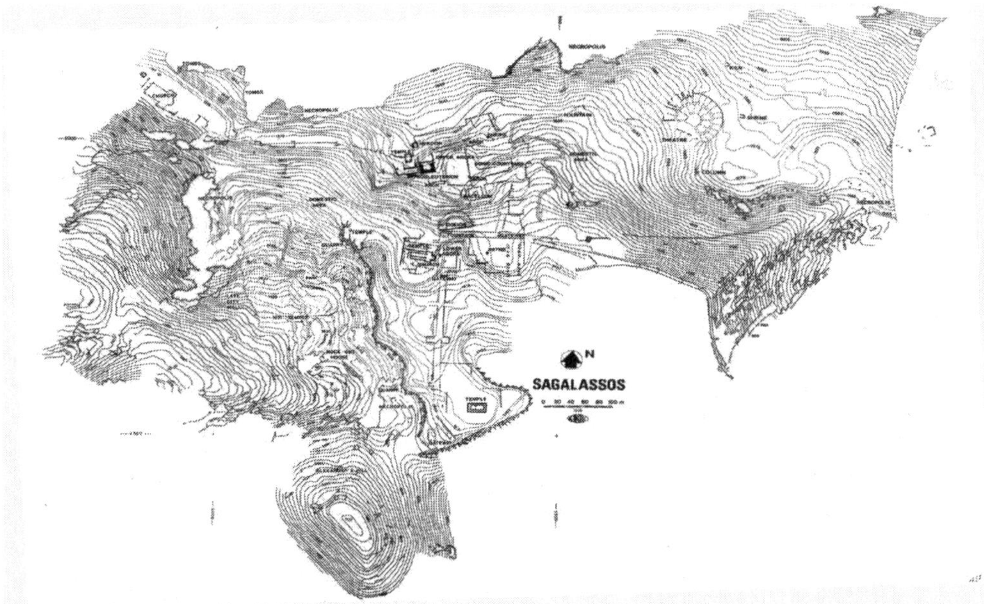

Figure 1: General plan of the town centre of Sagalassos.

The research at Sagalassos is not confined to the mere analysis of its monuments. Broad interdisciplinary research is being conducted in order to reconstruct the history of the town as well as the socio-economical and paleo-ecological framework of its historical development. Aside from archaeologists, the research team consists of geologists, geomorphologists, anthropologists, cartographers, archaeozoologists, botanists, architects, agricultural engineers and also computer specialists.

Several computer applications are presently being used in the study of the town and its territory. Apart from statistical methods, which facilitate the processing of the archaeological data (Poblome et al. 1993: 149-181; Ottenburgs et al 1995: 255-270) some interesting results have already been obtained by using Geographical Information Systems (GIS). Viewshed analysis has proven the efficiency of the city defence system of Sagalassos (Loots et al,1999), while tendencies in the settlement pattern on the territory of Sagalassos are made clear by the use of GIS. Also, the use of Computer-Aided Design (CAD) proved to be meritorious for the research on the ancient town of Sagalassos as will be demonstrated.

The Creation of the CAD 3D Reconstruction Models of the Buildings and Site of Sagalassos

The history of the creation of the complete 3D model of Sagalassos began in 1994 when two volunteers, Jos and Paul Legrand, offered to create a 3D model of the Hadrianic nymphaeum to the north of the Lower Agora at Sagalassos, of which a reconstruction drawing was available (Waelkens 1993a: 68, Fig.45). The basic modelling was done in AutoCAD R11. Details such as the texture of the building materials, the statues and the architectural decoration were added to the model using 3D Studio (Fig. 2). Since the model of the reconstructed nymphaeum was completed with a minimum amount of feedback from the archaeologists, a number of archaeological inaccuracies existed. Therefore it was decided to design a larger model but in closer collaboration with the archaeologists. This extended model containing many more reconstructed models of excavated or surveyed buildings at Sagalassos was created in AutoCAD R12. The models were positioned on their exact locations by means of a 3D mesh, covering most of the site. In order to check the accuracy of the model, perspective views of photographs taken at the site were reproduced in the computer model using the same camera and target positions and also the same lens characteristics. Overlays were then made by means of Adobe PhotoShop software. The model proved to be reasonably accurate, but the overlays also provided an interesting and vivid visualization of the reconstructed buildings within their physical environment (Fig. 7). More realistic overlays were obtained using 3D Studio R4 in which the mappings were based on photographs taken on the site. Currently the basic modelling is done in AutoCAD R14, whereas the models are rendered more visually attractive by using 3D Studio Max.

Figure 2: 3D Reconstruction model of the Hadrianic Nymphaeum to the north of the Lower Agora.

General Reliability and Possible Use of CAD Reconstructions of Ancient Buildings and Sites for Archaeology

The use of computer-aided design to reconstruct ancient buildings and archaeological sites is becoming commonplace in archaeological practice. (Forte and Silotti 1996) However, the actual potential of these computer reconstructions is still not fully realized (Gillings *this volume*). It is necessary to further explore and communicate the numerous possibilities of these computer applications. It is equally important, however, to question the reliability of these 3D reconstructions for archaeological purposes.

Concerning the reliability of the 3D models of reconstructed buildings one can distinguish two different kinds. Both should be taken into account when evaluating a particular model. First there is the extrinsic, metrical reliability depending on the accuracy of the measurements taken at the site as well as on the geometrical errors created during the construction of the model. It is clear that a conscientious attitude towards the accuracy of the initial archaeological reconstruction drawings and during the construction of the model is highly desirable. As with any research, when the need for accurate measurements is not being appreciated, the validity of all other information given will be doubtful (Hogg 1980: 289).

The intrinsic reliability answers the question of whether the model fulfills its requested purpose or not. The main purpose for creating 3D models of reconstructed buildings, following a survey or long-term excavations, is often that of presenting a lively image of the archaeological remains to the general public. It can be questioned, however, whether these 3D models can also function as a methodological tool for archaeological interpretation. A particular purpose will imply a specific degree of complexity within the model, ranging from metrically accurate but simplified models to complex models, presenting a very detailed reproduction of a reconstructed building. For educational purposes a rather simplified model of the reconstructed building may suffice. Such uncomplicated models can be made more attractive by simply pasting the aspect of surface, architectural decoration or sculptures to the building (Fig. 2). A more complex 3D reconstruction, however, is probably better suited to instruct the truly interested public on the discovered evidence. In such models it is important that the tentatively added elements are distinguished from the authentic parts by adding a different mapping. This kind of honesty towards the public corresponds with the common rules of actual archaeological reconstructions and publications (Barker 1977: 228)[1]. These complex, archaeologically highly accurate models present a very detailed reproduction of a reconstructed building, but usually only display one particular phase of the proper diachronic evolution of a building. When assembling such single-phase reconstructions of the different buildings of a site into one complete model of the town, the results are a simplified and rationalized image of the periods of occupation of the site. In reality, the situation is kaleidoscopic, with single buildings being replaced while other buildings on the site remain or are being repaired. Such a presentation of the building history of a site, however, is difficult to achieve mainly because of the limitations in the ability to date the building and demolition of all structures of a site. Some of these buildings may only be recorded by means of survey implying that chronological interpretations concerning these structures may be modified by long-term excavation. Moreover, since the building history of a site is hardly ever the result of consequent complete rebuilding activities across the site, it is particularly difficult to demonstrate the horizontal relationships between several buildings and their different phases of construction. The detailed presentation of all phases and sub-phases of the different buildings of a town would not only be confusing for the general public, but it would also be exceedingly costly to create (Barker 1977: 213-214). The same objections apply to the creation of 3D models which present a diachronic evolution within one particular building, not to mention the additional computer technical difficulties of the creation of the model itself. Therefore, complex single-phase reconstruction models, based on highly detailed excavated evidence can be very useful for educational purposes, but it is of the utmost importance that the public is informed on the complete building history of the construction, as well as on the possibility of alternative interpretations.

[1] This topic of distinguishing reality from tentative interpretations in reconstructed models is also discussed by John Kantner in this volume.

As mentioned before, one should question whether these 3D reconstruction models can be useful for archaeological interpretation. Here, a distinction should be made between the stratigraphical analysis of an excavated building and the interpretation of the character and the role of a building within its urban context. As far as the stratigraphical analysis is concerned, the superposition of different building phases of a structure within a 3D model could be very interesting for the archaeological interpretation of the historical evolution of a construction. During excavations every unit of stratification is being recorded in single-layer plans, each of which may represent a building phase. Several units can be compiled into one composite plan, which is the usual form in which archaeological plans are published. Of course when creating these composite plans in 2D, only those parts of the underlying units of stratification can be recorded, which appear at the surface and are not being overlapped by later units (Harris 1989: 86). On sites with a complicated stratigraphy this selective way of recording will result in a simplified image, seldom useful for archaeological interpretation since such plans cannot be broken down again into individual single-layer plans. Concerning this particular problem, we have to conclude that simply because of the morphological characteristics of 3D models created within AutoCAD, these reconstructions are not suited for the purpose of analysing the historical evolution of an excavated construction. For such an analysis specific software should be developed, which would enable the archaeologist to visually superimpose the successive strata discovered during excavation, without losing information because of the overlapping of units. The principle merit of a 3D model consisting of such a superposition would then be the fact that the stratigraphical relationships could be read from all sorts of viewpoints and that the subsequent strata could be peeled off in chronological order, without losing information on the individual layers. Likely the further development of structural, solid modelling in archaeology will also allow such use of 3D reconstructed models of ancient buildings (Daniel 1997: 4).

If not suited for the analysis of the historical evolution of a building, can 3D models of reconstructed buildings be useful for certain topics of urbanistic research? Important data for urbanistic research are the positions of buildings within the town, their orientation and morphological characteristics. For this type of research the traditional two-dimensional methods of data recording may prove to be inadequate in terms of accuracy and detail for the wealth of data produced and required. (Daniel 1997: 1.2) Particularly when reconstructed models of ancient buildings are inserted into the model of the complete town, this 3D representation of the data may prove to be of great benefit for urbanistic research. To answer specific questions concerning spatial relationships of buildings in relation to their urban context, simplified models of the reconstructed buildings may already suffice. And as an added advantage, it will take the computer program less time to run a certain test on such a simplified model.

Possible Use of CAD Reconstructions of Ancient Buildings and Sites Illustrated by Means of the 3D Models of Sagalassos

The initial purpose of the creation of CAD reconstructions of the buildings of Sagalassos was to present the discovered data in a vivid way to the interested public. The attractive visual character of the CAD reconstructions makes them especially suitable for this educational purpose (Fig.3). As such, the models have been used in lectures and on the explanatory panels, which have been positioned in front of the excavated buildings on the site itself.

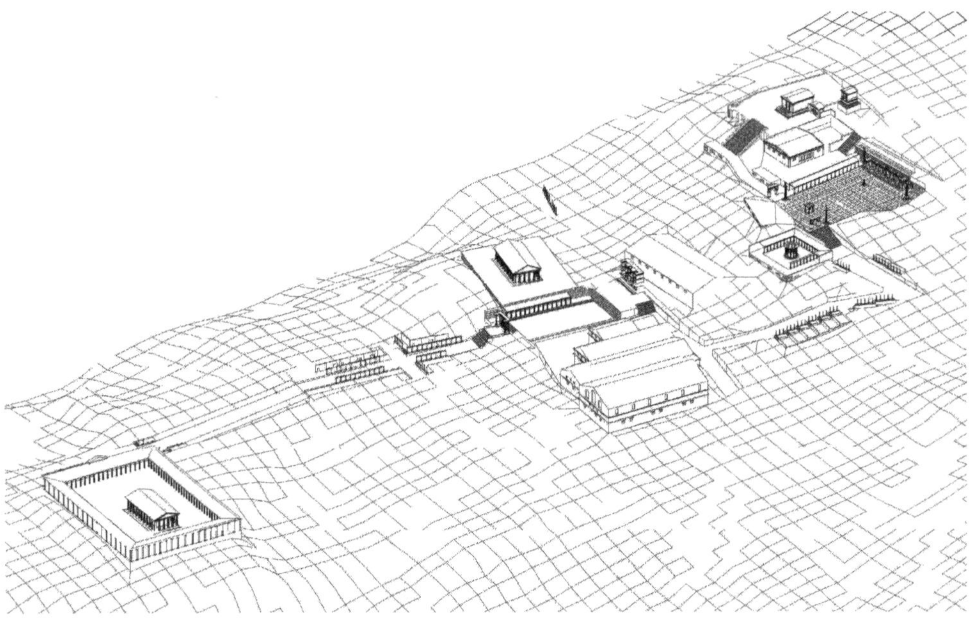

Figure 3: 3D Reconstruction model of the area surrounding the Upper Agora (model anno 1999).

Figure 4: 3D Reconstruction model of the topography and the buildings in the town centre of Sagalassos (model anno 1999).

Besides this obvious educational aspect we have tested whether the complete 3D model could also provide a methodological tool for the research concerning visibilities within the town and the influence of the physical environment upon the specific character of the buildings and upon the town planning itself. The buildings discovered at Sagalassos so far date from the third century BC until the seventh century AD, when the town was finally abandoned. Not all of these monumental buildings, dating from different periods (Vandeput 1997: 14-24), nor the different phases of their building history have been included in the model yet. Since the reconstructed model of the town of Sagalassos thus consists of single-phase models of the surveyed or excavated constructions, a brief chronology of the buildings surrounding the Upper Agora and Lower Agora will provide some more information on the general building history of the town and its monuments (Fig.5: 1-11).

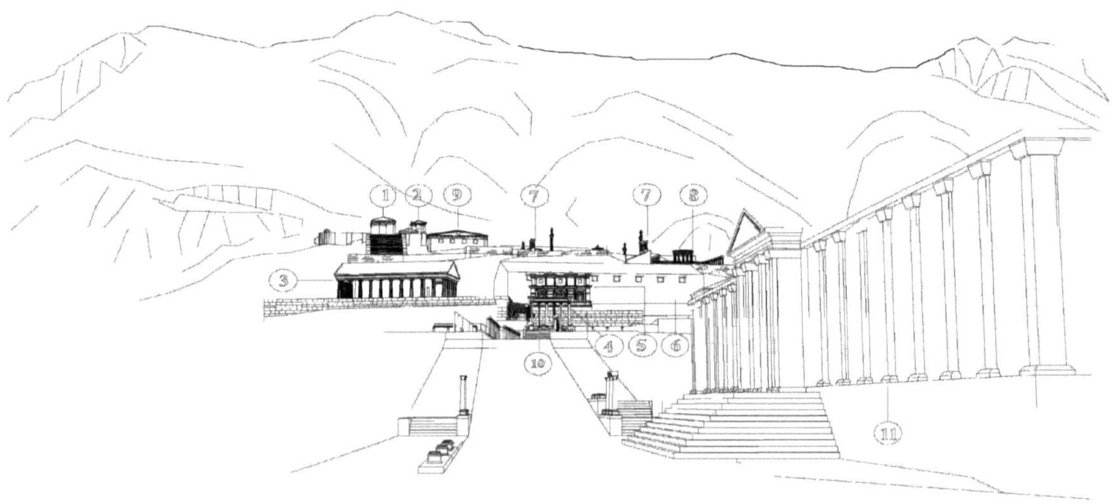

Figure 5: 3D Reconstruction model of the view of the southern approach to Sagalassos in antiquity (model anno 1999).

The earliest buildings of the town were mainly concentrated around the Upper Agora (Fig. 3). The arrangement of this trapezoidal open area goes back to the second century BC and probably even earlier, but the actual pavement dates from the Roman Imperial period (Waelkens 1993b: 15). The layout of this pavement was clearly not the result of a single operation (Waelkens et al 1995: 23). Originally the Upper Agora was bordered to the north by a structure, which may have been a market building and was dated to the third century BC on the basis of its building technique. Later, during the reigns of Augustus and Tiberius, the western part of the structure was transformed into a terrace building, and between 160 and 180 AD a Nymphaeum was erected against its facade. The terrace building itself was internally altered several times during the second and the early fifth centuries AD until it was finally subdivided and transformed into a kind of oriental bazaar during the sixth and seventh centuries AD (Waelkens et al. 1997: 127-173). Because of its complex building history, this terrace building to the north of the Upper Agora has been presented in the 3D model as a plain rectangular structure. To the west of the Upper Agora the Bouleuterion was built during the second half of the second century BC, preceded by a walled courtyard constructed at the end of the second century BC or in the first years of the first century BC (Fig. 5: 9; Fig. 3). The rectangular building to the southwest of the Upper Agora, the so-called Agoranomion, could be dated to around the middle of the first century BC. The next monumental building to be constructed in the late-Hellenistic or even early-Imperial period, was called the Doric Courtyard and may have been the Gymnasion of the town, situated along the eastern side of the Upper Agora (Waelkens 1993a: 45). Excavations may shed more light on the function and building history of this monument, but because of its present ruinous state it is not yet possible to fit a reconstructed model of this structure into the 3D reconstruction of the town. To the northwest of the Bouleuterion, the Doric Temple (Fig. 5: 1; Fig. 3) was constructed in the last years before the reign of Augustus, as well as a propylon of Augustan date and the northwest Heroon attributed to the late Augustan period (Fig. 5: 2; Fig. 3). During the imperial period the Upper Agora was embellished with several honorific monuments and two arches on its southeast and southwest extremities. (Fig. 5: 7; Fig. 3)The original portico which bordered the Agora to the west (Fig. 3) was rebuilt during the fourth or fifth century AD and its northwest extremity was incorporated into a Christian chapel some time during the fifth or sixth century (Waelkens et al 1995: 27), an alteration which is also not included in the model.

The Upper Agora and the middle Antonine Macellum to the southeast (Fig. 5: 8) were connected to the lower town by a north-south road of late Hellenistic date (Fig. 4). This led on to an east-west street, which provided access to the Lower Agora (Fig. 4). The late Hellenistic layout of this square was confirmed by the fragments of honorific monuments found along the longer sides of this Agora (Waelkens 1993b: 16). During the Imperial period porticoes were built along the eastern, western and southern edges of the Lower Agora. The portico on the eastern side was built in front of a row of shops, dated around the middle of the first century AD (Waelkens 1995: 27), the portico to the west was dated during the second half of the first century AD and the southwest entrance to the Lower Agora was controlled by an elegant gate built during the reign of Tiberius (14-37 AD) (Fig. 5: 4). Probably towards the end of the first century AD the Odeion was built to the north of the Lower Agora (Fig. 5: 6) and nearly half a century later a monumental aediculated nymphaeum was positioned in front of this covered theatre (Fig. 5: 5). The temple of Apollo Klarios bordered the Agora to the west (Fig. 5: 3). Originally constructed during the reign of Augustus, it was rebuilt around the transition of the first to the second century AD and even transformed into an Early Christian basilica in the second half of the fifth or the first half of the sixth century. To the east of the Lower Agora the Roman Baths were constructed in the second century AD (Fig. 4). The late Hellenistic colonnaded street continued further to the Sanctuary of Antoninus Pius in the southern extremity of the town (Fig. 5: 11; Fig. 4), which was completed in the second quarter of the second century AD.

Urbanization in ancient times implies the development of a complex settlement, functioning as a central place within a certain region and even beyond (Vittinghoff 1978: 549-550). The complexity of such an urban society is also reflected in the physical complexity of a town. Especially in larger towns, the organization of space to provide easy, mostly visual recognition of the urban facilities is as important to the inhabitants as to visitors (Perring 1991: 273). Analyzing the 3D reconstruction model of Sagalassos in this respect, it is clear that the late Hellenistic street, which became a colonnaded street in Imperial times and which dominated the entrance to the town from the south, was constructed to welcome residents and visitors into a certain aspect of urban life, which may have been commerce (Fig. 5). Indeed, the focus of this north-south axis was a public open space, called the Lower Agora which likely had a commercial character (Waelkens et al.1995: 27). This kind of axiallity, created here by the late Hellenistic street leading to an important urban location, as well as the great value attached to visual effects became common features of Roman urban planning in the East (Martin 1974: 159-163). Under Roman rule the cities of the eastern provinces were monumentalized and through the careful location of buildings artificial vistas were created (Owens 1991: 145). When studying the reconstructed model of the lower city of Sagalassos (Fig. 5) the importance and the visual effect of such vistas is clearly illustrated by the specific location of some of the early Roman constructions on the axis created by the colonnaded street. It became clear that both the Tiberian gate (Fig. 5: 4), giving entrance to the Lower Agora from the south as well as the aediculated nymphaeum (Fig. 5: 5) bordering this square to the north, were not only built to beautify this square but were positioned there in order to direct and control the spectator's vision, approaching the town from the south.

This view of the southern approach to the town of Sagalassos presented within the 3D model (Fig. 5) also demonstrates the awesome impression this town must have imposed upon its visitors. The architectural emphasis of the upper and lower town of Sagalassos leaves little doubt that visitors were to be expected into the urban area and what is more, already when entering the lower part of town, these people were confronted with the grandeur of the local elite who were the driving force behind all this magnificence. Indeed, as a result of the purposeful embellishment of the town during the Augustan period four honorific columns, carrying statues of local benefactors, were positioned in the four corners of the Upper Agora (Fig. 5; Fig. 3) (Waelkens 1993b: 15; Mitchell et al 1988: 63 ; Vandeput 1997: 46-49). Remarkable, however, is the fact that the two northern columns stood on pedestals, which were at least two metres higher than the southern ones. From the viewpoint of people approaching the town from the south reproduced within the 3D model, it becomes clear that these northern elevated pedestals likely served as a means to visually display all four of the statues upon these columns to the visiting public.

The same purpose of maximum visibility and impressiveness must have been the basis of the design of the fourteen metre high northwest Heroon. This late Augustan monument was built to the northwest of the Upper Agora (Fig. 3) and must have dominated the entire town from that period onwards. The perspective view towards the upper town of Sagalassos produced by means of the 3D model showed that the Heroon was clearly visible from the lower part of the town (Fig. 5: 2).

The 3D reconstructed model of Sagalassos also provides interesting views upon the orientation of buildings with regard to other structures within the town plan. Particularly interesting in this respect is the divergent orientation of the Odeion when compared to that of the Lower Agora and the aediculated nymphaeum, partly hiding the southern wall of this small covered theatre (Fig. 5: 5-6; Fig. 4). Most likely the specific location of the Odeion was imposed by the topographical suitability of the terrain there, as can be stated for most of the monumental buildings of Sagalassos (Vandeput 1997: 12). However, the reconstructions of both the Nymphaeum and the Odeion are based on evidence recorded by means of survey, implying that this hypothesis may still be altered by proper excavation.

By exploring the numerous perspective views, which can be produced by means of the 3D model of Sagalassos, an interesting hypothesis concerning the general urban planning of Sagalassos could also be tested. The complete 3D model of Sagalassos, bringing together both the topography and the information on the buildings, clearly shows that the town planners of Sagalassos took advantage of the specific characteristics of the terrain (Fig. 4). In fact, the sightly differing orientations of the monumental buildings constructed on several terraces (Fig. 6) and the integration of these buildings into one coherent urban plan is clearly reminiscent of the urban concept of the town of Pergamon on the west coast of Asia Minor (Vandeput 1997: 12). This ancient town is the most important example of a certain type of urban planning which incorporated the irregularities of the terrain in order to create visually attractive townscapes (Ward-Perkins 1987: 18-19; Owens 1991: 75). Moreover, the comparison between the urban planning of Sagalassos with that of Pergamon is particularly interesting since the latter city temporarily ruled over Pisidia in the second century BC . Although this reign only lasted for a short period, the cultural impact of this city in western Asia Minor must have been considerable (Radt 1988: 309-312).

Another interesting possibility of CAD reconstructions of ancient buildings is that of inserting reconstructed buildings into their actual physical environment by using overlays. When positioning the temple of Apollo Klarios by means of an overlay on its exact location within its physical environment at Sagalassos, there appears to be a striking resemblance between the rather steep slope angle of the gable of this temple and the mountain top behind it (Fig. 7). This view supports the presumption that the ancient architects took such elements of the natural environment into account when designing their monuments. Of course, such speculations can rarely be proven.

Figure 6: 3D Reconstruction model of the topography and buildings in the town centre of Sagalassos viewed from the east (model anno 1999).

Therefore, strong reservations should always accompany any tentative reconstruction (Barker 1986: 172) and in the same manner one should always be careful with interpretations based on these 3D reconstruction models. It is not the models themselves, which are deceptive, but rather their visual attractiveness, which allows the uncritical spectator to all too easily accept them as reality. Reconstructions such as these are convincing even when wrong and may perpetuate errors for generations. A critical evaluation of the extrinsic and intrinsic reliability of the created models is always required

Figure 7: Overlay of the wire model of the reconstructed temple of Apollo Klarios upon the preserved archaeological evidence of this building.

Evaluation of the 3D Reconstruction Models of Sagalassos

As stressed above, it is important to regard these 3D reconstruction models with the appropriate criticism. The 3D reconstruction models of the buildings of Sagalassos were initially created for educational purposes. They present one particular building phase, which for most reconstructions demonstrates the architectural form which is presumed to be the original design and construction. As explained, however, each of these constructions has its own building history which should be taken into account and it is also important that the public is informed on this evolution as well as on the possibility of alternative interpretations. In this way people are confronted with the data which will enable them to evaluate the models themselves. For the same reason it is necessary that the interpretative elements of a reconstruction are clearly distinguishable from the initial excavated evidence. This can be obtained by adding a different mapping to original and tentatively reconstructed elements.

The 3D reconstruction models of the buildings of Sagalassos also proved to be useful methodological tools for testing hypotheses concerning the specific location and character of some buildings, as well as the general layout of the town. As far as the reliability of the reconstruction models of Sagalassos is concerned, the extrinsic metrical reliability was tested by means of overlays and proved to be reasonably accurate. When evaluating the intrinsic reliability of the complete model of the reconstructed town it can be stated that for true archaeological interpretations a major shortcoming is the fact that it presents an almost artificial assembly of not always contemporary buildings. It is important, therefore, not to regard this model as an objective publication of the excavated evidence, but as an intermediate interpretative illustration of what the Roman town of Sagalassos may have looked like, based upon objectively recorded archaeological evidence. Reconstruction models should be capable of standing up against rigorous criticism and consequently the considered reliability should be indicated by accompanying comments. In this way CAD reconstruction models certainly can be very valuable for educational purposes when showed to the general public and useful to stimulate discussion, whenever presented to a scholarly audience.

The interesting aspect of designing reconstructions of ancient buildings is the fact that the archaeologist is being forced to place himself in the position of the ancient architect, to think in terms of structures and to suggest solutions to certain structural difficulties. He has to pose questions about the height of walls, the connection between buildings by mounting roads or staircases or the possible run-off and disposal of rainwater for instance. By posing all these questions new insights may arise. A great advantage of computer modelled reconstructions over materialized maquettes, is that such new insights then can easily be included in the computer model without having to rebuild the entire reconstruction.

In this way, regarding CAD reconstruction models as tools, their scientific value and possibilities can increase significantly, not only for visibility tests or educational purposes, but also for projects such as the actual conservation and restoration of sites.

Acknowledgements

This research is supported by the Belgian Programme on Interuniversity Poles of Attraction initiated by the Belgian State, Prime Minister's Office, Science Policy Programming (IUAP IV/12), by the Concerted Action of the Flemish Government (GOA 97/2) and the Fund for Scientific Research- Flanders (Belgium) (FWO) (G.2145.94). Scientific responsibility is assumed by the authors. Femke Martens is a Research Assistant of the Fund for Scientific Research-Flanders (Belgium) (FWO).

References Cited

BARKER, Philip, 1977, Techniques of Archaeological Excavation. London

BARKER, Philip, 1986, Understanding Archaeological Excavation. London.

DANIEL, R., 1997, The Need for Solid Modelling of Structure in the Archaeology of Buildings. *Internet Archaeology,* vol. 2, 2.3 (http://intarch.ac.uk/journal/issue2/daniels_index.html)

HARRIS, Edward, 1989, *Principles of Archaeological Stratigraphy.* London.

HOGG, Alexander Hubert Arthur, 1980, *Surveying for Archaeologists and Other Fieldworkers.* London.

LOOTS, Lieven, Kris NACKAERTS and Marc WAELKENS, 1999, Fuzzy Viewshed Analysis of the Hellenistic City Defence System At Sagalassos, Turkey, In *Proceedings of the 25th Aniversary Conference of Computer Applications and Quantative Methods in Archaeology, held at the University of Birmingham, 10th - 13 th April 1997 (BAR)*, Oxford.

MARTIN, Roland, 1974, *L'urbanisme dans la Grèce antique.* Paris.

MITCHELL, Stephen, and Marc WAELKENS,1987, Cremna and Sagalassus 1986. *Anatolian Studies*, vol. 37, pp: 37-43.

MITCHELL, Stephen, and Marc WAELKENS, 1988, Cremna and Sagalassus 1987. *Anatolian Studies*, vol. 38, pp. 53-65.

OTTENBURGS, Raoul, Willy VIAENE, Roland DEGEEST and Marc WAELKENS,1995, Statistical Analysis of Clays and Heterogeneous Sherds from Sagalassos. In Waelkens, Marc and Jeroen Poblome (eds). 1995. Sagalassos 3. Report on the Fourth Excavation Campaign of 1993. *Acta Archaeologica Lovaniensia Monographiae* 7. Leuven, pp. 255-270.

OWENS, Eddy, 1991, *The city in the Greek and Roman World.* London.

PERRING, Dominic, 1991, Spatial Organisation and Social Change in Roman Towns, In Rich John and Andrew Wallace-Hadrill (eds.) *City and Country in the Ancient World.* London

POBLOME, Jeroen and Roland DEGEEST, 1993, A Model of Ceramic Evolution. The pottery Found at Site N, In Waelkens, Marc and Jeroen Poblome (eds). 1993. Sagalassos 2. Report on the Third Excavation Campaign of 1992. In *Acta Archaeologica Lovaniensia Monographiae* 6. Leuven, pp. 149-181

RADT, Wolfgang, 1988, *Pergamon. Geschichte und Bauten, Funde und Erforschung einer antiken Metropole.* Köln.

VANDEPUT, Lutgarde, 1997, The Architectural Decoration in Roman Asia Minor. Sagalassos: a Case Study. In *Studies in Eastern Mediterranean Archaeology* 1. Turnhout.

VITTINGHOFF, Friedrich, 1978, "Stadt" und Urbanisierung in der Griechisch-Römischen Antike. In *Historische Zeitschrift*, vol. 226, 2, pp. 547-563.

WAELKENS, Marc, 1993a, Sagalassos. History and Archaeology. In Waelkens, Marc (ed.). Sagalassos 1. First general report on the survey (1986-1989) and Excavations (1990-1991). In *Acta Archaeologica Lovaniensia Monographiae* 5. Leuven, pp. 37-81.

WAELKENS, Marc, 1993b, The 1992 season at Sagalassos. A Preliminary Report. In Waelkens, Marc and Jeroen Poblome (eds). 1993. Sagalassos 2. Report on the Third Excavation Campaign of 1992. In *Acta Archaeologica Lovaniensia Monographiae* 6. Leuven, pp. 9-41.

WAELKENS Marc, Dirk PAUWELS, Jullie Van Den BERGH, 1993, The 1993 Excavations on the Upper and Lower Agora. In Waelkens, Marc and Jeroen Poblome (eds). 1995. Sagalassos 3. Report on the Fourth Excavation Campaign of 1993. *Acta Archaeologica Lovaniensia Monographiae* 7. Leuven, pp. 23-46.

WAELKENS, Marc, Pierre-Marie VERMEERSCH, Etienne PAULISSEN, Edwin J. OWENS, Burcu ARIKAN, Marleen MARTENS, Peter TALLOEN, Leen GIJSEN, Lieven LOOTS, Chris Peleman, Jeroen Poblome, Roland Degeest, Teresa C. PATRICIO, Semih ERCAN, Frans DEPUYDT, 1997, The 1994 and 1995 Excavation Seasons at Sagalassos. In Waelkens, Marc and Poblome, Jeroen (eds). 1997. Sagalassos 4. Report on the survey and Excavation Campaigns of 1994 and 1995. In *Acta Archaeologica Lovaniensia Monographiae* 9. Leuven, pp. 103-216.

WARD-PERKINS, John, 1987, Cities of Ancient Greece and Italy: Planning in Classical Antiquity. In G.R. Collins (ed.). *Planning and Cities*. New York

VIRTUAL MODEL OF THE BASILICA OF EMMAUS-NICOPOLIS

Mikko Louhivuori* and *Aaro Soederlund

Israel Antiquities Authority (Jerusalem),
Helsinki University of Technology and Micro Aided Design, Finland
Mikko@israntique.org.il
aaro.soderlund@hut.fi

The paucity and complexity of the evidence concerning the churches at Emmaus-Nicopolis pose a practical and theoretical challenge for computer-aided virtual modeling. Modeling requires exact field measurements, accurate use of ground plans, incorporation of maximum number of surviving elements into the models, and critical use of analogies. The finished model resembles a working hypothesis with a given level of validity giving coherence to the facts and providing valuable hints for further archaeological research.

The models were created using the ArchiCAD 5 architectural software package with objects. Use of objects gives advantages that are not available when modeling with vector primitives only. However, better rendering tools for creating complex surfaces would enable us to create the lavish interiors of the once so magnificent basilica of the Bishop of Emmaus.

Figure1 The virtual Basilica "in situ" at Emmaus (without Baptisterium)

The Site and Renewed Excavations

Emmaus-Nicopolis is located about halfway between Tel Aviv and Jerusalem. The architectural analysis of these badly damaged churches is among the more difficult tasks in the study of Byzantine structures in the Holy Land. With the lack of hard evidence, computer-aided virtual modeling becomes an indispensable research tool by making possible to consider alternative solutions. Accurate elevation measurements, size calculations based on standard Roman-Byzantine period aspect ratios, the mirroring of elements and other such special tools are of great help in unraveling the history of the buildings.

One of the famous pioneer students of the Holy Land, pere L.H. Vincent, excavated the Basilica of Emmaus-Nicopolis during the 1920s and laid the foundations for the archaeological and architectural study of the site.* Renewed excavations have been conducted at the site since 1993 with the kind permission of Dr. Yizhaq Magen, the Archaeological Staff Officer for Judea and Samaria and from the Carmelite sisters who own the site. The work is under the auspices of the Franciscan Bible School, professor Micelle Piccirillo, excavations directed by Mikko Louhivuori (Israel Antiquities Authority, Jerusalem) and Karl-Heinz Fleckenstein (University of Rome, Italy). Field work in different sectors has been led by Eero Junkkaala and Anna-Liisa Talaskivi (Finnish Theological Institute, Helsinki), Vincent Michelle (University of Sorbonne, Paris) and Gunter and Birgitta Oertel (Jesus Brothers, Germany).

Aaro Soderlund from Helsinki Technical High School created the virtual models of the Late Byzantine Basilica, the Baptisterium and the Crusader Chapel accompanying this paper. The models were made using ArchiCAD 5.0 architectural software package

* VINCENT, L.H. ABEL A.F.M. 1932, *Emmaus. Sa basilique et son histoire.* E. Leroux Paris.

on a PowerMac. MacIntosh G3 250 MHz computer, Sony Mavica FD7 10x digital camera (3.5-inch floppies) and a scanner.

Complexity of the Site

The building history at Emmaus-Nicopolis begins in the Hellenistic period and continues, with a few breaks, through Roman to Byzantine and Early Arab periods. (The entire Byzantine period in the Holy Land covers the time from Constantine the Great to the Arab Conquest or the "Early Byzantine period" in more generic terms). The site was abandoned after the infamous plague of Emmaus and largely forgotten until the Crusaders created a chapel on the ruins of the basilica in the 12th century AD. The chapel was destroyed and the site has been abandoned till modern days. The exact location of the city of Emmaus-Nicopolis itself is unknown although we do now have some indications where it may have been.

The archaeological layers representing various phases in the history of structures at the site are quite close to each other. The layers represent almost seven hundred years of continuous building and rebuilding on the same spot. In the Hellenistic-Roman period the eastern part of the area was a cemetery, while in the west there were some civilian structures. Sometime during the Early Byzantine period the first apsidal church was constructed on the site, perhaps as a Martyrion for St. Cleopas. Very little from these early phases have been exposed so far.

Builders of the large Late Byzantine basilica (see the model) destroyed much of the earlier church leaving only fragments of walls and unrelated pieces of mosaics in the fills under the church. The "domus dei" is in the classical basilica form with three aisles and the building had a tiled roof on wooden structures (numerous roof tiles have been discovered). The church has a rare triple apse that has survived until today. The basilica probably dates to the Justinian period in the 6th century AD and was probably destroyed during or after the Arab conquest. The church also had a baptisterium indicating its high status.

Figure 2 Virtual model of the Crusader chapel in French style

Twelfth-century Crusaders erected a chapel over the central nave of the Byzantine basilica reusing the old central apse and many stones from the ruined basilica for this purpose. Foundations for the Crusader chapel cut deep into the Early Byzantine and Roman layers. Also the numerous burials around the chapel damaged the mosaics and walls surviving under the building. The chapel was probably abandoned soon after the collapse of the Crusader Kingdom and its roof may have broken in one of frequent earthquakes in this area (the bedrock is seismically weak).

The complexity caused by the long period of occupation, frequent rebuilding, intrusions by later builders and soil shifts by earthquakes has been made even more difficult to unravel by the local inhabitants of the village of 'Imwas. For centuries they have taken ready-cut building stones from the ruins of "el-Kniseh" to make their houses. Here and there, soil-color shadows indicate where there once was a wall but more often huge parts of the structures have vanished without a trace. The result of all this is an archaeological site with a very convoluted building history and quite uncomfortable level of lack of hard evidence.

Basic Principles of Modeling

When L. H. Vincent studied the site he faced the same badly destroyed and complex set of structures that we have been studying with the help of modern computers. In order to make sense of the limited evidence Vincent used his considerable artistic skills to create analytical ground plans using color pens and paper. On the basis of the plans he drew pictures of how the baptisterium, basilica and Crusader chapel may once have looked. He also drew the ground plan of a pre-Byzantine structure, "Villa Romaine".

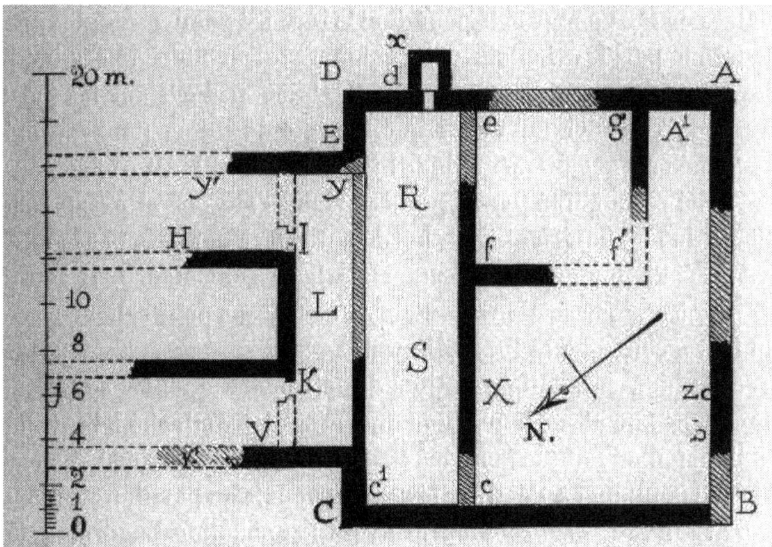

Fig. 79. — Schéma de la villa romaine antérieure à la basilique. Cf. pl. II s.

Figure 3 The famous "villa romaine" virtually created from the wall fragments at the site (VINCENT L.H. 1932:Fig.79)

Creating a drawing is an easy task when there is enough evidence. But what to do when the remains are as badly damaged and as paltry as at Emmaus-Nicopolis? In order to present his interpretation of the facts Vincent followed these basic principles in creating "virtual drawings" of how the churches may have looked:

* use of accurate measurements and elevations
* careful analysis of the association between remaining walls and floors
* assignment of elements into different archaeological periods on technical and stylistic grounds
* visual distinction between existing and assumed wall lines (using hatching and color coding)
* proper use of analogies where evidence is missing

The same principles are still valid today when preparing isometric drawings or computer models of structures that are not standing anymore. However, vivid imagination and strong artistic vision combined with a rather rigid architectural preconception led Vincent (and a generation of scholars after him) astray. The only model that we have been able to accept is the drawing of the Crusader chapel in early Medieval French style. The baptisterium and basilica are problematic and the "Villa Romaine" is non-existent.

Warning Signs in a Virtual Model

While creating the virtual models of the buildings we realized that the same force of logic and the same preconception of architectural models that led Vincent astray threatened us, as well. There is a real temptation to straighten wall lines to fit a particular form or to ignore elements that do not seem to belong. And while it is extremely important, it is still not easy to maintain clear and consistent color or other coding to separate architectural facts from assumed volumes and shapes.

Closer examination of the evolution of Vincent's ground plans from accurate early recording to "streamlined" versions demonstrates some typical warning signs that the model is not good:

* fundamental errors in dating architectural elements
* changing the alignment on the plan of difficult wall lines
* erroneous associating of walls and floors
* there are many structural elements that have no clear place in the final model
* use of inappropriate structural analogies

In order to avoid these kinds of methodological errors the excavation team worked in close cooperation with the architect who made the models. The creating of the computer model raised a number of new questions that also guided fieldwork to some degree in an attempt to gain coherent results. Many possible ideas in the models were, on the other hand, destroyed by the hard facts on the ground.

Evaluation of the Computerized Models

Regardless of all our efforts to gain as realistic and valid images as possible, the virtual church models of Emmaus-Nicopolis are, and remain, working hypotheses. As such they have limited value as an actual source of information for research but they do point to areas that require further research. For a visitor to the site or to a reader about Emmaus-Nicopolis the computer-generated images, fly-overs and walk-through do give an excellent understanding and feeling for the history of the site.

Our model of the Crusader church closely follows Vincent's original drawing. Unfortunately, we do not have any evidence of windows (all loose stones have been stolen from the site) or of the original roof. The suggested windows, barrel vaults and roofing are based on still existing examples in a Ramle mosque that was originally a church and in Jerusalem's St. Anna Church.

Figure 4 Virtual model of the suggested atrium and a view from inside

The model of the Byzantine basilica has many uncertainties. Since most of the structures to the west have disappeared without trace we do not know exactly where the main western wall with the entrances was. The length of the building is estimation. Also, it is not certain that there was an atrium although it is quite possible that there was.

The virtual model of the basilica shows existing wall fragments that probably were associated with the building in a separate layer from the assumed hypothetical parts of the structure. The red color is based on small fragments of paint still visible on the apsis wall. The modeling of the columns is based on the huge examples found at the site and now in the Latroun monastery garden (two are in a museum in Istanbul). The height of the columns is calculated from the diameter of the capitals. There probably was only a single pulpit in the church instead of the two shown in the model.

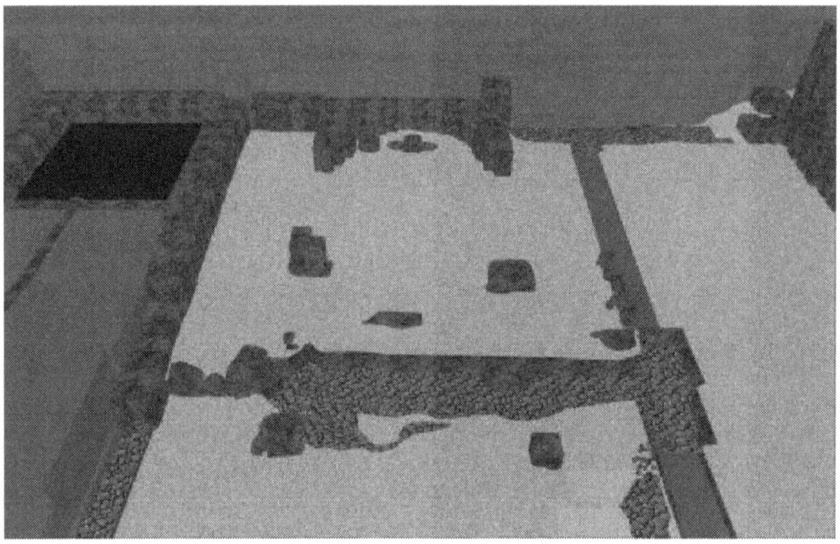

Figure 5 Existing structures from the Baptisterium

The baptisterium has been almost totally destroyed, so the reconstruction is quite hypothetical. Today, we are not yet able to establish the problematic architectural relationship between the baptisterium and the basilica. However, the reconstruction of the baldachin is probably quite accurate since the location and size of the four columns and the baptismal font itself have survived.

The Byzantine church models are missing the beautiful floor mosaics and lavish wall decorations that were in the originals, making them look from inside like splendid jewel boxes. We have found scattered individual glass tesserae with gold leaf on them telling about artworks on church walls and there are many beautiful fragments of floor mosaics. The newest version of ArchiCAD 6 has better realistic rendering tools and it is now easier to create complicated decorative patterns and to use digitized photographs to the models to make them more life-like.

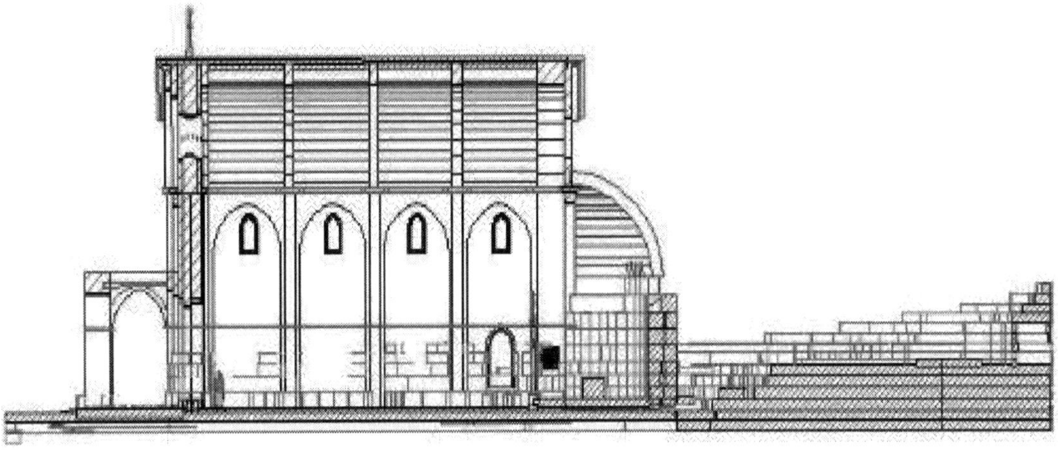

Figure 6 Virtual section of the Crusader Chapel

Future

The models may require revising and changes when the research continues. Creating more realistic interiors with new tools is important. The greatest future promise by the virtual modeling technology for advancing the research at Emmaus-Nicopolis is in the analysis of the earlier phases of the site. The many structural fragments that predate the Late Byzantine basilica imply a very interesting and many-faceted history. However, under the circumstances at Emmaus-Nicopolis it is almost impossible to understand the surviving pits and pieces of structures without using accurately measured computerized models as a working hypothesis.

MEDIEVAL TURKU: THE LOST CITY
A PROJECT TRYING TO RECONSTRUCT A MEDIEVAL TOWN IN FINLAND

Kari Uotila and Minna Sartes

Building archaeology, Muuritutkimus ky, Finland; Aboa Vetus & Ars Nova Museums, Finland
kari.uotila@kolumbus.fi,
minna.sartes@utu.fi,

A thriving commercial network was established in the Baltic Sea region during the Middle Ages, influenced mostly by the German merchants of the Hanseatic League. Well-organized towns were established on the southern coast of the Baltic Sea already by the 12th century, and from the beginning of the 13th century also in Sweden, Finland and Estonia. It was typical of these towns that the majority of the leading merchants were Germans and that the towns each had an impressive church, a town hall and many stone buildings.

The only significant medieval town in Finland—Turku—was one of these regional centers, through which furs and other products of the northern forests were exported to Europe.

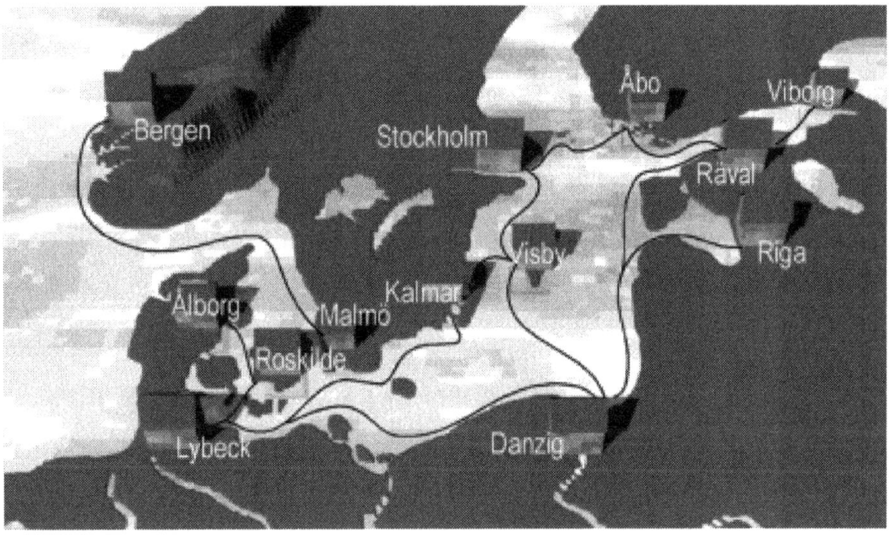

Figure 1. Turku (Swedish name Åbo) developed into a town during the 13th century and during the Middle Ages became one of the northern centers of the widespread Hanseatic trade. The products of the northern forests, such as furs, were exported to the European markets through these centers

As well as being the only important medieval town Turku is also the oldest town in Finland. It developed into a town during the 13th and 14th centuries. In the late medieval period there were about 2000 inhabitants in Turku and it occupied an area of 15 hectares. That means Turku was as big as Kalmar and, after Stockholm, Kalmar and Turku were the two biggest towns in the whole Swedish realm. In relation to the other medieval merchant towns in the Baltic region, Turku was medium-sized.

The medieval town plan of Turku was preserved until the beginning of the 19th century, when a great fire burned the entire city to the ground. The remains were buried under a 2- to 3-meters-thick layer of rubble and the new empire-style town was built on top of the old town.

Presenting a Vanished Town

Because the medieval town no longer exists, it is difficult to present it. We know about the medieval street plan from written sources, old maps and archaeological excavations. The archaeological excavations have also provided information on the medieval buildings. Througout the 20th century, archaeologists and historians worked on reconstructing a complete plan of medieval Turku. The result has been that several drawn maps exist from this research work.

In the beginning of the 1990's a large excavation in the old part of Turku revealed several ruins of medieval stone houses and streets. A museum called Aboa Vetus was built around these finds in order to present and preserve them. One of the aims of the museum is to exhibit the results of the research with the help of computers and multimedia programs.

Figure 2 Archaeological excavations at the site of the Aboa Vetus museum were carried out in 1992-1995. The excavated area is approximately 2000 square meters in size, and some 10,000 cubic meters of archaeologically excavated soil has been removed from the site. Several dozen foundations of buildings, as well as almost 40,000 artefacts, have been discovered at the site.

The researchers at the museum site used digital measuring equipment (total station) during the excavation. This was the first time that it was possible to take exact measurements of medieval buildings in Turku. The excavated area was quite large, altogether about 1600 square meters. The plan of the houses and streets could be compared with the oldest maps of Turku. The oldest map is from the year 1634 and the other map that has been used is also among the oldest ones, from the year 1743. Several recovered buildings, streets and alleys could be identified on the maps. In this connection the idea of creating a new reconstruction of the medieval Turku was born.

From a 2D Model to a 3D Model

To the digital material from the Aboa Vetus excavation was added all previously recorded archaeological material from various sites in medieval Turku, basically stone buildings and streets. The resulting CAD model was complemented by adding to it that material from the earliest maps of Turku which concern the medieval parts of the town.

The 2D model was further complemented with the data concerning the original or medieval topography including the level of the river Aurajoki and a small lake which was situated in the middle of the town. All known private stone buildings, streets, alleys, bridges and public buildings (such as the church, the town hall and the guild halls) were added to the topographical model. Historically recorded differences in the social status of different parts of the town and their influence on the buildings were also noted.

It was decided that a model of the town at the end of the 15th century would be reconstructed. This was a clearly distinct period and would enable the use of historical data about fires and other events. The exact timeframe placed demands on the model in terms of the layering of the constructional history of the town; some buildings were old and tattered, some were usable, while others were new and in a good condition. In the model all wooden houses are new, because we know that there was a disastrous fire in Turku in the 1470s. It is very probable that after the fire all the wooden houses had to be built again.

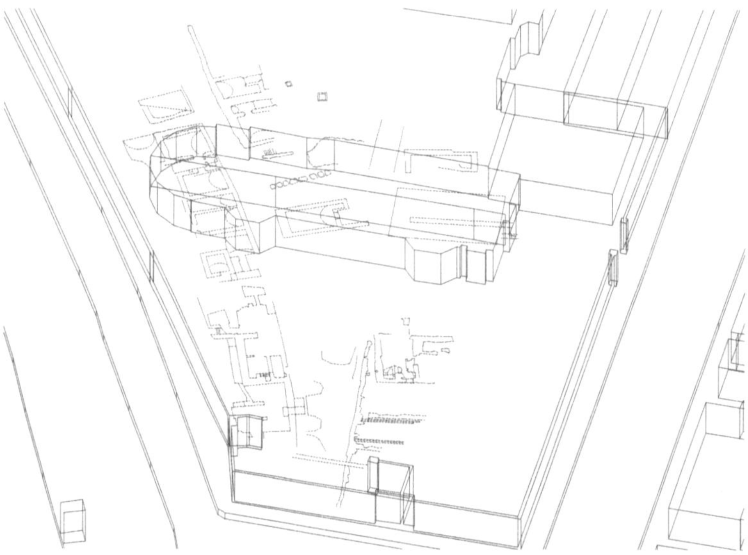

Figure 3 In the excavations of the Aboa Vetus museum more than ten old stone and brick houses were discovered, of which four can be dated to the Middle Ages with certainty. The main building material of these houses was brick, which was a very unusual building material in Finland at that time. According to an earlier view in research, during the Middle Ages there were only a few brick buildings in Finland, such as Turku Cathedral, Häme Castle and Hattula Church. However, it is possible that in towns, especially in Turku, there were several buildings made of brick.

Figure 4. After the excavations at the Aboa Vetus museum site, a modern museum where visitors can see the lost town was built on the location. The Convent Riverfront is one of Turku's oldest streets, which has connected the Cathedral, the market square and the Dominican convent already since the 14th century. Today one can walk along medieval streets in the museum's premises and see the ruins buried under ground after the great fire of 1827.

From all the digitized archaeological, historical and geological information a 3D model was created. The model includes also the botanical environment model provided by the results of research done by natural scientists. The results indicated that the forests surrounding the town were chopped down for timber and fuel during the Middle Ages, and that the present forests and parks are a result of the active development of the 19th and 20th centuries.

Presenting a 3D Model to the Public

The next stage in the project was to develop a 3D model in such a way that it could be presented to the public. Overviews in the form of still pictures can easily be done from the model. They are like aerial photographs and their quality is good. But we would also like to offer the audience the possibility of walking along the streets and experiencing the atmosphere of medieval Turku. We would like to offer a possibility of experiencing how narrow the streets were, from which points you could see the Cathedral and from which points you could not see it, what you could see if you stood at the main entrance of the Cathedral, what did the town look like if you climbed up on one of the nearby hills and looked down, or if you came to Turku by boat along the river Aurajoki?

To make all this possible the model has to be as detailed as possible and this demands quite a lot of work. In the first stage only a small part of medieval Turku was made into a detailed model. This part was the area by the river Aurajoki through which the street Luostarin jokikatu (Convent Riverfront) runs and in which the Aboa Vetus museum is now situated.
The stone houses in this area were researched in as much detail as possible, and the CAD reconstruction of them was then made. When making the reconstruction, information about Finnish medieval stone house building was used, as well as comparisons with buildings from other parts of the Baltic area. Research on Finnish stone houses is restricted by the fact that the only medieval stone houses which have remained whole are in Viborg and it has been impossible to research them since 1944. That is why most of the analogies are from the other towns near to Turku, mostly from Stockholm and Tallinn (Reval).

As well as the stone houses, there were a lot of wooden houses in the medieval town yards. Wooden houses have been used as living quarters and as store houses. The information on the construction of the wooden houses and their placement within the yards came from archaeological and ethnographic sources.

A Computer Model Is a Generalization

It has to be remembered that a computer model which is based mostly on archaeologically recorded information can only present a generalization. Firstly, the large computer capacity demanded when creating a lot of little details set limits to the work. Secondly, the technique on which the computer presentations are based is not designed to present details. In the real world every stone house and every yard was unique and this cannot be presented by a computer model

The VRML technique offers a possibility to move freely in the medieval town. This technique demands a considerable amount of computer memory because the computer has to update the image of the town all the time while the user is moving around. In this model it is almost impossible to use surface materials and textures, because the updating would demand so much capacity and time. Instead, textures have to be replaced with colors, which can be updated faster. With these colors the town does not look as authentic as it does in the videos with the surface materials, textures and the possibility to change the light from for example daytime to evening light. Despite these disadvantages of the technique we felt we needed to use it as well as the videos, because we wanted to give the user the possibility of moving freely in the medieval Turku. The user can for example walk over the bridge, stop in the middle and look around.

Figure 5. Medieval Turku (Åbo) was born to the western bank of the river Aurajoki in a low valley, where the Cathedral, consecrated in 1300, was built on the sole, small hill. The wealthy merchants' (mainly German-born) quarters with their stone houses formed a long band along the riverside, and the ecclesiastic center of all Finland developed around the Cathedral. Another important religious center was the convent of the Dominicans, located downriver, who came to Finland already in 1249. The outskirts of the town were made up of the shores of the swampy lake near the Cathedral and the low bank on the other side of the river. The two sides of the town were connected by a wooden bridge from 1414 onward.

Figure 6. The place shown in Figure 4 has been made into a 3D model, where the streets and buildings discovered in the excavations have been reconstructed as they can be thought to have looked in the Middle Ages. In addition, typical aspects of everyday life in a medieval town have been added to the model. In depicting the buildings and the milieu, attention has also been given to how the buildings have would looked after a long period of use—not just when they were new. The aim has been to depict everyday life on a medieval merchant street, and now only human and animal figures are missing from the model.

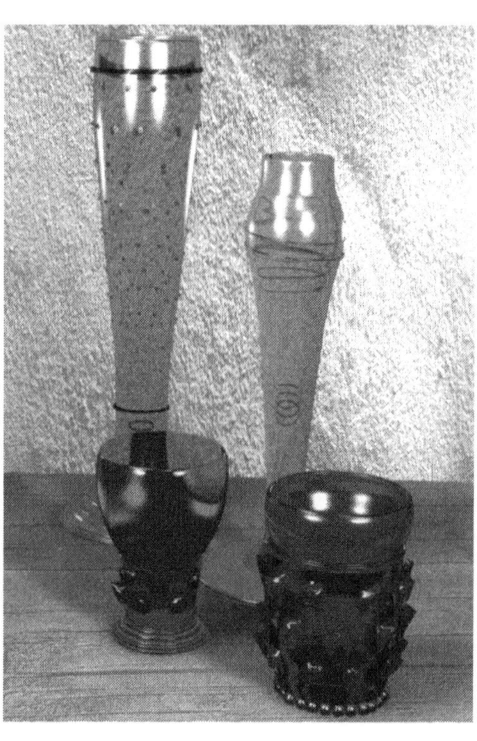

Figure 7. The making of 3D models has been extended to artefacts. For the summer of 1999, Aboa Vetus museum produced, together with other Nordic and Estonian medieval museums, an exhibition on medieval glass objects. In addition to the actual finds, the exhibition also used 3D models of glass vessels, based on the original finds. Also a CD-ROM was made to accompany the *Fragments from the Middle Ages* exhibition

The model done at the Aboa Vetus museum is based on two different presentation techniques. In one of them the user's moves are directed from one place to another with the help of a video. In the other the user moves freely in the medieval Turku. The technique using the videos allows more details, surface materials and textures to be seen. A restriction with the videos is that the user cannot interact with the program when the video is running, she or he can only look at it.

The other problem with the VRML program is the size of the model. Usually the VRMLs which are being done include a couple of houses or other objects, whereas we have a model of a whole city. Should we have more advanced computer technology available, the size would not be a problem. Due to financial realities we are, however, bound to use normal PCs instead of, for example, Silicon Graphics machines. Our PCs' limited memory capacity is a hindrance, but we have decided to do the project in any case. One of our goals is to show that it is possible for a museum to do projects that usually are done by expensive consultants.

Discussion

The work on the 3D reconstruction of medieval Turku has now lasted altogether for about three years and we think we still are in the very beginning. We have learned a lot and the computer technology has developed a great deal also. All the time there will be more and better oppotunities to make realistic-looking virtual realities on different themes.

One important thing to remember is that virtual reality cannot take us with it to past times, and all that we are able to show, for example, about medieval Turku is based on research results that are not in any sense complete. So, the look of our medieval Turku will change every time we get new information from the research projects. And however detailed our virtual reality programs are, we can never say that Turku really was like that. This is a fact that we also have to let the audience know. We can only say that it quite probably would have been a little like this, but that we never can know for sure. In our opinion there is nothing wrong in giving the audience visual stimuli and letting their imaginations work freely afterwards. That is also how they get interested in finding out more.

A wide database which includes about 500 sheets of information on the Middle Ages and research work concerned with this period is linked to our virtual reality multimedia. There are seven main themes which divide up into several sub-themes. We are also going to use the database with schoolchildren.

The software used in the project was comprised of various versions of the AutoCAD program, which was used to create the basic model. The basic model was then transformed into the 3D Studio Max environment which was utilized to create different animated sequences of the town. These include both aerial and street-level videos and views. The VRML model was created by using Max technology and it is run with Cosmo Player software.

The Lost City virtual presentation multimedia was opened at the Aboa Vetus museum in April 1998. After the summer of 1998 it goes to other Nordic medieval towns: Stockholm, Bergen, Roskilde, Lödöse and Trondheim.

VIRTUAL REALITY AS AN EXTENSION OF THE ARCHAEOLOGICAL RECORD: RECONSTRUCTION OF THE IRON AGE FORTRESS ELS VILARS (ARBECA, CATALONIA, SPAIN)

E. Junyent and J. Lorés
(Co-ordinators)
N. Alonso, D. Muñoz, E. Junyent, A. Lafuente, J.B. López, J. Lorés, M. Pérez and E. Tartera
(Authors)

University of Lleida, Spain

Arqueologia@historia.udl.es
Jesus@eup.udl.es

Introduction

The 26th International Congress "*Computers Applications in Archaeology*" held in Barcelona in March 1998 was an excellent setting for the presentation to the scientific community and the public at large of the first results of the "Vilars Virtual" project[1], which has been under joint development by two teams form the University of Lleida since 1996. These teams are the *Grup d'Investigació Prehistórica* (Prehistoric Research Group) from the Department of History, and the *Grup de Recerca Interacció Persona - Ordinador* (Research Group on Human Computer) of the Department of Computing and Industrial Engineering.

The research carried out over these last two years has been materialized in a video which synthesizes the state of the archaeological research in the site that lends its name to the project (Els Vilars), as well as the first trials in the area of three-dimensional reconstruction, application of textures and virtual animation.

However, this work, also presented and well-received in 1999 in the "*1er Festival International du Multimedia pour l'Archéologie: Archéo Virtua*" held in the *Archéodrome de Bourgogne* (France) only represents the first step of a much more ambitious project with longer term scientific objectives.
The reason for this article is to present these general objectives, the internal structure of the project, its components and the precise mechanism employed to obtain the optimum development of the computer resources and to submit these to debate. In this sense, it is necessary to emphasize that the two teams, whose disciplines are defined by the disparity of their intrinsic objectives (historical knowledge and industrial science), are facing a common research challenge that supposes, first and foremost, overcoming any epistemological prejudices and, from constant information feedback, jointly working towards the final aim of the project. That aim is to convert virtual reality into an instrument for scientific research.

The special nature of "Virtual Vilars" resides precisely in this basic principle. Beyond the consideration of virtual reality as an instrument for social diffusion, a concept which we obviously share and try to strengthen, the project presented here is aimed at generating a scientific document which rigorously synthesizes the results obtained from all the disciplines involved in the historical-archaeological research process. In other words, virtual reality must become simply an extension of the record, integrated into the general methodological system. The only difference is that it is aimed at supplying those elements that field research is unable to achieve directly owing to the fragmentary nature of the information preserved on the site. This will always be under the strictest conditions and bearing in mind the specific state of conservation of the site and its pertinence to the different chronological periods represented therein.
From a functional perspective, "Virtual Vilars" also has another specific characteristic. It is conceived as a dynamic product, capable of synthesizing new research under way and automatically and systematically incorporating this as soon as the results are obtained.
In the following paper, these proposals and their formal concretion are explained in more detail.

The Fortress of Els Vilars: General Characteristics

Els Vilars is located in the northeastern part of the municipality of Arbeca (300 m above mean sea level) in the Garrigues district (Catalonia, Spain), on a wide plain of Quaternary accumulation which owes its origins to the action of the various tributaries of the left bank of the River Segre, and more precisely to the alluvial activity in the alluvial fan of the River Corb (Fig. 1). Geologically, the area is situated in the eastern section of the Ebro basin

Discovered in 1975, the site has been since 1985 the object of systematic annual digs by the University of Lleida's *Grup d'Investigació Prehistorica,* the team responsible for directing and co-ordinating the work on the fortress as a whole[2].

A total of 25 publications in different specialized magazines (Alonso et. al. 1998: 355-372, with references to the rest of the bibliography), different studies and articles for the general public

[1] "Virtual Vilars" is registered in the general framework of the project: "A singular model of the transformation of segmented societies into complex societies: the valley of the Segre (2nd and 1st millennium BC)". This receives financial support and scientific recognition from the Ministry of Education and Culture in Madrid (DGES PB96 - 0419).

[2] The different excavations have been carried out under the sponsorship of the *Servei d'Arqueologia* of the *Generalitat de Catalunya,* the regional administration.

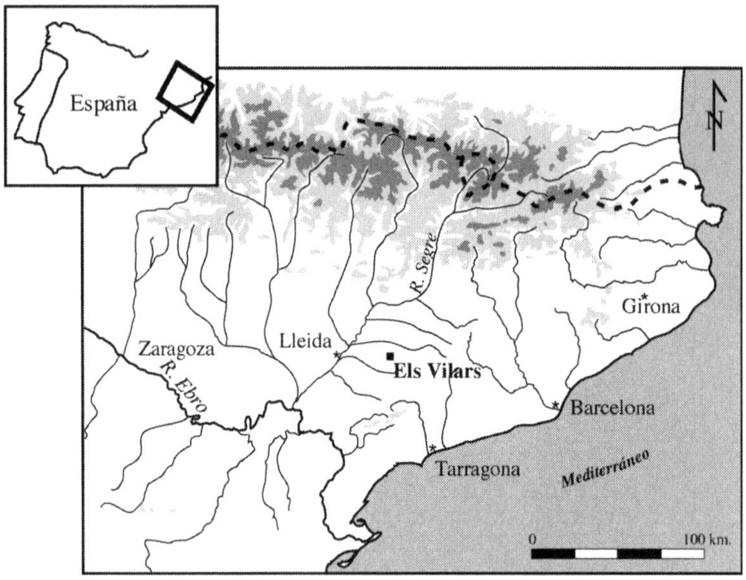

Figure 1. Situation of the fortress of Els Vilars.

(Garcés et al. 1997), a web site, (www.vilars2000.com), and the edition of a CD-ROM[3] have converted it into a classic site for research into the Iron Age in the Iberian Peninsula. This has also led to recognition by the public administration of the site's importance as heritage, and it was declared *Bé Cultural de Interés Nacional* (BCIN) (Site of National Cultural Interest) in the category of archaeology in 1996. Recently (1999), it has also been included in the project called "The Route of the Iberians," promoted by the *Museu d'Arqueologia de Catalunya.* This has led to the signposting of the accesses[4] and the installation of informative panels inside the site, which can now be visited all year round.

Topography and urbanism

The fortress is built on a vast plain, surrounded by fertile farmland and near a small stream, the Aixaragall, today practically dry. Without modifying its limits while inhabited, it was converted into an authentic archaeological *tell,* reaching a height of four metres. Unfortunately, levelling work carried out in the 1960s and '70s to extend the existing fields destroyed a large part of the tell, with the result that the most recent levels, from the high Iberian period (450-350 BC), have only survived in a narrow 3- to 6-meter wide strip. Nevertheless, the foundation levels, corresponding to the early Iron Age and the early Iberian period, have survived intact.

The projects carried out until now, through the excavation of the defensive system, have led to the thorough delimiting of the perimeter and the general features of the internal urban layout. This excavation is of an area of approximately 1,000 m^2, corresponding to a north-south section (18 x 44 m) situated in the central part of the site and limited by the structures located in the eastern part where the main gate is situated (Fig. 2).

The plan of the enclosure presents a trend towards an oval shape although the principal facade to the east is almost completely straight. The interior habitable area is around 2,300 m^2.

The principal peculiarity of the fortress resides in its spectacular defensive system, formed by a triple belt that includes a 5-metre thick wall with twelve towers, a standing stone barrier *(chevaux-de-frise)* and a paved moat which is 13 metres wide and 3 metres deep and is lined with stone walls.

There were two gates and a postern. The oldest gate was located to the east. It is the frontal type and had an access corridor formed of 2-metre thick walls, which were probably the faces of a hollow tower. In the opposite extreme to this main gate there was a postern protected by a small lateral bastion. Later, towards the middle of the sixth century BC, a second gate was built on the north side. This was defended by two towers. One belonged to the initial phase and the other was built *ex novo* slightly further forward so as to define a corridor with a slight twist with respect to the frontal axis of the opening, but without forming a *chicane.*
The street plan of the interior of the enclosure was organized radially around a space or central square presided over by a monumental cistern. This later structure was lined with stone and had a corridor or ramp to allow access to the variable water level. Documented with some certainty from the middle of the fifth century BC, it is more than probable that the cistern obscures some other similar structure used during previous phases.

The street plan is simple, being structured to function as a principal artery that ran parallel to the wall, defining two nuclei of housing on either side: one row of housing up against the fortifications and a second set of constructions on the opposite side, between the street and the central square. Other shorter streets were set perpendicularly to this main route, permitting access to the gates of the enclosure and internal communication between the perimeter neighborhoods and the central space. This

[3] This CD-ROM, *Vilars 2000. Una fortalesa ilergeta d'ara fa 2700 anys,* contains the contents of the publication by the same name in four languages (Catalan, Spanish, English and French) (Garcés et al., 1997) and includes a video of the virtual reconstruction of the fortress. It was financed jointly by the Arbeca Town Council, the University of Lleida and the Lleida City Council.

[4] The Arbeca town council, for its part, has asphalted the road that leads directly to the foot of the fortress.

Figure 2. General view of the dig from the south.

distribution remained almost unchanged, with minor modifications to the layout and those connected with the construction of the north gate, throughout the earliest phases (775-550 BC).

The housing was rectangular, long and narrow, separated by dividing walls. Its evolution is complex throughout the different phases, without an established linear evolutionary model with respect to a greater or lesser degree of sophistication in the organization of the internal space or in the distribution of the domestic structures found. The complete sequence of a row of different houses along 25 metres of the southern part of the site is known (zone 4).

PHASES AND GENERAL CHRONOLOGY

The foundation, occupation and abandonment of the fortress has three different cultural horizons as a temporary framework. Included in this are five urban and architectural renewals, which only affect the internal space and details in the defensive system, without implying, as already mentioned, an amplification of the inhabited space in the extramural zone.

- Early Iron Age (later Urn Fields or Iron).

This takes in the *ex novo* foundation of the fortified settlement (Vilars 0: 775-675/650 BC) and a first urban renewal which only affected the distribution of the buildings (Vilars I: 675/650-550/525 BC).

- Early Iberian period.

This corresponds to Vilars II (550/525-450/425 BC). Though the perimeter was not modified, in this period, the western postern was annulled and the north gate was built. The stone barrier and the pit gradually filled up with earth and by the end of period were practically out of service. The housing presented a greater compartmentalization and doubled its area.

- High Iberian period

This covers two phases: Vilars III (450/425-375 BC) and Vilars IV (375-350/325 BC). As mentioned above, all that remains of this period is a narrow strip of land that separated two holdings. At the beginning of the former period an important urban remodelling took place which affected the general distribution and orientation of the spaces for circulation and the great central cistern with the access ramp was also constructed. Outside the walls, a great trench was dug at the expense of the old one, and it was lined with a thick stepped wall. Vilars IV refers to the occupation prior to the abandonment. This is the phase about which least is known, and which small domestic repairs and the intentional obliteration of the cistern-well are linked to.

The Global Investigation Project and the Computerization of the Archaeological Record

The Vilars project revolves around three principal axes: the characterization of the historical-archaeologic evolution of the fortress and the community that inhabited it for over 400 years; the paleo-ecological reconstruction of its environment and the economic activity of its inhabitants and, finally, the patrimonial recovery of the monument as a whole.

With reference to the first part, the reference data come from the excavations themselves, which, in this case, have not been limited only to inside the enclosure, but also to the external defences. This has led to the finding of an area located between the wall and the pit that was also used by the inhabitants of the fortress for productive activities, possibly the stabling of the livestock. Similarly, apart from allowing a stratigraphic and architectural reconstruction of the evolutionary sequence of the site, certain ritual practices in the interior, such as child burials, the functional characterization of the spaces or the analysis of the data obtained, have made it possible to interpret Vilars as a center of power linked to a regional process of territorial hierarchization, that situates it on the threshold of the appearance of the archaic Ilerget state[5].

The paleo-ecological and paleo-economic reconstruction, in the current state of the research, has been carried out from *in situ* data. The team made up of archaeologists and specialists in archaeo-botanics (anthracology, carpology, palinology) archaeo-zoology (micro- and macro-fauna, malacology), geo-archaeology (geomorphology, micro-morphology) and paleo-metallurgy have been working since 1987 on a sampling system parallel to the excavation process. This system has led to a primary diachronic characterization of the subsistence activities (agriculture and stockbreeding) and the characterization of the resources found in the exploitation catchment of the settlement.

Leaving aside the third section, inasmuch as it does not directly affect the virtual reality project, the first reflection is that the research has generated such a large volume and variety of information, that it might have been impossible to manage it and exploit it as a whole without a prior rationalization process and the implementation of a rigorous and operative record system. In this case, this has been carried out since 1987 by means of computer support.

The above-mentioned system, previously presented to the scientific community (Garcés et al. 1991: 189-210), is mainly based on the Harris record method (Harris 1979) inasmuch as the "stratigraphic units" (SU or context) are used as the basic elements from which the rest of the record is structured and the stratigraphic sequence is reconstructed. The concept of "Feature" has also been added, following adaptations carried out in the south of France (López, 1991 11-64; Py 1997). "Feature" is understood as all the SUs which make up the structure, and which can be identified as such (walls, fireplaces, benches, etc.)

The system, which includes the novelty of the spatial attribution of the SU and Features to "zones" and "sectors" coherent with the urbanistic organization of the site, has been shown to be widely operative. Evidence of this has been its rapid diffusion throughout the archaeological community in Lleida (Junyent et al. 1992, 184-275).

Currently almost a thousand SU and more than 300 Features make up a documentary database structured in individual mono-files, mutually interrelated from the numbering of the SU. This configuration is carried out with FileMaker Pro 3.0 by Claris for the Apple environment.

Similarly, the graphic records that include mapping and general (zones), secondary (sectors) and precise (features) sections, after many trials and experiments often conditioned by the means available on the market, have been fully digitized. The process has been optimized with the use of a pantograph and a theodolite for drawing in the field and scanning, recopying and subsequent mounting in the laboratory. In this case, the program used is Adobe Illustrator 7.0.

[5] Iberian people widely cited in classic sources (Pliny, Tito Livio, Estrabon...) who inhabited the western plains on both sides of the middle and lower basin of the River Segre.

To sum up, the integration of virtual reality in the record has the support of a considerable computerized reference and a methodology for the management and development of the working data. The challenge now is to create a link between the base of the record of the different SU and Features and their virtual representation.

The "Virtual Vilars" Project

From what has been presented up until now, it can be deduced that the application of infography and virtual reality in the reconstruction of the fortress has certain advantages, but also more than a few limitations. The first phase of the work, which led to the above-mentioned video, required a process of prior reflection about the objectives of the project and the most suitable technical resources to achieve this end. The result was an infographic reconstruction of the fortress which mixed asynchronous elements, did not include the environmental data and was presented as a finished product that was impossible to modify without a laborious process (Fig. 3). By and large, however, the experience was highly positive inasmuch as it supposed a primary contact between both teams and led to the inclusion of many details of all types, but mainly architectural, which had not previously been directly considered. Today we are able to present a second phase of the project that differs qualitatively from the first, and which is already underway.

BASIC PRINCIPLES

As has already been mentioned in the introduction, several fundamental proposals guide the current phase of work:

A) Assumption of virtual reality as an extension of the record.

This supposes that the virtual reconstruction is carried out by faithfully integrating the whole of the field documentation (SUs, features, mapping, interdisciplinary results) and respecting the diachronic evolution of the fortress. The three-dimensional and individualized restoration of the different features must also constitute an instrument for the study and typological analysis of the aforementioned structures.

B) Differentiated visualization of the reconstruction of missing elements.

The virtual reconstruction incorporates those elements that have disappeared (elevations of the walls, roofs, etc.) in accordance with the clear evidence for their earlier presence in the moment of operation. Such recreations will be effected by analogies with other sites from the same cultural environment or, at least, by current ethnographic parallels. The elements added will be differentiated visually from the original elements.

C) The product obtained has to be interactive and reversible.

Given the fact that the field research is unfinished, it is necessary to anticipate the modification and incorporation of new restoration work as this becomes necessary. This work, on the other hand, must be able to be done automatically and with the basic experience of an advanced user.

D) The interface has to be easy to use by people without computer expertise, anticipating different levels of use (toolbox and navigator).

E) The system has to guarantee the orderly management of space and time and to permit the recognition of sets in both dimensions.

Figure 3. Virtual reconstruction of the fortress. Overall view.

SPECIFIC OBJECTIVES AND THEIR MATERIALIZATION

Starting from the previous proposals, the present phase of the project can be defined through the following objectives:

A) The reconstruction of the fortress

This will be carried out diachronically, including 4 phases: Vilars 0, I, II and III-IV, given that the upper levels do not allow individualized restoration. A virtual reconstruction of the elements of the post-depositional processes that have affected the enclosure after its abandonment will also be incorporated, with the aim of illustrating the causes of its current state.

The reconstruction will include two levels of detail: firstly at a macro level, affecting the principal urbanistic elements (defences, street plan, habited spaces); secondly, at a micro level, permitting a virtual visit to the interior of some of the houses with enough elements to differentiate the functional use of the space.

The materialization of these objectives will imply the design of different three-dimensional models according to the established phases (Fig. 4) and the creation of a dictionary of virtual objects from the existing mapping, structured in accordance with the different features. This dictionary will constitute the first step towards the creation of a database that allows the integration of all the information, both graphic and written.

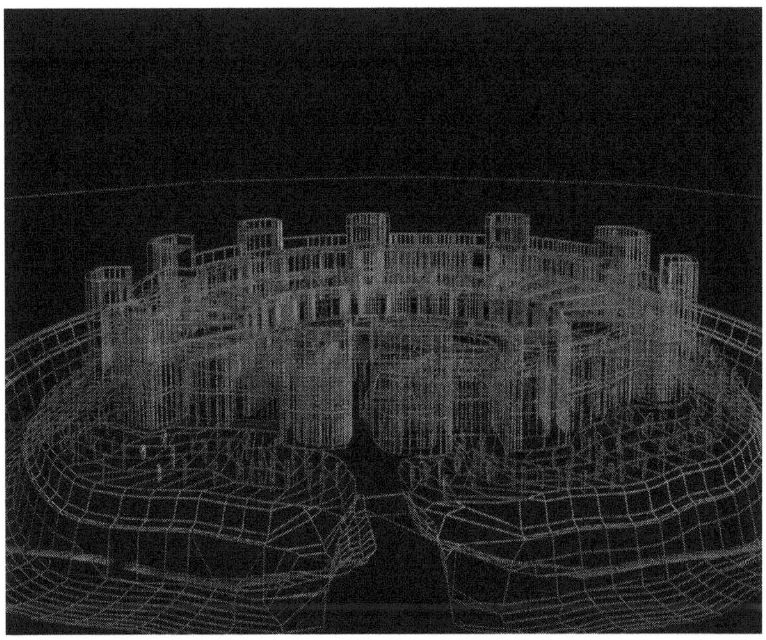

Figure 4. Three-dimensional model of Vilars

B) The reconstruction of the paleo-topography

This will be centered on the area of the immediate surroundings of the site (a radius of 5 km), given that the scope of current research does not permit longer-range reconstruction.

The process will consist of two phases: the volumetric reconstruction from current digital cartography (scale 1:5000) and the subsequent incorporation of the necessary modifications. These will be in relation to the research projects currently underway, based on geomorphologic and documentary studies (ancient cartography and aerial photography).

C) The reconstruction of the environment

Information about the use of the lands around Vilars constitutes the most awkward aspect for the researcher when it comes to situating the different elements that appear. Nevertheless, the existing information permits a reconstruction of the types of the crops, livestock and the hunting resources, as well as the mineral and forestry resources exploited. A large quantity of information, in fact, which it is impossible to ignore and whose situation in the space has to be as logical as possible. The restorations, on the other hand, will also be carried diachronically.

To carry this out, as with the structures, a virtual dictionary will be created with the different types of plants and animals that appear. This will be integrated into the general database.

D) The user interface.

The user interface is a fundamental element in any computer system and more so in the type of interactive system proposed here. The interface is the contact surface with the system, where the bytes and the people meet. This presents a real-time three-dimensional environment combined with visual elements for direct manipulation in two dimensions (fig. 5). This type of environment allows us to respect the infography, which has been applied to interactivity up to now in a non-immersion virtual reality system.

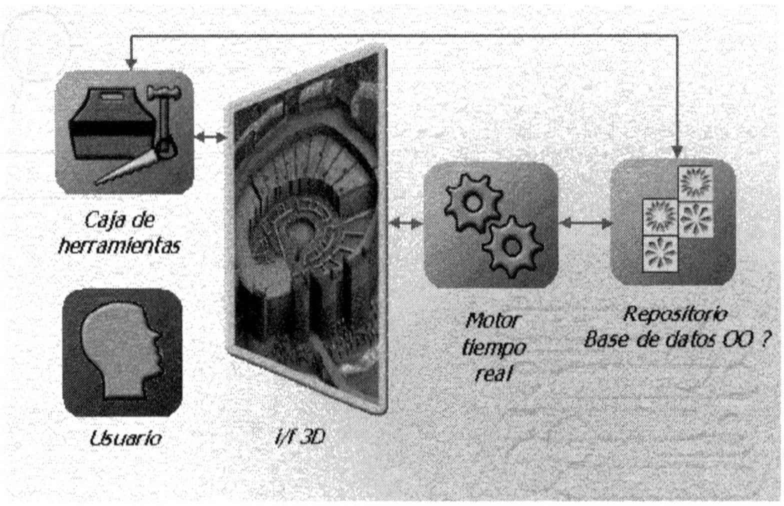

Figure 5. The user interface

One of the important aspects of the project is to reduce the cognitive load necessary to use the system and to adapt it to a simple mental model and to use by a non-computer-literate user. We are referring, on the one hand, to the wider public and its use as an instrument and, on the other hand, to the archaeologists and its use in a research environment.

The global metaphor that we use in the first case is that of navigating—a very easily understood metaphor that is widely used in today's computers. Navigating the dictionary tells us how to go from one site to another.

The mental model that stems from an archaeological dig is a model based on archaeological objects manipulated by tools. This is the global metaphor that we will add to the navigator metaphor, that of the archaeological toolbox that allows the addition and modification of virtual archaeological objects from familiar concepts that are intuitively understood.

Representing historical hypotheses graphically supposes asking what the graphic methodology will be. We believe that the disciplines that can help us here are restoration and historical geography. Both work with different levels of texture to represent different degrees of information. In the case of restoration, the use of different textures allows one to distinguish between the old and the restored. In the case of cartography, we have the framework of legends where the graduation of colour is correlated with statistical information. We thus believe that it is necessary to define one or more texture menus that allow us to represent the different levels of hypotheses graphically. This visualization can be combined with the photorealist one.

THE TECHNOLOGIC RESOURCES

The system is designed for use on PCs with sufficient graphic capacity, using standard devices (mouse, trackball, joystick, keyboard and screen) as interactive devices at the lowest level. The archaeological record is implemented around the relational system, accessible for manipulation via Internet, and multi-platform.

The system interface is based on a style of interaction by direct manipulation using windows, icons, menus and pointers (WIMP) with a three-dimensional content. The kernel of the system is an engine that collects the information supplied by the dispatcher and displays it on the screen. The engine is linked to the database by means of a dispatcher. This is the only process connected directly to the database. The system complements the archaeological facts with a store of 3D objects of the site, textures, elements, etc.. The different modules of the system have been developed using C++ and Open Inventor.

Conclusion

Fruits of a first experience, we have presented the protocols of a new project where virtual reality ceases to be conceived solely as an instrument of entertainment and is presented as one more research tool. Evidently, both functions—research and publication—are not contradictory, but what is certain is that the first archaeological applications of this type developed have all too often been aimed at the wider public, frequently grazing the limits of vulgarity. Perhaps it is the moment to recall that an image not only can be worth a thousand words but also can lie more than a thousand words; in using virtual reality we need to be careful, to be rigorous in our approximations and in creating from new recording systems, thus reclaiming virtual reality as a reliable mirror on past history.

References Cited

AGUSTÍ, B., ALONSO, N., GARCÉS, I., JUNYENT, E., LAFUENTE, A., LÓPEZ, J.B., 1999, "Una inhumación múltiple de perinatales en la fortaleza de Els Vilars (Arbeca, Lleida) y las prácticas de enterramiento en hábitat durante la I™ Edad del Hierro en el valle del Segre (Cataluña)", *Monographies d'Archèologie Mèditerranenne*, 5, Lattes, in press.

ALONSO, N., JUNYENT, E., LAFUENTE, A., LÓPEZ, J.B., 1998, "Poder, símbolo y territorio: el caso de la fortaleza de Arbeca", *Actas del Congreso Internacional. Los Iberos. Prìncipes de Occidente*, Fundación "la Caixa", Barcelona, pp. 355-372.

GARCÉS, I., JUNYENT, E., LAFUENTE, A., LÓPEZ, J.B., 1991, "Sistema de registro y tratamiento autom˙tico de la información en el yacimiento protohistórico de Els Vilars (Arbeca, Lleida)" *Complutum*, 1, Madrid, pp. 189-210.

GARCÉS, I., JUNYENT, E., LAFUENTE, A., LÓPEZ, J.B. (Coords.), 1997, *Vilars 2000. Una fortalesa ilergeta d'ara fa 2700 anys*, Universidad de Lleida, Lleida.

HARRIS, E.C., 1979, *Principes of Archaeological Stratigraphy*, Academic Press, London.

JUNYENT, E., LÓPEZ, J.B., OLIVER, A., 1992, "Strategy, stratigraphical analysis and registration of archaeological research in Lleida in the eighties. The Harris Matrix", *Harris Matrix. Recording Systems in Archaeology*, vol. II, Universidad de Lleida, Lleida, pp. 184-275.

LÓPEZ, J.B., 1991, "Principes generaux de l'enregistrement", *Lattara*, 4, Lattes, pp. 11-64.

PY, M., 1997, *SYSLAT 3.1. Systéme d'Information Archeologique. Manuel de Rèfèrence*, Lattara, 10, Lattes.

RECONSTRUCTION OF THE INTENDANT'S SECOND PALACE, QUEBEC CITY, AROUND 1730

Richard Lapointe

Université Laval, Quebec, Canada
Richard.Lapointe@scg.ulaval.ca
www.microtec.net/~richar

The archaeological site of the Îlot des Palais is located at the mouth of the St. Charles river, on the St. Lawrence river in Quebec City, Canada. The archaeological site of the Intendant's Palace was excavated by the Université Laval's archaeological summer school between 1982 and 1990, under the direction of Marcel Moussette. Today, these architectural remains are located under a tent in order to give the public the opportunity to visit this archaeological site and to learn about the local history.

Localisation of "L'Îlot des Palais, Québec"

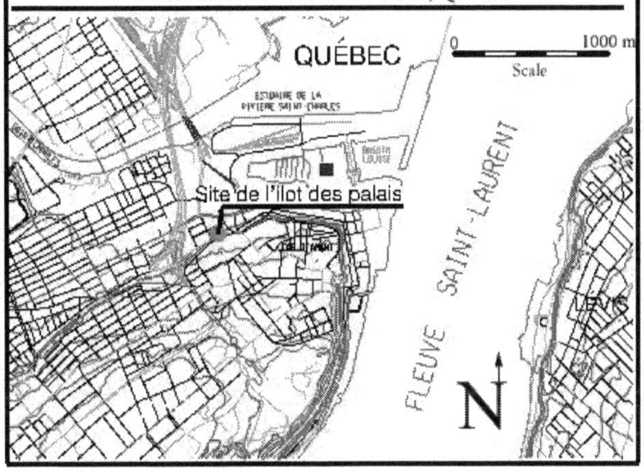

We have decided to reconstruct this site in virtual three dimensions to give a better comprehension of the site and to test the possibilities and limit of actual modelling software. We think that virtual reconstruction of an archaeological site is a useful new approach for the site's comprehension, visualization and interpretations.

For the conference, the reconstruction was presented as a multimedia document on a CD-ROM. This presentation gave us the opportunity to incorporate different types of data together: historic and recent maps, images of the 3D reconstruction, ancient painting, recent drawings and a little animation. The methodology used is an occasion to relate old maps and plans of the site to recent interpretations and actual elements.

History of L'Îlot des Palais

This site holds a very important place in the history of the colonial world of "Nouvelle-France. In fact, the Intendant represented the king of France in America and he played an important economic role. The buildings in which he lived where the economic and judiciary center in Quebec, and they had to demonstrate his prestige in the colony. These buildings were quite impressive for a city still in development, and many important activities were linked to this place.

The historical documentation and the archaeological remains offer researchers the possibility to identify five distinct phases of occupation on the site (Moussette. 1994. p.22).

1666-1675 Jean Talon Brewery

The first building constructed on the site was a brewery. This building served as foundations for all the other buildings, built later at the same place.

1685-1713 The Intendant's First Palace

When the Intendant decided to build his first palace, he used the brewery and added an annex, in which we can still find the underground prisons.

1716-1760 The Intendant's Second Palace and stores of the king

The first palace burned down in 1713 and the Intendant in office decided to build a different palace about 100 meters in front of the first one. This one was bigger and of French monumental tradition. The first palace's foundations where reused for the construction of the stores of the king, where the trading goods were stored.

The two latest periods of occupation—the reorganization and construction of many new buildings (1780-1845) and the Boswell Brewery (1852-1968)—are not being considered in the actual working project.

The Virtual Modelization

We decided to recreate the site as it was in approximately 1730. We have decide to reconstruct this phase of the Intendant's second palace and the stores of the king because of the abundant documentation related to the palace, the main building, the stores and the other annexes.

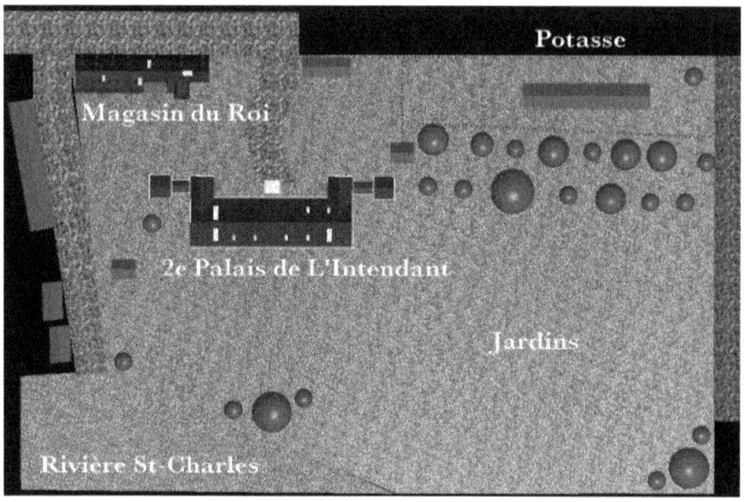

The documents used for the creation of the reconstruction are:

- The maps of the archaeological remains found during excavation;
- The modern reconstruction plans and interpretations;
- The historic maps and plans of the buildings in elevation;
- Historic maps showing the position of the building;
- Old drawings;
- A three-dimension virtual model of Quebec City.

Results

With these data, it was possible to virtually reconstruct the site of the Intendant's second palace. It is the stores of the king, the part of the site concerned with the archaeological research that mainly served the reconstruction study. In fact, for the second palace, only the volumes were reconstructed. More details and time were devoted to the storage building.

It is uncommon to identify the different levels of a building on an archaeological site, but such details are needed in order to create a three-dimensional reconstruction. With the help of the old plans and maps, we were able to recreate the stores of the king in elevation and to reconstruct the divisions of the building's different levels.

When we compared the mapping of the archaeological remains with the old maps and plans of the stores of the king, we observed that there are many differences in the position of the walls. We made corrections in the reconstruction process based on the archaeological evidence. Because of a lack of time and because this was not the main goal of our research, we did not digitize the archaeological elements with great precision and detail.

With a three-dimensional virtual model of Quebec City, we were able to localize the ancient building in the context of the city. This model gave us an idea of the Intendant's second palace in the city context with the fortifications in the background and modern roads around the site.

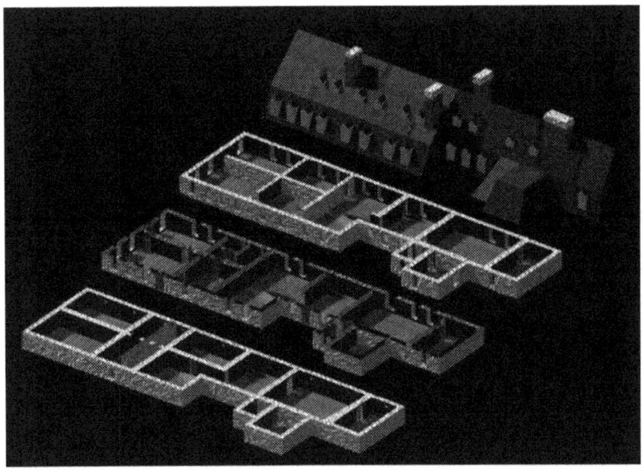

Some animation tests were made to see the rendering possibilities of the software used (Microstation). These tests where a good learning experience in terms of production methodology of computer animation. We worked with texture mapping, defining the camera path, lighting the scene and final rendering.

Finally, we developed a multimedia version, on CD-ROM, for the presentation of the different documents used and the modelling results. Multimedia provides an occasion for the user to interact with presented data, depending on his/her own interests or needs.

Conclusion

In conclusion, this project demonstrates the possibilities of a virtual reconstruction of an archeological site from the North American historical period. With the maps of the archaeological remains and those from the eighteenth century, we can now recreate the historic monuments thought to be lost forever.

We think that these reconstructions can be very useful for the diffusion of knowledge to a general public. Archaeological sites are not always easily understandable for everyone, and we think that it is easier to explain the remains of a lost building or monument visually, with a reconstruction of the building.

The future development of technology will also give the opportunity to recreate the different phases of occupation, and that will give a new temporal dimension to the three-dimensional reconstruction. These reconstructions can even be made in virtual reality to give the possibility of a fully immersive visit to a long-lost historic site. As archaological sites are not always easy to visit, the Internet could then be used for the diffusion of the virtual models. We think that this could be an interesting development for cultural tourism and for the diffusion of information.

References Cited

CHAUSSEGROS de Léry, 1722, Élévations de la face du côté du nord, *Archives nationales du Canada* , ANC, PH/350/Québec, 1722.

CHAUSSEGROS de Léry, 1732, Plan du terrain du Palais, *Archives nationales du Canada*, APC/M/Québec/1732.

Élévations et plan du nouveau Palais de l'Intendant, 1715. *Archives nationales du Canada*, ANC, PH/350/Québec, 1715, c-16036)

FILLION, Danielle., 1994a « Plan des vestiges structuraux des magasins du roi mis au jour par les archéologues. 1716-1760 ». *in* Moussette, 1994, p.83

FILLION, Danielle., 1994b « Élévation nord des magasins détachés recontitués d'après les plans de La Guer de Morville de 1716-1718 » *in* Moussette, p.122.

Le GUER de MORVILLE, 1716, Plan, Profil et Élévation des Magasins & Prisons du Roy de Québec. *Archives nationales du Canada*. AN, DFC, Amérique septentrionale, Portefeuil V, no 403B, 9 novembre 1718.

Le GUER de MORVILLE, 1717, Plan des terrains joignant celui du palais, *Archives nationales du Canada.* ANC, F/350/Québec, 1717)

MARTIN, M., FILION D., MORIN, M.-C. & R. BILODEAU., CeEt-30. Le site du Palais de l'Intendant, plan composite 1882-1990, Université Laval, *in* Moussette p.14.

MOUSSETTE, Marcel. 1994., *Le site du Palais de l'intendant à Québec*, Ed. Septentrion, Québec, 230 pages.

Plan de l'Intendance du Palais, 1750., *Archives nationales du Canada*, ANC, PH/340/Québec,1750)

SHORT, Richard, 1759, Vue du nouveau Palais et de la cour de l'Intendance, 1759. *Archives nationales du Canada*, C-19318.

VILLE de QUÉBEC., 1993, *Un parcours en cinq temps*, Québec, 36 pages.

THE ESTENSE CASTLE OF FERRARA (ITALY): MULTIMEDIA PROJECT AND VIRTUAL RECONSTRUCTION

Maurizio Forte
CNR ITABC (Inst.of Technology Applied to Cultural Heritage), Rome, Italy
forte@mlib.cnr.it

Davide Borra
No Real - archaeological and historical digital representation, Turin, Italy
noreal@citras.it

Introduction

The Ferrara "Estense" Castle is one of the most important monuments in Europe (and a Unesco property). Its history reflects the history of Ferrara itself (and, in part, of Europe), from the early Middle Ages when it functioned as the city's main defensive structure, until the times when Ferrara, under Ercole I, reached its most splendid period as one of the greatest cultural centres of Italy and Europe, with the castle still as its central nucleus (Righini, Bergellesi Severi 1971). In 1996 a multimedia project was undertaken by M. Forte to reconstruct the history of Estense Castle, mainly through the four principal phases of building and including also all the information and data concerning the architecture and the relationships between the castle and the evolution of the city of Ferrara. Specifically, we created the first virtual 3D reconstruction of the castle, starting from the architectural aspects of the monument (plans, sections, views), analysing and comparing the historical sources, and studying the volumes in order to make detailed 3D models of the monument through the four periods of building: tower (I), stronghold (II), fortress (III), palace (IV) (about the Ferrara castle, see the essential bibliography at the end of this paper).

In 1997, under the direction of the Provincia di Ferrara (arch. Marco Borella) and the Soprintendenza ai Beni Storici e Artistici di Ferrara-Bologna (arch.Carla Di Francesco), the company ARCHE' srl was charged with carrying out the multimedia project[1], including also the virtual reconstruction; the final goal was to produce a publication on CD-ROM in two languages, Italian and English, and for PC and Mac.

Multimedia Project and Interface

The multimedia project has been developed on Director Multimedia Studio 6 (for PC and Mac) and it has been completed in one year of work with a team of eight persons.

The principal multimedia graphic interface chosen involves the 3D reconstruction of the castle: using an animation of the 3D model as metaphora, it is possible to find the main hyperlink and themes:

- The castle and the city
- The architectural history
- Archaeological treasures
- Castle frescoes
- The house of Este
- Castle images
- The virtual castle
- Virtual panoramas
- Glossary

MULTIMEDIA INFORMATION LAYER

Considering the complexity of the project, it was very important to use different 2D-3D devices in order to obtain the best cognitive impact compared to many didactic approaches to multimedia information. In fact a visualisation in multiple levels permits every user to choose the best multimedia path in accordance with his/her own knowledge. Therefore the system must educate, employing key-concepts and key-words, but using images and animations for communicating information.

The project development carefully considered how best to correlate the distinct information layers of the architectural periods with the multimedia aims; in particular, the multimedia system has involved the following main stages in accordance with three targets: the first one dynamic-scientific (3D virtual processing/3D animations), the second one dynamic-interactive (VR panomamas and stitching techniques), the third one dynamic-didactic (2D color animations from drawings made by hand)

- 3D modelling (reconstruction of one virtual model for each period). In order to visualise in detail the special quality of model and rendering, we have produced high-quality rendered mages of the castle in different views; in this way the architectural space becomes a cognitive space

- 3D architectural animations: one animation around the castle (360°) for each phase and all the four reconstructions simultaneously (so it is easy to understand the architectural evolution). Moreover there are very impressive animations concerning a presentation of the castle in night and day versions.

- 3D archaeological animations: based on the archaeological excavations under the castle, we have reconstructed a virtual

[1] The multimedia team was composed by: Maurizio Forte (multimedia project and direction), Chiara Ronconi (multimedia system manager and 2D animation), Davide Borra (3D modelling and animation), Sofia Pescarin (graphic and computer graphic), Corrado Re (drawings and 2d animation), Elisabetta Pietrobon and Enrichetta Simioli (texts and bibliographic researches). Scientific consultants: Carla Di Francesco, Marco Borella.

stratigraphy, so that every user can simulate an archaeological dig with instruments and tools.

- VR (virtual reality interaction) stitching of photos of 360° panoramas of Ferrara and the Estense Castle. We have used a PC software, Photovista, with a plug-in for Director. PhotoVista creates spectacular 360° panoramas, and produces extremely compact, high-quality images optimised for Macintosh and Windows platforms. It can support stitching images taken with fisheye lenses of 16mm focal length or greater and supports stitching images taken with wide-angle rectilinear lenses of 13mm focal length or greater. To resize the image manually, we can perform a full stitch, convert the panorama to a cylinder, and save the panorama as a bitmap (BMP), or in QuickTime VR format. It is also possible to view "hot spots" in the scene, clicking there to cause an action on screen, such as switching to another panorama. This technique has been applied for showing panoramas of the castle and of the town, and for visualising the frescoes in the interior of the monument. In this last case the VR stitching has allowed us to show in one full view the articulated paintings of the ceilings, looking at them in real time.

- 2D plans, sections, views: in every type of reconstruction it is very important to check and to compare the virtual model with the original data (in this case digital CAD data) for keeping the reproduction always to scale. In the system it is possible to visualise all the plans (floor by floor), sections and views of the castle processed by CAD drawings.

- 2D animation: we have also used color drawings made by hand and sounds, in order to present the dynamic events in a didactic way.

The hypertext links of the multimedia system are organised on the basis of the importance of the information and, mainly, on the basis of the "distance" of the hot or key-words from each multimedia module. Thus we have different colors for distinct levels of information:

1 blue = internal link (in the same module), distance 1.

2 green = link to curiosity, distance 2.

3 yellow = link to internal glossary, distance 3.

4 red = link to another, different main module and interface, distance 4.

This distinction and classification is very important because it allows the user to know immediately the significance of an interactive action, answering the questions: where I am, where I am going, what is the next ?

Integrated with this information is a complete hypermap in which it is possible to find all the links and themes of the multimedia system.

The building of the castle: A few historical notes

"Marquis Nicolò Zoppo, Lord of Ferrara, had the building of San Michele Castle commence near to Porta dei Leoni. Alberto, who was appointed marquis by Nicolò, laid the first of the building's foundation stones and laid a golden ducat under it; he gave another ducat to the bricklayer. The castle was built because of what happened to Tomaso da Tortona in 1385 as described above." (Equicola d'Alveto, "Annali di Ferrara")

The architect Bartolino da Novara's idea was to add three new towers to the already existing fortress Rocca dei Leoni, in order to form a square structure which would be closed all around with walls somewhat lower in height than the towers themselves. He put up defensive decorations consisting of "beccatelli" (arched ridge supporting an overhanging structure), great battlements and a sloping tile roof, described as followed by Jacopo da Marano: "1387. How the building of the castle was finished at the Porta dei Leoni after 16 months and 8 days. Four magnificent towers with barbicans; its drawbridge and its fortifications, near to the Porta dei Leoni; they made up a wonderful courtyard: infinite number of rooms and halls." (Jacopo da Marano)

According to the chroniclers the building was completed after 16 months. The castle was accessible through five different entrances that gave direct access to the courtyard. All entrances were in the stretches of wall in between the towers and could be reached passing the barbicans and drawbridge towers.

When the building of the castle had arrived at the first foundation ring, the Este had their artillery positioned on top of it, pointed towards the city. "Having finished the construction of the first foundation ring, the marquis at night had some of the artillery, which he had already acquired some years before, positioned on top of it. Now finally he put it in use, which, the next morning when it was noticed, frightened the people."

The first foundation ring of the castle stretched from the fundaments to the ground floor. An ornamental border all around indicated the line where the foundation ring and the top structure met. Together with the bas reliefs on the towers, this was probably the only decorative element of the castle exterior.

The Este princess had a special bridge connection made to get from the residential palazzo on the piazza to the castle—for security reasons. Although the fortress was equipped with more than sufficient weaponry to go to war, the building has never functioned to confront enemies from outside the city. For about 70 years the fortress remained unchanged in its outspoken and strictly military appearance, housing the Este troops and damp, gloomy prisons.

All in all, the presence of this very military and intimidating new castle did not exactly enrich the city with a sense of peacefulness and harmony. There was a deliberate reason for this, of course: to intimidate the citizens, to let them know that at any time they could be taken under fire. This confirms again that the power of the Este was not so much based on consensus as it was on oppression.

Building a 3D Virtual Model

Project tutors

The composition of an interdisciplinary team is fundamental for beginning a project of a 3D virtual reconstruction, and a good final result depends mainly on this. In a team there are three main operating roles: Scientific Tutor, Modeller and Communication Manager. There is also a Project Coordinator, integrating results of modelling work in a hypermedia project.

The Scientific Tutor is competent in giving historical and architectonic information in checking the results and furthermore decides the "formal detail level" (how much detail to include in the visually rendered forms) in concert with the Communication Manager and the Modeller. With the last he also verifies the formal quality of the represented geometry.

The Modeller builds up the virtual model; sets scenes, points of view and animations; and produces renderings. He receives technical information from the Scientific Tutor and supplies outputs in the ways described by the Communication Manager. He verifies with both of them all the model elements. He particularly determines the ideal "operating level."

The Communication Manager will decide, in accord with the

target, the aesthetic language to be used and its detail level in order to achieve best communication. He verifies with the modeller the quality of the textures applied, animation sequences, and points of view.

A correct modelling is the result of the unceasing involvement of these characters, of the union of formal, operational and aesthetical analyses. The lexicon used by the Scientific Tutor, the Modeller and the Communication Manager should include common terms, to allow a good knowledge exchange. The Scientific Tutor should be free to modify the formal aspect of a project due to strong operative limits and aesthetic needs.

The Modeller should supply feedback to the Scientific Tutor and the Communication Manager on the average level of his/her hardware and software equipment and of his/her experience regarding speed and management level, in order to apply the necessary corrective parameters to formal analysis.

The Communication Manager should be aware of the software's expressive potential available for the aesthetic project interface and communicate them to the modeller. He furthermore interacts with the Scientific Tutor to underline the aesthetic needs in order to determinate the best possible formal detail level.

DETAIL LEVEL

Another key factor is the detail level to be used. It should seem, at first glance, a simple measuring parameter, identifying which of the real particulars should be modelled. A deeper analysis brings us to distinguish three components (fig.1):

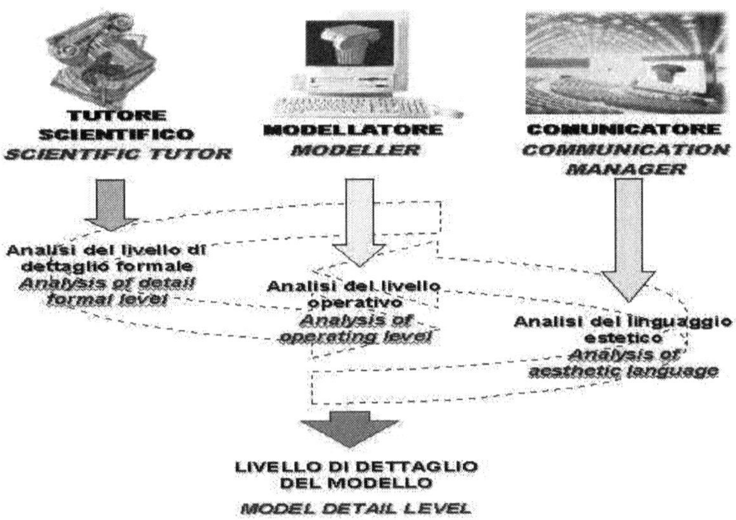

Determining the detail level consists of identifying the categories of elements that are not useful for the expository language. The elements belonging to these categories will not be modelled. This part of the job is not concerned with the predisposition of a minimum measurable threshold, but with the distinction into different formal categories. Different levels of detail can be used within the same model, due to the distance between the single elements and the point of view. Elements set close to the point of view will share the higher formal detail level used, while further distances will allow a lower level. Elements set at the same distance should be modelled with the same formal detail level.

The operating level concerns the fixing and measuring of the quality and quantity possibile with the operating equipment of the project, in relation with the foreseen aims of the project. In other words actual potentiality should always be kept in mind. Operating levels can be distinguished as low, intermediate and high levels

The level of aesthetic detail, in which the depth of aspects concerning the aesthetic language based upon the target is chosen. The rendering of a model in which no texture has been used will be helpful for all those people managing to receive information just by the intersection of volumes, while for a more heterogeneous public, textures, reflections and environmental simulation should be applied.

We can distinguish three further levels within the formal detail:

outline (level 1): this is the lowest detail level characterized by the least possible geometries, with the exception of these necessary to the correct identification of the form and of the described element.

simplification (level 2): this is the detail level offering the best decisional flexibility, with more formal pieces of information in comparison with the outline. The planners' duty is to adjust the detail level in order to provide a correct perception while maintaining the aesthetic language and the operating versatility.

reality (level 3): this includes all the real forms perceivable in the model representation

SCALE

The detail levels interact within a more general detail level characterising the modelled object representation. Powerful computers (high operating level), for instance, allow an improvement of the formal detail level, but if the modeller has not enough experience, the detail level should be restricted in order to avoid production delays. In different situations it might be necessary to present a virtual model rendering with an outlined formal detail level without simulation of materials: in this case less powerful equipment will be sufficient.

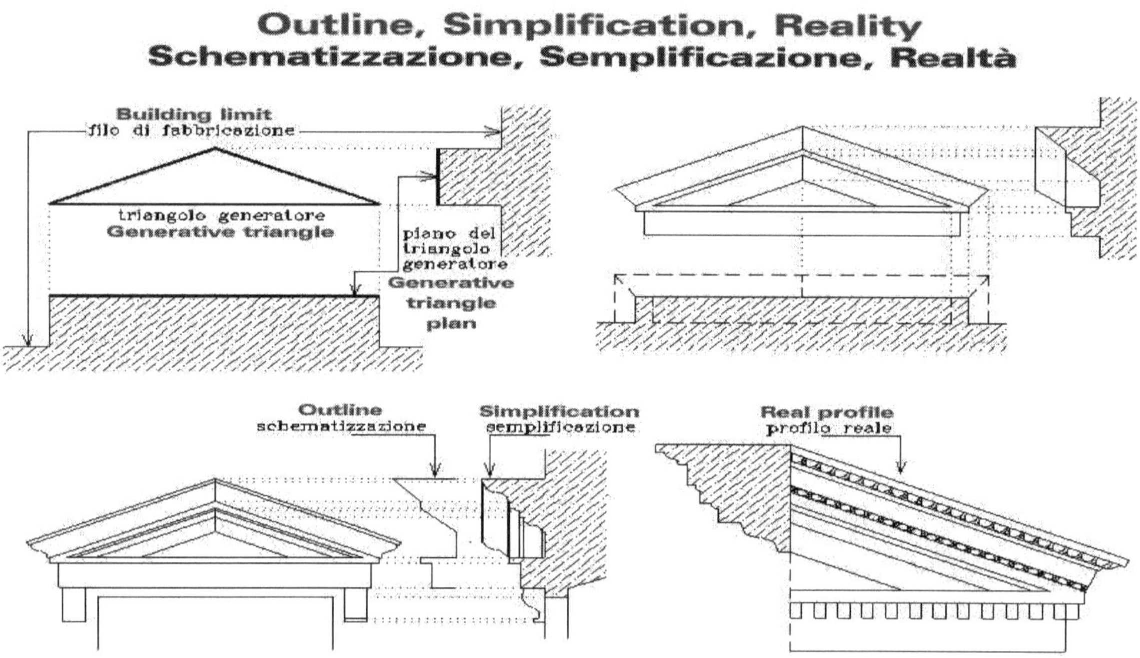

Figure 2 Varying levels of formal detail

The Virtual Model of Castello Estense di Ferrara

The aim of the virtual model was to produce images and animations representing the historical evolution of Castello Estense's architecture. Since the predetermined target was common users, the renderings were to be of a good degree of verisimilitude.

Four different historical ages have been determined for the building, and consequently four virtual models were developed.

PHASE 1 "Tower" : in the 13th century A.D. a tower stands beside the "Porta del Leone" (the town entrance), within the castle wall, at the time placed north of the town, on the shores of the "Canale della Giovecca".

PHASE 2 "Stronghold" : in the 14th century A.D. a fortification is added to the tower, simulating a small castle with four angular towers.

PHASE 3 "Fortress" : in 1385 three more towers are built to form a quadrilateral with the "Torre dei Leoni", linked by wings with battlements and a supplementary defence rampart.

PHASE 4 "Palace" : between 1471 and 1505 the fortress is gradually transformed into a residential palace, by losing the fortifications and elevating wings and niches level above the four towers.

The great amount of accurate technical data available has been a good operating advantage. Being in a vectorial format, it required no further conversion or corrections. The modelling has been developed at a high formal detail level (it is a high-quality level 2, close to a level 3) for each element.

The modelling process was started with Phase 4; afterwards subsequent removals of the central building and possible addition in the early stages was carried out.

A simplified model was first of all composed in order to prevent rough mistakes. Each part of the model was subsequently detailed. Every model was divided into different parts referenced to each other and to the different models, in order to easily manage to exchange elements and data characterising each of the four phases. A tridimensional outline was necessary to this aim so that each part of the castle had its own boundary and was identified by a file name. The outline is present in every file. The four models have become therefore puzzles whose elements were linked together in order to automatically have an updating version of the model whenever a new version of an element had to be created.

Although the castle, at first sight, shows a strong radiocentricity in the main building and several copies of equal elements (such as the battlements), in order to have a verifiable architectural result each element has been drawn according to the original survey. The model's precision derives from the performed surveys.

The modelling of brackets, for instance, has respected the differences between the elements present in a single tower, but also the differences evidenced by the comparison of the four towers. Any element which might be repeated has been defined as a block and copied by modifying eventual dimension and orientation. In this way 25 different frames, 3 kinds of mutules, and 2 sets of balustrades have been identified.

Once all of the four phases had been modelled, the work on textures and their application could be started. The first renderings were carried out with a set made up by four standard lights. The next step was to correct both the textures and the lighting of the scene. Each texture used has been created *ex novo* and customised for every different part of the castle, e.g., 6 different brick textures, 3 wood textures, two stone textures, etc.

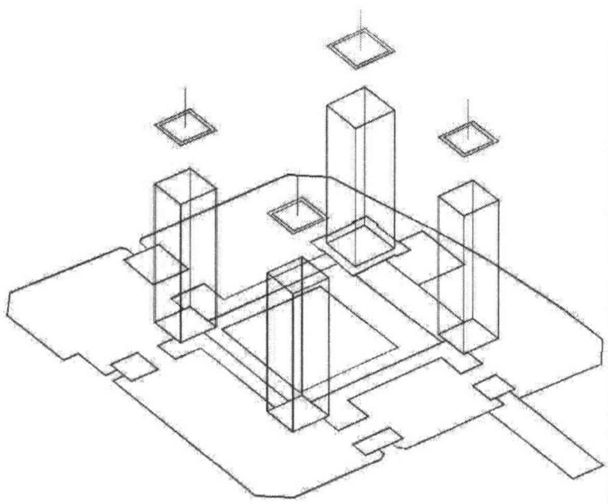

Figure 3 : 3D outline: a vector file defining spaces by principal volumes.

One of the most interesting aspects was the co-modelling on-line, by Internet: a continuous exchange was conducted through three poles: the modelling was carried out by Davide Borra in Turin, with direct cooperation of colleagues at the Castle of Ferrara. At the same time the results were checked both in Bologna by Maurizio Forte and in Ferrara by Marco Borella.

The net organization had two operative levels: a modelling one (Turin-Ferrara), and a controlling one (Turin-Bologna-Ferrara).

The co-modelling strategy was carried out this way:

one of the basic requirements for the operating net is a direct, unambiguos communication. Therefore all the involved people have been supplied with the codified communication rules used for the data exchange. This includes the ordering of file names, being linked to parts of objects which every modeller faces, to the check dates, to the modeller's name and so on; no special telephone lines were required, because the data exchange was carried out in planned times, often during the night

the massive data exchanges, on the whole, did not require communications lasting more than an hour and were carried out through the exchange of many compressed files rather than with a small amount of big files

the entire project development should be preserved, so that it will be possible to start again within a certain model at any time, even after further modification. It is furthermore compulsory to codify "blocks" or "cells", i.e. the matrix of those elements which will be copied many times, so that no confusion will take place and it will be easy to recall them for further modifications

the reference outline has been the guide for each modelled element. This way, no mistakes could be made, unless a modification of the space position of the reference outline had taken place.

Hardware and software used:

Pentium 100Mh, 64 Mb of Ram, Video-board Matrox IP 2Mb Ram

Pentium 200Mh, 32 Mb of Ram, Video-board SVGA 1Mb Ram

Modelling software: Autodesk AutoCAD r12

Rendering software and animation : Autodesk 3Dstudio r4

	PHASE 1 "Tower"	PHASE 2 "Stronghold"	PHASE 3 "Fortress"	PHASE 4 "Palace"

Nr. Elements	*5*	*5*	*14*	*15*
Nr. Objects	*121*	*122*	*290*	*504*
Nr. Vertex	*23.235*	*28.169*	*104.978*	*177.640*
Nr. Faces	*41.729*	*50.675*	*200.146*	*341.750*
Light Sets	*Ambient Light+3 Spot + 6 Omnidiretional+1 Projector*			
Nr. Materials	*17*	*19*	*23*	*23*
Rendering time (Pentium 100) 640x480x24bit	*14' c.ca*	*14'30" c.ca*	*45' c.ca*	*1h30' c.ca*
DWG file	*7.371 Kb*	*8.921 Kb*	*21.227 Kb*	*36.679 Kb*
3DS file	*1.021 Kb*	*1.161 Kb*	*4.341 Kb*	*8.201*

Figure 4. Information concerning the four virtual models.

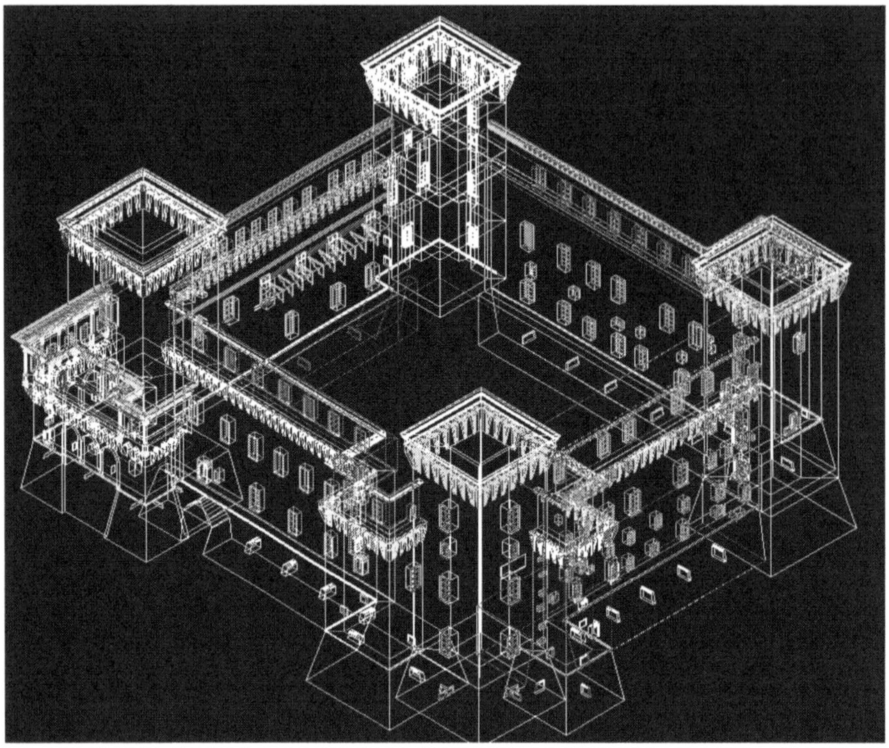

Figure 5. Wireframe representation of the model

Figure 6. Frontal view

Figure 7. Rendering with night light

Figure 8. Aerial view

New Developments of the Project

After the publication of the CD-ROM, we plan to extend the multimedia aspect of the castle project in two directions:

- a VRML version of the 3D model on-line on the Internet.
- The creation of an Information Multimedia Monumental System (IMMS)—a kind of a multimedia GIS applied to three-dimensional structures, linking all the data to each part or structure of the monument. For instance, it would be very important to include the documentation about the architectural restorations of the castle, describing and monitoring the materials of any single part (state of conservation, etc.), and organizing the data (images, databases, 3D reconstructions, animations, and so on) so as to select and connect referenced information in 3D. 3D components (from the single brick to the towers) could be used to correlate significative information from many different sources. The final result should be a 3D map, taking apart and reconstructing the monument, and visualising many collections of data layers simultaneously, each representing significative relationships of 3D structures.

References Cited

BARGELLESI SEVERI, A., Il Castello di Ferrara, 1985.

BOCCHI, F., Il Castello come struttura di potere, Il Castello. Origini, realtà, fantasia (a cura di P. Portoghesi e F. Bocchi), 1985.

BORELLA, M., *Il castello estense di Ferrara*, Milano 1990.

CHIAPPINI, A., *Introduzione a Il castello Estense rilievo 1978*, Amm. Prov. di Ferrara 1980.

DI FRANCESCO, C., *I frammenti di intonaco della chiesa di S. Giuliano, Ferrara prima e dopo il Castello.* Testimonianze archeologiche per la storia della città, Ferrara, 1992, 151-155.

GELICHI, S., (ed.) *Ferrara prima e dopo il Castello. Testimonianze archeologiche per la storia della città, Ferrara*, Spazio Libri, 1992.

RIGHINI, G., BERGELLESI SEVERI, A., *Il castello di Ferrara*, 1971

Concluding Address

ABOUT *VIRTUAL ARCHAEOLOGY*: DISORDERS, COGNITIVE INTERACTIONS AND VIRTUALITY

Maurizio Forte

CNR (National Research Council) Institute of Technology Applied to Cultural Heritage, Rome
forte@mlib.cnr.it

Introduction

What is effectively *virtual archaeology* (hereafter: VA)? And what is virtual (Levy, 1992, 1996, 1997; Reilly 1990; Forte 1996a)? In the ontological sense, as translated from Greek *dunaton*, it is "that in potential" (Aristotle, *Analitici primi*); in fact, in scholastic philosophy it is that which exists in potential form and not in reality. According to Levy it is the "transformation of a condition of being to another... one of the possible ways of being, in contradiction not to *reality* but to *actuality*... The virtual tends to actualise itself, without having gone through a real or formal realisation... virtuality and actuality are only two different ways of being" (Levy, 1997).

In a period of great technological-digital evolution in all scientific fields, it is even more important to try to decipher, monitor and critically describe the state of the art, giving particular attention to those interdisciplinary areas which will mark the avant garde of future research. The great communicative impact that archaeology offers in itself is highly enhanced by the possible digital interfaces and by the comprehensibility that these provide for much more than the scientific community.

During the CAA'98 (*Computer Applications in Archaeology* 1998 conference) in Barcelona, there was an entire congress session and a cinemagraphic-digital festival dedicated to the topic, with a great number of non-specialised participants. It is enough to look at a research tool such as Altavista, capable of finding over 200 pages (and who knows how many more by the time this article is published) relating to the key words "virtual archaology" (cfr. for example http://www.ukans.edu/~hoopes/virtual.htm) to understand just how many projects and applications are dedicated in various degrees to the virtual reconstruction of the ancient world, even if with very diverse applicative procedures and results. Therefore, considering what has been noted in this introduction and what will be discussed below, virtual archaeology can be defined as digital reconstructive archaeology, computational epistemology applied to the reconstruction of three-dimensional archaeological ecosystems, therefore, cognitive ecology. The epistemological aspect is key in the assessment of computational processes and accordingly, in archaeological activity. To the out-going elaboration one must increase the cognitive significance of the in-going data ("augmented" reality). The context is cognitively greater than the sum of its components and we must identify the "environment" of the VA in a structuralist sense.

Therefore in the assessment of the application of VA it an epistemological measurement is essential; if, in fact, we try to "measure" the cognitive quality of models there is a risk of completely destructuring the information in respect to the context. For example: during SIGGRAPH '99 (Congress and world wide exhibit of computer graphics held in Los Angeles in 1999), Silicon Graphics (creators of applications of immersive virtual reality) dedicated is exhibition space to a project on the virtual reconstruction of the Roman Forum. The models used an incorrect reproduction scale and the building phases were not clearly reproduced. Lacking the appropriate navigational instruments, the cognitive maps (computational cartography) used for navigation and the appropriate hypermedial tools, it was almost impossible for a classical archaeologist to orient himself in the three-dimensional spaces. Therefore in this case, the virtual reconstruction distanced the user from the representative memory of the context (the Forum), interfering in any type of literacy diffusion. All in all, we can say that the application, with the sole purpose of a technological exercise, caused a complete cognitive de-territorialisation of the user, lacking orientation and without any informative increase, rather an informative loss.

Moreover it is evident that virtual space, in the archaeological dimension, must be contextualised and hierarchically restructured in order to allow for the identification of the logical units of information in the geometry of the models; theoretically one should "undo" and "redo" the context to completely verify the geometric and functional system.

Key concepts here might be 3D, interaction, virtual models—below we will see with what other variables (Cremaschi, Forte, 1999). More specifically there are two macro-classes of applications to refer to: computer graphics (photorealistic rendering without interactivity with the models) and virtual reality with the associated variables (navigation in real time). The first class includes synthetic movies with algorithms (raytracing, Gourad, radiosity) that increase the degree of photorealism but also increase the calculation time; the latter instead covers all immersive type interactive applications (in different degrees): flythrough, with movement directed by the user in real time off line and on line (for example VRML). In the first case, even with very long rendering times, they can be operated even on a PC or on a medium-sized machine (the calculation will always be frame by frame). In the second case, however, rendering cannot be as completely photorealistic as in the first, yet it can be in real time. In this case it would be necessary to have a machine with excellent graphic performance and elevated calculation power. The most common algorithms used by graphic accelerators are the Gourad and the Phong. Raytracing is too demanding to be used in applications in real time (18-20 frames per second for a fluid visualisation of animation) and radiosity is used in primarily statistical settings (requiring a very long pre-elaboration time). Gourad assigns a luminosity value to every vertex of the polygon; the information of the remaining pixels is produced from the interpolations of the individual values of each vertex, the result being very soft shading, especially of curved surfaces. Phong, besides the interpolation between vertexes, introduces reflected light in the calculation, representing reflections on surfaces in a very realistic way. It is not possible to calculate a reflected image with this method (for example the reflection of an object on water), but it can be simulated using specific maps (reflection mapping), leaving an even more realistic impression (see also Barcelo, *this volume*).

For the 1990s it is possible to say that the major part of VA applications tended toward computer graphics, whereas instances of virtual reality were more rare, the latter almost exclusively concentrated on high-capacity workstations. For example, the reconstructions of the Colosseum (fig.1), the tomb of Nefertari (fig. 3), and St. Peter's Basilica (fig.4) were done in Infobyte on ONYX 2 Silicon Graphics; the cave of Lascaux was constructed by B. Britton (fig. 2) using Intergraph stations (personal workstation). It is therefore evident that the noticeable increase in the potential of Personal Computers and the low cost of these have had a double effect in the last two or three years: greater development of the applications and above all, active participation (even if still too sporadic) of archaeologists in the role of user-developer. The growth of on-line applications on the Internet, seeing that it will be in this digital territory that virtual reality will find capillary distribution with visibility and effective exchange of information will be interesting to follow.

Figure 1: Virtual reconstruction of the Collosseum (Infobyte)

Figure 2: Virtual reconstruction of the Lascaux Caves (B. Britton)

Figure 3: Virtual reconstruction of the tomb of Nefertari (Infobyte)

Beyond the definitions, the analysis of the state of the art shows a considerable increase of study cases and applications, with the effect, possibly unexpected, of having unfortunately passed from a pioneering phase, when everything caused clamour and excitement, to a more habitual phase or better yet one of the standardisation of the technology and its contents. This negative tolerance, in my opinion, was contributed to by an inadequate communicative-cognitive level of the applications and in an even more marked way, by the lack of valid archaeological projects that preceded these types of computer elaborations. It is useful, in fact, to notice that the major part of VA applications so far developed do not have important archaeological "contents", nor, as would be worthwhile, respond to precise questions. Instead they tend to float in a generically popular and multimedial sphere, or they are used as technological exercises or as a means of rendering the archaeology more spectacular; completely separate from the research context and from the exegesis of the data. Noticeable gaps are represented by the fact that the models are not "transparent" in respect to the initial information *(what were the initial data?)* and by the use of the peremptory single reconstruction without offering alternatives (*it could have been like this but we can also offer other models...*). The all too often missed occasions by VA are due to the clear and unbridgeable separation between the capacities of the archaeologists and computer scientists and to the lack of any interdisciplinary figure. The archaeologists involved in the projects must not only know the digital technology in detail but must participate in all of the data elaboration phases, beginning with the planning and when possible the digital acquisition of data in the field. The final risk of VA is to stagnate in evolutionary paths that are similar to those of quantitative archaeology, that is: "...in close relation to the theoretical debate tied to the processural method and that post-processural or anti-processural" (Moscati 1996; Clarke 1998). In respect to quantitative statistical methods, VA must define itself through new tools of archaeological standardisation, taking a fundamentally cognitive or "neutral" path in regards to technological capacity.

We do not want to downplay the many innovative results of VA, particularly in the comparative analysis between reality and reconstruction, between physical geometry and virtual models with these considerations because in the end the new visual digital representations also create new cognitive models (Forte 1996, 1996a).

Instead it is important to underline the yet unexpressed potential of VA especially if the research is aimed at the study of possible models and computational cognitive models integrated with the most advanced instances of Cognitive Archaeology (Renfrew, Zubrow 1994), and *Archéologie introspective* (Gardin 1996: "*...comment validons-nous reconstitutions du passé ?"*) which define the analysis of these anthropological process as *Cognitive Virtual Archaeology,* computational ecology. Even if computational experiments of artificial life should provide new applicative potential through the so-called intelligent agents (computational elements that develop within the artificial ecosystem interacting with the environment) in the next decades, the contribution of the study of artificial intelligence will still need to be verified (Doran 1996).

Below I will discuss the cognitive aspects of virtual archaeology, with investigation and theoretical-philosophical references (I would like to thank Roberta Beltrami, professor of philosophy, for discussions) which will allow us to better assess the epistemological complexity of virtuality and the role, in my opinion all but negligible, of archaeological science as an experimental sphere of the avant garde. In this sense, to decipher the present from the anthropological-cognitive point of view, I believe, provides new and unalterable instruments of discussion.

Figure 4: Virtual reconstruction of St. Peter's Basilica, Vatican City (Infobyte)

Definitions

Towards a virtual archaeology is the title of an article published by Paul Reilly in 1990, in which the author described some of the possible methods open to future archaeology, with some examples of three-dimensional visualisations relative to the virtual reconstruction of stratified contexts. Yet is VA solely a consequence of the development of digital technology or does it represent in itself also an evolutionary theory of archaeology?

I would propose the second hypothesis to avoid finding ourselves in front of a purely technological phenomenon, without important consequences on an epistemological level. Wasn't *New Archaeology* born as a systematic reflex for the need to discriminate, re-elaborate and rationalise archaeological information? We can therefore think of VA as a process of the three-dimensional modelling of information that becomes, in synthesis, visual information (Gregory, 1998). This type of visual information permits us to remodel and amplify the visible field. The need to virtualise data, with ever more advanced modelling, is a "natural " consequence of the strong informative increase, more data, more digital elaborations. The need to catalogue and archive increasing quantities of archaeological information introduces computer applications as a methodology that has been completely integrated in archaeological research, so much so that we speak commonly of computational archaeology. The capacity to render an archaeological model significantly visual becomes a compilation of interpretations, the essential base to describe the informative contents by geometry and context.

Therefore the possibility to virtually reproduce the entire explorative phase, or part of it and its relevant archaeological pattern-model, becomes the cognitive tool, par excellence, which allows us to respond to the question: how much and what do we reconstruct? The quality of the psycho-perceptive and representative-symbolic factors depends on the level of interaction upon which one can measure the quality of the model.

COGNITIVE INTERACTION

The value of a virtual model is represented by its cognitive interaction, a rule also valid for reconstructions of archaeological contexts.

"The environment acts on the system and the system in turn reacts with an output. The behaviour of the system therefore can be considered as the interaction between input and output. The behaviour depends in the first place on the structure of the system, by which is intended the organisation of links between its elements." (Malina, Vasicek, 1997, 78).

The perception of objects and/or three-dimensional virtual ecosystems provides for different grades of interaction with the virtual space: and perceptive phenomena provide an interaction level, or better an "exchange" or absence of behaviour between the actor and receiver; in this area we can identify mainly two levels of interaction in real time:

- a passive cognitive interaction where navigation/movement in 3D space takes place without the behaviour exchanges of the objects (events). This is the case with the major part of archaeological applications, where navigation (such as walking or flythrough) permits the passive exploration of the model (i.e., figs.3, 4, 5).
- An active cognitive interaction where navigation in 3D space takes place with behavioural exchange between the environment and the events. This type of interaction is possible only in the case of three-dimensional virtual models and represents the most advanced level of perceptive-cognitive increase (still rare in archaeological application). For example we can try to virtually reconstruct excavation phases and field exploration, removing in real time the stratigraphic layers, moving the artefacts, using virtually a "trowel", attributing subsequent behaviour also to the virtual objects of the scene. Moreover, the use of haptic technologies on a digital level can allow for the perception of our action with great realism, such as weight, size and thickness of an object.

Attempting to continue a macro-classification of the maximum of the possible interactions in 3D space, it is possible to construct a computational hierarchy with the following divisions (number 1 has the maximum degree of interaction):

- 1. Real-time 3D with rendering and texturing of surfaces (at different degrees of immersion), walkthrough (3D models, VRML)
- 2. Real-time 3D wire frame, transparent model, without rendering
- 3. Real-time 2D - pseudo 3D non immersive, photographic (virtual panoramas of the type QTVR)
- 4. Real-time 2D (multimedia)
- 5. Computer graphic 3D and passive animation (.avi, movies, guided pathways)

Models and Virtual Reconstructions

Why make virtual reconstructions? What is the goal of virtual models? What is the cognitive gain from a virtual reconstruction in archaeology (see also Barcelo, Sanders and Kantner, *this volume*) ?

These questions may seem banal, but in reality in many of the numerous reconstruction projects they are not asked and unfortunately remain unanswered. On the contrary, the entire reconstructive process should clarify its aims and objectives, notwithstanding its technological means and take into consideration a fundamental assumption: the contextual information of that "reconstructed" must cognitively exceed the sum of its parts, exploiting as much as possible the potential of dynamic perception.

Summarising the work of recent years, the primary fields of application of VA are: communication, education, simulation, and research with obvious integrations and overlapping between the various fields.

The following is an attempt at a preliminary classification of the possible archaeological applications of VA:

- Reconstructions of conserved archaeological sites
- Reconstructions of sites that have not been conserved but of which remains ample documentation.
- Reconstructions of sites that have been completely destroyed that are based on comparative analysis, iconographic analysis, etc. (i.e., fig.13).
- Reconstructions of sites of which remain only the foundations, that are on the basis of planimetric mapping.

- Reconstructions of archaeological sites well conserved but inaccessible (for example caves with prehistoric cave paintings).
- Chromatic and material reproductions (frescoes, terracottas, pediments, painted tombs, etc…).
- Contextualisation of material or finds.
- Landscape reconstructions (e.g., Forte, 1992; Cremaschi, Forte 1999).
- Dynamic events of anthropic, morphologic or geologic nature.
- Functional reconstructions of finds and mechanisms.
- Reconstructions or integrations of collections.
- Destructuring-recomposition of contexts (for example, the excavation as a metaphor of a digital and reconstructive logical elaboration).
- Reconstructions and/or simulations by telematic networks (metaphor of the VRML and JAVA languages)
- Reconstructions done on a GIS base (VRGIS, Virtual Reality Geographical Information System) and a remotely sensed base (navigations through remotely sensed models: Cremaschi, Forte, 1999).
- Virtual Museums. The concept of the virtual museum is based on a multimedial collection of digital data accessible telematically (Forte, Franzoni, 1998). As a structure-system the virtual museum is a cognitive space, therefore it increases in significance on the basis of the context it recomposes, that is the sum of information and associations that it unifies. The exchange (with other real and virtual environments) increases its narrative capacities, that is, the possibility for the virtual museum to render legible not only the works, finds or objects, but also the dynamic episodes (for example the hypothesis of a museum dedicated to battles of the ancient world).

The requirements that the VA projects fulfill include numerous variables; the complexity of these variables determine the enhancement of the applications:

- Multimedia-interaction: the visibility of the project uses different communication sources.
- Multidisciplinary: the project makes use of many different expertise.
- Multisensorial: the more senses involved, the more effective the interaction.
- Multidimensional: the project can integrate different geometry and scales of modelling.
- Multitemporal: the project can include four dimensional (4D) elements when it takes diachronic factors into consideration (i.e. NUME Project, see Guidazzoli, Bonfigli, *this volume*)
- Connection among multiusers: in the case that there are interactions or exchange of information between more users.
- Hypertextual: when the VA project provides links or hierarchies of data.
- Dynamic: data and models must interact in real time.
- Contextualisation of data (with reference to other levels of interaction, URL, etc)
- De-territorialisation (the information does not belong to a territory if not the context).
- Polisemicity: the models subtend meanings distributed according to the geometry of the models.
- Meta-literacy: the navigation is guided by metaphors of complex data (i.e. see the contribution of Rieko Kadobayashi, Kazushi Nishimoto, and Kenji Masein, *this volume*).
- Cognitivity-reality increase: the perception of the model becomes a complex interpretative horizon and enhances the significance of the model.
- Literacy: the introduction to the virtual territory is guided by educational systems and by virtual communications that noticeably increase the informative level.
- Graphic-symbolic representations (computational cartography): the VA project becomes a cognitive map, referenced by virtual spaces and territories with new contextual topographies.

How to Reconstruct

The relationship between the real and virtual, considered to be epistemologically dichotomous in the scientific world, on the contrary must be revised (Levy, 1997) for that concerning archaeological applications. Archaeological data are in themselves (ontologically) virtual since their nature is incomplete and subject to multiple interpretations, representing therefore a virtual context, for example an excavation or archaeological landscape. Therefore, the further virtualisation of archaeological data by computer, as a reconstructive-symbolic process, should be considered a passage from the virtual to the virtual and not from reality to virtuality, from photorealism to simulation. I believe it important to clarify this point seeing that a few "poor interpretations" can mislead the representitive-reconstructive process, manufacturing virtual contextualisation without control, or worse, raising the latter to cognitive metaphor notwithstanding the contents.

In the already vast field of virtual reconstruction there are different approaches that reflect (unfortunately too literally) almost always the technological properties of the hardware. It is evident that the technical quality of the models depends on the faculty of modelling and the software resources, but this should not be a problem; the archaeologist must first define a clear and data-saturated methodological-reconstructive approach, possibly directing the research beginning from the acquisition of data in the field (when possible):

- *What and why reconstruct ?* It is not essential to reconstruct always virtually, but it is important to use virtual technologies when we can obtain significative increments of information (*augmented reality*).
- Project: defining in detail the aims and target involves good communication of the VA applications, mainly to have important scientific results; the reconstruction is an interpretative hypothesis but also as a communicative project
- Pre-elaboration and standardisation of data in the fieldwork in digital form, planning the following virtual processing.

- Mapping dedicated to 2D-3D. The creation of "perceptive" archaeological textures (Healey, Interrante, Rheingans, 1999), studying materials and surfaces, increase very much the information level. New investigation of methods for choosing color, texture, orientation, shape, and other features will visualise different types of multidimensional datasets. Specific visualisation techniques will display data in a manner that will take advantage of the low-level human visual system.
- Who should reconstruct in 3D: archaeologists, architects, computer scientists, graphic artists, multimedia experts ? The best results will be obtained by an interdisciplinary work "in team", but the archaeologists should coordinate the VA project.
- There should exist not only the final reconstruction, but also a reconstructive method. In fact the model must be "transparent"—that is, contain reconstructive hierarchies of the modelling and original data, so as to verify the whole process of virtual reconstruction.
- Reconstruction as a metaphor of hypermedial navigation. In this case the final objective of the reconstruction is not access to more complex information, but rather the reconstruction is only a medium, an interface for hypermedial navigation.
- Other than the graphic impact there should be a real increase of information (3D editing).
- Study of the interfaces: the creation of specific graphic interfaces for VA applications represents a cognitive factor for the correct perception of the models.

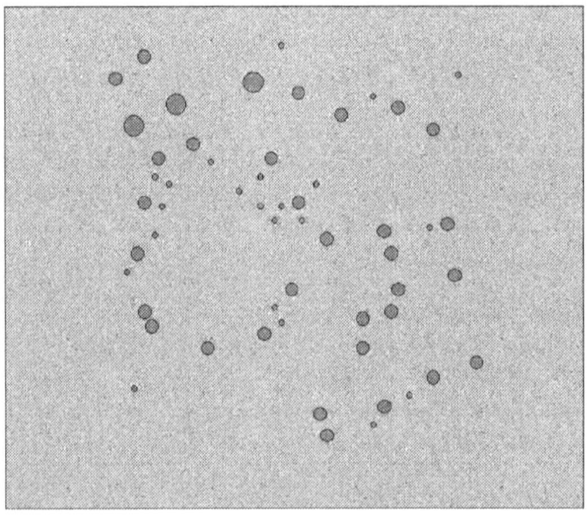

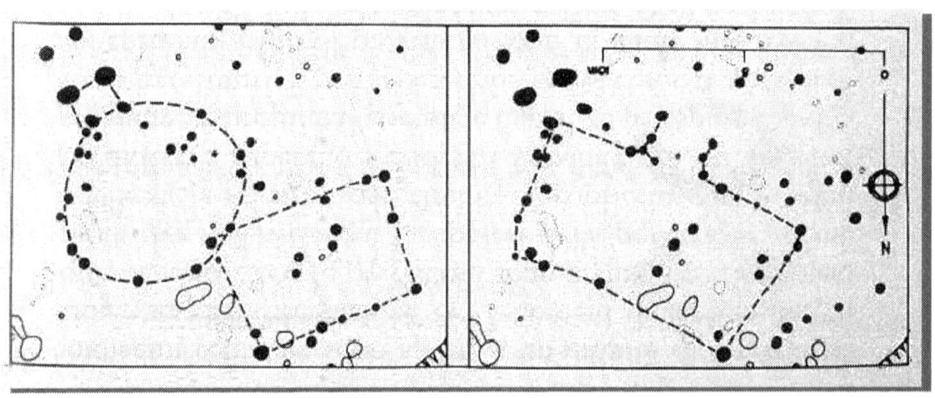

Figures 5-6: Observing the archaeological traces on the ground (post holes, top) it is possible to suggest different interpretations on the basis of the typological comparisons. So the connection of the post holes determines the next possible archaeological reconstruction (bottom, see also Gregory, 1998).

The methodological approach in reconstructing archaeological models can be outlined in the following classes:

- Virtual find*:* reconstruction of finds and/or relative functions;
- Virtual intra-site*:* a) reconstructions of structures, sites or architectural elements b) stratigraphic reconstructions; both within the sphere of intra-site analysis.
- Virtual landscape: reconstruction of archaeological landscapes, GIS links, remotely sensed data, landscape navigation.
- Virtual context: multi-dimensional that contain the 3 previous types.

GENETIC ALGORITHMS AND ARTIFICIAL LIFE

Genetic Algorithms is a technique which springs from the fundamental mechanisms of natural evolution. They are able to induce evolution of solutions to complex problems releasing the programmer from the necessity to precisely define all the necessary steps for the solution of the problem in consideration. Their effectiveness was demonstrated in numerous successful practical applications.

In nature, live organisms are able to solve complex problems which effect their livelihood using mechanisms of natural evolution. Through many generations, populations of organisms are capable of evolving—that is, to positively adapt to the changeable environment which hosts them, in order to have the capacity to survive. In the future the development of these techniques could make interesting contributions to archaeology, specifically for the reconstruction of virtual ecosystems.

Some Languages of Virtualisation 2D-3D

The *on-line* applications—that is, on the Internet, represent a distributed level of "interactivity", a sort of disseminated virtual reality for obtaining, in our cases, a global archaeological communication. Here I have described, in a few words, the most interesting and used Internet interactive "metaphors" of visual information.

–QTVR (QuickTime Virtual Reality, created by Apple as part of the Macintosh package but also useable on a PC, file with extension .mov), permits the interactive visualisation of photographic and photomosaic panoramas (of scenes or objects) real and virtual (that is, created by computer graphics). The photographic sequences, mounted in sequence in a virtual reality, represents an immersive, pseudo-three-dimensional panorama, that the user can explore in an interactive way. Metaphors of this type are often used on Internet for the virtual visiting of museums and exhibitions, archaeological digs and for the navigation within virtual models.

–Realspace-Photovista (produced by Livepicture, file with extension .ivr), with similar functions as the above (even if created for PC) integrates however real three-dimensional objects and solids created in the VRML format with the photographic panoramas. For example, in virtual space photographic panoramas (even if created with QTVR) can be associated, as a background, with three-dimensional elements such as the subjects of the scene, which at that point are in the foreground. In the case of reconstructing an ancient urban complex, for example, one can envision in the centre the architectonic anastilosis of three-dimensional buildings, while in the background is a panoramic photograph mounted by the stitching technique (panorama photo) obtained with Realspace-Photovista.

–Metastream. This is a plug-in created by Metacreation to interactively visualise three-dimensional models on-line, created beforehand with Canoma software.

–Flash. This is a software created by Macromedia to create multimedial presentations on-line very similar to those accessible off-line (for example on CD-ROM)

–QuickTime, Movie (file with extension .mov, .avi), is the canonical form of movies and animation, including particular algorithms in order to be seen on-line. In archaeology they are metaphors utilised for the virtual tours of museums, but also as documents themselves, excavation documentation films, computer graphic elaborations, etc.

–FLASHPIX (produced by Livepicture, with file extension .fpx), is a new visualisation format which allows for the access of high resolution images (or better of variable resolution) also on line through progressive zoom-ins. They are extremely useful applications for the visualisation of images of finds or decorative details of a certain complexity which require a high level of visualisation.

–Meta Content Framework (created by Apple, file with extension .mcf), is the metaphor of the hypertextual map of an Internet site, visualised in three dimensions. All of the hypermedial associations are represented by three-dimensional labels distinct from the thematic title (which indicates where one arrives clicking on it with the mouse) and by different colours according to the hypertextual hierarchy. The user can navigate in the three-dimensional space of the map immerging himself within it in order to visualise the information in detail; they could represent the future standard of the hypertextual maps on line.

–JAVA is a compilator of programs, defined as *applets*, that are created to function and interact on line, independently from the hardware package or operator system. Some applications of Java have also been used for drawing the hypermedial maps of important museums, such as the Louvre. Other interesting applets were developed for GIS applications, such as the 2D-3D visualisation of thematic maps or of georeferenced satellite images.

–VRML (Virtual Reality Modelling Language) This is a language for describing three-dimensional (3D) image sequences and possible user interactions with them. Using VRML it is possible to build a sequence of visual images into Web settings with which a user can interact by viewing, moving, rotating, and otherwise interacting with an apparently 3D scene (i.e., fig.7). For example, it is possible to view a room and use controls to move the room as you would experience it if you were walking through it in real space.

The Future

The future of VA depends essentially on the following series of factors: the technological evolution of hardware-software and of the networks, the digital elaboration of archaeological data, and the theoretical discussion by the archaeological scientific community. Apart from the technological limits, in respect to the actual state of the art it is possible to do much more, addressing research to telematic applications and multilevel reconstructions.

- Connecting multiusers in 3D. Telematic evolution will permit more users (by using avatars) to be able to simultaneously interact with the same model or virtual territory, exchanging data, information and simulations.
- On-line creation of virtual worlds by the merging of VRML and Java 3D (see also Sanders, *this volume*).
- VR Networks. The high-velocity networks could become the instrument dedicated to three-dimensional interactions in real time (like VRML), supporting ever more detailed and complex models.
- Immersive interactivity with an increase of the graphic performance.
- Digital Graphic Archives and 3D data banks. The development of VA projects should include the creation of 2D-3D digital graphic archives, established on a chrono-typological basis; the access, for example telematic, to this class of resource, will also allow for a certain standardisation of the models and a consequent expansion on the cognitive level.
- Behavioural exchanges between objects and models (coordinated visualisation of 3D models)—that is, the

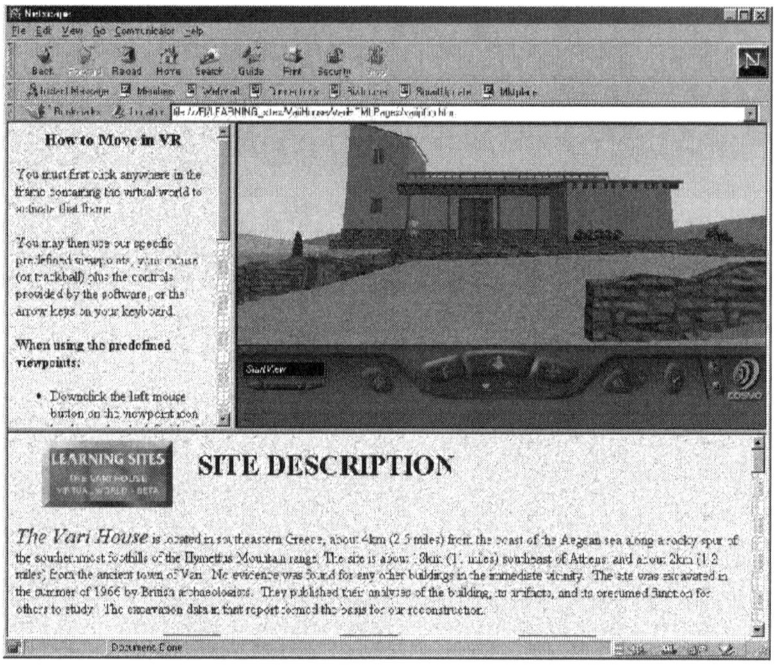

Figure 7: VRML reconstruction of the archaeological site of Vari (D. Sanders, Learning Sites, Inc.)

creation of tools of dynamic behaviours programmed object by object (e.g., as in some video games).

- Development of artificial life. In the field of the simulation of virtual ecosystems, the entity of artificial life (models, settlement systems, virtual communities) can grow, evolve and reproduce in virtual space in a random and unpredictable way.
- Computational cognitivity: virtual knowledge through the interaction in real time will produce new perceptive degrees of visual information that I call "mindscapes", mind landscapes (in particular in the applications concerning the virtual reconstruction of archaeological landscapes).
- Architecture for communication agents and ecosystems (cognitive ecology) and analysis of meta-communications. The use of virtual communication agents (guide on line) allows to study the socio-psychological factors in human-computer interactions (social agents).
- Development of perceptive textures (as I have mentioned before, C. Healey, V. Interrante, P. Rheingans, 1999).
- Increase of the level of photorealism and of the graphic performance in real time: prompt 2D-3D mapping in the field to allow for better visualisation and interpretation of data.
- VRGIS (Virtual Reality Geographic Information System, fig.8): Integration of GIS, networks and multimedia in order to create complex VR applications on line (Internet) – (more than VRML, Virtual Reality Modelling Language).
- Integrations of models of different kind and geometry: 3D, photographic stitching, billboard, movies, VRML, 3D surrounding sound etc.
- New visualisation and interactive devices (immersive, semi-immersive, non immersive).
- 3D data banks available on line: creation of archaeological graphic libraries aimed to the geometrical reconstruction of virtual worlds. This approach will permit new possibilities for publishing archaeological data on multimedia platforms.
- 3D tactile perception of the virtual worlds: new tools and devices will permit to navigate interactively perceiving and touching really the virtual objects.
- Multimedia presentation by MPEG 4 pemitting real-time distance education and video-conferencing (Sanders, *this volume*).

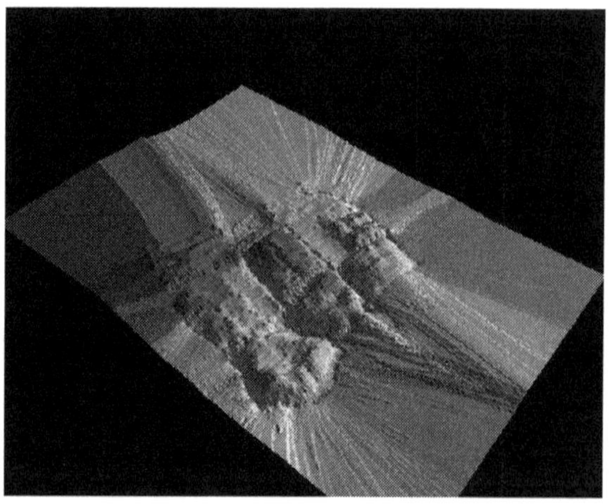

Figure 8: Vrgis Reconstruction Of A Terramara (Middle Bronze Age Site) By Total Laser Station (M.Forte

REALITY CENTERS AND VIRTUAL THEATERS: TOWARDS IMMERSIVE VIRTUAL ENVIRONMENTS

The term 'virtual theatre' (fig.9) is used to denote a physical space where a group of people can navigate in a virtual reality environment. If necessary, the visitors may be provided with polarised eyeglasses for a stereophonic view of the projected image. In figure 9 there is a general plan for setting up a virtual theatre housing an audience of up to 50 people.

The Virtual Theater can be designed to allow to visit a virtual reconstruction of archaeological areas on the basis of an "acceptable" interaction in terms of display speed for every type of user. Clearly an archaeologist needs a more detailed 3D visualisation than the average virtual tourist. On the other hand a virtual tourist, who is connected to the Internet with a standard PC and modem is likely to give preference to speed of access rather than to the careful reproduction of too much detail. So a project of integrated communication will provide two different ways of accessing this Virtual Environment by the Internet and hopefully in an immersive environment, but the data visualised in both the models will be equally validated by archaeological research

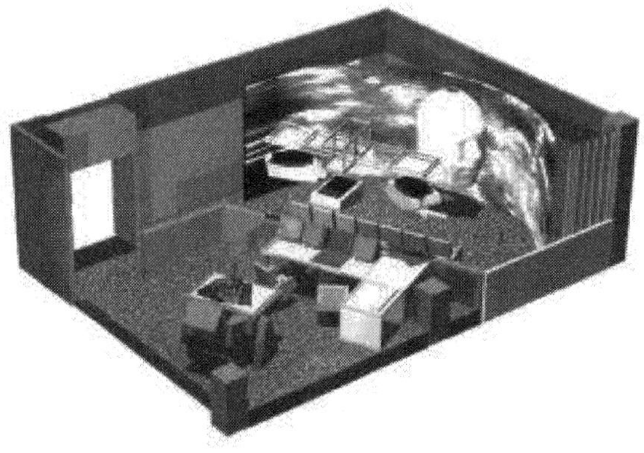

Figure 9: A virtual theater for cultural heritage and archaeological applications (CINECA, Bologna)

Fig. 10: Reality Center Walls (SGI System)

In order to allow more complex behaviour depending on outside data or user interaction, it is possible to use External Authoring Interface (EAI) to control the VRML world externally with a Java applet. The choice of VRML and Java guarantees equal conditions of access for all platforms.

From the technological point of view, two essential characteristics must be considered:

1 immersion and interaction,

2 high-quality graphics with photo-realistic characteristics.

There is reason to believe that the virtual theatre could be the natural development of archaeological high-resolution models.

REALITY CENTER DESKS

Reality Center Desks are ideal for hands-on applications—that is, grabbing and moving 3D models and data sets with the hands. The desks are self-contained and transportable, and they easily fit into an office or laboratory. Desks provide stereo graphics for scientific visualisation, digital prototyping, engineering simulation, factory simulation, mission planning, and educational applications.

REALITY CENTER WALLS

Reality Center walls (fig.10) suit groups of five to 50 viewers. By using flat or curved screens, it is possible to walk up and point to life-size visualisations. Walls can be rear- or front-projected using mono or stereo graphics. They are used for product design reviews, plan and process walk-throughs, site planning, collaborative engineering analysis, scenario visualisation, sales and marketing, public relations, recruiting, training, and enterprise decision support.

REALITY CENTER ROOMS

Reality Center rooms are surfaces that surround the environment with stereo graphics and sound. Rooms are used for multidisciplinary science and technology research, hands-on big-data interaction, computational steering, collaborative data analysis, interdepartmental communication, education, and recruitment.

THE FAKESPACE IMMERSADESK R2

Based on groundbreaking research by the Electronic Visualization Lab at the University of Illinois, Chicago, the ImmersaDesk R2 (fig.11) is a leading choice for visual supercomputing applications in scientific visualisation, engineering analysis, and other high-performance, real-time graphics projects. This stand-alone, transportable system includes a rear-projected, adjustable-angle screen that provides an ideal drafting-table work environment. A tracked handheld wand allows intuitive and direct data manipulation, while a pair of StereoGraphics™ CrystalEyes™ active shutter glasses, with integrated tracker, enables continuously corrected stereo image perspectives in real time. Four additional pairs of CrystalEyes glasses are provided for stereoscopic group viewing.

Figure 12: A new discovery of a mysterious topographic fresco concerning a roman town. It is painted on a wall of the Domus Aurea, the very same wall that was incorporated into Trajan's Baths after a demolition of the Domus Aurea. The fresco came to light during the excavations undertaken by Monuments and Fine Arts Office in Rome for the year 2000 Jubilee. The corresponding virtual 3D reconstruction gives new information about the topography of the ancient town (ACS Studio).

Fig.11: ImmersaDesk R2

COGNITIVITY, INFORMATIVE LANDSCAPES AND COMPUTERS

"Knowledge is power " summarizes the significance in the adventurous voyage toward knowledge. From Bacon to the modern developments of natural sciences, the aim of man's research has been ever more clearly defined: to decipher the language of phenomena in order to foresee its course and modify it to their pleasing. It is an ambitious aspiration that will never be completely accomplished. The final aim is that of knowledge, the term to which we slowly approach without ever being able to reach. The first obstacle is formed by the limits of our capacity: "...without sensitivity no object would be given us and without intelligence no object would be thought. Thoughts lacking content are empty, and intuitions lacking concepts are blind...." (Kant, *Critique of Pure Reason).* We know what experience offers us, therefore the amount of information is always limited to a particular moment and place. The process of knowing consists of exceeding these limits, to which sensation is subordinate—that is, the transformation from simple isolated impressions into "concepts". They have nothing in common with the initial event, however they allow us to explain these and others which have yet taken place and that may never come to pass.

The study of the process of knowledge is aimed at "discovering" or "creating" laws which permits us to monitor it step by step and to amplify its potential. Computational information is increasingly affected by this mechanism. The study of the perception of objects in real space is indispensable once we begin to create synthetic space that must transmit even more information yet always through the senses. A clear expression of this project is "computational simulation"—that is, the synthetic reconstruction of a physical or conceptual phenomena. Through the collection of multiple forms of data otherwise lost, that become homogeneous after calculation, a model of the event can

Figure 13: Virtual reconstruction of the Domus Aurea: the octagonal room (ACS Studio)

be constructed. This allows for the step-by-step visualisation of all phases, providing humanity with extraordinary predictive power, since each level is the necessary condition for the next one.

In this way the "interactive-computational simulation" becomes the methodical ideal of the scientist: reason and observation permit the break down of an event into its primary elements and from these it is reconstructed. A tight link is established between computational information and the "architecture of thought", because both embody man's desire to be the "architect" of the "world". In fact the different metaphysics that have flourished in western thought are similar to buildings constructed brick-by-brick according to precise construction rules. Each of their parts is a level of reality that is not real nor arbitrary since they exhibit a law of the real. Synthetic images which populate the world of virtuality have the same role: they are intermediary beings between the world of ideas and the perceptible reality. They represent a "non-reality" which exists since they are the visualisation of the truth of the real. Computational information tends to fulfill man's childhood "dream" finding motivation in his stupor of looking at the world. However, the moment that they began to express themselves exploiting the instruments that technology put at their disposal (that is, the computer visual simulation techniques) as well as the mathematical development of fractal geometry and inversion, they went well beyond the first objective. A portion of the real is no longer represented by a chain of ideas in which all pertinent information is housed, instead it is reconstructed in a way that the observer can immerse himself, react to it and be reacted to.

When D'Alambert and Diderot decided in the eighteenth century to collect into the *Encyclopaedia* all knowledge of reality, scattered throughout the different fields of knowledge, they planned a new image of reality adequate to man's needs. With the present means it would be possible to virtually undertake this project. It would require the construction of a large symbolic space that would represent the general framework of reference, in which there would be many symbolic spaces, the various disciplines or in our case, various archaeological fields. The "Preliminary Discussion of the *Encyclopaedia*" offers precious information on the meaning and aim of the work, that allows for the maintenance of the dream of its being rewritten in the virtual language. "...the encyclopaedic order of our consciousness is made up of the collection of them in as little space as possible, in being able to make the philosopher assume a position raised high above this labyrinth...able to embrace in a glance the objects of his speculation and operations....It is a type of globe that must indicate the more important countries, their position and mutual dependence, the straight path from one country to the next: a path often filled with obstacles that only the inhabitants of the individual countries know....and are possible to be indicated on specific detail rich maps. These specific maps will be the different articles of the *Encyclopaedia*, while the whole figurative system the globe...." (J. B. D'Alambert, *Discours préliminaire de l'encyclopédie*).

We can take the *Encyclopaedia* as a metaphor for virtual reality in that it is a great synthetic space. It is the image of images, in which all knowledge that we have on reality is found. These are distributed in different elements, that in turn correspond to specific images. Like in virtual space, icons are linked to each other since each one reproduces the whole series. These icons are constructed according to fractal theory, where every element is the starting point for a reconstruction of reality. Therefore there is a common need to reconstruct reality beginning from any point, but in this case this is expressed in alphabetical order, by the use of fractals which have auto-reflexibility. "...the form of the encyclopaedic tree will depend on the point of view the philosopher will use in considering the literary universe. We can therefore imagine many different systems of human consciousness, as many globes of different projections that can be constructed, each one presenting advantages that the others lack..." (J. B. D'Alambert, *Discours préliminaire de l'encyclopédie*).

These lines offer topics of further reflection: the entirety of the relationships that we define are not "guaranteed" by the correspondence with reality, because it does not offer us relationships but individuals and single objects. The validity of our network is based on its easy comprehension and at the same time on the greatest possible number of links it can establish. In the same way the symbolic space does not pretend to exhaust the complexity of the real, but only to allow for a better classification of information and their increased use by the observer. Both are "open" creations—that is, revisable by new complexes of relationships that are not arbitrary because they are founded on two principles, alphabetical order and the laws of mathematics comparable in every way. In other words, they do not need any form of external "guarantee".

Not only the *Encyclopaedia* ou *Dictionnaire raisonné des sciences, des arts et des métiers, par une Société de Gens de lettres* (subtitle of the *Encyclopaedia*) provides a useful comparison between the construction process of computational information and that of the architecture of knowledge, but also the extraordinary cornerstone of Leibnizian metaphysics as well as the idea of a universal *Encyclopaedia* of knowledge, realised through the *caratheristica universalis.* In this way Leibniz states in *Discours de Metaphysique*" "...every substance is like an entire world, it is like a reflection of God, or the whole universe, that expresses in its own particular way, more or less like the same city represented differently according to the position of who observes it....and since all other substances express in turn that substance, it can be said that it expands its power on all the others..." (Leibniz, *Monadologia e discorso di metafisica, Laterza 1986*). Every *monad* occupies the same role of a synthetic image: it reproduces in its unity the multiplicity, and the various *monads* like different images, are linked by their capacity of reproducing the whole. The only difference is in principal: for Leibniz it is the "life force", in the world of computational information it is the construction according to mathematical principals and geometric models.

Even more useful for establishing a parallel are the Disputatio de arithmetica de complexionibus and the Dissertatio de arte combinatoria (Leibniz, Scritti di logica, Laterza, 1992). Here the reconstruction of reality is entrusted to a finite number of "primary ideas', derived from the analysis of all worldly knowledge, combined by algebraic laws. Starting from here we arrive at an open collection of compound ideas that are always controllable within the system since they are always devisable by the primary ideas. This project is animated by the same "spirit" that inhibits virtuality: a collection of information from very different sources, selection and classification of them and their visualisation in synthetic images. The final element is that which differentiates the two systems, because in the Leibnizian Encyclopaedia there are only formulas which link one to the other according to relations of derivative logic, and there is no project for their subsequent conversion in images.

The world of cognitive virtuality is therefore much less technical than it seems to be because it responds to an ancient need of man: that of understanding truth beyond its appearance, identifying the first in unity and the second in multiplicity. The dream of all western mysticism seems to be accomplished through the cooperation of theory (developments in mathematics, geometry, studies of perception) and technological applications. Among these the world of perception is the least explored yet most important. Here one must abandon every "laplacian" expectation of a complete prediction of the future by the collection of past data. The world of consciousness does not seem to be reducible to a simple material substratum—that is, the brain. This is essential for its "emergence", but once the thought is formed, it does not allow itself to be completely explained by neurophysiological laws. In the face of this shortcoming, research has turned to determining the "principals" of perceptive mechanisms. They do not investigate "what" we perceive but "how" we perceive it. Creating a model on the functioning of perception allows for the reconstruction of a space in which everyone can be at ease, without having the number and the quality of the computational information be established beforehand for the individual case. This is the "open" quality of the synthetic image: it can be used by a large number of individuals without compromising the detail of the contents of their perception. This double nature allows for the closure of the gap between the world of ideas and that of events perceivable by the senses, between the fixed world and that of change, because it is the mathematical model made visible. The long path of the history of western thought that tends to reconcile the universal and the particular has reached an end ?

Plato and Plotinus discovered the "medium" of truth and reality whereas before them the Pythagorians had defined the structure of reality. In "modern" times the theories of art and natural sciences, in their elaborations of the 1500s and 1600s, discovered the meeting point between liberty and necessity in the concept of "law". This is also the world of Galileo and Descartes, where mathematics is no longer the basis of reality but only a more simple way of expressing the relationship between ideas, therefore the "structure" of the real. In fact it is enough to look at the various cosmological images that appear in "Principals of Philosophy" to understand the role that mathematics has acquired. The value that an image of this sort has does not lay in the rich detail with which it reproduces reality, but in its ability to explain it with a few well defined elements. It does not matter if the world of lines and points is nonexistent in reality because they serve only to explain its sounds and colours. Moreover, notwithstanding the clarity and univocity of meaning, images of this sort have a limit: they are able to transmit a greater quantity of information only at the cost of the perception contents' vivacity and richness. The size of the synthetic image depends on reconciling these two requirements. This is due to the fact that they act on the senses of the observer communicating information "as if" it is in contact with the real image (Gregory, 1998). Or better still, they evoke a representative memory that may not necessarily be geometric but is essentially conceptual or perceptive-symbolic.

The techniques of immersion, interaction, sensorial interaction are all based on perceptive mechanisms (Gregory, 1998). They represent instruments that permit the user to operate in synthetic space, that is, to be able to understand synthetic space in all of its richness through the shifting of points of view. This world created by an imagination restrained by reason is expanding in all fields of knowledge, since it offers windows on a world otherwise invisible; that is, it offers the conditions for making better use of reality without the desire to substitute it.

Conclusions

As a final consideration, being on the threshold of the next millennium, I have recently reflected on what could be a general definition of *computational archaeology* or *digital archaeology* (or the computer elaboration of archaeological data) and if this scientific field has brought about significant progress in the discipline, in methodological and theoretical terms. Do we need therefore to consider the existence of digital archaeology, technological, post-(hyper)processual, and cognitive, separately from *archaeology* tout court ? Is digital archaeology, in itself, an applicative field? For many of us ("computational archaeologists") it would auspicable, but it is not so: historically, the first applications of computerised archaeology go back to the 1960s, almost contemporary with the development of New Archaeology (Malina, Vasicek, 1997). However it is obvious that the great development of "computerised" archaeology reflects primarily technological-digital developments, in particular the revolutionary period of the personal computer.

Progressively I have been convinced that digital or computational archaeology represents a necessary path (in many ways revolutionary) and inescapable for the methodological evolution of the archaeological sciences. Yet the revolutionary and hyperprocessual significance of digital archaeology is as a research instrument and tool.

I also believe that the archaeology of the third millennium will be, without a doubt, digital; it will not be able to be otherwise, yet it will nevertheless remain archaeology, or as Foucalt says, *archéologie du savoir* (Foucalt 1980).

Acknowledgments

Very special thanks are due to Gianna Ayala for the important support in the English translation of the text and to Roberta Beltrami for the fundamental phylosophical and theoretical discussions.

We thank also Infobyte, ACS Studio, Learning Sites Inc., Mondadori Editore, CINECA, B. Britton, for the images and the documentation.

References Cited

CLARKE D.L.1998, *Archeologia analitica,* Milano, 1998 (I edizione 1968).

CREMASCHI M., FORTE M., 1999, *Reconstructing a fossil landscape by Remote Sensing and GIS applications: sites, virtual models and territory during the Middle Bronze age in the Po plain (Northern Italy),* in "Archeologia e Calcolatori", X, 1999.

DORAN J., 1996, *Artificial societies and cognitive archaeology*, in "Archeologia a calcolatori", 7, III Convegno Internazionale di Archeologia eInformatica, 1996, 1231-1245.

FORTE M., 1992, "Image processing applications in archaeology: classification systems of archaeological sites in the landscape". In *Computing the Past.* Edited by J.Andresen, T. Madsen & I.Scollar. Aarhus (DK): Aarhus University Press, pp. 53-61

FORTE,M., 1996, "Il Progetto ARCTOS. Verso un GIS Multimediale". *Archeologia e Calcolatori* 7, (1), pp. 179-192.

FORTE M.1996a (ed.), *Archeologia. Percorsi virtuali delle civiltà scomparse*, Milano, 1996.

FORTE M., FRANZONI M., 1998, *Il museo virtuale: comunicazione e metafore*, in "Sistemi Intelligenti", Anno X, numero 2, agosto 1998, 193-240.

FOUCALT M., 1980, *L'archeologia del sapere*, Milano, 1980.

GARDIN J.C., 1996, *La révolution cognitive et l'archéologie*, in "Archeologia a calcolatori", 7, III Convegno Internazionale di Archeologia eInformatica, 1996, 1221-1230.

GREGORY R.L., 1998, *Occhio e cervello. La psicologia del vedere,* Milano, 1998.

HEALEY C., INTERRANTE V., RHEINGANS P., 1999, *Fundamental Issues of Visual Perception for Effective Image Generation*, "Course Notes", 6, SIGGRAPH '99, 26th International Conference on Computer Graphics and Interactive Techniques, Los Angeles 1999.

LEVY P.1992, *Le tecnologie dell'intelligenza*, Bologna, 1992.

LEVY P., 1996, *L'intelligenza collettiva. Per un'antropologia del cyberspazio*, Milano, 1996.

LEVY P., 1997, *Il virtuale*, Milano, 1997

MALINA J., VASICEK Z.1997, *Archeologia. Storia, problemi, metodi*, Milano, 1997.

MOSCATI P. 1996, *Archeologia quantitativa: nascita, sviluppo e "crisi"*, in "Archeologia a calcolatori", 7, III Convegno Internazionale di Archeologia eInformatica, 1996, 579-590.

REILLY,P., 1990, "Towards a virtual archaeology". *Computer Applications in Archaeology 1990*, Edited by K.Lockyear and S.Rahtz. oxford: British Archaeological reports (Int. Series 565), pp., 133-139.

RENFREW C., ZUBROW E.B.1994, (ed.), *The ancient mind. Elements of cognitive archaeology*, Cambridge, 1994.

VR Terminology

(SOURCES: M. FORTE AND HTTP://WWW-EUROPE.SGI.COM/VIRTUAL_REALITY/OVERVIEW/GLOSSARY.HTML)

absolute values: Position and orientation within a virtual space as measured from a single, constant point of origin. If a real or virtual object is moved, its previous coordinates are ignored, and new position and orientation measurements are taken.

actuator: Usually mechanical (hydraulic) or electric means used to provide force or tactile feedback to a user.

ambient light: Naturally occurring illumination arising from outside the apparatus (e.g., HMD).

articulation: Objects composed of several parts that are separately movable.

artificial reality: Simulated spaces created from a combination of computer and video systems. Coined by VR pioneer Myron Krueger in 1974.

aspect ratio: Ratio of width to height of the field of view.

assistive agents: Artificial intelligence algorithms developed to guide participants through a VR world, and to coach on available choices within the world.

augmented reality: The use of transparent glasses on which a computer displays data so that the viewer can simultaneously view virtual and physical objects. As general definition, the variety of techniques that combine computer-generated images and other objects with real scenes, creating augmented reality.

avatar: A participant's graphical persona inside a virtual world.

back clipping plane: A distance beyond which objects are not shown.

backdrop: The stationary background in a virtual world. The boundary of the world which cannot be moved or broken into smaller elements.

backface removal: The elimination of those portions of a displayed object that are facing away from the viewer.

bi-ocular: Displaying the same image to each eye. Sometimes done to conserve computing resources when depth perception is not critical. See also: stereoscopic.

biosensors: Sensor devices that monitor the body's electrical activity for purpose of computer input.

clue conflict: A kind of motion sickness caused when the body tries to interpret conflicting clues being received by the senses. Usually attributed to faulty calibration of eye devices or delay between the sensory inputs and output display.

concept map: Terms, definitions, or icons arranged in semantic proximity.

convergence: Occurs in stereoscopic viewing when the left and right eye images become fused into a single image.

convolve: To filter and intertwine signals (e.g., sounds) and render them three-dimensional. Used in VR applications to recreate sounds that give directional cues.

coordinates: A set of data values that determine the location of a point in a space. The number of coordinates corresponds to the dimensionality of the space.

culling: Removing invisible pieces of geometry and only sending potentially visible geometry to the graphics subsystem. Simple culling rejects entire objects not in the view. More complex systems take into account occlusion of some objects by others, e.g. a building hiding trees behind it.

data sonification: Assignment of sounds to digitized data which may involve filtering to give illusion of localized sound.

data spatialization: Assignment of orientation (yaw, pitch) and position coordinates (x,y,z) to digital sounds assigned to data.

DataGlove: A glove wired with sensors and connected to a computer system for gesture recognition and navigation through a virtual environment. Known generically as a "wired glove".

depth cueing: Use of shading, texture, color, interposition, or other visual characteristics to provide a cue for the distance of an object from the observer.

digital prototype: Simulation of an intended design or product to illustrate the characteristics before actual construction. Usually used as an exploratory tool for manufacturing designers/engineers or as a communications tool for persons reviewing proposed designs.

Doppler effect: An apparent increase in the frequency of sound or light as its source approaches an observer or a decrease if it moves away.

Deformable Object Technology (DOT): Virtual objects which bend and deform appropriately when touched. dynamic lighting: Changes in lighting effects as objects or the observer move.

dynamics: The rules that govern all actions and behaviors within the environment.

DVEM: Digital Virtual Elevation Model

effectors: Interfacing devices used in virtual environments for input/output, tactile sensation and tracking. Examples are gloves, headmounted displays, headphon and trackers.

egocenter: The sense of one's own location in a virtual environment.

environment: In VR terms, this is a computer-generated model that can be experienced by an observer as if it were a place.

exoskeleton: mechanically linked structure for control of and feedback from application.

eye clearance: The most accurate figure of merit used to describe the HMD positioning relative to the eye.

eye tracking: Measurement of the direction of gaze.

eyeball in the hand: A metaphor for visualized tracking where the tracker is held in the hand and is connected to motion of the projection point of the display.

field of view (FOV): The angle in degrees of the visual field. Since a human's two eyes have overlapping 140 degree FOV, binocular or total FOV is roughly 180 degrees in most people. A feeling of immersion arises with FOV greater than roughly 60 to 90 degrees.

force feedback: Output that transmits pressure, force or vibration to provide the VR participant with the sense of resisting force, typically to weight or inertia. This is in contrast to tactile feedback, which simulates sensation (e.g., texture) applied to the skin.

fractal: A self-similar graphical pattern generated by using the same rules at various levels of detail. That is, a graphical pattern that repeats itself on a smaller and smaller scale.

frustum of vision: Three-dimensional field of view in which all modeled objects are visible.

gesture: Hand motion that can be interpreted as a sign, signal, or symbol.

haptic interfaces: Use of physical sensors to provide users with a sense of touch the skin level, and force feedback information from muscles and joints.

head tracking: Monitoring the position and orientation of the head through various tracking devices.

head-coupled: Displays or robotic actions that are activated by head motion through a head tracking device.

head-related transfer function: A mathematical transformation of sound spectrum that modifies the amplitude and phase of acoustic signals to take into account the shape effects of the listener's head.

heads-up display: A display device that allows users see graphics superimposed on their view of the real world.

hidden surface: A surface of a graphics object that is occluded from view by intervening objects.

head mounted display (HMD): A set of goggles or a helmet with tiny monitors in front of each eye to generate images seen by the wearer as three-dimensional. Often the HMD is combined with a head tracker so that the images displayed in the HMD changes as the head moves.

immersion: The observer's behavioral (subjective) reaction to the virtual world as being part of it, or virtual model as being actual.

interaural amplitude: Differences between a person's two ears in the intensity of a sound, typically due to the location of the sound.

interaural time: Differences between a person's two ears in the phase of a sound, typically due to the location of the sound.

interface: Any device, software, or technique that allows people to perform task with a computer.

inverse kinematics: A specification of the motion of dynamic systems from properties of their joints and extensions.

kinesthesis: Sensations derived from muscles, tendons and joints and stimulated by movement and tension.

kinesthetic dissonance: Mismatch between feedback or its absence from touch or motion during VR experiences.

latency: Lag between user motion and tracker system response, sometimes measured in frames. Delay between actual change in position and reflection by the program. Delayed response time.

Liquid Crystal Display (LCD): Display devices that use bipolar films sandwiched between thin panes of glass. They are lightweight and transmissive or reflective, and are often used in HMDs.

level of detail (LOD): A model of a particular resolution among a series of models of the same object. Greater graphic performance can be obtained by using a lower LOD when the object occupies fewer pixels on the screen or is not in a region of significant interest.

metaball: A surface defined about a point specified by a location, a radius, and "intensity." When two metaballs come in contact, their shapes blend together.

metallic distortion: Noise interference or degraded performance in electromagnetic trackers when used near large metallic objects.

mindscape: mind landscapes or cognitive archaeological landscape; 4D dynamic perception of virtual archaeological landscapes through a 3D digital navigation.

model: A computer-generated simulation of something real.

motion parallax: A means whereby the eyes can judge distance by noticing how closer objects appear to move more than distant ones when the observer moves.

motion platform: A controlled physical system that provides real motion to simulate the displayed motion in a VR world.

navigation: Purposeful motion through virtual space.

objects: Discrete 3-D shapes within the virtual world with which an operator can interact.

occipital cortex: The back of the brain receiving retinotopic projections of visual displays.

occlusion: Hiding an object or a portion of an object from sight by interposition of other objects.

pan: The angular displacement of a view along any axis or direction in a three-dimensional world.

parallax: The difference in viewing angle created by having two eyes looking at the same scene from slightly different positions, thereby creating a sense of depth.

parietal cortex: An area of the brain adjacent and above the occipital cortex, thought to process spatial location and direction information.

perspective: The rules that determine the relative size of objects on a flat viewing surface to give the perception of depth.

pitch: The angular displacement of the lateral axis about a horizontal axis perpendicular to the lateral axis.

portal: Polygons or icon that a user can pass through in a virtual space to automatically load a new world or execute a user-defined function.

position sensor: A tracking device that provides information about its location and/or orientation.

position trigger: A hotspot, sensitive spot, or button that causes a change in the application when touched in some way.

presence: A feeling of being immersed in an environment, able to interact with objects there. A defining characteristic of a VR system.

radiosity: A diffuse illumination calculation system for graphics based on energy balancing that takes into account multiple reflections off many walls.

ray tracing: A technique for displaying a three-dimensional object with shading and shadows by tracing light rays backward from the viewing position to the light source.

real time: Action taking place with no perceptible or significant delay after the input that initiates the action.

real-time imaging: Graphics or images synchronized with real-world time events.

refresh rate: The frequency with which an image is regenerated on a display surface.

roll: Angular displacement about the lateral axis.

scene view: Virtual display viewed on a large screen or through a terminal window rather than with immersive devices.

shutter glasses: Glasses that alternately block out the left and right eye views in synchrony with the computer display of left- and right-eye images to provide stereoscopic effect.

simulator sickness: Various disturbances, ranging in degree from a feeling of unpleasantness, disorientation, and headaches to extreme nausea, caused by various aspects of a simulator. Possible factors include sensory distortions such as abnormal movement of arms and heads because of the weight of equipment; long delays or lags in feedback, and missing visual cues from convergence and accommodation.

six degrees of freedom (6DOF): Ability to move in three spatial directions and orient about three axes passing through the center of the body. Thus the location and orientation are specified by six coordinates.

spatial navigation: Self orientation and locomotion in virtual worlds.

stereopsis: Binocular vision of images with different views by the two eyes to distinguish depth.

tactile displays: Devices that provide tactile and kinesthetic sensations.

telemanipulation: Robotic control of distant objects.

telepresence: Virtual reality experienced from remote locations. Remote control with adequate sensory data to give the illusion of being at that remote location.

terrain: Geographical information and models that can be either randomly generated or based on actual data.

texture mapping: A bitmap pattern added to an object to increase realism.

tracker: A device that provides numeric coordinates to identify the current position and/or orientation of an object or user in real space.

universe: The collection of all entities and the space they are embedded in for a VR world.

viewpoints: Points from which raytracing and geometry creation occurs. The geometric eye point of the simulation.

virtual environments: Realistic, interactive, immersive simulations of places and scenes.

virtual human: Robotic humanoid or photo-realistic, animated character; may be embedded with neural networks/AI-based autonomous behavior for training simulation or telepresence tasks, or may be a properly proportioned representati of a human figure for purposes of human factors/ergonomics analysis.

virtual museum: on line museum, the virtual museum is a cognitive space, therefore it increases in significance on the basis of the context it recomposes, that is the sum of information and associations that it unifies; the exchange with other real and virtual environments increases its narrative capacities.

virtual surgery: Use of computer models and specialized interaction devices that mimic surgical tools to allow medical personnel to practice surgical procedures.

virtual world: Whole virtual environment or universe within a given simulation.

voxel: A cubic volume pixel for quantizing three-dimensional space.

VRGIS: Virtual Reality GIS; virtual reality applications through GIS models

world in the hand: A metaphor for visualized tracking where a tracker is held in the hand and is connected to the motion of an object in a display.

yaw: The angular displacement about the vertical axis.

NOTE: the CD-ROM includes a complete version of all papers with full colour pictures, video and interactive virtual models, and also some additional papers. All files should be read using Netscape Navigator 4.0 or higher and Internet Explorer 4.0 or higher. The additional software (plug-ins) included should also be installed. Please, consult the readme file at the beginning of the CD.*

*The CD referred to above (and in the text) has now been replaced with a download available at www.barpublishing.com/additional-downloads.html

www.ingramcontent.com/pod-product-compliance
Lightning Source LLC
LaVergne TN
LVHW072251300926
849160LV00018B/1639